ARTIFICIAL INTELLIGENCE
AND INFORMATION-CONTROL SYSTEMS
OF ROBOTS

Third International Conference on
Artificial Intelligence and Information-Control
Systems of Robots
Smolenice, Czechoslovakia, June 11-15, 1984

sponsored by
the Sciencetific Board for Artificial Intelligence
of the Systems Analysis Committee of the
Presidium of the Academy of Sciences
of the USSR
and
the Institute of Technical Cybernetics
of the Slovak Academy of Sciences

NORTH-HOLLAND
AMSTERDAM • NEW YORK • OXFORD

ARTIFICIAL INTELLIGENCE AND INFORMATION-CONTROL SYSTEMS OF ROBOTS

Proceedings of the Third International Conference on
Artificial Intelligence and Information-Control Systems of Robots
Smolenice, Czechoslovakia, June 11-15, 1984

edited by

IVAN PLANDER

Institute of Technical Cybernetics
Slovak Academy of Sciences
Bratislava, Czechoslovakia

1984

NORTH-HOLLAND
AMSTERDAM • NEW YORK • OXFORD

© ELSEVIER SCIENCE PUBLISHERS B.V., 1984

All rights reserved. No part of this publication may be reproduced, stored in a retrieval system, or transmitted, in any form or by any means, electronic, mechanical, photocopying, recording or otherwise, without the prior permission of the copyright owner.

ISBN: 0 444 87533 6

Published by:
ELSEVIER SCIENCE PUBLISHERS B.V.
P.O. Box 1991
1000 BZ Amsterdam
The Netherlands

Sole distributors for the U.S.A and Canada:
ELSEVIER SCIENCE PUBLISHING COMPANY, INC.
52 Vanderbilt Avenue
New York, N.Y. 10017
U.S.A.

PRINTED IN THE NETHERLANDS

PREFACE

It is hard to find a place in the world today where computing technique would not be used in various areas and aspects of human activity. At present we are eyewitnessing the gradual transformation of the proceeding scientific-technical revolution into a computer revolution and AI and robotic systems implementation. Thereby this stage renders invaluable services to man, liberating him from heavy drudgery and unwholesome activities.

The stormy development in microelectronics and in the technology of computer production has provided real prerequisites for the application of the results achieved in artificial intelligence(AI) theory and theoretical robotics to practice in form of actual systems exhibiting attributes of AI.

Hitherto it has been practically impossible to utilize in practice the results achieved in AI since the efficiency and capacity of contemporary computer memories do not allow to implement in real time such large-scale processings as AI algorithms require.

The situation has now developed in the way that AI theory, in addition to other areas, immediately assists in automating computer systems and VLSI circuits design. It is already known that VLSI integrated circuits of a complexity of several hundred thousand up to several millions of transistors per chip will be designable only with the help of intelligent CAD VLSI, completing the abilities of the human designer.

All these problems referred to are covered by the International Conference ARTIFICIAL INTELLIGENCE AND INFORMATION-CONTROL SYSTEMS OF ROBOTS held biannually at the House of Scientists of the Slovak Academy of Sciences at the Castle of Smolenice near Bratislava. The organizers of this Conference are the Scientific Board for Artificial Intelligence of the Systems Committee of the Presidium of the Academy of Sciences of the USSR, Moscow, and the Institute of Technical Cybernetics of the Slovak Academy of Sciences in Bratislava. The Conference is attended by a limited number of scientists and experts in the area of artificial intelligence, computer science and information-control systems of robots.

The Conference is aligned upon the most progressive areas of computer science, such as artificial intelligence and theoretical robotics. The Conference has become the forum also presenting the results achieved by the Working Group WG 18 "Knowledge representation in man-machine and robotic systems" of the Board for Scientific Problems of Computer Science of the Academies of Science of socialist countries. The Conference is also closely tied up with the International Basis Laboratory for Artificial Intelligence associated with the Institute of Technical Cybernetics of the Slovak Academy of Sciences in Bratislava.

The International Program Committee led by G.S. Pospelov is responsible for the scientific program of the Conference and its organization is supervised by the Czechoslovak National Organizing Committee with I. Plander in charge. The 3rd Conference is devoted to the following major topics:

1. Theoretical problems of artificial intelligence
2. Expert systems
3. Perception and pattern recognition
4. Robotics
5. Specialized computer systems for artificial intelligence and robotics

The volume includes 9 invited papers of top experts in the field of Artificial Intelligence and theoretical robotics.

The paper of L. Aielo and D. Nardy (Italy) illustrates how techniques developed in AI find applications in office automation. The most relevant problems of office automation are mentioned and problems arising in the construction of an expert system for an office information system are investigated.

W. Bibel (FRG) brings a new first-order model for reasoning about knowledge and belief. In the model different agents act in separate worlds so that they do not share any knowledge at all and the factual aspect of what is believed and the procedural aspect of how to use beliefs are strictly separated. Applications of there results are also discussed.

L. Bolc (Poland) and his collaborators present the experimental version of the deductive system DIALOG for natural language communication. The system answers questions about a precisely defined domain - now it is some fragment of medical knowledge.

In the paper of M. Draganescu (Romania) an AI scheme for a general theory of information is discussed and phenomenological processes of matter are proposed.

Y. Kodratoff (France) and his co-authors present a unified approach to concept learning. Authors promote together a definition of a concept, a methodology for discovering these concepts and an algorithm which realizes this discovery.

In T. Kohonen´s paper (Finland) it is argued that the principles underlying biological intelligence may be completely different from those applied in AI. Using an idealized model of a self--organizing system, the author offers an explanation for the ability of the brain to form "feature maps" and abstractions of sensory signals. As an example the automatic formation of a 2D map of speech elements is given.

D.E. Okhotsimsky (USSR) and his co-authors describe an approach to the problem of automating an industrial assembly process with the aid of robots with simple sensors and auxiliary devices.The application of a vision systems for testing the correctness of the assembly process is investigated and experiments in automatic multi-operation assembly are presented.

In the paper of G.S. Pospelov (USSR) three topics are discussed: AI as simulation of cognitive processes, AI as the theory of interface in the interactive systems and AI as the theory of goalprogrammed robot behaviour. Special attention is given to the second topic.

In the paper of E.H. Tyugu (USSR) on knowledge-based programming the object-oriented language NUT is presented. It is highly interactive and combines the feature of SMALTAK, UTOPIST and PROLOG languages. The new language is a step in the direction of building intelligent software for a wide class of users.

In addition, the volume contains 72 selected papers from 15 countries, Section 1 "Theoretical Problems of Artificial Intelligence" includes twenty-nine submitted papers.

Many of them (10) deal with various aspects of natural language understanding and generation. Another group contains papers on different approaches to knowledge representation. Inference processes, decision-making and heuristics learning are topics of the next five papers. Papers on problem solving, planning and execution systems are also included. The last group of papers within this section deals with program correctness and logic programming (inclusive of experience gained in using the programming language PROLOG).

Within Section 2 "Expert Systems", eight papers have been selected for inclusion into the volume. Three contributions present an empty expert system, two of them running along medicinal, one along technical lines. Additional three contributions are theoretical studies on knowledge base architectures. Out of the remaining two papers one covers natural language interface to an expert system and the other deals with inferences on rule-based expert systems.

Section 3 " Perception and Pattern Recognition" includes 8 contributions. Their authors present two real-time industrial vision systems, one of them being of the Ist, the other of the 2nd generation, that is it works with a grayscale of brightness and also allows object overlap in the scene. Another of the presented systems is an interactive image processing system for solving artificial intelligence problems which contains an SM-4 control computer and a specialized grayscale colour terminal. The rest of contributions deals with the segmentation of object in 2D-holes, with texture analysis, the computation of the weak visibility polygon and with the acquisition and representation of data for 3D vision systems.

Section 4 "Robotics" includes nineteen papers thematically covering a considerable part of the problems connected with intelligent robots and robotic sites. Most papers are focussed upon solving multicomputer control systems and their sensoric portions, robotic programming languages, software systems of manufacturing shops, the automatic generation of assembly sequences from the viewpoint of carrying out the assembly with an intelligent robot. Most of the papers center around the solution of these problems from the viewpoint of artificial intelligence and adaptive control. This concerns mainly robot operation planning in dynamic scenes, that is the planning of collision-free trajectories and object grasping for robots.

In Section 5" Specialized Computer Systems for Artificial Intelligence and Robotics" there are eight contributions. They present efficient methods of the structural solution of complex tasks on semantic networks and graphs based on a concept of active data networks that may serve as a theoretical model for the construction of parallel computers. Dynamic correctness of control devices functions realization, systolic arrays dedicated to some typical parallel problems aimed at VLSI realisation are also dealt with. An additional area are parallel algorithms with an assessment of the efficiency of their implementation. In contributions dealing with the architecture of parallel computers the design is presented of a dedicated numerical coprocessor and an associative SIMD-type parallel computer is described designed for the fast computation of parallel algorithms.

Special thanks go to all members of the International Programme Committee and to the referees who have read and evaluated the manuscripts. The organizer's thanks are also due to the North Holland Publishing Co. for the publication of this volume.

Ivan Plander
editor

The views, opinions and findings contained in these PROCEEDINGS are those of the authors and should not be construed as an official position, policy or decision of the sponsoring organizations.

NATIONAL ORGANIZING COMMITTEE

Chairman: I. Plander
Members:
- J. Chudík
- R. Fiby
- N. Frištacký
- F. Gliviak
- J. Gruska
- P. Hatala
- J. Mikloško
- Ľ. Molnár
- M. Postulková
- K. Richter
- F. Sloboda

INTERNATIONAL PROGRAM COMMITTEE

Chairman: G.S. Pospelov, Moscow, USSR
Members:
- W. Bibel, Munich, FRG
- L. Bolc, Warsaw, Poland
- H. Coelho, Lisboa, Portugal
- M. Draganescu, Bucharest, Romania
- G. Guida, Milano and Udine, Italy
- W. Händler, Erlangen, FRG
- B.H. Khang, Hanoi, Vietnam
- Y. Kodratoff, Orsay, France
- T. Kohonen, Helsinki, Finland
- Z. Kotek, Prague, Czechoslovakia
- V.P. Masnikosa, Belgrade, Yugoslavia
- J. Mikloško, Bratislava, Czechoslovakia
- A.S. Narinyani, Novosibirsk, USSR
- D.E. Okhotsimsky, Moscow, USSR
- D. Parkinson, London, UK
- V.L. Perchuk, Vladivostok, USSR
- I. Plander, Bratislava, Czechoslovakia
- V.M. Ponomaryov, Leningrad, USSR
- E.P. Popov, Moscow, USSR
- D.A. Pospelov, Moscow, USSR
- V.I. Rybak, Kiev, USSR
- V. Sgurev, Sofia, Bulgaria
- G. Stanke, Berlin, GDR
- E.H. Tyugu, Tallin, USSR
- T. Vámos, Budapest, Hungary

TABLE OF CONTENTS

Artificial intelligence and office automation (Invited)
    L. Aiello, D. Nardi   1

On first-order reasoning about knowledge and belief (Invited)
    W. Bibel   9

Deductive question answering system Dialog (Invited)
    L. Bolc, K. Kochut, P. Rychlik, T. Strzalkowski   17

Information, heuristics, creation (Invited)
    M. Draganescu   25

Concept learning (Invited)
    Y. Kodratoff, J.G. Ganascia, B. Clavieras, G. Tecuci   31

Self-organizing feature maps and abstractions
    T. Kohonen (Invited)   39

A contribution towards forming relations between the linking space and executive level of robotic systems
    Vukašin P. Masnikosa   47

Automatic multioperation assembly and application of visual control (Invited)
    D.E. Okhotsimsky, S.S. Kamynin, E.I. Kugushev   53

The role of artificial intelligence for scientific and engineering progress (Invited)
    G.S. Pospelov   61

NUT - an object oriented language (Invited)
    Enn H. Tyugu   69

Adaptive natural language generation
    G. Adorni, M. Di Manzo, F. Giunchiglia   77

An approach to intelligent action execution
    G. Airenti, M. Colombetti   81

Inference processes in everyday reasoning
    Bruno G. Bara, Antonella G. Carassa, Giuliano C. Geminiani   87

The multiprocessor control system of a mobile robot with elements of artificial intelligence
    N.E. Bogomolov, Yu. M.Lazutin, V.S. Yaroshevsky   91

A second generation real-time industrial vision system
    Alan H. Bond, Roger S. Brown, Chris R. Rowbury   97

The system performance of the SM 54/30 vision
system
    V.Britanak, M.Kuchta, F. Sloboda,I.Treba-
    ticky   101

A quaternion representation of rotation and
robot motion synthesis
    F. Čapkovič   105

A new approach to texture
    D. Chetverikov   109

Logic programming paradigm at work:the case of
a civil engineering environment
    H. Coelho   113

Interpretation of natural language queries via
pattern-action rules
    R. Cudazzo, L. Lesmo, C. Randi   119

Knowledge representation and deduction in
extended Priz
    Peep V. Eomois   123

Picture segmentation and feature extraction for
automatic surface inspection
    A. Friedrich, K. Fritzsch, W. Uebel   129

3-D object recognition with location constraints
    P. Florath   135

Inferential reasoning in natural language
processing
    D. Fum   139

Inference processes:a mean to shape knowledge
control
    Cristian A. Giumale   143

Decision planning systems
    V.P. Gladun   147

A manufacturing cell management systems CEMAS
    F. Gliviak, J. Kubiš, A. Mičovský,
    E. Karabinošová   153

Application of attributed grammar and algorithmic
sensitivity model for knowledge representation and
estimation
    V.I. Gorodetzki, V.V. Drozhzhin, R.M.Yusupov   157

Combining functions in consulting systems and
dependence of premisses (a remark)
    P. Hájek   163

Linguistically motivated representation of
knowledge as a basis for inference procedures
    E. Hajičová, M. Hnátková   167

Natural language access to the data base of the
AIDOS/VS information retrieval system
    H. Helbig   171

Proving/testing module correctness
    J. Hořejš   175

Hierarchical - regressive generating and executing
robot's plans
    P. Hrivík   179

A R C - a modular approach to advanced robot
programming and control
    J. Huebener   185

A generalized approach to inductive inference
    Klaus P. Jantke   189

Off-line planning of collision-free trajectories
and object grasping for manipulation robots
    W. Jentsch   193

Automatic generation of assembly sequences
    W. Jentsch, F. Kaden   197

The ATNL-based macroprocessor - a software tool
of communication modules implementation
    Vladimir F. Khoroshevsky   201

On the synthesis of image matching algorithms
    Hoang Kiem, G. Podhájecký   207

Off-line programming for robot painters
    A. Klein   211

Problem-oriented representations for development
of knowledge base for expert systems
    Alexander S. Kleshchev   215

German language questioning of relational
databases
    D. Koch   221

Control of four-legged running-type robot
    V.V. Lapshin   225

Robots - skill and sensitive behaviour
    Dan Mandutianu, Serban Voinea   229

ROUND-S: an experiment with knowledge driven
semantics in natural language understanding
    S. Mandutianu   233

A reasonable compromise between straightforward
and feedback laws in a combined system for robots
control
    Ognian B. Manolov, Nedko S. Shivarov   237

On the intellectual program packages
    V.M. Matrosov, S.N. Vassiljev, O.G. Divakov,
    G.A. Oparin   241

Data optimization in natural language based systems
    W. Menzel   247

A formal approach to verb semantics
    G. Mihailova, G. Gargov   251

SM-4-"OMEGA" interactive image processing system in solving artificial intelligence problems
    E.G. Mikhaltsov, V.P. Pjatkin   255

Universal systolic array processors for fast matrix operations
    J. Mikloško, B. Zaťko   259

Hierarchical parallel algorithms
    N.N. Mirenkov   265

Results of implementation of the first version of medical expert system "Consultant"
    Olga S. Molokova, Mary Ju. Chernyakovskaja   269

Advanced control system for industrial robots
    E. Oprea, D. Nedelea, B. Udrea, A. Moanga   273

Natural language interface to an expert system
    J. Panevová   277

Software system of robotized manufacturing shop
    V.A. Pavlov   281

A domain independent framework for problem solving
    B. Petkoff   285

Functional approach to knowledge representation
    J. Pokorný, P. Materna   289

Dynamic correctness of control devices functions realization
    V.M. Ponomarev, A.N. Domaratsky, V.V. Nikiforov   293

CODEX: A computer-based diagnostic expert system
    M. Popper and F. Gyárfáš   297

A limited vocabulary speech recognition system
    J. Psutka   301

"LAOCON" control systems of robots
    István G. Rákóczy, László Frittmann, Erika Kovács   305

A parallel computer system SIMD
    K. Richter   309

Solving tasks on semantic networks and graphs by active distributed structures
    Peter S. Sapaty   315

Highly parallel algorithms and the architecture of
a computer system for solving large matrix problems
    S.G. Sedukhin 319

Representation and generalization of
transformationsbetween relational structures
    J. Selbig 325

Artificial intelligence and semantics
    P. Sgall 329

Decision-making in conditions of fuzzy
uncertainties and opposing factors, using human
specifics
    D.I. Shapiro 333

Applications of a microcomputer-based robot
vision system
    A. Siegler, M. Bathor 337

Knowledge presentation in the form of role
structures
    I. Sildmäe, R. Käi 341

From sentences to attribute networks
    Michael W. Sobolewski, Zenon Kulpa 345

A method of the execution of fuzzy programs
    Zenon A. Sosnowski 349

A magnetic sensing microsystem for assembling
robots
    Aurelian M. Stanescu, Mihai M. Atodiroaiei 353

Acquisition of data for 3-D vision systems
    G. Stanke, P. Florath 359

Improving the structure of logic programs
    P. Štěpánek, O. Štěpánková 363

A framework for constructing knowledge-based
planning systems
    Gheorghe Tecuci 369

Area-time complexity for VLSI
    Clark D. Thompson 373

A fast SVD image restoration on an associative parallel
computer
    M. Vajteršic 383

Dedicated numerical coprocessor for matrix handling
throughput enhancement
    K. Vlček 389

The computation of the weak visibility polygon
    Günter Werner 393

A plan generating system of an intellectual robot
using a frame representation of the information
    Nely P. Zlatareva   399

A new approach to the design of expert system
architectures (Invited)*
    G. Guida, C. Tasso   405

---

* This paper was submitted at too late a date to be included in its correct session position.

ARTIFICIAL INTELLIGENCE AND OFFICE AUTOMATION

Luigia Aiello and Daniele Nardi[°]

Dipartimento di Informatica e Sistemistica
Università di Roma "La Sapienza"
Roma, Italy

The purpose of the present paper is to illustrate the relationships between Artificial Intelligence (AI) and Office Automation (OA). In particular we show how techniques developed in AI find a natural application in OA. In fact, a system for a real OA must embody a certain degree of "intelligence" about the office, that is to say the Office Information System (OIS) should be an Expert System (ES) as well. After a brief introduction to ES, the most relevant problems of OA are sketched and some of the possible applications of AI within OA are examined. Particular attention is paid to the problem of office modeling and to the problems arising in the construction of an OIS-ES.

1. ARTIFICIAL INTELLIGENCE AND EXPERT SYSTEMS

Artificial Intelligence is a challenging field. Even though it is often criticized and there is no general consensus even on its objectives and on its achievements, years of research and experimentations have yielded to extremely meaningful results, both in terms of methodologies and techniques and in terms of practical results. Here we refer in particular to the so-called Expert Systems: some of them perform in an "intelligent" way, their responses being comparable to those of a human expert in the domain of application of the system itself.

Various definitions of Expert System can be found in the literature, here we consider two of them:

- Buchanan in /5/ defines ES a reasoning program that can be distinguished by other AI programs in its utility, performance and transparency.

- Nau in /8/ defines ES a problem-solving program whose performance compares with that of a human expert in a specialized problem domain. He points out that the main difference between application programs and ES is in that in most ES the model of problem-solving in the ap-

---

[°] The work of Daniele Nardi is supported by TECSIEL

plication domain is explicitly wiewed as a separate entity named "knowledge base", rather than being implicitly embedded into the coding of the program. In addition, the knowledge base is manipulated by a separate and clearly identifiable control strategy.

The definition proposed by Buchanan is an attempt to characterize an ES in terms of its behaviour, rather than of its internal organization, and it doesn't distinguish clearly between a sophisticated application program and an ES.

Conversely, the characterization proposed by Nau tends to identify ES with Knowledge Based Systems (KBS), hence binding the definition of ES to the software architecture of most of the present ones.

Up to some years ago the names ES and KBS were used in very restricted environments. More recently they have become very common: this is mostly due to the glamour of some very meaningful practical results achieved by some ES in fields considered domain of human high specialization and expertise. Among them we mention various branches of medicine, chemistry, geology, circuit design, etc..

Here we sketch the structure of an ES organized around a knowledge base. As it is shown in Fig. 1, knowledge is logically organized as a data base divided into two parts: facts and rules. By facts we mean assertions that are true in the domain of application of the ES itself. Rules embody the knowledge that allows the automatic deduction of new facts.

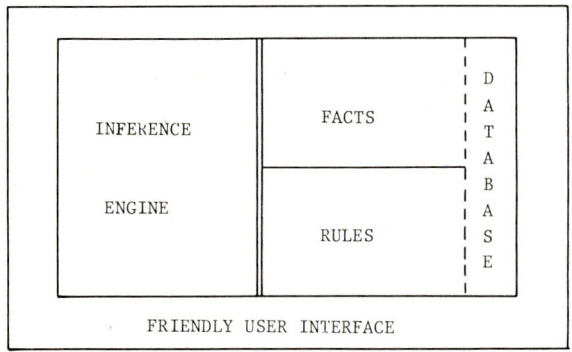

Figure 1
Architecture of a Knowledge Based System

Besides the knowledge base, that has a passive role, we have a deductive apparatus, i.e. an inference engine that uses facts and rules to draw conclusions in the object domain.

A detailed analysis of the various formalisms and methods used both for knowledge representation and for the deduction techniques is out of the scope of the present paper. The interested reader can find more details in /5,8,11/ and in a vast literature.

2. OFFICE AUTOMATION

Office Automation is a key problem in the development of our society, since it involves a great amount of workers and it seems deemed to bring a considerable evolution in the organization and in the quality of office work.

It is not possible to give a commonly accepted definition of OA, in fact the field attracts the attention of a very heterogeneous crowd of researchers and producers /3,6,10,12/. However, a vast activity in this area has led to what we may call a first generation OA systems. These systems are being successfully marketed because they solve, often in a brilliant way, some of the typical office problems, allowing certain office functions to be performed in a much more efficient and precise way than it could be done before. Here we refer to the possibility of better and quicker communication provided by electronic mail systems, to the effectiveness of automatic document production, to the agenda programs, etc.. However, the "software package" for OA often consists in a set of non-integrated tools and, moreover, enters into the office on a dedicated hardware not integrated with the pre-existing EDP systems. This of course creates many problems and doesn't satisfy the need for automation.

It has been claimed /3,6/ that a system, in order to candidate for a real office automation must have some fundamental features: among them we point out the integration of hardware and software tools, the uniformity of the interface and its friendlyness.

The integration of tools is fundamental because it allows to move with continuity from an action to another one and to make a tool visible and usable from within another one, without creating opaque contexts of activity. As an example, think about the need of consulting various databases from within the document preparation system, in order to insert data into a document.

As far as the human interface is concerned, its ease of use, ease of learning and an ergonomic design are essential in order for the user to be at ease in the dialogue with the system.

The above requirements are very important, but they are minimal in the sense that they are not sufficient to guarantee the effectiveness of the OA system. To this end two factors are determinant: from the one side the set of tools has to be rich and provide good features to help the user in specific tasks, on the other side the system must include among its tools one that allows to analyze, control and evaluate the office itself and to plan its organization and evolution. In fact, the office structure is a complex and dynamic reality, because of delegations, replacement of personnel during their absence or when their roles have been changed, reorganizations due to new regulations or new production requirements. It is clear that the system must be flexible and reconfigurable on the basis of the evolution of the office structure and it must keep track of these reconfigurations.

The core of a system that embodies tools for the description, analysis and modification of the state and the structure of the office organization must be a model that provides a compact and uniform description of the office itself. This model should provide also a basis for the integration of the various tools specific for the various office activities. Recently the problem of office modeling has been tackled by various authors. A description of the research in this area may be found in /4/: in the sequel we refer to a model we have proposed in /2/.

3. ARTFICIAL INTELLIGENCE AND OFFICE AUTOMATION

In this section we point out some relationships between AI and OA. In particular, we attempt to individuate those parts of the integrated OA systems where more intelligence should be embedded.

3.1. Man-Machine Interface

The friendlyness of the interface that the system offers to the user is always crucial, in particular in the office environment where users are usually non-expert and often, mostly at the managerial level, not inclined to an interaction via the traditional keyboard.

As already observed, essential features of the interface are its uniformity and its ease of use and learning. Besides that, in man-machine interaction, the richness and the quality of I/O media are determinant. Traditional character displays are often replaced by high-resolution displays. They offer, among other things, the possibility of graphic display and of animation, which can be very useful in offices. Modern printers allow for the printing quality usually only achieved in typographies.

As far as input is concerned, along with a keyboard the system can provide a pointing device as a mouse or a joystick, which makes the interaction with the display more immediate, while the presence of an optical reader improves both the speed and the quality of data entry.

In the future, an increasingly important role will be played by vocal I/O which, in the office environment, is very useful. The development of sophisticated I/O media has been and still is an area of research in many AI laboratories.

However, the most significant contribution of AI to man-machine interaction has not to be looked for in the technology of I/O media, but in the possibility of embedding intelligence into the system in order to enable it to accept not highly formalized input, possibly in natural language.

The need for an intelligent interaction is a must in the case of ES: the expertise shown by the system on a problem domain has to be completed by intelligence in the understanding of assertions and queries about the domain itself.

3.2. Intelligent Tools

Designers and producers have paid much attention to devise quality tools to automate specific office activities, such as document preparation systems, mail systems, and so on. Nevertheless, they cannot yet be considered intelligent tools. As an example, a document preparation system may be more or less sophisticated according to the level of abstraction of its commands and according to the level of typographical and structural knowledge it embodies about the type of documents. Some of them provide also spelling correctors and tools for quantitative analyses of the texts. An intelligent document preparation system, however, can "understand" the contents of a document hence being able to correct errors in a much more effective way (by locating them through a synctactic+semantic analysis of the text) and guide the user in adopting a style appropriate to the type of document he is preparing.

Analogously, an electronic mail system, instead of classifying and retrieving mails on the basis of the sender, date or key-words (i.e. by string matching), might be able to classify/retrieve documents on the basis of their contents. The same considerations hold for any data base of non structured data, i.e. of textual data.

Another tool that may show some intelligence is the data base management system. To provide this tool with a deductive power means to enhance its possibilities from many viewpoints. As an example, if deduction rules are embedded into the system, the number of facts explicitly recorded may be minimized, since new facts can be derived from them, when needed. The embedding of derivation rules into a data base positively influences both the design and the use of the data base itself. In fact, the rules constitute a big help in the understanding of the data base and, through deductions, both its consistency and its organization can be checked. Even on this subject the interested reader may find more in the literature, in particular /7/.

Besides the above mentioned intelligent tools, specific tools may be tailored on the specific office activities. Hence ES can be devised for various application domains, which deal with the particular activity supported by the office.

4. THE OFFICE INFORMATION SYSTEM - EXPERT SYSTEM

As observed in section 2, the organization and the structure of the office are crucial aspects the OA system has to deal with. Hence a knowledge representation formalism is needed to describe the office structure and organization, i.e. to build a model of the office.

An office model must guarantee:

- a compact and minimal description of the office;

- the integration of tools and an uniform interface;

- a description on whose basis the office can be measured, hence its structural organization can be dinamically planned and controlled.

Several office models have been proposed, but they are often incomplete and cover only partial aspects of the office reality. We again refer to /4/ for a classification of the various office models presented in the literature.

The model we propose in /2/ is based on the notion of agent, hence an office is described in terms of a collection of agents. An agent is defined as a pair: its structural description and a set of functionalities. The structural description is composed by an identification part, a domain of action, a set of relations between the agent and other agents in the office, and a working area reserved to the agent. The set of functionalities consists of some basic ones that allow the agent both to operate and to analyze the model itself, and some specific ones.

The agent, basic element of our model, embodies all the fundamental characteristics of an office. In fact, besides the description of functionalities, it contains information about the access to resources, and the structure of communication and control within the office. Offices of various sizes and with different organizations can be described in terms of agents: a small office being possibly described through a single agent, a large one through several agents. The interactions and the hierarchy links among these agents are specified in their definition. This entails a great uniformity in the description of an office. In fact, the formalism allows to describe it (and the evolution of its structure) in terms of elementary components that are all of the same type. The detalis of the formalism can be found in /2/. Here we show how our model may constitute the basis for the Office Expert System.

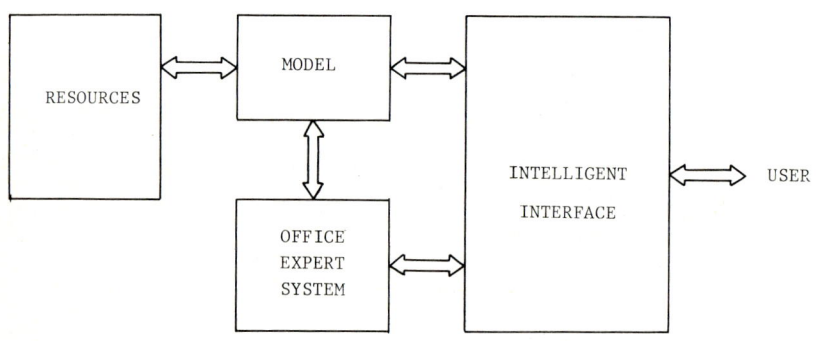

Figure 2
Architecture of the OIS-ES

The core of the system shown in Fig. 2 consists of the model, through which the user has access to the resources, among them there are both hardware and software tools. The Office Expert System incorporates the deductive apparatus which can infer facts about the office (on the basis of the information embedded into the model) and on the status of the resources. The characteristics of the intelligent interface have already been sketched in section 3. We only notice that it has to be independent of both the I/O media and of the various components of the software environment.

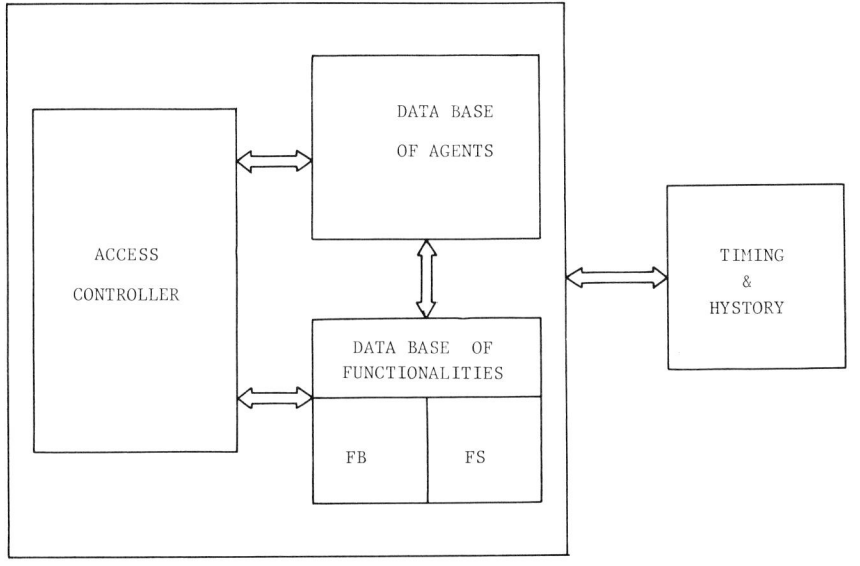

Figure 3
Architecture of the office model

Figure 3 shows in more details the structure of the model. In it we distinguish a data base of agents DBA, that contains the description of all the agents present in the office, and a data base of functionalities DBF, that contains all the functionalities present in the office, each agent being assigned some of them. DBF is divided into two parts: FB, the basic functionalities, and FS, the functionalities that are specific of the given office. The double arrow connecting DBA to DBF indicates that, on the one side the agents find in DBF the functionalities associated with their descriptors, on the other one, that the basic functionalities (FB) "read and write" in DBA, that is to say they operate on the data base of agents (hence on the model). The access controller "reads" in DBA and checks the access rights, by using the constraints described in it, namely it incorporates the protection mechanism. The block "timing and history", that appears in Fig. 3, provides both a timing facility to allow for the triggering of actions subject to temporal constraints and a tool for recording meaningful facts, among them the updates of the model. This block has been represented outside the core of the model. In fact, in a sense, it is not part of the model itself: nevertheless its presence is needed to keep track of the events and of the temporal evolution of the office structure.

The structure of the Office Expert System should be that of a Knowledge Based System (Fig. 1). All the knowledge about the office contained in the model (Fig. 3), constitutes an essential part of the knowledge base of facts. Along with it, a base of rules has to be devised, that allow the system to draw conclusions about the office. In this way the system may suggest actions to the user, on the basis of the conclusions it has reached. In some cases, decisions can be made automatically by the system.

5. CONCLUSIONS

The paper contains some indications on possible applications of AI into OA. In particular we have pointed out the importance of an office model, both for the integration of (possibly intelligent) tools, and for the construction of an intelligent interface, and for a description of the office on whose basis the Office Expert System can operate. Such an ES has as its domain of expertise the structure and the organization of the office, on which it is able to draw conclusions and make modifications and updatings.

BIBLIOGRAPHY

/1/ Aiello L. and Nardi D., Intelligent Man-Machine Interfaces, in: Bolognani M., Ferrari G. and Goguen J. (eds.), Theory and Practice of Software Technology (North-Holland, 1983) 1-20.

/2/ Aiello L., Nardi D. and Panti M., Structural Office Modeling: a first step towards the Office Expert System, to be presented at the Second ACM Conf. on Office Information Systems (Toronto, Canada, June, 25-27, 1984).

/3/ Attardi G., Office Information Systems Design and Implementation, Report Cnet 47 (December 1981).

/4/ Bracchi G. and Pernici B., Design Requirements of Office Systtems, in: Proc. of the Fourth Int. Conf. on Information Systems (Houston, Texas, December 1983).

/5/ Buchanan B.G., New Research on Expert Systems, in: Machine Intelligence 10 (Ellis Horwood, 1982) 269-299.

/6/ Ellis C.A. and Nutt G., Office Information Systems and Computer Science, ACM Computing Surveys 12, 1 (1980) 27-60.

/7/ Gallaire H. and Minker J. (eds.), Logic and Data Bases (Plenum Press, 1978).

/8/ Nau D.S., Expert Computer Systems, IEEE Computer 2 (1983) 63-82.

/9/ Newman W., Office Models and Office System Design, in: Naffah N. (ed.), Integrated Office System - Burotics (North-Holland, 1980) 3-10.

/10/ Proceedings of the ACM Conference on Office Information Systems (Philadelphia, June 1982), in: SIGOA NEWSLETTERS vol. 3, n. 1-2.

/11/ Stefik M. and others, The organization of Expert Systems, a Tutorial, Artificial Intelligence 18, (1982) 135-173.

/12/ IEEE Transactions on Communications, COM-30 (1982).

ON FIRST-ORDER REASONING ABOUT KNOWLEDGE AND BELIEF

W. Bibel

Institut f. Informatik
Technische Universitaet
Muenchen, FR Germany

In this paper a new first-order model for reasoning about knowledge and belief is proposed. It is based on the following two natural assumptions. (i) Different agents act in separate worlds (as humans in fact seem to do) so that, in a very strict sense, they do not share any knowledge at all; (ii) the two aspects of beliefs, namely the factual aspect of **what** is believed and the procedural aspect of **how** to use beliefs, are strictly separated. These assumptions allow a simple classical first-order treatment, and thus avoid the complications inherent in the possible-worlds model as well as the intuitively complicated distinctions between objects and the concepts of them.

INTRODUCTION

In various applications advanced reasoning systems need to take into account the knowledge and beliefs of several agents. Essentially two different ways have been proposed to formalize such a general situation.

One is based on Hintikka's adaption [Hin] of Kripke's possible-worlds model for modal logics; e.g. [Kon], [Moo], [Nil] follow that route. Humans quite effectively reason about other humans' knowledge and belief states; it appears to be unlikely that they do so with anything like a possible-worlds model in mind. This suggests that there might be a simpler and more "natural" solution to this problem.

With such a motivation in mind McCarthy proposed a Fregean first-order formalization in [McC] which initiated a number of further investigations, e.g. [Bar], [Cre], [Mai]. This approach, however, requires the introduction of an (infinite) hierarchy of orders of concepts, wherein a clear distinction has to be made between an object and its concept; e.g. the person Mary and the concept of Mary are to be distinguished in this way. It is felt that such a distinction is artificially sophisticated and unnatural as well. Hence there remained the motivation to keep looking for a simpler or more intuitive solution.

In this paper we propose a classical first-order formalism dealing with this situation in a conceptually rather simple way. The simplicity is a consequence of an apparently more appropriate structure of the model capturing this type of situation. This structure grew out of the analysis of the problem of knowledge representation given in [Bi3]. In fact, the results of the present paper provide further evidence supporting the position taken in [Bi3], in particular the reservedness against "exotic logics". The essential features of this model, distinguishing our approach from others such as those mentioned above, are the following two.

First, we take the view that each agent lives in its own separate world. For instance, consider the situation that two agents a and b refer to the person

Mary. What they in fact have to refer to are their own inner representations of Mary (cf. section 2 in [Bi3]) which is different for each agent, say to constant $mary^a$ for agent a and to $mary^b$ for agent b. As with Mary, any constant, function, or predicate requires a distinct denotation in a and in b which will be achieved by the respective indices a and b the way just demonstrated. Now, if a wants to refer to some knowledge of b, say to $mary^b$, in his own world this again requires a new constant which we denote by $[mary^b]^a$, i.e. the constant $mary^b$ indexed by a. Note, that $mary^a$, $mary^b$, $[mary^b]^a$, all are syntactically different constants, although their mnemonic structure carries helpful information, e.g. the outermost index identifies the actual agent in question. This kind of indexing scheme may be iterated for arbitrary many agents. This way, an agent's reasoning about other agents' states of knowledge simplifies to classical first-order reasoning in its own world.

Second, the factual and procedural aspects of beliefs are treated separately, very much in analogy with logic programming where the descriptive or logic part is independent from the control part (cf. section V.2 in [Bi1]). For instance, if agent a believes that Mary is married then the literal $MARRIED^a(mary^a)$ is part of a's knowledge base; a's reasoning and acting will rely on this fact. Whenever possible, however, agent a would better avoid using this literal in a chain of reasoning because of the uncertainty that goes with beliefs. But avoiding the literal's usage is a matter of controlling the reasoning, not a matter of the facts laid down in the knowledge base. Since it is well known how to amalgamate language (describing the knowledge) and meta-language (describing the control) within a first-order setting (e.g. see [BoK] or [Wey]), the indexing scheme described before may be extended to such an amalgamated language. This way we obtain a pure first-order formalism for reasoning on other agents' knowledge and beliefs.

Apparently, the main task in the introduction of this formalism lies in the specification of the index scheme which is the subject of section 2. The rest relies on standard first-order techniques which may be found in various textbooks such as [Bi1]. Section 3 outlines the respective techniques handling the meta-language and procedural aspects in beliefs.

It seems to be amazing that such a simple approach has not been proposed earlier. Perhaps it is hard for humans to overcome the illusion, what we see, hear, know **were** the outside reality rather than some individual inner representation thereof. This shows how important it is to have an adequate model of our own world for which reason we begin in the next section with an outline of the author's model of a knowledge-based system.

1. A STRUCTURAL MODEL FOR KNOWLEDGE-BASED SYSTEMS

A fundamental principle of science is its division into disciplines. Any phenomenon may therefore be studied from a variety of aspects. For instance, we may analyse a natural tree exclusively under physical aspects or focus on its chemistry or treat it as a biological organism. This principle evidently is a very fruitful one (although of course only a subsequent interdisciplinary synopsis will provide us with a full account of the phenomenon under consideration).

Knowledge-based systems - KBSs - are complex phenomena as well; hence it is very likely that the same principle would further our understanding of their nature. In this section we will identify several of the "disciplines" which bear some relevance on KBSs; they are shown in figure 1. We will speak of a **layer** when considering the system under the aspects of one of these "disciplines".

In the discussion we will use the notions "knowledge", "representation", "logic" in the sense analysed in [Bi3]; familiarity with that paper might therefore be of some help.

The basic layer of any KBS consists of the **factual knowledge** (see figure 1 for the following discussion). Its entries are statements like "Mary is married" or "any married woman has a husband" or Goedel's theorems or the definition of entropy or a set of statements outlining the history of Bavaria, and so forth. Note that we included the fact about married women in this list which in the (from our point of view misleading) expert systems terminology would have been called a "rule"; we will see shortly that rules controlling the reasoning process definitely should be identified in a different layer. At the present layer we include factual knowledge also without taking notice of the degree of certainty about the truth; for instance, at

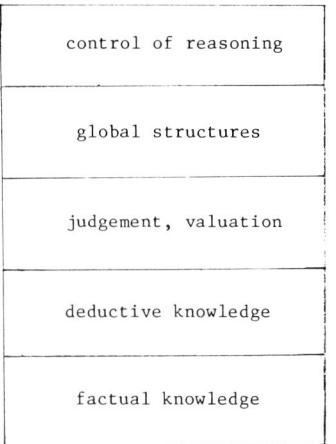

Figure 1. Several layers of a KBS

this layer there is no distinction between "I know that Mary is married" or "I believe that mary is married", both represented as "Mary is married", and the remaining information in these sentences taken care of at a different layer. The representation itself is assumed to be a logic representation in the sense of [Bi3].

The layer consisting of **deductive knowledge** determines the space of possible deductions. It consists of (a net of) potential connections relating literals in the statements of the factual knowledge, as shown in the following example.

MARRIED(mary) , WOMAN(x) & MARRIED(x) -> HUSBAND(h(x),x)

Here is not the place to go into any details of the theoretical background provided by the **connection method** in automated deduction for which the reader is referred to [Bi1] or [Bi2]. We only mention a few features of relevance for the present context.
(i) It is possible and feasible to determine all potential connections of the factual knowledge in advance (but in large knowledge bases this information might also be gathered dynamically).
(ii) Deductions consist simply in an identification of a subset of all connections (with potentially multiple occurrences) fulfilling certain criteria.
(iii) The factual knowledge together with the deductive knowledge provides a representation of all knowledge deducible from the factual knowledge with the connections given in the deductive knowledge (e.g. without the literal WOMAN(x) the previous two statements with the depicted connection also represents the statement HUSBAND(h(mary),mary)).

In the third layer information of **judgement, valuation**, degree of importance (of statements, literals, connections) or belief is gathered. The way of handling beliefs is discussed in some more detail in section 3. This is the layer also providing information for default or autoepistemic reasoning and handling principles like circumscription (see section 6 in [Bi3]).

Global structures, identified on the basis of the information provided by the previous two layers, are stored in the forth layer. These consist of macro-connections abbreviating deductive nets of connections, of clusters of connected statements (or frames), of information about the presense or absense of contradictions in (parts of) the factual knowledge, and the like (see section 5 in [Bi3]).

On top of all this information we find the layer responsible for the **control of the reasoning** process which operates on the set of connections in a way compatible with or suggested by the information in the previous two layers.

Any layer except the basic one contains information talking about the information (i.e. the statements) in previous layers. The meta-language required for their formalization may be assumed to be the same as the language used for the basic layer which will be illustrated in section 3.

We claim that these five layers are relevant for any intelligent KBS. On the other side our model is certainly not exhaustive; further layers or components might be of importance (supervisor, interface, etc.). But these five are sufficient for a coherent view of our topic.

Under this topic we assume that several agents are involved. Each of them is now assumed to be structured the way captured in figure 1.

2. KNOWLEDGE IN SEVERAL AGENTS

In the present section we are going to present the main technical contribution of this note, namely a formalism for reasoning about knowledge in various agents. For simplicity and clarity we restrict the discussion here to factual knowledge in the basic layer only (in the sense of the previous section).

It was already pointed out briefly in the introduction that we adopt the view outlined in more detail in [Bi3] that the reasoning of any agent in fact deals with a representation of reality rather than with reality itself. For each agent this representation is absolutely private and not directly addressable by other agents. In this sense, if agent **a** has knowledge about a person Mary, it does not refer directly to Mary in reality but rather to a symbolic object, say **mary**^{a}, within **a**'s world or formalism. The same applies to agent **b** (different from **a**), and there is no reason for **b**'s symbolic object referring to Mary being identical with **mary**^{a}; however, in order to indicate the joint referential real world object Mary, we keep the constant and only change the index for the distinction, hence **mary**^{b}. From a syntactic point of view of the first-order language we are about to develop, **mary**^{a} and **mary**^{b} are to be regarded as distinct symbols with nothing in common; however, we of course can take advantage of the inner syntactic structure of such an indexed constant as will be seen later.

What we pointed out for the case of a constant, apparently applies to functions and predicates in the same way under our view. In fact, it even applies to any expression in a way to be explained shortly. How realistic this view actually is might be experienced in such cases like when people disagree whether a certain colour should be called green or blue. Hence there is good reason to make a clear distinction between GREEN^a (a predicate in **a**'s world) and GREEN^b (a predicate in **b**'s world).

From the viewpoint of agent **a**, agent **b** is part of the real world; the same applies to **b**'s knowledge. Hence, as with Mary, agent **a** has to use its private symbols for the representation of such knowledge. For agent **a** the person Mary and **b**'s symbolic representation **mary**^{b} obviously cannot be the same in its own representation. Hence, using the same denotational method as before, **mary**^{b} will be indexed by a for this purpose. Using brackets in this case of multiple indexing we obtain $[mary^b]^a$, a constant in a's world distinct from $mary^a$. Thus our formalism is based on the following first-order language.

We take alphabets for basic n-ary function and predicate symbols, $n \geq 0$, and for variables, as usual (e.g. see [Bil]); in addition we assume an alphabet for denoting agents. n-ary function symbols are then defined inductively:
they include the basic ones; further,
if f denotes an n-ary function symbol and a is taken from the agents' alphabet then $[f]^a$ is also an n-ary function symbol.
The same applies to predicate symbols. For the following let a , b denote any two distinct agents.
Terms in a's world are defined inductively as follows:
they include the constants indexed by a and the variables; further
they include the terms of the form $[f]^a t1...tn$ where f is an n-ary function symbol and the ti are terms in a's world, i=1,...,n.
Atomic formulas in a's world are expressions of the form $[P]^a t1...tn$ where P is an n-ary predicate symbol and the ti are terms in a's world, i=1,...,n.
Formulas in a's world are defined inductively as follows:
they include the atomic formulas in a's world and
the formulas of the form $[F]^a$ where F is a formula in b's world;
further if $[F]^a$, $[G]^a$ are formulas in a's world then the same holds for $[-F]^a$, $[F \& G]^a$, $[F \vee G]^a$, $[F \rightarrow G]^a$, $[\forall x F]^a$, $[\exists x F]^a$.

In order to make the notation somewhat more comfortable we adopt the following conventions. The brackets around basic symbols will always be deleted. In a formula $[F]^a$ the outermost index of any symbol will not be written explicitly if it is identical with a . For instance, $[MARRIED(mary) \& \exists x \; HUSBAND(x,mary)]^a$ abbreviates $[MARRIED^a(mary^a) \& \exists x \; HUSBAND^a(x,mary^a)]^a$.

From a formal point of view this is a first-order language as usual, except for the indexed brackets around formula parts; hence to some extent it may be subject of any classical reasoning system in existence in a way to be discussed shortly. Our claim is that this language has enough representational power to cover any of the examples in the literature which are concerned with reasoning about the knowledge of several agents. We will illustrate this claim with a couple of examples.

Obviously it holds that $[[F]^b \vee [G]^b]^a$ and $[[F \vee G]^b]^a$ mean different things as it in fact should be; hence a default discussed in section 2 of [Moo] certainly does not apply here. Also note the following subtle distinction. $[[GREEN^b]^a[object^b]^a]^a$ is intended to express that a knows that the object is green where both the predicate GREEN and the term object are understood in a's representation of their representation in b . In contrast, $[[GREEN^b object^b]^b]^a$ means that a knows about b's knowledge, namely that the object is green considered in b's world.

McCarthy in [McC] begins with the simple example of Pat knowing Mike's phone number which is incidentally the same as Mary's phone number, although Pat does not necessarily know this. It exposes one of the alleged difficulties of reasoning about knowledge, namely the problem of inhibiting substitution of equal terms for equal terms in referentially opaque contexts.

Apparently, the example is to be treated from the viewpoint of an agent, the narrator, different from pat , say a . Mike's phone number in Pat's view would be represented as phone#^{pat}(mike^{pat}) in our formalism which is a term in pat's world. The equality holding for the two phone numbers, phone#^{a}(mike^a) =^{a} phone#^{a}(mary^a), however, is an equality among terms in a's world which, strictly speaking do not share even a single symbol with the previous term; thus a substitution is clearly not possible under any reasonable circumstances, in accordance with what we want to have.

What, however, if Pat does in fact know the equality of the two numbers? Obviously, in this case he would be able to use this fact in an inference, and a would have to take this into account in what he knows about Pat's knowledge. In order to achieve such a reasoning for a, we need the following inference rule

(r)   [[F1]^b,..., [Fn]^b, [F1,...,Fn |- F]^b |- [F]^b]^a

In words, if b knows Fi, i=1,...,n, and also knows a proof inferring F from F1,...,Fn then he knows F, obviously a valid rule.

Let us now formalise the problem just posed in the following way. [DIAL(phone#(mike))]^{pat} will be regarded as an instance of [F1]^b in (r), [phone#(mike)=phone#(mary)]^{pat} as an instance of [F2]^b, and [DIAL(phone#(mary))]^{pat} as an instance of [F]^b. As indicated in the previous section, any agent is supposed to have the deductive knowledge which enables it to eventually carrying out a proof of F1, F2 |- F in this particular instance. For example, with the connection method we would have the following connection proof (see section V.3 in [Bi] for equality connections).

DIAL(phone#(mike)) & phone#(mike)=phone#(mary) -> DIAL(phone#(mary))

Thus under the assumption that such a proof has been established by Pat, a would now be able to conclude [F]^b on the basis of (r), exactly what we wanted to have. Incidentally, if a is read John, we have the same example as one given in [Mai]. Note that this example involves an iterated propositional attitude. Hence our approach allows to combine the deductive power of a classical proof system with the performance characteristics (listed in III.A of [Mai]) of non-standard systems like those described in [Cre], [Mai], and others. Namely, via rule (r) any classical proof may be lifted to any higher conceptual level, which technically means simply a change in the indices.

Perhaps we should mention that, of course, our formalism can be made subject to restrictions like a **consistency axiom scheme** [F^a]^b -> F^a. Also, the formalism allows the transfer of knowledge from one agent to another by specifying appropriate conditions as axiom schemes such as [F^b]^a & TRUST^a(b) -> F^a for any formula F. It also allows the meta-reasoning of an agent a about its own knowledge, e.g. by introducing an agent ego^a, for any a. We also can take syntactic advantage of the inner structure of our symbols and use formulas like $\forall$a BLUE^a(sky^a). Possibly it would increase the flexibility to allow the indexing also for the variables which certainly could be done. Further, " a knows whether P " may be formalized as [F & (F = P v F = -P)]^a.

In summary, this simple approach appears to provide all the capabilities necessary for reasoning about the knowledge of several, say n, agents, degenerating to the usual first-order logic formalism in the special case n = 1.

3. BELIEFS

The main purpose of the present paper is the presentation of our approach to formalising reasoning about knowledge as given in the previous section. The model outlined in section 1 shows, however, that a general reasoning formalism has to deal not only with the basic layer of knowledge but also with a number of layers containing meta-knowledge. As we pointed out in the introduction formalizing meta-knowledge with first-order logic as meta-language and amalgamating language and meta-language as a joint formalism is a familiar technique. Thus if we treat this kind of joint formalism the way shown in section 2 we will achieve the desired generality.

This is not the place to give a full account of such a general approach. We only want to discuss briefly the way to handle beliefs as an example in this direction.

The difference between "Mike knows that Mary is married" and "Mike believes that Mary is married" becomes manifest in Mike's reasoning and actions only. In both cases the fact "Mary is married" is taken into account; but if it is just a belief then Mike will better not rely too much on this fact in his reasoning or actions whenever possible. Under this view
(i) the difference between knowing and believing is just a gradual one, the scale being
         know-that-not | don't-believe | don't-know | believe | know
(ii) knowing as well as believing amounts to extra-information on a given fact, the nature of which is that of meta-knowledge.

Because of the latter fact we naturally treat this meta-knowledge in a layer separate from the factual knowledge layer. In accordance with usual practice, knowing is assumed to be the standard case being assumed by default for which therefore no extra information has to be put into the respective layer. Similarly with the don't-know case which applies for a fact by default whenever this fact is by none of the available mean the result of some chain of reasoning. Hence only the believe and don't-believe cases have to be treated explicitly.

This may, for instance, be done by way of a meta-predicate BELIEVE (or DON'T-BELIEVE) applicable to references to formulas in the factual knowledge. Thus "Mike believes that Mary is married" would be represented by $[MARRIED(mary)]^{mike}$ in the factual knowledge layer together with $BELIEVE^{mike}('[MARRIED(mary)]^{mike'})$ in the judgement layer. The effect of this entry is one on the control of the reasoning only. Namely, in presence of this entry the control tries to avoid this statement as far as possible, otherwise taking the statement as a fact. Note that in the first-order formalism the whole quotation $'[MARRIED(mary)]^{mike'}$ is to be treated as a constant.

Also believing can now be iterated in the case of several agents, possibly mixed with knowing. For instance, "John believes that Mike believes that Mary is married" would be represented by

$$[[MARRIED(mary) \& BELIEVE('[MARRIED(mary)]^{mike'})]^{mike}]^{john}$$

- abbreviated by F - in John's factual knowledge layer together with $BELIEVE^{john}('F')$ in John's judgement layer. Note that such abbreviations would certainly be used in the actual system as well so that the entries do not become more bulky than the natural text.

Of course, the believe-scale may also expose a finer structure than that shown in (i) above (STRONGLY-BELIEVE, etc.) with respective complications for the control of reasoning. But matters like that are purely technical complications which may be taken care of in a straightforward way (possibly quite lengthy in all details though).

What we have illustrated for beliefs similarly applies to the other meta-level concepts assumed in our model of section 1.

CONCLUSIONS

Our discussion has in fact yielded an - admittedly very sketchy - outline of the surface structure of a major part of a knowledge-based reasoning system involving several agents, for which our main focus, however, has been on the propositional attitude of knowing; in particular we have outlined a new conceptually simple first-order formalism for dealing with it. Clearly, substantial work of detail has to be invested still, in order to clarify many obvious questions, too many to be considered in the very limited time available to the author for the preparation of this paper. One of these questions, for instance, is how our formalism relates to the previously proposed ones. On the surface they look certainly quite different; but on a deeper level there may be much closer, perhaps revealing relationships.

It is obvious that the topic of this paper has numerous applications. For lack of space we simply mention a few of them. Of course, expert systems are among these applications. In particular one might think of expert systems with remote components, or less ambitious, remote data bases with some reasoning capabilities. An area par excellence certainly is robotics where reasoning about other agents obviously is crucial. But we may even think of applications to the social sciences, with which remark we have in mind a formal approach in this area like the one outlined in [Els].

Acknowledgements. I thank E. Eder for several discussions on the topic and an anonymous referee for helpful comments pointing out several defaults in an earlier version.

REFERENCES

[Bar] Barnden, J.A., Intensions as such: an outline, Proceedings IJCAI-83, Kaufmann, Los Altos, 280 - 286 (1983).
[Bi1] Bibel, W., Automated theorem proving, Vieweg, Wiesbaden (1982).
[Bi2] Bibel, W., Matings in matrices, Comm. ACM 26, 844 - 852 (1983).
[Bi3] Bibel, W., Knowledge representation from a deductive point of view, Proceedings IFAC Symposium on Artificial Intelligence, Leningrad, Oct. 1983, Pergamon Press, Oxford (to appear).
[BoK] Bowen, K.A. and Kowalski, R.A., Amalgamating language and metalanguage in logic programming, In: Logic programming (Clark, K.L. and Taernlund, S.A., eds.), Academic Press, London, 153 - 172 (1982).
[Cre] Creary, L.G., Propositional attitudes: Fregean representations and simulative reasoning, Proceedings IJCAI-79, Kaufmann, Los Altos, 176 - 181 (1979).
[Els] Elster, J., Logic and society, Wiley, Chichester (1978).
[Hin] Hintikka, J., Knowledge and belief: an introduction to the logic of the two notions, Cornell University Press, Ithaca (1962).
[Kon] Konolige, K., A deductive model of belief, Proceedings IJCAI-83, Kaufmann, Los Altos, 377 - 381 (1983).
[Mai] Maida, A.S., Knowing intensional individuals, and reasoning about intensional individuals, Proceedings IJCAI-83, Kaufmann, Los Altos, 382 - 384 (1983).
[McC] McCarthy, J., First-order theories of individual concepts and propositions, In: Expert systems in the micro-electronic age (Michie, D., ed.), Edinburgh University Press, 271 - 287 (1979).
[Moo] Moore, R.C., Reasoning about knowledge and action, Proceedings IJCAI-77, Kaufmann, Los Altos, 223 - 227 (1977).
[Nil] Nilsson, M., A logical model of knowledge, Proceedings IJCAI-83, Kaufmann, Los Altos, 374 - 376 (1983).
[Wey] Weyrauch, R.W., Prolegomena to a theory of mechanized formal reasoning, Artificial Intelligence Journal 13, 133 - 170 (1980).

DEDUCTIVE QUESTION ANSWERING SYSTEM
DIALOG

L. Bolc, K. Kochut, P. Rychlik, T. Strzałkowski

Institute of Informatics
Warsaw University
PKiN, pok. 850
00-901 Warszawa, POLAND

The experimental version of the DIALOG system is presented in this work. It was designed as the deductive system with natural language communication. The purpose of the system is to answer questions about precisely defined domain. Now, the domain is the certain fragment of medical knowledge. The system is devided into two main subparts: the natural language component and the deductive component. The first one is coded with the use of the Cascaded ATN grammars. The latter one works as the backward deduction system for first-order logic.

1. INTRODUCTION

The DIALOG system is to play the role of the doctor's "collaborator", being in a position of informing and advising him in certain fields of medical knowledge.

The current, yet experimental, version of the system was developed on the basis of the narrow part of medicine - gastroenterology /more precisely - pancreas pathology/. Having acquired of the knowledge contained in the professional natural text, the system is able to answer questions about this very domain.

The big module TESS is the language interface of the system. It performs the transformation of the professional natural language text to the possibly most equivalent formal notation. As this formal notation the First Order Predicate Calculus language is used.

The programme of the analyzer was coded with the use of CATN /Cascaded ATN/ mechanism, deviding the whole processing to syntactics and semantics.

The deductive module of the system administers the data base that is devided to the extensional /EDB, containing facts - ground literals only/ and intensional /IDB, containing axioms/ parts.

The administration of DB consists in data manipulation /adding, deleting, introducing changes, etc./ and in answering questions about the represented domain as well. The extracting of knowledge proceeds on the basis of the information represented in DB explicitly and implicitly. In the latter case the deductive programme is used that operates as a backward deduction system.

The deductive module was worked out with the use of ideas presented in papers by E. Konrad and N. Klein /TUB, West Berlin/.

The current version of the system was implemented in the LISP programming language on the IBM 370 computer under the VM 370 operating system.

2. NATURAL LANGUAGE INTERFACE

The Natural Language Transformation Expert System /TESS/ translates written Polish sentences of the professional text into formal representations that express their meanings in context of a dialogue subject. In present realisation, TESS transforms natural language medical descriptions into logical form.

TESS is divided into two main parts: the analytical stage /AS/ and the interpretational stage /IS/. First of them is almost completely domain-independent and syntax plays the most important role in it. AS is, however, enriched by selected elements of semantics. AS maintains a syntactical dictionary that provides the lexical level of the analytical process. The latter subcomponent is to assign meanings to sentences. The process is strongly dependent on the conversation subject. The most important part of IS consists of the so-called experts that keep the elementary knowledge in the subject of discourse. This knowledge together with the content of a semantical dictionary enables the system to act as a qualified specialist in the field. It enables each sentence to be really understood.

The core of TESS is constructed as a CATN net. Both stages of the system correspond to the couple of CATN cascades. The first stage produces grammatical analyses and TRANSMITs them to the latter one, which attempts to give them appropriate interpretations. If such interpretation cannot be found for a given sentence the analytical stage is asked to derive another syntactically correct parsing. This procedure is repeated until AS puts forward a suitable issue or fails. In the latter case the sentence is regarded as meaningless.

Both stages are equipped with several additional devices. The conversational spelling corrector helps the analytical grammar by examining each entering sentence with regard to its lexical correctness. A user is advised of every misspelling or using an unknown word, and he has the possibility to correct the utterance. The interpretational stage is endowed with a special context register. It keeps some information about the recently transformed sentence necessary to solve the pronominal references problem.

2.1. ANALYTICAL STAGE

The analytical subcomponent of TESS is applied to a sentence to distinguish such propositional elements as verb/action, subject, object, indirect object, prepositional phrases and so on. All this constituents are moved into their underlying positions according to the canonical scheme of a sentence. Aspectual and temporal properties of sentences that represent the speaker's attitude are also placed in the final structure.

The syntactical grammar comprises quite a wide subset of Polish language. AS can recognize simple indicative sentences and questions, complements, relative clauses, and certain types of complex sentences. A number of special properties of the medical dialect have been taken into account. It covers most of medical expression that seldom occur in a common conversation. These facilities are located in the AS dictionary rather than directly in the grammar. The grammar must remain mostly invariant without regard to changes of the discourse subject. The grammar strongly utilises the regularities of the natural language so it is able to capture most of the linguistic generalizations such as passivations, NP-movements, conjunctions and so on.

AS transforms a natural language sentence into an ordered and unflex-

ional form called o-form. The o-form gives a first approximation of
the deep structure of the sentence. It expresses the underlying construction of the sentence where each constituent has sharp boundaries. A sentence is divided into a collection of embedded clauses
that are then cut into phrases. Each clause expresses the least
prepositional constituent of a sentence that describes a particular
event. It corresponds to the construction of a simple indicative
sentence that has a subject, a verb and other necessary elements.

The analytical grammar consists of five ATN nets that can recognize
different types of syntactical constructions: sentences, nominal
groups, adjectival groups, adverbial groups and interrogative expressions.

2.2. INTERPRETATIONAL STAGE

When the analytical phase is completed the interpretational stage
attempts to find out a meaning of an o-form in context of the given
subject. Each clause is interpreted as a description of an elementary event. The meaning of the whole sentence combines meanings of all
its clauses.

IS maintains a collection of semantical rules that describe elementary events. A rule consists of an event symbolic name and type, a
phrasal pattern and a scheme of an atomic formula. The pattern is
matched against a clause. If it is done successfully, the appropriate formula is generated. The pattern determines which phrases may
be expected round its predicate and which of them must occur. Each
pattern slot is specified by a name limiting its semantical role.
The slot itself consists of the description of syntactical, semantical and pragmatical conditions that must hold true during the
matching process. The concept part of a rule is a notion that represents a meaning of a clause. The final form of the TESS outputs is
partially estabilished at this point. In the framework of the DIALOG
system TESS produces formulae of the first-order logic.

The core of IS includes ten ATN nets that may be divided into three
levels. The highest one consists of the main net arranging the
clauses processing. This level controls the general correctness of
the interpretational process and combines logically formulae comming
from the lower level. The second IS level is involved when a pattern
slot is to be filled. This level checks wheather the syntactical
constraints of the slot are satisfied and if so selects an expert
net from the third IS level to give the phrase a suitable meaning.
Experts are selected according to the semantical and pragmatical
requirements of the pattern slot. When the semantical constraints
are less restricted several experts may be called by turns until the
term falls into the proper one.

Experts match professional terms against their own knowledge and the
one included in the semantical dictionary. Sometimes when a term is
more complex, the help of other experts is required. Thus experts
can support each other and finally they prepare the completed filler
for the pattern slot. Occasionaly a quantity of additional information is also picked up to the second IS level. Such information is
generated when the considered term depicts a nonterminal concept.

Experts are constructed as ATN nets. There are seven expert nets in
TESS. They can recognize special medical expressions such as names
of diseases, symptoms, organs, treatments and so on. The number of
experts may be changed if necessary and experts themselves may be
replaced by others when one intends the cardinal alteration of the
discourse subject. This operation, including the reestabilishment of

the dictionary and semantical rules, is not necessary in other TESS components.

Finally, TESS produces a first-order formula that corresponds to the input sentence. The formula is then transferred to the next DIALOG component.

3. DEDUCTIVE MODULE

The role of this part of the system consists in administrating acquired knowledge. It goes on through a suitable operating of the data base. Below, the general schema of this module is presented.

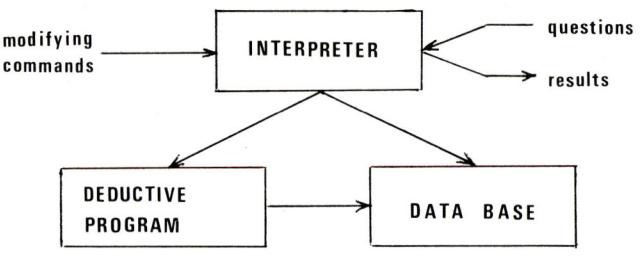

Figure 1
General schema of the deductive module

3.1. DATA BASE

As it was mentioned earlier, the formal notation used to describe data is the First Order Predicate Calculus language. Natural language sentence is then represented by the FOPC formula as precisely as allows first-order logic. For the most precise rendering of the idea of the sentence different sorts of individual variables are introduced. In this sense many-sorted logic is used, however it does not give any more power to first-order language. The sorts create special hierarchy with one dominating. It may be represented by simple tree structure.

The whole knowledge of the system is stored in the two parts of the data base: extensional and intensional. The experimental medical text, after being analysed by TESS, gave only FOPC formulae that were put into the IDB as axioms used by the deductive process. The extensional part had to be fulfilled during the initialization of the system. The set of elementary facts, valid in the represented domain, was the main subpart of the EDB. Extensions of sorts were also put into this very part of DB.

Elementary facts had to be discovered during the special analysis not only of the presented experimental text but of the peculiarity of the entire field of knowledge as well.

The information contained in the EDB, called the kernel later on /Konrad '76/, was divided into many relations. This partitioning was introduced after the analysis of the subject and renders the relationships among many concepts in the field.

The information contained in the IDB, called the amplifier /after Konrad/, consists of the formulae of three different types:

    a/ conditioned rules
        they may be represented as below:

$$\forall x_1/S_1 \; \forall x_2/S_2 \; \ldots \; \forall x_n/S_n \; A(x_1,x_2,\ldots,x_n) \rightarrow \pi(x_1,x_2,\ldots,x_n)$$

x_i - individual variables
S_i - corresponding sorts
A - premises - FOPC formulae
π - conclusion - atomic formulae

b/ unconditioned rules

$$\forall x_1/S_1 \; \forall x_2/S_2 \; \ldots \; \forall x_n/S_n (\pi(x_1,x_2,\ldots,x_n))$$

c/ restrictive rules

$$\forall x_1/S_1 \; \forall x_2/S_2 \; \ldots \; \forall x_n/S_n \; (\neg\pi(x_1,x_2,\ldots,x_n))$$

Reasuming, the IDB introduces the partition of the whole knowledge, not represented in the kernel, to the implicitly defined /by the formulae/ relations.

The part of the data base, called filter, keeps the FOPC formulae securing the integrity of data base contents. The form of the integrity formulae is as follows:

$$\forall x_1/S_1 \; \ldots \; \forall x_n/S_n \; \pi(x_1,\ldots,x_n) \rightarrow (S_1(x_1) \wedge \ldots \wedge S_n(x_n))$$

The protector, taking care of data base confidentiality, includes two kinds of rules:

a/ conditioned protective rules, which are of the form:

$$\forall x_1/S_1 \; \ldots \; \forall x_n/S_n \; \pi(x_1,\ldots,x_n) \rightarrow A(x_1,\ldots,x_n)$$

Keeping in secret the information unifiable with atomic formula $\pi(x_1,\ldots,x_n)$ is conditioned by satisfaction of the relation A, defined by the right hand side of the above implication.

b/ unconditioned protective rules

$$\forall x_1/S_1 \; \ldots \; \forall x_n/S_n \; \neg\pi(x_1,\ldots,x_n)$$

Such rules permit the system to keep in secret facts unifiable with the atomic formula $\pi(x_1,\ldots,x_n)$.

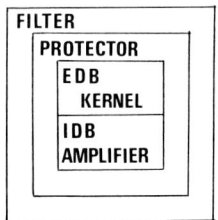

Figure 2
The schema of the data base partition /Klein '78/

3.2. DATA MANIPULATION LANGUAGE

Data manipulation language is used by the special monitor that, after analyzing the natural language sentence by TESS, constructs a suitable expression in DML and starts the deductive module. First of all, DML is a tool designed to enable a user to communicate with the module /we mean the deductive module, not the whole system with which he may communicate in the natural language/. It accomplishes the following functions:

- secures the ability of:
    - adding new facts to the kernel
    - adding new theorems to the amplifier
    - introducing the integrity rules
    - introducing the protective rules
- gives the ability of deleting data and rules from DB
- answers the stated questions.

The above functions are realized with the use of the special commands of the DML. The argument of every command is a formulae describing the request. The corresponding commands are: ADD, ADDAXIOM, ADDFILTER, PROTECT, DEL, DELAXIOM, DELFILTER, FREE, and TEST and FIND.

Realization of the last two commands is most important for functioning of the system. They are used to retrieve the information from DB. Before they are described presentation of the internal form of the formulae is necessary.

As it was mentioned, the whole system is implemented in LISP. Because of this every formula is coded as a list structure.

Transformation of the facts, elements of the kernel, to the internal form is immediate and obvious. The formulae stored in the other parts of the data base are represented in less natural way.

Theorems in the amplifier are transformed in such a way so that testing the premises could start the recursive process of going backward in the deductive process /it is described later in details/. Premises are then put into the normal form and transformed to a suitable LISP form, causing the subsequent backward steps /quantifiers are not dropped/. As an example consider the formula having the following matrix:

$$P(x,y) \longrightarrow P(x,M) \quad x,y - \text{variables}, M - \text{constant}.$$

It is transformed to the LISP form presented below:

```
(OR (NOT (TESTE (QUOTE P) (QUOTE (X Y))))
    (TESTE (QUOTE P) (QUOTE (X M))))
```

The function TESTE is to deduce the, given as argument, fact /at the time of the above form evaluation variables x and y would be valuated by the constants of the proper sorts/.

Each formula is then stored in the following form:

(⟨conclusion⟩ ⟨premises-testing-form⟩)

Each question is presented to the system as a list of the form:

(⟨prefix⟩ ⟨matrix-realising-form⟩)

Because of the domain character every implication is sanctioned as true only if it leads from true premises to true conclusion.

The TEST command is used to give answers to the questions, representated as FOPC formulae, that may be answered by YES or NO.

TEST (⟨question-representing-formula⟩)

The FIND command serve as a way to answer the questions about the concrete objects. Such questions can be answered by giving the list of constants or information about unsuccessful search.

FIND (⟨list-of-questioned-variables⟩⟨formula⟩)

If we ask about any constant, satisfying the conditions of the question, the variable is bound by the quantifier THIS, otherwise by THOSE.

FIND is different from TEST in that it returns the valuation of questioned variables as its response.

3.3. DEDUCTION

As it was mentioned earlier, every formula is transformed to a suitable LISP form. This form is constructed only of the functions ANS, OR and NOT and TESTE. The last one is destined to test ground literals only. Its functioning is as follows:

We proove fact E:

1. If the formula being proved appears to be protected then the answer is NO; there is no proof of this fact. Otherwise go to 2.
2. Search the extensional DB /the kernel/ for this fact. If it is found then the answer is YES. The proof of E exists. Otherwise go to 3.
3. If the amplifier is empty - the answer is NO. Otherwise go to 4.
4. Choose the next axiom from the amplifier whose conclusion is unifiable with the fact being proved. Let it be AF. Go to 5. If there is no such axiom - the answer is NO.
5. If AF is marked as an unconditional rule then the answer is YES. The proof does exist. Otherwise go to 6.
6. If AF is marked as a restrictive rule then the answer is NO. Otherwise go to 7.
7. Evaluate the LISP form associated with the rule AF. If it evaluates to T /true in LISP/ then the answer is YES. Otherwise go to 3.
   Evaluation of that LISP form may cause the recursive application of the function TESTE and to avoid an infinite loop the fact E is stored in a special buffer of facts being still proved.

4. CONCLUSION

The results of our efforts seem to sanction our experiments. The future work will concentrate on the subsequent improvement of the existing modules. It is planned to introduce some elements of the second-order logic - deductive module is already adopted to it; and to distinguish the answer NO and DON'T KNOW. Because of the great amount of information to be kept in the system it is necessary to make improvement in data base organisation. Simultaneosly, the work on other deductive modules using such methodes as resolution, fuzzy sets, frames and semantic networks will be continued.

REFERENCES

1. Bolc, L. /1980/ (ed.) "Natural Language Based Computer Systems" Hanser-Verlag and MacMillan Press, London 1980
2. Bolc, L. /1980/ (ed.) "Natural Language Question-Answering Systems", Hanser-Verlag and MacMillan Press, London 1980
3. Bolc, L. /1980/ (ed.) "Representation and Processing of Natural Language", Hanser-Verlag and MacMillan Press, London 1980
4. Bolc, L., Strzałkowski, T. /1982/ "Transformation of Natural Language into Logical Formulae", Proceedings of the Ninth International Conf. on Comp. Ling. COLING'82, North-Holland Pub. Comp. 1982

5. Bolc, L. /1983/ (ed.) "The Design of Interpreters, Compilers, and Editors for Augmented Transition Networks", Springer-Verlag, Berlin, Heidelberg, New York, Tokyo 1983
6. Grosz, B., Haas, N., Hendrix, G., Hobbs, J., Martin, P., Moore, R., Robinson, J., Rosenschein, S. /1982/ "DIALOGIC: A Core Natural-Language Processing System", Proceedings of the 9th Int. Conf. on Comp. Ling. COLLING´82, North-Holland Pub. Comp., 1982
7. Klein, N. /1978/ "Implementierung eines Frage-Antwort-Systems auf der Basis der Predikatenlogik II Stufe", TUB, Berlin, 1978
8. Konrad, E. /1976/ "Formale Semantik von Datenbanksprachen", Doktor Ingenieur genehmigte Dissertation, TUB, Berlin, 1976, D83
9. Marcus, M. M. /1980/ "A Theory of Syntactic Recognition for Natural Language", The MIT Press, Cambridge Ma, London, 1980
10. Moore, r. c. /1981/ "Problems in Logical Form", Proc. of the 19th Annual Meeting of the ACL, Stanford Ca., 1981
11. Woods, W. A. /1980/ "Cascaded ATN Grammars", American Journal of Computational Linguistics, vol 6, no 1, 1980

INFORMATION, HEURISTICS, CREATION

Mihai Drăgănescu

Central Institute for Management and
Informatics

Bucharest, Romania

A general scheme for a general theory of information taking into account artificial intelligence and phenomenological processes of matter is proposed.

INTRODUCTION

Today it is easier to speak about the technology of information and of the economy of information than about a science of information. What is information from a scientific point of view? Fortunately, the advent of artificial intelligence (AI) and its similarities and differences with the natural intelligence (NI) of man may help get an answer. Since NI has a biological substratum and in any biological being information plays an important role, it is necessary to investigate the reason why the living matter uses information, the natural non-living matter does not use it (if this is quite true), and the artificial technological matter may also use it as can be seen in intelligent robots.

For a general scheme of a theory of information it is supposed that:

  I. Matter is of four kinds: a) profound matter; b) non-living matter; c) living matter; d) intermediate matter

 II. Information always manifests itself on a material substratum

III. Although matter is fundamental, information is nearly at equality with matter, therefore information is present beginning with the profound matter.

Profound matter, after Aristotle [1] [2], has two principles, which may be interpreted now as nonstructured matter and matter which can give form to the previous one by information. This informational matter, in which information cannot be originally structural in the usual sense, has been called informatter [3]. The information in the informatter is supposed to be of the nature of the phenomenological senses of the human mind and perhaps of any living being. The phenomenological information of the informatter is a physical process with a special property of sensibility of this profound matter. The phenomenological sense of the mind is of the same nature and therefore it is supposed that any living being has, in a way, access to the informatter of profound matter. On the contrary, the non-living matter gives no access, the informatter being covered by the structured (formed) matter. Therefore, both non-living and living matter are built with the same ingredients, but the living matter still has, for some reasons, access to informatter. Seen from the outside, non-living matter is structural and, may be said, formal.

Living matter is structural-phenomenological or formal-nonformal. Non-living matter has also at its origin an informational phenomenological source; living matter is always informational [4].

COMPONENTS OF INFORMATION

Alongside with the phenomenological information (profound senses and mental senses) and the structural information, which needs no other explanation, a third component of information is significance. The importance of such a component is tested in AI where significance acquired by semantic networks, frames, etc. is a formal meaning.

For NI, meaning is formed by two components, significance (formal meaning) and phenomenological sense [5], where significance has, in its turn, according to Mario Bunge [6] two components

significance
(M.Bunge's meaning, in fact, formal meaning)
— context significance (M.Bunge's sense)
— reference significance (M.Bunge's reference)

Significance is built into AI systems and it may exist in the neuronic machine of the brain. The most complete information is then [7],

$$I = <S, M> \quad (1)$$

where S is the structural information and M is the meaning of information

$$M = <G, \mathcal{S}> \quad (2)$$

In (2), G is the significance and $\mathcal{S}$ the corresponding phenomenological sense. Because

$$G = <\mathcal{C}, \mathcal{R}> \quad (3)$$

where $\mathcal{C}$ is the context significance and $\mathcal{R}$ the reference significance, then, from the above expressions it follows

$$I = <S, \mathcal{C}, \mathcal{R}, \mathcal{S}> \quad (4)$$

Such information characterizes a human mind. Artificial intelligence is characterized by information without phenomenological sense

$$I_{AI} = <S, \mathcal{C}, \mathcal{R}> \quad (5)$$

AI is born from NI, even if afterwards AI can develop its own information content. Therefore (4) is mental-psychological information and (5) is reduced AI information. In most cases (4) and (5) are equivalent because there is a static correspondence between G and $\mathcal{S}$, but when one manifests structural or phenomenological heuristics there is a transitory period before a new correspondence between G and $\mathcal{S}$ is established. AI may know a structural (formal) heuristics but not a phenomenological heuristics. NI may know both, formal heuristics and phenomenological heuristics, and more, formal heuristics may induce new phenomenological senses and viceversa.

Some more reduced information is the structural information under its syntactic form

$$I = <S> \quad (6)$$

but this information has a reason only in connection with NI or AI. It is the usual form in which information has been considered until recently.

From (4) to (5) and to (6) the components of information are reduced and only having in mind such a reduction, the expression (5) and especially (6) are still called information.

OTHER CASES OF INFORMATION

If informatter is generating phenomenological information by physical fluctuations, when informatter is coupled with nonstructured matter, a physical universe is born. The physical universe is based on the information of the form

$$I_{Univ} = <\mathcal{S}_{Univ}, S_{Univ}> \qquad (7)$$

where $\mathcal{S}_{Univ}$ is the generated phenomenological information and S_{Univ} is the corresponding physical structure of the Universe, playing the role of the structural information to be implemented physically. The programs or the laws of an Universe may be considered as given by the profound information $I_{Univ} = <\mathcal{S}_{Univ}>$ or by the corresponding structure of the universe $<S_{Univ}>$. Man and society can understand this structure as information by knowing the structural, that is, the physical laws of the Universe.

For a biological universe, through the "free" informatter of the living beings, new phenomenological senses may appear, induced by a structural-phenomenological interaction or by the processes in informatter itself. Then

$$I_{Biol\ Univ} = <\Delta, \mathcal{S}_{Univ}, S_{Univ}, \mathcal{S}_{Biol}, S_{Biol}> \qquad (8)$$

where $\mathcal{S}_{Univ}$ and S_{Univ} have the same significance (or meaning) as before; $\mathcal{S}_{Biol}$ and S_{Biol} are the new senses and the corresponding physical and informational structures; Δ is a symbol for the physical availability of senses of informatter. At any moment new senses $\mathcal{S}_{Biol}$ appear and disappear. They can be maintained only when they are transposed into structural information which can regenerate these senses.

A biological cell has the information,

$$I = <S_{fiz}, S_{inf}, \mathcal{S}, \Delta> \qquad (9)$$

where S_{fiz} is, for instance, the genetic information, S_{inf} is the dynamic information of the cell due to its functioning, $\mathcal{S}$ are the corresponding phenomenological senses and Δ is the availability for new phenomenological senses.

In (7), (8) and (9) a formal significance is lacking and consequently it is doubtful that any of these objects has an intelligence. The phenomenological senses cannot be used to process their own information, on the contrary, processing of information may be done by some type of computer, therefore by physical or informational structures. So, the condition of **significance** is obligatory for intelligence. This condition may be fulfilled only by objects with a nervous system or with some other types of processing structural information with significance, that is by NI and AI.

The biological cell and the plants are not intelligent although they know structural-phenomenological interactions. The physical universe is not intelligent, the profound matter is not intelligent, only the biological universe may be intelligent if it con-

tains animals with nervous system that works and builds AI.
A special case concerns the information at the social level, but
this is a very large theme in itself.

HEURISTICS AND CREATION

Heuristics may be of two types: a) structural heuristics; b) phenomenological heuristics.

A structural heuristics is described in artificial intelligence as informal rules of thumb to solve a problem, that is to change the structure of an initial state into the structure of a goal state [8] . Phenomenological processes are nonformal. Structural heuristics applies to old structures giving new structures using informal rules, which are in fact formal. The heuristic rules formalise what is not coming from a complete formal theory, and with this significance the heuristic rules are informal. But, in fact, structural heuristics is still formal heuristics.

What is obtained by structural (formal) heuristics, although it may be new, is not a creation. It is the result of a play with formal structures. An AI system with heuristics does not create. When the creative insight of a man becomes a rule of thumb, an informal procedure for heuristics, it is not heuristics that creates a new structure, but the creative man. It may happen that a new structure generated by an AI system to be created by a man, by a phenomenological or a creative procedure (as described below). In such a case the formal heuristics looks like a creation. But it is not a creation yet, because of the formal internal procedure. Sometimes, in such cases, the formal heuristics is called creation of the third species [4].

Formal heuristics may also be used by NI, not only by AI. But in the case of NI (of man), because of a structural-phenomenological interaction, it is very difficult to distinguish between formal and phenomenological heuristics. It is to be expected that the formal heuristics is enhanced by the phenomenological heuristics. Phenomenological heuristics may take place even independently of formal heuristics, due to the property of generating phenomenological senses. These are then crystallized as neuronic structures. Because of the advanced degree of novelty brought about by phenomenological heuristics, this may be called a creation of the second species.

Creation (true creation, creation of the first species) implies a conscious control of formal heuristics and phenomenological heuristics, an **iterative** interaction between these two types of heuristics, in order to obtain the new phenomenological sense and the corresponding significant structure that satisfy a tendency, a desire, an expectation. Creation is a conscious imbrication and **iteration** of the two types of heuristics. Creation does not come from anything, but its result may be very far of what is known, although the point of departure is old structure and old phenomenological senses, respectively.

AI does not have creation because it does not have phenomenological senses (because AI is not alive). AI has only structural heuristics. A biological cell does not have creation because it does not have consciousness; it cannot have a conscious control of the structural-phenomenological interaction. But the cell still has a non-conscious structural-phenomenological interaction and phenomenological heuristics may bring new structures. The cell has a creation of the second species, that is, phenomenological heuristics. This could have contributed to the process of evolution together with mutations (structural heuristics) in the frame of the natural selection process. The profound matter does not create because it does not have consciousness and it does not have consciousness because it does not process structures with significance.

FORMAL AND NONFORMAL SOLVING PROBLEMS

For a class of problems to be solved, if it is to build an AI system, this is conceived by a man or by a human team. This man or this team does not only function in a formal way, they have phenomenological heuristics and creation as two important functions. Their behaviour is formal, informal and nonformal. Their problem is to build a problem solver using AI methods. But he or the team is a natural problem solver, that is they represent NI. After NI has built an AI system, the latter is not let work alone. In terms of the "problem space", the AI system may be confronted with formal subspaces but also with nonformalized subspaces of the problem space. In order to formalize the nonformalized subspaces AI may use structural heuristics and if it does not succeed NI must be called for. Therefore, in general, AI and NI are working in symbiosis. We do not have a theory of this symbiosis. NI has not only intelligence in this symbiosis for solving problems: it has also intuition, creation and reason. NI and AI determine together a new social intelligence [9] . Solving problems at social level and at global level is one of the challenges of the social intelligence. The intermediate matter made of non-living matter and intelligent information, that is information with significance, will it help us build a socio-human civilization? We hope that this will be the case.

REFERENCES

[1] Aristotel, Fizica (Physics), (Editura ştiinţifică, Bucureşti, 1966)

[2] Aristotel, Metafizica (Metaphysics), (Editura Academiei R.S. România, Bucureşti, 1965)

[3] Drăgănescu,M., Profunzimile lumii materiale (The depths of the material world), (Editura politică, Bucureşti, 1979)

[4] Drăgănescu,M., Ortofizica (Orthophysics), (Editura ştiinţifică şi enciclopedică, Bucureşti, to be printed)

[5] Drăgănescu,M., Semantică şi subiect (Semantics and subject), (Institutul central pentru conducere şi informatică, Bucureşti, May 1983)

[6] Bunge,M., Treatise on basic philosophy,vol.I,Semantics I: Sense and reference; vol.II, Semantics II: Interpretation and truth (D.Reidel Publishing Comp., Dordrecht-Holland,1974)

[7] Drăgănescu,M., Spre o teorie generală a informaţiei (Towards a general theory of information), (Institutul central pentru conducere şi informatică, Bucureşti, May 1983)

[8] Lenat, D.B., The nature of heuristics,Artificial Intelligence, 19 (1982) 189-249

[9] Drăgănescu,M.,Social intelligence, in: Drăgănescu,M.a.o.(eds), Inteligenţa artificială şi robotica (Artificial intelligence and robotics),(Editura Academiei R.S.România,Bucureşti,1983).

CONCEPT LEARNING

Y. Kodratoff, J.G. Ganascia, B. Clavieras
E.R.A. 452 du C.N.R.S.
Laboratoire de Recherche en
Informatique - Bât. 490
Université de Paris-Sud
F-91405 Orsay Cédex (FRANCE)

G. TECUCI
Institutul Central
Pentru Conducere si
Informatica
Bucaresti, B-Dul Miciurin 8-10,
(ROMANIA)

This paper tries to show a unified approach to concept learning. "Unified" means here that we want to promote together a definition of a concept, a methodology for discovering these concepts and an algorithm which realizes this discovery. Besides, we claim that this methodology has direct consequences in the way counterexamples can be used in concept discovery and in the way conceptual hierarchies may be built.

INTRODUCTION

A description of the main ideas relevant to concept learning has been given by Dietterich and Michalski [Dietterich & Al. 81] in a particularly understandable paper. We shall here consider that the reader is aware of [Dietterich & Al. 81] since our own paper criticizes and refines the generalization concept used by these authors. A comprehensive survey of concept learning is also found in [Handbook 82] and [Holte 84].

As shown in [Kodratoff 83] and [Kodratoff & All 83] one must, as far as possible, try to put the formulas to be generalized in "structural matching". The idea is that one should generalize together formula that are as close as possible of each other. This may be done by use of logical AND idempotency or of logical AND neutral element TRUE (see [Kodratoff & All 83]).

This method allows to put into evidence links between variables that are usually forgotten in generalizations. For instance given the expression (ON B A) & (ON C B) & (ON D C) where ON is known as a function on which no generalization should occur and A,B,C,D are constants, one can notice the following :
1- B and C appear in two litterals
2- Both of them occur once in first position, once in second position
3- The same instance never occurs into one litteral (i.e. there is no (ON A A) for instance)
4- The same instance never occurs into two litterals except B and C
5- There is some alphabetic ordering of the names of the instances. A generalization that takes into account these links is :
(ON x w) & (ON y x) & (ON z y) & (DIFFERENT_FROM_EACH_OTHER w,x,y,z)
& (ALPHABETIC_ORDERING $\bar{w},x,\bar{y},z$)
Other examples will be used either for further generalization, e.g. replacing the two occurrences of y by different variables, or for further particularization, e.g. when the variable z is instantiated by A in all examples, deleting z and replacing it by A.

1- GENERALIZATION ALGORITHM

The generalization process may be divided into two main steps. The first is intended to detect structural matchings between examples belonging to the learning set.

The second one, the generalization step can be easily realized : it simply detects the common variables links of all the structurally matching formulae.
Overview of the algorithm : The algorithm may be roughly described as a sequence of two alternate operations. The conjunction of these two operations leads to introduce new variables with common occurrences in all the examples. All these variables are called Generalization Variables (GV). Links between variables, or between variables and constants keep track of the instantiations of each variable in each example. The first operation consists in choosing one constant or one variable which is not a GV in each example and turning it into a new GV. This choice as we shall see is a crucial step of the process, we therefore need to use heuristics in order to lead it. The second operation is a partial structural matching. One considers the set of predicates containing GV and attempts to realize a structural matching of this subset of the example predicates. Each variable of the GV must be at the same instance of the same predicate in all the examples. Otherwise, the structural matching is considered as faulty and a new one is looked for.
Description of the algorithm: Each of its steps is exemplified by a very simple example for which our algorithm is not really useful.
Let
E_1 = (ON A B) E_2 = (ON C D) & (NEAR D F). The predicates ON and NEAR have their intuitive meaning. Their properties are expressed by rules R1 and R2:
R1 : $\forall x \forall y$ (NEAR x y) $\rightarrow$ (NEAR y x)   R2 : $\forall x \forall y$ (ON x y) $\rightarrow$ (ON x y) & (NEAR x y)
Operation 1 is divided into two steps
Step 1: According to some heuristics we choose one constant (or non GV variable) in each example. Let us suppose that our heuristic requires to choose firstly the second occurrence of the predicate ON, secondly the first occurrence of ON, and then the first and the second occurrence of NEAR. Applying this heuristic to our examples leads us to turn B and D into a GV.
Step 2: We create a new Generalization Variable and we substitute it to the constants and to the variables chosen at Step 1. One keeps track of this substitution by using links between variables. Applying Step 2 to our examples gives:
E_1 = (ON A x_0) [(= x_0 B)] E_2 = (ON C x_0) & (NEAR x_0 F) [(= x_0 D)] where the formula inside [ ] states the links between variables.
Operation 2 is intended to force the partial structural matching between examples. Let us consider again our example : x_0 appears once in E_1 (at the second occurrence of the predicate ON) and twice in E_2 (at the second occurence of the predicate ON, and at the first occurrence of the predicate NEAR). There is a common occurrence of x_0 in E_1 and E_2, and one occurrence which appears in E_2 and not in E_1. Operation 2 is divided into two steps :
Step 3: Detects the occurrences of the variables substituted in step 2 and checks that these occurrences belong to all the examples.
Step 4: If this not the case, step 4 tries to generate them using transformations introduced in section 4. For instance the first occurrence of NEAR being x_0 in E_2, we try to generate it in E_1. Rule R2 with instantiation x$\leftarrow$A and y$\leftarrow x_0$, is applied to E_1. One obtains E_1 =$_\varepsilon$ E_1' = (ON A x_0) & (NEAR A x_0) [(= x_0 B)] x_0 appears now in E_1' at the second occurrence of NEAR, and we want to generate it in the first occurence of x_0, which is possible using rule R1. Therefore, E_1' will be rewritten as
E_1'' = (ON A x_0) & (NEAR x_0 A) [(= x_0 B)].
Lastly, if step 4 did not manage to generate some occurrence of the variable substituted in step 2, then step 4 kills this occurrence by introducing a new variable. Let us go on applying this algorithm to our example.
Step 1: Suppose that we choose A et C which are first occurrences of ON.
Step 2: E_1'' = (ON y_0 x_0) & (NEAR x_0 y_0) & [(=x_0 B) & (= y_0 A) &($\neq x_0$ y_0)]
E_2 = (ON y_0 x_0) & (NEAR x_0 F) & [(=x_0 D) & (= y_0 C) &($\neq x_0$ y_0)]
Step 3: Occurrence of y_0 shared by all examples : (ON y_0 x_0)
Occurrence of y_0 belonging to E_1'' and not to E_2 = (NEAR x_0 y_0)
Step 4: In order to generate (NEAR * y_0) we use rules R_1 and R_2 so E_2 is rewritten as

$E''_2 : E''_2 = (ON\ y_0\ x_0)\ \&\ (NEAR\ x_0\ y_0)\ \&\ (NEAR\ x_0\ F)\ \&\ [(=\ x_0\ D)\ \&\ (=y_0\ C)\&(\neq x_0\ y_0)]$

Step 1: The last constant is F.
Step 2: $E''_1 = (ON\ y_0\ x_0)\ \&\ (NEAR\ x_0\ y_0)\ \&\ [(=\ x_0\ B)\ \&\ (=\ y_0\ A)\ \&\ (\neq\ x_0\ y_0)]$
$E_2 = (ON\ y_0\ x_0)\ \&\ (NEAR\ x_0\ y_0)\ \&\ (NEAR\ x_0\ z_0)\ [(=\ x_0\ D)\ \&\ (=\ y_0\ C)$
$\&\ (=\ z_0\ F)\ \&\ (\neq\ x_0\ y_0)\ \&\ (\neq\ z_0\ x_0)\ \&\ (\neq\ z_0\ y_0)]$

Step 3: The only occurrence of z_0 is $(NEAR\ x_0\ z_0)$ in E_2
Step 4: We can obtain a similar occurrence of z_0 in E''_1 due to the use of & idempotency on $(NEAR\ x_0\ y_0) =_\varepsilon (NEAR\ x_0\ z_0)[(=\ z_0\ y_0)]$.

$E''_1 = (ON\ y_0\ x_0)\ \&\ (NEAR\ x_0\ y_0)\ \&\ (NEAR\ x_0\ z_0)\ \&\ [(=\ x_0\ B)\ \&\ (=\ y_0\ A)$
$\&\ (=z_0\ y_0)\ \&\ (\neq\ x_0\ y_0)\ \&\ (\neq\ z_0\ x_0)]$

$E''_2 = (ON\ y_0\ x_0)\ \&\ (NEAR\ x_0\ y_0)\ \&\ (NEAR\ x_0\ z_0)\ \&\ [(=\ x_0\ D)\ \&\ (=\ z_0\ F)$
$\&\ (\neq\ x_0\ y_0)\ \&\ (\neq\ z_0\ x_0)\ \&\ (\neq\ z_0\ y_0)]$

Now the algorithm stops because there is no constant or variable not being a GV in formulae E''_1 and E''_2. One can easily verify the structural matching of E''_1 and E''_2.

2- LEARNING A CONCEPT FROM EXAMPLES AND COUNTEREXAMPLES

Since our methodology detects links between the variables of the generalization, counterexamples will be used to attempt their matching with the generalization. Since both "speak about the same kind of things" they must have some kind of (at least partial) structural matching. The general principle we shall follow is that firstly, links present in both are not very significant and secondly that links producing a matching failure are, on the contrary, very significant. Their matching failure or success may happen within two different syntactic contexts. In the first place, the counterexample may be "shorter" (i.e. contains less predicates) than the example generalization. One could then use theorems or idempotency in order to "increase" the counterexample size. This is not so useful because we are looking for a partial matching only. This is enough to detect the links needing some reaction.

Example 2-1. : Suppose one starts form the generalization
$SQUARE(x)\ \&\ RED(x)\ \&\ TRIANGLE(y)\ \&\ BLACK(y)\ \&\ CIRCLE(z)\ \&\ BLACK(z)$ to which $SQUARE(A)\ \&\ BLACK(A)$ is a counterexample. One can nevertheless write the counterexample as $SQUARE(A)\ \&\ BLACK(A)\ \&\ BLACK(A)$ in order to "improve" its matching with the generalization, but as we have said this is useless. One can see that the two subexpressions $SQUARE(x)\ \&\ BLACK(y)$ and $SQUARE(x)\ \&\ BLACK(z)$ can match $SQUARE(A)\ \&\ BLACK(A)$, with the two substitutions $\sigma_1 = (x \leftarrow A,\ y \leftarrow A)$ and $\sigma_2(x \leftarrow A,\ z \leftarrow A)$. These should therefore be forbidden and one should add $Different\ (x,y)\ \&\ Different(x,z)$ to the generalization. In the second place, the counterexample may be "bigger" than the example generalization. One must not use idempotency in the generalization since this would produce trivial failures of the matching by instantiating the same variable by different constants.

Example 2-2. : Let an example generalization be $SQUARE(x)\ \&\ BLACK(x)$ and a counterexample be $SQUARE(A)\ \&\ BLACK(B)\ \&\ SQUARE(B)$. Using idempotency on $SQUARE(x)$ would of course lead to the contradictory substitution $(x \leftarrow A,\ x \leftarrow B)$. This failure says no more that the counterexample is bigger than the generalization. On the contrary, one must again attempt partial matching. When they succeed, one can conclude that the corresponding part of the counterexample is not significant. When they fail, the failure indicates the important links in the generalization since these links reject the counterexample as an instance of the generalization.

Example 2-3. : Consider again Example 2. The matching of $SQUARE(x)\ \&\ BLACK(x)$ fails with the subpart of the counterexample $SQUARE(A)\ \&\ BLACK(B)$. This shows that SQUARE and BLACK must really refer to the same object, the fact that x appears as a variable of this two predicates is not due to chance. The matching of $SQUARE(x)\ \&\ BLACK(x)$ succeeds with the subpart $BLACK(B)\ \&\ SQUARE(B)$ and this simply shows that "SQUARE(B)" is an anecdotal part of the counterexample. We shall now give two

substantial examples.
Example 2-4. : We shall use the example of [Vere 80]which shows examples of "stacking, transfer and unstacking actions for uniform cubic blocks on a table ...". The counterexamples "illustrate that a block 1 cannot be moved on atop another block 2 if there is a block 3 on block 2" [Vere 80]. The formula generated by Vere 's system is : [(on t TABLE) & ¬((ON u z) & ¬((ON y v) & ¬((ON z TABLE) & (ON w u))))] (ON x y) → (ON x z) where x,y,z,t,u,v,w are variables that can be instantiated by the name of a block or the constant "TABLE", where the → shows the modification to be done to the blocks and the expression inside the brackets is the context in which this modification is allowed. This formula takes the value TRUE for all the examples and the value FALSE for all the counterexamples but anyone will agree that it illustrates very badly the concept of "stacking, unstacking but two blocks cannot be on a third one". We shall not use exactly the same examples as Vere because they are somewhat uselessly complicated, but it easy to check that our examples convey the same idea (and they are nothing but some simplification of Vere's examples).

$$E_1 : \underline{A \quad B} \to \underline{B \atop A} \qquad E_2 : \underline{G \atop F \atop E} \to \underline{F \atop E \quad G} \qquad E_3 : \underline{J \atop I \atop H \quad J} \to \underline{J \atop I \atop H}$$

We shall use Vere's notation which describes these examples by :
E_1 : = [(ON A TABLE)](ON B TABLE) → (ON B A)
E_2 : = [(ON E TABLE) & (ON F E)] (ON G F) → (ON G TABLE)
E_3 : = [(ON H TABLE) & (ON J H)] (ON J I TABLE) → (ON J I)
Using our methodology, the reader will easily find that G : [(ON t TABLE) & (ON t' u) & Different ((x,(y,z,t,t',u))(y,(z,t)), (z,u),(t',u))] (ON x y)→(ON x z) is a generalization of E_1, E_2, E_3, where, for instance, Different ((y,(z,t)))is a short way of saying Different(y,z) & Different(y,t). As we shall see, G has also no instance such that two cubes are over a third one. Of course, G is less ugly than Vere's formula but we are not still satisfied since much of its information is useless relative to the concept. Let us now consider the following counter-example :

$$CE_1 : \underline{M \quad N}^{P} \to \underline{M}^{P \quad N}$$
which is written as :

CE_1 : = [(ON M TABLE) & (ON P M)] (ON N TABLE) → (ON N M)
     (M1)   (M2)   (M3)
This counterexample is "nearly" in instance of G with the instantiations : x←N, y←TABLE, z←M,t'←P, u←P, u←M, t←M. This succeeds only if z, u and t are the same. From the set of Different in G, one sees that u and t may be the same therefore the "link" M1 = M2 may be present in both examples and counterexamples ; z and t may be the same, therefore the link M1 = M3 may be present in both examples and counterexamples ; z and u cannot be the same therefore the link M2 = M3 is the link which rejects the counterexample as an instance of G. This link expresses precisely that a new block cannot be put on an other which is not already clear. Our concept is therefore contained in the formula : G' : [(ON t TABLE) & (ON t' u) & Different (z,u)] (ON x y) → (ON x z) which is contained into G.
Example 2-5. : We use again the examples of Example 2-4,but give a different counterexample,

$$CE2 : \underline{Q \quad S}^{R} \to \underline{S}^{R \atop Q}$$

in order to forbid the transfer of two blocks together. It is written
CE2 : = [(ON S TABLE) & (ON R Q)] (ON Q TABLE) → (ON Q S)
This formula is almost matched by G with the substitution x←Q, y←TABLE, z←S, t←S, t'←R, u←Q. As in the preceeding example the fact that z and t may be the same shows that this property has no great importance. On the contrary, the link Different(x,u) is stressed by this counterexample since it causes the matching failure. One concludes that, relative to the two counterexamples so far seen, the generalization
G" : [(ON t TABLE) & (ON t' u) & Different((z,u),(x,u))] (ON x y) → (ON x z) stresses two concepts. The meaning of Different(z,u) has already been given and Different (x,u) says that if t' is on u then u cannot be moved on an other block. This is the

concept, "a block must be clear to be moved".

3- CHANGE OF DESCRIPTION LANGUAGE

Transforming the description language is certainly the most difficult and the most efficient way of learning. In the other sections it is always implicitely known that the desired information is somewhere included in the language, and we have shown how to improve the discovery of hidden or implicit information. In many cases this information is not at all present in the chosen description and our methodology becomes helpless. We claim that one can use this failure as a language modification test. This modification cannot be performed without a good knowledge of the universe in which learning is proceeding. We suppose here that this knowledge is put under the form of a tree which can be a "fuzzy" generalization tree as built in section 4. In that case, one can modify quite straighfordwardly the description language. Given a present language, change it by using the fathers (or the sons) of the words of the present language. A detailed example will now show the efficiency of this proposal.
Example : Consider the following 4 examples and counterexamples inspired by [Bongart 70], where it is said that a shape presence or absence only is significant.
E1 = $(\nabla,\Delta,\star)$, E2 = (∇,Δ), E3 = $(\star)$, E4 = $(\nabla,\square)$,
CE1 = $(\nabla,\Delta,\star,\square)$, CE2 = $(\nabla,\star)$, CE3 = $(\Delta,\uparrow)$, CE4 = $(\Delta,\star)$ where Ei's are examples and CEi's are counterexamples to the concept they are supposed to illustrate. Much learning work has been done on this example [Sallantin 83, Clavieras & All 83, Kodratoff & All 83], finding many formulas able to "recognize" the examples and "reject" the counterexamples. Nevertheless, no real concept was discovered. We now claim that this set of examples and counterexamples describe at least one clear, simple concept and we ask the reader to try finding it by using his intuitive concept discovery abilities. The description language we use is dictated by the sentence "shape presence or absence only is significant" : a variable x_i is associated to each shape, this variable takes the numerical value n when the shape is n times present in an example (n may be equal to 0). Associating x_1 and ∇, x_2 and Δ, x_3 and $\star$, x_4 and $\square$, x_5 and $\uparrow$, one obtains the following descriptions.
E1 := $(x_1 = 1, x_2 = 1, x_3 = 1, x_4 = 0, x_5 = 0)$, E2 := $(x_1 = 1, x_2 = 1, x_3 = 0, x_4 = 0, x_5 = 0)$, E3 := $(x_1 = 0, x_2 = 0, x_3 = 1, x_4 = 0, x_5 = 0)$, E4 := $(x_1 = 1, x_2 = 0, x_3 = 0, x_4 = 1, x_5 = 0)$. CE1 := $(x_1 = 1, x_2 = 1, x_3 = 1, x_4 = 1, x_5 = 0)$, CE2 := $(x_1 = 1, x_2 = 0, x_3 = 1, x_4 = 0, x_5 = 0)$, CE3 := $(x_1 = 0, x_2 = 1, x_3 = 0, x_4 = 0, x_5 = 1)$, CE4 := $(x_1 = 0, x_2 = 1, x_3 = 1, x_4 = 0, x_5 = 0)$. We already have given details [Clavieras & All 83, Kodratoff & All 83] explaining how to find a formula which recognizes each E_i and rejects all CE_i. But this formula is quite complicated and, worse, is not an impressive improvement over the trivial "generalization" : (E1 v E2 v E3 v E4) & $\neg$(CE1 v CE2 v CE3 v CE4). Since no concept has been discovered, one can attempt to change the representation. Among the knowledge about the shapes, one must have   triangle   . One can therefore attempt to

transform the description language by associating "triangle" to the variable x_{12} and leave x_3, x_4, x_5 as before. The formulas Ei' and CEi' would then read like Ei and CEi except that x_1 and x_2 are replaced by x_{12}, computed by adding the values of x_1 and x_2 (for instance, in E'_1, $x_{12} = 2$). One can show that still no concept is discovered. The research must go on into the knowledge tree of the shapes. After some (may be long) time, one can use the following trees :

Associating now x_a to "polygon" and x_b to "one-dimensional-shapes" one obtains the descriptions E1" := (x_a = 2, x_b = 1), E2" := (x_a = 2, x_b = 0), E3" := (x_a = 0, x_b = 1), E4" := (x_a = 2, x_b = 0), CE1" := (x_a = 3, x_b = 1), CE2" = (x_a = 1, x_b = 1), CE3" := (x_a = 1, x_b = 1), CE4" := (x_a = 1, x_b = 1). It follows that the examples are such that x_a = 0 or 2, and the counterexamples such that x_a = 1 or 3. Supposing that some ^{a}knowledge of the parity function (see [Utgoff ^{a}83]) or of automatic synthesis from input-output examples (see [Kodratoff 79]) has been given to the system, it is now possible (if not easy) to discover that x_a is even in the examples and odd in the counterexamples. We therefore claim that we have been able to change the description language up to the point where one can find a possible concept contained in the examples and counterexamples. This concept is the following : scenes which, among other shapes, always contain an even number of polygons.

4- CLUSTERING BY PRE-LEARNING

This section wants to show a clustering algorithm linked with what has been called "syntaxic distance" by [Michalski & All 81]. We shall implicitly define a distance and its associated clustering algorithm by considering the size and the nature of changes to be made to a description in order to put it in structural matching with the others. This section describes a clustering algorithm with the help of an example the presence of which will be denoted by /*... */.
/* consider the following description of a toy-robots world containing axles, wheels and car-bodies.
AXLE 1 (A1) : RELATION(ATTACHED) & RELATION(THRU) & ACTION(GRASP) & ACTION(INSERT) & POSITION(P1) & GRASPING(G1) & APPROACHING(A1) & SUBPART(SOLID CYLINDER(5 1) R1) & SUBPART(SOLID CYLINDER(10 4) R2) & SUBPART(SOLID CYLINDER(5 1) R3)
AXLE 2 (A2) : RELATION(ATTACHED) & RELATION(THRU) & ACTION(GRASP) & ACTION(INSERT) & POSITION(P2) & GRASPING (G2) & APPROACHING(A2) & SUBPART(SOLID CYLINDER(7 3) R4) & SUBPART(SOLID CYLINDER(12 6) R5) & SUBPART(SOLID CYLINDER(7 3) R6)
WHEEL 1 (W1) : RELATION(ATTACHED) & ACTION(PUSH) & ACTION(GRASP) & POSITION(P3) & GRASPING(G3) & APPROACHING(A3) & SUBPART(SOLID CYLINDER(2 8) R7) & SUBPART(HOLE CYLINDER(2 1) R8)
WHEEL 2 (W2) : RELATION(ATTACHED) & ACTION(PUSH) & ACTION(GRASP) & POSITION(P4) & GRASPING(G4) & APPROACHING(A4) & SUBPART(SOLID CYLINDER(4 10) R9) & SUBPART(HOLE CYLINDER(4 3) R10)
CARBODY 1 (C1) : RELATION(BLOCKED) & RELATION(UNBLOCKED) & ACTION(BLOCK) & ACTION (UNBLOCK) & POSITION(P5) & SUBPART(SOLID CUBOID(30 20 12) R11) & SUBPART(HOLE CYLINDER(20 6) R12) & SUBPART(HOLE CYLINDER(20 6) R13)
CARBODY 2 (C2) : RELATION(BLOCKED) & RELATION(UNBLOCKED) & ACTION(BLOCK) & ACTION (UNBLOCK) & POSITION(P6) & SUBPART(SOLID CUBOID(45 30 18) R14) & SUBPART(HOLE CYLINDER(30 9) R15) & SUBPART(HOLE CYLINDER(30 9) R16).
We willingly agree that this description is not complete but it will enough to see that a little more complication leads to "real-life" problems. The symbols R1, P1, A1, G1 for instance are constants (the "names" of the subparts) and the numbers are their dimensions on a given scale. For instance, SUBPART(SOLID CYLINDER(5 1) R1) means that the subpart R1 is a solid cylinder of height 5 and of diameter 1.*/
1- Let E1,..., En be a set of examples./*A1,A2,W1,W2,C1,C2 are 6 examples */ Compute the pairs of examples S_i^o, $1 \leq i \leq n(n-1)/2$.
/* $S_1^o = \{A_1, A_2\}$, $S_2^o = \{A_1, W_1\}$,..., $S_{15}^o = \{C_1, C_2\}$ */
2- For each $S_i^o = \{E_p, E_q\}$, $1 \leq i \leq n(n-1)/2$, compute 4 lists.

L_i^1 : list of predicates that will have to be dropped when "generalizing" Ep and Eq (recall that our definition of generalization excludes the use of the dropping rule which generates "fuzzy" generalizations).

L_i^2 : list of predicates common to Ep and Eq.

L_i^3 : predicates introduced by using theorems when generalizing Ep and Eq.

L_i^4 : predicates introduced by use of idempotency when generalizing Ep and Eq.

Concept learning 37

/* Since S_1^o = {A1,A2}, L_1^1, L_1^3 and L_1^4 are empty, L_1^2 contains the predicates of A1 and A2. In this example, we shall admit that no theorem is known about the system. Therefore no predicates will be introduced by using theorems and L_j^3 will always be empty. Consider now S_4^o = {A1,C1}. L_4^1 = (GRASPING, APPROACHING), L_4^2 = (RELATION, ACTION, POSITION, SUBPART), L_4^3 = ( ), L_4^4 = ( ). On the contrary, for S_2^o = {A1,W1}, L_4^2 is empty but L_4^4 = (RELATION, SUBPART). */

3- Associate a partial ordering to each of these four types of lists. This partial ordering can be linked for instance to the number of predicates in each list. Some knowledge about the system can also be introduced at this step by giving more "weight" to some predicates /* We shall give a weight of 1 to each predicate and therefore associate an integer to each list. The weight of L_4^1 is 2, the weight of L_4^3 is 0 etc... The ordering will be the one of the integers. */

4- When lists are different but have the same weight, we shall denote it by $L_i^j <> L_i^k$(they are not comparable). When a list L_i^j has less weight that a list L_i^k we shall denote it by $L_i^j < L_i^k$. /* $L_i^3 <> L_j^3$ if $i \neq j$. $L_4^1 < L_4^2$. */

5- Call L_i^5 each quadruplet $<L_i^1, L_i^2, L_i^3, L_i^4>$ and associate a partial ordering to the set $\{L_i^j, 1 \leq i \leq n(n-1)/2\}$. Here again semantic information may be introduced in order, for instance, to favor common predicates relative to absent predicates. /* We shall not use explicit semantic knowledge and define $L_i^5 < L_j^5$ by

if $\neg(L_i^1 <> L_j^1)$ then $L_i^1 < L_j^1$ else if $\neg(L_i^2 <> L_j^2)$ then $L_i^2 < L_j^2$ else
if $\neg(L_i^3 <> L_j^3)$ then $L_i^3 < L_j^3$ else if $\neg(L_i^4 <> L_j^4)$ then $L_i^4 < L_j^4$ else $L_i^5 <> L_j^5$

which means that, for instance, if L_i^1 and L_j^1 are comparable then $L_i^5 < L_j^5$ takes the value of $L_i^1 < L_j^1$. S_1^o is such that $L_1^1 = 0$, $L_1^2 = 6$, $L_1^3 = 0$, $L_1^4 = 0$ and S_{15}^o such that $L_{15}^1 = 0$, $L_{15}^2 = 4$, $L_{15}^3 = 0$, $L_{15}^4 = 0$. Since $L_1^1 = L_{15}^1$ and $L_{15}^2 < L_1^2$ then $L_1^5 < L_{15}^5$. S_3^o = {A1,W1} and S_4^o {A1,W2} have the same L_j^1, then $L_3^5 <> L_4^5$. */

6- This partial ordering defines <u>levels</u> (of some generality) as follows : level 1 contains all the pairs associated to the incomparable L_1^5's that are the lowest. Level i+1 contains the least incomparable pairs with a L_k^5 greatest than at least one of the L^5 of level less than or equal to i. /* Level 1 contains S_1^o = {A1,A2}, S_{10}^o = {W1,W2}. Level 2 contains S_{15}^o = {C1,C2}. Level 3 contains S_2^o = {A1,W1}, S_3^o = {A1,W2}, S_6^o = {A2,W1}, S_7^o = {A2,W2}. Level 4 contains S_4^o = {A1,C1}, S_5^o = {A1,C2}, S_8^o = {A2,C1}, S_9^o = {A2,C2}. Level 5 contains S_{11}^o = {W1,C1}, S_{12}^o ={W2,C1}, S_{13}^o ={W2,C1}, S_{14}^o= {W2,C2}. */

7- Using these levels, one can build a hierarchy of concepts as we shall define in the following. This definition will be a little complicated, we therefore insist on the fact that it simply tells that the partial ordering relation associated to couples is compatible with some inclusion relationship relative to sets of examples.
<u>Maximal subset</u> : For each S_i^o belonging to level j, compute the <u>maximal subsets</u> $MS_k^j = \{E_e,...,E_m\}$ as follows. Choose a first pair {Ep,Eq} of level j and put Ep and Eq in MS_o^j. All other pairs in level j that contain Ep or Eq are put into MS_o^j. This process is iterated on each newly included pair. When it stops, if all pairs are not in MS_o^j, then a new pair is chosen as starting point for filling up a MS_1^j. The process is iterated as long as some pairs do not belong to some MS_k^j. /* The maximal subsets are in Level 1 : MS_1^1 = {A1,A2}, MS_2^1 = {W1,W2}. In level 2 : MS_1^2 = {C1,C2}. In level 3 : MS_1^3 = {A1,A2,W1,W2}. In level 4 : MS_1^4 = {A1,A2,C1,C2}. In level 5 : MS_1^5 = {W1,W2,C1,C2} */ <u>Father</u> Suppose that the Maximal subset MS_v^k of

level k contains the elements of MS_u^i, MS_w^j, etc... of level less than k. Then MS_v^k is called a father of MS_u^i, MS_w^j, etc... if and only if there is none of MS_u^i, MS_w^j etc... which has already found a father in a level less than k. Building one (or several) conceptual hierarchies is now easy.
8- Apply the Maximal subset procedure to Level1. If all the examples are not contained in the MS_u^1, add to them the Maximal subset of higher levels that contain only the examples not in MS_u^1. These are the "basis concepts". /* In Level 1 one finds the maximal subsets MS_1^1 and MS_2^1. One must add to them MS_2^2 in order to have all the examples contained in the basis concepts. In a future step, this concepts will be made of the generalizations of the examples they contain */
9- The fathers of these basis concepts in the upper level are the "second generation" concepts. This process is iterated up to the last level. If a common father to all examples is not found in the last level, a really last one is made of a last maximal subset containing all the examples. /* The basis concepts are made of MS_1^1, MS_2^1 and MS_2^2. In Level 3 MS_1^3 is a father of both MS_1^1 and MS_2^1, therefore it is the next hierarchy father. In Level 4 MS_1^4 contains C1 and C2 but it contains also {A1} which is in a set which has already found a father. In Level 5 MS_1^5 contains C1 and C2 but it contains also {W1}. One has therefore to add a Level 6 containing all the examples, MS_1^6 = {A1,A2,A3,A4,C1,C2} which is the father of MS_1^2 and MS_1^3 (because MS_1^3 had no father of course). One has obtained the following clustering

{A1,A2,W1,W2,C1,C2}

{A1,A2,W1,W2}

{A1,A2} {W1,W2}   {C1,C2}.

Notice that there was no alternative hierarchy to be found. But suppose that for some reason we find that MS_1^4 is actually at level 3, let us call it MS_2^3. Then one could also find the clustering   {A1,A2,W1,W2,C1,C2}

{A1,A2,C1,C2}

{W1,W2} {A1,A2} {C1,C2}

which would be an alternative to the first one. */ In general, more than one clustering may be possible and all of them must be kept since each of them is of equal interest. Since the predicates "Different" we introduce during the generalization are not inherited, one cannot insure that a father will be really more general than all its sons. It may be that it is only "almost" more general because a "Different" has changed. Each concept must therefore be obtained as the generalization of all the examples the associated Maximal Subset contains. In a sense we introduce here some "logical fuzziness" linked to the fact that a father contains all the examples its son contains, but the formula of a father may be slightly different from the formula describing its sons.

BIBLIOGRAPHY :[Bongard 70] Bongard, N., Pattern Recognition (Spartan Books, New-York, 1970). [Clavieras & Al. 83] Clavieras, B., and Ganascia, J.G., Lemerle-Loisel, R., Actes Journées sur les outils de l'apprentissage à partir d'exemples, Orsay, 1983. [Dietterich & Al. 81] Dietterich, G.T., and Michalski, S.R., Artificial Intelligence 16, pp. 257-294, 1981. [Handbook 82]The handbook of Artificial Intelligence, Cohen, P.R. and Feigenbaum, E.A. (Eds.), vol. 3, Pitman, London, 1982. [Hayes-Roth & Al. 78] Hayes-Roth, F. and Mc Dermott, J., Com. ACM 21, pp. 401-411, 1978. [Holte 84] Holte, R.C., in Advanced Digital Information Systems, I. Alexander (Eds.) Prentice Hall, 1984. [Kodratoff 79]Kodratoff, Y., Interntl. J. Comput. Info. Sciences 8, pp. 489-521, 1979. [Kodratoff 83] Kodratoff, Y., Computers and Artificial Intelligence 2, pp. 417-441, 1983. [Kodratoff & Al. 83] Kodratoff, Y. and Ganascia, J.G., Proc. Internatl. Machine Learning Workshop, Monticello (1983), pp. 81-91. [Michalski & Al. 81] Michalski, R., and Stepp, R.E., Proc. 7th IJCAI ; pp. 460-465, Vancouver (1981). [Mitchell 83] Mitchell, T.M., Proc. IJCAI 83, pp. 1139-1169. [Plotkin 70] Plotkin, G.D., in Machine Intelligence, B. Meltzer & D. Michie eds., American Elsevier New-York, 1970. [Sallantin 83]Sallantin, J., Actes Journées sur les outils de l'apprentissage à partir d'exemples, Orsay, 1983. [Utgoff 83]Utgoff, P.E., Proc. IJCAI-83, pp. 447-449. [Vere 80] Vere, S.A., Artificial Intelligence J. 14, pp. 139-164, 1980. [Vere 81] Vere, S.A., unpublished draft, 23, Feb. 1981.

SELF-ORGANIZING FEATURE MAPS AND ABSTRACTIONS

Teuvo Kohonen

Department of Technical Physics
Helsinki University of Technology
Espoo, Finland

It is argued in this paper that the principles underlying biological intelligence may be completely different from those applied in AI. One of the most fundamental properties of the brain is its ability to form "feature maps" and abstractions of sensory signals. This paper offers an explanation for this ability, using an idealized model of a self-organizing system. Automatic formation of a two-dimensional map of speech elements is given as a practical example. The process, however, is more general and the formation of many other kinds of abstractions have already been demonstrated by computer simulations.

INTRODUCTION

The concept of "machine intelligence" was originally, before 1960, attributed to certain elementary learning machines, believed to describe the operation of neural networks formally. After an initial optimism it was soon felt, however, that in order to develop efficient *applications*, one has to forget the network models and to concentrate on high-level computing languages and procedures. After 1970, Artificial Intelligence (AI) has generally been restricted to mean the application of computers to automatic handling of complex tasks which earlier was possible for human beings only. Nonetheless there are researchers who are not quite happy with this development, and who would like to pose at least the following questions: (1) Because the neural networks seem to be completely different from digital computer networks structurally, functionally, as well as by their organization, why should the biological brain be doing similar things as the computers do? (2) Could it be that for the execution of certain difficult tasks such as generalization, extraction of invariances, creation of abstractions etc., one needs operations which have not been known in Computer Science and AI?

Even though it were agreed that the theories of intelligence are only intended to describe mental operations without any need to specify the physical systems underlying them, there still remains the big mystery of how the biological brain operates. In spite of masses of physiological data, however, many of its fundamental principles have remained unknown. In the light of present knowledge, it is much easier to state what the brain is *not* doing: (1) There does not exist any brain code in the sense of binary codes or even DNA; it seems that the brain is an analog computer, although a very sophisticated one. (2) The elementary operations of the brain are not controlled by machine instructions which are fetched from memory in a sequence and executed; the very concept of machine instruction in the biological realms does not exist. (3) There do not exist any units which would be called memories, and which would hold coded data or operation codes; all the adaptive functions of the neural network together comprise the memory. (4) The information-processing operations are not centralized or even disseminated, and no back-and-forth traffic of operands, characteristic of the operation of digital computers, can be detected.

If none of the basic computer principles can be found from the brain, how is it then possible that the computers and the brain resemble each other on the software level? One obviously needs a highly developed computer architecture and sophisticated programming systems to imitate even the simplest mental functions. It is necessary to realize that such computing procedures are mere analogies, more or less accurate, to the high-level functions of biological intelligence, whereas the underlying arithmetic and logic operations of computers may have little in common with the elementary functions of biological intelligence.

Even a bit more pointed comment might be presented: it seems that the theories of AI, and of intelligence in general only aim at describing *results* of information processing, not the processes themselves.

The unavoidable counterquestion is what then might account for the ability of biological beings to infer rather complicated relations from elementary sensory experiences. The answer is in fact very simple: the brain has an ability of forming *internal models* of the environment and its history. The existence of such models is evident from many instances: subjective experiences, psychological experiments, and physiological recordings. It is obvious that the brain represents such a "miniature environment" using the states of activity of the neural network, as well as stores and recalls these states by adaptive changes induced in such a network. The changes, together with the mapping which produces the internal models, then constitute the *biological memory* in the most general sense. The internal model, or the "memory", is not very faithful, however. During recall, many details of visual and aural experiences are dropped, while only the most important spatial and temporal relations between representations ("concepts") are usually preserved. Such internal models may reflect a very complex behavior because a brain state is able to evoke another state selectively, conditional on the prevailing context (background), and the state sequences can then branch in an immense number of variations.

The purpose of the present paper is to demonstrate the existence of a very simple network principle by which various kinds of concrete internal models can be formed automatically. Such a mechanism is then also able to form "abstractions", i.e., ordered images or "maps" of features of the sensory experiences, whereby the dimensionality of the representations is radically reduced. It is believed that this principle is most fundamental to all information processing in the brain, and combined with a mechanism for *associative memory* (which is also a network property) it then explains many characteristics of biological intelligence [1]. Naturally the artificial demonstrations must still be restricted to idealized examples. They would be implemented more effectively by special computers, but the latter should then be fundamentally different from the conventional or von Neumann computers. The development of such new computers has not yet begun.

At the end of this paper it will be demonstrated that at least in one example, namely, recognition of natural speech waveforms, the simple "map principle" is already able to produce results of practical value.

FEATURE MAPS IN THE BRAIN

Before the brain can perform any inference, it must have somewhere available ultimately compressed representations (abstractions) of the sensory data. The two tough questions to be answered are: (1) Where and in what form do such representations exist? (2) What is the physical process or system principle by which such representations are formed automatically, i.e., without external control?

Although many different views are held about the operation of the brain, nonetheless it will be possible, in view of the present experimental knowledge, to give a plausible answer to the first question. The brain tissue is organized in laminar sheets of neural cells which are densely interconnected by neural fibers. It seems that many important sensory qualities are described by *feature maps*, *i.e.*, they have a *two-dimensional, metrically and topologically organized representation* on a respective piece of such sheets. A very illustrative example can be found from the auditory cortex of mammals: it receives neural signals from the cochlea of the ear, and by virtue of resonance phenomena taking place in the basilar membrane of the cochlea, a rude decomposition into acoustic frequencies of the perceived sound is performed before the neural signals enter the cortex. These signals, roughly representing the frequency components, are connected to the cells of a piece of cortex, approximately one square centimeter wide. So called *tonotopically organized maps* can be recorded over such an area which means that pure monochromatic sounds produce neural responses in a particular set of cells, the location of which depends on the pitch of the sound; higher frequencies evoke responses on the anterior side of the map, and lower frequencies on the posterior side, respectively. Moreover the scale of frequencies is continuous and almost logarithmic. The tonotopic map is an example of a pure feature map. Other examples of observed feature maps which represent important qualities of sensory signals are a direct representation of *color* in the chromaticity diagram on a certain part of the visual cortex; topographic representation of *environment* in the hippocampus (recorded from the rat); metric representation of *echo delays* on the cortex of the bat, etc. There is a well-known, almost one-to-one representation of the various parts of the body on the somatosensory and motor cortices, and the retina is also known to be mapped on the primary visual cortex. There exist further experimental data which support the view that topographically organized maps, in a more or less clear form, of almost any important sensory qualities can be found. It is also plausible that some kind of maps relate to the higher levels of abstraction, too.

It has recently become possible to demonstrate, mathematically as well as by computer simulations, that *a universal and very simple principle alone may be responsible for the formation of such maps*. There are two important aspects thereby to be noted: (1) Although the feature maps can be realized in one, two, or more dimensions, it is most natural, in view of the structure of the brain networks, to consider mainly *two-dimensional* feature maps. On the contrary, the abstract space of sensory signals may have an arbitrary, and usually very high, dimensionality ("degrees of freedom"). (2) Although the set of sensory signals thus may have variations in a huge number of feature dimensions, it can be demonstrated that the mapping principle described in this paper is automatically able to pick up two of the most important feature dimensions, namely, those "directions" in which the density function of the sensory signals has the greatest variance, and to organize the feature map using these dimensions as the basis of the map. This may be regarded as a kind of abstraction. Moreover, the selection of feature dimensions is dynamic in the sense that different feature dimensions may be chosen to different parts of the map, whereby the map actually starts to reflect topological structures of the signal distribution.

Although the formation of different kinds of feature maps may be one of the most fundamental phenomena in biological information processing, of course the maps alone do not yet explain the whole thinking process. Therefore, one should augment this principle at least with the *associative memory function* [1]: patterns of activity also leave memory traces on these maps, as adaptive changes of the neural connections. "Memorized" response patterns can be recalled associatively, which means that a part of the prevailing activity pattern is able to reconstruct also the rest (i.e., responses which had earlier occurred together with the part used as key excitation). Another function which must be added to this model is *sequential operation*. The brain network is known to have many kinds of feedback loops and recurrent signal paths. A delay is associated with every signal path so that the neural system will then automatically generate timed sequences of activity patterns, relating to present as well as memorized information. It will be necessary to realize how complex such sequences in a large system can be, and that the brain state can be made to branch into many alternative sequences depending on the evoking conditions, memory traces, background, and internal state of the organism. *For intelligent behavior it is only necessary that such sequences follow meaningful rules; these rules, however, are formed adaptively and they can thus be implemented without any computer circuits.*

A SYSTEM MODEL WHICH AUTOMATICALLY GENERATES FEATURE MAPS

This section contains the description of a self-organizing principle which is believed to be embodied in neural networks, and according to which various kinds of feature maps will be formed automatically, without external supervision, by the effect of received signals only. Such a self-organizing mapping is able to reduce the dimensionality of input signal vectors in a way which is apparently equivalent to the formation of their *abstractions*. We shall not yet aim at the demonstration of very complex processes; it will be more important to understand the basic operation. It seems, however, that this principle has a potential for the creation of much more complex information structures than exemplified here; up to time the demonstrations have only been limited by the computational capacity of general-purpose computers available to us.

Consider a two-dimensional network composed of elementary processing units, schematically represented in Fig.1. Every unit can be imagined similar to an adaptive linear element which has a number of inputs, each one provided with a variable weight, and one output. In the idealized case, each unit receives a set of external signals, denoted by vector $x = (\xi_1, \xi_2, \ldots, \xi_n) \in R^n$. In addition there shall exist lateral interconnections between the units, not explicitly shown in the simplified picture, however. In the present paper, the function of the lateral connections cannot be discussed explicitly; let it be referred to a more detailed representation published elsewhere [1]. It is only assumed here that, as a result of these lateral couplings, the adaptive process taking place in the network is describable by the following simplified system equations (which, on the other hand, could easily be implemented by special parallel computing circuits). The set of input weights of unit i shall be denoted by another vector $m_i = (\mu_{i1}, \mu_{i2}, \ldots, \mu_{in}) \in R^n$.

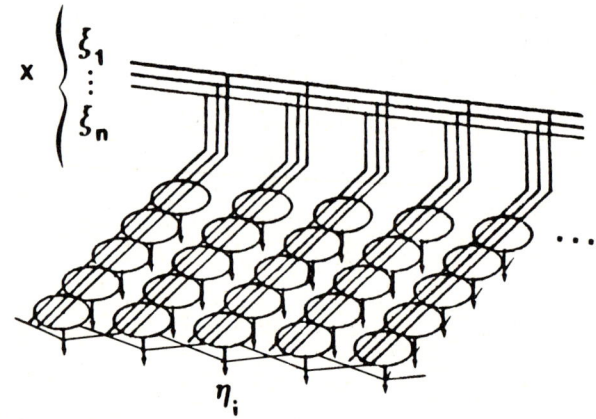

Figure 1
The Self-Organizing Network

Assume tentatively that the input weights of the units have already been determined as shown later on. Every unit then acts like a matched filter, tuned to a particular value combination of the input signals. In the simplest case the same set of signals was connected in parallel to every unit; *the wanted result is that different units become sensitized to different input vectors* x *in an orderly fashion* which means, for instance, that if all possible input vectors can be ordered according to, say, two independent parameters, then *localized output responses* will be obtained from the network around a unit the index of which is proportional to the above pair of parameter values (cf. the feature maps of the brain, discussed earlier). It then seems as if a coordinate system, with these parameters as axes, were created over the network.

The output response from unit i, denoted by η_i, may be assumed to have the following linear form in the simplest case (it is also possible to obtain organized maps using nonlinear transfer functions):

$$\eta_i = \sum_{j=1}^{n} \mu_{ij} \xi_j \ . \tag{1}$$

Next we shall define an adaptive process which updates the input weights and in which an ordered mapping, or formation of the feature coordinate system over the network in the sense defined above, is indeed realized. Assume that the different values of x are realized with a probability density p(x) ; this function may have an arbitrary form, and if the input signals are derived from the observation of natural objects, p(x) usually has plenty of "branches" in the signal space. For convenience, we shall discuss this process in the discrete-time formalism whereby x = x(t) is a function of the integer-valued time parameter t , and the $m_i(t)$ are the corresponding time-variable weight vectors of the different units.

There are also many possible choices for the adaptation law of which we take the following simple one; it has a bearing on the early learning machines. There is a characteristic feature in this law which distinguishes it from all previous models: adaptive changes are restricted to occur only in a constricted subset of units, denoted N_c , and this subset shall be centered around that unit c for which the output response is maximum. For different x(t) the maximum response will be obtained at different units, whereby in a long run, changes at all units shall occur iteratively. The exact definition of N_c has been presented elsewhere [1]; in the simplest case N_c comprises unit c and its local neighbors in the network.

The initial values of the m_i can be arbitrary, and they are usually selected as random numbers. The *updating* of the weight vectors shall be defined by the formulas

$$m_i(t+1) = m_i(t) + \alpha(t) \cdot \left[x(t) - m_i(t) \right] \quad \text{for} \ i \in N_c ,$$

$$m_i(t+1) = m_i(t) \quad \text{for} \ i \notin N_c . \tag{2}$$

Here $\alpha(t)$ is a scalar adaptation gain coefficient, similar to the gain factor used in stochastic approximation problems.

The nature of the process which is defined by Eqs.(1) and (2) may not be quite obvious, and indeed its mathematical solution has turned out cumbersome. One might observe rather easily, however, that Eq.(2) describes a corrective process in which, at a particular iteration step, all the weight vectors belonging to the subset N_c will change towards x(t) ; this in effect then increases *continuity* of the values of neighboring weight vectors (weights belonging to locally neighboring units in the network). From many iterative steps, each one increasing local continuity of the m_i, there finally results a two-dimensional order of these values. The final result, however, is still more intriguing, and it can be proved mathematically: after adaption, *the asymptotic point density of the m_i vectors tends to approximate the probability density function* $p(x)$; thus there will be formed an ordered image of $p(x)$ in the network.

As the above result might otherwise still remain a little obscure, the organizing power of the process defined by Eqs.(1) and (2) shall further be illustrated with the aid of the following practical example.

CASE EXAMPLE : FORMATION OF PHONOTOPIC MAPS

The term *phonotopic map* introduced here refers to a two-dimensional display of speech elements. This new representation of phonological features of the natural speech waveforms, actually that of the phonemes (of the Finnish language) has been developed in connection with our speech recognition experiments [2] . The purpose was to find a method by which short-time spectra of speech waveforms, or maybe even other types of pattern vectors representing speech signals, could be displayed in a feature coordinate system which directly indicates their metric similarity relations. The above self-organizing mapping has thereby shown very effective, and it has further led to a new pattern recognition method. The two-dimensional network consisted in this experiment of *hexagonally* arranged units. We used *short-time spectra of a continuous speech signal* as the input patterns $x(t)$. These spectra were evaluated every 10 ms, with a window of 25.6 ms. The spectra were computed for natural speech by the Discrete Fourier Transform, and only 15 frequency channels were used. Channels 1 though 12 were equally spaced in the frequency range 200 Hz to 3 kHz, and channels 13, 14, and 15 equally spaced in the range 3 kHz to 5 kHz, respectively. Thus the dimensionality of $x(t)$ was 15.

In a previous article [3] which described a similar experiment we had picked up the spectral samples from the points of best stationarity of the waveforms and presented them to the algorithm in a random order. This time all spectral samples,

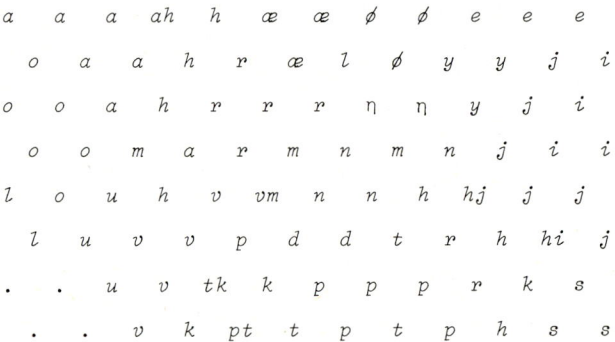

Figure 2
Self-Organized Phonotopic Map

even from the regions of phonemic transitions, were employed and they were presented to the algorithm in the natural order of their utterance (whereby each iteration step corresponds to an interval of 10 ms of the waveform). The resulting map was calibrated using known stationary phonemes to lay a scale to the map. The 8 by 12 positions shown in Fig.2 correspond to the locations of the adaptive units in the network, and the labels at these positions indicate that test phoneme which caused the maximum response. As there were 30 independent samples of each test phoneme, a statistical spread of the responses is discernible. If certain samples of different phonemes caused the maximum response at the same unit, this is shown by double labels. Those units in which none of the test phonemes caused a response are shown by dots.

FURTHER IMPLICATIONS

It will be mentioned only briefly that the following other simulations of self-organizing maps have succeeded [1,3] :

- a one-to-one ordered topographic mapping (e.g., retinotectal or somatotopic mapping);
- tonotopic map;
- feature map of light bars in width-displacement coordinates;
- topographic mapping of the environment using different kinds of sensory channels (feeler mechanism, direction of gaze, elementary retina) and
- hierarchical (tree-like) clustering of taxonomic data.

The self-organizing algorithm expressed in Eqs. (1) and (2) has usually worked rather reliably and with wide margins of the system parameters. For details of experimental conditions, see, e.g., [3] .

REFERENCES

[1] Kohonen, T., Self-organization and associative memory (Springer, Berlin-Heidelberg-New York-Tokyo, 1984).

[2] Kohonen, T., Riittinen, H., Reuhkala, E., and Haltsonen, S., On-line recognition of spoken words from a large vocabulary, to be published in Information Sciences (1984).

[3] Kohonen, T., Clustering, taxonomy, and topological maps of patterns, Proc. 6th ICPR (1982) 114-128.

A CONTRIBUTION TOWARDS FORMING RELATIONS
BETWEEN THE LINKING SPACE AND EXECUTIVE LEVEL OF ROBOTIC SYSTEMS

Vukašin P. Masnikosa
Institute "Mihailo Pupin"
Belgrade, Yugoslavia

In this paper the problem of connecting executive organs of a robotic system to the linking space in order to provide control is dealt with. The basis for solutions of the problem is the action principle theory (1).

1. INTRODUCTION

Solution of the problem connected with the control of robotic systems has been based, up to now upon the model synthesis principle, and many different methods have been applied (3,4,6). An exceptional success was achieved by the application of the synergy approach (2,8). The approach used here is complemetary to the approach which is very actual today, although these two approaches do not overlap in any of their parts. The basis of the solution suggested here is the linking space theory; the linking space is considered as being congruent with the nerve system. The tendency in the solution is to approximate its characteristics to the characteristics to the characteristics of the natural one (6,7).

2. TASK SETTING UP

The use of a robot is acceptable only if its preparation for the execution of a certain job is as simple as possible. Task set up in this paper is to find solution for the problem of training and the repetition of the task to be performed without pre-knowledge and conflict with the environment.

3. TASK SOLVING

Application of the action principle is possible only by applying the linking space theoury as well.
In fact, input/output mechanisms have to be adapted to the conditions required by the linking space. In figure 1, a block diagram showing a computer system, by which linking space may be initiated, is presented. The jointed system, subject of control, is shown in figure 2. In figure 4 a practical solution for the control of motor required for the motion of jointed system is presented. Figures 3 and 4 shown two classes of links over which the motion of action and provocations are possible.

3.1. Connecting the Executive Organs with the Linking Space

In accordance with the linking space characteristics and corresponding semantics (1), a formal description of action motion is given. Thanks to the feature of computer system operational organ, contents of the exit element are easely transcribed into the KR register, i.e., IR register and SR counter. This part of action motion is to be described in the following way:

$$v_i = d(\{@\}) = d(\{kr\}_i) \quad @ V = V @ KR @ V = V @ M_i \qquad (1)$$

where:
v_i = linking element,
$d(@.)$ = sign for action (field),
$d(\{kr\}_i)$ = distributive action by the array of links,
KR = command register
M_i = executive motors,
V = linking space sign,
$\triangle$ = equality sign,
@ = action sign,
( ) = denoting contents,
{ } = sign for the set.

Statement (1) may also be writteh in the following way:

$$v_i \ominus d(\{kr\}_i) \oplus KR \oplus M_i \qquad (2)$$

where:
$\ominus$ = layered transmission of provocation,
$\oplus$ = unique and permanent linking.

```
┌─────────────────────┐
│ input-output units  │
└─────────────────────┘
           ↕
┌─────────────────────┐
│     processor       │
└─────────────────────┘
      ↕         ↕
┌──────────┐ ┌──────────┐
│program's │ │ linking  │
│ memory   │ │ space's  │
│          │ │ memory   │
└──────────┘ └──────────┘
```

Fig.1. Computer system block diagram, for the realization of linking space.

In figure 4 a rigid connection of motors with the return action is shown. This return action from the transducer S is transmitted, over unique and permanent connections, over the register IR. This part of the path may be described as:

$$M_i \ominus S_i \oplus d(m_i) \oplus IR \qquad (3)$$

Action from IR may cause the existence of action inside the environment of the entry linking element, but it is obvious that this action is not strong enough for forming a link between this element and any other one. The given clossed chain of links:

$$v_i \ominus KR \oplus d(\{kr\}_{ij}) \oplus \{M_i\} \quad \{S_j\} \oplus d(\{m\}_i) \oplus IR \ominus v_i \qquad (4)$$

Motion of the tactile element carrier is under restriction until the moment of contact with a body inside the environment, causing the following state:

$$NT \ominus A \oplus d(\{a\}_{ij}) \ominus TE \oplus d(\{te\}_p) \oplus TR \ominus v_j \qquad (5)$$

From the element v_j action occurs, i.e., linking field in the environment. According to the features of linking space (1), the conditions for forming the links between elements v_j and v_i will set in. By establishing this link between elements v_j and v_i the following chain for the motion of provocation and action will be established:

$$NT \ominus A \oplus d(\{a\}_{ij}) \ominus TE \oplus d(\{te\}_p) \oplus TR \ominus v_j \oplus v_i \ominus$$
$$\ominus KR \oplus d(\{KR\}_{ij}) \oplus M_i \ominus NT \qquad (6)$$

Statement (4) stands for the internal closed chain of provocation. Statement (5) shows that the external action $/d(\{a\}_{ij})/$ is transmitted to the element v_i, and appears as the source of the field, while v_j, transmitted towards the chain (4) is the inflow of the field. This is a sufficient and required condition for unique link forming $(v_i \oplus v_j)$ between elements v_j and v_i. The consequence of forming this link is the forming of the chain given by statement (6). Request to provide for the training assumes the existence of a chain of links which is established over a second class of external actions. Such a chain will have

$$B \oplus d(\{b\}_{ij}) \ominus PB \oplus d(\{pb\}_{ij}) \oplus RB \ominus v_z \oplus v_k \ominus BR \oplus$$
$$\oplus d(\{b\}_{ij}) \oplus U \ominus PB \tag{7}$$

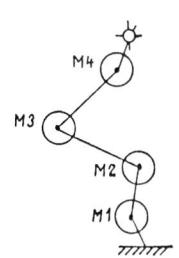

Fig.2. Graphic representation of a jointed system.

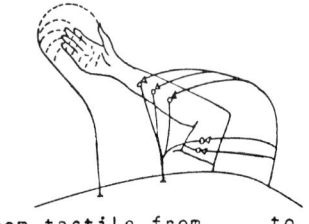

from tactile   from   to
elements   muscules   muscules

Fig.3. Links of nerve system between CNS and "arm", and between the tactile elements and the CNS.

In both cases, in statements (6) and (7), elements v_j and v_z, respectively, occur as the source of the linking field, and the elements v_i and v_k as the inflows of action. It is assumed that between the linking space receiving external action from the tactile elements, and the corresponding one responsible for the receipt of acoustic actions, there is a linking interspace, so that on it actions from elements v_j and v_z will be acting as well. If the element inside the interspace is denoted by v_{mv}, the internal link between external actions may be established in the following way:

$$v_j \oplus v_{mv} \oplus v_k \ominus BR \oplus d(\{bk\}_{ij}) \oplus U \ominus PB \oplus d(\{pb\}_{ij})$$
$$\oplus v_k \oplus v_z \oplus v_k \tag{8}$$

i.e.,

$$v_z \oplus v_{mv} \oplus v_m \oplus KR \oplus d(kr_{ij}) \oplus \{M_i\} \oplus \{S_i\} \oplus d(\{m\}_i) \oplus$$
$$\oplus IR \ominus v_i \oplus v_j \oplus v_i \tag{9}$$

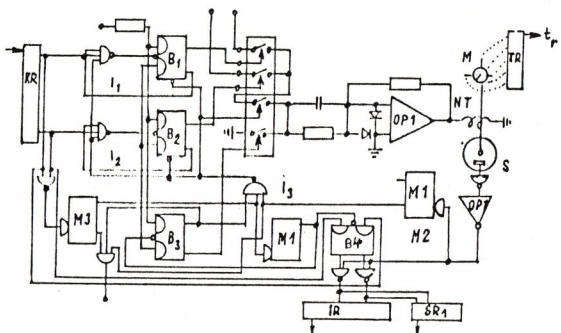

Fig. 4. Solution for connecting linking space with the executive motors and of the executive motors with the linking space.

Statement (6) represents the training process, i.e., forming the description of external object, and statement (9) the process of jointed system executing the work in accordance with the algorithm learned, by repetition of motion of the jointed system in accordance with sequence of commands. Searching starts with the action from one of input/output elements and lasts until following conditions are met: u1: (TR) $\neq$ 0, u2: (NE) $\neq$ 0. In both cases the motion of the jointed system is stopped. In case of condition under u1 being satisfied the system is the one which determines the starting requirements of touch. Should one of the following conditions u3: (TR) = 0, u4: (NE) $\neq$ 0 set in the system is stopped because it has to change the control information, in fact, action from another element. In case of existing command being repeated m times, provided m is ≥ 2, the condition for forming the initial linking element is satisfied. Connection of input/output element to the linking and interlayer one is effected in a manner shown in figure 5. The advantage of the solution suggested for the termination of repetition lies in that there is a dialog with the system, i.e., this is not a mechanical solution but a conceptual one, in so far as it simulates the features of natural intelligence.

4. DISCUSSION AND CONCLUSION

Association of executive organ and linking space, made possible by the aid of a program system /processor/, is congruent with the association of nerve system in living beings and the executive organs. Executive organ motors, found satisfactory for the practice, are quasi-stepped ones. This property of the motors is completely congruent with the property of the muscles. Work of the motors is performed, in both cases, under the action of a series of pulses. Manifestation of the linking space are identical

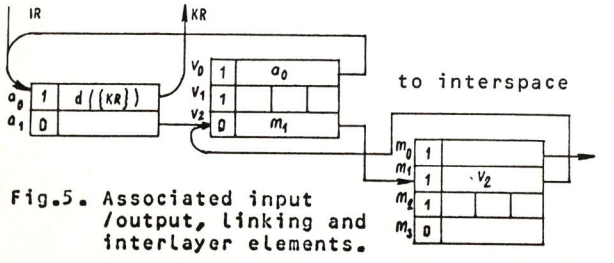

Fig. 5. Associated input /output, linking and interlayer elements.

to the manifestations of the nerve system, and so are the information (signals) flows.

BIBLIOGRAPHY

1. V.P.Masnikosa: "Action Principle", A monography in preperation for publishing.
2. M.Vukobratović: "Dynamic Stability of Unstable, Legged Locomotion Systems", Mathematical Bioscience, Vol. 24, No. 1-2.
3. A.Barto, R.Sutton: "Landmark Learning: an Illustration of Associative Search", Bibliogical Cybernetics, No. 42, No. 1-8, 1981.
4. T.Kohonen: "Associative Memory", in Russian, "Mir" - Moscow, 1978.
5. V.P.Masnikosa: "One Solution of Artificial Visual Perception Problem", Computers and Artificial Intelligence, Vol. 2, No. 1, Febr. 1983, pp. 75-86, Bratislava, ČSSR.
6. A.Barto, R.Sutton, P.Brouwer: "Associative Search Network, A Reinforcement Learning Associative Memory", Biological Cybernetics, No. 40, 201-211, 1981.
7. V.P.Masnikosa: "Simulation of CNS Operations by a Program Organized Linking Space", Paper to be published the journal "AUTOMATIKA" - Zagreb.
8. M.Vukobratović: "Legged Locomotion Robots and Anthoropomorphic Mechanisms", Monography by M.Vukobratović, Institute "Mihailo Pupin", Belgrade, 1975.

AUTOMATIC MULTIOPERATION ASSEMBLY
AND APPLICATION OF VISUAL CONTROL

D.E. Okhotsimsky, S.S. Kamynin, E.I. Kugushev

Keldysh Institute of Applied Mathematics
USSR Academy of Sciences
Moscow

The paper describes an approach to the problem
of automation of industrial assembly process
with the aid of general purpose robots equipped
with simple sensors and auxiliary devices and
controlled by a minicomputer. The application
of a vision system for testing the correctness
of assembly process is investigated. Results
of experiments in automatic multioperation
assembly are presented.

INTRODUCTION

This paper describes an approach to the problem of industrial
assembly automation by using manipulating robots. An experimental
automatic assembly system developed at the Keldysh Institute of
Applied Mathematics of the USSR Academy of Sciences is described.
Main principles used to construct the algorithms for automatic
assembly implementation are considered. The results of experiments
on the assembly of some industrial articles are given. The main
purpose of these research and experiments with the automatic assembly system was to demonstrate the feasibility of rather complex
multioperation assembly with the aid of general purpose manipulators controlled by a minicomputer and equipped with simplest sensors, tools and auxiliary devices. Also the development of vision
data processing algorithms was carried out. The attention was paid
to the inspection vision system aimed for testing the correctness
of performance of assembly operations during the automatic assembly
process.

1. ASSEMBLY ROBOT

A laboratory breadboard model of the assembly robot [1] was used
as a technical basis for the research. It included two electrome-
chanical 2-kg load-carrying capacity manipulators UEM-2 that were
developed at the Bauman's Institute. Each manipulator had six degrees of freedom (plus the seventh one of a gripper) and was connected to the M-6000 minicomputer. The indications of the potentiometric sensors of the manipulator link positions were entered into
the computer via a 10-bit A/D converter. The computer was included
in the manipulator motor control loop and used to vary the motor
control parameters with a frequency of about 30 Hz. A special robot
control interface was employed to convert digital signals of the
computer into pulse-duration outputs to control the manipulator
motors.

The manipulator grips were changable. There were both nonsensitized grips and the ones equipped with simple force sensors. In particular, spring-loaded fingers with sensors of linear shifts were used.

The robot may be connected to a technical vision device. It was developed by the Institute of Information Transfer Problems of the USSR Academy of Sciences on the basis of a standard Electronica L-50 TV-camera [2].

The UEM-2 manipulators operate with a rather modest positioning accuracy. The accuracies which may be achieved by manipulators seem to be often lower than those needed for mating the assembled parts. So in any case methods of adaptive control should be developed with applying the force feedback, search motions and other means to manage assembly operations successfully.

2. SOFTWARE

The automatic assembly system software is comprised of a number of modules to provide the robot control in a basic operating mode (automatic assembly mode) as well as to allow preliminary planning of the robot operation by a programmer-operator [3]. The latter plans the assembly at three levels:

1. Composes an assembly plan where a sequence of assembly operations to be fulfilled is specified, and the response to faulty executed operations is provided.

2. Composes a plan of each operation where a sequence of manipulator motions necessary to fulfil an operation is specified, and where the conditions, under which the transfer from one motion to another is possible, are described. Besides the operation plan contains a response to faulty executed motions.

3. Composes programs of motions listed in the operation plans.

An alphabet-digital Videoton-340 display was used as an operator terminal. The motions may be specified also by "choreographic" programming, i.e. by sequentially placing the manipulators (by hand or with the aid of a special console) at the positions across which they must pass.

In accordance with what is said above the following software modules were developed [4].

1. Module for assigning and editing the assembly plan.

2. Module for assigning and editing the assembly operation plans.

3. Module for assigning and editing the condition plans.

4. Module for assigning and editing the motion contours.

5. Module for assigning and editing the servosystem coefficients.

6. Module for the automatic assembly control.

Modules 1 through 5 operate at the assembly planning stage. A programmer-operator can refer to them in any order convenient for him. The planning must result in the assembly plan, the operation plans, the condition plans and the motion contours. It is of no importance in what order these data are prepared, so the operator may carry out programming in a "bottom-up" or "top-down" mode, or in any other way.

Module 6 executes the automatic assembly control and is composed of two processes. The first one, basic, is a part of the servosystem operation. It starts by timer's interruptions with frequency of about 30 Hz. During this process the sensor indications are scanned and the commands to servomotors are produced and transmitted to provide the given programmed motion. The second process is a background one. It uses a residual of the time cycle. It includes inspection of the assembly plan and operation plans, necessary preparations and start of a current motion in the main process as well as testing of the conditions of the transfer from one motion to another.

Thus the automatic assembly comes to the effect that the assembly robot performs sequential motions required for the assembly. Transfer from one motion to another is performed in accordance with the assembly plan and operation plans. Simultaneously with the start of each motion, testing of the condition assigned to the given motion begins. By involving simplest sensing devices, a robot control system analyzes current situation, and when satisfying given conditions, organizes completion of a given motion and transfer to another one, etc.

3. EXPERIMENTS

In experiments with the assembly automatic system the assembly of some units and articles was performed. In particular, the assembly of an oil gearing pump was implemented.

The pump consists of the following parts: a base, a cover, two gears, a gasket, four bolts, four nuts, four spring rings - all in all seventeen parts. A clearance between the gear axle and the walls of a hole in the base is about 30 μ m. The pump assembly was performed by two manipulators whose simultaneous motions were coordinated. An electropower nut-driver was used as a tool to screw nuts on the bolts. The total assembly time was about 4 min 17 sec.

Since an accuracy in positioning the manipulators used for the automatic assembly was about 3 to 5 mm, the assembly could be performed only due to interaction between mated surfaces of parts and their utilization as stops and guides. The compliance of grippers was also used.

From the above it follows that an important problem to be solved by the robot sensors is to detect the touching of the stops. Rather simple sensors can do it. Note that touching of the stop may also be detected by the position sensor indicating the manipulator's interlink angles. If indications of the sensor do not change in time, though the control signals are being sent to the respective motor, the situation may be interpreted as the contact with the stop. Thus the robot equipped only with the position sensors proves to be sufficiently sensitized and capable to use adaptive behavior and rather developed control logic.

The automatic assembly system was also used for the assembly of a case of the motor for a light motocycle. In this experiment the assembled parts were a base, a cover, a gasket, and ten screws.

Since the cover was rather heavy and bulky it was mounted on the base with the aid of both manipulators. An electrical screw-driver was used as a tool for setting screws. The total assembly time was about 4 min 30 sec.

The idea was to manage the above experiments with applying a minimal set of sensors. An adaptive behavior of the robot in assembling the pump and the motor case was based on indications of the potentiometric sensors of the manipulator link positions without use of the force-moment sensors or any technical vision system.

4. SYSTEM OF INSPECTION VISION

The system of inspection vision is a part of the experimental automatic assembly system described above. It is aimed to verify the correctness of operation execution in the course of automatic assembly of industrial articles. Its use considerably enhances reliability of the assembly process.

The system hardware is based on a commercial TV-camera "Electronica L-50" which is connected with the M-6000 control minicomputer via an interface developed by the Institute of Information Transfer Problems and the Keldysh Institute of Applied Mathematics (USSR Academy of Sciences). The interface allows any rectilinear fragment of raster to be fed into the computer memory. The TV-camera raster consists of 128x128 elements. The luminance of each element is coded by a ten-digit binary number.

The concept of the inspection vision system operation is based on good organization of an observed scene. At the correctly performed assembly operation each part always found at the same assigned position in a working zone of the assembly robot and, hence, in the picture. So for verifying the correctness of assembly operation the inspection vision system should conform fragments of a current image with some standard fragments, stored in advance, which correspond to the correct assembly. The fragment comparison is carried out element by element which allows to construct compact and fast algorithms for the inspection vision system.

During the automatic assembly the inspection vision system tests a certain condition, and depending on the testing results the operation plan is branched, i.e. the transfer to some or other manipulator motion takes place.

It should be noted that in each specific case small informative spots can usually be selected in the picture of parts being manipulated, which look significantly different depending on whether the situation is correct or no. Therefore, the size of conformed fragments may be rather small (of 20x20 raster dots). The ability of using small fragments speeds up the inspection system operation and allows to manage with rather little amount of data.

This selection of fragments to be conformed during the assembly as well as their feeding into the image processor are made at the planning stage by a programmer-operator. When teaching the system he shows the assembly objects in correct and incorrect versions which are memorized automatically.

ALGORITHMS FOR FRAGMENT CONFORMANCE.

To ensure smooth operation of the inspection vision system the algorithms for fragment conformance must be stable against disturbances occurring in real conditions.

Three main categories of such disturbances may be named.

1. Variation in the scene illumination.

2. Small shifts of the scene image caused by a varying raster grid, errors in positioning the TV-camera as well as small displacements of objects in the scene.

3. Variation in the object characteristics (due to oil spots, glares, admissible changes in object orientation, etc.).

In order to make the conformance algorithms stable against varying illumination the fragments have to be normed.

The normed luminance of each element is calculated by the formula

$$b_i = (B_i - M)/D ,$$

where B_i is the luminance of i-th element, b_i is its normed luminance, and

$$M = \sum_{i=1}^{N} B_i / N , \qquad D = \sum_{i=1}^{N} (B_i - M)/N ,$$

(N is the number of fragment elements).
By norming the elements, invariance of the image under linear variation in the element luminances B_i is ensured.

Small shifts in the image may be compensated in two ways. First, the elements are assumed to conform with the standard ones if

$$b_{i\,min}^{s} \leq b_i \leq b_{i\,max}^{s} ,$$

where b_i is the normed luminance of i-th element of a current fragment, $b_{i\,min}^{s}$ and $b_{i\,max}^{s}$ are, respectively, the minimal and maximal normed luminances of elements in a standard fragment taken from a certain small vicinity of i-th element.

Second, the current fragment is selected from an area somewhat larger than the standard fragment. The conformance is performed for the current fragment in all its positions in the area. The conformance with the standard fragment is assumed to be acceptable if the conformance conditions are satisfied even for one position of the current fragment.

Stability against disturbances of the third kind may be achieved if the conformance of the current and standard fragments is made not in all elements but only in those which are conserved best in correct situations under these disturbances and most changed in incorrect situations. The choice of these most informative elements is made at construction of a standard fragment during the system learning. The number of such highly informative elements is usually much less than a total number of elements in a fragment, it may be equal to 20-30 for a fragment of 20x20 elements.

TEACHING

This process when standard fragments are constructed, takes place at the assembly planning stage and consists of the following steps.

1. The fragment size and location on the raster are chosen. It is performed either from the operator terminal or by indicating the coordinates of the fragment rectangle or by introducing a contrast object (usually a small piece of white paper) in an appropriate place of the scene to distinguish the fragment. In the last case the fragment coordinates are determined by comparing two images - with and without the introduced object.

2. A series of correct situations is shown (correct positions of assembled parts) representative with respect to the disturbances caused by variations in the object characteristics (the third type of disturbances). By using this information obtained in the shows the fragment elements are selected which are best conserved in correct situations.

3. A series of incorrect situations (incorrect positions of assembled parts) sufficiently representative is shown. By using this information only the elements of those selected at step 2 are kept which change most in incorrect situations.

The coordinates of a standard fragment defined at step 1, and the elements selected at steps 2 and 3 are stored in the computer memory.

EXPERIMENTS

The inspection vision system is implemented on the base of the M-6000 minicomputer and the ELECTRONICA L-50 TV-camera mounted on a stand with two controlled degrees of freedom. In terms of automatic assembly the inspection system is an universal contactless sensor allowing to evaluate the situation in the assembly zone and answer the question if they correspond to the given ones. Depending on the answer a branching may take place in the assembly plan.

The inspection vision system was used to check the correctness of performing the operations of gear insertion into the oil pump case and putting the gasket onto guide pins. In the last case a fragment of 12x12 elements was employed, which included the image of a guide pin. Also, the system checked the presence of a nut (the pump part) in a feeder. This checking operation may be applied after the nut was grasped by a manipulator with an electrical nut driver.

The experiments demonstrated high reliability of the inspection vision system. Correct recognition of the situation took place in a wide range of illumination variations (by a few times), at optic defocusing of TV-camera and shifts of parts in the assembly zone (within 1 cm).

The time of fragment conformance was about 0.1 sec. The size of a program to enter the fragment and conform it with a standard one is about 2K of 16-digit words.

The time taken for construction of one standard fragment in the system teaching was about 5-10 min.

CONCLUSION

The algorithms for assembly robot control in multioperation

assembly of industrial articles are described.

The algorithms developed provide adaptive control of an assembly robot with a minimal set of sensors, rather simple auxiliary devices and tools. Their use allows to carry out automatic assembly of workpieces.

The inspection vision system algorithms allow to considerably enhance the reliability of the assembly process. Being compact and fast they proved their efficiency under significant disturbances in the observed scene.

The algorithms efficiency in automatic assembly operations is demonstrated by a short film.

REFERENCES

[1] Smol'yanov, Yu.P., Vakhlin, V.V., Volkov, A.V., et al., Laboratory breadboard model of an assembly robot. Preprint IPM im.M.V. Keldysha, AN SSSR, 1981, N 91.

[2] Andreev, V.P., Sokolov, S.M. The interface between a commercial TV-camera and a computer, its construction and software. Preprint IPM im.M.V. Keldysha, AN SSSR, 1982, N 181.

[3] Okhotsimsky, D.E., Platonov, A.K., Smol'yanov, Yu.P., et al., The investigation of multioperation assembly with the aid of an experimental robotic system. Preprint IPM im.M.V. Keldysha, AN SSSR, 1982, N 76.

[4] Grimailo, S.I. The assembly robot software. Preprint IPM im.M.V. Keldysha, AN SSSR, 1982, N 81.

THE ROLE OF ARTIFICIAL INTELLIGENCE FOR SCIENTIFIC AND ENGINEERING PROGRESS

G.S.Pospelov

The Computer Center of the Academy
of Sciences of the USSR
Moscow
U S S R

Some problems of the theory of Artificial Intelligence are discussed. Especially, three interdependent fields are described: AI as simulation of cognitive processes; AI as the theory of interface in the interactive systems and AI as the theory of goalprogrammed robot behavior. Special attention is paid to the second field.

At the present time three interdependent fields could be outlined in the theory of artificial intelligence (AI):
1. Artificial intelligence as simulation of cognitive processes.
2. Artificial intelligence as the theory of interface in the interactive systems.
3. Artificial intelligence as the theory of goal-programmed robot behaviour.

Although the role of artificial intelligence theory for the scientific and engineering progress is quite evident here we concern with the first two fields in more detail. Special attention will be paid to the second field.

1. SIMULATION OF COGNITIVE PROCESSES

The simulation of cognitive processes in games (chess, draught, callakh...), music, theorem proving etc. has been launched almost simultaneously with the use of computers for solving computational problems.

The following problems solved to some extent could be mentioned now.

Game problems: chess, draught, callakh, domino ...

Synthesis of musical compositions [1]

Synthesis of texts by templates (fairy tales) [1].

Theorem proving.

Automatical synthesis of programs.

Analysis and synthesis of speech texts. Automatic translation [2,3].

Situation control [4,5].

- decision making under time defficiency and stress situations.

Simulation of human reasoning [6,7].
- modelling the thinking of state activity persons;
- predicting the goals of group leaders.

Two psychological models of thinking hypothesis could be viewed when programming the most cognitive problems.

1. Labyrinth thinking hypothesis proposed by E.Torndike early in this century.
2. The psychological thinking model of the Soviet psychologist V.N.Pushkin proposed at the end of sixties, which is called semantic model [1].

The first hypothesis is consistent with the fact that solving any cognitive problem is a search of a way in some labyrinth of the possibilities for attaining the goal. Obviously this approach is associated with selective choice from the great number of ways in theorem proving, game proceeding etc. This approach stimulated the theory of heuristic search and heuristic programming. In solving each problem the success is defined by perfectness of the heuristic tools (algorithms) capable to cut off the non-promising and to select promising versions for attaining the goal. Thus the labyrinth model has its drawbacks. However the labyrinth model and the theory of heuristic search are the main tools in the artificial intelligence applications. The chess programs demonstrate clearly the possibilities of heuristic search theory.

The semantic model of reasoning is described as relations of the structural descriptions of the initial and final situations in any cognitive process. This means that a labyrinth of possibilities is created (but not given beforehand) in which the way to problem solution lies.

If the structure is considered as a single indivisible carrier of some image, phenomenon or concept, one immediately arrives to Minsky's frames and knowledge representation in the form of quanta. The knowledge representation systems are known to be the high problems in the modern artificial intelligence.

The semantic model of reasoning refers directly to the logical-linguistic modelling and situation control [4,5].

Now on human reasoning. Dr. D.A.Pospelov in his paper "On human reasoning in the intellectual systems" [6] has mentioned the formal systems

$$F = \langle T, P, A, \Pi \rangle \qquad (1)$$

and semiotic systems

$$S = \langle T, P, A, \Pi, \Psi_P, \Psi_A, \Psi_\Pi \rangle \qquad (2)$$

here T is the set of initial base elements, P is the set of syntactic rules from which the correct syntactic combinations could be constructed (M_Π). $A \subset M_\Pi$ is the set of axioms, Π is inference rule (semantic rules) for deriving other correct syntactic combinations from A. The formal system with the same T, P, A, Π includes all types of logical inference from Aristotel's sillogistics to mathematical logics.

It is also obvious that when P, A and π change in the course of inference the semiotic system "S" should follow the logics of human reasoning. A simulation of such reasoning is consistent with formalizing ψ_P, ψ_A, ψ_π. In this view S.Yu.Maslov has proposed the probablistic canonical calculus [8,9]. The canonical calculus is a partial case ($K = A, P, \{a_o\}, \pi$) of a formal system in which A and P are alphabets having no common characters, a_o is axiom and $\pi = \{\pi_1,...,\pi_m\}$ is the list of unireferenced inference rules. The calculus K as well as the formal system F are the mathematical models of final results of human reasoning (they describe "what the brain accepts as truth").

Within the inference search theory S.Yu.Maslov (formalizing ψ_π) comes closer to solving the problem "how to discover the truth". For such purpose on the set of inferences π he introduced a probabilistic measure.

In analysing the text and its related automatic translation problem in general one has to solve the problem of formalizing the morphology, syntax, semantics and pragmatics of the particular sentences. The first two items are formalized to a sufficient detail. In the third component only semantics is analyzed. Of all four components pragmatics is least formalized (Yu.D.Apresyan, [9], p.159). Meanwhile the formalized language model attained enables the computers "to understand" an actual sence of sentences and thus design sufficiently effective question-answering and other dialogue systems [2,3] and also provide sentence-by-sentence automatic translation of sufficient quality. In this case one deals with some problem oriented language subset whose sentences are sufficiently unequivocal. Further modification of the language model, elucidating the inner sence of a sentence, transfer from sentence to text analysis are necessary not only for improving the question-answering systems and automatic translation systems but mainly for procedures of knowledge aquisition from texts. These problems could be solved with the help of logical inference systems in linguistics. Mutual collaboration of the specialists in linguistics and logics is helpful here. In this sence the school "Telavi-83" on 29.10 - 6.11 [9] was quite representative where specialists in linguistics and logics have discussed the logical structural of natural languages and means of enriching the logics with natural language facilities (heuristic reasoning).

II. ARTIFICIAL INTELLIGENCE AND INTERACTIVE SYSTEMS

This field of artificial intelligence led directly to a design of intelligent computer facilities and to a novel data processing technology [10].

This technology is based on the fact that with the use of special hardware-software facilities of AI the computers became available to many non-programming users: engineers, designers, managers, planners, scientific and medical staff etc. Now the final users may solve their problems via the special terminals (with text, graphical and speach processing) asking no help from analysts, applied programmers, specially trained operators and data processing staff. The following means of intelligent computer interface should be implemented. Within their own problem oriented language (natural language dialect) the specialists will have possibilities:

1) to use computers with data bases as inquiry-advising systems,

hypothesis validation and new theory derivation systems,
2) to solve the design, planning, management and svientific problems over their statement and initial data with regard of any complexity of their mathematical models. In this case the final user may control all steps of a computation process.
3) of an automatic design of the mathematical model and working software from problem description in the problem-oriented language.

Possibility 1) is implemented via the artificial intelligence question-answering and expert systems.

Possibility 2) is provided by logical calculus systems including the intellectual application software packages.

Property 3) is implemented in reformulating systems are as an extension of logical calculus systems. We point out that the logical calculus systems and reformulating systems increase drastically the efficiency of the automatic management and design systems.

The need for the final user to have a direct computer access is satisfied by commercial production of personal computers as well as by development of the special software with minimum effort for training the final users (superhigh-level languages, request languages, report and application program generators). However the AI software-hardware facilities with minimum effort for training the final user solve the problem of computer interface in a more drastic fasion.

Now we have to explain why one should attract the great number of final users to the modern data processing technology constituting 14% of the national total output in the USA against 13% portion of the high-current power industry [11] . In fact in the highly developed countries there exists a certain disbalance between the power capacity and industry automation as well as industry management automation. Thus within the last 100 years in the developed industrial countries the number of people occupied with data processing (science, investigations, planning and management) is increasing continuously. Thus in the USA the number of staff in data processing attains 50% against 5% 100 years ago. In spite of such growth in the data processing staff and developed computer facilities the data processing is still a bottleneck in the growth of social labour efficiency and in the progress of science and engineering. This led to an idea of data processing crisis and the reserves concealed by data processing automation are considered as data processing resources - insufficiently comprehended economical item. The data processing crisis may still go further. Advances in microelectronics and robotics allow to design flexible automated industries. In this case the labour efficiency, rates of material flows in the industry are incresing and the main factor of scientific and engineering progress would be the rates of innovation and expanding the list of goods and facilities. However the increasing possibilities of robotized and programmed industry will be kept by the same data processing medium.

The problem could be solved by supplementing flexible production with flexible design and planning. It is hard to overestimate the role of the above mentioned artificial intelligence systems. Of the great importance will be the logical calculus and reformulating systems since their software-hardware facilities provide an intellectual interface with computing processes in the computer.

With another aspect of the data processing technology, paperless informatics [12] in mind it becomes evident that in the near future there would be highly automated enterprises in which the production, design and planning processes produce a common dynamical system with the computers actually participating in the human relations in the course of their mutual activity.

Now we descuss the main software-hardware AI computer facilities which enable to design the above mentioned interactive AI systems employed in management, planning, design and scientific investigations. The four components could be outlines.
- the sensible semantic model of the problem area (outer three-dimensional world for a robot) based on the knowledge representation systems in a computer. The problem of knowledge representation in computer is the main problem of artificial intelligence.
- the program-planner for planning computations using the final user requests.
- a linguistic processor software-hardware implemented providing the final user interface in the natural language professional dialect.
- software-hardware logical inference facilities not only for solving user problems, but also for implementing knowledge aquisition procedures from the sources, knowledge generalization and validity checking.

The AI software-hardware facilities provide the basis to the four above mentioned classes of systems. Of them question-answering and expert systems have received broad application. The expert systems have first appeared in the mathematically weakly formalized sciences: medicine, biology, chemistry etc. We make remarks on the expert systems:
1. The expert system should contain an explanation subsystem. The user must have an explanation why acting interactive with the computer he came to such or other conclusion.
2. Of the great significance is the use of computer graphics in expert systems because of image reasoning in brain right semisphere. Examples could be cited [13,14] when visual analysis of the specially structured data arrays leads to discoveries and new theories.

The logical calculus systems are less known than question-answering and expert systems although they are quite important for planning solution support and design systems. The "Priz" system [15,16] is the first representative of this class. Then the DILLOS [3] system has been developed along with question-answering system.

In the logical calculus systems the main function is played by semantic network as biparitate graph. Some vertices of the graph are different parameters which are the subject of calculation and solution. Other vertices are mathematical objects: formulas, operators or complex mathematical models transforming some variables to others.

In general one deals with the nondirected mathematical objects and semantic network of relations as a nondirected graph.

Semantic network of the mathematical relations is a mathematical model of problem area. This may produce mathematical models of different mathematical problems for the study of problem area.

The problem mathematical model is always a directed graph selected by a program-planner from the nondirected relational graph. For such purpose all network relations should be resolved and placed in a program module library. Then any problem is posed in the following manner. The vertex - the problem solution and that of initial data are noted. The planner-program derives all the ways in the graph from "result" vertex to that of "initial data". Deriving a directed graph means producing a chain of program modules for solving the problem.

When the number and types of problems are known beforehand along with the data flows between modules one way aviod the common relational network but produce semantic program network in the form of directed graphs.

The semantic program networks are convenient for the automatic management systems (AMS). Combining different AMS problems into semantic network with its data base converts AMS into the fast reacting systems for the final users. In AMS the order of interactions between subsystems is known (or found) in the course of decision making and plan coordination. Thus semantic network is a directed graph with vertices as mathematical model programs of the partial planning and management problems [17,18]. If each planning unit would have its own micro- or minicomputer for solving their mathematical models then semantic network and program planner would derive an algorithm for functioning the local network of a given planning unit or enterprise.

However if designed technological systems of the same class would have different morphology (different subsystem content, subsets and relations between subsets and subsystems) then the approach described is unsuitable. In such case each morphological version should have its semantic network of mathematical relations. Here one may use reformulating systems. In this case a mathematical model of designed system could be drawn automatically in the from of semantic network of mathematical relations from morphology description in the problem-oriented language. Then on posing some problem by the final user in its own language a directed graph of the problem should be separated with generation of a working program as described above. This may be implemented using a three-level knowledge base: problem level knowledge base, mathematical level base and program level knowledge base. In a problem level base the fragments could be the process computation frames implemented via some part of a designed system. Thus in thermostatic systems such frames would be "compression", "heat exchange", "drosselling", "detending" etc. Now in describing morphology of a designed system (set composition and their links) a network of frames is generated automatically as problem level semantic network. Since each problem fragment in a knowledge base has its mathematical counterpart then a reformulation block will automatically derive the respective mathematical model in the form of a nondirected graph of mathematical relations.

In our opinion this approach to reformulation systems could be used for devising the flexible production programming systems as a tool for technologist as a final user.

REFERENCES

1. R.Kh.Zaripov. Computer flow of versions in modelling cognitive process. Moscow, 'Nauka', Fizmatgiz, 1983 (In Russian).
2. E.V.Popov, Natural language access to a computer, Moscow, 'Nauka', Fizmatgiz, 1982 (In Russian).
3. Dialog systems in ASU. D.A.Pospelov ed. Moscow, Energoizdat, 1983 (In Russian).
4. D.A.Pospelov, Logical linguistic models in control systems, Moscow, Energoizdat, 1981 (In Russian).
5. Situational control and semiotic modelling. D.A.Pospelov ed., 'Voprosy Kibernetiki', Acad,Sci. USSR, Scientific Council on Complex Problem "Kibernetika", Moscow, 1983 (In Russian).
6. Logics of reasoning and its modelling. D.A.Pospelov ed., 'Voprosy Kibernetiki', Acad.Sci.USSR, Scientific Council on Complex Problem "Kibernetika", Moscow, 1983 (In Russian).
7. V.Ya.Propp, Fairy tale morphology, 2-nd Ed. Moscow, 'Nauka', 1969 (In Russian).
8. S.Yu.Maslov, Theory and search of inference and problems of cognitive psychology. Semiotika i Informatika, 1979, N°13, p.17-46 (In Russian).
9. S.Yu.Maslov, Possibilities of using the probabilistic canonical calculus. Semioticheskie aspekty formalizatsii intellektual'noi deyatel'nosti. Shkola-seminar "Telavi-83", Moscow, 1983, p.87-90 (In Russian).
10. G.S.Pospelov, Artificial intelligence. New data processing technology, Moscow, Vestnik Akad. Nauk SSSR, N° , 1983, p.31-42 (In Russian).
11. G.R.Gromov, Modern data processing industry, Izv, Akad. Nauk SSSR, Tekhnicheskaya kibernetika, 1982, N°5, (In Russian).
12. V.M.Glushkov, Fundamentals of paperless informatics. Moscow, 'Nauka', Fizmatgiz, 1982 (In Russian).
13. Oliver Gilli "Is cancer mechanism discovered", Moscow, 'Literaturnaya gazeta', Nov.23, 1983 (In Russian).
14. A.L.Zenkin, Viverikh theorem extension to the case of natural terms, Moscow, Doklady Akad. Nauk SSSR, 264, N°2, 1982 (In Russian).
15. B.G.Tamm, E.Kh.Tyugu, Software packages, Izv. Akad. Nauk SSSR, Tekhnicheskaya kibernetika, 1977, N°5 (In Russian).
16. M.N.Kokhra, A.P.Kolva, E.Kh.Tyugu. Instrumental system of ES computer ("Priz"). 'Finansy i Statistika', Moscow, 1981 (In Russian).
17. G.S.Pospelov, Some problems of dialog planning and design systems, Preprint, Moscow, 'Nauka', 1980 (In Russian).
18. Problems of programmed goal planning and management. G.S.Pospelov Ed., Moscow, 'Nauka', 1981 (In Russian).
19. G.S.Pospelov, Yu.E.Antipov, K.N.Shikhaev, A.I.Potemkin, V.M.Solodov, Dialog system of perspective planning "Granit". 'Voprosy radioelektroniki', Seriya ASU, 1981, N°2 (In Russian).
20. W.S.Mark, The reformulation model expertise, USA: MII/LOS/TR-172, 1976.
21. S.R.Rodin, A.I.Erlikh, Interactive system of block modelling of engineering systems, Moscow, VINITI, 1981, N°6, (In Russian).

NUT - AN OBJECT ORIENTED LANGUAGE

Enn H. Tyugu

Institute of Cybernetics
Academy of Sciences of the Estonian SSR
Tallinn, U.S.S.R.

An object oriented language is presented which
is highly interactive and provides facilities
for the knowledge based programming. It combines
the features of SMALLTALK, UTOPIST and PROLOG
languages.

1. INTRODUCTION

The NUT language has been developed from UTOPIST (NUT is New UTopist)
which is an object oriented language for automatic program synthesis
(Kahro (1981)). The new language is more flexible due to completely
dynamic handling of types. UTOPIST was designed ten years ago for
implementation on mainframes like IBM/360, whereas NUT is designed
for implementation on new computers with tagged architecture, high
speed and large virtual memory.

An important feature of the new language is using production rules
for expressing general knowledge. This enables to write programs in
PROLOG-like style, if needed for the generality, and to preserve high
performance by using more specific knowledge representation which has
been developed in UTOPIST.

The basic concept of the NUT language is **object**. The user manipulates
objects when using a computer. Programs, data types, files etc. are
objects. There are predefined programs for handling objects (for handling files, generating programs, etc.), but most of useful programs
appear during the computations, and quite a number of them can be
generated automatically using structural synthesis of programs (Tyugu
(1981), Mints (1983)).

2. KNOWLEDGE BASE AND MODES OF COMPUTATION

At any moment the user works in a computational environment which
consists of a **knowledge base** and of a (working) **context**. The knowledge base includes all objects which are permanently stored in the
computer. The knowledge base can be modified only explicitly using
predefined programs. The context is generated at the beginning of a
session and it is modified explicitly and implicitly (due to side
effects) during the computations. The context disappears when the
session ends.

There are several operating modes of the NUT system. When a session
is started, an **initiation mode** is selected automatically. This is a
predefined mode for starting and ending a session. Another predefined
mode is **editing mode**. In this mode only text processing is possible.

No text can be interpreted (i.e. used as a program or as some other kind of knowledge).

The other modes are __computational modes__. Generally speaking, they must be specified by the user. Every mode has its own window on a multiwindow screen. Generation of windows and the multiwindow screens are similar to those of SMALLTALK.

All operations on objects (except the text processing) are performed in the computational modes. In particular, such operations are: generation of new objects, storing the objects in the knowledge base, changing and deleting the objects. Since the programs are objects, they are handled in computational modes. Some modes for program handling (for compiling, debugging) are predefined.

3. CLASSES

What has been an abstract object in UTOPIST is called a class in NUT, because the class which was introduced in SIMULA-67 seems to be a generally accepted concept. Disregarding some details, the classes in NUT are being built and used in the same way as in SMALLTALK.

Classes are objects used for defining other objects. A class is a carrier of the knowledge about the common properties of the objects belonging to the class. There is only one object - the class of classes which does not belong to any class. The class of classes specifies operations applicable to classes, in particular, the operations for building new classes. About an object belonging to a class T we also say that the object is of the type T.

3.1. PRIMARY CLASSES AND THE OBJECT nil

The primary classes are numbers, text, programs and the class of all objects, denoted as follows: __num__, __text__, __prog__, __any__.

The properties of these classes are predefined, i.e. the operations are defined which are applicable to the objects of these classes. If we look at the classes as the sets of objects belonging to these classes, the following relations hold: __num__ $\subset$ __prog__ $\subset$ __text__ $\subset$ __any__. This means that any number can be regarded as a program and any program has a standard representation in the form of a text. The class __any__ contains all objects of all classes.

__nil__ is an object which belongs to every class. __nil__ is interpreted as a completely undefined object and also as the falsity constant.

3.2. DEFINITION OF NEW CLASSES

In the class of classes an operation exists which enables us to specify new classes:

                    __let__ <id> : <class specification> ,

where <id> is an identifier which becomes the name of the new class, and <class specification> is a text which is very similar to the specification of an abstract object in UTOPIST. Actually the class specification is an extension of the specification of abstract objects in UTOPIST by the following: variables which are not components of objects; definition of initial values of objects; production rules for generating new objects. There are two ways to specify a new class: 1) explicit specification, 2) using a superclass.

3.3. EXPLICIT SPECIFICATION OF CLASSES

Explicit specification has the following form:
<class specification>::= (<components>
                          [var <variables>]
                          [<relations>]
                          [<rules>]).

The only obligatory part is <components> where names and classes of components are given, for instance,

    let *point* : (x : num; y : num)

specifies a class of points with two numeric components x and y.

Variables differ from components so that their values are not determined when a new object is generated.

    let *compl0*: (*re*:num; *im*:num; var *arg*:num; *mod*:num)

specifies a class of complex numbers which have components *re* and *im*. The variables *arg* and *mod* can be used for computations if needed, but any function computing an object of the type *compl0* computes only values of *re* and *im*.

To make use of *arg* and *mod* we can add some relations and build a new class:

    let *compl*: (*re*:num; *im*:num; var *arg*:num; *mod*:num;
                 r1:cos *arg* = *re*/*mod*;
                 r2:*mod* ↑2 = *re* ↑ 2 + *im* ↑ 2);

The relations r1 and r2 can be used for computing *re* and *im* as soon as *arg* and *mod* are given. We shall denote such computability as follows: *arg*, *mod* → *re*, *im*. There exist some other computations for the class *compl* :

        re, *im* → *arg*, *mod*
        re, *mod* → *arg*, *im*
        re, *arg* → *im*, *mod*
        im, *mod* → *arg*, *re*.

The programs for such computations are built automatically, using structural synthesis of programs (Tyugu (1981)). This will also be discussed in Section 5.

There are different ways of specifying relations in NUT. The following example illustrates using programs for representing relations:

    let *set*: (*value*: any;
        var: *elem*: any; *key*: any; *nr*: num;
        nrselect:*value*, *nr* → *elem* [prog A];
        keyselect:*value*,*key* → *elem*[prog B];
        put:*value*, *elem* →   *value*[prog C]);

The relations *nrselect* and *keyselect* are applicable for finding an element of a set by its number or by its key. The relation *put* is for adding new elements into a set.

The last part of the class specification can contain rules of the following form: $P,\ldots,Q \to R$, where $P,\ldots,Q,R$ are atomic formulas with constants or variables as terms.

Predicate symbols of the formulas are built from the names of classes, components and variables. In the following example a rule is presented which defines grandfather as a predicate binding son and father of a person.

> let *person*:(...
>
> >   var *son: person;*
> >   *father: person;*
> >   ...
> >   rules *son* ($x), *father* ($y) → *grandfather* ($x, $y));

3.4. USING SUPERCLASSES

A new class can be specified using any other class as a superclass. In this case the properties of the superclass are inherited by the new class. New properties are added if amendments are specified. This is analogous to copying of abstract objects in UTOPIST.

In this case the class specification contains the name of the superclass, for example,

> let *pair* : *point*

is a specification of a new class *pair* which has exactly the same properties as the class *point*.

Amendments can be added after the name of a superclass:

> let *unit* : *compl mod* = 1.

Here a class of complex numbers with *mod* = 1 is defined.

The amendments enable to bind classes together in various ways:

> let *points*: *set elem* = *point*

specifies a set of points using the superclass *set* and filling a slot *elem* : any in it with another class *point*.

4. OBJECTS

All data and knowledge exist in the form of objects in NUT system. Objects can be created, deleted and changed. They can exist in the working context and they can be stored into the knowledge base.

The following predefined objects (constants) exist:
- numbers,
- strings,
- some predefined objects which contain system functions (class of classes, for instance).

New objects are generated during the computations. The two predefined functions let and new are of special interest for generation of objects.

Executing the statement

> let <id> : <class specification>

generates a new class (it is also an object) as it was described in Section 3.2.

Executing the statement

> <id> = new <class name>

generates a new object of the designated class. For example, execu-

tion of the statement
$$Z = \underline{\text{new}}\ point$$
generates a new object Z of the class $point$.

When an object is generated, memory is reserved for it and initial values are assigned to all its components. The default values are $\underline{\text{nil}}$, but it is possible to specify relations for generating initial values of components in a class specification.

In our example the value of Z is initiated to $(\underline{\text{nil}}, \underline{\text{nil}})$.

Amendments can be added after the class name:
$$Z1 = \underline{\text{new}}\ point\ x = 0$$
generates a point $Z1$ with the value $(0, \underline{\text{nil}})$. The most usual way to generate an object is to evaluate an expression. The resulting object can be assigned to some other object, then the value of the latter and the value of its components are changed. For instance,
$$Z := (\underline{\sin}(30), \underline{\cos}(60))$$
changes the value of Z from $(\underline{\text{nil}}, \underline{\text{nil}})$ to $(0.5, 0.5)$. (The dynamic type checking protects us from disasters.)

Objects can be generated implicitly when specifications are processed. In particular, equations are regarded as program specifications and therefore objects of the type $\underline{\text{prog}}$ are generated when an equation is added to a class specification or to the working context. For example, from the equation $u = i * r$ the following three objects are generated:

$(i, r \rightarrow u)$ $\underline{\text{begin}}$ $u := i * r$ $\underline{\text{end}}$,

$(u, r \rightarrow i)$ $\underline{\text{begin}}$ $i := u/r$ $\underline{\text{end}}$,

$(u, i \rightarrow r)$ $\underline{\text{begin}}$ $r := u/i$ $\underline{\text{end}}$.

Programs are discussed more specifically in the next Section.

5. PROGRAMS

Programs are objects, they can be created, changed, deleted and assigned as values.

In the end of the previous Section we presented an example of the implicit generation of programs.

A program can also be generated from an explicit specification of the following form:
$$<id> = \underline{\text{new}}\ \underline{\text{prog}}\ <type><body>.$$

For example, the program SUB which computes a subset $S1$ of a set S, such that the elements of $S1$ satisfy the condition $cond$, is specified as follows:

$SUB = \underline{\text{new}}\ \underline{\text{prog}}\ (T, S \rightarrow S1)$
  $\underline{\text{begin}}\ i:\ \underline{\text{num}}\ ;$
  $\%T = \underline{\text{on}}\ context\ \underline{\text{comp}}\ of.select,\ of.val \rightarrow is.elem,\ cond\%$
  $i := \overline{1};$
  $L:\ \underline{\text{do}}$
    $T(i);$
    $\underline{\text{if}}\ is.elem = \underline{\text{nil}}\ \underline{\text{then}}\ \underline{\text{exit}}\ L;$
    $\underline{\text{if}}\ cond\ \underline{\text{then}}\ \overline{is.put};$
    $\overline{i := i + 1}$
  $\underline{\text{od}}$
$\underline{\text{end}}.$

This program has a parameter T of the class prog. The type of the program T is described in a comment between two symbols %. The program T computes the values of the object $cond$ and of the component $elem$ of the object is from the given values of the components $select$ and val which belong to the object of. Besides, an external object $is.put$ (which is also a program) is used in SUB. The program SUB is designed for representing a relation in a class $subset$ which we now specify, as follows:

   let subset: (of:set; is:set; cond: any ;
         r1:(of.select, of.val → is.elem, cond),
         of.val → is.val [prog SUB]).

When the program SUB is executed as the realization of the relation $r1$ its parameters T,S and $S1$ will be bound, as follows: 1) the value of T will be a program for computing $is.elem$ and $cond$ from $of.select$ and $of.val$; 2) S will be bound to $of.val$; 3) $S1$ will be bound to $is.val$. As a result, the value of $is.val$ will be computed applying repetitively $is.put$ each time the computed value of $cond$ is not nil.

6. COMPUTATIONS

The user can describe his own computation modes by generating a new object of the class $window$. This feature of NUT is copied from SMALL-TALK. Every object of the class $window$ provides some general input-output facilities, common control structures and directly executable statements which are inherited from the class specification. Furthermore, new functions and other facilities can be added to a computation mode by making amendments to the specification when a new window is generated.

6.1. PROGRAM SYNTHESIS

The implementation of several statements of NUT language requires automatic synthesizing of programs. The structural synthesis method (Tyugu (1983)) is used which enables to build a program schema from a given set of axioms $\mathcal{A}$ and from a formula of the form

$$x_1,\ldots,x_m \to y_1,\ldots,y_n$$

which expresses the following goal: "compute the values of $y_1,\ldots,y_n$ from the given values of $x_1,\ldots,x_m$". The program schema is transformed into a program using predefined interpretations of function symbols from the axioms. (The following axiom was presented in the subset specification in Section 4:

   (of.select, of.val → is.elem, cond), of.val → is.val.

Also an interpretation of the function SUB for this axiom was presented there.)

6.2. compute-STATEMENT

If the statement
           compute
is used in a direct computation mode, all axioms of the working context are used to build a set of axioms $\mathcal{A}$ and on the basis of these axioms a program is built and executed which computes the values of all objects computable in the working context.

If the statement
           compute $y_1,\ldots,y_n$ from $x_1,\ldots,x_m$

is used in a direct computation mode, all axioms of the working context are used to build a set of axioms $\mathcal{O}\!\mathcal{L}$, for this set of axioms and for the goal

$$x_1,\ldots,x_m \to y_1,\ldots,y_n$$

a program is synthesized and executed.
If the statement

$$\underline{on}\ M\ \underline{compute}\ y_1,\ldots,y_n\ \underline{from}\ x_1,\ldots,x_m$$

is used where M is the name of a class, a program is synthesized for the set of all axioms of the class M and for the goal

$$x_1,\ldots,x_m \to y_1,\ldots,y_n.$$

This program can be used as a part of another program or as an independent program, depending on the context of the <u>compute</u>-statement.

6.2. <u>recompute</u>-STATEMENT

This statement can be used only in a direct computation mode. It has the following form:

$$\underline{recompute}\ x_1 = v_1,\ldots,x_n = v_k,$$

where $x_1,\ldots,x_n$ are the names of objects from the working context and $v_1,\ldots,v_k$ are expressions.

The execution of this statement is, as follows:
1) the relations from which the previous values of $x_1,\ldots,x_n$ were directly computed are deleted from the working context;
2) new relations

$$x_1 = v_1;\ \ldots;\ x_n = v_k$$

are introduced into the context;
3) the statement <u>compute</u> is executed.

7. CONCLUDING REMARKS

We presented a language called NUT which contains almost nothing new as compared to the existing languages PROLOG, SMALLTALK and UTOPIST. The general schema of computations is taken from SMALLTALK (though we do not call " + " and " - " messages). Abstract objects of UTOPIST are called classes now, but constructing new classes and creating objects is very similar to the corresponding facilities of UTOPIST, structural synthesis of programs is also being used as in UTOPIST. The semantics of <u>rule</u> statements is taken from PROLOG. These statements have a more restricted form in NUT, but in combination with the structural synthesis, at least theoretically, they provide the same facilities as PROLOG does.

An eclectic approach to the language design is deplorable, generally speaking. Nevertheless, we hope that the new language will be a step in the right direction in building intelligent software for a wide class of users. Combining structural synthesis of programs with rule-based programming has been our goal for some time already. Some examples on this topic can be found also in (Eomois (1984)). The experiences of our group in using personal computers show that a computational environment which is similar to SMALLTALK can be very convenient for various users, if the efficiency problem can be solved, and using the compute-statement in an indirect computation mode enables compilation of large efficient programs.

REFERENCES

[1] Eomois, P., Knowledge representation and deduction in extended PRIZ (in the present edition).

[2] Kahro, M. et al., Instrumental programming system for ES computer (PRIZ) ("Finansy i statistica", Moscow, 1981, in Russian).

[3] Mints, G., Tyugu, E., Justification of the structural synthesis, Science of Computer Programming, vol. 2, No. 3 (1983) 215-240.

[4] Tyugu, E., The structural synthesis of programs, Lecture Notes in Computer Sciences, vol. 122 (1981) 290-303.

[5] The Xerox Learning Research Group, The Smalltalk-80 System, Byte No. 8 (1981) 36-48.

ADAPTIVE NATURAL LANGUAGE GENERATION

G. Adorni, M. Di Manzo and F. Giunchiglia

Department of Communication, Computer and System Sciences
University of Genoa
Viale Causa 13, 16145 Genoa, Italy

Language generation plays an important role in expert systems which must provide user friendly interfaces. In this paper an approach to sentence generation is presented focusing on the problem of self adaptation to changes in the conceptual representation formalism or in the known lexicon, in order to allow a great degree of flexibility in tuning the system to new application areas.

INTRODUCTION

The problem of language generation did not receive in the past the same attention devoted to language understanding, probably because some experiences made in the early seventies showed that it was possible to obtain nice dialogues using rather simple techniques (6,8,12,14). The recent development of expert systems with natural language interfaces is raising a new interest in the generation problem (5,7,9,10,11,13). Despite some current attempts to strongly integrate the process of producing surface syntactic forms with the planning of illocutionary acts(4), in most systems these two phases are kept separated; this allows a higher degree of modularity and therefore an easier requirements updating and system portability, even if an obvious shortcoming is the inability to take into account the influence of syntactic constraints on the planning of speech acts. This approach has been followed also in the development of the PRISE system for the Italian language (2). This paper, after a brief introduction to PRISE, is focused on the discussion of some facilities for the self-generation of the translation rules and the updating of the vocabulary, which result in a great degree of flexibility in learning new words and redefining the conceptual representation formalism to cover new applications.

SYSTEM OVERVIEW

System outputs are generated in a Conceptual Description Language (CDL) which is independent of the actual natural language used to communicate with the human operator.

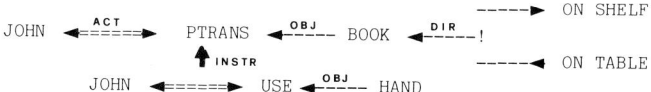

Figure 1: Conceptual Representation of:"John moves the book from the table to the self"

This language describes a Conceptual Network (CN) whose nodes and arcs represent primitive actions, states and relationships in a Conceptual-Dependency-like form (1). An example is shown in fig.1.

The translation process from the CDL to the Italian language is organized in two steps. The first step performs basic operations as word selection, syntactic groups formation and relationships definition, rewriting the deep CN into a Surface Network (SN) in which all the syntactic components are related each to other, the SN corresponding to the CN of fig.1 is shown in fig.2.

```
VERB:= (Shift V1) ----->  ---------------   ---------------   -----------------
REGG:= (TRUE) -           !FORM:=FINITE !   !GENDER:=MALE !   !GENDER:=FEMININ !
SUBJ:= (John V2) -----!   !MODE:=IND.   !   !ART:=DET.    !   !ART:=DET        !
OBJ := (Book V3) ... !    !TEMPER:= ... !   !NUMB:=SING   !   !NUMBER:= SING   !
FROM:= (Table V4) ... !   !........     !   ---------------   -----------------
TO  := (Shelf V5) ... !   ---------------          ↑                  ↑
INSTR:= (Hand V6)--!  !!--------------------------!                   !
                   !_____!
```

Figure 2: Surface Network for: "John is moving ....."

The second step generates the final Italian sentence, making choices about the best sequence of the syntactic components, the use of pronouns, the suppression of components which are commonly left the listener's inference (for instance, subject repetition in coordinate phrases), the active or passive form and other structural details(2). The mayor advantage of the use of an intermediate SN is that all the syntax and morphology dependent processing is separated from the conceptual one; so, all the rules needed for the final assembling of the sentence are not affected by any modification in the CDL. The generation of the SN is based on a set of rules which associate words to proper subset of the CN. These rules are grouped in two sets of decision trees, namely Discrimination trees (D-trees), which associate words to single-primitive subnets, and Merging trees (M-trees), which associate words to multi-primitive subnets. The difference between D-trees and M-trees is not significant for the following considerations and will be neglected from here on. An example of D-tree for subnets containing the PTRANS primitive is shown in fig.3c.

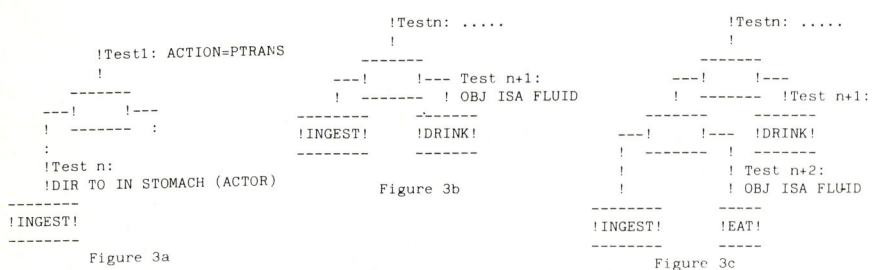

Figure 3: PTRANS D-tree

Decision trees are highly sensitive to the CDL and the vocabulary; therefore, an automatic generation of this kind of rules is necessary in order to let the system learn new words and to adapt the CDL syntax to new requirements.

SELF-GENERATION OF DECISION TREES

Each D-tree organizes the set of tests required to select one word among those whose meanings are based on a given primitive; all these words can be distinguished each other looking at the restrictions imposed on the connected conceptual cases. Hence, a different D-tree must be defined for each primitive. D-tree generation is carried out in two steps. During the first step all the viable subgraphs which are relevant to the same D-tree are selected and inserted into a list. Subgraph selection is performed scanning the vocabulary and looking at the conceptualization associated to each word. In the second step every subgraph list is processed to built the corresponding D-tree. D-trees are binary trees and the building criterion is quite simple. At first, the intersection of all the subgraphs is computed in order to obtain the minimal common subset of features (it is never empty, because all the subgraphs within the same list share at least the same primitive); this minimal intersection defines the set of tests associated to the root of the tree. Then the last discarded feature is selected and the set of subgraphs is subdivided in two new sets, characterized respectively by the presence and absence of such a feature; this rule is applied again to every new set until all the obtained sets contain no more than one full subgraph. A trivial example of D-tree generation for a vocabulary containing 3 words is shown in fig.3. The vocabulary is stored as a set of lists created by means of a user-friendly interface (see fig. 4). Rules for D-trees generation are implemented in PROLOG (a detailed description is omitted for sake of brevity); they do not interpret the CDL, so both the CDL syntax and the list of known words can be freely modified. The user interface is based on an interpreted language which accepts concepts defined in a higher level formalism, generating all the required data structure. The analysis is made by means of an attribute grammar based on a fixed context length LL(1) parser. CDL is centered around a set of THOUGHTs with associated descriptions. A thought is a frame like structure within which new data are interpreted in terms of concepts acquired through previous experience (3). An example of construction of the three words used in the previous example is given in figure 4.

Figure 4: Word description in CDL

CONCLUSIONS

The PRISE system is a language generation module which accepts as input a semantic network describing the concepts to be uttered. The basic design constraint has been the ability of self-defining its own decision rules, in order to make PRISE implementation independent of any particular choice about the syntax of the CDL. Therefore, PRISE learns what conceptual primitives and relationships are used to build the SN and how Italian words can be associated to them simply by exploring the vocabulary; only the knowledge related to the syntactic rules of the Italian language, is embedded in the system, since surface rules can be assumed to be much more stable than the CDL syntax. PRISE is part of a larger conversational system currently under development; it is implemented in PROLOG and LISP on a DEC VAX 11/750 under Unix.

REFERENCES

1. Adorni,G., Di Manzo,M., and Ansaldi,W., "NAUSICA: Natural language Understanding System; the Italian Case Analysed", Rivista di Informatica XI (1981). (in Italian) **39 — 88**.

2. Adorni,G. and Di Manzo,M., "PRISE: Production of Italian Sentences", Proc. AICA Congress (Naples 1983).

3. Adorni,G. and Di Manzo,M., "Top-Down Approach to Scene Interpretation", CIL-83 (Barcelona, June 1983).

4. Appelt,D.E, "Planning Natural Language Utterances to Satisfy Multiple Goals", Tech. Note 259, SRI International (1982).

5. Clancey,W.J., "Dialogue Management for Rule-Based Tutorials", Proc. 6th IJCAI (1979).

6. Goldman,N., "Conceptual Generation ", in Schank,R,C. (ed.), Conceptual Information Processing (North Holland, Amsterdam, 1975).

7. Von Hahn,W., Hoppner,W., Jameson,A., and Wahlster,W., "The anatomy of the Natural Language Dialog System HAM-RPM", in: Bole,L. (ed.), Natural Language Based Computer System (Hauser-MacMillan, Munich, 1980).

8. Herskovits,A., "The Generation of French from Semantic Structure", Tech. Report 212, Stanford Artif. Intell. Lab. (1973).

9. Mann,W.C. and Moore,J.A., "Computer Generation of Multiparagraph English Text", AJCL 7 (1981).

10. Mc.Donald,D.D., "Subsequent References: Syntactic and Rethorical Constraints", TINLAP-2 ACM (1978).

11. Mc.Donald,D.D., "Natural Language Production as a Process of Decision-Making under Constraints", Ph.D. Thesis, Dept. of Elect. Eng. and Comp. Science M.I.T. (1980).

12. Simmons,R.F. and Slocum,J., "Generating English Discourse from Semantic Net", Comm. ACM 15 (1972) **891 — 905**.

13. Waltz,D.L., "An English Language Question Answering System for large Relational Database", Comm. ACM 21 (1978) **526 - 539**.

14. Winograd,T., "Understanding Natural Language", (Academic Press, New York, 1972).

AN APPROACH TO INTELLIGENT ACTION EXECUTION

Gabriella Airenti[°], Marco Colombetti[°°]

[°] Unità di ricerca di intelligenza artificiale, Università di Milano
[°°] Progetto di intelligenza artificiale, Politecnico di Milano

>In this paper we delineate a representation of action as
>a component of intelligent action execution. In particu-
>lar our representation allows an actor to attribute the
>reason of a possible execution failure to a specific
>element of his action plan. To this purpose, the relevant
>features of the representation we propose are: basic
>actions, the sequencing of actions in a plan, the relation
>of realization between actions, and the enabling conditions
>of realizations.

INTRODUCTION

Aim of this paper is to develop conceptual tools for the analysis of action. Act
ing involves several intelligent activities: forming a plan in order to achieve
specific goals, executing the plan by means of motor and perceptual skills, recognizing the effects of actions and recovering possible failures.

Plan formation has been investigated in artificial intelligence with interesting
achievements, both for highly artificial problems of robot planning and for
human planning in real life situations.
Plan execution seems to have received less attention than plan formation. The
most relevant problem here is dealing with possible failures occurring during the
execution of an action plan, due either to errors of the actor or to the partial
unpredictability of events in the external world. In general, such a problem is
very effectively faced by humans; on the contrary, no artificial system realized
so far is able to achieve a comparable performance in this regard (Kempf, 1983).
Therefore, an advance in the analysis of action seems to be a relevant step towards
the realization of intelligent artificial actors.

In this paper we propose a treatment of action aimed at accounting for an actor's
ability to cope with execution failures. To this purpose, we make use of the basic
concept of levels of abstraction introduced by Minsky (1963) and Sacerdoti (1977)
for decomposing plans.

THE REPRESENTATION OF ACTION

In this section we delineate a representation of action which we believe to be a
necessary component of intelligent action execution.

Intuitively, an <u>action</u> is an event actuated by an actor. We define an <u>event</u> as a
change in the world over an interval of time (think for example of the slamming
of a door). An event is actuated by an actor if it results from the execution of
an action plan. This defines action as intentional behavior (e.g. someone slams a
door closed) and distinguishes it from non intentional behavior (e.g. someone

accidentally causes a door to close).
The event associated to an action defines what an action is, but not how it can be performed. As regards its execution, an action can be directly linked to a perceptual and motor skill of the actor, like for example opening one's eyes or raising one's arm. Such actions will be referred to as <u>basic actions</u>. In order to perform a basic action an actor can run the skill which <u>results into</u> the associated event, provided that some <u>enabling conditions</u> hold (for example, one cannot raise his arm if this is <u>fastened</u>). However, not all actions are basic; for instance it cannot be assumed that writing a book is directly associated to a skill.

To be executed, nonbasic actions must be reduced to basic actions only. Therefore, in order to perform a nonbasic action A_1 the actor must perform another action A_2 whose associated event he knows to cause the event associated to A_1. In this case we say that A_2 <u>realizes</u> A_1. If A_2 is a basic action there is no need for further decomposition. Otherwise, a realization for A_2 must be found. This process iterates until a basic action is reached. As in the case of skills, a realization is viable under given enabling conditions which assure the causal link between the events actually holds. For example, turning the switch is a realization for putting the light on provided that electric current flows in the circuit, the bulb works, etc.

Our approach is related to the classical AI representation of action in terms of preconditions and effects. The traditional use of preconditions and effects merges the logical definition of the action and a specific way of performing it. On the contrary, we introduce the following distinction :
- an action is defined only by the logical preconditions and the effects of the associated event (in the previous example the precondition is 'the light is off' and the effect is 'the light is on')
- additional preconditions and effects are introduced with the realization of the action. These fall in two categories: preconditions and effects which logically define the event associated to the realization ('the switch is off' is the precondition and 'the switch is on' is the effect), and preconditions necessary for its viability, i.e. its enabling conditions ('electric current flows in the circuit', etc.). If the action is basic, only the preconditions corresponding to the enabling conditions of its realization by the skill are introduced.

As we shall argue in the next section, this taxonomy is relevant for failure analysis as it permits to identify the reasons of failure.

In general actions do not stand alone, but are organized into action plans which present a two-dimensional structure:
- horizontal dimension: actions are arranged in a temporal sequence by concatenating their effects and preconditions
- vertical dimension: actions are decomposed into lower level actions which realize them.

An action plan can be executed if all actions in the plan are decomposed along the vertical dimension down to basic actions only. The process of execution consists of the activation of the skills associated to such basic actions in the order defined by the horizontal dimension of the plan.

FAILURES IN THE EXECUTION OF ACTIONS

A sound theory of action must include a treatment of execution failures; these arise when an attempted action does not achieve the results expected by the actor.

The two basic problems with failures are their recognition and their recovery. In fact, failure recovery falls within the area of plan formation and does not seem to pose qualitatively new problems. On the contrary, failure recognition demands a specific inquiry. The main difficulty here is the acknowledged impossibility of predicting all possible failures in advance. In the following we delineate a way to cope with this problem.

In failure recognition we can distinguish two phases. First, it is necessary for the actor to detect that a failure occurred. This task may be not trivial, for instance when some effects of the action are not under direct control of the actor. Second, the actor must attribute the responsibility of the failure to a specific point of his action plan. It follows that an actor's ability to recognize the failure of actions relies on the structure of their representation. In this regard the relevant features of the representation we propose are: i) basic actions; ii) the sequencing of actions; iii) the relation of realization; iv) the enabling conditions of realizations. Any of these elements can be responsible for failure.

We conform to Norman's terminology (1981) in distinguishing among accidents, mistakes and slips as possible causes of failure.

When an action A_2 succeeds but failes to realize the action A_1 for which it was planned we say that:
- an <u>accident</u> occurs if an enabling condition, assumed to hold by the actor, in fact does not hold
- a <u>mistake</u> is made by the actor if A_2 cannot possibly realize A_1 even if all the enabling conditions held.

The term <u>slip</u> refers to failures for which the execution process is responsible. Slips fall into two categories:
- a skill is activated but does not run properly
- the sequence of actions in the plan is uncorrectly executed.

In the next section we shall show how an actor detects a failure and attributes it to the appropriate point of the plan.

THE RECOGNITION OF FAILURES

In the figure we show a possible plan for putting on the light.

Suppose that after the actor's attempt to execute this plan it happens that the light is not on. If the light is under his direct control, the actor detects the failure of the action PUT ON THE LIGHT. The actor tries then to attribute such a failure to a specific point in this plan. Firstly the actor tries to determine whether the action TURN ON THE SWITCH, intended to realize the action PUT ON THE LIGHT, has succeeded or failed. Let us suppose that the former alternative takes place. The actor has therefore individuated the failure point. The actor tries to attribute the reasons for the failure to the fact that at least one of the enabling conditions assumed in the plan does not hold. If the actor is able to ascertain that the electric current is missing or either the bulb or the switch do not work, then the recognition of the failure ends with its attribution to an accident. If this is not the case, the actor may guess that the plan is uncorrect, for example because he chose the wrong switch. This amounts to acknowledge a mistake.

A different possibility is that the actor detects the failure of the action TURN ON THE SWITCH. In this case the analysis previously described is performed on such an action. An interesting difference here is that the enabling condition 'the finger is on the switch' is not assumed: the plan for putting on the light contains a subplan intended to achieve such a condition. In this case the failure of the action TURN ON THE SWITCH, due to the fact that such an enabling condition does not hold, is not an accident but derives from a failure of the action PLACE FINGER ON SWITCH.

The scheme we have described applies to all abstraction levels in the plan above basic actions. On the contrary, when a basic action has been attributed the failure, the treatment is partially different: while the concept of accident is still valid, it is not possible for the actor to acknowledge a mistake, because the link between the basic action and its skill, like the skill itself, is not represented conceptually. Therefore, if no accident can be detected, the responsibility of the failure must be attributed to an inadequate running of the skill itself. This corresponds to one of the two types of slip we have introduced.

The last case still to be analyzed is the slip due to uncorrect sequencing of the execution of actions in the plan. A model of motor skills which accounts for this kind of slip is presented in Rumelhart and Norman (1982). We shall not deal with this topic here, as a model of skills lies outside the scope of this paper.

When the process of attributing the responsibility for the failure has been completed, the actor can plan a recovery strategy. We expect such a strategy to be strongly influenced by the fact that the failure has been recognized as an accident, a mistake, or a slip.

CONCLUSIONS

In this paper we have presented a representation of action which allows an actor to attribute the reason of a possible execution failure to an element of his action plan. A major step in the development of our treatment is the establishment of the necessary connections between our representation and the actor's general knowledge (action schemes, causal laws, etc.).

In our opinion, the most challenging question concerns the difference between the enabling conditions which are assumed by the actor and the ones for which a subplan is built. A good suggestion can be found in Wilensky (1983) with regard to 'implicit preconditions' of plans. The proposal is that preconditions should be stored at the proper place along an event hierarchy; for each event, the preconditions stored at the corresponding node are considered for planning, while all preconditions stored at higher levels are in general assumed.

REFERENCES

Kempf K.G., Artificial intelligence application in Robotics - A tutorial, 8th IJCAI, Karlsruhe (1983).

Minsky M., Steps toward artificial intelligence, in: Feldman J. and Feigenbaum E.A., eds., Computers and thought (McGraw-Hill, New York, 1963).

Norman D.A., Position paper on human error, NATO Conference on human error, Bellagio (1983).

Rumelhart D.E., Norman D.A., Simulating a skilled typist: a study of skilled cognitive-motor performance, Cognitive Science, 6 (1982)

Sacerdoti E.D., A structure for plans and behavior (Elsevier, New York, 1977).

Wilensky R., Planning and understanding (Addison Wesley, Reading, Mass. 1983).

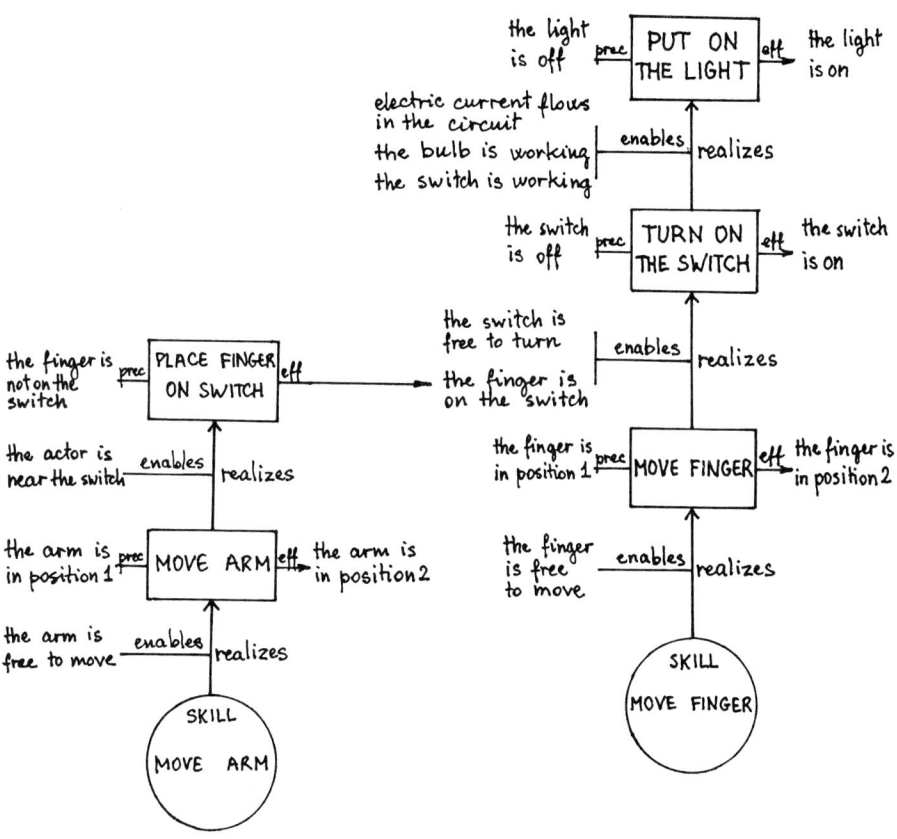

The plan for putting on the light

ACKNOWLEDGMENTS

This research has been supported by the Consiglio Nazionale delle Ricerche, Comitato di Biologia e Medicina, Gruppo di Scienze del Comportamento, for the year 1983.

AUTHORS' ADDRESS

Istituto di Psicologia della Facoltà Medica
Via Francesco Sforza, 23
20122 Milano
Italy

INFERENCE PROCESSES IN EVERYDAY REASONING

Bruno G.Bara[°], Antonella G.Carassa[°°], Giuliano C.Geminiani[°°]

[°] Unità di ricerca di intelligenza artificiale, Università di Milano
[°°] Istituto di Psicologia della Facoltà Medica, Università di Milano

This paper is concerned with the analysis of the processes of mundane inferences when performed on linguistic propositions. We single out as a fundamental point the manipulation of causal relations. We classify human inferences in two types (chain and constructive inferences), focusing on the problem of how cause-effect relation is represented in a mental model. We present our model through the discussion of a sample protocol of a 9 years old subject.

INTRODUCTION

We suggest that the way human beings perform the processes of mundane inference is by postulating causal relations among events and checking their validity.

When A.I. researchers depart from formalized problems like theorem proving, they are confronted with the frustrating puzzle of the real world, where both the vastity of the knowledge requested and the complexity of the natural and social laws governing it, are critical features.
Similarly, an artificial system leaving a laboratory must deal with the surrounding open environement, handling information with an expertise not too inferior to the one exhibited by human beaings in mundane reasoning.

How people represent causal relations is a crucial point for both a theory of comprehension (story understanding) and a theory of production (planning and problem solving).
Rieger (1976) claimed that: "Plan synthesis and language comprehension are two sides of the same coin, because they both rely on a cause and effect algorithmic knowledge about how to do things and how things work".

A distinctive feature of everyday reasoning inferences is how they can be interfaced with a general representation. We refer to the knowledge representation system proposed by Airenti, Bara, Colombetti (1982). This system consists of two interacting subsystems named K-theory and K-model, playing the role of conceptual and episodic knowledge, respectively. Particularly, in this system there is a data structure that describes stereotypic situations, similar to frames as introduced by Minsky (1975). Frame concept accounts for how easily we can accede to a chain of informations which allow to get a context and to infer events not expressly mentioned.

Acknowledgments: This research has been supported by a grant of the Ministero della Pubblica Istruzione, for the year 1984.
We thank Philip Johnson-Laird for many helpful discussions in developing the ideas and the research project and Marco Colombetti for comments and criticisms of a draft of this paper.

As argued by Johnson-Laird (1983), we assumed that the reasoner constructs mental model of the states of affairs described in the sentence he has to analyze in order to draw a plausible inference.
Mental models present structures isomorphic to the conceived structures of the state of affairs that mental models are meant to represent. In a domain related with the mundane reasoning, Johnson-Laird and Bara (1984) proposed that in syllogistic inference reasoners construct mental models of the premises, formulate informative conclusions about the relations in the model, and search for alternative models that are counterexamples to these conclusions. In the following, we shall try to extend this theory from formal to mundane reasoning.

A THEORY OF MUNDANE CAUSALITY

On the base of a qualitative analysis of a series of experiment on everyday reasoning, we have postulated two types of inferences: chain inferences and constructive inferences.
In order to define the two types of inferences just mentioned, we have to introduce a few basic concepts.
We define fact as the representation of a property holding for an individual, or of a relation holding among a number of individuals.
We define state as a collection of facts which keeps itself unchanged in a fixed time interval.
We define event the occurring of a change in the state of the world. This change occurs in an interval of time one cannot furtherly split.
We consider the cause-effect relation as a basic relation between the two events event (cause) and event (effect).

When the cause-effect relation is used in the area of everyday reasoning, it can never be considered as necessary (while it is possible to determine in a necessary way, for instance, the thermodynamics of an isolated system).
In fact, no mundane inference is ever certain, but always probable.

From the point of view of the cognitive processes, establishing a cause-effect relation is a creative activity, based not on necessity, but on a subjective judgment.
In particular, we claim that the event (effect) follows the event (cause) with a high degree of expectation when some enabling conditions subsist.
Both the establishing of the relation cause-effect and the introduction of different enabling conditions depends upon the general knowledge of the system.

A scheme of the cause-effect relation in everyday reasoning is depicted below.

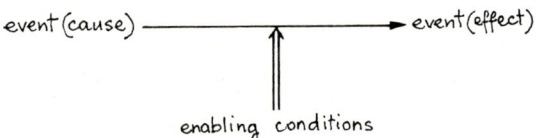

In other words a cause-effect relation needs to be "justified" by an evaluation of the considered enabling conditions. Furthermore the degree of expectation of the same link event (cause)→event(effect) changes in relation with the number and the weight of the enabling conditions assumed.

The decisive point for the mundane inference reasoning is, in our opinion, the construction of mental models embedding a cause-effect relation.

TYPES OF INFERENCES IN EVERYDAY REASONING

In the semantic domain we focused on, the reasoner is requested to produce an inference (I), drawn on the basis of two given sentences, A_1 and A_2.

Chain inferences

The reasoner postulates a cause-effect relation between A_1 and A_2 and tries to confirm it in two alternative ways:

a) He finds the postulated relation already structured within his knowledge representation. He introduces an enabling condition I to justify the cause-effect relation between A_1 and A_2, i.e. to increase its confidence.

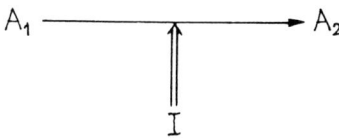

example : A_1 = Charles was bitten by a snake.
A_2 = Charles died.
I = The snake was poisonous.

b) The reasoner does not find such a structured relation. He has to introduce an event I so as to generate two relations $A_1 \to I$ and $I \to A_2$.
The reasoner breaks the relation in a two steps one, in order to increase the global degree of expectation.
Only the two-step relation can be considered as a cause-effect one, while each single step is weakly related in a causal way.

$$A_1 \longrightarrow I \longrightarrow A_2$$

example : A_1 = Today there is a railway strike.
A_2 = John cooks a chocolate cake.
I = John stays at home.

The distinctive feature of chain inferences is that the reasoner tries to explain the situation described by the two assigned propositions.

Constructive inferences

The reasoner does not postulate a cause-effect relation between A_1 and A_2. He tries to construct a cause-effect relation producing an event effect I, proceeding from $\overline{A_1}$ and $\overline{A_2}$.
He recognizes some relation (different from causal ones) between A_1 and A_2. He looks for an event (effect), assigning the role of event (cause) to one of the two propositions and the role of enabling conditions to the other one.

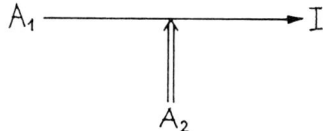

example : A_1 = Both John and George have asked for Mary's hand in marriage.
A_2 = Mary is love with George.
I = Mary marries George.

A CASE STORY

In an experiment we carried out, our subject were presented with a pair of sentences, and they were asked to say what in their opinion could reasonably follow. For instance, one of the pairs of sentences was:

A_1 - Stephen played poker last night.
A_2 - This morning he is in a bad mood.

After the first answer (in our example it was always: "Stephen lost"), subjects were asked if they could think an alternative answer, or more than one.
What we found was that subjects were able to construct a wide range of different models, gradually moving from the most obvious one to the very improbable ones.

E.g., one of our subjects, Barbara (9 years) produced this series of answers:
- He lost all his money
- They have promised to give the winner a prize, he won but they did not give it.
- The night before he had drunk a lot, so in the morning he was sleepy and he did not feel like getting up
- They had said: "We will eat a good cake while playing poker". He brought a bad cake and somebody had the nerve to tell him that the cake was disgusting.

DISCUSSION

A theory based on a fixed manipulation of stereotyped situations, as for instance Schank's theory (1982), cannot explain the variety of solutions given by our subjects to a single pair of sentences. Even the most sophisticated implementation of this type of theory (see Lebowitz, 1983) do not allow the system to go beyond a pre-determined number of reconstructions-explanations-interpretations of an event described in a few sentences.

Our theory, based on mental models, accounts for the potentially infinite number of inferences one can draw from the informations contained in a short text, and for their order of presentation. The different models subjects build can be ranked according to their actual order of occurrence. Roughly speaking, this order corresponds to the degree of confidence subjects assign to the resulting model.

A system aiming to simulate human ability in everyday reasoning has to reproduce not only the simplest performance (i.e. the first inference), but the full one (i.e. all different inferences). Moreover, we consider relevant both the output (the what) and the way this output is produced (the how).

REFERENCES

[1] Airenti G., Bara B.G., Colombetti M., Semantic network representation of conceptual and episodic knowledge, in: Trappl R., (ed), Progress in Cybernetics and System Research, vol. VI (Hemisphere, Washington, 1982)
[2] Johnson-Laird P.N., Mental Models (Cambridge University Press, Cambridge, 1983)
[3] Johnson-Laird P.N., Bara B.G., Syllogistic Inference, Cognition, (1984)
[4] Lebowitz L., Memory-Based Parsing, Artificial Intelligence, 21, 4 (1983)
[5] Minsky M., A Framework for Representing Knowledge, in: Winston P.H. (ed), The Psychology of Computer Vision (McGraw-Hill, New York, 1975)
[6] Rieger C., An organization of knowledge for problem solving and language comprehension, Artificial Intelligence, 7 (1976)
[7] Schank R.C., Dynamic memory (Cambridge University Press, 1982)

THE MULTIPROCESSOR CONTROL SYSTEM OF A MOBILE ROBOT
WITH ELEMENTS OF ARTIFICIAL INTELLIGENCE

Bogomolov N.E., Lazutin Yu.M., Yaroshevsky V.S.

Keldysh Institute of Applied Mathematics
USSR Academy of Sciences
Moscow, USSR

A mobile robot control system includes a few simultaneous interacting processes. In this work the control complex using a network on the basis of the six minicomputers have been examined. A structure of such a control system, distribution of the processes among the processors, functions carring out by each system block are discussed. Problems which have been solved during preparation of the software are described.

Two directions may be distinguished in the development of mobile robots (MR). The first one is a creation of the automatic means of transportation which are intended to solve industrial and economical problems. The robots of this class deal with completly or partially regulated environment. It is rational to construct them with the wheel chassis (they will be referred to as wheel transport vehicles - WTV). The kinematic complication level of the WTV may be different. However, in order to adapt an universal transport robot to the equipment available without considerable modification it must have higher ability for manoeuvre that requires kinematic abundance.

The creation of the means of transportation usable in unregulated environment with complex relief is the second direction of the development of mobile robots. Legged or wheel-legged vehicles (LV) are preferable in this case.

The solution for the motion construction and control problems of the above devices is not unique because of the driver complexity and the kinematic abundance. So the problem arises as to choosing a possible solution. To form motion close to the optimal one it is necessary to have in mind the information about:

- environment in which the robot works,
- the current state of the vehicle,
- a general task given for MR.

So the control system (CS) must include the blocks for the processing of the indicated information, the blocks for planning and performing of the motion.

The function blocks mentioned above are the closely interacting simultaneous processes. The simulation which have been carried out at the Keldysh Institute of Applied Mathematics of the USSR Academy of Sciences and the experience available in the organization of parallel-serial processing in robototechnical devices show that to enable MR to work in real time, and not in the start-stop mode it is necessary to provide a parallel data processing [1].

The MR control system may be constructed using either analog or digital units. The latter is more noiseprooved. Besides, during research and test of the whole complex the alteration in the algorithms of all the levels should be made. Modifications of the program for digital computer may be done quickly and without much labour consumption.

Taking into account the above considerations it is reasonable to design a control complex using several digital computers. In this paper the control system of mobile robot constructed with six interacting microcomputers "Electronika-60" have been examined. We will study in detail the organization and the structure of such CS. First we shall describe briefly kinematics of the drivers and the sensors of control objects.

The wheel transport vehicle model that have been investigated in the Keldysh Institute of Applied Mathematics is a rectangular platform with four wheels [2]. Each wheel can independently turn around the vertical axle (the angle of turning). The two wheels mounted diagonally are leading, the two others are free rolling. The potentiometers placed on the vertical axle of each wheel allow to determine the angle of turning. Two paired potentiometers are intended for the measurement of the angle of rotation. The long-range vision system (LRVIS) built in Leningrad Mechanical Institute on the base of the laser distance gauge is used to collect the environmental data [3]. The contact safety system is based on the wire tactile sensors placed on the corners of the platform.

The legged vehicle model [4] is a flat rectangular platform with six identical three-link legs with three degrees of mobility each. The potentiometers placed in every moving element allow to determine the angles of turning of these elements. All feet are supplied with the contact sensors of touch. The long-range vision system is analogous to the system of the WTV model.

The **system was constructed** using **hierarchical principle**. The high level (1) computer carries out the following:

- connection with the operator console, through which the general task is introduced (in case of the supervisor control this is the direction and the velocity, the state of the body and so on). The operator console is used also for diagnostic check of the equipment,
- interaction with peripheral units attached to the control complex. These units execute the loading of the programs into CS,
- work of the channel with the auxiliary computer. At the stage of debugging and research of CS the complex is connected with the universal minicomputer M-6000 which has a developed disk operating system, means for editing, translation and loading the programs. Such an organization of the work allows to quickly make alterations in the programs of CS using large external memory to store different versions.

The general monitor of the system which will arrange the interaction of all levels is also based on the level-1 computer. On the basis of the instructions received from the operator the monitor gives a task to the system on the choice of the route. So far as the system under description provides supervisor control the block of the automatic route choice is absent and its functions are carried out by the operator. This level of the MR control system is the same for LV and WTV.

The block diagram of the control system and the distribution of the processes among the processors is presented in the Figure

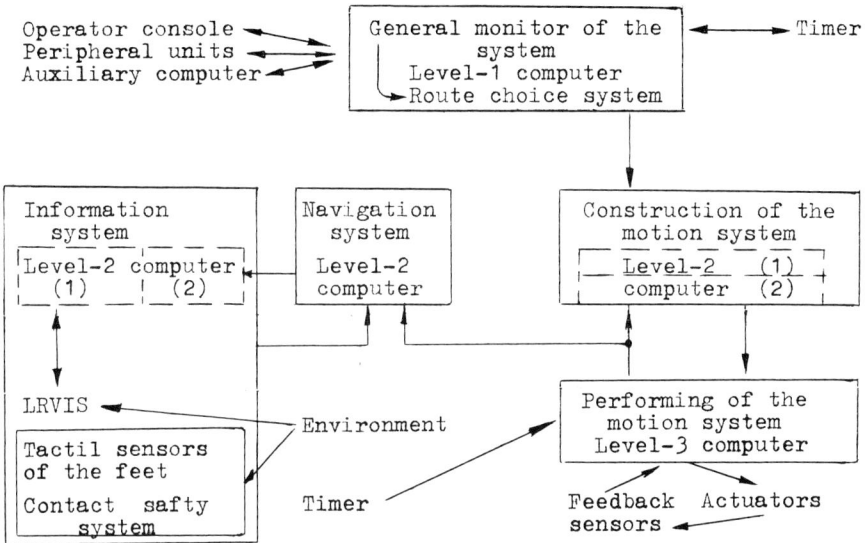

Figure
Block diagram of the mobile robot control system

The LV motion system is based on two computers. The first computer forms a gait and footprint points in accordance with the linear and angular velocities of the machine centre of mass, roll and pitch angles received from the system route choice and information about current state of the robot. According to the results of its work the second computer builds program values for all 18 LV degrees of mobility, the given program velocities being corrected in conformity with dynamics and stability of the machine. The above initial information in case of WTV serves for the calculation of the angles of turning and the rolling velocities of all wheels. The program values of 6 degrees of mobility are also an output of the WTV motion construction system. So far as the wheeled robot has a simpler kinematic scheme the construction of the motion system of WTV may be done with one computer.

According to the program values and on the basis of the feedback sensor readings the level-3 computer forms a control over the actuators of the machine. The control is carried out by pulse-width modulation of voltage of the direct-current motor. The control signals are generated in cycles. On the control cycle the following operations are performed for each degree of mobility:
- interrogation of the sensors, filtration and preprocessing of the measurement results. For example, the WTV model has two potentiometers on each wheel to determine the angle of rolling. This is conditioned by the fact that the working zone of the potentiometer is only $330°$. Two sensors with shifted insensitive zones allow to measure full rotation of wheels (360), but then an additional data

processing is required;

- prediction of the value of controlling parameters on the basis of the motion model with the corresponding degree of mobility, the measurements performed and previous control;
- determination of control over the actuators on the basis of the formed prediction and given motion program.

The motion performance system is the same for LV and WTV. In order to provide smooth motion and to make the terminal position (placement of foot, angles of turning of wheels) more precise, the control cycle must be minimum.

Information about current state of the actuators is transmitted into the motion construction system and into the navigation system (NS). Due to the errors in the turning angle adjustment of the wheels there may occur a wheel slipping. Therefore and due to miscalculations in the definition of rolling velocity of the wheels the real trajectory of the machine differs from the planned one. The errors in the LV leg stepping also lead to the deviation from the fixed trajectory. Values of these deviations are determined by the navigation system based on one level-2 computer. Its function is to determine the state of the machine in space on the basis of the data from the motion performance system, environment model formed by the information system and data from the safety sensor system. A request may be given to the information system for the detailed examination of a part of the environment.

Two blocks may be distinguished in the information system: 1) contact safety block, 2) block for the environment data collection. The first one is built on the basis of tactile sensors. The second one includes two level-2 computers and LRVIS [3]. One of them arranges the initiation of LRVIS, control of the survey block drivers and reception of information. The second one is intended to form the model of the environment. An individual computer is allowed for the work with LRVIS due to the following factors.

- rate of data reception is very high (the time of a single measurement is less than 500 μs),
- the storage time of the data from LRVIS is little,
- there is no data buffer in LRVIS.

Application of a more sophysticated LRVIS with its own preprocessors for data preprocessing, data storage, control of survey block sensors will eneble one to manage with a single computer in the MR data system. The model of the environment is formed using the results of the NS work that allow to correlate and to interpret the data obtained by LRVIS. The most complicated and important problem arising during the construction of such a multiprocessor control system is preparation of the software. The following tasks should be solved.

- organization of the interaction between computer and peripheral units,
- elaboration of the programs for carring out supervision functions, relation with operator, control over the lower levels,
- elaboration of the programs for loading of the processors. After the power supply is on, it is necessary to load the computers with the programs from the external medium (punched tape, magnetic tape, disk, channel to the auxiliary computer, etc.). It is not reasonable to store the programs in ROM at the stage of the CS

elaboration. So far as only the level-1 computer is connected with the peripheral units, the level-2 processor must be loaded through the first one. The level-J processor may be loaded also only through the computers of the high levels.

The means to test the efficiency of the elements and the diagnostics to define the failures should be provided, the interaction and parallel operation of a few processors should be arranged. The timing during the interaction of the processors is done by interruption. The control time of the level-3 computer is organized by means of a timer initiated by the level-1 processor. Besides, with some period which is formed also by the timer the high level processor interrogates the elements of the complex to determine their efficiency. The operation of the computer responsible for the interaction with LRVIS is defined by the rate of information coming from the measurer. The rest of processes are repeated after termination.

At the present time distribution processes among the processors are defined beforehand. The next stage of the software elaboration should provide the redistribution of the processes in case of a failure and reloading of the complex which insreases the reliability of the system. This paper represents one of the stages in the research of the principles of multiprocessor control system construction for complicated robotic machines.

REFERENCES.

[1] Okhotsimsky, D.E., Platonov, A.K., The problems of creation of legged vehicles in biomechanics, In: Biomechanics (USSR, Riga) 1975, 594-599.

[2] Kiril'chenko, A.A., Kugushev, E.I., Plotnikov, A.M., Yaroshevsky, V.S., Use of the long-range information in control system of a mobile robot, In: Problems of the machine vision in the robotics (USSR, Moscow) 1981, 48-60.

[3] Information system of the mobile robot model. Preprint of Institute of Applied Mathematics (USSR, Moscow) 1982, N (45).

[4] Efimov, V.A., Kudryavtsev, M.V., Titov, A.F., Physical model motion of the ledded vehicle, In: Investigations of robototechnics systems (USSR, Moscow) 1982, 96-92.

A SECOND GENERATION REAL-TIME INDUSTRIAL
VISION SYSTEM

Alan H. Bond, Roger S. Brown and Chris R. Rowbury
Artificial Intelligence and Robotics Laboratory
Queen Mary College
Mile End Road, London E1 4NS
England

We describe an industrial vision system which has been implemented and tested in software. It has been designed to be implemented in special purpose hardware, using a modified form of video stream technique. The system uses 256 x 256 x 8 bit grey scale images of industrial parts which may overlap or touch. It is based upon 5 x 5 edge templates followed by exhaustive matching of each pair of segments of each stored model separately, the weighing of evidence and the extraction of identity and location of each part in the scene. The expected speed in hardware is of the order of a second.

INTRODUCTION

We report here on a two and a half year project which is part of the British Science and Engineering Research Council's Robotics Initiative. The aim was to produce a second generation industrial vision system i.e. one using grey scale images and allowing overlapping parts (Bond et al (1983a)(1983b)).

The project started with the assumption that a commercially viable vision system would involve using a video stream implementation technique (Tenenbaum (1980)). That is, the image and subsequent data derived from it would be held in a frame store. The frame store would allow fast read out in video raster order. Processing would be achieved by special purpose function boards and the data would be streamed at video rates from the frame store through the boards and back into the same or similar frame store.

We used an Intellect frame store provided by Microconsultants Ltd. A diagram of our system is given in Figure 1.

THE SYSTEM DESIGN

The system operates as a simple sequence of processing starting with the captured image and ending with the identity and position of the recognised objects in the scene. The overall strategy is to extract a set of curves from the image and then to exhaustively match a set of model segments onto these curves. Places where good fits occur produce votes of evidence as to the identity and location of a part in the scene.

EXTRACTION OF CURVES

This follows the Nevatia-Babu approach (Nevatia and Babu (1978)); it has four stages.

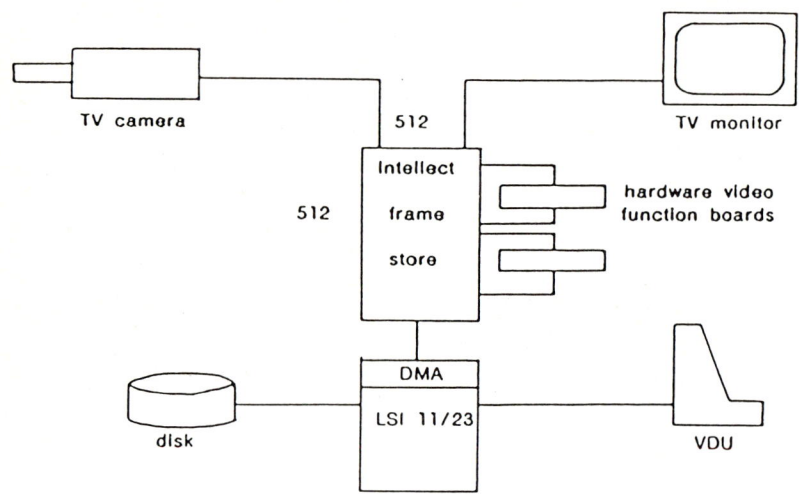

Figure 1
Intellect System and Hardware Design Concept

1. <u>Edge detection</u> uses a set of 5 x 5 edge templates at 45 degree intervals giving a strength and direction for each potential edge point. By using 45 degree intervals, the matrix elements are only 1, 0 or -1 and hence convolution involves only additions.

2. <u>Thinning</u> removes redundant adjacent edge points using a 3 x 3 template depending upon the direction at the edge point.

3. <u>Linking</u> generates the data which connects each edge point to its neighbours along the edge. This is achieved by a 3 x 3 template generating results into an image sized array. We call each connected list an edgepoint chain.

4. <u>Gap filling</u> in chains, where single pixels may be missing, is accomplished by a 3 x 3 template. This is a slight streamlining of the Nevatia-Babu method.

The (s,θ) representation of each chain is then computed.

MODEL MATCHING AND WEIGHING OF EVIDENCE

Since the system was meant to recognise highly overlapped parts, we adopted an approach to modelling and matching that allows each meaningful fragment of each model to be matched exhaustively over the image. The set of matches of model fragments constitutes the evidence to be weighed as to what the scene comprises.

The system has a set of stored models which are segmented and held as s,θ curves. The image chains are not segmented. Instead, we match each model fragment separately to each chain, at every point in the chain.

The meaningful model fragments were taken to be each contiguous pair of model segments. The discrepancy function for matching was

$$\int (\theta_{model} - \theta_{image})^2 \, ds \Big/ \int ds$$

This function gave a high value except at a small number, usually less than 10 for each fragment, of chain points. Where the value dropped below a threshold, we had a good fit and each good fit produced a vote as to the identity, location and orientation of the part giving an interpretation of this point in the image. The good fits for the set of model fragments for a given model voted into a set of ϕ, X and Y buckets for that model. This produced a distribution with a clear peak for each object of that type in the scene. This peak could be separated by a simple threshold, and the location and orientation found to good accuracy. Figure 2 shows the recognised model overlaid onto the image.

Figure 2
Projected Solution

PERFORMANCE

The system has been demonstrated to be accurate and flexible. We have published a systematic study (Bond et al (1983b)) of the effect of environmental variation. The system is robust under variations of lighting angle and intensity, camera angle and aperture, background reflection and vibration. It can also tolerate 50-70% obscurement of objects by overlapping.

HARDWARE IMPLEMENTATION

We have developed a hardware design for the vision system, which is a modified video stream type. The system would use two 16 bit frame stores, built from RAM. These would share data and address buses with, although be isolatable from, a serial processor with its own RAM for program and working data. Video stream boards would be attached to the buses.

The implementation is in eight phases, given in Table 1. As already mentioned, the 5 x 5 convolution for edge point finding only involves additions. The next three processes are simple 3 x 3 table lookups. The end result is a matrix of linking information. In order to follow the links to produce a linearised form of the chain in the raster, we use the serial cpu which can follow the chain of pointers very easily in RAM. Each chain comprises at most 1000 pixels.

Having the model fragments and the chains in raster order, we can now stream them at video rates through a special video stream board implementing the matching function. For this, we have to store many copies of the fragments

Process	Hardware Implementation	Estimated Time
1. Edgepoint finding	5x5 convolution v-s board	1/25 sec
2. Thinning	3x3 convolution v-s board	1/25 sec
3. Linking	3x3 convolution v-s board	1/25 sec
4. Gap filling	3x3 convolution v-s board	1/25 sec
5. Linearising	RAM + cpu	1 millisec
6. Matching	special v-s board	1/25 sec per model
7. Histogram projection	RAM + cpu	1 millisec
8. Calculation of location	RAM + cpu	1 millisec

Table 1
Hardware Implementation

in different registrations to achieve efficient use of the frame time. The estimated time for this process is linear in the number of models.

Finally, the histogram projection and calculation of location and orientation involve only a few good fit points and are rapidly computed using the serial cpu.

It would be possible to achieve 1 second by pipelining of the first 4 processes.

REFERENCES

[1] Bond A.H., Brown R.S. and Rowbury C., "An industrial vision system recognising overlapping industrial parts using grey scale images under a wide range of lighting conditions" Society of Photo - Optical Instrumentation Engineers, Conference, San Diego, August (1983a)

[2] Bond A.H., Brown R.S. and Rowbury C., "The effect of environmental variation upon the performance of a second generation industrial vision system" Intelligent Robots: Third International Conference on Robot vision and Sensory Controls ROVISEC3, Cambridge, Massachusetts, pp 711-718, November (1983b)

[3] Tenenbaum J.M., "Video stream processors: a cost effective computational architecture for image processing" Stanford Research Institute, Technical Report ETL-0229 (1980)

[4] Nevatia R. and Babu K.R., "Linear feature extraction and classification" Computer Graphics and Image Processing, Vol. 13, pp 257-269 (1978)

Artificial Intelligence and Information-Control Systems of Robots
I. Plander (editor)
© Elsevier Science Publishers B.V. (North-Holland), 1984

THE SYSTEM PERFORMANCE OF THE SM 54/30 VISION SYSTEM

V.Britanak,M.Kuchta,F.Sloboda,I.Trebaticky

Institute of Technical Cybernetics
84237 Bratislava,Dubravska 9,Czechoslovakia

The SM 54/30 vision system [1,2] is a general-purpose vision system which have adequate flexibility for advanced applications. In this paper the system performance of the vision system is described and some experimental results with several sets of geometric figures are published. The influence of the image size /128x128, 256x256/ on the total processing time investigated.

INTRODUCTION

The SM 54/30 vision system [1,2] can be considered as a general-purpose vision system which have adequate flexibility for advanced applications such as inspection, materials handling and automated assembly. The hardware of the vision system consits of TV-camera, 16-grey-scale level A/D convertor, histogram module, binary image memory, monitor interface and 16-bit microcomputer SM 50/50. The image is read in, encoded and stored in the coder buffer and the image memory in one TV frame /20 ms/. The vision system converts the 16-grey-scale level image into the binary one and extracts all necessary information from the silhouettes of the objects. For real time applications a run-length hardware encoder was developed /with single noise rejection in a row/ so that the image /128x128, 256x256/ is read in, encoded and stored into the buffer and the image memory in one TV frame. One to four TV-camera can be connected to the system through the computer controlled analoque switch. The 16-grey-scale image is converted into binary one using optimal threshold level which is obtained by the histogram evaluation or adjusted by the operator. All processing hardware modules are connected to the internal bus of the video-processor. Internal bus is through the interface bidirectionally connected to the microcomputer SM 50/50.

The vision software is stored in the SM 50/50 28 K word memory and includes connectivity analysis which is performed on the encoded binary image in a single top-to-bottom pass. This procedure breaks a binary image into its connected components, performes component labeling and enables to count objects in the scene and to distinguish a hole from the background. During the connectivity analysis important values are calculated such as the number of blobs, the number of holes in a blob, the area of a blob, the first and the second order moments of a blob, the coordinates of the perimeter points. The connectivity analysis module can be set up so that only those values are calculated which are needed for the given application. From the values calculated during the connectivity analysis important features can be obtained: the perimeter length, the maximum and the minimum radius vector length, the ratio between the maximum and the minimum radius vector length, the ratio between the perimeter length and the area, the trace of the second order moments matrix, the determinant of the second order moments matrix, the maximum and the minimum eigenvalue of the second order moments matrix. According to the values calculated during the connectivity analysis the following alternatives for the angular orientation can be calculated: the angle of the minimum inertia axis, the angle of the maximum or the minimum radius vector, the angle towards the centre of the largest hole, the angle of the maximum or the minimum radius vector of the largest hole.

In the training phase for each stable position of an object a statistical model is built up. This model is defined by the selected invariant features. In the operation phase the recognition is performed by the nearest neighbour method. The solution is then verificated by the confidence intervals.

SYSTEM PERFORMANCE

The software of the vision system consits of the following three main parts:

    Set up
    Training
    Optimization.

These modules enable interactive communication between the operator and the vision system in order to set up the system and to optimize the system for a given application.

Module Set up

The module Set up is devoted to setting up the basic parameters which have influence on the system performance. The following basic parameters is possible to set up:

    The color of the background which can be white or black

    The size of the field of view which can be 256x256, 128x128 or 64x64 picture elements

    The threshold for the minimal blob area according to which during the connectivity analysis only those blobs are accepted whose area is greater than given threshold

    The threshold for the minimal hole area accordint to which during the connectivity analysis only those holes are accepted whose area is greater than the given threshold

    The optimal threshold for binarization which is defined automaticaly if the histogram is bimodal or is selected by the operator

    The calibration parameters which enable to calibrate the TV camera and which enable by subsequent processing to calculate the are rea and the length of the perimeter in mm^2 or mm respectively.

Module Training

The module Training is devoted for the training of the vision system. Each object in each stable position is shown several times to TV camera. According to each stable position corresponding data base of features is created. There are three different types of data bases:

- to create new data bases
- to add a new data base to the given set of data bases
- to remove a data base the given set of data bases.

The following parameters can be set up:

- the sign for the mirror symmetry
- the number which indicates how many times a picture should be processed
- the alternative for the angular orientation.

Module optimization

The module Optimization provides the ability to select the most suitable features for the recognition. The selection is performed by the discrimination matrix or by the operator. The connectivity analysis is set up according to the selected features, so that only those features are calculated which are necessary for the given application.

VISION SYSTEM LANGUAGE

The vision software is written in the ASSEMBLER language. For easy of operation with the vision system a special low-level language has been developed. The language enables communication with the main three modules in order to set up the system for a given application. The control structures are similar to those in BASIC language /for..next,gosub..return,if..then,goto/. IO operations are performed as in BASIC language. The vision system commands are of two different types: picture processing commands and picture display commands. Picture processing commands are as follows:

PICTURE /Camera number/ - is devoted for picture processing, for calculation of selected features and for object recognition.
LOCATE /Name/ - is devoted for finding and object in the scene.
HISTOGRAM /Camera number/ - for set up the optimal threshold.
SETTHRESHOLD - for set up an arbitrary threshold.
BLOBINFORMATION /Blob number/ - makes available all features of a prototype which has been trained by teaching by showing.

Picture display commands are

DRAWIMAGE - displays a binary image ecoded in the run-length code.
DRAWBLOB /Blob number/ - draws the perimeter points of a blob and coordinates of the center of gravity of a blob.
DRAWRECBOX /Blob number/ - draws the rectangular boundary box.
DRAWMINBOX /Blob number/ - draws the minimal rectangular boundary box.

As a high-level lenguage, for writting special application programs, the language PASCAL will be used in the future.

EXPERIMENTAL RESULTS

Several sets of geometric figures were used as test patterns for evaluating a few major performance factors of the vision system. The performance of the vision system using these sets of test patterns was investigated and the influence of the size of view /128x128, 256x256/ on the total time required for processing the image and for recognition was tested. In order to compare our results with those recently published we have used the same patterns as in [3]. For the set of patterns, shown in Fig. 1, several important features have been calculated /area, first and second order moments/ and the execution time is shown in Fig. 2 and Fig. 3. The size of view /128x128, 256x256/ influences the execution time approximately by factor 2 which is in correspondence with the fact that the length of a linear segment has no influence on the execution time of selected features in the case of run-length encoded binary images.

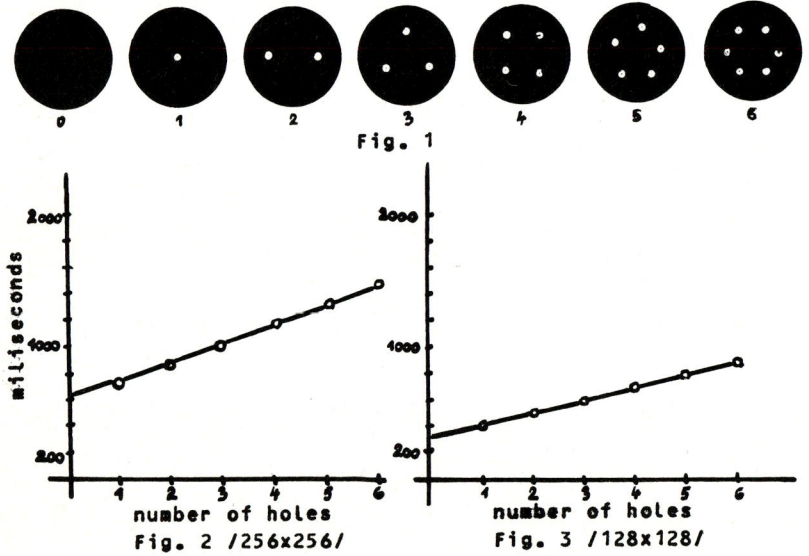

Fig. 1

Fig. 2 /256x256/   Fig. 3 /128x128/

REFERENCES

1. V.Britaňák,F.Sloboda,I.Trebatický,: A Modular Vision System For Inspection, Materials Handling and Assembly, Proc. of the II. Intern. Conference on Artificial Intelligence and Information-Control Systems of Robots, Smolenice, 1982, 24-29.
2. V.Britaňák,F.Sloboda,I.Trebatický: A Modular Vision System for inspection, Materials Handling and Assembly Proc. of the III. Scandinavian Conference on Image Analysis, Copenhagen, 1983, 199-203.
3. C.A.Rosen,G.J.Gleason: Evaluating Vision System Performance, Robotics Today, 1981.

A QUATERNION REPRESENTATION OF ROTATION
AND ROBOT MOTION SYNTHESIS

František Čapkovič

Institute of Technical Cybernetics
Slovak Academy of Sciences
Bratislava
Czechoslovakia

The possibility of a special representation of
the rotation by quaternions is discussed and its
application to a description of a robot end effector orientation is shown. The main advantage of
the representation of rotation by four parameters
instead of the nine elements rotation matrix lies
in its use for computing the result of successive
rotations. To demonstrate it, the straight line
motion synthesis of the robot hand is performed
in such a way.

INTRODUCTION

It is generally known that six parameters are needed to specify
a location and orientation of a robot end effector in a three dimensional /3-D/ Euclidean space. Usually, the location of a point
of the end effector expressed in some fixed Cartesian coordinates
system is given by a position vector $\hat{p}$ /three degrees of freedom/
and the orientation of the end effector is specified by the Euler
angles /the other three degrees of freedom/. Without doubt the
Euler angles are the most common but definitely not the most useful for robot applications. Because of the need to handle with a
/3x3/ rotation matrix $\hat{R}$, they require the longest processing time
among all available choices of rotation representations. This paper is devoted to a special representation of the rotation by quaternions and its application to a robot motion synthesis.

POSITION AND ORIENTATION OF THE END EFFECTOR

To describe the kinematics of a robot it is customary to define a
/4x4/ transformation matrix $\hat{T}$, combining operations of translation
and rotation as follows.

$$\hat{T} = \begin{bmatrix} \hat{R} & \hat{p} \\ \hat{0} & 1 \end{bmatrix} \qquad \begin{array}{l} \hat{R} = /3x3/ \text{ rotation matrix} \\ \hat{p} = /3x1/ \text{ position vector} \\ \hat{0} = /1x3/ \text{ zero-vector} \end{array}$$

Matrix $\hat{T}$ is derived by taking the product of N matrices $\hat{T}_1$, $\hat{T}_2$, ...
..., $\hat{T}_N$ of similar type, the elements of each being known functions
of one of the N robot joint angle coordinates q_1, q_2, ..., q_N. Rotation matrix $\hat{R}$ is orthonormal. It can be variously expressed as a
product of three matrices of similar type, each depending on one of
the three Euler angles. The position and orientation of the end ef-
fector /the hand/ in based coordinates system S: /$\hat{x}$, $\hat{y}$, $\hat{z}$/ is fully

described by the position vector $\hat{p}$, unit normal vector $\hat{n}$, unit slide vector $\hat{s}$, and unit approach vector $\hat{a}$, according to Fig. 1, where the meaning of the Euler angles α, β, γ is also shown. Thus

$$\hat{R}_\alpha = \begin{bmatrix} c\alpha & -s\alpha & 0 \\ s\alpha & c\alpha & 0 \\ 0 & 0 & 1 \end{bmatrix}, \quad \hat{R}_\beta = \begin{bmatrix} 1 & 0 & 0 \\ 0 & c\beta & -s\beta \\ 0 & s\beta & c\beta \end{bmatrix}, \quad \hat{R}_\gamma = \begin{bmatrix} c\gamma & -s\gamma & 0 \\ s\gamma & c\gamma & 0 \\ 0 & 0 & 1 \end{bmatrix} \qquad /1/$$

where $c\alpha$, $s\alpha$ symbolize trigonometric functions $\cos\alpha$, $\sin\alpha$, respectively. After multiplying $\hat{R}_\alpha$, $\hat{R}_\beta$, $\hat{R}_\gamma$ we obtain

$$\hat{n} = \begin{bmatrix} c\alpha.c\gamma - s\alpha.c\beta.s\gamma \\ s\alpha.c\gamma + c\alpha.c\beta.s\gamma \\ s\beta.s\gamma \end{bmatrix}, \quad \hat{s} = \begin{bmatrix} -c\alpha.s\gamma - s\alpha.c\beta.c\gamma \\ -s\alpha.s\gamma + c\alpha.c\beta.c\gamma \\ s\beta.c\gamma \end{bmatrix}, \quad \hat{a} = \begin{bmatrix} s\alpha.s\beta \\ -c\alpha.s\beta \\ c\beta \end{bmatrix} \qquad /2/$$

where $\hat{n}$, $\hat{s}$, $\hat{a}$ represent the columns of $\hat{R}$.

REPRESENTATION OF ROTATION BY FOUR PARAMETERS

Matrix $\hat{R}$ rotates the position vector of each point in the 3-D Euclidean space by the angle of rotation δ about a directed rotation axis $\hat{o}$ whose points are invariant with respect to this rotation. The rotation angle δ and the direction cosines c_1, c_2, c_3 of the positive rotation axis are given [1] by

$$\cos\delta = (n_1 + s_2 + a_3)/2 \qquad /3/$$

$$c_1 = (s_3 - a_2)/2\sin\delta \;;\; c_2 = (a_1 - n_3)/2\sin\delta \;;\; c_3 = (n_2 - s_1)/2\sin\delta \qquad /4/$$

where $\hat{n} = (n_1, n_2, n_3)^T$, $\hat{s} = (s_1, s_2, s_3)^T$, $\hat{a} = (a_1, a_2, a_3)^T$

The angle $\delta > 0$ corresponds to a rotation in sense of a right-handed screw propelled in the direction of the positive rotation axis. Either the sign of δ or the positive direction of the rotation axis may be arbitrarily assigned. Some image gives Fig. 2.

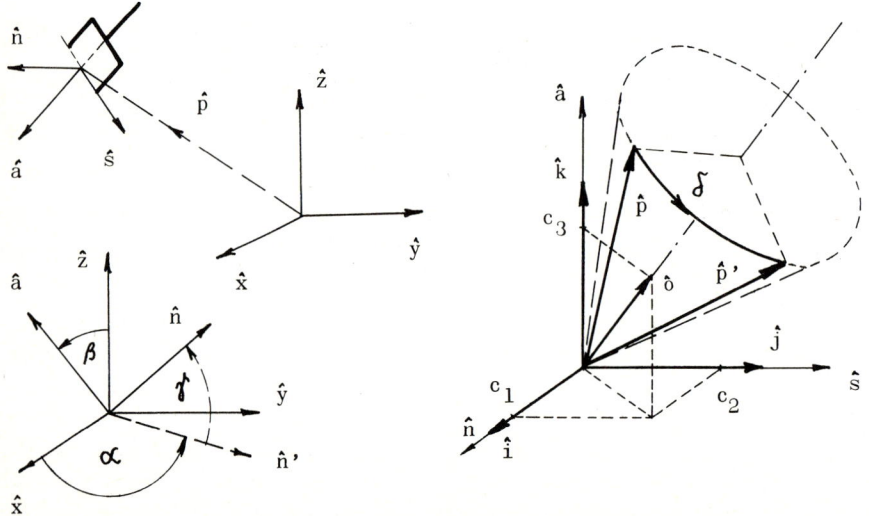

Figure 1   Figure 2

The direction of the positive rotation axis is that of the eigenvector corresponding to the eigenvalue $\lambda_1 = +1$ of $\hat{R}$ /the remaining eigenvalues of $\hat{R}$ are $\lambda_{2,3} = e^{\pm i\delta}$/. It can be easily shown, because $\hat{R}.\hat{o} = \lambda_1.\hat{o} = +1.\hat{o} = \hat{o}$.

Hence, it can be said that the nine elements of the matrix $\hat{R}$ contain the same amount of information on rotation as the four elements /δ, c_1, c_2, c_3/ do. This fact leads to an idea concerning the possibility of utilizing the so called quaternions algebra /also Hamilton's algebra or H-algebra/ [2].

H-ALGEBRA AND ITS MODIFICATION

H-algebra is [3] a real four-dimensional associative and noncommutative algebra with a real unit. Its base is defined by four elements $\{1, i, j, k\}$. The multiplying is defined by the following rules.

$$i^2 = j^2 = k^2 = -1$$
$$ij = k = -ji \; ; \; jk = i = -kj \; ; \; ki = j = -ik \qquad /5/$$

Each quaternion Q is represented by four elements /Q_0, Q_1, Q_2, Q_3/ as follows.

$$Q = Q_0 + Q_1 i + Q_2 j + Q_3 k \qquad /6/$$

The inverse element to the Q is defined as $Q^{-1} = (1/N(Q))\bar{Q}$, where $\bar{Q} = Q_0 - Q_1 i - Q_2 j - Q_3 k$ is the conjugate element to the Q. The $N/Q/ = Q\bar{Q}$ is a norm of quaternion Q. The product of two quaternions U, V can be derived by the application of multiplications rules /5/. We obtain

$$W = U \circ V = U_0 V_0 - (U_1 V_1 + U_2 V_2 + U_3 V_3) + V_0 (U_1 i + U_2 j + U_3 k) +$$
$$+ U_0 (V_1 i + V_2 j + V_3 k) + (U_2 V_3 - U_3 V_2) i +$$
$$+ (U_3 V_1 - U_1 V_3) j + (U_1 V_2 - U_2 V_1) k \qquad /7/$$

After some analysis of /5/ and /7/ we can modify /6/ into the form

$$Q = (Q_0, \hat{Q}) \; ; \; \hat{Q} = Q_1 \hat{i} + Q_2 \hat{j} + Q_3 \hat{k} \qquad /8/$$

where $\hat{i}$, $\hat{j}$, $\hat{k}$ are the orthonormal vectors - the unit vectors of the 3-D Euclidean space. Thus

$$U = (U_0, \hat{U}) \; ; \; V = (V_0, \hat{V}) \; ; \; W = (W_0, \hat{W})$$
$$W = (U_0 V_0 - \langle \hat{U}, \hat{V} \rangle, V_0 \hat{U} + U_0 \hat{V} + (\hat{U} \times \hat{V})) \qquad /9/$$

where $\langle \hat{U}, \hat{V} \rangle$ is a scalar product of $\hat{U}$, $\hat{V}$ and $(\hat{U} \times \hat{V})$ symbolizes a vector /cross/ product of $\hat{U}$, $\hat{V}$.

QUATERNION REPRESENTATION OF ROTATION

In order to utilize H-algebra for a robot motion synthesis, the four parameters /δ, c_1, c_2, c_3/ cannot be straightly used, but they must be somewhat modified. For example the unit quaternion q /its norm $N/q/ = 1$/ in the form

with
$$q = (q_0, \hat{q}) = (\cos(\delta/2), \sin(\delta/2).\hat{o}) \qquad /10/$$
$$\hat{o} = c_1\hat{i} + c_2\hat{j} + c_3\hat{k} \qquad /11/$$

is suitable for the quaternion representation of the rotation. The elements of quaternion q are called Euler's symmetrical parameters. Although having to store four parameters of q is more advantageous than that of nine parameters of $\hat{R}$, a system of three parameters is preferred. Such a set of parameters is called Rodrigues-Cayley parameters or also the Gibbs vector. They are given by dividing /10/ by q_0. The major drawback of the Gibbs vector is that it becomes infinite when $\delta = 180°$. In the same case the magnitude of $\hat{q}$ in /10/ becomes insensitive to variations in δ which are then reflected in variations of q_0. The main advantage of q lies in its use for computing the result of successive rotations.

STRAIGHT LINE MOTION SYNTHESIS

If we wish to move hand of the robot along the straight path in the based coordinates system $\bar{S}$ from point A to point B in time T, we envision this path as consisting of the translation of the coordinates system /$\hat{n}$, $\hat{s}$, $\hat{a}$/ origin from $\hat{p}_A$ to $\hat{p}_B$, coupled with the rotation of this coordinates frame from $\hat{R}_A$ to $\hat{R}_B$. The situation is shown on Fig. 3.

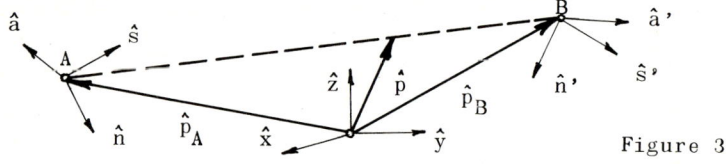

Figure 3

Let $\mathcal{M}/t/$ be the fraction of the motion segment still to be traversed at time t, i.e. $\mathcal{M}/t/ = (T - t)/T$. The displacement and the rotation of the hand at the time t /$t_0 = 0$/ are given by
$$\hat{p}/t/ = \hat{p}_B - \mathcal{M}/t/.(\hat{p}_B - \hat{p}_A) \qquad /12/$$
$$\hat{R}/t/ = \hat{R}_B.(-\mathcal{R}/T, t/) = \hat{R}_A.\mathcal{R}/t_0, t/ \qquad /13/$$
where $\delta = \delta_B - \delta_A$ and the rotations are expressed by quaternions. Thus $\hat{R}_A, \hat{R}_B \longrightarrow q_A, q_B$; $-\mathcal{R}/T, t/ \longrightarrow (\cos(\mathcal{M}\delta/2), -\sin(\mathcal{M}\delta/2).\hat{o})$ and $\mathcal{R}/t_0, t/ \longrightarrow (\cos((1 - \mathcal{M})\delta/2), \sin((1 - \mathcal{M})\delta/2).\hat{o})$.

REFERENCES

[1] Korn, G.A. and Korn, T.M., Mathematical Handbook for Scientists and Engineers (Mc Graw-Hill, New York, 1968).

[2] Blaschke, W., Kinematics and Quaternionen (Technische Verlag, Leipzig, 1960, in German).

[3] Collective of authors, Applied Mathematics (SNTL, Prague, 1978).

A NEW APPROACH TO TEXTURE

Dmitry Chetverikov

Computer and Automation Institute
Hungarian Academy of Sciences
Budapest, POB 63.
H-1502 Hungary

Structural approaches to texture concentrate on spatial interaction of elementary regions, local features, or intensities. Most of them assume that the texture pattern being analyzed is highly regular, and fail to cope with the gradual transition from regularity to randomness. We choose the contrast curve (the first moment of a co-occurence matrix plotted as a function of the intersample distance) as a texture descriptor, and suggest a new uniform model approach which enables us to model the contrast curves of regular and rangom textures. The model curves are fitted to the experimental ones, and several combinations of the best fitting model parameters are suggested as the possible measures of regularity.

INTRODUCTION

From the viewpoint of texture regularity, two categories of approaches to texture are usually distinguished, namely statistical and structural approaches. Statistical approaches compute a set of scalar features describing the distribution of intensities or local features neglecting their spatial interdependence. The strength of statistical methods is in their robustness, relative simplicity and low computational cost, in their adaptability to dedicated hardware and, finally, in the fact that they may be used for any type of texture, random or not.

Structural approaches, on the opposite, concentrate on spatial interaction of elementary regions, local features, or intensities. Pixel-based structural approaches usually compute the dimensions of periodicity parallelogram of regular pattern. The methods [1,2] trying to catch the spatial relationship of gray levels in the image through the spatial dependence of a gray-level co-occurence matrix are examples of pixel-based structural analyzers.

The principal weakness of most pixel-based structural analyzers is their unability to provide a description of both regular and random textures in a framework of one, conceptually uniform model. A description that can cope with the gradual transition from regularity to randomness must contain a measure of degree of regularity which is easily interpretable in terms of global geometry (spatial arrangement), local geometry (shape and orientation of local features), and in terms of painting function (region intensity).

Conners and Harlow [1] used inertia feature computed on co-occurence matrices, as a function of interpixel distance, to detect structure in natural textures. Let gray-level co-occurence matrix of texture be denoted by $c_{ij}(d)$. Its entries are the estimated probabilities of going from gray level i to gray level j given that the interpixel distance is d. The moments of $c_{ij}(d)$ are given as

$$M_n(d) = \sum_{ij} |i-j|^n \cdot c_{ij}(d), \qquad n=1,2,\ldots \qquad (1)$$

where $\sum_{ij}$ stays for $\sum_{i=0}^{N_g-1} \sum_{j=0}^{N_g-1}$, with N_g being the number of gray levels.

Regular pattern exhibits its periodicity through any of its moments $M_n(d)$ plotted as a function of d. Following the terminology adopted in [1], we call the second moment $M_2(d)$ "inertia" saving the word "contrast" for the first moment.

Zucker and Terzopoulos [2] applied chi square test to co-occurence matrices $c_{ij}(d)$ to find interpixel distances which yield matrices that maximally capture the regularity in a texture. Using analogy between contingency tables of a random process and the co-occurence matrices, they measure the degree of regularity observed for a range of values of d, and then select the largest value of the measure of regularity. However, no attempt is made to compare the values of the regularity measure computed for different textures with different degrees of regularity. The question whether the approach can be used to measure pattern regularity remains open.

Modestiono et al. [3] consider a mosaic model for texture based on rectangular partition of the plane by two mutually independent stationary renewal processes with common interarrival distribution. Geometry of the model is specified by an edge density parameter and a randomness parameter. The latter provides theoretical possibility to control mosaic randomness. But the mathematical complexity of the approach leads to the necessity of simplifying the model when it is used to estimate the parameters of real-world textures. The parameter estimation procedure assumes a distribution of edges which containes no randomness parameter.

This note describes a beginning study which attempts bridging the gap between random and regular texture analyzers. We suggest a new model approach based on a simple, well-parameterized one-dimensional stochastic process which enables us to model the contrast curves of regular and random textures in a uniform way. The model curves are fitted to the experimental ones and several combinations of the parameters of the best-fitting model curve are suggested as the possible measures of regularity.

I. Contrast curve and zebra

In the present study we choose modelling texture descriptor rather then the texture itself. We use contrast curve, i.e. normalized first moment of GLCM plotted as a function of interpixel distance d, as a texture descriptor. Contrast measure is defined as follows:

$$CON(d) = \frac{M_1(d)}{CONMAX} = \frac{\sum_{ij} |i-j| \cdot c_{ij}(d)}{CONMAX} \quad (2)$$

where $CONMAX = i_{max} - i_{min} + 1$, and i_{max}, i_{min} are maximum and minimum gray level of the image, respectively; all other entry symbols are specified in eq.(1). The magnitude of the normalized contrast falls into the range of values [0,1].

Consider textures that have no hierarchical structure and no drastic gray-level changes inside elementary regions. Consider then idealized contrast curves describing three degrees of regularity of this class of textures. The contrast curve of a regular pattern is periodic, with the curve amplitude gradually decreasing as distance d grows. The curve of a pattern posessing very weak regularity has a single maximum. Finally, a purely random pattern is describded by a monotone contrast curve.

To obtain more realistic plots, one must add a slow drift resulting from nonhomogeneity of real-world textures. Note that the position of the extrema of a contrast curve describes pattern periodicity, while the rate of the amplitude decrease reflects the degree of pattern randomness.

Now we shall briefly describe an algorithm for generation of the model contrast curves which can be fitted to the real ones. Consider the sequence of pulses of unit height and varying length. Let each blank of the pattern contain the constant part ℓ_0 and the random part whose mean length is a_0. Analogously, let the corresponding parts of each pulse be ℓ_1 and a_1. The pulse pattern that has both random and regular parts will be called zebra pattern.

Since we intend to apply the zebra scheme to digital images, we shall assume that ℓ_0 and ℓ_1 are non-negative integers. The mean values a_0 and a_1 need not be integers, although the length of each particular blank and pulse is assumed to be so.

If the random parts are generated by two mutually independent Poisson processes, we can derive a recursive expression for the contrast function of an arbitrary zebra pattern. By varying zebra parameters ℓ_0, a_0, ℓ_1 and a_1 we can generate zebra curves which are very similar to the contrast curves of random and regular textures.

II. Contrast curve fitting

The remaining part of this note describes an experimental study aimed at fitting artificially generated zebra curves to real contrast curves.

By adjusting zebra parameters ℓ_o, a_o, ℓ_1 and a_1 we found theoretical curves that best correlate with the contrast curves of two texture patterns, Netting and Coffee beans. The best-fitting zebra curves are shown in Fig. 1, superimposed on the real curves.

We see that the quality of the fitting is quite good. The curves of a regular and an almost random pattern were approximated with reasonable accuracy in the framework of a uniform approach. The approach is sensitive to weak regularity also. This is illustrated by the successful attempt to catch the regularity in Coffee beans pattern.

Let us finally consider two of the possible combinations of zebra parameters that can serve as regularity measures of real textures. We introduce

$$R_{\pm} = \left| \frac{\ell_o + 1}{\ell_o + a_o} \pm \frac{\ell_1 + 1}{\ell_1 + a_1} \right| \qquad (3)$$

R_+ is a general measure of texture regularity, while R_- describes the difference in the degree of regularity between the placement rules, on one hand, and the element shape, on the other.

REFERENCES

[1] Conners R.W., C.A. Harlow, "Toward a structural texture analyzer based on statistical methods", Comput. Graphics Image Processing, vol.12, pp. 224-256, 1980.

[2] Zucker, S.W., D. Terzopoulos, "Finding structure in cooccurence matrices for texture analysis", Comput. Graphics Image Processing, vol.12, 1286-308, 1980.

[3] Modestino, J.W., R.W. Fries and A.L. Vickers, "Texture discrimination based upon an assumed stochastic testure model", IEEE Trans. PAMI, vol. PAMI-3, pp. 557-579, 1981.

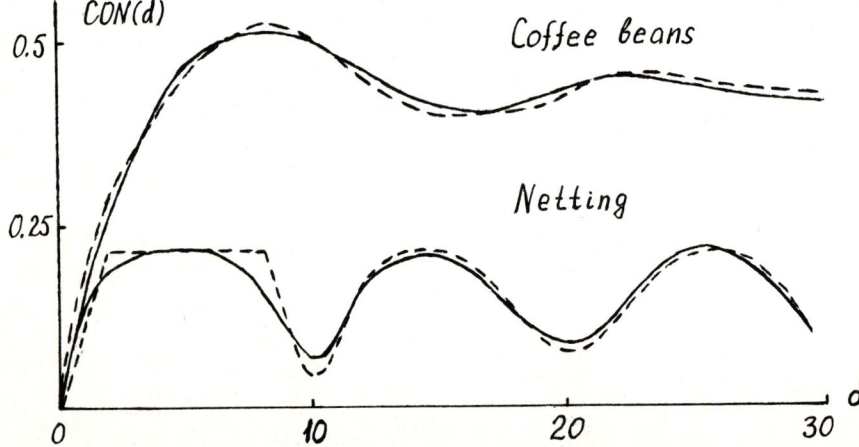

Fig. 1. The best-fitting zebra curves for Netting and Coffee beans.

LOGIC PROGRAMMING PARADIGM AT WORK:
THE CASE OF A CIVIL ENGINEERING ENVIRONMENT

Helder Coelho

Laboratório Nacional de Engenharia Civil (LNEC)
Centro de Informática
101, Av. Brasil
1799 Lisboa CODEX
Portugal

> PROLOG was selected at LNEC in 1975 as an experimental frame-
> work to enlarge the scope, flexibility and versatility of ci-
> vil engineering computer programs. After 9 years of research,
> either on PROLOG implementations side or on putting PROLOG in
> pratice, we draw some conclusions and we argue the case for lo
> gic programming paradigm in general.

INTRODUCTION:

Today only few people have been trained to build knowledge systems in PROLOG. This situation is even worst when we search for real applications in industrial and in comercial environments. Also, there is a lack of reports on experimental trips on how to solve it with PROLOG [1]. Apart of some information on the work carried out in Hungary [2], as far as we know, there is no other report giving insight about the use of such powerful technique for representing and testing knowledge in compu ter programs.

We are convinced the above bottleneck constrains the scope and impact of knowledge engineering in PROLOG, even after its choice by the Japanese as the core computer language for the Fifth Generation Project. The reasons are straigntforward: the num ber of good ideas that are propagated is reduced, the number of problem domains that can be tried is conditioned, failure and successful applications are not known, and the knowledge that is learnt by doing is not communicated. The output result, as we see it at our Laboratory, is very poor and with little chances to influence the way that others (in our case, civil engineers dominated by the imperative pro-gramming paradigm) perceive the field of logic programming.

Along the present paper we give account on our experimental courses, stressing our own conclusions about our failures and progress.

EXPERIMENTAL TRIP AROUND PROLOG:

Training in knowledge engineering usually requires several years of study after a tool is selected. At LNEC, PROLOG was imported from Edinburgh in 1975 (Marseille FORTRAN IV version), and after one year developping a geometry theorem-prover.Feed back about the learnability of PROLOG and its deficiencies was collected and sup-ported the definition of a new interpreter and compiler (Edinburgh version for DEC-system-10), in a R&D project based upon the cooperation between Edinburgh Universi ty and LNEC.

At that time our goal was to improve a tool and to prove, by writing small programs, its suitability to a civil engineering environment dominated by the imperative sty le à la ALGOL. Also, our belief was built up by comparing PROLOG to ALGOL-60 and to POP-2, at that time strong enough at LNEC and Edinburgh, respectively. First im - pressions gave us a list of outstanding features that impressed us deeply, in par-ticular a declarative semantics inherited from logic in addition to the usual pro-cedural semantics, the same uniform representation (Horn clauses) for program and data, a readable and machine independent representation for data objects, a high level form of iteration allowing multi-purpose to procedures, an easy way to treat structured data (pattern-matching in stead of selector and constructor functions), no declaration of record types and no type restrictions, the freedom procedures have to return partially defined results (containing variables) which are completed by other procedures (the logical variable power), non-determinism, and no need of "go to", "do for", "while" loops, assignment, and reference (pointers). The exercises we made, trying to enhance our ideal, justified our bet. Unification machinery, behind the PROLOG interpreter, was a generalization of pattern-matching, and finally, but not the last, the effect of executing a program was completely defined in all cases, with no illegal or undefined operations.

Having in mind PROLOG as a tool, we started studying the typical problems in our environment, and we concluded the available programming tools were quite insufficient, covering only numerical analysis and statistical methods. We found that even in those typical problems there were plenty of symbolic manipulation tasks, such as those requiring deductive capabilities, either in knowledge engineering or in natural language processing. In fact, knowledge was so strongly present that civil engineers had difficulties to look at, on account of the nature of algorithmic languages they used and the procedure-oriented programming paradigm they were attached. During 1976 we discovered the need to handle real data bases, by selecting two typical LNEC computer applications, measurements done on physical models and regular checking of structures (eg. dams). But that was not possible by PROLOG inability to handle clauses stored in secondary memory (disks and diskettes). Although, experiments were carried out concerning interfaces to our DBMS stored in our DEC-10. We concluded PROLOG programs could handle the data definition schema and generate the COBOL code necessary to access it. This fact stressed that PROLOG could be either the data definition or the data manipulation (query) language. Such discover convinced us to proceed our trip, in spite of attacks we suffered by the computer science community unable to find a missing link between knowledge and software engineering.

The following two years were fully dedicated to natural language (Portuguese) understanding, and it was produced our first generation of systems. Two prototypes were written, the one providing an AI library service [3] and the other supporting question-answering to the civil engineering legislation [4]. The last one was installed at LNEC library and all interactions were recorded. The study collected demand and requirements for the man-machine next generation of natural language systems.

During 1979, the Ministry of Public Works commissioned us a study regarding the distribution of portuguese families by steps of income. The nature of the problem behind was combinatorial and we faced the challenge by choosing PROLOG. The match was correct, however we found the efficiency of the application was heavily dependent on optimization (the care involved in writing it). Apart of the interest in using PROLOG for Combinatorics, the other branch of the Mathematics of Computation, we discovered an obvious link to Architecture. And, therefore, we reinforced the impact of programming in PROLOG at LNEC. But, this field is generally connected to CAD, and it requires a lot of computer graphics. So, we developped an extension to PROLOG, allowing its access to a picture book stored in our graphic display GT42.

By the begining of the 80's, our R&D program around PROLOG was set up: our trip was at a crossing of roads. Several directions were necessary to pursue at the same time, namely: 1) the development of a new PROLOG system with a capability to handle data stored on secondary memory, 2) linguistic engineering necessary to support friendly interfaces and front-ends, 3) knowledge engineering connected to civil engineering applications (expert systems), information systems and decision-support systems, and 4) the integration of multiple programming paradigms. All these projects needed computer resources, man power, and publicity to make PROLOG more widely accessible. The first requirement was obtained gradually, but the others were closed connected, and we faced difficulties to untangle the circle.

NEW PROLOG SYSTEM:

The knowledge brought up by the cooperation with the Edinburgh University during the development of DECsystem-10 PROLOG, and our access to the source codes of al - most all the implementations around, allowed a full understanding of the best programming environment.

During the experimental test-sides we did over several PROLOG systems, in our DEC--10 timesharing environment, we discovered that the priority of the priorities was to implement efficient and reliable machinery to make direct access to secondary memories. This new PROLOG feature is necessary and sufficient to support a wide use of PROLOG at LNEC, in particular for the development of mini-R systems, nowdays popular but yet difficult to implement. Current research is done with PASCAL and upon the use of B-trees, and having in mind the absolute need of designing a universal PROLOG system, ie. with easy portability to micros and super minis and a dedicated programming environment. So, the design is modular and architectured around layers ("onion" model). C will be the implementation language to be selected later on. The layered design will allow the user may choose easily several components of the new PROLOG system, and even the most suitable syntax to his applications and desires.

LINGUISTIC ENGINEERING:

The first generation of Portuguese language understanding systems was built upon definite clause grammars (DCG's), an extension of the so-called Colmerauer's metamorphosis grammars. The experiments we carried out with the first systems showed the need to go deeply in the knowledge of Portuguese language before to improve the parsing machinery. Also, we discovered that the option to put syntax plus semantics was good in certain cases, but could constrain the extensions to the grammar, in particular the pronoun resolution facility. Man-machine communication was handled by a grammar of dialogues [3], written with DCG's and cascaded with the Portuguese grammar.

After 1980, we pursued research around cognitive and perceptual aspects, always present during conversations, and we refined our own computational model of intelli - gent behaviour. The need for discussing the adopted linguistic machinery was recognized after studying in detail an extension of DCG's the so-called extraposion grammars (XG's), and its application to data base queries [5]. Also, this case showed the appropriate use of planning to improve efficiency during the processing of interactive queries expressed in logic [6]. Our bet now is to enlarge tne use of planning machinery to other aspects of man-machine communications, in particular for automatizing conversations.

KNOWLEDGE ENGINEERING:

By representing knowledge in computer programs, and by extending and debugging small knowledge systems we realized PROLOG kas not only a tool. The logic programming paradigm behind PROLOG was present as a method of problem-solving and as a style of writing programs.

During the three last years we promoted PROLOG use across a spectrum pf applica - tions, trying to disprove an important principle of knowledge programming, the one stating different paradigms are appropriate for different purposes.

Along the Architecture road, a first program was written to generate alternative layouts of rectangular spaces with dimensions. This program can be now extended to design movable walls and partitions taking into account the complex inter relation ship between ergonomics, space economy, flexibility, people desires, efficiency and requisites of a pleasant work environment. Another program was written for generating flat layouts and buildings layouts (elevation and level planes), and later on improved with a graphic output able to contain furniture symbols. A new project is starting now around CAD for Architecture, trying to improve the link between the previous knowledge engineering work and computer graphics.

Along the problem-solving road, several puzzles and games were tackled: missionaires and cannibals, 8-puzzle, tic-tac-toe, chess, naval battle and treasure search. Such research allowed a consistent checking of PROLOG adequacy to implement searching machinery, and in some cases planning machinery. This last aspect is very important to give more power to Portuguese interfaces and front-ends, and we are now giving more attention to it by approaching CAM (robotics) applications.

Along the information systems road, and after the construction of the two prototypes implemented during the 70's, we were commissioned by a Department of LNEC to design a system able to fill specific forms. PROLOG was also adopted to support the writing of knowledge bases for a sports club, a cooking book and INFOLOG (a methodology of information systems) specifications [7]. This last application was envisaged as a case study of information engineering: the construction of a systems specification support system. The knowledge base captured and encoded human expertise about the INFOLOG model and INFOLOG specifications, and its attached intelligent knowledge-based system might be considered a work bench for information system designers.

Along the road of CAI, we started by writing small programs to be used in secondary schools for helping the teaching of Mathematics, History, Natural Sciences and Portuguese. Work in progress covers the preparation and management of classes, by helping the teacher and the students. This last application was selected in order to disprove the idea that PROLOG is unable to handle files, and therefore to support word processing in general. The main target now consists of discovering deficiencies of PROLOG to deal with these tasks, present in an office environment.

This research project around knowledge engineering is a prerequisite to prepare two R&D programmes, the one on logic programming and management information, and the other on intelligent knowledge-based systems for civil engineering.

INTEGRATING MULTIPLE PROGRAMMING PARADIGMS:

Experimental work was carried out to obtain two major objectives: comparing different programming paradigms and interfacing different programming languages. The first objective has been concerned to make PROLOG more widely understood. And, we are collecting feedback by pursuing benchmarks around groups of problems written in PROLOG and PASCAL. The second objective concerned the known difficulties to assemble programs written in different languages, including PROLOG. A front-end written in PROLOG helps currently the exploration of a SIMULA program that was already available for delivering information in tabular form. The goal consisted of achieving an extension of the previous program by automatic writing of the missing code. Another application, around graphic displaying of a scene in 3D, was built for a town fragment and a computing room. It is processed either in a dynamic mode or in a static mode, and with the view point defined by the user. It showed the possibility to interface PROLOG with SAIL, FORTRAN and FRAIL. In this example, the PROLOG program made easier to the user the definition of the data base with the information on the scene, generating the surface coordinates of the primitive objects, and allowing the user to give the minimum of information on a scene. This application is currently used by civil engineers in urban environment studies to generate axonometric drawings, either in a graphic display, or on a plotter. Finally, an extension to DECsystem-10 PROLOG allowed output graphic displaying in a GT-42. PROLOG was interfaced with the picture book written in FORTRAN IV and PDP11 ASSEMBLER.

CONCLUSION:

Artificial Intelligence, long a topic of basic Computer Science research, is now being applied at LNEC to problems of scientific, technical, and commercial interest. The successes achieved to date have been modest. However, they hold great promise because the logic programming paradigm synthesizes current trends in the otherwise disparate fields of software engineering, data base systems and natural language processing. The research efforts have led so far to a substancial body of experimental knowledge on how to solve it with PROLOG, taking into account an engineering-oriented goal, the development of computer programs that can solve problems normally thought to require human intelligence.

REFERENCE:

[1] - Coelho, H., Cotta, J.C. and Pereira, L.M., How to solve it with PROLOG (LNEC, Lisboa, 3th edition, 1982).

[2] - Sãntãnẽ-Tõth, E. and Szeredi, P., PROLOG applications in Hungary, in: Clark, K.L. and Tarnlund, S-A. (eds.), Logic Programming (Academic Press, London, 1982).

[3] - Coelho, H., A program conversing in Portuguese providing a library service (LNEC, Lisbon, 2nd edition, 1980).

[4] - Cotta, J.C., A Portuguese Question-answering system for civil engineering legislation: overview and experimental results, in: Proc. of the First International Workshop on Natural Communication with Computers, Warsaw (September, 1980).

[5] - Pereira, F.C.N., Logic for natural language analysis (SRI, Stanford, 1983).

[6] - Warren, D.H.D., Efficient processing of interactive relation data base queries expressed in logic, Proc. of the International Conference on Very Large Data Bases, Cannes (1981).

[7] - Coelho, H., Rodrigues, A.J. and Sernadas, A., Towards knowledge-based INFOLOG specifications, in: Proc. of the Knowledge Representation and Organization Theory, Lisbon (September 1983).

INTERPRETATION OF NATURAL LANGUAGE QUERIES VIA PATTERN-ACTION RULES

Raffaele Cudazzo, Leonardo Lesmo & Claudia Randi

Dipartimento di Informatica
Università di Torino
C.so M. D'Azeglio 42 - 10125 TORINO
ITALY

A natural language query system is introduced and described. The basic assumption on which the design of the system is based is that in semantically constrained domains, such as data base query, no explicit representation of the syntactic knowledge is required. On the contrary, a set of pattern-action rules is provided to translate the command into an internal form. The rules are grouped in packets associated with some content words which can appear in the input commands. The feasibility of the approach is discussed and some examples are reported.

INTRODUCTION

The present paper deals with the analysis of natural language commands to a computer system. The limitation of the interaction to the interpretation of commands is fundamental in the design of the system which will be described in the paper. In fact, the basic assumption is that such a system does not require a syntactic knowledge base covering all the phenomena characteristic of the natural language to which it has to be applied /1/. This does not mean that the system is not able to accept and analyze the sentences where these phenomena occur, but that in many cases a command can be correctly interpreted without checking that all the rules characterizing the correct sentences are respected. Consider, as an example, the agreement in number between the subject and the verb; the claim is that even if the agreement rule is not respected the command can be interpreted. Consequently, it is not necessary that the knowledge source embodies such a rule.

The system which we are going to describe deals with commands allowing to access a relational data base and the application domain concerns airplane booking management. The choice of data base access as the test bed for the proposed methodologies presents two advantages:
- a practical one, in the sense that one of the main problems of data base management is the availability of the data and the more and more widespread use of data base systems leads to an increasing number of casual users. It seems that the adoption of a natural language front-end fully meets the requirements of casual users (however, in spite of the fact that some NL front-ends are currently operating /3,4/, this view is not held by everybody; see /5/ for a discussion)
- a methodological one, in the sense that data base access is not a "toy problem". In particular, the specification of the data which the user is interested in can require complex natural language expressions, so that, even if the domain of discourse is semantically restricted, the validity of the proposed methodologies cannot be questioned on the sole basis of the simplicity of the domain itself.

The final result of the interpretation of a command consists in a sequence of operations on the relations and attributes composing the data base. This transla̲tion is obtained in two steps:
- a syntactic/semantic analysis generates a deep representation of the command by extracting the useful pieces of information
- the internal representation is fed to a second module which produces the desired sequence of operations.

The present paper describes the first module. In the next section the knowledge structures used in the interpretation process are introduced. The subsequent sec̲tion describes the control structure of the interpreter. Finally some examples are reported.

KNOWLEDGE STRUCTURES USED BY THE INTERPRETER

The system includes two main sources of information: a dictionary and a set of rule packets used to express the correspondence between a surface construct and its interpretation (meaning).

As regards the dictionary, its entries are:
- function words (articles, prepositions)
- content words (nouns, verbs, adjectives)
- shorthands (for example "Sat" for "saturday" and "Jan" for "january")

The main point to be stressed regards the structure of the entries referring to content words. Each of them contains the root of the word, the syntactic/semantic category, the set of allowed endings and the name of a rule packet. The category can be a classical one (as "noun" or "verb") or a more specific one (e.g. DAYSPEC and MONTHSPEC are the categories, respectively, of "Sunday" and "January"). The most characteristic datum stored in a lexical entry is the name of a rule packet. A rule packet describes both the way in which the various specifications of the concept associated with the packet have to be given in the input command (e.g. the required cases of a verb) and the way in which the construct has to be interpreted. In fig.1 some examples of dictionary entries are reported.

The second and more important knowledge source used by the system is composed of a set of rule packets. Each of them consists in a set of pattern-action rules/2/. The pattern part describes the surface form which a component may assume in the input command, whereas the action is a program which implements the translation of the component into its internal form. Actually, there are two types of packets, de̲pending on whether the packet describes components which can contemporarily appear in the command (OR packets) or which are mutually exclusive (EXOR packets).

An example of OR packet is the one associated with the "volo" (flight) con̲cept. In order to identify a particular flight the user can specify the flight code, or the departure airport together with the departure time and, possibly, some other data which, even if not necessary for the identification, are often supplied by the user and may be useful to detect incorrect requests (e.g. the des̲

BIGLIETT	NOUN	E5	TICKET
VOL	NOUN	E5	FLIGHT

PRENOTAZION	NOUN	E8	TICKET
CANCELL	VERB	E12	RELEASE

Fig.1 - Example of dictionary entries: "biglietto" (ticket), "prenotazione" (re̲servation), "volo" (flight) and "cancellare" (to cancel). Notice that the packet name of the first two entries is the same: this means that the two nouns are "synonimous" in our domain, i.e. that they admit the same speci̲fications and are translated in the same way.

NAME	TYPE	PATTERN	ACTION
FLIGHT	OR	FLIGHT_CODE DEP_TIME ARRIVAL_TIME DEP_AIRPORT DEST_AIRPORT REL_PRON	FLIGHT_IDENTIF TIME_CODING_D TIME_CODING_A AIRP_CODING_DP AIRP_CODING_DS SUSPEND_ACTIVATE

Fig.2 - The FLIGHT rule packet

tination could not correspond to the flight code). The FLIGHT packet is depicted in fig.2. An example of EXOR packet concerns the verb DESIDERARE (to wish), where different requests can be issued (e.g. reservations, information , etc.) but only one of them may appear in a single command.

The patterns whose name appears in the FLIGHT packet are very simple. A more interesting example concerns the pattern USER_NAME, which is shown, in a transition network style, in fig.3. It allows to recognize, among others, the patterns:
     a nome di Rossi   (on the behalf of Rossi)
     per il Signor Rossi (for Mister Rossi)
     per Rossi   (for Rossi).
The action part has the purpose of extracting from the input pattern the useful data. In the case of USER_NAME the associated procedure builds the specification: (PASS name), i.e. "the passenger is 'name'".

INTERPRETER CONTROL STRUCTURE

The strategy of analysis is partly bottom-up and partly top-down. The switching between each other depends on the concept of "context". A context is an activated packet. As we have seen in the previous section, the various packets are associated with particular content words; when such a word is encountered in the input command, the pattern parts of the packet are "activated" and they are matched (in OR or EXOR way) against the sequences of words occurring in the input. This kind of processing would imply that all the patterns specified in the packet follow the activating word. Actually, this is avoided by saving the portions of the input command which do not match a pattern; when a pattern is activated, the save list is inspected in order to recover the constituents occurred before the activation.

The analysis starts in a bottom-up fashion. The scanned words are saved without being interpreted until an activating word is reached. At that time the processing mode switches to top-down and the constituents present in the save list are

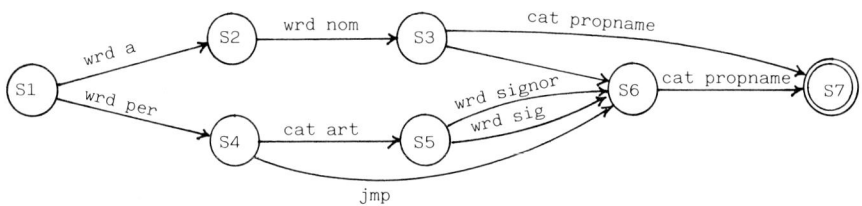

Fig.3 - The USER_NAME pattern

recovered (the save list is not necessarily exhausted in this phase).

In some cases the activated packets could be nested (for example the "volo" - flight - packet can be activated when the "prenotare" - reserve - verb is active); in this case the processing is basically the same as described above, but the currently active patterns are the ones belonging to the packet at the lower level of nesting. When a packet is disactivated (i.e. as soon as a pattern is matched in an EXOR packet or as soon as a portion of the input cannot be matched by at least a pattern of an OR packet) the control is returned to the packet at the immediately higher level, or, in case no such packet exists, the bottom-up processing mode is resumed.

EXAMPLES

- Posso prenotare un posto per andare a Torino, domani, su di un volo proveniente dall'aeroporto di Fiumicino? (May I book a seat to go to Torino, tomorrow, on a flight leaving from the Fiumicino airport?)
  Result: ((OP pren) (NUMP 1) (DEST trn) (DATA 83/12/7) (PROV fco))

- Per favore, disdici il posto prenotato a nome di Rossi, ieri, sul volo Pisa Torino, relativo al giorno 11/12/83. (Please, release the seat booked on behalf of Rossi, yesterday, on the flight Pisa Torino, relative to the day 11/12/83).
  Result: ((OP disd) (NUMP 1) (PASS Rossi) (PROV pis) (DEST trn) (DATA 83/12/11))

CONCLUSIONS

A system for the analysis of natural language commands to a relational data base has been described. The system interprets the commands by using packets of pattern-action rules; each packet is associated with a particular content word and the rules of the packet are activated when that content word is encountered in the input command. We do not claim that this very simple methodology for natural language analysis can be used in all domains (for a more complex and complete approach see /6,7/), but that in some cases, particularly in building interfaces to databases (and, perhaps, to operating systems), it may be adopted with good performances. In other words, the paper has shown the feasibility of robust and efficient natural language interfaces also in case a very limited computing power is available. A first version of the system was in fact implemented in PASCAL, even if the current one is implemented in LISP on a VAX 11/780.

REFERENCES

/1/ P.J.Hayes, J.G.Carbonell : "Multi-Strategy Construction Specific Parsing for flexible Data Base Query and Update". Proc.7th IJCAI (1981) 432-439.
/2/ R.Wilensky, Y.Arens: "A Knowledge-Based Approach to Natural Language Analysis". Electr.Research Labs. Memo M80/34, University of California at Berkeley (1980).
/3/ L.R.Harris: "User-Oriented Data Base Query with the ROBOT Natural Language Query System". Int.J.Man-Machine Studies 9 (1977) 697-713.
/4/ D.Sagalowicz (ed.): "Mechanical Intelligence: Research and Applications". SRI Final Tech. Report, Menlo Park (Dec.1980).
/5/ B.Shneiderman: "A Note on Human Factors Issues of Natural Language Interactions with Database Systems". Information Systems 6 (1981) 125-130.
/6/ L.Lesmo, D.Magnani, P.Torasso: "A Deterministic Analyzer for the Interpretation of Natural Language Commands". Proc.7th IJCAI (1981) 440-442.
/7/ L.Lesmo, P.Torasso: "A Flexible Natural Language Parser Based on a Two-Level Representation of the Syntax". Proc.1st Int. Conf. ACL-Europe (Sept.1983).

KNOWLEDGE REPRESENTATION AND DEDUCTION
IN EXTENDED PRIZ

Peep V. Eomois

Institute of Cybernetics
Academy of Sciences of the Estonian SSR
Tallinn, U.S.S.R.

An extension of the PRIZ system is proposed.
Logical background of the solution is discussed
and some examples of knowledge representation
are given.

1. INTRODUCTION

It is widely accepted that automatic program construction or program synthesis is intended to be one of the main part of an intelligent programming system. A number of actually working program synthesis systems operate according to the schema as follows:
    SPECIFICATION → PROOF → PROGRAM
This approach is called deductive synthesis. An existence proof is constructed from a given specification for the solution. The program required is derived from the constructed proof.

The main differences between deductive systems are in knowledge representation and reasoning methods. For instance, in PROLOG systems specification of a problem is given in the form of logical formulae - Horn's clauses. And only one inference rule - resolution - is used to obtain a target program. On the other hand, in the PECOS system (Barstow (1979)), there are hundreds of refining rules. In the PRIZ system (Tyugu (1977)), knowledge is represented in the form of computability relations, and three inference rules are used (Tyugu, Harf (1980)).

From an another point of view, when programming in PROLOG is called logic programming writing programs in source language of the PRIZ system may be called conceptual programming. These approaches of programming are quite widely appreciated. Even some programming systems are tried to provide by such a facilities. Let us name LOGLISP (Robinson, Sibert (1982)) and GLISP (Gordon, Novak (1983)).

In this paper, a program synthesis system is proposed. Actually it may be viewed as an extension of the PRIZ system. The extension is needed to expand a class of problems solved in the PRIZ at present time. Comparing with PROLOG systems the PRIZ has some drawbacks as well as some positive features. The main advantage is its effective deduction system. Actually it is linked with the main restriction of the system - individual variables cannot be used in the computability relations.

A solution is suggested which allows to retain efficiency of the logical level of the PRIZ system. The approach is illustrated in the 4th Section with examples. Logical background of the solution is considered in the 5th Section.

In the next Section, a general background of the idea is given. The third part of the paper is intended to recall programming in source language of the PRIZ system. Some concluding remarks are given in the 6th Section.

2. TWO LEVELS OF REASONING

It is supposed that a human being solves problems on two levels of reasoning. He starts on sublogical level where the problem to be solved is specified in terms of problem domain and knowledge expected to be correct is used. On this level a human being operates with units of knowledge which may be viewed as concepts of the problem domain. Therefore, sublogical level can be considered as conceptual or specific level of reasoning. Reasoning process on this level is quite fast because there are direct associations between objects.

If the problem is not solvable on the conceptual level the reasoning goes on on the logical level. The knowledge about the domain is presented here in a more general form. On the logical level a human being tries to obtain some more specific knowledge about the problem. It can be viewed as expanding the preliminary specification of the problem. Now, the expanded specification is taken and the problem is treated again.

In this paper, an idea is proposed how to extend the PRIZ system in order to cover the reasoning processes in full. The system is illustrated in Figure 1.

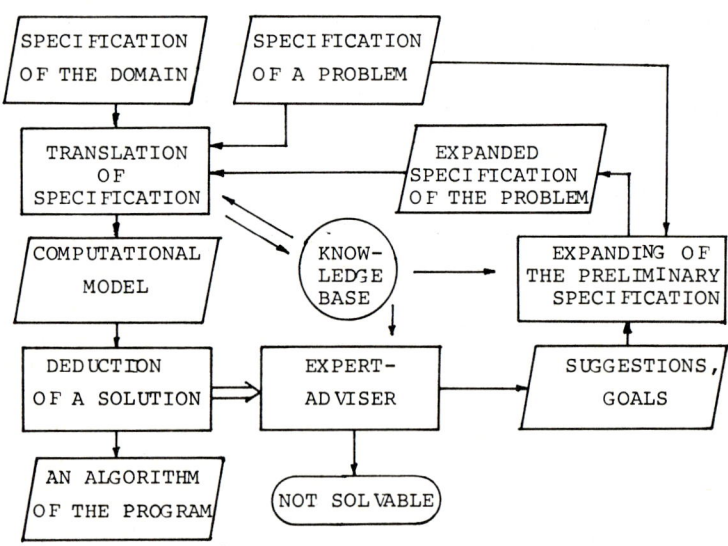

Figure 1

3. SPECIFICATIONS IN UTOPIST

The source language of the PRIZ system, called UTOPIST, is considered in (Tyugu (1979)). Here an example is presented in order to illustrate programming in UTOPIST.

EXAMPLE 1. Some concepts for describing linear elektrical circuits are specified. They are used for representing a circuit given of Figure 2. As an example, the whole resistance of the schema is computed.

$\underline{let}$ $res:(i,u,r:$ $\underline{real}$;

$\quad\underline{rel}$ $i = u/r)$;

$conn: (r_1, r_2, r: res)$;

$seq : conn$ $r.i=r_1.i, r.i=r_2.i, r.u=r_1.u+r_1.u, r.r=r_1.r+r_2.r$;

$par : conn$ $r.i=r_1.i+r_2.i, r.u=r_1.u, r.u=r_2.u, r.r=r_1.r \times r_2.r /$
$\qquad\qquad\qquad (r_1.r + r_2.r)$;

$\underline{let}$ R1, R2, R3: res ;
$\quad$ P: par $r_1 = R2, r_2 = R3$;
$\quad$ C: seq $r_1 = R1, r_2 = P.r$;

$\underline{act}$ R1.r = 5; R2.r = 10; R3.r = 10;
$\quad$ $\underline{compute}$ (R1.r, R2.r, R3.r → C.$r.r$) ;

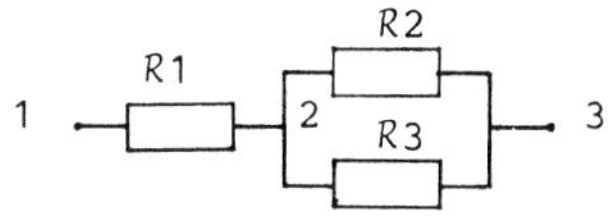

Figure 2

4. ADDING PRODUCTION RULES

Production rules are introduced to increase the level of knowledge representation of the PRIZ system. Using production rules allows:
- to represent more general knowledge than it is enabled by computability relations,
- to specify families of computability relations. Adding production rules we do not change logical bases of the PRIZ system. These rules are used only for expanding the source specifications. In this Section, only some examples are given to show programming in extended UTOPIST language.

EXAMPLE 2. A person is specified. The last two lines of the specification conatin rules for finding the grandfather of a person.

$\underline{let}$ $person:$ (name: $\underline{string}$;
$\qquad\qquad\qquad$ age : $\underline{integer}$;
$\qquad\qquad\qquad$ male: $\underline{string}$) ;
$\quad father:$ (c, f: $person$) ;
$\quad mother:$ (c, m: $person$) ;
$\quad grandf:$ ($gs, gf: person$);

$\underline{rule}$ $gf(x,z)$ ← father(x,y) ∧ father(y,z);
$\underline{rule}$ $gf(x,z)$ ← mother(x,y) ∧ father(y,z);

EXAMPLE 3. Let us change the specification of a resistor for convenient representation of production rules. In this example, a special predicate $\underline{true}$ is used. This is the only predicate evaluated during deduction process (more presidely see in the 5th Section).

$\underline{let}$ $port: (i,u,r: \underline{real}$;
$\qquad\qquad \underline{rel}$ $i = u/r)$;
$\quad res : (a, b: \underline{integer}; r: port)$;
$\quad conn: (r_1, r_2, r: res$);

$$seq : conn\ r.r.i = r_1.r.i,$$
$$...$$
$$r.a = r_1.a,\ r.b = r_2.b;$$
$$par : conn\ r.r.i = r_1.r.i + r_2.r.i,$$
$$...$$
$$r.b = r_1.b,\ r.b = r_2.b;$$

rule $par(x,y) \leftarrow res(u,v,x) \wedge res(u,v,y);$

rule $seq(x,y) \leftarrow res(u,v,x) \wedge res(v,w,y) \wedge \underline{true}\ (nomore,u,v) \wedge$
$\wedge \underline{true}\ (nomore, v, w);$

rule $res(p.a, p.b, p.r) \leftarrow par(x,y,p);$

rule $res(p.a, p.b, p.r) \leftarrow seq(x,y,p);$

Using the new specification of resistor with production rules the circuit on Figure 2 may be specified as follows:

rule R1. $res\ (1,2,,,5.);$

rule R2. $res\ (2,3,,,10.);$

rule R3. $res\ (2,3,,,10.);$

rule S. $res\ (1,3);$

The production system works out a description of the problem like that given in Example 2.

5. LOGICAL BACKGROUND

Logical background of the PRIZ system is thoroughly discussed in (Tyugu, Harf (1980), Mints, Tyugu (1982)). Logical bases of the extension of UTOPIST language is briefly considered here.

The source language of the PRIZ system is extended with production rules. They are intended to be logical formulae as follows:

$$B \leftarrow A_1 \wedge A_2 \wedge ... \wedge A_n,$$

where B, A_i, $i = 0,...,n$ are atomic formulae. These formulae may contain individual variables. An atomic formula consists of a predicate symbol and a list of variables. Functional symbols are not allowed in the formulae and, considering deduction, there is only one special predicate to be evaluated:

$$\underline{true}\ (f, x_1, ..., x_n).$$

Here f is a name of preprogrammed procedure and $x_1,...,x_n$ are it's input parameters. The output value of f is logical $\underline{true}$ or $\underline{false}$.

Predicates used in production rules are derived from the specification of a problem. Let us have a description in UTOPIST language as follows:
$$x: (x_1:t_1, ..., x_n:t_n);$$

To write production rules we can use 2^n predicates: x, $x(x_1)$, $x(x_2),...,x(x_1,x_2),...,x(x_1,x_3),...,x(x_1,...,x_n)$. Variables used in atomic formulae have the same type as their conceptual variables in problem specification. Substitution of conceptual variables and constants may be shown positionally or by means of keywords.

6. CONCLUSIONS

Using production system as deduction mechanism, consequent of a production rule need not be an atomic formula. Any construction of UTOPIST language can be used in its place. In particular, a specification of computability relation may be used as the conclusion of a produc-

tion rule. On the other hand, for each atomic formula $P(x_1,\ldots,x_n)$ there exists a specification in UTOPIST language as follows:
$: P$ $a_1 = x_1,\ldots,a_n = x_n;$, where $ denotes an identifier and $a_1,\ldots,a_n$ are conceptual variables.

Considering the project proposed, modifications of the source language of the PRIZ system are not considerable. To specify production rules a new keyword <u>rule</u> is added into UTOPIST language.

One of the decisive problems of the approach is setting up the goal for expanding of the prelimenary specification. From the solution of this problem the efficiency of deduction of the logical level will depend a great deal.

REFERENCES

[1] Barstow, D.R., Knowledge-Based Program Construction, Programming language series: 6 (North-Holland, New York, 1979).

[2] Tyugu, E., A programming system with automatic program synthesis, in: Lecture Notes in Computer Sciences. vol. 47 (Springer-Verlag, Berlin, 1977) 251-267.

[3] Tyugu, E., Harf, M., Algorithms for the Structural Synthesis of Programs, in: Systematic Programming and Computer Software 4 (1980) 3-13 (in Russian).

[4] Robinson, J.A., Sibert, E.E., LOGLISP: an alternative to PROLOG, in: Machine Intelligence 10: Ellis Horwood Ltd. (1982) 399-419.

[5] Gordon, S., Novak, Jr. GLISP: A Lisp-based Programming system with Data Abstraction, in: AI Magazine, vol. 4, No. 3 (1983) 37-47.

[6] Tyugu, E., UTOPIST language, in: Report of WG.04 of the ICSG, Definition of Specialized Languages, p. 2, Technische Universität (Dresden, DDR, 1979) 168-205.

[7] Mints, G., Tyugu, E., Justification of the Structural Synthesis of Programs, in: Science of Computer Programming 2 (North-Holland, 1982) 215-240.

PICTURE SEGMENTATION AND FEATURE EXTRACTION FOR AUTOMATIC
SURFACE INSPECTION

Friedrich, A.; Fritzsch, K.; Uebel, W.

Central Institute for Cybernetics and Information Processes
AdW der DDR
DDR - 1086 Berlin
Kurstr. 33

A method for the automatic surface inspection is
proposed in cluding three main steps: 1. selection
of the region on the part to be checked, representing the regions by a quadtree method, 2. preprocessing the picture segments with the aim of
statictical feature extraction. 3. classification
of the picture segments as belonging to a good or
bad part. The application of the method to the
problem of automatic surface inspection of castings
is described.

INTRODUCTION

In loading and unloading machines with industrial parts a human
operator usually does the visual inspection. The human operator
can be replaced by a robot only if the robot is equipped with
visual sense.

A typical problem is inspecting the surface of castings. This can
be divided into three main steps:
- selection of the region on the part to be checked
- preprocessing the picture segments with the aim of feature extraction
- classification of the picture segments as belonging to a good or
  a bad part.
All necessary data for the running phase, especially the segmentation, the feature extraction and the classification of parts to be
checked, have to be prepared in a teaching phase.

REPRESENTATION OF PICTURE SEGMENTS WITH THE AID OF QUADTREE STRUC-
TURES

As a rule the surface inspection is done on selected areas of the
part surface. Therefore the picture segments be to checked, are
taught in the teaching phase by framing these picture segments on
a raster display with the aim of a cursor control. Each picture
segment is interpreted as a binary picture whose blackpoints describe the position of the segments in the raster display. The binary picture is represented by a quadtree. The position of the
terminalnodes in the quadtree allows a transformation from the
quadtree to the raster picture representation and vicer versa. Because the failure extension in the picture segments may be very
small, the picture segments are subdivided in subsegments with a
minimal and maximal number of picture points. The segmentation is
accomplished in such a way that subsegments of the same size should
avise where possible. From the segmentes quadtree a list structure
is produced, which is the basis for the further feature extraction.

The position of the part in the coordinate system of the camera is in generally different for the working phase and the teaching phase respectivally. Therefore, a positional segment with a well discriminable feature is taught. From the difference of the center of gravity of this feature in both phases a correctional term can be calculated.

FEATURE EXTRACTION AND CLASSIFICATION

It is proposed that statistics of a first and second order i. e. histograms and coocurrence matrices, are sufficient as basic data arrays for feature extraction. The histogram is a linear array of bins, each consisting of the coocurences of a certain gray level. In the coocurence matrix the coocurences of all possible pairs of gray levels at neighbour points are included. The grid pattern for the coocurrence is isotropic and is shown in fig. a. Histogram and coocurrence matrix are computed separately for each subsegments. This is done sequentially, going through the list of quadrants representing a subsegment.

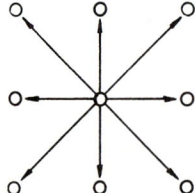

Neighbour points for calculation of the cooccurrence matrix

Figure a

On the basic of the histogram, the following features are proposed:

mean gray value $\qquad \bar{g} = \dfrac{\sum_{i=0}^{g} i \cdot h_i}{\sum_{i=0}^{g} h_i}$

mean square variation $\qquad \bar{g}_s = \dfrac{\sum i^2 \cdot h_i}{\sum h_i} - \bar{g}^2$

weighted mean gray value $\qquad h_{mj} = \dfrac{\sum h_i \cdot w_j(i)}{\sum h_i} \qquad j = 1, 2$

$$w_1(i) = (g-i+1)^N, \quad N \geq 2$$
$$w_2(i) = (i+1)^N, \quad N \geq 2$$

upper quantile $\bar{g}_r$, defined by

$$\sum_{i=\bar{g}_r+1}^{g} h_i \leq r \sum_{i=0}^{g} h_i \leq \sum_{i=\bar{g}_r}^{g} h_i$$

lower quantile $\underline{g}_r$, defined by

$$\sum_{i=0}^{g_r-1} h_i \leq r \cdot \sum_{i=0}^{g} h_i \leq \sum_{i=0}^{g_r} h_i$$

From the coocurrence matrix the following features are derived:

a) Intermediate results:
$$SUM = \sum_{0}^{GW} \sum_{0}^{GW} c[I,J]$$

$$Q = (GW+1)^2$$

where $c[I,J]$ — element of the cooccurece matrix
GW — maximal gray level

First order Moments:
$$M_x = \sum_{0}^{GW} \sum_{0}^{GW} I \, c[I,J] / SUM$$

$$M_y = \sum_{0}^{GW} \sum_{0}^{GW} J \, c[I,J] / SUM$$

where $0 \leq M_x, M_y \leq GW$

Second order Moments:
$$S_{xx} = \frac{\sum\sum(I-M_x)^2 c[I,J]}{SUM}$$

$$S_{yy} = \frac{\sum\sum(J-M_y)^2 c[I,J]}{SUM}$$

$$S_{xy} = \frac{\sum\sum(I-M_x)(J-M_y)c[I,J]}{SUM}$$

Energy:
$$e = \sum\sum c[I,J]^2$$

b) features:

Variance:
$$s_c = \frac{1}{ANZ}\left[e - \frac{1}{ANZ} SUM^2 \right]$$

where ANZ — number of rows and columns of the scanned picture

Homogenity:
$$h_c = \sum_{0}^{GW} \sum_{0}^{GW} \frac{1}{1+(I-J)^2} \cdot c[I,J]$$

Inertia:
$$i_c = \sum_{0}^{GW} \sum_{0}^{GW} (I-J)^2 c[I,J]$$

Contrast:
$$d_c = \frac{(\frac{1}{ANZ-1}(e - \frac{1}{ANZ} SUM^2))^{1/2}}{SUM/Q}$$

Correlation: $$K_c = \frac{S_{xy}}{(S_{xx} \cdot S_{yy})^{1/2}}$$

Histogramlike arrays can be achieved by projecting the value of the coocurrence matrix on a straight line, perpendicular to the main diagonal as shown in fig. b and c

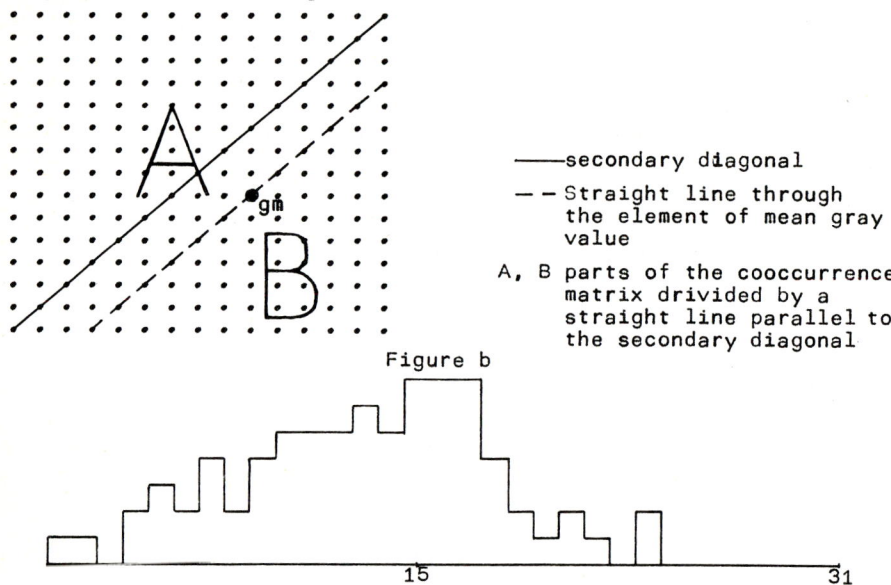

———secondary diagonal

– – Straight line through the element of mean gray value

A, B parts of the cooccurrence matrix drivided by a straight line parallel to the secondary diagonal

Figure b

Example for projecting the part A of the cooccurrence matrix onto the secondary diagonal

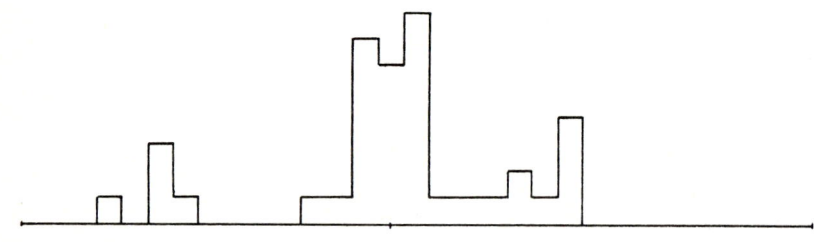

Example for projecting the part B

Figure c

Features are the quantiles as in the case of the histogram and the differences between minimum and maximum. The gray level features are assumed to be sufficient for classification. It can be shown that the gradient histogram delivers almost the same information as the projection array of the coocurrence-matrix on the normal to the main diagonal.

APPLICATION OF THE SYSTEM FOR AUTOMATIC SURFACE INSPECTION TO CASTINGS (proposal)

The completeness of the cluster of castings is checked and the surface of the castings is inspected on taking up of the cluster of castings from the automaton with industrial robots. The system structure is shown in fig. d. It consists of two CCD-matrix cameras. First camera scans the complete cluster with a dissolution of

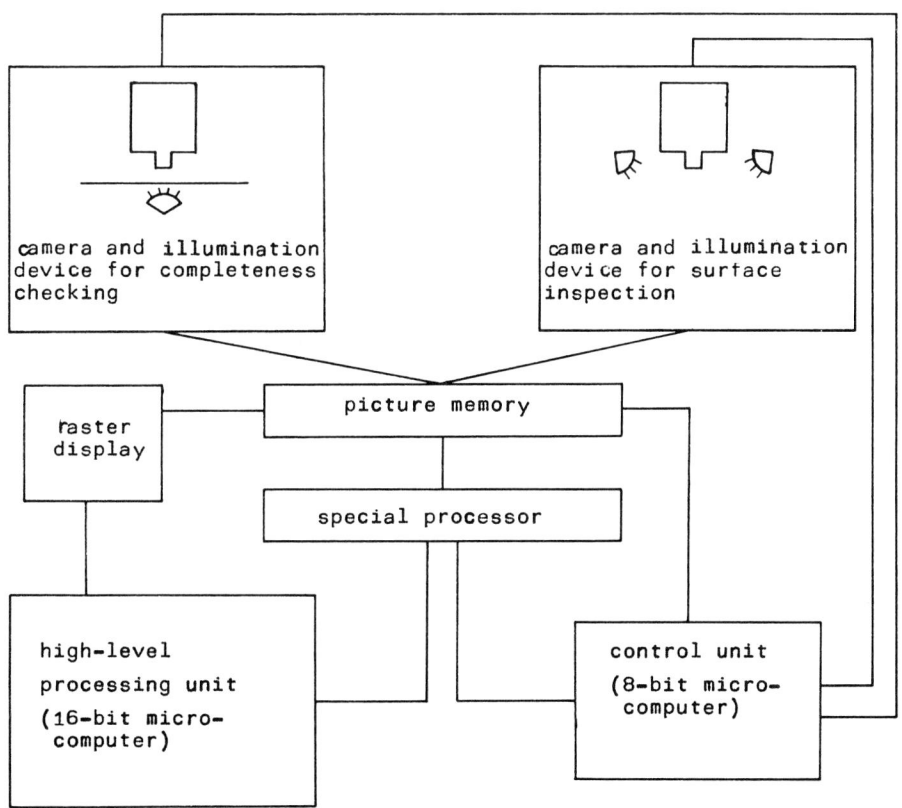

Figure d
Visual system for surface inspection

1 pixel/mm. The completeness of the cluster is checked by measuring the area of picture segments that were taught in the teaching phase. If incompletness is given a stop signal is released. The second camera for automatic surface inspection scans the castings with a dissolution of 6 pixel/mm. The picture size is 380 x 488 pixel on 16 gray levels. A special processor for all subsegments calculates the gray level histogram and the cooccurence matrix. The cameras and the special processor are controlled by the 8-bit-microcomputer K 1520 from the GDR. For the input of picture segments in the teaching phase a raster display with cursor is used. Feature extraction in the subsegments and classification are per-

formed with a 16-bit-minicomputer in the PASCAL language. The bad castings are divided into three subclasses with light, moderate and dark surfaces. The same is done with the good parts including a further class: dark with light blobs.

For the feature set of mean gray value, mean square deviation from mean gray value, difference between upper and lower quantile of gray value histogram, correlation, contrast, the differences between the minimum and maximum value and between the upper and lower quantile of projected coocurrence matrix, a error rate of 0% in the learning sample set (20 samples) and of 15% in the test set (11 samples) was achieved.

3-D OBJECT RECOGNITION WITH LOCATION CONSTRAINTS

Peter Florath

Dept. of Artificial Intelligence, Central Institute
of Cybernetics and Information Processes of the Academy of Sciences
1086 Berlin, German Democratic Republic

> This paper describes an approach to object identification and location based on three-dimensional object models and a model of restrictions on possible object locations. As an essential part a generalized Hough transform is used based on iterative prediction, 3D-orientation estimation and restriction verification of local features. Recognition of objects lying in a stable position on a supporting plane slanted with respect to the viewing direction is given as an example.

INTRODUCTION

Important tasks for a vision system are identification and determination of location (i. e. position and orientation) of objects in 3D space. Simplifications arise if the possibly appearing objects are known and models are available for these objects. Additionally, there can be known restrictions regarding the possible locations of objects and the viewing conditions. This leads in its extreme variant to the case of two-dimensional recognition or verification which is characterized by the fact that a small set of (2D-) image models (as templates or feature models) describing an object is sufficient for recognition. Otherwise, 3D-object models are necessary even in these cases where the object location is substantially restricted.

A SPECIAL PROBLEM CLASS FOR 3D-RECOGNITION

An interesting class of location constraints is where the full variability within the n degrees of freedom (d. o. f.; 6 for location in general, 3 for orientation) can be described by

- a small number of location classes which are described with respect to a so-called "restriction environment" and

- a variability with m < n d. o. f. within each location class.

In particular, that class of 3D recognition problems is regarded where for each location class the number of rotational d. o. f. is 1 and the number of translational d. o. f. is maximally 2.

Practical examples for restriction environments leading to the defined class are

- a supporting plane slanted with respect to the viewing direction (parts are lying in stable positions on this plane)

- an overhead conveyor (parts hung on hooks)
- a vice
- a parallel gripper of a manipulation robot
- (sometimes) an assembly context.

In general in these cases the description of an object by a small set of image models is not sufficient for recognition. Only supposing additional constraints leads to such simplification. For example, assuming the camera axis and supporting plane normal to be collinear and orthographic projection the 3D recognition reduces to a 2D or 2½D one.

THE GENERAL APPROACH

For computational reasons the recognition algorithm is a two-stage one. During the first stage an algorithm is applied which discriminates coarsely between different combinations of object class/object location range. The particular regime for deciding which features to extract and which decisions to make is fully specified during the training phase on the basis of 3D object models and known location restrictions. A simple binary decision tree classifier with multiple class decisions is used. Features used are global morphometric features like area, perimeter etc. and the visibility of relevant local features. The training algorithm for the regarded specific class of 3D recognition problems includes the computation of stable states and an appropriate tree construction algorithm /1/.

The principle of the second stage is a generalized Hough transform method /2/ followed by a verification part /3/. It is characterized by the following main steps:

1. Definition of a suitable accumulator array having a cell for each combination of object class/object location with a particular discretization level. Filling a particular value into all cells which correspond to those object class/object location-combinations suggested by the first stage algorithm.

2. Choosing a recognition relevant model feature which
   - could be visible according to the known location constraints and to the current contents of accumulator array
   - should have evidence within the image data.

   Searching for an image feature which could have been originated by this model feature.

3. Estimation of all possible spatial locations of the model feature assuming that it originates the particular image feature. The solution set can be empty, unique or ambiguous; there can remain degrees of freedom.

4. Converting derived feature location solutions into those for location of relevant objects.
   Removing remaining degrees of freedom for object location by regarding the a priori given object location constraints. Eliminating those solutions for object location inconsistent with the constraints. Calculation of a reliability value for all local admissable solutions.

5. Adding the reliability values to the corresponding accumulator cells. The regarded model feature/image feature - pair is asso-

ciated with each of these cells.
If additional feature pairs should be regarded goto 2.
6. Searching for peaks withon the accumulator array.
Constructing a compatibility graph for each peak with the nodes being the associated feature pairs.
7. Searching for maximal cliques within the compatibility graph. "Good enough" ones characterize reasonable hypotheses for the presence of specific objects.
8. Verification of the total solution.

The following two paragraphs discuss steps 3 and 4 in more detail. A longer presentation can be found in /4/.

ESTIMATION OF 3D LOCATION OF LOCAL FEATURES

Given an object model feature and an observed image feature, position and orientation of the model feature in the camera coordinate system have to be determined such that for a given optical projection the model feature will cause the image feature.
This problem will be extremely simplified if the image feature description contains local 3D information - e. g. as result of analyzing structured light images.
If the image feature is only a 2D projection of the model feature possible model feature locations are coded in the location and shape of the projection.

Theoretically, an exact algorithm exists but for computational reasons approximative methods are necessary. These should be able to estimate different location variables separately which together determine the location completely.

With respect to the Hough transform approach.it is reasonable to concentrate on feature orientation only. The dimension of the accumulator array should be small and orientation is especially suitable for sparse updating of the accumulator because an estimated feature orientation directly defines an object model orientation.

Feature orientation estimation can easily by reduced to that for orthographic projection /4/ if the so-called perspective normal projection /5/ holds approximately. But even for perspective projection in general the resulting failure will be small if the camera opening angle is not to large and only relative size parameters are considered.

Orientation estimation in the outlined recognition algorithm concentrates on specific, particularly planar (open or closed, real or virtual) boundary features as edges, corners and hole contours. Estimation for planar features of general shape /6/ can mostly be reduced to that for specific features if distinguishing points are detectable.

VERIFICATION OF FEATURE MATCHING BY MEANS OF KNOWN OBJECT ORIENTATION CONSTRAINTS

The relations in terms of coordinate transformations between the relevant coordinate systems for recognition are shown in Fig. 1.

Obviously, supposing model and location class are correctly chosen, with

$$M =_{def} M_{RC} \cdot M_{CF} \cdot M_{FM} \cdot M_{ML},$$
the matrix equation $M = M_{RL}$ should be valid.

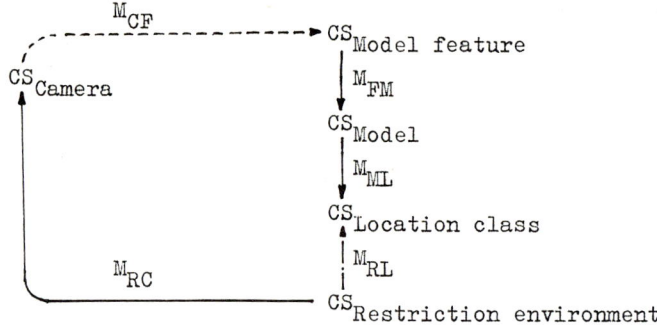

Fig. 1

Because of noise in the location (especially orientation) estimation the constraints according to the location coded in the equations can only be approximately fulfilled. That's why the solution of the resulting equation set is not a solution in a standard sense but a solution here would be such a set of variable values that the equation set as a whole is fulfilled as well as possible (for instance in the least mean square sense). In order to be able to effectively update the Hough accumulator the resulted deviations should lead to a range of possible values for the free location variables in M_{RL} as well as to a reliability parameter correctness measure) for these values. This requires the whole number of d. o. f. in the matrices to be smaller than 6 respectively 3 (for orientation only).
A possible solution for the defined special recognition class (e.g. slanted supporting plane) is given in /4/.

OUTLOOK

Implementation of a system for 3D recognition is going on. Besides algorithms for high level vision as described in this paper it will especially include programs for extracting local 3D information from structures light images. The algorithms will be included into a modular image recognition system oriented to robotic applications.

REFERENCES

/1/ Florath, P.; A Two-Stage Sequential Pattern Classification Approach, Proc. 2. AIICSR, Smolenice 1982, 80 - 83.
/2/ Ballard, D., Generalizing the Hough Transform to Detect Arbitrary Shapes. Pattern Recognition 13 (1981), No. 2, 111 - 122.
/3/ Bolles, R. C., Robust Feature Matching Through Maximal Cliques. Proc. SPIE 182 (1979), 140 - 149.
/4/ Florath, P., Three-Dimensional Recognition of Objects with Location Constraints, Conf. Autom. of Industr. Proc., Turin, 1983.
/5/ Brooks, R. A., Symbolic Reasoning Among 3D-Models and 2D-Images. Artificial Intelligence 17 (1981), 285 - 348.
/6/ Fisher, R. B., Using Surfaces and Object Models to Recognize Partially Obscured Objects. Proc. IJCAI 1983, 989 - 995.

INFERENTIAL REASONING IN NATURAL LANGUAGE PROCESSING

Danilo Fum

Laboratorio di psicologia dell'eta' evolutiva
Universita' di Trieste (Italy)

Inferential reasoning represents a very important activity in language use and its understanding constitutes a starting point to design natural language processing systems capable of human-like performances. The paper gives an outline of a research project aimed at studying inferential reasoning in the context of knowledge acquisition via text comprehension. A general overview of an experimental system is provided with the description of its specifics and basic methodologies. After presenting the acquisition algorithm, topics connected with inferencing in knowledge acquisition are briefly discussed.

INTRODUCTION

Drawing inferences constitutes one of the most important activities in language comprehension, and inferencing is practically implied in every phase of understanding. By inferencing we mean the process whereby people are enabled to go beyond the information explicitly stated in a piece of text. A lot of what we understand comes in fact from what we infer; most of what is derived from a given text (where "text" is used as an omnicomprehensive term that can refer to discourse as well as to a written passage) is constituted by information that is not directly expressed in the text itself but that must be reconstructed by the language user. Inferential reasoning is then needed to establish the internal coherence of seemingly irrelated segments of text (3), to discover what the speaker intended in uttering what he did, to understand "between the lines" and get some information that te writer did not necessarily mean to convey with a particular sentence, to critically compare and evaluate a passage. But it is often necessary to resort to inferencing even to do very elementary operations: capture the particular meaning of a polysemous word, identify the antecedent of an anaphoric reference, disambiguate the syntactic structure of a sentence, not to mention the case when it is necessary to guess the meaning of an unknown word. It is evident that any system which wants to achieve human-like performances must support a very sophisticated treatment of inferences.

In the paper the problem of how it is possible to model inferential reasoning is examined and presented in the context of a research project whose long term goal is to design and implement an experimental system capable of acquiring new information through the processing of natural language texts. Automatic knowledge acquisition via text comprehension has not been sufficiently studied in artificial intelligence. There have been in fact very few attempts to develop computer models that, after understanding the linguistic input, could store it in memory and integrate it with the existing knowledge in order to learn it. In the following sections a general overview of a new system is provided with a brief description of its specifics, basic methodologies, and modes of operation. A discussion of some problems connected with inferential reasoning is also provided.

SPECIFICS AND BASIC METHODOLOGIES

The system is designed to receive in input a series of introductory scientific texts in Italian (the domains chosen for the initial experimentation are chemistry and electronics) and gives as output a knowledge base (KB) containing all the information acquired by processing them. It is necessary to distinguish between the KB (i.e. the output of the process) and the knowledge sources (basic vocabulary and encyclopedia) that are utilized during operation. Whereas the KB produced is a function of what the system has received in input, the basic vocabulary and the encyclopedia are domain independent and constitute the necessary background for the acquisition activity. Even if they are conceptually distinct, KB and encyclopedia are functionally integrated since the KB is open to inspection and is effectively used as an additional data base. The system is therefore enabled to utilize the previously acquired knowledge in order to process a text in the same domain and to acquire new knowledge. This feature represents an attempt to implement one of the most important characteristics of the way humans learn, i.e. the capability to understand texts of increasing degree of conceptual difficulty with the progress of learning.

As a side effect of augmenting the KB, the system improves also its lexical knowledge. A very important part of learning a new subject is constituted by mastering the technical lexicon, i.e. learning new terms and new definitions. It is impossible to supply the system with the vocabulary necessary to gather information in every domain so the system itself must be able to recognize a new technical term defined in the text, and to learn its meaning. When a word that is not defined in the basic vocabulary appears in a text, the system tries to infer its meaning and some of its morpho-syntactic features by the context in which it appears, and then puts it as a new entry in the vocabulary. In this way the basic vocabulary is more and more transformed by the insertion of new words into a specialized lexicon.

The choice of deriving the meaning of new words directly from the text has imposed some constraints on the kind of knowledge representation utilized. It was decided to adopt what Rieger (5) has called the "compressionist" approach and to represent knowledge in concise form. All the information is declaratively represented in the KB through a propositional language (2) whose building blocks (concepts expressing predicates and arguments) are not decomposed into semantic primitives. Even the procedural knowledge (concerning principally the kind of inferences that is possible to draw starting from a given piece of information) derived from a text is expressed in the same format and needs an interpreter to be executed.

THE ACQUISITION PROCESS

The process of knowledge acquisition by natural language processing can be split

into three activities (separated here only for expository purposes, since the system runs as a single integrated module):
- parsing
- matching
- integrating.

The parsing process (in which a lexical functional grammar is used) is essentially devoted to map the natural language input text into the propositional representation that is utilized in performing the other activities. This process is devoted also to the above mentioned task of inferring (through the morphologic and syntactic analysis) the grammatical characteristics and (through semantic analysis) the meaning of the new words, and is closely integrated with the remaining activities. In particular, since it is possible to work with new and not completely defined words, it is compulsory to access the encyclopedia and the information stored in the KB to perform a semantic checking for the correctness of the interpretation the parser gives to a sentence.

The matching phase is principally devoted to find the right portion of the KB to which the just parsed information must be attached. A critical choice to be made is that of deciding how (i.e. with what key/s) to access the KB. It is possible to distinguish intuitively, in every sentence, between what different authors have called local focus or theme, or given part of the sentence (the part that conveys known information) and the comment ot rheme (the part that conveys known information). The theme states what the sentence is about, the comment states something about the theme. The grammatical subject of a sentence represents usually the theme whereas the predicate expresses the comment. It seems reasonable therefore to access the KB using the concept/s related to the grammatical subject as a key. If the search fails, the key is changed and the KB is accessed through the concept/s expressed in the new part of the sentence. If both searches fail, then the sentence to be learned does not share any coreferential relationship with the previously stored knowledge, and inferential activity (3) must be performed in order to establish the missing links.

The main problem to be solved with integration deals with the global component of this activity. We can in fact distinguish two distinct aspects of integration (4): the specific component, related to the number of links between the new facts and the specific existing concept nodes in the KB to which they refer, and the global component, related to the fact that learning new information about a node is not necessarily limited to that specific concept node but can serve to establish links among a variety of other concepts in the KB as well: new facts have a global influence on the memory structure. New facts may be linked with an existing concept node in either of two ways. First, whenever a piece of new information related to a concept wich already exists in the KB is encountered, the new information is linked and directly attached to the existing concept node, i.e. no functional separation between old and new information exists. Alternatively, new facts may be attached to the existing node via a subnode which contains all the newly learned facts about a particular concept. While the first way is simpler and deals quite well with the global aspect of integration (property inheritance is straighforward, for instance) it presents the disadvantage that newly learned information can interfere (i.e. slow down) with the retrieval of already known facts. Another disadvantage of attaching new information directly to existing nodes is that it is impossible to discriminate between permanent and episodic knowledge, i.e. knowledge the system must consider always true and knowledge derived from processing a particular piece of text. Information that needs to be frequently used or that is relative and true only in a particular context is then integrated in the KB according to the second approach.

INFERENCING IN KNOWLEDGE ACQUISITION

In order to model human cognitive capabilities and to construct natural language understanding systems capable of human-like performances we must be able to describe computationally how people apply previously gained knowledge to infer information that goes beyond the content of a given text, i.e. to realize how, when and what kind of inferences people draw. A complete solution to this problem would require, according to Charniak (1) answering the following questions: (a) how is it possible to represent the huge amount of knowledge people use in dealing with language and the meaning of natural language expressions, respectively? (b) under what circumstances and for what reasons do people draw inferences? (c) on which knowledge people rely in making inferences; which concepts and in what combinations are used in drawing them? (d) how is it possible to retrieve - efficiently and apparently without effort, as humans do - exactly the information needed to draw a particular inference or a set of inferences? (d) which reasoning rules are applied to a given piece of knowledge in order to draw a particular inference?

Lots of researchers both in artificial intelligence and cognitive science have tried to answer these questions and different temptative solution have been offered. The project here reported represents an attempt to tackle the inference problem in a unitary way and according to an integrated approach. Inferential activity is present in every phase of the acquisition process (parsing, matching, and integrating) and the compressionist approach adopted relies heavily on inferencing since it make less of an attempt to have interrelationships among concepts be transparent from the data structures themselves. As open problems for future research remain the devising of more sophisticated integration algorithms and the speed up of the search and match processes.

References

(1) Charniak, E., Inference and knowledge, in: Charniak, E. and Wilks, Y. (eds.), Computational semantics (North-Holland, Amsterdam, 1976).
(2) Fum, D., Guida, G., and Tasso, C., A propositional language for text representation, in: B.G. Bara and G. Guida (eds.), Natural language processing (North-Holland, Amsterdam, to appear).
(3) Hobbs, J.R., Towards an understanding of coherence in discourse, in: W.G. Lehnert and M.H. Ringle (eds.), Strategies for natural language processing (Erlbaum, Hillsdale:NJ, 1983).
(4) Peterson, S.B. and Potts, G.R., Global and specific components of information integration. Journal of verbal learning and verbal behavior 21 (1982) 403-420.
(5) Rieger, C., Five aspects of a full-scale story comprehension model, in: N.V. Findler (ed.), Associative Network: representation and use of knowledge by computers (Academic Press, New York, 1979).

INFERENCE PROCESSES:
A MEAN TO SHAPE KNOWLEDGE CONTROL

Cristian A. Giumale

Computer Science Department
Bucharest Polytechnic
RUMANIA

Apart from a versatile reprezentation framework, a
knowledge processing system (KPS) should provide
control facilities powerful enough to cope with as
wide an application area as possible. It is well
known that a KPS gets much of its power from the
control heuristics it uses. Therefore, one way
towards a more general KPS is to provide basic
control elements which can be used to program various heuristics. The paper sketches some results
along this line, obtained with a rule oriented KPS.

INTRODUCTION

In KISS (Giumale (1983)) the effort was directed towards a more natural and unified method for reprezenting both the application
knowledge and the reasoning based on this knowledge. In KISS, knowledge means not only a modular collection of rules, which may be
viewed rather as the static part of KPS, but, in addition, as a set
of cooperating inference processes, which are the live part of the
system, used to slove concurrently different goals or the same goal by various methods.

That is like humans usually solve problems. Often we think many
possible solutions that can then be refined to solve subproblems.
At each stage of this process some solutions seem more promising
than others as a result of dynamic changes in the state of the
problem context and, also, due to the total or partial failure of
other solutions. This way of problem solving can easily be shaped
to capture control heuristics and cuts drastically the pure backtracking search space.

The attributes of inference processes, their control primitives,
and the structure of their working environment are of major importance for the flexibility of control scheme as a whole. They are
rather an independent part of a KPS but, for clarity, the discussion is anchored on KISS reprezentation framework.

KNOWLEDGE REPREZENTATION IN KISS

Besides the different structure of terms and other irrelevant
anatomic peculiarities, the knowledge reprezentation in KISS is
similar to PROLOG. For example, the PROLOG rule
    on(_x,_y):- create(global,_process,50.,work,on(_x,_y)).
is written in KISS
(>x on >y)
    (create GLOBAL >process merit 50. in WORK for (>x on>y)).

where $>x$, $>y$ and $>process$ are variables and $(>x\ on\ >y)$, $(create...)$ are sentences (terms) matched by templates $-(>on\ >)$ and $(create\ >>\ merit\ >\ in\ >\ for\ +)$ - which, as a matter of fact, are distributed functors.

The slots of a template $(>, +)$ can be replaced with objects - constants and variables - of the following types: simple, which stand for atoms or lists and substitute the $>$ slot, and compound, which stand for none or more objects and substitute the $+$ slot. In turn, each object within a sentence may be matched by a template (the object is said transparent) or may have an undefined structure (the object is opaque). The object transparency can be controlled dynamically.

The templates and the sentences they match can be grouped to form independent working spaces, named contexts. Contexts are a good base to structure knowledge semantically for each context has a meaning corresponding to the information it stores and to the role it plays vis-a-vis the problem solving strategy (i.e. the set of inference processes the context creates or accomodates). The communication between contexts is achieved by means of templates. A template can be associated with a context or a function (system or user defined). The goal matched by the template is solved by the associated context or function. For example, all goals matched by

$$(create\ >>\ merit\ >\ in\ >\ for\ +) \# CREATE.$$

trigger on the system function $\#CREATE$, to create an inference process each time.

INFERENCE PROCESSES

A process is a labelled dynamic object which runs in a context to satisfy an associated goal. In addition, a process has a merit, a type and a list of properties (a LISP property list). The solving of the process goal starts in the specified working context but, of course, it can unwind recursively through many other contexts. From the programming point of view, processes behave like coroutines. If a process runs in a private copy of its working context, then it is LOCAL. Processes which share their working contexts are GLOBAL. Local processes can be used to implement encapuslated data types, while global processes are usually used to solve concurrently a given goal.

A process can be active or suspended (interrupted). It can be suspended at any time from within itself in order to resume some other process, eventually the BEST (i.e. the process with the highest merit value) or the WORST (to simulate the 'fail first' heuristic). There are system functions to create, destroy, suspend, resume, and modify the attributes of processes. Essential is the identification mode of a process. The process name is important only as a programming facility. More important is the goal the process solves. There are functions to obtain the names of those processes satisfying goals with a given structure, specified using meta-templates. The need for metas arises from the fact that processes can create and destroy both, templates and rules. The set of contexts can be structured hierarchically to generate and control hierarchies of inference processes. The solving activity can then start with general strategies and end with detailed schemes for knowledge processing.

The example in the Appendix illustrates a possible solution of the
blocks world problem. The program observes the strategy: if >x must
be on y then move >x on >y only when >y is already positioned
as wanted. Initially, the context CONSTR stores the given state of
the blocks world and, finally, the wanted state, which is specified
by the processes creation goal. There is an inference process for
each final relation between two blocks. The program prints the sequence of moves necessary to reach the specified model of the
blocks world.

CONCLUDING REMARKS

The process approach to implement knowledge control is not only a
mean to program various heuristics in a KPS but, moreover, it is a
gate towards simulating inexact reasoning and reasoning with limited resources. It is also possible to build solving plans and
learning devices.

APPENDIX

Start of comment.
    The program uses the following system functions:
        #CREATE creates an inference process;
        #RESUME interrupts the current process, if there is any,
                and resumes a process;
        #KILL kills an inference process;
        #SELPROC selects a process which solves a given goal;
        #MERIT fetches or updates the merit of a process;
        #GENP generates an unit rule;
        #REMP erases an unit rule;
        #PRINT prints a sentence.
    In addition, the following control symbols are used:
        #   on backtrack fails the rule which contains it;
        @   fails the rule whcih contains it and forces the repeti-
            tion of the goal received by the current context.
    End of comment. ##

CONTEXT INIT.
TEMPLATES
  (> on >)
  (create >> merit > in > for +) # CREATE.
  (resume >) #RESUME.
  (kill >) #KILL.
  (>).

RULES
  (>x on >y)
          (create GLOBAL >process merit 50. in WORK for (>x on >y)).
  (do)
          (create LOCAL STOP merit 0 in HERE for (kill THIS))
          (resume BEST).

CONTEXT WORK.
TEMPLATES
  (> on >).
  (free >).
  (move > on >).
  (wait +) WAIT.
  (in CONSTR ?) CONSTR.
  (delete + from CONSTR) CONSTR.
  (insert + in CONSTR) CONSTR.
  (kill >) KILL.
  (resume >) RESUME.
  (print +) PRINT.
  (>).
 •
RULES
  (>x on >y)
     (wait (>y on >>))#
     (>x on >y in CONSTR ?)
     (kill THIS)
     (resume BEST).
  (>x on >y)
     (free >x)
     (free >y)
     (move >x on >y)
     (kill THIS)
     (resume BEST).
  (free table).
  (free >x)
     (>z on > x in CONSTR ?)
     (free >z)
     (move >z on table).
  (free >x).
  (move >x on >y)
     (>x on   z in CONSTR ?)
     (delete >x on >z from CONSTR)
     (insert >x on >y in CONSTR)
     (print move >x on >y).

CONTEXT WAIT.
TEMPLATES
  (wait +).
  (merit >>>) # MERIT.
  (resume >) # RESUME
  (any > with +) # SELPROC.
 •
RULES
  (wait > goal)
     (any > process with > goal)
     (merit > process = >mP)
     (merit THIS = >mP)
     (merit THIS - 1)
     (resume BEST)
     @
  (wait > goal).
 •

CONTEXT CONSTR.
TEMPLATES
  (> on >).
  (> on > in CONSTR ?).
  (insert + in CONSTR) # GENP.
  (delete + from CONSTR) # REMP.
 •
RULES
  (>x on >y in CONSTR ?)
     (>x on   >y).
  (c on a).
  (a on b).
  (b on table).
 •

##The main goal which specifies the final state of CONSTR is##
       ? (a on b)(b on c)(c on table)(do).
##The moves printed by the program are##

              (move c on table)
              (move a on table)
              (move b on c)
              (move a on b)

REFERENCES

[1] Giumale,C.A., KISS - a Knowledge Inference Simple System - reference manual, Dept. of Comp. Sc., Bucharest Polytechnic (December 1983).

DECISION PLANNING SYSTEMS

V.P. GLADUN, Dr.Eng.Sci.
V.M. Glushkov Institute of Cybernetics
Ukrainian Academy of Sciences
252207, Kiev 207, USSR

INTRODUCTION

One of the most important trends in the development of computer-aided design systems is represented by automation of the functions which nowadays are considered as a prerogative of a human being. The decision making processes aimed at choosing the design components and parameters on the basis of analysis of design specification as well as the processes of formation of a sequence of actions ensuring the project realization are the key points of the creative activity of a designer. So far as the decisions on the choice of components and parameters are usually stipulated by realization of similar decisions, the decision making process as well as the process of formation of the sequence of actions require the development of the plan determining the order of making the decisions or executing the actions. Because of this the decision and action planning is realized practically in all modern expert systems. A number of systems were created in which the planning is carried-out on the basis of functional semantic networks simulating the designing environment [1,2]. However there is a lot of applied environments with the great number of objects and communications for which it is impossible to construct such a network due to the great variability of actions and decisions at each stage of design and to the difficulies involved in the situation transformations during realization of actions and decisions. In these cases it is necessary to define actions and decisions applicable to classes of situations rather than to individual specific situations. This complicates considerably the processes of choice, realization and recognition of applicability of actions and decisions. Complex environment which eliminates the possibilities for the predefinition of variants of actions and decisions with the help of tables and functional semantic networks are characteristic not only of design but of scientific studies and of problems of operation scheduling of robotics complexes.

TRENDS IN THE DEVELOPMENT OF PLANNING SYSTEMS

Some important trends in the development of decisions and actions planning systems are investigated with the help of APROS system (Adaptive Problem Solver)[3,4]. Let us remind them.

1. Systems must include the developed means of adaptation to new problems and to changes of problem environment since only in such a way it is possible to prevent their rapid moral ageing. The automatic adjustment of systems to environment and problems is provided due to realization of the <u>principle of adaptive decision</u>

making (Fig.1). The usual mechanism of decision making requires

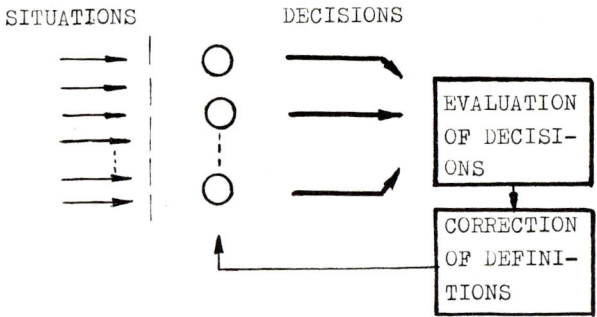

Fig.1

the fixation of an agreement between classes of situations and decisions. To recognize situations the definitions of classes of situations are used. Changes of the environment result in the change of a set of situations and, as a consequence, in the disagreement between classes of situations and decisions. Therefore, adaptive systems must contain means providing the redistribution of situations according to classes and the change of definitions of classes of situations. This may be achieved by realizing in systems the functions of estimation of the quality of made decisions and by correcting the definitions of classes of situations when revealing the disagreements between decisions and situations. The automation of these processes provides the reconstruction of the mechanism of decision making.

The principle of adaptive decision making may be realized both for single-step and multistep decisions. Organization of the processes of adaptation on the basis of this principle in action planning systems is described in [7]. In action planning systems the problems correspond to situations. Decision schemes which define principal stages of plan formation are connected with definitions of classes of problems. Decision schemes are formed automatically by generalization of plans and are used for accelerating the process of their construction. The correctness of choosing a decision scheme is estimated by the results of solving the problem. In case of failure the definitions of classes of problems are corrected.

2. Realization of the principle of adaptive decision making requires the use of such means of knowledge representation for which the processes of classification and formation of definition of classes of situations are defined. In this connection, the apparatus of growing semantic networks [6] of a pyramidal structure [5] is developed, i.e. the apparatus of such semantic networks in which the formation of new concepts and relations between con-

cepts is possible. This is a step to automation of the process of simulating the applied environment, the most complex part of the process of problem solution.

3. In the developed decision and action planning systems operating in complex environment with a large variety of problems it is advisable to use libraries of planning strategies rather than one "universal" strategy [8] . Strategies are chosen by a user or as a result of a man-machine dialog.

EXAMPLES OF SYSTEMS

Let us consider as an example of decision planning system the system of planning the assembly technology and the system of designing the composition of computer complexes. These systems are constructed by adjusting the APROS system to the appropriate application fields.

The planning of assembly technology for robotics complexes is a multilevel process. At the highest level a technological scheme of the assembly is constructed. This scheme defines a sequence of joining the construction units, a sequence of joining the parts in each unit (assembly plans), the distribution of assembly operations among manipulators with regard to their specialization. Each operation of joining the parts, in its turn, is a sequence of manipulations with parts being joined (grasping, transposition, orientation, connection, clamping). The part manipulation is realized by executing a sequence of movements and rotations of different parts of the manipulator. When joining separate parts, robot-manipulator actions are usually capable of unification. Therefore, the planning process at lower levels could be organized on the basis of a library of standard programs. At the higher level a variability of plans depends on diversity of constructions and therefore the standard programs application is expedient only when the manipulator is intended for long-term employment for assembly of the same units .

The assembly planning automation is advisable if the process of formalization of the planning problem is simpler for a human being than the planning process itself.

In the system of assembly technology planning [9] a drawing is the original document for description of the construction. Each connection of two parts is described by the expression where names of parts, connected surfaces, the type of connection (butting, enclosure, stringing, etc.) and the type of joints (threaded, bayonet, spline, etc,) are indicated. A retrosynthetic method is used. It consists in planning of disassembly order according to the drawing where the assembly plan is constructed as a result of inversion of disassembly plan. The order of parts disconnection is determined by comparing their special characteristics which are numerically equal to the sum of limitations on the part transposition in six defined directions(to the left, to the right, upwards, downwards, forwards, backwards). The limitation on part transposition results from its connection with other parts. The part with the minimum sum of limitations is chosen for disconnection. Two types of operators, DISCONNECT and DISFASTEN, modelling the disconnection of part or unit from construction and disfastenning the joint, respectively, represent the action models.

Technological constraints affecting the assembly order which are stored in the knowledge base are taken into account at each step of planning. The technological constraints are the main source of information for determination of priority in the cases when there are a few parts with the same degree of access.

After forming the plan of assembly, its debugging is performed. The correction of the construction model and the replanning are carried out in the case of necessity.

The system was used for planning the assembly of constructions consisting of more than 40 components. The drawings are described according to the instructions by a specialist of an average qualification. In principle, it is possible to automate the process of describing the drawing with the help of recognition devices.

The system of designing the composition of computer complexes [10] relates to the class of the development decision planning systems which choose the design components by the design specification.

Design specification of a computer complex contains a list of values of the complex parameters. Operators correspond to the individual devices. Each operator contains the values of parameters which are conditions and results of choosing the device to which it corresponds. The system sequentially chooses the devices on the basis of the analysis of design specification thus forming the complete set of the computer complex.

CONCLUSION

The further enhancement of the efficiency of the development work is connected with automation of creative processes, first of all the processes of decision and action planning. Practicability of decision and action planning systems results from the automation of the processes of their adjustment to the applied environments. The considered suggestions such as the principle of adaptive decision making, the growing semantic networks, libraries of planning strategies are aimed at solving this problem.

REFERENCES

1. Tyugu, E.Kh., Computer frames and structural synthesis of programs. Izvestija AN SSSR, Tekhnicheskaja kibernetika, 6 (1982) (in Russian).

2. Pospelov, G.S., Artificial intelligence, the basis for new information technology, In: International Symposium on Artificial Intelligence (Leningrad, October 4-6, 1983), Leningrad, 1983 (in Russian).

3. Gladun, V.P., Galagan, N.I., Vashchenko, N.D., Action planning systems for complex environment, Kibernetika, 5 (1982) 88-94 (in Russian).

4. Gladun, V.P., Galagan, N.I., Biba, I.G., Drjuchin, Ju.L., Chernykh, N.A., Robot planning systems for real environments. In: Advances in CADICAM: Proceedings of the 5 International IFIP/

IFAC Conference PROLAMAT'82 (Leningrad,USSR, 16-18 May 1982) Amsterdam, 1982, 535-554.

5. Gladun, V.P., Rabinovich, Z.L., Formation of the world model in artificial intelligence systems. In: Machine Intelligence 9. Ellis Horwood Ltd., Chichester, 1980, 299-309.

6. Biba, I.G., Vashchenko, N.D., Galagan, N.I., Gladun, V.P., Data representation in problem solving systems, Izvestija AN SSSR, Tekhnicheskaja kibernetika, 6 (1982), 170-175 (in Russian).

7. Gladun, V.P., Vashchenko N.D., Adaptive problem-solving systems, Kybernetes, 1980, v.9, 181-188.

8. Galagan, N.I., A library of strategies for problem solving in action planning systems, Izvestija AN SSSR, Tekhnicheskaja kiber netika, 5 (1983) (in Russian).

9. Gladun, V.P., Galagan, N.I., Drjuchin, Ju.L., Automation of assembly by drawing description. In: International Symposium on Artificial Intelligence (Leningrad, October 4-6, 1983), Leningrad, 1983.

10. Biba, I.G., Galagan, N.I., Gladun, V.P., Kurgaev, A.F., On automation of solution of problems of formation of hardware set of a problem-oriented complex, Upravljajushchie Sistemy i Mashiny, 5 (1982) 45-52 (in Russian).

A MANUFACTURING CELL MANAGEMENT SYSTEMS CEMAS

F.Gliviak[1], J.Kubiš[2], A.Mičovský[1], and E.Karabinošová[1]

[1] Institute of Technical Cybernetics, Slovak Academy of Sciences, Dúbravská cesta 9, 84237 Bratislava, Czechoslovakia

[2] Institute of Technology and Rationalization, Nevädzová 2, 82613 Bratislava, Czechoslovakia

> The CEMAS system has been designed to supervise a manufacturing cell. It was designed as an empty expert system. It contains data base, knowledge base, knowledge acquisition block and explaining block. The main activities of the CEMAS system involve the recording of dynamically changing situation, the scheduling of tasks to particular workplaces as well as detection and resolving of critical situations. The system is at the stage of program implementation in the LISP language extended by data structure array.

PROBLEM FORMULATION

We handle a design of a manufacturing cell management system for a cell working under the condition of small-lot production. We assume that manufacturing, welding and assembling processes can go on in the cell. Moreover, we suppose that the following technical conditions are satisfied:

1/ Each machine tool /e.g. a lathe, a borer, a robot/ is controlled by a microcomputer. Manual workplaces as the cell input and output, technical inspection are linked to a central minicomputer via terminals.
2/ The transport of pre-forms and products between working places and stores is automatic, being controlled by a microcomputer.
3/ All microcomputers and terminals of the cell workplaces are linked to a central minicomputer. The latter supervises the cell operation through receiving the data, analysing them, and sending its commands to particular workplaces.

Additional conditions are the following:

4/ Each working machine can perform in parallel solely one technological operation, wheras a new operation can begin only with the preceeding one having been completed.
5/ Each operation is associated with a group of machines for which a technology to execute this operation is prepared.

The manufacturing cell management has three levels: execution /controlling the moves of the machine tools/, information /recording the actual state/, and decision /scheduling work to the workplaces/, [5]. We assume the execution level to be ensured /see condition 13/. Our aim is to design and build a system for both information and decision levels of the cell management.

In Czechoslovak industry there exist some data-base systems for managing smaller manufacturing cells, e.g. TAVSO [4], DYNAR [6]. Critical points of such systems are:
a/ system's adaptability to changes of cell configuration as well

as production program
b/ choosing the criteria of selection from among numbers of tasks
c/ a timely detection and solution of critical situations
d/ learning of the management system in the course of operation

Our management system CEMAS contributes to resolving the problems a/, b/, c/ and experiments concerning point d/ will be carried out later.

MAIN PARTS OF THE CEMAS SYSTEM

The CEMAS management system has been created as an empty expert system, see [1], [2], [3]. Its main parts are data base, knowledge base, inference mechanism, knowledge acquisition block and explainer. We shall give a short describtion of them.

DATABASE contains models /data structures/ that serve as general prototypes for describing both the actual state and actual tasks of a particular manufacturing cell. These models are the following.

- A workplace model is a frame-like data structure containing "slots" for describing its name, internal manipulation places, actual task, set of tasks waiting for the workplace, etc.

- A store model on every manipulation place contains a record whether the place is either free or occupied or reserved, and a pointer to the name of a transport lot which occupies or reserves the place.

- Model of technological processes contains dynamic data structures of changeable length which allow to record precise technological procedures including assigning the operations to relevant workplace and their time characteristics.

- Model of production and transport lots represents a structure which serves to describe the actual production and transport lots, the stage of their manufacturing, and their movement in the cell.

- Operation plan model is employed for recording the time of begining and terminating the production lots and their actual realization.

- Model of message protocols serves to record and send information between particular blocks of the system, as well as between the system and the workplaces, thus allowing to maintain the actual image of the cell state.

KNOWLEDGE BASE contains several groups of concrete knowledge as well as knowledge on the mode of utilizing the concrete knowledge /control block/. Concrete knowledge groups are knowledge about input and output of production lot to the cell, the system working at the begining and end of a working day, selection of task among the tasks to be executed, controlling a workplace while handling a production lot, store organization, system reaction on results of technical inspection, solution of disturbing accident, cell state prediction and some statistics and surveys on cell activities. We shall give here only a few remarks on the knowledge groups.

-Selection among the tasks to be executed is realized in accordance with various different criteria. Trerefore we have proposed a list of criteria along with some macro-views (intensions) which are realized with the aid of a suitable subset of criteria. Having chosen a particular intension (macro-view), a user can decide on its suitable realization and the system will accordingly choose the demands to be executed.

- Reaction of the system to disturbing accidents. Examples of these are failures of either machines or means of transport, a store overfilling, supply of in-appropriate material, a delay in supplying material, absence of workers, occurrence of a rather high percent of detective products, etc. Each of these disturbances is recorded, attended, or a modification of the cell schedule is done.

- Cell state prediction for a certain period of time is necessary for ensuring the preparation of special production devices, and for timely detection of possible critical situations, e.g. machine or transport overloading, and store overfilling. Prediction of a cell state is made by simulating the work of the CEMAS system in an appropriate period of time on the basis of actual data.

- The control block receives information and requests both from workplaces and superior part of the factory. It evaluates them and, if necessary, conveys a working command and information relevant knowledge base block. To exemplify the input information to the control block we indicate: workplace is prepared, workplace is disturbed, production lot is at input or output, operation on a transport lot is finished, transport task is started or finished, massage about results of technical inspection, changes of scheduled output time, cell plan for a week or a month.

KNOWLEDGE ACQUISITION BLOCK. Loading and modification of knowledge and data into knowledge base is realized via communication language. Changes in data base are realized either by the system during its operation or by a cell manager either key-words or a prepared dialogue scheme in natural language. The movement among the question groups during dialogue is guided by a cell manager's answers, which have a priori defined and checked syntax. In case of ambiguities the user can ask for instructions.

EXPLAINER. On a cell manager's demand the system explains lucidly and briefly its conclusions derived from the data base. For example, it gives reasons for choosing a task from among the number of tasks, or it can give information regarding the contents of items in data base.

THE CEMAS SYSTEM OPERATION

The system operation is devided into two user classes. In the first one a cell supervision of the system is realized, i.e. analyzing the information from particular workplaces, dicision regarding the assignment of work to a workplace, sending commands to workplaces, and a continuous updating of the cell state record.

In the second class cooperation between the cell manager and CEMAS is realized. The system creates in advance a cell schedule for a chosen period of time, analyzes possible critical situations and suggests alternatives for solving them. Cell manager definitely approves one alternative. Then the system either makes or cancels the order for materials and tools in a reasonable time beforehand, shifting the significant cell manager's demands to the first user class. Both part of the system have an accese to a common actual data base.

CEMAS is at the stage of program implementation on the PDP 11/40 computer under the operation system RSX 11M in the LISP language extended by "array" data structure. The system will be tested in manufacturing cell at Institute of Technology and Rationalization, Bratislava.

REFERENCES

1. Aikins,J.S.: Prototypes and Production Rules, A Knowledge representation for Computer Consultation. Stanford University, Report No.STAN-CS-80-814, 204pp.
2. Barr,A. and Feigenbaum,E.A. /eds./: The Handbook of Artificial Intelligence, Vol.2, W.Kaufmann Inc., Los Altos, CA, 1982, 428pp.
3. Buchanan,B.G., and Duda,R.O.: Principles of Rule-Based Expert Systems. Stanford University, Report No.HPP-82-14, 55pp.
4. Chromec,S.: Application Programming Tools TAVSO for Manufacturing Cell Managing. Internal Research Report, UTAR Bratislava, 1983, 134pp. /in Czech/.
5. Fox,M.: The Intelligent Management System, An Overview. Carnegie-Mellon University, Report No.CMU-RI-TR-81-4, 35pp.
6. Herman,J. and Šafka,Z.: Dynamic Scheduling System DYNAR. In: ASŘ Sešity, INORGA Praha, 1982, No.88-89, pp.124-162 /in Czech/.

APPLICATION OF ATTRIBUTED GRAMMAR AND ALGORITHMIC
SENSITIVITY MODEL FOR KNOWLEDGE REPRESENTATION AND
ESTIMATION

V.I.Gorodetzki, V.V.Drozhzhin, R.M.Yusupov

USSR

Nonlogic formal calculus for knowledge representation of dynamic environment are discussed. A class of attributed translation web-grammars is introduced. Algorithmic sensitivity models for the analysis of knowledge representation systems are suggested. The main features of the approach under consideration are the compactness of knowledge description by means of generation schemes, the feasibility of joint use of various mathematical formalisms, the evident description of the evolution of knowledge representation structures in time, the feasibility of assignment of arbitrary depth of environment description detail by means of using the metagrammar concept and grammar substitution operations.

INTRODUCTION

The notion of attributed grammars was introduced by Knuth (1968) for the description of programming languages semantics. The main idea of describing semantics is that the "value" (the meaning, characteristics in range interpretation) of formal language elements is found byvalue calculation of synthesized and inherited attributes, assigned to given elements. The rules of attribute value calculation are ascribed to grammar productions. Thus, if terminal and nonterminal elements as well as production system present formal system syntax, then the attributes and rules of their calculation constitute semantics.

The number variables are traditionally used as attributes. In addition, symbol variables, mathematical structures, semiotical systems (in particular, semantic networks, frames, procedure names, etc.) can be used as attributes, which requires the correct underdetermination of attributed grammars apparatus. In this case the attributed grammars formalism can be used for the representation of declarative and procedural knowledge.

Let us consider the production of common type:

IF A , THEN B ,

where A is the description of some designated situation, and B is the decisions made in this situation. Such productions are widely used for knowledge representation in expert and calculative-logical systems. The main difficulty in using production systems is that the observed situations, as a rule, do not coincide with situation descriptions, presented in the left portions of productions. This results to considerable growth of the amount of productions (up to several thousand in complex systems). The construction of comparison and situation recognition systems, the generalization and formation of **multilevel** production systems, the adoption of certain strategy **of** productions use. In addition, the means of conflict removal are **necessary** in conflict situations. All these problems are effectively solved when used for formalism knowledge representation, based on the attributed grammars notion extention.

ATTRIBUTED TRANSLATION WEB-GRAMMARS

The attributed translation web-grammar (ATWG) is given as

$$G = \langle V_N, V_T, S, P, A', B' \rangle \quad ,$$

where $V_N \neq \emptyset$ is the alphabet of nonterminal symbols; $V_T = V_{T,1} \cup V_{T,2}$ is the alphabet of input terminal symbols $V_{T,1}$ and action (output) terminal symbols $V_{T,2}$, $V_{T,1} \cap V_{T,2} = \emptyset$; $S \in V_N$ is the starting symbol; P - the productions systems; $A' = \langle A, \Omega \rangle$ - the attributed component; $B' = \langle B, \mathcal{U} \rangle$ - the web-component of grammar. Here A is the set of attributes, ascribed to terminal and nonterminal grammar symbols; Ω is the set of rules of attribute value calculation; B is the set of webs ascribed to input terminal symbols; $\mathcal{U}$ is the web combination and exception conditions in web-structures. The attributes are ascribed to corresponding grammar symbols as lower indexes. The time attribute t is introduced as a special attribute. The time is considered as discrete and changes every next step of using one of the productions in the ptocess of string inference $\alpha\beta \in L(G)$ from the starting symbol S. Note that the time interval between two successive steps may be arbitrary from step to step. The terminal symbols of string $\alpha \in V_{T,1}^*$ determine the set of webs, from which the time-variable web-structures ascribed to action terminal symbols of the string $\beta \in V_{T,2}^*$ are "composed". In this case the webs of the string α play the role of structural components for string β time-variable web-structures.

Let us consider the graphs as an example of webs. Note that in general case the finite algebraical systems may constitute webs. Let the graph D_i, $i \in N_n$ correspond to the symbol α_i, $i \in N_n$ in the string $\alpha = \alpha_1 \ldots \alpha_n$, and the graph $D(t_j)$, $j \in N_m$ correspond to the symbol β_j, $j \in N_m$ in the string $\beta = \beta_1 \ldots \beta_m$. Then the equation of structural dynamics will be as follows:

$$D(t_j) = \Phi(D_i, i \in I_j) , \quad j \in N_m ,$$

where I_j is the set of string α symbol indexes derived by the time instant t_j.

Thus, the sequence $D(t_j)$, $j = 1, \ldots, m$ will correspond to the string $\beta = \beta_1 \ldots \beta_m$. The number of such sequences exactly equals the number of words of the language generated by ATWG. The recursive ATWG generate infinite calculative languages, therefore their potential for modelling various evolution versions of dynamic environment is rather great. The situational conditions and uncertainty factors, the time and resources limitations are taken into ac-

Attributed grammar and algorithmic sensitivity model 159

count by means of attributes in the process of the string α and β syntactic inference.

Let us give an example of one of the possible determinations of ATWG G. Let $V_N = \{S, E, C\}$, $V_{T,1} = \{b, c, d, e\}$, $V_{T,2} = \{f, g, h\}$. The structural attributes presented as marked graphs correspond to the starting nonterminal S and to terminal b, c, d, e. They are shown in Fig.1.

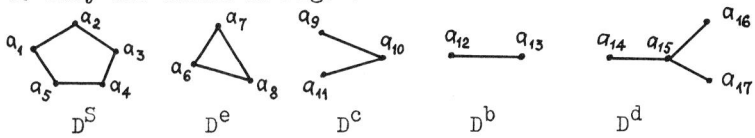

Figure 1
Webs of Symbols S, e, c, b, d.

The common time attribute t and the structure D(t) are ascribed to the terminals f, g, h. Nonterminals S, E, C have the time attributes t_S, Δt_E, Δt_C, respectively. All attributes are inherited.

Let us introduce designations:
$a_i: = a_j$ — graph vertices with numbers a_i and a_j are "stuck" and ascribed the number a_j;
D_a — undergraph of the graph D containing the vertex a and the arks incidental to it;
$D(t) \setminus D_a(t)$ — the extraction of the undergraph $D_a(t)$ from the graph D(t);
$D^b \cup D^c$ — the union of graphs.

Grammar productions:

1) $S_{[D^S, \, t_S]} \longrightarrow {}^b[D^b] \; {}^e[D^e] \; {}^E[\Delta t_E] \; {}^C[\Delta t_C] \{ f[D(t), \, t] \}$,
$t = t_S + \Delta t_E + \Delta t_C$, $D(t) = (D^S \setminus D^S_{a_3}) \cup D^b \cup D^e$, $a_2 := a_7$, $a_4 := a_6$, $a_{12} := a_1$, $a_{13} := a_8$;

2) $E_{[\Delta t_E]} \longrightarrow {}^c[D^c] \; {}^E[\Delta t_E] \{ g[D(t), \, t] \}$,
$t = t + \Delta t_E$, $D(t) = (D(t) \setminus D_{a_4}(t)) \cup D^c$, $a_9 := a_1$, $a_{11} := a_5$;

3) $E_{[\Delta t_E]} \longrightarrow {}^d[D^d] \{ g[D(t), \, t] \}$,
$t = t + \Delta t_{E_2}$, $D(t) = (D(t) \setminus D_{a_7, a_8}(t)) \cup D^d$, $a_{14} := a_1$, $a_{17} := a_6$;

4) $C_{[\Delta t_C]} \longrightarrow {}^b[D^b] \{ h[D(t), \, t] \}$,
$t = t + \Delta t_C$, $D(t) = (D(t) \setminus D_{a_7}(t)) \cup D^b$, $a_{12} := a_6$, $a_{16} := a_{13}$.

The first line in the description of the productions corresponds to syntax component of the production and the second — to semantic component.

This grammar generate the languages $L_1(G) = \{bec^k db / k = 0,1,2,...\}$ and $L_2(G) = \{fg^n h / n = 1,2,...\}$. Nonattributive tree of string inference becdb and corresponding string fggh are represented in Figure 2. Sequence of evolutions in time of graph $D(t)$ corresponding to string fggh is shown in Figure 3.

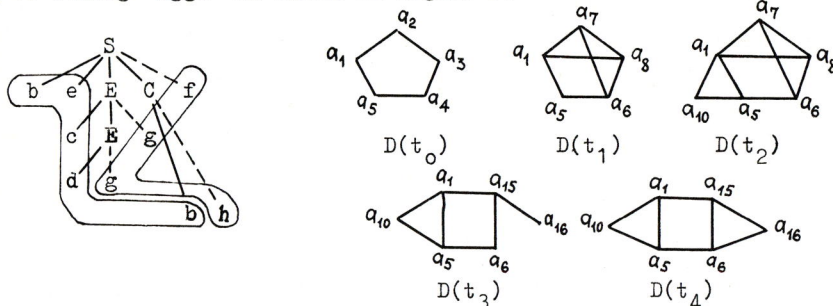

Figure 2
Nonattributive Tree of Strings becdb and fggh Inference

Figure 3
Evolution in Time of Graph $D(t)$, $t = t_0, t_1, ..., t_4$ Corresponding to String fggh

Symbols f,g,h are the names of metaprocedures of structural transformations of initial graph $D(t_0)$.

MULTILEVEL KNOWLEDGE REPRESENTATION MODELS

Let us consider the attributed translation web-grammar as metagrammar provided the terminal symbols be the starting nonterminal symbols of the other ATWG and the attributes of terminal symbols - the inherited attributes of the starting nonterminal in the corresponding grammar.

Thus metagrammar is such a ATWG in which the operation of grammar substitution is permitted and the limitations on its use by fixing in the substitution of all pairs of the type <terminal symbol> ⟶ <grammar name> are given.

The introduction of metagrammars gives some essential advantages in the development of the complex knowledge representation systems. The main advantage is that metagrammar in the compact form contains the generative schemes of aggregative objects descriptions which correspond to the terminal grammar symbols. The generalized characteristic of these objects is represented by the terminal symbol attributes. And the description of the infrastructure of the corresponding aggregative object model is performed by means of ATWG which is substituted for the corresponding metagrammar terminal.

The structure of the "up-down" relations is represented by the syntax inference tree and the one level relations are described by the attributes and rules of their calculations.

It is evident that each grammar can be treated as metagrammar relative to such grammars the names of which take part in the substitution used for the symbols of the terminal string.

ALGORITHMIC SENSITIVITY MODELS

The common approach to the dynamic control systems sensitivity analysis deals with the construction of the state and observation equations and the formation of the differential sensitivity models (Rosenwasser, Yusupov (1981)). In this case the system model as well as the sensitivity models are given evidently by the certain functional relations.

The knowledge models described in terms of attributive grammars unlike the dynamic systems models are not functional but algorithmetic. They represent a generative scheme the realization of which results in obtaining the separate knowledge fragments provided that the corresponding situational conditions of the production applications and the attribute meaning calculations be given. So the sensitivity models will be given algorithmetically and thus will be named algorithmetic (Gorodetzki and al. (1983)).

Now let us take the production system of an attributive grammar:

1) $S_{[Z,R/I]} \longrightarrow A_{[Z_1,R_1/I_1]} \; B_{[Z_2,R_2/I_2]}$,

   $Z_1 = f_1(Z)$, $R_1 = g_1(R,Z_1)$, $I = \varphi_1(I_1,I_2)$;

2) $A_{[Z_1,R_1/I_1]} \longrightarrow a_{[Z_{11},R_{11}/I_{11}]} \; A_{[Z_1,R_1/I_1]}$,

   $Z_{11} = f_{11}(Z_1)$, $R_{11} = g_{11}(R_1,Z_{11})$, $Z_1 = \varphi_2(I_{11}, Z_{11}, R_{11})$;

3) $A_{[Z_1,R_1/I_1]} \longrightarrow a_{[Z_{11},R_{11}/I_{11}]}$,

   $Z_{11} = f_{11}(Z_1)$, $R_{11} = g_{11}(R_1,Z_{11})$, $I_1 = \varphi_2(I_{11}, Z_{11}, R_{11})$;

4) $B_{[Z_2,R_2/I_2]} \longrightarrow b_{[Z_{22},R_{22}/I_{22}]} \; B_{[Z_2,R_2/I_2]}$,

   $Z_{22}=f_{22}(Z_2)$, $R_{22}=g_{22}(R_2,Z_{22})$, $I_2= \varphi_3(I_{22},Z_{22},R_{22})$;

5) $B_{[Z_2,R_2/I_2]} \longrightarrow b_{[Z_{22},R_{22}/I_{22}]}$,

   $Z_{22}=f_{22}(Z_2)$, $R_{22}=g_{22}(R_2, Z_{22})$, $I_2= \varphi_3(I_{22},Z_{22},R_{22})$.

The attributes of the grammar symbols are written in square brakets. Inherited are those with symbols Z and R (with indexes). They may be interpreted as the state and object resource variables or the corresponding aggregative level. The object characteristics is represented by the synthesised attributes I, I_1, I_2, I_{11} and I_{22}. The initial meanings of attributes Z, R and I_{11}, I_{22} are suggested to be given.

The inference tree of any string $\alpha \in L(G)$ gives the possibility to construct the recursive calculation scheme of the sensitivity algorithmetic functions (SAF) of the inherited and synthesised attributes. SAF of the inherited attributes are calculated according to the inference tree by the "up-down" method. As an example let us take string ab. Then the order will be as follows:

1) $\dfrac{\partial Z_1}{\partial Z} = \dfrac{\partial f_1(Z)}{\partial Z} \cdot \dfrac{\partial R_1}{\partial Z} = \dfrac{\partial g_1(R,Z_1)}{\partial Z_1} \cdot \dfrac{\partial Z_1}{\partial Z}$, $\dfrac{\partial R_1}{\partial R} = \dfrac{\partial g_1(R,Z_1)}{\partial R}$;

2) $\dfrac{\partial Z_{11}}{\partial Z} = \dfrac{\partial f_{11}(Z_1)}{\partial Z_1} \cdot \dfrac{\partial Z_1}{\partial Z}$, ... ;

3) $\dfrac{\partial Z_{22}}{\partial Z} = \dfrac{\partial f_{22}(Z_2)}{\partial Z_2} \cdot \dfrac{\partial Z_2}{\partial Z}$, ...

SAF of the synthesized attributes are calculated by the "down-up" method:

1) $\dfrac{\partial I_1}{\partial I_{11}} = \dfrac{\partial \varphi_2}{\partial I_{11}}$;   2) $\dfrac{\partial I_2}{\partial I_{22}} = \dfrac{\partial \varphi_3}{\partial I_{22}}$;

3) $\dfrac{\partial I}{\partial I_{11}} = \dfrac{\partial \varphi_1}{\partial I_1} \cdot \dfrac{\partial I_1}{\partial I_{11}}$, $\dfrac{\partial I}{\partial I_{22}} = \dfrac{\partial \varphi_1}{\partial I_2} \cdot \dfrac{\partial I_2}{\partial I_{22}}$.

Thus the parametrization of the discrete formal knowledge representation models performed by means of attributes and attribute calculation rules introduction permits the construction of the algorithmetic models and the sensitivity functions. These models may be used in the knowledge analysis for the construction of the optimizational solution search procedures and etc. The ATWG application allows to perform the sensitivity analysis not only according to the inference tree but also to the network structures.

REFERENCES:

[1] Knuth, D.E., Semantics of Context-Free Language, Mathematical Systems Theory 2(1968) 127-146;

[2] Rosenwasser, E.N. and Yusupov, R.M., The Control Systems Sensitivity (Nauka, Moscow, 1981 - In Russian).

[3] Gorodetzki, V.I., Drozhzhin, V.V. and Yusupov, R.M., Algorithmetic Function and Sensitivity Models of Complex Systems, in: Theses of 9-th All-Union Conference on Control Problems (Moscow, 1983 - In Russian).

COMBINING FUNCTIONS IN CONSULTING SYSTEMS AND
DEPENDENCE OF PREMISSES (A REMARK)

Petr Hájek

Mathematical Institute, ČSAV
115 67 Prague, Czechoslovakia

In the framework of algebraic foundations of propagation of uncertain information in consulting systems, the problem of dependence of premisses of rules is discussed. It is shown how MYCIN-like systems can handle this problem.

1. INTRODUCTION AND PRELIMINARIES

We shall investigate rule-based consulting systems. The knowledge base B of such a system consists of rules of the form

IF (antecedent) THEN (consequent) with weight (weight).

In symbols, $A \Rightarrow C\ (w)$. The rule means: If you are cartain that A then give the contribution w to the belief that C (= to the weight of C). There is a function $CTR(a,w)$ (contribution with uncertain assumption) telling us which contribution we have to give to the belief that C if our belief that A is only a. And there is a binary operation $\oplus$ (commutative and associative) such that if there are exactly n rules (in B) with the consequent C and we know their contributions $c_1, c_2, \ldots, c_n$ then the global weight of C is
$c_1 \oplus c_2 \oplus \ldots \oplus c_n$.

There are various possibilities of defining $\oplus$, see /1/ for a probabilistic definition of one choice of $\oplus$. (For a synthesizing review of various approximate reasoning techniques see /5/.) Probabilistic derivations of the operation $\oplus$ of combining weights suffer by the necessity of assuming conditional independence, i.e. if $A_1 \Rightarrow C\ (w_1)$ and $A_2 \Rightarrow C\ (w_2)$ are two rules in B and if P denotes probability one has to assume $P(A_1\ \&\ A_2\ /\ C) = P(A_1\ /\ C).P(A_2\ /\ C)$ and similarly for C replaced by $\neg C$. (Cf. the discussion in /4/.) On the one hand, this is certainly not always satisfied; on the other hand, consulting systems with carefully prepared knowledge bases and with a usual operation $\oplus$ (PROSPECTOR's or other) perform well as experience shows. The present paper is not more than a remark (both theoretical and practical) concerning careful preparation of the knowledge base keeping in mind the possibility of some kind of dependence of antecedents of rules.

In /3/, /2/ we developed algebraical foundations for combining weights in consulting systems. They cannot be repeated here, we only remember very basic facts. As usual, we assume that the domain D of weights is linearly ordered, has a greatest element $\top$ (certainly yes), a least element $\bot$ (certainly no, an element called "unknown" and various other elements. $\top$ and $\bot$ are extremal elements; the behaviour of the operation $\oplus$ (for computing global weights) can be described as follows: For each $x \neq \bot$, $\top \oplus x = \top$; for each $x \neq \top$, $\bot \oplus x = \bot$; $\top \oplus \bot$ is undefined and $\oplus$ makes non-extremal elements of D to an ordered Abelian group, i.e.

it is commutative, associative, "unknown" is the neutral element, each (non-extremal) element has an inverse and $\oplus$ is monotone, i.e. $u \leq v$ implies $u \oplus w \leq v \oplus w$. We showed that under some assumptions on D (D is the closed interval $[-1,1]$), $\oplus$ is determined uniquely up to an isomorphism (thus isomorphic to both PROSPECTOR's and EMYCIN's operation) but for other D's we can have substantially other operations, even non-Archimedean ones, capable of practical use. The reader may keep his favorite operation $\oplus$ (e. g. PROSPECTOR's, which, in the case of $D = [-1,1]$, is as follows: $x \oplus y = (x + y)/(1 + xy)$, keeping only in mind that for non-extremal weights $\oplus$ behaves as a group operation.

2. THE PROBLEM - AN EXAMPLE

Imagine a miniature knowledge base B consisting of three rules:

$$P1 \Rightarrow C \ (w1),$$
$$P2 \Rightarrow C \ (w2),$$
$$P1 \ \& \ P2 \Rightarrow C \ (w3).$$

If the user is **certain** that P1 and does know anything about P2 (denot this information by q1) then the global weight $W_B(C/q1)$ of C given by B and q1 is w1 - only the first rule applies. Similarly for 1 replaced by 2. Now assume that the user is certain that both P1 and P2 is true; denote this information by q. Then, of course, the global weight $W_B(C/q)$ of C is $w1 \oplus w2 \oplus w3$. If all w1, w2, w3 are positive (i.e. bigger than "unknown") then $W_B(C/q) > \max(w1, w2, w3)$. Bur this may not correspond to the user's intuition: rather, he would like his knowledge base to give $W_B(C/q) = w3$ without changing $W_B(C/q1)$ and $W_B(C/q2)$. This is indeed possible - one has to change the third rule to

$$P1 \ \& \ P2 \Rightarrow C \ (w3 \oplus -w1 \oplus -w2)$$

(assuming that $w3 \oplus -w1 \oplus -w2$ is defined).

<u>Moral</u>. If A is a conjunction of two or more conjuncts and if the domain expert says "Knowing A and nothing else, my degree of belief that C is w" then interpret w as $W_B(C/q)$ (where q is the knowledge that A holds) rather than the weight of the rule $A \Rightarrow C$; compute the weight of this rule from w and from weights of rules of the form $A_o \Rightarrow C$, where A_o is a proper subconjunction of A.

<u>Caution</u>. Then a rule $A \Rightarrow C \ (w)$ is to be interpreted carefully: as <u>yielding</u> a <u>correction</u> to simpler rules.

The reader may ask whether this approach is general enough. The theorem in next section gives a preliminary answer.

3. A REPRESENTABILITY THEOREM

Here we use the framework developed in /3/, i.e. we work with propositions 1, 2, ..., n, rules have the form $A \Rightarrow C \ (w)$ where A is an elementary conjunction of propositions, C is a proposition not occuring in A and $w \in D$ where $D \subseteq [-1,1]$; a <u>consulting system</u> is given by a loop free set B of rules and by an operation $\oplus$ which makes $D \cap (-1,1)$ to an ordered Abelian group. A question is a proposition not occuring in the consequent of any rule in B; a goal is a proposition not occuring in the antecedent of any rule in B. A questionnaire is a mapping q of the set of all questions to D. (In fact, this is a questionnaire with answers to questions.) The global weight $W_B(P/q)$ of a proposition P given by a questionnaire q is defined inductively using combining functions; in particular, if P is a question then $W_B(P/q) = q(P)$ and if P is not a question and w1,.. ..,wn are contributions of all rules having P as the consequent (wi given by q) then $W_B(P/q) = w1 \oplus ... \oplus wn$.

Now let us start with propositions 1,...,n and let a subset Quest $\subseteq \{1,...,n\}$ be declared as the set of future questions of a consulting system. Investigate mappings q of Quest into the three-element set $\{-1, 0, 1\}$ (three-valued questionnaires). These correspond uniquely to elementary conjunctions of questions, e.g. 2 & ¬4 corresponds to the q such that $q(2) = 1$, $q(4) = -1$ and $q(P) = 0$ otherwise. Let a set Goal $\subseteq \{1,...,n\}$ disjoint from Quest be declared to be the set of goals of a future consulting system. A system of conditioned weights is a function W associating with some three-valued questionnaires and some goals $P \in$ Goal a weight $W(P/q) \in D$. We may write $\{W(P/q), \langle q,P \rangle \in \Gamma\}$ instead of W. Such a system represents domain expert's evaluation of goals in various more or less complicated situations expressed by longer of shorter elementary conjunctions of questions, i.e. the result of a particular knowledge acquisition. W is consistent if the following holds: Let qi correspond to an elementary conjunction Ai (i = 1, 2) and let A1 be a subconjunction of A2. Then if $W(P/q1) = 1$ or -1 then $W(P/q2) = W(P/q1)$. (If a shorter conjunction gives certainty then its prolongation gives certainty too.)

Let a group operation $\oplus$ be given in the sequel. A system W of conditioned weights is realized by a consulting system $(B, \oplus)$ if for each pair $\langle q,P \rangle$ from the domain of W, $W(P/q) = W_B(P/q)$, i.e. the global weight of P given by the system and by the questionnaire q is just as prescribed by W.

Theorem. A system W of conditioned weights is realizable by a consulting system if and only if W is consistent.

Proof is easy using the techniques of Section 2.

Concluding remarks. (1) One can understand a system of conditioned weights as a system of conditional probabilities if one likes; the theorem just shows that each such system is realizable by a consulting system and thus consulting systems do not present any inherent unavoidable probabilistic restrictions.
(2) The system produced in the proof of our theorem is simple-minded -   the rules just connect questions and goals (there are no intermediate propositions). Thus we gave a mere proof of existence; elaborated systems usually have various intermediate propositions and therefore better reflect the process of expertise.
(3) We hope to have shown in /2/, /3/ and here that MYCIN-like consulting systems can have mathematical foundations not dependent on probability theory. To avoid misunderstanding, this does not say that probability theory is useless for such foundations. The question is: given non-probabilistic foundations, what is their probabilistic meaning? A good answer could deepen our understanding of expert systems.

REFERENCES

/1/ R. O. Duda, P. E. Hart, N. J. Nilsson: Subjective Bayesian methods for rule-based inference systems, SRI Technical Note 124, Stanford 1976

/2/ P. Hájek: Combining functions for certainty factors in consulting systems, Artificial Intelligence and Information-Control Systems of Robots, Smolenice (Czechoslovakia) 1982, p. 107-110

/3/ P. Hájek: Combining functions for certainty factor in consulting systems (full paper), submitted.

/4/ E. P. D. Pednault, S. W. Zucker, L. V. Muresan: On the independence assumption underlying subjective Bayesian inference, Artificial Intelligence 16 (1981) 213-222

/5/ H. Prade: A synthetic view of approximate reasoning techniques, Proceedings IJCAI 1983, Karlsruhe, p. 130-136

LINGUISTICALLY MOTIVATED REPRESENTATION OF KNOWLEDGE AS A BASIS FOR INFERENCE PROCEDURES

Eva Hajičová, Milena Hnátková

Department of Applied Mathematics
Faculty of Mathematics and Physics
Charles University
Prague
Czechoslovakia

The paper describes different kinds of inference rules that operate on representations of meaning of sentences conceived as dependency trees. The described inference procedures form one of the main parts of the question answering system based on the method TIBAQ (Text-and-Inference Based Answering of Questions) developed by the group of mathematical linguistics at the faculty of mathematics and physics, Charles University, Prague, under the leadership of Petr Sgall.

An experiment based on the method TIBAQ (Text-and-Inference Based Answering of Questions) is under preparation. The system converses the natural language input (for both new pieces of information and questions) into the representations of meaning (tectogrammatical representations, TR´s) to retrieve suitable answers in the stock of the stored TR´s (organized as a semantic network) as well as in the set of those gained from these TR´s by rules of inference, and to transfer these answers (i.e. their TR´s) into the output form of Czech sentences (for an overall description of the system, see [3], [5]).

The system consists in several basic procedures implemented partly in PL/1 and Assembler, and partly in Colmerauer´s Q-language [1]. The first experiment is being carried out by the group of algebraic linguistics at Charles University, Prague, on a computer EC 1040 (compatible with IBM 360).

The TR´s are based on an original approach to syntax and semantics, including a dependency based stratificational description; the form of a TR is illustrated in Fig. 1, where one of the TR´s of the sentence "An operational amplifier is designed to perform mathematical functions" is presented; the edges are labelled by names of kinds of the dependency relation (deep cases: Actor, Objective, Effect, and free modifications: General Relationship and others), the nodes are labelled by complex symbols consisting in (a) the lexical part (instead of which we use - for the ease of reference - only the graphemic shape of English words) and (b) a sequence of grammatemes or morphological meanings: with nouns, these are the values of number and delimitation, with verbs - of tense, aspect, modality, etc.; the grammatemes are complemented by the category of contextual boundness. In Fig. 1 we present only the marked values of the grammatemes, so that Def stands for Definite, Pl for Plural, and b for contextually bound; the non-marked values are supplied by default conventions: Specifying, Singular, Present, Indicative, contextually non-bound, etc. The symbol Gen stands for a General Actor. For the linguistic background of this approach we refer to [2], [4], [6] and [7].

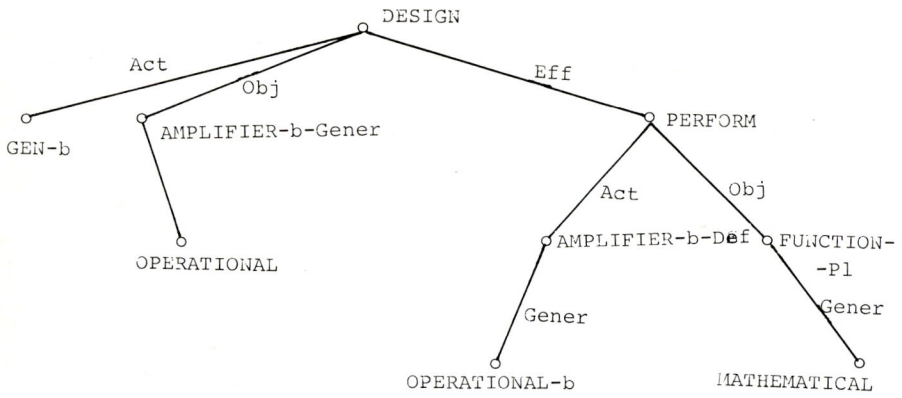

Figure 1

First, the system analyzes the sentences of the input texts, i.e. it produces a semantic network consisting in TR´s of the input sentences, interconnected by links associating word tokens with items of a semantic lexicon in which the relations of synonymy and hyponymy are reflected. When a question is given by a user, it is handled by the same procedure of analysis and the system then selects from its semantic network (stock of knowledge) such a subset that (according to the lexical parts of the labels included in its TR´s) can be relevant to the given question.

A set of rules of inference was formulated, which operate on this set of relevant TR´s to yield an enriched set of TR´s. This enriched set then serves as a domain in which a suitable answer can be found, even if it does not fully correspond to any sentence of the input text; in this way we attempt to model natural language comprehension including that layer of natural language inferencing that a reader of a technical text performs without being fully aware of it.

The inference rules are programmed in Q-language, which is one of the higher-type programming languages developed for the analysis and synthesis of sentences (see [1]). A Q-system is a set of rules that carry out transformations of oriented graphs; it operates on oriented graphs in which over each edge there is a tree written as a bracketed expression. Another interesting feature of the Q-language is the possibility to concatenate more Q-systems in one whole: each consequent system takes as its input data the output of the immediately preceding system.

The basic unit of the Q-language is a tree containing certain parameters; the parameters consist in the letter p followed by an asterisk and by a figure $c \in \{1,2,3,...9\}$. If $p \in \{A,B,C,D,E,F\}$, then the parameter represents a value; if $p \in \{I,J,K,L,M,N\}$, then the parameter represents a tree; if $p \in \{U,V,W,X,Y,Z\}$, then the parameter represents a list (i.e. a sequence of trees separated by commas).

The following four kinds of relations obtain between lists and trees: =, ≠, -DANS-, -HORS-. Let z_1, z_2 be two arbitrary values, s_1, s_2 be two arbitrary trees, and v_1, v_2 be two arbitrary lists; then the relation -DANS- is defined as follows:

Linguistically motivated representation of knowledge   169

$$-\text{NUL}- \quad -\text{DANS}- \quad v_1 \quad = \underline{\text{true}} \text{ (where } -\text{NUL}- \text{ represents an empty list)}$$
$$v_1 \quad -\text{DANS}- \quad -\text{NUL}- \quad = (v_1 = -\text{NUL}-)$$
$$s_1, v_1 \quad -\text{DANS}- \quad v_2 \quad = s_1 \ -\text{DANS}- \ v_2 \ \underline{\text{and}} \ v_1 \ -\text{DANS}- \ v_2$$
$$z_1(v_1) \quad -\text{DANS}- \quad z_2(v_2) \quad = (z_1 = z_2) \ \underline{\text{and}} \ v_1 \ -\text{DANS}- \ v_2$$
$$s_1 \quad -\text{DANS}- \quad s_2, v_2 \quad = s_1 \ -\text{DANS}- \ s_2 \ \underline{\text{or}} \ s_1 \ -\text{DANS}- \ v_2$$

(where $z_1(v_1)$ denotes that the elements of the list v_1 immediately depend on the root labelled by z_1).
The relation -HORS-, which is not a precise negation of -DANS-, is defined as follows:

$$-\text{NUL}- \quad -\text{HORS}- \quad v_2 \quad = \underline{\text{false}}$$
$$v_1 \quad -\text{HORS}- \quad -\text{NUL}- \quad = \underline{\text{false}}$$
$$s_1, v_1 \quad -\text{HORS}- \quad v_2 \quad = s_1 \ -\text{HORS}- \ v_2 \ \underline{\text{and}} \ (v_1 \ -\text{HORS}- \ v_2 \ \underline{\text{or}} \ v_1 = -\text{NUL}-)$$
$$s_1 \quad -\text{HORS}- \quad s_2, v_2 \quad = s_1 \ -\text{HORS}- \ s_2 \ \underline{\text{and}} \ (s_1 \ -\text{HORS}- \ v_2 \ \underline{\text{or}} \ v_2 = -\text{NUL}-)$$
$$z_1(v_1) \quad -\text{HORS}- \quad z_2(v_2) \quad = (z_1 \neq z_2) \ \underline{\text{or}} \ v_1 \ -\text{HORS}- \ v_2.$$

The Q-language applies given transformation on the <u>string graphs</u>, consisting of a set of strings (finite sequences of symbols, which are separated by the separator +).

The string graph must meet the following conditions:
(i) it does not contain a loop,
(ii) one node is called the input and one is called the output; every edge is oriented in the direction from the input to the output; the graph must be connected, i.e. it must contain a path from the input to the output.

The <u>rules</u> then have the following form:
$a_1 + a_2 + \ldots + a_p == b_1 + b_2 + \ldots + b_q$.
where a_i, b_j ($i=1, \ldots, p$; $j=1, \ldots, q$) are arbitrary trees, == is read "is rewritten as" and the fullstop denotes the end of the rule. The transformation is performed in two different stages: in the first stage a new edge (i.e. the right-hand side of the rule applied) is added to the graph, and in the second stage those edges that are considered as superfluous (i.e. the left-hand side of the rule applied) are deleted.

A <u>system Q</u> is a set of rules and commentaries; the rules may contain parameters and conditions (separated by slashes). The part of a rule that is identical with a part of the immediately preceding rule may be replaced by a double dash. The system is considered to be inverted if it is preceded by -INV-.

A <u>procedure Q</u> is a sequence of phases (consisting in an application of a system Q or of its inverse -INV-), which are separated by the symbol -REG-.

Some of the typical inference rules used in the present version of the system can be characterized as follows:

(a) Relatively very simple rules perform the deletion of certain parts of TR´s; thus one of the rules deletes a part of a TR, if this part is introduced by the expression "i.e." (formally treated as apposition).

(b) Such a part of a TR that is expressed by a dependent (embedded) clause of cause or effect is transformed into an independent TR (assertion) by the rule illustrated in Fig. 2, if certain conditions are met (the governing clause is not negated, or else the main verb

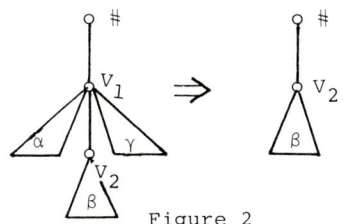

Figure 2

of the dependent clause is contextually bound: "He came, since the weather was nice" → "The weather was nice"; "Since the weather was nice, he came/didn't come" → "The weather was nice"; however from "He didn't come since the weather was nice" it does not follow that the weather was nice; the sentence can be continued by "This time he stayed at home, because his wife was ill").

(c) An assertion stating that a device can function in a certain way is transformed into an assertion stating that such a device functions in that way (the texts underlying our experiment deal with electronic devices as types).
(d) Some of the inference rules operate on two TR's, e.g. from two assertions of the forms (i) and (ii) an assertion of the form (iii) is derive where "does" stands for any action verb:
    (i) X is Y   (ii) X does Z   (iii) X is Y that does Z
(e) TR's of definitions (of the form "X is called Y") serve as a basis for the substitution of X by Y and vice versa in all other TR's.

Also rules concerning the distributivity of conjunction and disjunction ("and", "or") are included, as well as several groups of other rules of various degrees of generality.

The retrieval of an answer in the enriched set of assertions (TR's) is performed in the following steps:
(a) first it is checked whether the lexical value of the root of the TR is identical with that of the TR of the question, or, if the question ha the form "What is performed (done) by X?", then the TR from the enriched set must include an action verb as a label of its root;
(b) the path leading from the root to the wh-word is checked (yes-no questions are excluded from the first experiment); the rightmost path the relevant TR must coincide with the wh-path in its lexical labels, co textual boundness, grammatemes and labels of the edges (with some cases substitutability: Singular - Plural, Manner - Accompaniment, etc.); the wh-word in the question must be matched by a lexical unit of the potential answer, where the latter may be further expanded;
(c) if also the rest of the two compared TR's meets the conditions of identity or substitutability, the relevant TR is marked as a full answer to the given question; if this is not the case but at least one of the nodes depending on a node included in the wh-path meets these condition then the relevant TR is marked as an indirect (partial) answer.

REFERENCES:

[1] Colmerauer,A., Les systèmes Q ou un formalisme pour analyser et synthétiser des phrases sur ordinateur, mimeo, without date. Montréal. Germ.translation: Prague Bull.of Math.Linguistics 38 (1982) 45-74.
[2] Hajičová,E. and Sgall,P., A Dependency-Based Specification of Topic and Focus, SMIL 1/2 (1980) 93-140.
[3] Hajičová,E. and Sgall,P., Towards Automatic Understanding of Technic Texts, Prague Bull.of Math.Linguistics 36 (1981) 5-23.
[4] Sgall,P., Functional Sentence Perspective in a Generative Descriptio in: Prague Studies in Mathematical Linguistics 2 (1967) 203-225.
[5] Sgall,P., Towards a Fully Automatic System of Communication with Dat Bases, Computers and Artificial Intelligence 1 (1982) 35-45.
[6] Sgall,P., Nebeský,L., Goralčíková,A. and Hajičová,E., A Functional Approach to Syntax (American Elsevier, New York, 1969).
[7] Sgall,P., Hajičová,E. and Benešová,E., Topic, Focus, and Generative Semantics (Scriptor, Kronberg/Taunus, 1973).

NATURAL LANGUAGE ACCESS TO THE DATA BASE
OF THE AIDOS/VS INFORMATION RETRIEVAL SYSTEM

Hermann Helbig

VEB Robotron, Zentrum für Forschung und Technik
Dresden, German Democratic Republic

Natural language interfaces (NLI) mark one border-
line between research in the field of Artificial
Intelligence and its commercial application. Considering the fact that in the next decade the so-
called "naive users" will become typical users of
information systems, the realization of natural
language access to data bases will become a necessity. This paper discusses the structure of a NLI
for the AIDOS/VS information retrieval system.
Particular attention is paid to the operation of
the linguistic processor.

1. INTRODUCTION

To meet the needs for natural language communication with the computer, especially with information bases, there are, in principle,
two major lines of development:
(1) long-term: Creation of question-answering systems - QAS -
    (see [3], [4]), which are able to "understand" natural language
    information and to store it in a semantic form of representa-
    tion (teaching phase), and which are able to respond to natural
    language queries with the aid of logical inference procedures
    (query phase).
(2) short-term: Development of natural language interfaces - NLI -,
    which permit to ask a question of a data base in natural lan-
    guage; the information of this base is, however, stored in a
    specific, computer-oriented form and is usually not entered in
    natural language.

As far as information retrieval systems are concerned, we consider
line (1) to be the strategic aim of development. However, the main
difficulty for commercial use of QAS is still the question of efficient storage management arising from mass data processing.
Conventional data base management systems (DBMS) with their, in
comparison with QAS, simple data models have solved the problem of
managing large data bases in a relatively good way. Consequently,
it is reasonable to develop special processors (NLI) for these
DBMS, which allow for natural language communication with the
system.
Following this idea, the VEB Robotron Zentrum fuer Forschung und
Technik is developing such an interface - called NLI/AIDOS - for
the AIDOS/VS Information Retrieval System (see [1]). This NLI is
the topic of our paper.

2. STRUCTURE OF THE NLI/AIDOS INTERFACE

Figure 1 depicts the global structure of the NLI/AIDOS Interface:

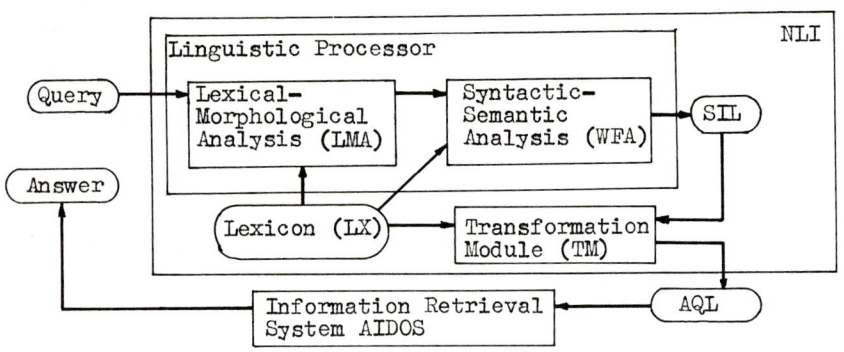

Figure 1 Global Structure of the NLI/AIDOS

The interface consists of four main components:
a) a lexical-morphological analysis (LMA);
b) a word-class-controlled functional analysis (WFA) translating the natural language queries into expressions of a semantic intermediate language (SIL) after the preparatory LMA-step;
c) a lexicon (LX) containing the grammatical-semantic background information;
d) a transformation module (TM) transforming SIL expressions into AIDOS Query Language (AQL) expressions.

3. THE LINGUISTIC PROCESSOR

The core of the linguistic processor is a word-class-controlled functional analysis (WFA). This analysis does not work, as often found, with a set of grammatical rules which are applied during the analysis by a central parser. The basic idea of the WFA-method is the following one: each-word-class is connected with a function for its own processing that is called when a word of the corresponding word-class appears in the surface structure of the sentence. During this process the fact is used that valencies (so-called SLOTs) are opened by certain word forms of the sentence, e.g., verbs, prepositions etc., which can be saturated by other words or constructions, e.g., adverbs, noun phrases etc. (the so-called FILLERs). Accordingly, the procedure makes use of three stacks: STACK, OP-STACK, CL-STACK, which are dynamically built up and reduced during the analysis.
All constituents of the sentence are stored in the STACK, whereas the OP-STACK contains only the elements that open slots, and the CL-STACK the constituents for which the analysis has been completed and which are available now as fillers for the corresponding slots. Figure 2 depicts a snapshot of the stack when analyzing the sentence: "Welche Firmen verkaufen Schreibmaschinen?" ("Which firms sell electric typewriters?") in that moment when all word forms of the sample sentence have been included into the analysis.
The STACK elements contain a representative, a partially analyzed structure, a morphosyntactic and a semantic characteristic (distinguished for slots and fillers), and the category (for fillers) or word-class function (for slots).

Natural language access to AIDOS 173

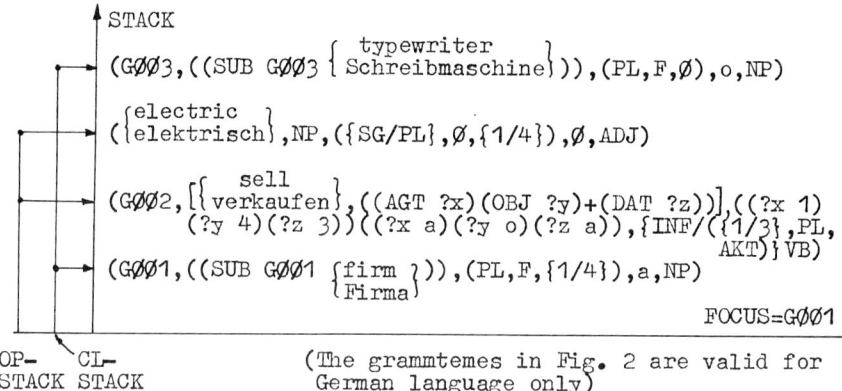

OP-   CL-   (The grammtemes in Fig. 2 are valid for
STACK   STACK   German language only)

Fig. 2 Snapshot from the analysis of a sample sentence

The symbols have the following meaning: SG - singular; PL - plural;
F - feminine; AGT, OBJ, DAT - the valences agentive, objective, dative, respectively; ∅ - non-differentiated feature; INF - infinitive; + - separation of obligatory and facultative valences; AKT - active; numbers - indication of cases for nominal constituents and persons for verbs; NP - noun phrase (opened or closed); ADJ - adjective; VB - verb; o - concrete object; a - object being able to act; ? - variables beginning with question mark designate slots.

Since the English language has a different system of morphological forms (namely, a much poorer one) than the German or even Russian language has, the analysis sketched above cannot be applied to other languages without modifications. As far as languages are concerned, in which checks for congruency are not so productive in finding suitable fillers for the slots, conditions of arrangement must be taken into consideration to a greater extent.
The objective of the analysis process is to translate natural language sentences (mostly queries in case of NLI) into expressions of the semantic intermediate language (SIL), which reflect the essential semantic relations of the input sentences. (A more detailed explanation of the intermediate languages of the system is given in [5]). The result of the syntactic-semantic analysis of the sample sentence (see above) has the following form:

[TYPE: SUPPL, FOCUS:GØØ1, SPEC:((SUBA GØØ2{sell/verkaufen})(AGT GØØ2 GØØ1)
(SUB GØØ1 {firm/Firma})(OBJ GØØ2 GØØ3)(SUB GØØ3 {typewriter/Schreibmaschine})
(PROP GØØ3 {electrical/elektrisch}))]

The indicator TYPE marks the type of the sentence (here: supplementary question); FOCUS specifies the point of interest the question is directed to. A detailed description of what is asked is given in the specification part (indicator SPEC).

4. THE TRANSFORMATION MODULE

Not all components for a specific NLI can be designed independently of the underlying data base system or application model. For each application, the relations between data base-independent SIL constructions and the data base-specific terms of the application field must be established. In the NLI/AIDOS, this task is solved by a transformation module (TM). It consists of a central control part, which uses a given set of transformations to translate universal linguistic deep structures into expressions pertinent to the specific application model. Let's assume that the treatment of the above example is based on a simple relational data model with the following table (relation) as target data structure.

TRADE HANDEL	SELLER VERKÄUFER	LOCATION ORT	PRODUCT ERZEUGNIS	PRICE PREIS	... ...
	MEYER TECHCOM	LONDON GLASGOW	ELTYPEWR PLOTTER	500 800	... ...

In this case, the system determines first by a menu-driven dialogue that the above question refers to the particular relation TRADE (HANDEL). After that, the transformation module establishes the relationship between <"Firma" (firm) + AGT-relation for "verkaufen" (sell)> and the attribute<"Verkäufer" (seller)>(this is a column name). Furthermore, TM infers that the partial structure of the SIL ((SUB GØØ3 Schreibmaschine (typewriter)) (PROP GØØ3 elektrisch (electric))) refers to the code ELTYPEWR (Engl. abbreviation for "electric typewriter") in the "Erzeugnis" column. The necessary transformations and background information are derived from the lexicon or from the thesaurus of the AIDOS system. Transformation problems are discussed in detail in [2]. After the transformation step, the query from the example has the following structure in the AIDOS query language AQL:

$$\left[(TABLE = \begin{Bmatrix} TRADE \\ HANDEL \end{Bmatrix}); (\begin{Bmatrix} FIRM \\ FIRMA \end{Bmatrix} = ?) \text{ AND } (\begin{Bmatrix} PRODUCT \\ ERZEUGNIS \end{Bmatrix} = ELTYPEWR) \right]$$

FINAL REMARK

At present, the system NLI/AIDOS is being implemented on a medium-performance ES1055 computer using the LISP language. The author thanks his collegues H. Böttger, P. String and F. Zänker for the stimulations he received from joint work on the project.

REFERENCES

(1) AIDOS - Automated Information and Documentation System (General Description), Technical Report H 2063-2002-2 VEB Robotron ZFT, Dresden, Nov. 1981
(2) Böttger, H. Probleme der natürlichen Anfrage an AIDOS/VS und DABA 1600, Tagungsberichte des Datenbankseminars in Gaußig, 1983, Schriftenreihe des WBZ der TU Dresden
(3) Bolc, L. Natural Language Based Computer Systems, Akademieverlag Berlin 1980
(4) Helbig, H. (et al.) FAS-80 - ein natürlichsprachiges Auskunftssystem, WIB Nr. 18, VEB Robotron ZFT, Dresden 1983
(5) Helbig, H. (et al.) NSI-AIDOS - ein natürlichsprachiges Interface für das Informationsrecherchesystem AIDOS/VS Tagungsbericht INFO-84, Dresden 1984

PROVING/TESTING MODULE CORRECTNESS

Jiří Hořejš

Computer Science Department
University of Brno
Brno
Czechoslovakia

Systems of considerable complexity - and almost
all systems within the area of AI share this feature - are always error-prone, both in specification
and in implementation. This paper offers an old
tool, namely finite automata, to relieve the
proces of proving and/or testing system reliability under fairly general circumstances. The
concept of stable partition is used to reduce the
number of test cases. There is an experimental
evidence that the method detects many errors with
only a little additional effort.

INTRODUCTION

Many systems can be specified by a predicate $Q(x_1,\ldots,x_r,y_1,\ldots,y_t, z_1,\ldots,z_s)$ relating values of inputs (input variables $x_1,\ldots,x_r$), states (memory variables $y_1,\ldots,y_t$) and outputs (output variables $z_1,\ldots,z_s$). It is assumed that each of the variables x_i (y_j,z_k) is restricted to corresponding domain X_i (Y_j,Z_k, respectively).
The specification is implemented by a module M with corresponding
inputs, states and outputs. The implementation is correct iff for
all admissible inputs and states ($x_i \in X_i, y_j \in Y_j$), the outputs
($z_k \in Z_k$), observed in proper time satisfy the predicate Q. That
this "proper time" really comes is also to be shown (i.e. we
consider so called "total" correctness).

The modules need not necessarily be programs. Due to space limitation we shall restrict ourselves, however, to this case, and use
terminology and an example from this area. Moreover we assume that
modules are reusable in the sense that their behaviour does not
depend on initial values of memory variables. It follows that
memory states do not appear in Q (but they generally do appear
in the proof/testing process); again, this assumption is not
substantial.

There is a plenty of methods for verifying and/or testing of
module correctness. Verification requires a formal proof, testing
requires a selection of proper test cases. What we propose is
a mixture of both approaches : by reducing the number of test cases
to a finite one we can sometimes replace the actual excercising
of testing by a proof.

The idea of finite testing was outlined in the paper by Henderson
and Quarendon (1974) and generalized to some extent in Hořejš
(1979). This contribution tries to show that the approach can be
applied to a considerably broader class of specification and

implementation problems.

THE METHOD

We propose to reduce the number of test cases, still retaining a sufficient level of reliability, by heuristical considerations of the meaning of particular variables.
A partition $\bar{X}_i = \{\bar{X}_{i1}, \ldots, \bar{X}_{in_i}\}$ of the domain X_i is said to be <u>stable</u> iff it is (manageably) finite and for every $\bar{X}_{ij} \in \bar{X}_i$ there is a stable value $x_{ij} \in \bar{X}_{ij}$ such that satisfying Q for x_{ij} implies that Q is satisfied for all $x \in \bar{X}_{ij}$. Formally: $\bar{X}_i$ is stable if it holds (for $1 \leq u \leq r$, $1 \leq v \leq s$):
$$\forall x_u \in X_u \ (u \neq i) \ \forall x_{ij} \in \bar{X}_{ij} \ (1 \leq j \leq n_i) \ \forall z_v \in Z_v \ Q(x_1, \ldots, x_{ij}, \ldots, z_s) \Rightarrow$$
$$\forall x_u \in X_u \ \forall z_v \in Z_v \ Q(x_1, \ldots, x_i, \ldots, z_s)$$

If all input domains happen to have a stable decomposition then to prove that M is correct, it is sufficient to test or prove it for all combinations of stable values. Usually this induces a natural finite partition of the state domain as well. If we are able effectively to find such finite (stable) partitions (and perhaps even some of the stable values), the testing/proving process can be performed automatically. We hope that the following example (simple, yet not trivial) will clarify the idea sufficiently.

THE EXAMPLE

Consider the program P of Figure 1 for bubble-sorting into increasing order an array of n+1 (n=0) real numbers. The program is borrowed from Manna (1974) (example 3-6, figure 3-10), but we depart from the proof methodology given there. (The symbol ↔ denotes mutual exchange of values). Input domain for the input variable n is the set N of all nonnegative integers, the input vectors x consist of all (n+1) - tuples of real numbers from R^{n+1}. Q requires that the values $z_0, \ldots, z_n$ of output variables are permutation of $x_0, \ldots, x_n$ and $z_0 \leq z_1 \leq \ldots \leq z_n$.

We claim (heuristically) that the following partitions of input domains are stable:
(a) $\bar{N}_3 = \{N\}$ (one-element partition), with a stable value (e.g.)n=2.
(b) $\bar{R}^3 = \{R_1, \ldots, R_m\}$, where every R_i consists of all n-tuples with the same inequality relation between the numbers (so that e.g. the vectors (1.1,3.3,2.2) and (0,5.6,4) belong to the same class; the number of classes m as well as some of them will turn out not to be important as discussed below). These stable partitions would be useful, when we wanted to test the module - program P. But, as we are now going to show, we can pass directly to a proof of P, using stability of $\bar{R}^3$ only indirectly. Namely, the input domains partitions lead to a simple characterization of memory states, which are given by the values of memory variables I,J,Y[0],Y[1], Y[2], the last three ones representing an array storing initially the input data, x_0, x_1, x_2, and changing their values during the program execution until they store the resulting output values z_0, z_1, z_2.

There are 7 important memory states induced by the input domains partitions and values of I and J; namely, the module is in the state:
S_0 iff I=2,J=0, the values of Y[i] being quite arbitrary;
S_1 iff I=2,J=1, Y[0] $\leq$ Y[1];
S_2 iff I=2,J=2, Y[0] $\leq$ Y[2], Y[1] $\leq$ Y[2];

S_3 iff I=1,J=2, Y[0]≤ Y[2], Y[1]≤ Y[2];
S_4 iff I=1,J=0, Y[0]≤ Y[2], Y[1]≤ Y[2];
S_5 iff I=1,J=1, Y[0]≤ Y[1]≤ Y[2];
S_6 iff I=0,J=1, Y[0]≤ Y[1]≤ Y[2].

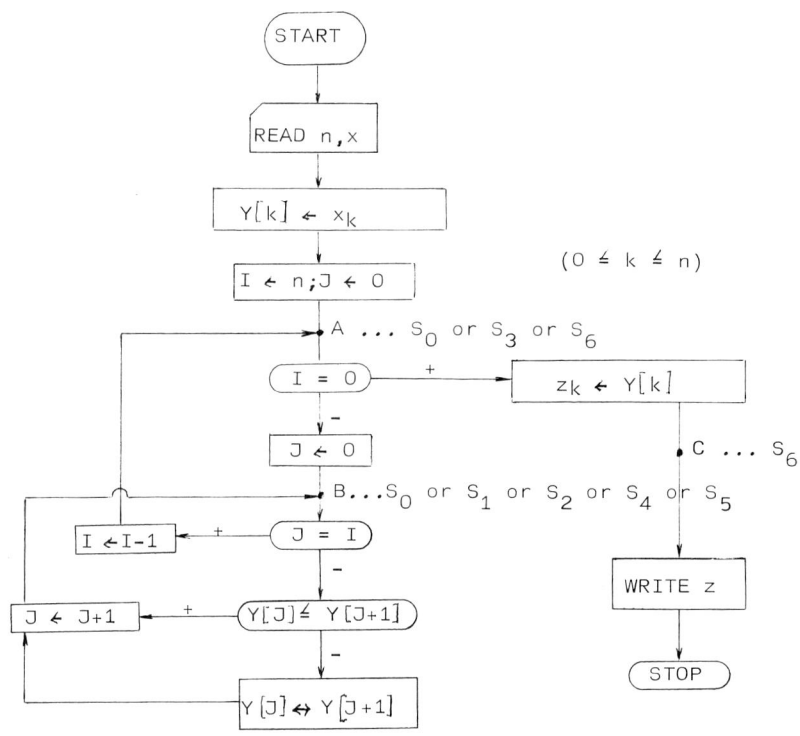

Figure 1

The program P.

These are the only characteristic states that can be reached during any computation (for n=2!), as is indicated by the following diagram, showing how the states change when traversing from one of the cutpoints A,B,C to the other:
$$S_0 \xrightarrow[AB]{} S_0 \xrightarrow[BB]{} S_1 \xrightarrow[BB]{} S_2 \xrightarrow[BA]{} S_3 \xrightarrow[AB]{} S_4 \xrightarrow[BA]{} S_5 \xrightarrow[BA]{} S_6 \xrightarrow[AC]{} S_6$$
The diagram indicates how the states $S_0,\ldots,S_6$ were "invented" — it was possible to do it by a sort of "Symbolic execution", automatically. Because we end with the state S_6 satisfying the predicate Q (array ordered), we have actually proved correctness of program P for the case n=2. (The OR-statements attached to the points A,B,C play the role of invariants, known from the

classical Floyd`s verification techniques). It would take only few
lines more to show correctness of P for any other small value of n.
Supposing that any such value of n is stable, the program is fully
proven.

The assumptions of stability that we made may be justified by
noting that the value of the problem does not require any special
properties of the number n (except that it should be large enough
to excercise all paths through the program) and any special
properties of input real vectors except for their relation concerning inequalities. In this way, what we do when establishing
stability is a sort of abstraction - an additional one, differing
from what is usually ment when speaking about the Principle of
Abstraction in ordinary modules design.

REFERENCES

[1] Henderson, P., Quarendon, P.: Finite Testing of Structured
    Programs, Lecture Notes in Comp.Sci.19, Springer Verlag 1974,
    72-80.
[2] Hořejš, J.: Finite Semantics: a Technique for Program Testing,
    in: Proc. 4th Int.Conf.Software Eng., Munich, IEEE Computer
    Society, (Sept.1979), 433 - 440
[3] Manna, Z.: Mathematical Theory of Computation, (McGraw - Hill,
    1974)

HIERARCHICAL – REGRESSIVE GENERATING AND EXECUTING ROBOT'S PLANS

Pavol Hrivik

Institute of Technical Cybernetics, SAS
Dúbravská cesta 9, 842 37 Bratislava
Czechoslovakia

The paper deals with a research project which is concerned with the development of advanced software control systems for industrial robots. The work focusses on implementing the special automatic regressive planning system HANEL into a control complex of a robot. The main aim of HANEL implementation is to create a robotic plan, to execute a generated plan and to provide automatic error recovery facilities in an existing industrial application.

INTRODUCTION

This paper describes a research project of implementing the automatic regressive planning system HANEL [5] into a control complex of a robot. The main aim of HANEL implementation is to create a robotic plan, to execute a generated plan and to provide automatic error recovery facilities in an existing industrial application.

The HANEL implementation scheme is shown in Fig. 1. Three basic control levels of a robot are considered: A, B and C. Each of the control levels has its specialized tool for programming corresponding algorithms: L_1, L_2 and L_3.

A model states hierarchy of the robot's world /SM-modules/ is defined. It involves the knowledge base of a given robotic task, parts, working tools or workplace.

The SM_1-module contains knowledge of an objects configuration including the names of parts and tools, their approximate positions, orientations and relationships, etc.

The SM_2-module involves knowledge of the geometrical size, weight and shapes of three-dimensional objects /parts, tools/ and the relationships between coordinate systems of the robot and the work space.

The SM_3-module contains expected positions and orientations of specific features of parts and tools, such as slots, surfaces, edges, corners and holes.

SM-modules also contain procedures for computing expectations and predictions of sensory data processed and evaluated in VSV-modules. This allows VSV-modules at each control level to compare expectations with observations, and to measure both the degree of correlation and the degree of difference. A strong degree of correlation means that the proper model is being matched with the incoming sensory data. On the other hand, a large degree of difference between expectations and observations derived from sensory data means that either an incorrect actual state of a world model has been made, or sensory data are incorrectly processed and filtered. In this case, VSV-modules must decide which type of error is being encountered and what is required to remedy the discrepancy.

THE CONTROL LEVEL A

Algorithms of this level correspond to the degree of tasks complexity solved by a robot independently of man. Through the KOM-module man communicates with all control levels of the robot. The central module of the level A is the automatic regressive planning system HANEL /the HANEL-module/. The aim of the HANEL-module is to find a plan for removing any difference between the required and the observed robot's world state. If found, the plan is step by step applied in the lower control levels; if not, HANEL ends its operation and applies to man /through the KOM-module/, or to some superior control system /through the JM-module/ for help.

The planning system HANEL is designed on principles of hierarchical planning and a goals regression mechanism. The resulting robotic plan is created by a combination of linear and nonlinear partial plan modification /see [5]/. During plan synthesis, HANEL makes use of knowledge of:
- actual model state of a robotic world /SM_1-module/
- inadmissible situations in a robotic world /ZRP-module/
- robot's actions /MVO-module/
- confinements of a planning process /POPP-module/.

The AZC-module analyses the validity of the given goal in the robotic world model state. If it holds, the robotic task is trivial; if not, HANEL is activated.

Each successful output of the HANEL-module is converted into a triangular form by the RVP-module /see [3], [7]/. The VOP-module controls operators choice from a robotic plan. The selected operator is first applied in SM_1 and then processed by algorithms of the control level B.

The VSV_1-module processes and evaluates feedback data from sensory devices /SP/ and from lower control levels. VSV_1 coordinates the operation of all modules in the level A. It adds new facts to the SM_1-module resulting from dynamic changes in the robot's environment, correlates observations against expectations, recognizes patterns, etc. If difference between observation and expectation is detected, the HANEL-module is activated.

As a programming language L_1 for the control level A an arbitrary language out of known AI languages can be theoretically used. For our purposes, LISP 1.10 was chosen /see [6]/.

THE CONTROL LEVEL B

The aim of the control level B is to convert each step of a robotic plan into a sequence of elementary robot's control commands. That means, the output from the level A, written in a language L_1, is transformed through executive procedures of a language L_2 into commands of a language L_3 for controlling a robot effector. A language L_2 must contain means for a "more detailed" description of a robotic world and robotic actions. As L_2, an arbitrary AI language or some out of known assembly languages /e.g. AL, LAMA, AUTOPASS, RAPT/ can served. For our need, LISP 1.10 and RAL [2] were used.

The transformation of each operator in a generated robotic plan into the executive procedure of L_2 is realized in two steps:
1. The PO-module finds a suitable one in the set of general executive procedures of the MVVP-module. /Each element of MVO has its corresponding procedure in MVVP/.
2. Creating a ground instance of the selected executive procedure in the SVP-module by instantiations:
    - corresponding to the competent operator being analysed in the PO-module
    - obtained in a unification process of executive procedure elements with facts in the SM_2-module.

The VSV_2-module /also VSV_3 in the control level C/ has a similar aim as the VSV_1-module. If expectations of executive procedure application are not achieved, VSV_2 sends a message to the SVP-module to create a new ground instance of the last chosen procedure taking account of unanticipated changes or errors in the workplace. If a suitable instance of the procedure is not found, VSV_2 applies to the VSV_1-module for help; otherwise the created ground instance procedure is decomposed by the DP-module into some sequence of elementary effector commands in a language L_3.

THE CONTROL LEVEL C

Algorithms of this level compute a robot end effector trajectory, compute desirable values of controlled variables for each degree of freedom and perform all prescribed robot effector motions.

The sequence of elementary control commands in a language L_3, obtained by decomposing executive procedures from the level B, are converted into desirable values for effector servo-controls.

The following languages can serve as a suitable programming tool for modules of the level C: WAVE, SIGLA, EMILY, VAL etc. For our purposes, the language for a robot effector control system MARS /PRE-module/ was chosen /see [4] /. Without any problems, the language of VAL [8] can be also used in our project.

The application result of each robot's action in the workplace is observed by a sensory subsystem /SP/, then gradually processed and evaluated in VSV-modules.

CONCLUSION

There appear to be advantages of our approach to implementing the automatic regressive planning system HANEL into a robot's control complex. The first is that it partitions the problem into simple, well-defined modules with clearly specified inputs, outputs, internal states and rules for state-transitions. The control problem is partitioned vertically with respect to task complexity and abstraction, horizontaly with respect to function. This simplifies the design and eases the synchronization of simultaneous processes in the many different computing modules.

The second advantage is that it facilitates the handling of error conditions. We are dealing mainly with physical errors and faults in the robots work cell environment. These include the robot itself, associated jigs, tools and feeders and the components being processed. A generated recovery sequence of actions will vary widely in complexity and feasibility but their success will depend upon the quality of robotic task knowledge that is available to the system.

REFERENCES

[1] Albus, J.S., Barbera,A.J., Fitzgerald,M.L., Hierarchical Control for Sensory Interactive Robots, in: Proc. 11th International Symposium on Industrial Robots, Tokyo, Japan (1981) 7-9.

[2] Blaťák,J., Justiňák,D., The RAL Language and its Compiler, Internal research report (in Slovak) VUMA, Nové Mesto n. Váhom, Czechoslovakia (1982).

[3] Fikes,R.E., Hart,P.E., Nilson,N.J., Learning and Executing Generalized Robot Plans, Artificial Intelligence Jrnl. 3 (1972) 251-288.

[4] Frankovič,B. et al., Algorithms of Adaptive Control of Robots and Intelligent Robotic Systems, Internal research report (in Slovak) ITC SAS, Bratislava, Czechoslovania (1983).

[5] Hrivík,P., Automatic Regressive Planning of Robot Actions, Ph. D. Thesis (in print, in Slovak) ITC SAS, Bratislava, Czechoslovakia (1983).

[6] Hulman,J., LISP for PDP-11/40, Programmer's manual, ITC SAS, Bratislava, Czechoslovakia (1981).

[7] Nilsson,N.J., Principles of Artificial Intelligence (Tioga Publ. Co., Palo Alto, 1980).

[8] Shimano,B., VAL: A Versatile Robot Programming and Control System, in: Proc. of IEEE Comp. Soc. COMPSAC, Chicago (1979) 878-883.

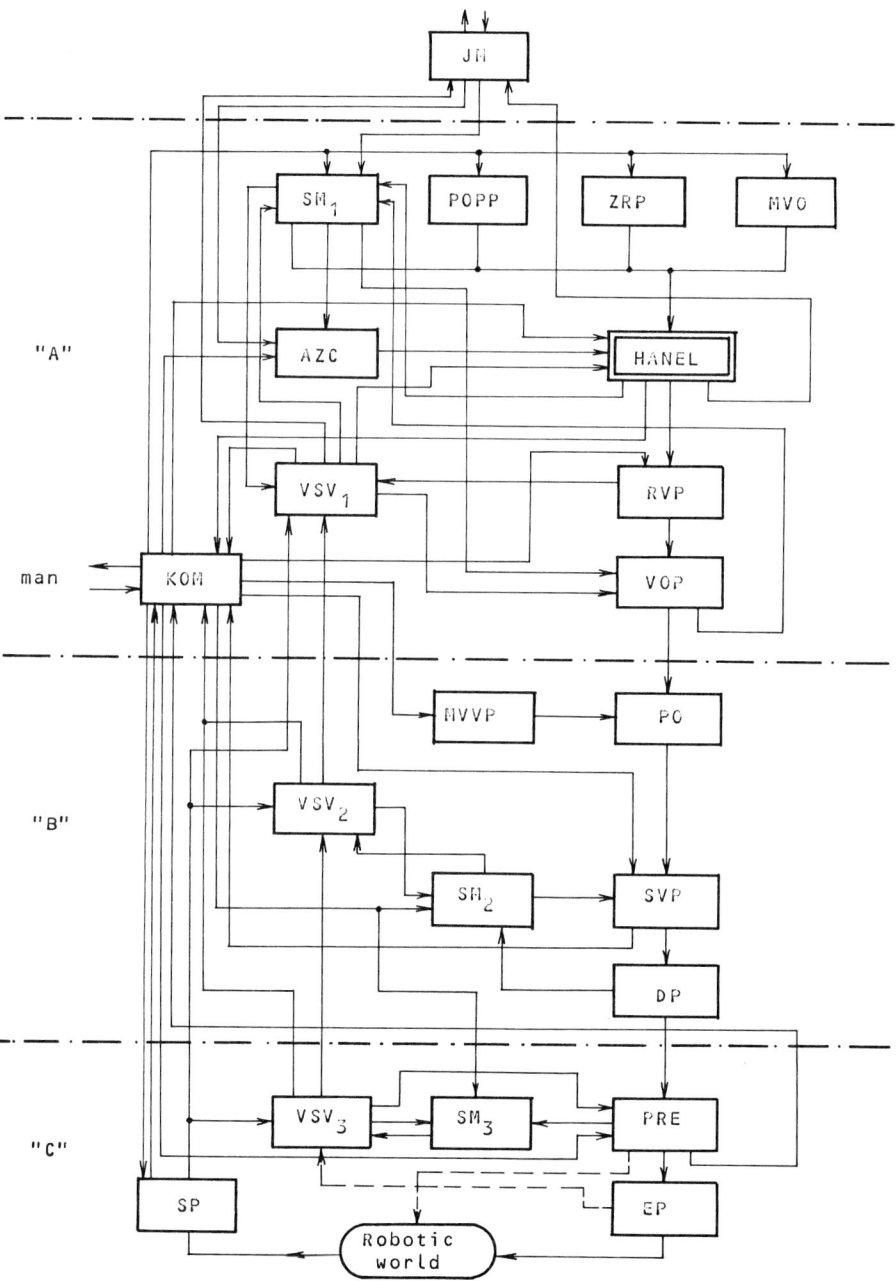

Figure 1
The HANEL implementation scheme

A R C — A MODULAR APPROACH TO ADVANCED ROBOT PROGRAMMING AND CONTROL

Joachim Huebener

Academy of Science of the GDR
Central Institute of Cybernetics and Information Processes
DDR - 1086 Berlin, Kurstr. 33
GDR

The functional decomposition of the complex problem of robot programming and control yields a hierachical design with each function realized in form of a module. Almost all modules are implemented in PASCAL to form a portable library of robot software. The system is running under a multitask operating system on a minicomputer or a distributed microprocessor system. The structure of the system is flexible and easy to change. Therefore the functional power of ARC may be increased or tailored to special applications.

INTRODUCTION

Programming and control of robots in the environment of flexible manufacturing systems is a problem of increasing complexity. The usual way of implementing software for an actual robot is programming of the specialized system in assembly language tailored to the microprocessor being used. In that way it is difficult to use the programs on different computers and for different robots. In addition it is a hard work to add new program parts to enlarge the functional power of the system.

The aim of the system ARC (Advanced Robot Control Software System) which is currently under development in the Central Institute of Cybernetics and Information Processes is to generate a portable software system of specialized modules for control and programming of robots. It supports programming, testing, editing, simulation and execution of application programs. The software should be as much as possible independent of the robot and computer system being used. The language PASCAL is used due to the inherent structured programming capabilities and the availability on several computers. The system is arranged in a multilevel architecture. On each level there is a set of functions realized in modular fashion. In the following sections the overall architecture is described followed by a short description of the lower levels (base level, control system, first level of the programming system). The system will be extended with new modules if new functions on each level are introduced. In this sense it is an open system which is used as a tool in robotic research (2nd and 3rd generation robots). The generation of tailored industrial application systems is intended.

OVERALL ARCHITECTURE

Due to the complexity of the robot programming task in flexible manufacturing environment the system is divided into hierarchical levels (decomposition). Each level performs several functions depending on input commands and the actual state of processing (model-information). A function is performed directly by a call to the corresponding module (procedure) or generates commands to the next lower level. The result of the function processing updates the actual state.

A rough distinction is made between programming system and control system. Each of these parts is itself divided into several levels. All parts of an application which are not part of ARC are treated as programming environment and located in the base level of the design. In ARC there are following levels:

- FMS-Level: Control of robots in flexible manufacturing systems
  Decomposition of the global task, integration of CAD/CAM
- Task-Level: Automatic action planning
  Interaktiv test system, problem solver, generation of robot programs in a higher-level language
- Object-Level: Manipulation of objects
  Compiler for the higher-level robot language, world model (objects, relation between objects)
- Manipulator-Level: Control of robot with respect to the effector
  Command language interpreter, teach-routines, base-language assembler (virtual machine VMR), interpreter of VMR-Code, simulation/execution of robot programs
- Base-Level (Software): Software environment
  Operating system: OS-Kernel (task management), I/O-System (resource management), tools (compiler, editor, ..)
- Base-Level (Hardware): Hardware environment
  Devices: Computer, manipulator, drives, effector, sensor system, process control system

The internal structure of each of these levels is defined in the progress of implementation. As the functions are realized in form of modules several structures are possible. The actual structure of a tailored system depends on the hardware being used.

SYSTEM ENVIRONMENT

The system ARC is running as an application program under control of an operating system with multitasking capability. The host system is a minicomputer and the target will be a distributed microprocessor system. Tasks (processes) are located on the same (pseudo-parallel) or different processors depending on processing demands. As task management is a function of the operating system and sequential PASCAL offers no task-control procedures one module (ARCOSK) of ARC is realized as interface to operating system calls in MACRO-Assembly-Language to provide these procedures to PASCAL-Programs. This interface module depends on the operating system and must be changed in transporting ARC. All tasks of ARC are running under supervision of the ARC-Monitor (ARCMON). These monitor creates the task structure and monitors processing.

THE CONTROL SYSTEM

Most of the present control systems are teach-in systems with location definition in joint coordinates on-line with the robot. In the future it should be possible to generate a program off-line with

the most locations defined externally. This is one of the design
goals of the ARC-System. Only a few unknown locations have to be
defined on-line while testing the program. The control system of
ARC includes the base level and a part of the manipulator level. As
a first step after starting the monitor, the ARC-Command-Interpreter (ARCCLI) is installed to communicate with the operator. Control
commands to the monitor are executed immediately by special processes to initialize the system, activate the sensor, drives and effector system. The main task of the control system is to execute
robot programs generated by the programming system. An EXEC-Command starts the VMR-Interpreter (ARCVMI) which loads the specified
program (VMR-Code and VMR-Data) and begins execution of VMR-Code.
The locations are stored and managed by the state-modelling routines (ARCWMO). Undefined locations are entered using the teach-routines (ARCTCH). The VMR-Interpreter controls the activities inside
of the control system and forms together with the state-modelling
routines and the teach-routines one of the following three internal levels of the control system:

- level of coordination and program interpreting
  (program management, state-modelling, teach-in)
- level of control in external coordinates
  (trajectory planning, dynamic state processing, interpolation,
  transformation between external and joint coordinates)
- level of control in joint coordinates
  (joint interpolation and servo, sensorprocessing,
  effector and process control)

On the level of control in external coordinates the trajectory
planning module (ARCTRP) controls the robot motion. According to
commands from the interpreter intermediate trajectory points are
generated (ARCAPX) and after conversion to joint coordinates
(ARCTRI) sent to the joint control routines on the next level.
Feedback from the sensor system is managed by the dynamic state
processing module (ARCDSP), which performs direct coordinate transformation from joint and sensor coordinates to external coordinates (ARCTRD) and monitoring of sensor information values. These information is used in the interpreter to alter program flow and in
the trajectory planning routine to modify path parameters. The lowest control level controls the actual devices e.g. joints
(ARCJNT), effector and process (ARCEFF, ARCPCC) and sensor system
(ARCSEN). The routines at the lowest level are dependent of the
hardware and are subject to change if other devices are used. Additional modules will be included if new devices are connected to
ARC or new algorithms are implemented.

THE PROGRAMMING SYSTEM

In this paper only the lowest level (manipulator level) of the
hierarchical programming system is described. The modules of the
programming system are running off-line from the control system
under control of the operating system or on-line under control of
the ARC-Monitor. The operator types the program text as input to
the editor (ARCEDI) or to the command interpreter (ARCCLI). The
resulting text file is placed in the file system or send to the
macro-assembler (ARCVMA) of the VMR-Language ARCL1. The output of
ARCVMA is in form of VMR-Code. The program and location files are
managed by the trajectory modelling routines (ARCVM1) and stored
in the file system for execution. The macro-facility enables the
user to build libraries of robot program subroutines. The level 1
command language ARCL1 has the capabilities of the VAL-Language (9)

with some extensions. More powerfull language constructs are implemented in the higher levels of the programming system. The language elements are described in later publications.

CONCLUSION

Some of the design criteria of the system ARC were described. The overall architecture is outlined and the lowest levels of these architecture are described in more details. All the system functions are realized in form of modules to ensure flexibility of the structure and expandability of the functional power. The system is used as a resarch tool in robotic research and is completed in progress of work. As there are some similar developments in other institutes a (not exhausting) list of references to the literature is appended.

REFERENCES

1/ Barbera, A.: An Architecture for a Robot Hierarchical Control System. Washington, 1977.
2/ Bison, P.; Lorenzin, G.; Pagello, E.: The Formal Definition of VML and a Proposed portable Implementation. 11th ISIR Tokyo, 1981.
3/ Blume, C.: A Structured Way of Implementing the High-level Programming Language AL on a Microcomputer Configuration. 11th ISIR Tokyo, 1981.
4/ Dillmann, R.: Weiterentwicklung der Steuerungs- und Bahnplanungsebene fuer Montageroboter mit hoeheren Programmiersystemen. VDI-Z 124 (1982) Nr. 8.
5/ Falek, D.; Parent, M.: An Evolutive Language for an Intelligent Robot. The Industrial Robot, Sept. 1980.
6/ Gini, G.; Gini, M.; Pagello, E.; Trainito, G.: Distributed Robot Programming. 10th ISIR Milan, 1980.
7/ Novatchenko, S. I.; Pavlov, V.A.; Yurevich, E.I.: Specialized Modular Software System of Sensitized Robot Control Computer. Mechanism and Machine theory, Vol 16. pp. 41-48
8/ Takase, K.; Paul, R.: A Structured Approach to Robot Programming and Teaching. IEEE Trans. SMC-11, Nr. 4, Apr. 1981.
9/ -,-: User's Guide to VAL, a Robot Programming and Control System. Unimation Inc., Danbury, Conn., 1980.

A GENERALIZED APPROACH TO INDUCTIVE INFERENCE

Klaus P. Jantke

Humboldt University Berlin
Department of Mathematics
P.O.Box 1297
DDR - 1086 Berlin

Inductive inference is a mathematical theory dealt with the problem of learning objects like languages or algorithms from possibly incomplete descriptions. The general approach being presented is aimed at the comparison of inductive inference approaches and results as well as at carrying over successful algorithms from one field to another. It is based on the framework of algebraic semantics. It enables to illuminate the key ideas of specialized inductive inference algorithms.

INTRODUCTION INTO INDUCTIVE INFERENCE

1984 is the year of the 20th anniversary of the foundation of the mathematical theory of inductive inference. Solomonoff's paper [9] published in 1964 was the first inductive inference publication. Nevertheless, Gold's seminal paper [5] has been the main source of further research work in the field of inductive inference. The reader not familiar with inductive inference ideas is referred to the surveys [2] and [8]. Because of the restricted space we can only present a considerably short introduction.

There are a lot of different approaches to the problem of learning or synthesizing objects like programs, for instance, from certain descriptions. The common feature of inductive inference approaches is that most emphasis is put on the incompleteness of information to be processed. Hence tasks as the synthesis of programs from input/output examples or as the identification of languages from finite samples are typical inductive inference problems. Every particular inductive inference concept is characterized by the following 5 parameters:
(1) The class of objects under consideration.
(2) The type of information taken as a basis for some learning or synthesis processes.
(3) The class of algorithms allowed as inductive inference methods.
(4) The space of possible hypotheses, i.e. the descriptions of objects generated by inference methods guessing objects.
(5) The concept of convergency, that means a rule describing in which cases an inductive inference method works successful.

For clearness we discuss a particular inductive inference concept. For further examples we direct the reader to the surveys mentioned above. The example discussed here can be found in the book [10].

The objects to be synthesized (identified, learned) are finite deterministic automata on fixed input and output alphabets X and Y, respectively. The information presented in the n-th step (for any positive integer n) is the full sample of input/output pairs up to the length n, i.e. the information to be processed in the n-th step consists of a finite set of pairs (x,y) such that x ranges over the set of all words over X of a length less than or equal to n and y is the word produced by a certain automaton in working up x. This underlying automaton is to be identified. As identification methods we consider arbitrary recursive devices of polynomial time complexity. Outputs are given as automata diagrams as usual. A finite deterministic automaton being presented by the sequence of full samples (for n = 1,2,...) describing its behavior is said to be synthesized by a certain inductive inference method in the limit if and only if there exists a certain number n such that the result of processing any full sample of words of a length exceeding n is a unique automata diagram defining a reduced automaton being equivalent to the one presented.

This inductive inference problem has been solved in [10]. In the 5th paragraph of chapter IV tne authors describe an inductive inference procedure which, in fact, is a certain tree matching procedure.

In the example above as well as in almost all other approaches (see [2],[8]) the information to be processed in the n-th step could be presented as a finite set of term equations. If these equations describe input/output examples they do not contain any variable. To allow the presentation of more general but incomplete information it is desirable to take into account arbitrary term equations possibly containing variables. This suggests to utilize the well-developed framework of algebraic semantics.

INITIAL AND FINAL ALGEBRA SEMANTICS

An inductive inference problem in the generalized form under consideration is mainly the problem of constructing algebraic structures from (possibly incomplete) equational descriptions. Before solving an inference problem one has to specify the "meaning" of admissible descriptions. This is a difficult problem as such an equational system understood as a system of first order axioms has a very large (normally infinite) model class, in general. We refer the reader to the standard reference [4] in this regard.

For our generalized approach to inductive inference we take the following concept as a basis. Objects to be synthesized are algebraic structures of a fixed underlying signature SIG. Note that a signature is allowed to be heterogenious, i.e. many-sorted. We define well-formed terms over SIG as usual. Assume a family X of sets of variables indexed by the sort names of the signature. By T(SIG,X) we denote the class of well-formed terms over SIG which possibly contain variables from X like constant names of the concerning sort. Conditional term equations are defined as follows:
a) For two terms t and t' from T(SIG,X) the expression
    t = t' is a conditional term equation.
b) For two terms t and t' as above and for any conditional term equation T the expression (t = t' $\longrightarrow$ T) is a conditional term equation, too.
CEQ(SIG,X) is the smallest set defined by the rules a) and b).
Finite subsets of CEQ(SIG,X) are taken as information on algebras.

Assume E to be a finite subset of CEQ(SIG,X). First we have to
specify the "meaning" of E. By ALG(SIG,E) we denote the class of
all algebras of the underlying signature SIG which are models of E
and which are finitely generated from SIG, i.e. for each element
there exists a term over SIG describing it. ALG(SIG,E) can be understood as a category with SIG-homomorphisms as morphisms. From
this viewpoint there may exist algebraically indicated algebras:
the initial and the final element. An element of a category is
called initial if for each other element of the category there is
a morphism from the initial element to it. Vice versa, an element
is called final if from each other element there is a morphism to
the final one. The term algebra factorized by the congruence relation induced by E is initial in ALG(SIG,E). The final object is
the unit algebra of the underlying signature. We remove this very
simple algebra (and all isomorphic structures) from ALG(SIG,E) and
ask for a final algebra in the remaining category ALG+(SIG,E). The
reader not familiar with the basic concepts should consult [4].

THE GENERALIZED APPROACH TO INDUCTIVE INFERENCE

We assume any finite heterogenious signature SIG and a corresponding family X of sets of variables. Assume that A is any given
algebra of this signature. A sequence E1, E2, E3, ... of finite
subsets of CEQ(SIG,X) describes the algebra A in the limit under
initial or final algebra semantics if and only if the initial resp.
final algebra of ALG+(SIG, ∪ Ei) exists and is isomorphic to A. The
inductive inference problem is to identify the target algebra A in
processing the sequence E1, E2, ... such that after working up a
finite initial segment of this description in the limit A is identified. The figure below shows this concept as a whole.

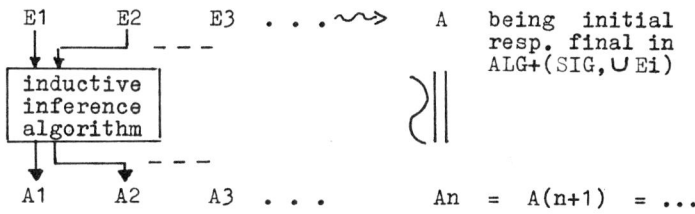

Ai denotes the algebra constructed by the inductive inference algorithm in working up E1, ... ,Ei . What powerful and efficient
inductive inference algorithms do exist? What are the main inductive inference ideas from the viewpoint of the general setting
introduced? What classes of algebras are synthesizable by a single
inductive inference method? We study these questions for the case
of final algebra semantics as quite interesting classes of objects
are specifiable within the framework of total algebras (possibly
with exception states) under final semantics (see [7]).

Assume A to be an arbitrary algebra described in the limit under
final algebra semantics by a sequence as above. As a consequence
of Gödel's completeness theorem each term inequality valid in A is
provable from ∪ Ei and the fact that A is not the unit algebra. A
similar result does not hold for equations, in general. Moreover,

as the usual deduction operator is of finite character each inequality turns out to be provable from some intermediate descriptions E1 , ... , En . This leads to the following result.

Theorem   For every finite signature there exists a universal inductive inference algorithm able to synthesize each finite algebra of this signature from any description in the limit under final algebra semantics.

We can prove a similar result for algebras with infinite parameters. The main work performed by these inductive inference algorithms consists in proving term inequalities.

SPECIALIZED INDUCTIVE INFERENCE ALGORITHMS

Indeed, the algorithm of [10] mentioned above is based on proofs of term inequalities by tree matching. From the general viewpoint proposed we can exhibit that the inference method for synthesizing Turing machine programs developed in [3] is exactly the algorithm for identifying automata of Trachtenbrot and Barzdin.

Finally, the polynomial time algorithm developed in [6] for solving a problem which remained open in [1] has been analyzed. It is possible to characterize its kernel method algebraically.

REFERENCES

[1]   Angluin, Dana   Finding patterns common to a set of strings, Journal of Computer and Systems Science 21 (1980), 46 - 62

[2]   Angluin, D. / Smith, C.H.   A survey of inductive inference: theory and methods, Yale Univ., Dep. Comp. Sci., Technical Report 250, October 1982

[3]   Biermann, Alan W.   On the inference of Turing machines from sample computations, Artif. Intelligence 3 (1973), 181 - 198

[4]   Goguen, J.A. / Thatcher, J.W. / Wagner, E.G.   An initial algebra approach to the specification, correctness, and implementation of abstract data types, i.: R.T. Yeh (ed.), Current trends in programming methodology, Vol. IV, Prentice-Hall Inc., 1978

[5]   Gold, E. Mark   Language identification in the limit, Inf. and Control 10 (1967), 447 - 474

[6]   Jantke, Klaus P.   Polynomial time inference of general pattern languages, Proceedings of STACS'84, april 11 - 13, 1984, Paris

[7]   Jantke, Klaus P.   The recursive power of algebraic semantics, submitted to EIK

[8]   Klette, R. / Wiehagen, R.   Research in the theory of inductive inference by GDR mathematicians - a survey, Information Sciences 22 (1980), 149 - 169

[9]   Solomonoff, R.J.   A formal theory of inductive inference, Part I,II, Inf. and Control 7 (1964), 1 - 22, 224 - 254

[10]   Trachtenbrot, B.A. / Barzdin, J.M.   Finite automata. Behaviour and synthesis (russ.), Moscow, 1970

OFF-LINE PLANNING OF COLLISION-FREE TRAJECTORIES AND OBJECT GRASPING FOR MANIPULATION ROBOTS

Winfried Jentsch

Central Institute for Cybernetics and Information Processes
AdW der DDR
DDR - 1086 Berlin
Kurstr. 33

The problem of geometrical planning for manipulation robots is considered. We get a description of the obstacles in the configuration space by a self-learning classification method. The path-find problem is resolved by a special path-graph construction and an A^*-search. The generation of suitable grasping and regrasping vectors is based on the correspondence between configuration and work space.

INTRODUCTION

Off-line programming of robots develops into the favorated option in assembly automation /1/. The human interaction will be changed stepwise by automatic generation of control programs. In this context the geometrical planning of collision-free trajectories is an basic research problem, which has been handled in different ways /5/, /4/, /3/, /2/. The task of the geometrical planning is to generate a collision-free trajectory of the manipulator with an object in the gripper between suitable start and end configurations, SC and EC, respectively. The knowledge for that generation process is completly given in the cinematic and geometric models of the robot and his environment.

At first we prepare an indexed point set system, which gives for each grid point GP in the work space WS the set of all colliding manipulator configurations in the configuration space CS. The mapping of a stationary obstacle into the CS is carried out by means of that indexation. The learning sample for a sequential clustering method consists of indexed configuration points CP. By a graph-theoretic method we get a certain hull description of the forbidden zones in the CS and construct a partition of the free space into convex segments. The path-find problem is globally resolved by the A^*-algorithm /2/. Suitable grasp-and, if needed, regrasp-configuration vectors of the manipulator are constructed by means of the correspondence of the WS with the CS. The generated trajectories for the manipulator will be fine-tuned by an emulation of the object movement in a collision-checking manner for the grided objects. The object collision may be attacked in the CS too.

PREPARING OF THE MAPPING INDEXATION

A manipulator configuration-vector CP is uniquely determined by a kinematic-geometric description of the robot and values for its joint variables $\mathscr{f}_i$, $i = 1, n$. The vector CP, CP = $(\mathscr{f}_1, \mathscr{f}_2, \ldots \mathscr{f}_n)$

defines a physical cover of grid points with the robot body. Let us perform a mental experiment to explain the idea of the indexation construction: In a very large matrix we index all potentially possible CP's in the rows and all grid points of the WS in the columns. We suppose, that a procedure is available for the computation of the physical covered GP's by a given robot configuration. If that procedure was running for all CP's, we have got the indexation of all $\mathcal{L}$ (GP)-sets of forbidden CP's for the GP columns.

Fortunately we can essentially reduce that point set system by means of
- subspace equivalencies and certain halfspace symmetries,
- epicyclic dependences for compriming of the $\mathcal{L}$-sets,
- a reduced grid description of the robot in the WS and
- the smoothing property of the overlying $\mathcal{L}$-sets.

Of course the rotation of the grasp around his own axis is not treated. For a 256 x 256 x 256 WS-grid a coarse evaluation gives a memory demand of $\sim$ 0.5 MB for a five-axes robot (ASEA-typ) and $\sim$ 30 MB for a six-axes robot (PUMA-typ).

The $\mathcal{L}$-set system is needed only on an external memory device. An additional cartesian degree of freedom DOF for a mobile affixment of the robot does not increase the memory demand. Keep in mind, that the generation of that indexation must be done only one time for a special robot-typ!

Now one can simple map any obstacle by means of the recorded indexation GP$\rightarrow \mathcal{L}$(GP). A compact obstacle is mapped onto a not necesserily connected forbidden zone FZ. The following figure is taken from /6/ and illustrates the high nonconformity of the map.

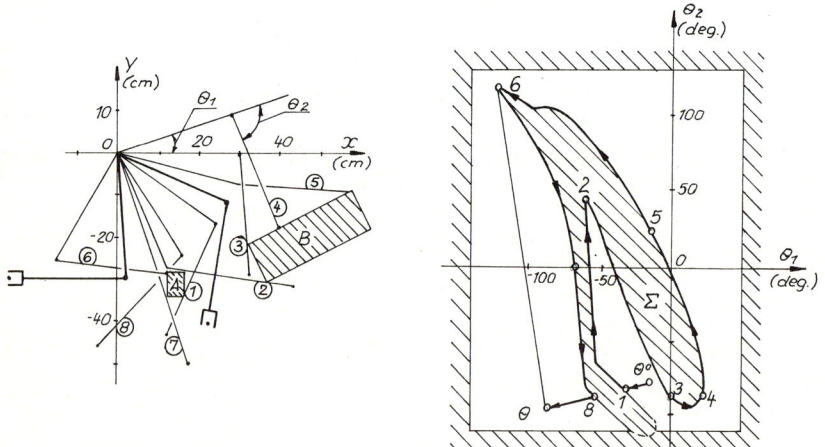

Figure 1
The work space of a 2-DOF manipulator (on the left) and the corresponding configuration space of its joint variables (on the right).

THE CONSTRUCTION OF THE FREE SPACE DESCRIPTION

Firstly we have to map the obstacles into the CS, recalling the $\mathcal{L}$-sets for all GP's which are covered from the obstacle surface. Simultaneously we envelope the incoming CP-vectors by a sequential clustering method /7/ in ellyptical or spherical volumes. The volume neighbourhood is analysed with a simple discrimination method: Any volume is discriminated against all others with a minimal set of linear discrimination functions /7/. If we describe each volume by its centre and the neighbourhood by an arc between the centres, we get a graph, whose connected subgraphs represent compact FZ's. For each such FZ-own subgraph we analyse the topological given cover with (n+1)-cliques (in the case of a n-dimensional space). We delete all edges, which are included in n different (n+1)-cliques and all vertices, which has been isolated by that erasing process. The resulting graph is a n-clique cover of the FZ margin (FZ-spanned subspaces are graph-theoretical recognized and handled). The resulting graph is a path-graph for obstacle by-passing. Now we have to complete the path-graph with edges between mutual visible vertices. We decompose therefore the free space in convex segments, e. g. piecewise -linear bounded segments, which are constructed by a discrimination method /7/ on the vertex set. The vertices, lying in the segment boundary, belong to a visibility clique. The path-graph is the intersection of all visibility cliques. It has to be constructed for a given robot in a stationary environment only one time.

THE PATH-FIND PROBLEM

Until now we have constructed
a) a hull-description of the free space and
b) a decomposition of the free space in convex segments.

Both free space descriptions are connected on the same reference-point sets. The path-find problem consists in a trajectory generation between the start and end configurations SC, EC of the robot through the free space.

We have
1. to determinate the segments, including SC and EC,
2. to accomplish a local path-graph extension between the vertix sets of those segments and SC, respectively EC,
3. to apply the A^*-algorithm, developing the path graph locally and beginning on both sides simultaneously and
4. to correct the trajectory by means of the geometric description of the volums , which are attached to the path covered vertices.

As A^* evaluation function we take the euclidian distance of the co-ordinate-transformed vertices of the path-graph in the WS. In this way we get the shortest collision-free object trajectory, which is performed by a simultaneously movement of all participated joints.

GENERATION OF GRASP AND REGRASP VECTORS

A path-finding is impossible, if SC and EC lie I) not in the free space or II) in an unconnected free space. In this case we have to generate a suitable SC/EC pair. Problem I) is resolvable, if among the machanical possible grasp- and put-frames in the WS there are such ones, which leads by their inverse coordinate transformation to SC and EC's in the free space, i. e. one has to generate mechanical allowed grasp frames and to test the correspondent CP's in the CS. For the generation process we use knowledge over the configuration of the free space in the CS. In case that the problem II) is not resolvable in such way, we ask for a suitable regrasp operation, i. e. more precisely, we ask for a suitable grasp position with at least two orientations, which leads to CP's in connected zones of the free space. An analogous problem is given, if the manipulator cannot move an object trough a bottle-neck between free zones.

TREATMENT OF OBJECT COLLISION IN THE CONFIGURATION SPACE

In our approach to off-line programming we can treat the obstacle avoidance for the robot arm in the CS and the collision of the moved object by emulation in the WS. We have two possibilities for a consideration of the object collision in the CS directly. The first one consist in a simple growing on ε of the physical volume of the robot body for the GP$\rightarrow\mathcal{L}$(GP) indexation. Then a security distance of ε is garanted for the manipulator. This imply an remaining security distance of $\varepsilon/2$ for an object with a radius of $\varepsilon/2$ too. The second one is based on a direct mapping of the cross-section of the grasped object in gripper direction into the CS by a virtual movement of the manipulator around the object. If the virtual drive-around operation can be performed by using only the last but ones two joints (e. g. with a PUMA), we get a CP independent object map in the $\mathcal{F}_4/\mathcal{F}_5$ subspace. Now we can directly move this two-dimensional image how a solid disk, which is centered by CP through the CS. The generation of collision-free trajectories is reduced to the upper one by such a growing of the forbidden zones, that the CP disk is shrinked to a point again.

REFERENCES

/1/ Dillmann, R., A Graphical Emulation System for Robot Design and Program Testing, Proc. ISIR 83, 7.1 - 7.15.

/2/ Nilsson, N. J., Principles of Artificial Intelligence (Springer, Berlin-Heidelberg-New York, 1982).

/3/ Lozano-Perez, T., Spatial Planning: A Configuration Space Approach, IEEE on Computers, vol. C-32 (1983), 108-119.

/4/ Brooks, R. A., Solving Find-Path Problem by Good Representation of Free Space, IEEE SMC-13 (1983), 190-197

/5/ Gouzenez, L., Generation of Collision-Free Trajectories for Mobile and Manipulator Robots, Proc. ISIR, Leningrad (1983), vol. II

/6/ Petrov, A. A. and Sirota, I. M., Control of a Robot-Manipulator with Obstacle Avoidance under Little Information about the Environment, Proc. IFAC VIII, Kyoto (1981), XIV-54-XIV-59.

/7/ Unger, S., Wysotzki, F., Lernfähige Klassifizierungssysteme (Akademie-Verlag, Berlin, 1981)

AUTOMATIC GENERATION OF ASSEMBLY SEQUENCES

Winfried Jentsch
Frieder Kaden

Central Institute for Cybernetics and Information Processes
AdW der DDR
DDR - 1086 Berlin
Kurstr. 33

High-level planning of assembling automation by robot should include the automatic computation of assembling sequences. In our approach we generate dismounting sequences for a geometrical described assembly, which is transformed into the so-called connection graph and blocking graph. Their analysis leads to a tree-ordered subassembly partition and to the set of all mechanical allowed assembling sequences.

INTRODUCTION

Assembling by robot is a problem that can be divided into several levels of automatic planning. High-level planning concerns the computation of a principal sequence of assembling. In the next levels this sequence has to be compiled by concrete actions the robot system is able to perform. The parts of the assembly are supposed to be described in a geometrical form /1/. Their positions in the desired assembly are given by transformations or geometrical relations /4/. Our aim is to compute a assembling sequence of the desired state from the given parts. A traditional method for this problem is presented in /5/. The basic idea of our approach is to find the assembling sequence by inverting sequences if dismounting according to backward chaining in problem solving.

THE CONNECTION GRAPH

Basing on a geometrical description of the assembly we define the so-called connection graph G, which describes all touches of parts of the assembly. The vertex set V of the connection graph G is the set of all parts. For graph-theoretic terminology not presented here see /2/. Two parts A and B are adjacent in G iff they touch each other. The type of contact is expressed by a label of the edge between A and B. We distinguish three types of touch, which are relevant to the desired applications restricted to translational dismounting only. The first relation $A \bar{n} B$ expresses that body A and body B touch each other so that at least one body has a tangent plane in a point of contact. The normal vector $\bar{n}$ of this plane is directed from A to B. The relation $A \bar{n} B$ corresponds to a directed edge (arc) from A to B in G. If the relations $A \bar{n} B$ and $B \bar{n} A$ hold, we use an undirected edge in $\underline{G}$. In order to express that body A cannot be moved in direction $\bar{a}$ without moving body B we use the notation $A l\bar{a} B$. Note that $A \bar{n} B$ implies $A l\bar{a} B$ for all directions $\bar{a}$ with $\bar{a} \cdot \bar{n} > 0$.

We use the notation $A c\bar{a} B$ to express that the bodies A and B touch each other in a regular cylindrical surface with axis $\bar{a}$ so that one body cannot be moved in a direction different from $\bar{a}$ and $-\bar{a}$ without moving the other one. This relation can be compared with the fits-relation of RAPT /4/.

The following list contains some implications between the relations defined above.

(1) $A \bar{n} B \Leftrightarrow B -\bar{n} A$ (4) $A c\bar{a} B \Leftrightarrow A c-\bar{a} B$
(2) $A l\bar{a} B \Leftrightarrow B l-\bar{a} A$ (5) $A \bar{n} B \wedge \bar{n} \cdot \bar{a} > 0 \Rightarrow A l\bar{a} B$
(3) $A c\bar{a} B \Leftrightarrow B c\bar{a} A$ (6) $A c\bar{a} B \wedge \bar{n} \cdot \bar{a} = 0 \Rightarrow A \bar{n} B$

Let x, y, and z be the unit vectors of a fixed coordinate system. For a detail of an assembly we construct the connection graph G', which is shown in figure 1. An edge of the connection graph (see edge D y⁻ F of graph G') is indicated by a minus sign in order to express that this edge can be removed, e. g. by elastic or rotational transformations.

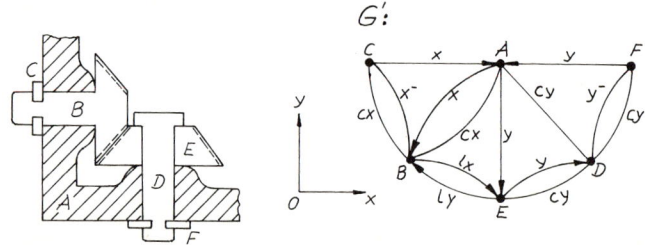

Figure 1
A two-dimensional subassembly

Figure 2 shows a three-dimensional problem of puzzle mathematics. It is difficult to construct the assembly when its parts are given. This problem can easily be solved by dismounting the goal state and inverting this sequence.

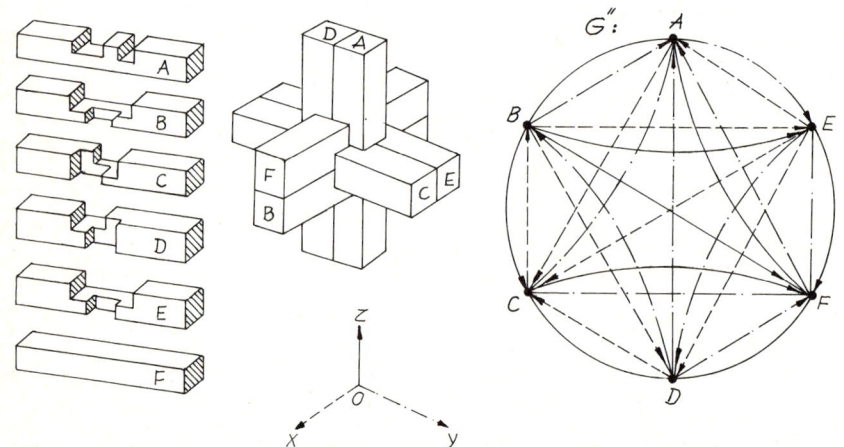

Figure 2
A three-dimensional problem of assembling.

In the next chapter a graph-theoretic method of finding dismounting sequences is presented.

DISMOUNTING SEQUENCES FOR SUBASSEMBLIES

A body A of a (sub-)assembly is fixed (in notation fix A) if it cannot be moved in any direction without moving another object, i.e.

(7) fix A $\Leftrightarrow$ $\forall a$ $\exists B$: A l$\bar{a}$ B.

The following implications contain sufficient conditions for a body to be fixed.

(8) A c$\bar{a}$ B $\wedge$ A l$\bar{a}$ C $\wedge$ D l$\bar{a}$ A $\Rightarrow$ fix A
(9) A c$\bar{a}$ B $\wedge$ A c$\bar{n}$ C $\wedge$ $\bar{a}$x$\bar{n}$ $\neq$ $\bar{0}$ $\Rightarrow$ fix A
(10) B $\bar{a}$ A $\bar{a}$ C $\wedge$ D $\bar{n}$ A $\bar{n}$ E $\wedge$ F $\bar{m}$ A $\bar{m}$ H $\wedge$ [$\bar{a}$ $\bar{n}$ $\bar{m}$] $\neq$ 0 $\Rightarrow$ fix A

Now we formulate two operations in order to produce dismounting sequences from the connection graph.
I) An edge of the connection graph can be removed if it is indicated by a minus sign.
II) A vertex of the connection graph can be removed if the corresponding body is not fixed.

Repeating these two steps up to one-point graphs we find the set of all potential sequences of dismounting. If it is impossible to obtain a one-point graph, the corresponding assembling problem is unsolvable. There might be dismounting sequences, which cannot be inverted to practical assembling sequences (forbidden dismounting sequences) because of mechanical or robot-specific impossibilities. Therefore we have to study the assembly as a whole.

DISMOUNTING SEQUENCES FOR ASSEMBLIES

Our aim is to generate all allowed dismounting sequences of an assembly. We have to find a partition into subassemblies and details that can be solved with the method described above. In a sequence of three steps we transform the connection graph to a blocking graph and the dismounting tree. In the first step we comprime the connection graph by means of the following operations:

a) replace C c$\bar{a}$ A l$\bar{a}$ B c$\bar{a}$ C, B c$\bar{a}$ A l$\bar{a}$ B, C c$\bar{a}$ A $\bar{n}$ B c$\bar{b}$ D and D c$\bar{d}$ B c$\bar{a}$ A c$\bar{d}$ D ($\bar{a}$x$\bar{d}$ $\neq$ $\bar{0}$) by A ag B

b) reduce vertices of degree two (homeomorphic reduction)

In the second step we search for the set L of all elementary circuits of the comprimed connection graph. We apply a graph-theoretic method /6/ or the A^{*}-algorithm /3/ with an evaluation function given by the euclidian distances of points of contact. In the third step we analyse each circuit C for the blocking-input I(C) and the blocking-output O(C). A blocking transmission C $\rightarrow$ C' holds for C, C' $\in$ L iff the sets I(C') and O(C) are not disjoint. The intersection analysis of L leads to a tree of blocking transmission. This blocking graph describes the decomposition of the whole assembly in subassemblies. A subassembly is mechanical closed, if the blocking transmission between C and C' is based on a vertex u with u = C$\cap$C'. The dismounting sequences are fitted together by means of the blocking graph. We cannot give a more detailed description here.

The abstraction of the concrete geometry by the connection graph and his stepwise transformation leads to a generalized description of a certain class of functional analogous assemblies. With the help of that description we can infer impossibilities of dismounting and possibilities for reduction or exchange of certain assembly details. This demonstrates the flexibility of our approach.

Further investigation should concern e. g. rotational assembly details.

REFERENCES

/1/ Binford, T. O., Visual perception by computer, IEEE Conf. Systems and Control, Miami (December 1971).

/2/ Harary, F., Graph Theory (Addison-Wesley Publishing Company, Reading-Menlo Park-London-Don Mills, 1969).

/3/ Hart, P. E., Nilsson, N. J., Raphael, B., A formal basis for the heuristic determination of minimum cost paths, IEEE Trans. Syst, Science and Cybernetics, SSC-4 (1968) 100-107.

/4/ Popplestone, R. J., Ambler, A. P., A language for specifying robot manipulations. DAI Research Paper No. 161, Dept. of Artificial Intelligence, Univ. of Edinburgh (September 1981).

/5/ Sacerdoti, E. D., Planning in a hierarchy of abstraction spaces, Artificial Intelligence 5 (1974) 115-135.

/6/ Tiernan, J., An efficient search algorithm to find the elementary circuits of a graph. Comm. ACM 13 (1970) 722-726.

THE ATNL-BASED MACROPROCESSOR - A SOFTWARE TOOL
OF COMMUNICATION MODULES IMPLEMENTATION

Vladimir F. Khoroshevsky

Computer Centre Academy of Sciences
of the USSR, Moscow
U.S.S.R.

The design of the practically useful
modules of man-machine communication
demands the implementation of special
discourse schemes. In the presented
paper the macroprocessor based on the
augmented transition network language
ATNL-2.0 is described and questions of
the dialogue schemes implementation
are discussed.

INTRODUCTION

The Augmented Transition Networks (ATN) have been actively used for the linguistic processors (LP) design for about ten years [1 ÷ 3].The main advantage of the ATN-approach is its "meta-levelness" for the description of the communication language.That is why it allows different theoretical models of the communication and LPs to be implemented by it.Several versions of the linguistic knowledge representation languages based on the ATN-method and called ATNL have been developed and implemented in the USSR [4,5].

Practical use of the ATNL has made evident that its basic tools are oriented to the natural language (NL) analyzers and generators programming.But nowadays it has become clear,that the design of the practically useful modules of the communication demands the implementation of special discourse schemes.This discourse description is based on the use of the non-simple sequences of ATNL-instructions.

PRELIMINARY REMARKS

In the present paper we shall describe the macroprocessor based on the ATNL-2.0 language and discuss the questions of the dialogue schemes implementation.The basic language,macrolanguage and the questions of the implementation of these tools are described in accordance with macroprocessor design [6].

BASIC LANGUAGE

Our macroprocessor (MATN) is a special macroprocessor. It actively uses the ATNL-2.0 [5] orientation.So, for the sake of further discussion, let us give some remarks about this language.

Generally, the ATNL-2.0 language is oriented on the LP mechanization design.All the knowledge necessary for the NL-communication module implementation are described in form of the ATNL-program. It includes four divisions: <u>module-division</u> (Its main purpose is describing the top-down technology of the LP design); <u>define-division</u>, in which the definition of the standard tools of the ATNL-compositions and the description of the nondefinite ATNL-tools are comprised; <u>vocabulary-division</u> (This division consists of the description of the structures used in the LP units and the description of all vocables and recommendations for its reflection on different types of memories); net-division (This last division comprises the definition of the analysis/synthesis text's net).

MACROLANGUAGE

As any practically useful macroprocessor MATN provides the text building in the basic language ATNL-2.0 by using the macrodeclaration from MATNL-program and macrolibraries.So, we need certain tools of identification of macrolibraries and macros definition. As it follows from the above overview of the ATNL-2.0,it is natural to extend this language by the new types of MACRO and MCLIB in the linkage section and macros definitions in the external development section.For these purposes the following declarations are used:

    external-object-description   ‖ IS-EXTRN ‖.
        type-group {, type-group}   ‖ ARE-EXTRN ‖

    type-group
        object-name {, object-name} WITH-TYPE object-type,
where object-name and object-type in addition to [5] may be macros or macrolibrary name and,respectively, MACRO or MCLIB.

    ATNL-external-development-section
        EXDEV-SECTION. ‖macros-description   ‖.
                                ‖other-language-interface-description‖

    macros-description
        macros {; macros}

    macros
        MACRO prototype MCDEF macroexpansion MEND

It is convenient to go through the further description of the macrolanguage in such a way: common characteristic,prototype syntax, conditional generation tools and implementation.At the end we shall discuss an example of the discourse description with MATNL.

As already mentioned, our main task is to develop simple,suitable and,at the same time, powerful macrotools for the problem domain specialists.But these requirements made evident the necessity of: (1) the simple and flexible tools of macrodeclarations; (2) good macrocompile-time diagnostics on the user level.

In our approach we use the idea of the syntactic macros of Leavenworth [7],whose declaration is connected with the description of the macrocall syntax on the prototype level and macros semantics on the macroexpansion level.It is possible to use any nesting level macros and powerful conditional generation tools in the MATNL.

The main declarative construction of MATNL is macros and procedural - macrocall.The last may be used not only in the vocab. and net-division, but also in the macrodeclarations.Prototypes have very simple syntax. It is based on the use of the delimiters which are defined by the user.But in this case the special marks of the macronames and parameter's values are necessary.The macroname in MATNL may be any sequence of the letters and/or digits with the special first symbol @ .The parameter may be a symbol of the variable (in this case the first symbol is &) or literal (then we use quotes).

So,we have the following syntax definitions:
    prototype
        [parameter-label]   macro-name   [{parameter}]

<u>parameter-label</u>
    & name

<u>macro-name</u>
    @ name

<u>parameter</u>
        delimiter {delimiter}   parameter-value

<u>parameter-value</u>
‖ &name ‖
‖ text ‖

Delimiter - this is any sequence of signs from the available alphabet. We can use the own signs of the macrolanguage (usual, square and angle brackets and slash) in the prototype descriptions. If there is need of these signs in the MATNL-program, we must use double quote in front of such signs. Own signs of MATNL have the following semantics: (1) construction in the usual brackets is repeated; (2) construction in the square brackets is facultative; (3) one of the elements of the construction in the angle brackets must be present (slash is the delimiter of the elements). Thus, we can describe prototypes with the variant parameters number, with facultative parameters and we can use alternative delimiters. In this way we can obtain natural extension of the basic language ATNL-2.0.

It is known that the powerfulness of the macrolanguage is connected with the available conditional generation tools. In the MATNL we use the symbols of the generation time and system macroses which define the values of the generation time, conditional statements and output statement.

Now we shall describe these tools with the use of the prototypes definition tools, which were mentioned above. We use system macros @ LET with the prototype

    @ LET   & VAR = & VAL (, & VAR = & VAL)

for the values definition in the MATNL. The & VAL-parameter is the name of the local variable in the current macroexpansion. The & VAL-parameter may be integer or text. It is possible to receive the first type of the & VAL-parameters by the composition of the integer & add ("+") and/or mult("*") operators. The text values are received by the use of the literals and/or concatenation (".") operator. We can use LET-macroses in the macroexpansions only.

The symbols of the generation time are prescribed in MATNL to the element prototype references and generation time labels determination. Element prototype pointer is marked as &&P&VAL, and generation time label - && L&VAL.

System macroses of the GOTO-type, IF-type and EXIT-type are the conditional statements of the generation time. They have the following prototypes:

    @ GOTO   & LAB ;
    @ IF & COND   THEN & LAB [ELSE & LAB];
    @ EXIT

The & LAB-parameter must be the generation time label, and the & COND-parameter - the composition of the generation time variables and their values being connected by the " $<$ ", " $\leq$ ", " $=$ ", " $\geq$ ", " $>$ " relations.

There is a single macros of the output in the MATNL.Its prototype is

@ NOTE &TEXT (,&TEXT)

The &TEXT-parameter may be the generation time variable or literal.

It is necessary to note that all generation time macroses are performed on the macroexpansion stage and are located on the current level of this macroexpansion.

IMPLEMENTATION

Up to now we have discussed the main tools of the macrolanguage MATNL.It is clear that macroprocessors of this language require recursive processing and powerful tools of symbol manipulation.We use here the metalanguage REFAL, which is the universal macrogenerator with the nonfixed input and output languages.

AN EXAMPLE

In conclusion let us exemplify the MATNL-language.Let us assume that we design the communication module which supports the discourse scheme shown in Figure 1.

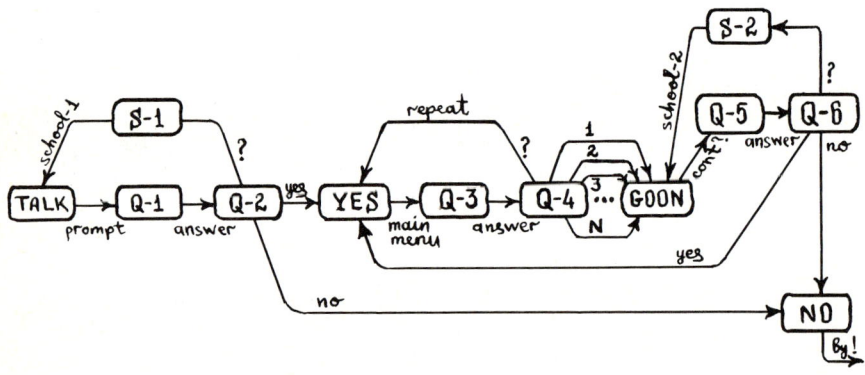

Figure 1.

Discourse scheme with the "menu"-type basic elements.

It is obvious that such a scheme may be described in the basic language ATNL-2.0. But the latter description will be more complicated than the macrodescription.

As it follows from the analysis of the discourse scheme (Fig.1), its main element is menu. Thus, we describe the macroarc @ MENU with the next macrodeclaration:

```
                MACRO
  &BEG    @MENU         TITLE= &TTL (,&TTL);
                        CASE   &RG:= &PROMPT  OF
                          &P-COND  : "( &ACT (; &ACT ) ")
                         (&P-COND  : "( &ACT (; &ACT ) ") );
                        [ ON-ERROR  "( &ACT (; &ACT ) ");]
                        NEXT = &T-ACT
```

```
                MCDEF
                @LET    N=3, K=100, LAB=$;
  &BEG          TST     T       PUT(&&PN);
  &&L1          @LET    N = N + 1;
                @IF     &&PN = 'CASE'       THEN    &&L2;
                @IF     &&PN = ';'          THEN    &&L1;
                @IF     &&PN = ','          THEN    &&L1;
                                          PUT(&&PN); @GOTO &&L1;
  &&L2          JUMP    LAB.K
  LAB.K         TST     T       PUT(&PROMPT);  &RG := GET;
                @LET    K = K + 1, N = N + 5;
  &&L7          JUMP    LAB.K
                @IF     &&PN = 'ON-ERROR'   THEN    &&L3;
                @IF     &&PN = 'NEXT'       THEN    &&L4;
  .................................................................
  &&L4          @LET    N = N + 2;
  LAB.K         TST     T       &&PN
                MEND
```

If we put such a macrodeclaration in the external development section we can write the next macroprogram of the communication block:

```
  TALK   @MENU    TITLE = 'invitation' ;
                  CASE  WORD := 'prompt' OF
                     WORD = 'yes'  :  (UP.WORD)
                     WORD = 'no'   :  (UP.WORD;  JUMP  NO);
                     ON-ERROR  ( PUT( 'strange-answer' );
                                      UP.WORD;  JUMP  Q-1 );
                     NEXT = JUMP YES
  YES    @MENU    TITLE = 'title-of-the-main-menu' ,
                             'string-1' , 'string-2' , ... ;
                  CASE  ANSWER := 'your-choise?' OF
                     ANSWER = 1 : ( UP.ANSWER; call  P-1 )
                     ANSWER = 2 : ( UP.ANSWER; call  P-2 )
                     .........................................
                     T : ( PUT ( 'again-ask' );
                                      UP.ANSWER;  JUMP  YES );
                     NEXT = JUMP GOON
  GOON   @MENU    TITLE = 'let us go on?' ;
                  CASE  SENT := '(yes, no)?' OF
                     SENT = 'yes' : ( UP.SENT;  JUMP  YES )
                     SENT = 'no'  : ( UP.SENT )
                     ON-ERROR  ( PUT('strange-answer' );
                                      UP.SENT;  JUMP  Q-2 );
                     NEXT = JUMP NO
  Q-1          TST    T    PUT( 'school-1' );    JUMP    TALK
  Q-2          TST    T    PUT( 'school-2' );    JUMP    GOON
  NO           POP         PUT( 'by!' );         T
```

Due to the space-limits of the paper the macroexpansion will not be exemplified here, but it is clear that our approach is more convenient to the discourse implementation.

CONCLUSION

This paper presents a special macroprocessor MATN, based on the language ATNL-2.0. In our opinion the use of the macrolanguage discussed above, is useful for intelligent man-machine communication modules design and implementation. Nowadays the software of the macroprocessor is under development and its instrumental base is the complex of the Problem-Oriented-Software-Of-High-level-communication (POSOH) design [8].

REFERENCES:

[1] Woods,W., Transition network grammer for natural language analysis, CACM vol.13,No.10 (1970) 591-606.

[2] Woods,E.,Cascaded ATN grammars, American Jrnl.of Comp.Linguistics vol.6 No.1 (1980) 372-386.

[3] Winograd,T., Language as a Cognitive Process, vol.1:Syntax (Addison-Wesley Publishing Company,1983).

[4] Khoroshevsky,V.F.,ATNL - jazik predstavlenia lingvisticheskih znanie v estestvennojazikovih sistemah, in: Kuzin,L.T. (ed.), Voprosi kibernetiki,55 (Sov.Radio,Moskva,1979) (In Russian).

[5] Khoroshevsky,V.F., ATNL-machine - Software and Hardware, Proc.of 1 Symp. IFAC and IFIP on AI, Leningrad, USSR, 4 - 6 october (1983)

[6] Brown,P.J., Using a macroprocessor to Aid Software Implementation, Computer J., vol.12 (1969) 326-331.

[7] Leavenworth,B.M., Syntax Macros on Extended Translation, CACM, vol.9 (1966) 790-793.

[8] Khoroshevsky,V.F., Development of the NL-communication systems on the base of the DBMS-software, Proc. II Int.Conf. "Artificial Intelligence and Information-Control Systems of Robots", Smolenice, Bratislava, Czechoslovakia, 18-22 oct. (1982).

ON THE SYNTHESIS OF IMAGE MATCHING ALGORITHMS

Hoang Kiem [+)]   G. Podhájecký [++)]

[+)] Basical Laboratory on the Artificial Intelligence, Institute of Technical Cybernetics, Bratislava; Institute of Informatics and Cybernetics - Hanoi
[++)] Institute of Technical Cybernetics - Bratislava

> In order to improve the efficiency of image matching, a lot of matching schemes have been proposed, based on various approaches. Here we discuss the efficient synthesis of algorithms for two types of most important image matching problems: the location problem and the identification problem. This research is toward the use of hierarchical schemes and those that use the combination of equivalent recognition algorithms.

I. Analysis and Synthesis of algorithms for the location problem.
The location problem or scene matching is: given a template of a scene, determine the location of this template in another scene. The method used to solve this problem, in its simplest form, is called template matching with the basic correlator, the statistical correlator (1,2). Later, some modifications using invariant moments for scene matching have been developed to solve the general problem involving geometrical and sensor variations (3,4).

Since a template of size (MxM) can be shifted into $(N-M+1)^2$ possible positions in an (NxN) image, the number of correlations can be extremely large.

The tendency in the current research is toward the use of hierarchical techniques for decreasing the number of search positions. In particular, coarse-fine techniques are logarithmically efficient and reduce the number of search positions to $K \cdot \log(N-M+1)^2$, where K is a constant (4,5,6).

However, at each level of search, the number of computations needed to obtain the beatures for scene matching (for example, invariant moments) can be still large. In our method, a synthesis using hierarchical technique and detection for decreasing the computation time at each shift position has been proposed:
- At first, a structured set of pictures at different resolution is defined. The level-K scene is reduced to a level-(K-1) scene with the agglomerative rule, for example, as follows:

$$f_{K-1}(i,j) = \frac{1}{4} \; f_K(2i,2j) + f_K(2i,2j+1) + f_K(2i+1,2j) + f_K(2i+1,2j+1)$$

where, $f_K(i,j)$ - the gray-scale of pixel (i,j) at level - K.
Note that, at the level K, number of possible test locations is $[(N-M+1) / (2^K+1)]^2$ and at level (K-1), only the locations selected in level K needed to be tested.

where ϕ' — the computational complexity of the detection at each location
ϕ — the computational complexity of the main - matching rule at each location
p — the probability of matching by the detection.

Theorical analyses and simulations with ζ - Test and ρ - Test in scene - matching by invariant moments indicated that a saving of computation time as weel as a high degree of precision in locating a region is possible.

II. Analysis and Synthesis of algorithms for the identification problem.

The identification problem or scene recognition is: identifying a pattern in a given position as being one of a given set of patterns. The basic recognition models may be used to solve this problem (7). Previously we have introduced a new description of recognition algorithms, indicating that almost all recognition algorithm are either M-algorithms or extr-algorithms. (8,9).

Here, we have proposed a synthesis system for scene recognition using a combination of equivalent recognition algorithms. The theoretical basis of this synthesis is based on the following results (9).

Theorem 1: With the condition f being a monotonic function of R and distribution of R being normal or exponential, the following scheme is correct:

$$\begin{array}{ccc} M_R \text{ - algorithm} & \xrightarrow{\text{prob}} & M_{f(R)} \text{ - algorithm} \\ \Big\downarrow \text{prob} & & \Big\downarrow \text{prob} \\ \text{Extr}_R \text{ - algorithm} & \sim & \text{Extr}_{f(R)} \text{ - algorithm} \end{array}$$

where, $A \sim B$ denote the equivalence of algorithm A and B

$A \overset{\text{prob}}{\sim} B$ denote the probable equivalence of algorithm A and B.

Theorem 2: The error probability of the synthesis system of N probable equivalent recognition algorithm using the majority decision rule values:

$$\varepsilon_S \leq \sum_{k > \lfloor N/2 \rfloor}^{N} C_N^k \cdot \varepsilon^k$$

where, ε_S — the error probability of the synthesis system
ε — the error probability of each recognition algorithm in the synthesis system.

In practice, we have designed a synthesis of the algorithms based on the methods: Nearest Neighbour, Potential function, Calculation of valuation and K-means. Some of them are modified to suit the concrete situations. The results in the experiments also have pro-

- A matching rule to guide the search from level K-1 to level K, must also be defined. In the scene matching with invariant moments, this rule is the moment correlation which is costly in computation, due to the calculations needed to obtain the invariant features. But it can be used to great advantage at the low resolution level at which other methods are not possible. Here, we use an approach as follows: Instead of matching each template of scene at every location, the templates are partitioned into "informative" and "irrelevant" templates by some simple test. Elimination of mismatching locations and termination of computation can take place at each level of test based on this partition.

In practice, we have used a detection that combined two simple tests matching the scene with the invariant moments:
 1. Test based on measure of the similarity of two gray-level distributions (γ - Test).
 2. Test based on the correlation coefficient of the joint distributions (ρ - Test). The γ, and ρ measures are computed for each location. If both γ, ρ are smaller than selected threshold, this location is rejected.

- Thus, let N_k^i be a set of test locations (u,v) at search level K, with a matching rule R_k^i such that

$$N_k^i = \left\{ (u,v) \mid R_k^i(u,v) \geq \theta_k^i, \quad 1 \leq u,v \leq M \right\}$$

where θ_k^i is the threshold selected to be used at search level K, R_k^i is some matching rule at test location (u,v), M^2 is the number of picture elements in the template. We can divide R_k^i into the preliminary rule (detection by simple tests) and the main rule (for example, the moment correlation rule).

let $N_k := \bigcap_i N_k^i$, For a search region of size NxN, an $(2N-2M+1)^2$ - matrix G_{K-1} was generated by

$$G_{K-1}(2i,2j) = \begin{cases} 1 & \text{if } (i,j) \in N_k \\ 0 & \text{if } (i,j) \bar{\in} N_k \end{cases}$$

All other entries of G_{K-1}, are set to zero. Tests are to be performed at the test locations for $G_{K-1}(u,v) = 1$. The search continues until one of two conditions is encountered:

 1. At search level L=n, $G_n(u,v)=1$ for one value of (u,v) location (u,v) is declared the matched location.

 2. At the level l=0, there exist several locations (u,v) such that $G_0(u,v)=1$. Select the location with the highest correlation with the invariant moments.

The condition for saving the computation time using this synthesis is following:

$$\phi' < \phi.(1 - p)$$

ved the efficacy of this synthesis.

We have presented the efficiency synthesis of algorithms for scene matching and image recognition. This approach can be developed in order to improve the efficiency of very large scale image matching and recognition.

REFERENCES:

1   Hall, E., Computer image processing and recognition. Academic Press.(1979) 468-554.

2   Rosenfeld, A., Image Pattern Recognition. Proceedings IEEE T-69, No 5/1981, 120-133.

3   Wong, Y., et al., Scene Matching with Invariant Moments. Comput-Graphics Image Process. 8. (1978) 16-24.

4   Ranade, S. at al., Shape approximation using quadtree. Pattern Recognition Vol. 15, No 1 (1982) 31-40.

5   Wong, Y. et al., Sequential hierarchical scene matching IEEE Transactions on Computers 27, (1978) 359-366.

6   Kanderbrug, G., Coarse-fine template matching. IEEE Trans-on Systems-Man-Cybernetics 7 (1977) 104-107.

7   Bach Hung Khang, Hoang Kiem., On the automatic generation System of efficient pattern recognition procedures and its applications. Proceedings Conference IFIF - Hanoi 1-1983.

8   Bach Hung Khang, Hoang Kiem., Classification of the problems of pattern recognition and the correctness of certain families of recognition algorithms. Preprint No 2 (1982). Institute of Informatics and Cybernetics - Hanoi.

9   Hoang Kiem., Combination of equivalent recognition algorithms research report No 9 (1983) Institute of Technical Cybernetics Bratislava.

OFF-LINE PROGRAMMING FOR ROBOT PAINTERS

Alexandr Klein

Computer and Automation Institute
Hungarian Academy of Sciences
Budapest, Hungary

Usual teach-in methods of robot painters programming depend on human factors and thus have some disadvantages (expensive "teaching" of robots, high paint losses etc.). This is why a new approach based on off-line programming is suggested and demonstrated on the example of coating a planar surface having holes in it. The coating thickness is visualized on a colour display and the operator can modify the parameters of spraying to obtain optimal coating quality. Robot joint angles as functions of the time are calculated from the resulted spraying gun trajectory, thus the optimal painting strategy can be realized for the given type of robot.

BASIC DEFINITIONS

Let the surface to be painted be an $L_1 \times L_2$ planar rectangle with possible rectangular holes in it. The coating thickness must be within the limits $h \pm \Delta h$ (drying up isn't taken into account). The spraying gun sprays $Q[m^3]$ of paint per second. It is assumed that paint forms a cone (Figure 1). To the unit square of the surface $q\ m^3/(m^2 \ast s)$ of paint is delivered per one second. It is obvious that $q = q(R, \phi)$, where R is the distance of spraying.

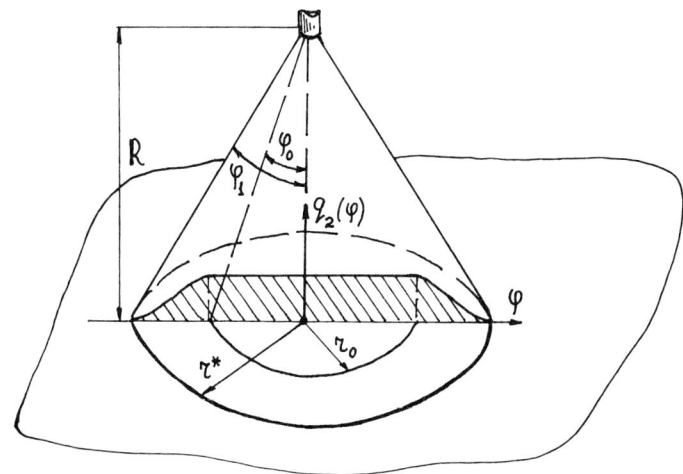

Fig.1 The Paint Cone and the $q_2(\phi)$ Function

We assume that
$$q(R, \phi) = q_1(R) \cdot q_2(\phi) \tag{1}$$
where $0 \leq q_2(\phi) \leq 1$.

The essential part of the task is the definition of the shape of function $q_2(\phi)$. Usually, if a perpendicular cross-section of the spraying cone is taken at some distance R from its peak, then paint distribution in such an intersecting circle is the following: within a certain inner circle the coating thickness is uniform and then it decreases outwards irregularly [1,2].

Let the radius of the circular section be $r^* = R \cdot \tan \phi_1$. We suppose that the decreasing of the function $q_2(\phi)$ is determined, namely it is sinusoidal, as it is shown is Figure 1.

Knowing the value of Q we can obtain the expression for $q^* = q(R)$ with ϕ = const:

$$Q = \int_0^{r^*} q(R,\phi) \cdot 2\pi r dr = 2\pi q^* \int_0^{\phi_1} R \tan\phi \cdot q_2(\phi) \frac{R}{\cos^2\phi} d\phi = 2\pi R^2 \cdot q^* \int_0^{\phi_1} \frac{q_2(\phi)\sin\phi}{\cos^3\phi} d\phi, \tag{2}$$

where $dr = R d\phi/\cos^2\phi$, $r^* = R \cdot \tan\phi_1$.

Hence, $q^* = C(\phi)/R^2$, i.e. paint thickness is inversely proportional to the distance of spraying R.

SPRAYING GUN TRAJECTORY AND COATING THICKNESS

Let us consider a simple painting strategy for the surface $L_1 \times L_2$ [3]. When the time t = 0, then the paint circle on the surface starting from the A position (Figure 2) moves with the constant speed v to the B position, where it stops and then moves rapidly to the C position, neighbouring with B, and so on.

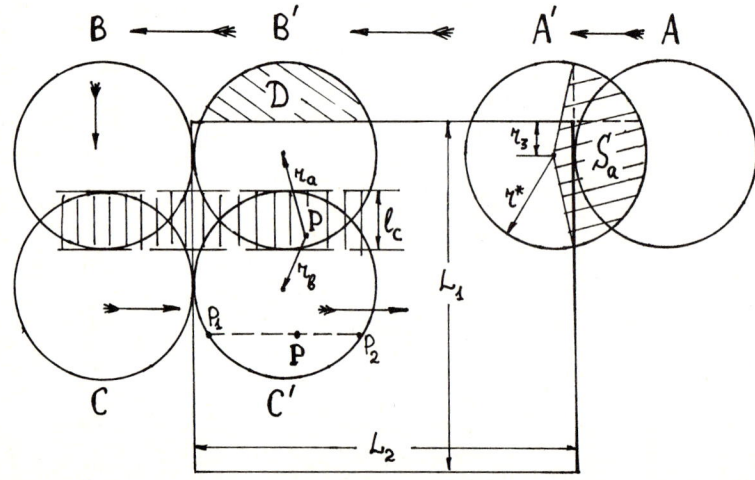

Fig.2. Motion of the Paint Circle on the Surface

Paint distribution within the paint circle is uneven. When the circle moves on the surface, its track is a stripe and on the central line of this stripe there will be much more paint than on a line close to its border. This is why paint circles must overlap. The segment of overlapping is shown in Figure 2, its width is $l_c = r^* - r_3$.

Let us find the thickness of coating H in some point P of the paint circle. The maximal time of paint delivered to a given point of the surface is $t_o = 2r^*/v$, if $v = $ const. Then

$$H = t_o \int_{p_1}^{p_2} q(R,\phi) d\phi = t_o q^* \int_{p_1}^{p_2} q_2(\phi) d\phi \qquad (3)$$

where p_1 and p_2 are the border points of the paint circle (see Figure 2).

When the point P in which we calculate the coating thickness is in the overlapping zone of paint tracks, then $H = H(r_a) + H(r_b)$, where $H(R_a)$ and $H(r_b)$ are calculated depending on the position of the point P within each of the two circles (see Figure 2). The value of H must satisfy the evident condition $h - \Delta h \leq H \leq h + \Delta h$.

THE QUALITY CRITERIA.

Three quality criteria are suggested.

1. Specific paint consumption (including losses) F [m³/m²].
2. Specific paint loss L [m³/m²].
3. Efficiency coefficient $\eta = (F-L)/F$.

To calculate F we assume that the number of passages of the paint circle from one edge of the surface to another edge is a whole number. Then

$$F = N.Q.T / (L_1.L_2) \qquad (4)$$

where T is the time needed for one passage of the paint circle.

Now let us see the calculation of losses.

While the paint circle is moving along the edge of the stripe, i.e. twice, the segment D is lost under the time T (see Figure 2). The amount of paint in the segment D is:

$$S = \int_{-\alpha}^{\alpha} \int_{\phi_3}^{\phi_1} q^* \frac{q_2(\phi).R\sin\phi}{\cos^3\phi} d\phi\, d\alpha \approx 2Rq^*\alpha_0 \int_{\phi_3}^{\phi_1} q_2(\phi).\phi\, d\phi. \qquad (5)$$

where $\phi_3 = \tan^{-1}(r_3/R)$, see Figure 2.

Let us consider the paint losses from the moment $t = 0$ (the whole paint is sprayed to the air) till the moment t_o when the whole circle is already on the surface. For the time t the circle moves to the distance $l = vt$, and the loss L is:

$$L(t) = \int_0^t dL(t) = \int_0^t S_a(t).q(R,\phi) dt \qquad (6)$$

The segment S_a is shown in the Figure 2. If $l < r^*$, then the definition $S_b = \pi r^{*2} - S_a$ is preferable. If $l \leq r^*$, then $S_a = 0.5 r^{*2}(\alpha - \sin\alpha)$, and if $l > r^*$, then $S_b = \pi \cdot r^{*2} - 0.5 r^{*2}(\alpha - \sin\alpha)$. The total loss is

$$L(t_o) = \int_0^{t_o} S_a(t)q(R,\phi)dt + \int_0^{t_o} S_b(t)q(R,\phi)dt \qquad (7)$$

The complete expression for the specific paint loss L:

$$L = 2.[N.L(t_o) + T.S]/(L_1.L_2)$$

where S was defined by (5).

AN INTERACTIVE PROGRAM FOR DESIGNING SPRAYING GUN TRAJECTORY

The host computer used in numerical experiments was a TPA 11/40 (an analogue to PDP 11/40). Two dysplays were used: a GD 80 graphic display for observing visually paint distribution on the surface and a Videoton AN display for control purposes and for obtaining numerical information (for instance, joint angles for a robot painter).

After drawing the surface to be painted on a graphic display screen, an operator sets the initial information: the range of a coating thickness, the distance of spraying and the speed of the spraying gun. An operator can "spray" paint onto the surface while moving the "spraying gun" (he can also move it with no spraying) and thus it is possible to see the result of "coating". For example, if less than $(h-\Delta h)$ [mm] of paint has been delivered to some pixel, this is shown in yellow colour; if the thickness is acceptable $(h-\Delta h \leq H \leq h+\Delta h)$, then in orange colour and if it is too high (more than $h+\Delta h$), then in red colour. An operator can erase unsuccessfull passages, change the distance and the speed of the spraying gun, as well as the width of the overlapping zone of two neighbouring paint stripes in order to obtain the optimal painting strategy for the given surface. Of course, the evaluation of paint consumption and losses becomes more difficult.

Simultaneously with each step of the "spraying gun", the set of joint coordinates for a particular type of robot painter is evaluated. Current values of joint angles together with the Cartesian coordinates and the orientation of the "spraying gun" are displayed on the Videoton terminal screen. The arrays of joint angles as time functions are formed and appended with each new step, so that after obtaining the optimal painting strategy we have all corresponding joint coordinates as discrete time functions stored on a disk. This information may be then translated to the format of the robot control device and then the chosen painting strategy can be realized by the robot.

Numerical experiments with different shapes of surfaces show among others that optimization of the painting strategy provides a decrease in paint losses from 50% (as it is in practice) to 25-30%. There can be reached also very good eveness of "coating" [3].

The author is very grateful to Dr.J.Marton who have suggested the idea of application of off-line programming methods to the field of robot painting.

REFERENCES.

[1] Grane K., Robots in spray painting, Product Finishing 6 (1982).
[2] Hauke W., Strömungstechnische Untersuchungen an Düsen für das Druckluftstrahlen., Maschinenbautechnik 31,2 (1982).
[3] Klein A.,Marton J., Off-line calculation of sraying gun trajectories (for painting robots), MTA SZTAKI Working Paper No GR/23 (1983).

PROBLEM-ORIENTED REPRESENTATIONS FOR DEVELOPMENT OF KNOWLEDGE BASE FOR EXPERT SYSTEMS

Alexander S. Kleshchev

Laboratory of program systems for AI
Automation and Control Processes Institute
Far-Eastern Research Center of Academy of Sciences
Vladivostok
U.S.S.R.

A method of problem-oriented representations designed for expert systems is described. Definitions of knowledge base schema, data base schema and their matching are given. By frame systems problem-oriented representations and problem-oriented knowledge representation languages are defined. Their use and implementation metodology is discussed.

Up to day in the practice of expert systems building two directions may be distinguished. The first deals with the building of systems, whose knowledge bases contain experts' heuristic knowledge - "what the masters really know is not written in the textbooks" [1]. The second one deals with the building of systems, whose knowledge bases contain scientific knowledge [2,3]. From the point of declarative approach [4] the paper presents a scientific knowledge problem-oriented representation method designed for expert systems.

The representation will be referred to as a triple $<D,K,R>$, where D is a set of expert system's data base states, K is a set of expert system's knowledge base states, and $R \subset D \times K$ is the matching relation. If $d \in D$ and $k \in K$, then $(d,k) \in R$ means that an expert system's data base state d matches with its knowledge base state k. The knowledge base state $k \in K$ represents the knowledge about a set $W_k = \{d \in D \mid (d,k) \in R\}$. Let $<D_1,K_1,R_1>$ and $<D_2,K_2,R_2>$ be two representations. The knowledge bases states $k_1 \in K_1$ and $k_2 \in K_2$ represent the same knowledge, if sets W_{k_1} and W_{k_2} are equivalent. The representations are equivalent, if there is such one-to-one mapping ψ of set K_1 onto K_2, that for every $k \in K_1$ the states of knowledge bases k and $\psi(k)$ represent the same knowledge.

Depending on the matching relation specification we distinguish procedural, syntactical or semantic representations. For procedural representation the relation R is defined with the algorithm which computes by $k \in K$ and by findings $d' \in D'$ such data base state $d \in D$, that $(d,k) \in R$. The syntactical representation corresponds to the calculus with the input in the sense that $(d,k) \in R$, if $d \in D$ is deduced in the calculus with the input $k \in K$. In semantic representation the R relation definition is based on a truth notion, namely $(d,k) \in R$, if substitution d to k reduces k to true.

The scientific knowledge formalization is based on the assumption that experts own a "natural" non-regular representation of their knowledge. In this representation "the knowledge base states" are associated with experts' domain knowledge, and "the data base states" are associated with experts' interpretation of reality fragments from the point of their knowledge. Knowledge base development or knowledge formalization consists of cooperative and coordinated translation of experts' "knowledge bases states" from a "natural" representation into the formal one which an expert system supports. The experts should know for certain that their "natural" representation is equivalent to the formal one in a non-regular sense. For such certainty to become available and labour-consuming formalization to be performed more easily, it is necessary to make formal representation similar to the "natural" one as much as possible. For a "natural" scientific knowledge representation the matching relation meets the principle "practice is the criterion of truth". Therefore representations which are "similar" to "natural" representation may be found only in the semantic representations class. The main demand to such representations is that the ones shouldn't, in principle, make rough a knowledge in the expert consultation area, because only on this condition one can reach for the expert systems to have the same depth of "understanding" as the experts demonstrate. Further search for representations which are similar to "natural" one may be associated with studying the experts' knowledge forms.

One of the specific forms of scientific knowledge is a notional representation in which knowledge takes modular structure, the modules are associated with notions, and the total knowledge is considered a system of certain definitions of notions. The notional representations may be considered as probable "natural" representations of the experts' scientific knowledge, and the frame systems [5] as the formal representations which are "similar" to the notional ones [6]. Every notion in a notional system is associated with a frame-prototype in the frame system. The latter may be regarded as a formal definition (a model) of the first. Each interpretation of the individual (object, effect, situation) as an example of the notion is associated with a frame-instance in the frame system. There is a declarative definition of the frame system as a semantic representation in [4]. In this definition the matching relation models match among notions instances and the "natural" representation notions themselves.

Further investigation into the experts' knowledge forms suggests to fix these forms as "knowledge about knowledge". Let $\langle D_1, K_1, R_1 \rangle$ and $\langle D_2, K_2, R_2 \rangle$ be representations. The knowledge base state $k \in K_1$ will be referred to as knowledge base schema in the representation $\langle D_2, K_2, R_2 \rangle$, if the sets W_k and K_2 are equivalent. Thus $k \in K_1$ represents knowledge fixed in representation $\langle D_1, K_1, R_1 \rangle$ about all potential knowledge base states in representation $\langle D_2, K_2, R_2 \rangle$. Within the framework of the notional representation class, a knowledge base schema is the meta-notion system describing the experts' notional knowledge. Each meta-notion is associated with a certain class of notions. Such a knowledge base schema may be formalized into the frame representation as it has been done for medical knowledge [3]. The form in which the result of situation analysis in expert consultation ought to be represented also suggests specific knowledge about it. The knowledge base state $k' \in K_1$ will be referred to as a data base schema of the expert system in representation $\langle D_2, K_2, R_2 \rangle$, if the sets W_k and D_2 are equivalent. Within the framework of the notional representations class the data base schema of expert system is a notion system describing situation analysis results in expert consultation [3].

The meta-notion systems of the knowledge base schema and the notion systems of the data base schema are isomorph in the following: if m is a meta-notion of the knowledge base schema, p is a corresponding notion of the data base schema, $W_m = \{p_1, \ldots, p_n\}$ are the notions of the knowledge base states matching the meta-notion m, and $W_{p_1}, \ldots, W_{p_n}, W_p$ - are all possible instances of notions $p_1, \ldots, p_n, p$, then $W_{p_1} \cup \ldots \cup W_{p_n} = W_p$. A triple $\langle k, k', R_2 \rangle$ defines a problem-oriented notional (frame) representation by means of general notional (frame) representation, R_2 being a reduction of matching relation for general notional (frame) representation on the sets W_k and $W_{k'}$.

As a rule the notation of general frame representation is hardly understandable by experts. Therefore its immediate use for knowledge formalization neither makes this procedure easier nor the results of formalization understandable to experts. And otherwise using of problem-oriented representation allows to build a natural problem-oriented notation for experts (for every domain). Such a notation not only simplifies formalization but also allows specialists to discuss formalized knowledge without fixing their attention upon reading a formal text but not a natural language text. The problem-oriented representations provided with an adequate notation are referred to as problem-oriented knowledge representation languages. When one designs such a representation, the knowledge base schema in frame representation plays the role of abstract notational syntax. The concrete syntax is developed by taking into account the following demands. The text structure in problem-oriented knowledge representation language should be separated explicitly in a manner conventional for scientific texts: by portitioning the text into dicisions, subdivisions, paragraphs, and so on; by separating out all parts through titles, subtitles, in-phrases, and so on. The application of every title or the in-phrase is an unequivocal definition of the following part content. The whole text must have a phrase structure satisfying demands of a business prose language [7]. As soon as the language designed by such a method appears to be extra hard the notation should be expanded by means of "syntactical sugar" to enhance its elegance: i.e. by conventional defaults, anaphoric references, and so on. The language MEDIFOR-3 [8] can serve as an example of a problem-oriented knowledge representation language. On compiling the text in a problem-oriented knowledge representation language into the frame representation, "syntactical sugar" may be deleted by preprocessor. The knowledge base schema defines a methodology of experts' work upon development a knowledge base. The meta-notions of the schema in their natural order are designing the notion definition according to the structure prescribed by the schema. Such a methodology can be formalized as a system of scenaries determining the experts' actions in developing the knowledge base state or the questions whose answer enables to build such a state on knowledge base schema. In the latter case similar scenarios may control a performance of the program system carrying out the experts´ questioning and automatically forming a knowledge base state according to their answers. On using a problem-oriented language for knowledge base description the methodology of the experts´ performance is determined implicitly by the notation structure. The development of knowledge base state asks for the experts to work on the systematization of knowledge in accordance with a knowledge base schema. The language allows to fix the results of this performance. In addition to the discussion of resulting description any specialists may be invited because reading and understanding the text doesn't need special skills. Furthermore, on using the program system carrying out the experts´ questioning, a problem-oriented knowledge representation language may serve as a documentation language. The periodic output of the documents describing already formed part of the knowledge base state may be an important form of experts´ selfcontrolling performance.

The implementation of problem-oriented representation may be accomplished by compiling a knowledge base state into equivalent production rules base. In this case a problem-oriented representation or a problem-oriented knowledge representation language plays the role of the external formalism directed to the expert, and the production systems play the role of inner formalism, directed at implementation. The compilation of one representation into another may be implemented also by means of the production systems [9].

REFERENCES:

[1] Feigenbaum,E.A., The art of artificial intelligence - themes and case studies of knowledge engineering, AFIPS Conference Proceedings (1978) 227-240.
[2] Szolovits,P., Artificial intelligence and clinical problem solving (MIT LCS TM N 140, Cambridge,1979).
[3] Černjahovskaja,M.Ju., Predstavlenie znanij v ekspertnyh sistemah medicynskoj diagnostiki (DVNC AN SSSR, Vladivostok, 1983): in Russian.
[4] Kleščev,A.S., Frejmovye modeli, ih primenenie v predstavlenii znanij, In: Kleščev,A.S. and Černjahovskaja,M.Ju.(eds.), Jazyki predstavlenija znanija i voprosy realizacii ekspertnyh sistem (DVNC AN SSSR, Vladivostok,1983) 3-12: in Russin.

[5] Minsky,M., A framework for representing knowledge, in: Winston,P.H.(ed.), The Psychology of Computer Vision (McGraw-Hill, New York, 1975) 211-277.

[6] Kleščev,A.S.,Predstavlenie znanij: metodologija,formalizmy, organizacija vycislenij i programmnaja podderzhka,Prikladnaja Informatika 1 (1983) 49-94, in Russian.

[7] Eršov,A.P. K metodologii postroenija dialogovyh sistem: fenomen delovoy prozy, Voprosy Kibernetiki 80 (1982) 3-20: in Russian.

[8] Gorbachev,S.B.,Kleshchev,A.S. and Chernyakovskaja,M.Ju., A problem-oriented language for medical diagnostic knowledge representation MEDIFOR-3, 2-nd International Conference "Artif. Intell. and Inform. Control Systems of Robots" (1982) 99-102: in Russian.

[9] Artemjeva,I.L.,Gorbačev,S.B.,Kleščev,A.S.,Lefšic,A.Ja., Orlov,S.I.,Orlova,L.D. and Uvarova,T.G. Instrunentalnyj konpleks dlja realizacii jazykov predstavlenija znanij, Programmirovanie 4 (1983) 78-89, in Russian.

GERMAN LANGUAGE QUESTIONING OF RELATIONAL DATABASES

Dietrich Koch

Central Institute for Cybernetics and Information Processes
AdW der DDR
DDR-1086 Berlin
Kurstr. 33

This paper gives a short outline of the DAD NLI-System. DAD has a high degree of portability: the SYSAN linguistic processor /1/ works only with typical linguistic features, and does not know anything about database application. The translation module creating the retrieval program from the linguistic structure is independent of the database management system and of the special data base. It uses only the database description. A logically oriented intermediate expression can be executed by our toy database system and is the origin for translation into several manipulation languages.

GOALS OF THE PROJECT

The main goal of the project is to make availbale German language interfaces for different database management systems (DBMS), whereby we likewisely stress a manifold use of the language in a dialog on a definite subject and logical completeness in the framework of relational systems. The system can reply only in table form not in natural language formulations. For the future it is planned to interface to a graphic module. The final goal is an applicable program package which can be adapted to the database by the user himself, if DAD supports the DBMS used. Knowledge of computer linguistic should not be necessary for this adaption, although an exact understanding of the database architecture would be demanded for this first generation step. The end user will be able to extend the lexicon in a simple way. Natural language update is not planned for the time being. A thorough discussion of the DAD version 1 can be found in /2/.

WHICH DBMS WILL BE SUPPORTED?

At the moment, we are dealing with such DBMS which are accessible (directly or indirectly) to us and such systems for which we have a good language description. The systems developed in the GDR (TOPAS and DBS/R) and the DATATRIEVE and MIMER systems belong to this class. Additionally, we are working on translation into the SEQUEL query language, which is used by different DBMS. The technical problem of interfacing with DBMS (i.e. process communication, subprogram call or off-line use) will be grappled separately for each application case. At present we have complete experiments (including retrieval) only with the self-made "mini-DBMS" for DAD.

ROUGH ARCHITECTURE OF THE SYSTEM

The SYSAN language processor comprises of lexical analysis, syntactic analysis, and semantic analysis in an inner linguistic

sense. All these components are independent of discourse and application. No reference is made to database application. The lexical analysis performs inflexional analysis and a partial word building analysis, if the form is not in the lexicon. A dialog module supports the user to define word forms which cannot be analysed. The human partner in this dialog is not supposed to be a linguistic expert, s/he needs only a good command of the language. A basic lexicon containing all functional words and representatives of open word classes belongs to the DAD standard equipment.
Translating the SYSAN-output into a logic expression, which is the origin for translation into several query languages, is performed by several steps. The distance between our executable DAD retrieval expression and this logic expression is very small.

DIALOG WITH THE USER

As mentioned above (lexical analysis), there is a system-controlled dialog besides the natural dialog controlled by the user. This system-controlled clarification dialog is very rarely initiated, because we assume the user is not willing to help the system more than absolutely necessary. For example, the user is not bothered with different meanings of his question, if there is more than one reading, but the first reading (very often the valid one) is chosen and executed, inclusively retrieval. Then s/he is encouraged to call for the execution of the other readings. The headline of the answer table usually gives sufficient information about which reading is executed.
For underspecified questions DAD tries to generate a program which supplies an answer containing all possible intentions of the user. For example, if the user asks for the salary of some employees, all attributes belonging to salary(e.g. net, gross) are included, if nothing specific is demanded. But if s/he puts in a comparative question, the system will ask him what he is refferring to: net or gross. All the questions put out by DAD are designed in such a way that the user has to respond either with yes or no, or to choose a number from an offered menu.

LANGUAGE EXTENSION, DIALOG COHERENCE

DAD covers a large area of language formulations. All customary syntactic means for specification of constituents of the question are permitted: left and right attributing, arbitrarily nested relative clauses and appositions. Every sentence that is closed by full-stop, an exclamation or question mark is understood as a query. Therefore, preludes to the question are not allowed. It is possible to put in two questions connected by "and". The conjuncts can be related in content by reference particles or deletions. Of couse, not all possible deletions are permitted. However, we think that all deletions usually occurring in such a dialog context are included. Positives, comparatives, and superlatives are permitted. We hope that restrictions in the use of these will never be noticed in the life time of this program. Although SYSAN covers a rather wide language range,we are not interested in translating every question into a retrieval program. Question acts of the form "I've an uttermost interest in learning the salary of my estimable boss" does not seem to be very typical. Whoever wants to ask in such a manner should not only have to pay with more typing effort, but also with some additional routine and more run time. We are focussing particularlyon enabling the system to process grammatically incomplete questions (e.g. "Miller's salary").
DAD permits some natural-language means for performing a coherent

dialog. References with the help of pronouns and deletions of before-mentioned sentence fragments is possible already in the current experimental version. The former question and the former answer can be referred to. Further reference possibilities will be developed step by step. To which degree our mechanism for dereferencing can be transported to real applications depends on the type of communication between DAD and the DBMS in question. If we have an off-line use, all such problems will disappear.

LOGICAL COMPLETENESS

The DAD retrieval language is equivalent to PC1. Because it is embedded in LISP, we can extend our language for special demands quite simply. All these possibilities should also be covered by the translation module. Every logical construction can be embedded independent of depth. In this way, the generation and computation of subtotals are possible (e.g. "Who earns more than the average income?"). Not all relational query languages have all these facilities. Therefore, the last translation step can not always be performed. But the reason for this shortcoming can be told the user, so that the NLI interface is freed of responsibility. With respect to arithmetical and statistical functions, we are restricted to the usual ones (sum over, count on, average, arithmetic predicates) and do not intend - up to now - to extend these facilities. We hold the opinion that high-level statistical functions should not be invoked by an NLI system.

IMPLEMENTATION

DAD is implemented in ZKI-LISP/F3, a considerably improved version of LISP/F3 /3/. The interpreter of ZKI-LISP/F3 is completely cons-free. The DAD test version runs in a virtual memory of 2 MByte. Application systems will be prepared for 300 KByte and 160 KByte real storage. The last size seems to be the lowest limit. From the set of very high level languages, we use ATN for syntactic analysis, and a reduced version of FUZZY /4/. "Reduced" means, we only use the deduction capability (for translation) and the pattern matcher (for retrieval).

AN EXAMPLE FOR DEMONSTRATING LOGICAL COVERNESS

We comment the examples by the text after semicolon.
  BITTE EINGEBEN:
WELCHE MITARBEITER PRODUZIEREN GENAU DIE SCHRAUBEN,
DIE MUELLER PRODUZIERT?
  ;Which employees produce exactly those screws, which Mueller produces?
  ;Syntax signs are separated automatically, input is finished if an end marker is recognized

Output of SYSAN:

  ;Nodes of the linguistic structures are GENSYMs, their p-lists
  ;are the carriers of subtrees(nets) (indicators STRU, BL, LEX, NAME) and of some characteristics of the subtrees (indicators NTYP, TYP, LOGFORM), most of which are left out here

    A00076   NTYP A   TYP ERG
              STRU ((V A00070) (AGT A00077) (OBJ A00069))
              ;Toplevel structure of the sentence
              A00070   NTYP G   LEX PRODUZIEREN

```
          A00077   NTYP G LEX MITARBEITER FPRON WELCH
          A00069   NTYP K BL (A00075 MODS A00071)
                   A00075   NTYP G LEX SCHRAUBE
                            LOGFORM $00000804
                            ;a compressed form of "genau die"
                            ;(exactly the), informed the trans-
                            ;lator to build the right logical
                            ;connection between the relativ clauses
                   A00071   NTYP A TYP AS
                            STRU ((V A00066) (AGT A00072) (OBJ A00075))
                            A00066   NTYP G LEX PRODUZIEREN
                            A00072   NTYP G NAME MUELLER
                            A00075   ;the same node as above,i.e. reference
                                     ;is solved exactly
                                     NTYP G LOGFORM $804 LEX SCHRAUBE

Intermediate language:
((SEARCH P ((P.P *? A00072) (P.N *ANY (*? IF0044) (MUELLER))))
  ;Look for the personellnumber of an employee with name MUELLER
  ;in the P-table
  (SEARCH P ((P.P *? A00077) (P.N *? IF0043)))
  ;look for someone's personellnumber
  (FORALL T ((T.T *? A00075) (T.N . SCHRAUBE))
           ;for all parts A00075, if A00075 is a
           ;screw(SCHRAUBE), it holds
           (IF-THEN H ((H.P *! A00072) (H.T *! A00075))
                       ;if this MUELLER A00072 produce part A00075
                       (DFETCH H ((H.P *! A00077) (H.T *! A00075))))
                       ;so "someone A00077" produces this part, too
           ;and
           (IF-THEN H ((H.P *! A00077) (H.T *! A00075))
                     ; if "somenne" produces this part
                       (DFETCH H ((H.P *! A00072) (H.T *! A00075))))
                       ;so this MUELLER produces this part, too
  (SET-RESULT (*! A00072) (*! IF0044) (*! A00077) (*! IF0043)))
  ;if every condition is fulfilled, put "someone" and MUELLER in
  ;the result-table, try the next someone, or, if everybody has
  ;been tried, take the next MUELLER, etc.

Result of retrieval:
```

VERGLEICH-ZU	NAME	PRODUZENT	NAME
P1	MUELLER	P1	MUELLER
P1	MUELLER	P5	MEIER
P3	MUELLER	P3	MUELLER
P3	MUELLER	P4	PIEFKE
P3	MUELLER	P6	KRAUSE

;the first attribute indicates what MUELLER is reffered to

REFERENCES
/1/ Koch, D. and W. Heicking (1982), SYSAN - Linguistischer Prozessor fuer FAS-80, ZKI-Forschungsbericht
/2/ Koch, D. (1983), DAD-1 - deutschsprachige Abfrage von relationalen Datenbasen, In: NLI - Arbeiten zur natuerlichsprachigen Abfrage von Datenbanken, hrsg. vom Zentralinstitut fuer Kybernetik und Informationsprozesse
/3/ Nordstroem, M. (1978), LISP/F3 User Guide, University Uppsala
/4/ Le Faivre, R. (1977), FUZZY Reference Manual, Rutgers University

CONTROL OF FOUR-LEGGED RUNNING-TYPE ROBOT

Lapshin V.V.

Keldysh Institute of Applied Mathematics
USSR Academy of Sciences
Moscow

The paper deals with the problem of
constructing the programmed motion and
stabilization of a four-legged robot running
with different gaits (trot, amble and gallop).
The DC simulation results are presented.

The change of statically stable motion of legged robot to dynamically stable motion is energy advantageous while the speed increases [1-3], like it is observed in animals [4].

It explains the interest to the problem of control for dynamical locomotion of legged robots and design of these robots [2, 5-8].

This paper deals with the problem of constructing the programmed motion and stabilization of a four-legged robot running with different gaits (trot, amble and gallop) over a horizontal surface. The programmed motion is so constructed that uniform load on both footholds is provided in support phase of motion. The motion stabilization is achieved by changing the control forces at the leg joints (reactions at footholds) and by varying the coordinates of foothold positions on the support surface.

The spatial motion of a robot consisting of a massive body and four weightless legs is studied. The axes of the body coordinate system Oxyz are directed along the major inertial axes. The body orientation in the absolute coordinate system $O_1 \xi \eta \zeta$ (where the $O_1 \xi \eta$ -plane is a horizontal support surface) is determined by the body's center-of-mass coordinates ξ, η, ζ, and the angles θ (pitch), χ (roll) and ψ (yaw).

The leg contact with the support surface is assumed to be at a point. The leg-to-support surface interaction is reduced to the reaction force of the support surface. By the foot we shall mean a leg's tip.

The robot body motion is described by motion equations for a solid body under the action of gravity and reaction forces of the support surface.

Let each leg have three degrees of freedom with respect to the body, which provide spatial motion of each foothold. Then there is one-to-one correspondence between reactions at the footholds and control forces at the leg joints; accordingly, it exists between the foothold coordinates and velocities in the Oxyz-axes and phase coordinates at the leg joints (except for some particular foot positions with respect to the body, which are forbidden in the robot motion). The above relations were explicitly written for some kinematic schemes of legs. All the below arguments are valid for arbitrary kinematic scheme of legs, the reactions at footholds being considered as controls.

<u>The robot's programmed motion</u>. The robot running with different gaits (trot, amble and gallop) over a horizontal surface is considered. Each two-leg support phase is followed by the flight phase. The gaits under consideration differ by combination of support legs:

trot - alternation of the support onto diagonally positioned legs (right fore leg and left hind leg or left fore leg and right hind leg) and the flight;

amble - alternation of the support onto the left and right legs and the flight;

gallop - alternation of the support onto the fore and hind legs and the flight.

One support phase of motion and the next flight phase will be called a step. Durations of the support and supportless phases do not change from step to step.

Dynamical models of walking at trot, amble and gallop are specific cases of the motion modes under consideration when the flight phase duration is equal to zero.

The programmed motion is so constructed that the body's center of mass projected on the horizontal plane moves rectilinearly and uniformly. The vertical coordinate of the center of mass at the beginning and end of each support and supportless motion phase is equal to the given value h. The motion law in the coordinate ξ is such that in the flight phase $\ddot{\xi} = -g$ (where g is the gravity acceleration). In the support phase $\ddot{\xi}$ = const, and $\dot{\xi}$ is determined by the given durations of the support and supportless motion phases.

By virtue of the motion equations for the center of mass in the support phase a sum of horizontal force reactions at footholds is zero, and a sum of vertical force reactions is constant. Let the horizontal force reactions be equal to zeros, and in order to equalize the load onto the support legs we demand that the reactions at footholds be equal to each other.

We assume that a lateral shift of the foothold positions, in projection onto the support surface, with respect to the center-of--mass trajectory remains constant (in module) for all legs throughout the robot motion.

Then, from the equations of the body motion about the center of mass the periodic modes may analytically be determined in terms of angular coordinates, which correspond to the given parameters of the robot gait (velocity, durations of the support and supportless motion phases, forward and lateral shifts of the foothold positions, etc.). The yaw angle is identically equal to zero for each of the gaits under consideration. For the trot and gallop the roll is identically equal to zero, and the periodic modes of the pitch motion are derived. For the amble the periodic modes of the roll and pitch motions are derived in the linearized problem statement, i.e. under the assumption of smallness of these angles.

Algorithm for the robot motion stabilization. The algorithm provides periodic programmed motion for each gait under various disturbances. In the flight phase the robot moves under the action of gravity and its motion is uncontrollable. In the support phase the motion stabilization is achieved due to the change of reactions at the footholds (controlled forces at leg joints) and by varying the coordinates of the foothold positions on the support surface in subsequent steps. It is assumed that all the phase coordinates of the robot body in the support phase are known from the navigation system.

We consider first the stabilization algorithms for the <u>trot</u> and <u>amble</u> gaits.

In the support phase by choosing the reactions at the footholds one may provide an arbitrary law of motion that would satisfy initial phase coordinates only in five variables: $\bar{q}^* = (\bar{q}, \gamma, \zeta, \psi, \theta)$. This is explained by the fact that one cannot produce a torque with respect to the line connecting the footholds.

In order to stabilize the motion in coordinate $\bar{q}^*$ the walking robot motion stabilization logic was applied [9]. By using the information on discrepances between current and programmed values of $\bar{q}^*$ and $\dot{\bar{q}}^*$ the path lines are constructed. By moving along these lines the robot performs programmed motion in coordinate $\bar{q}^*$ for a given time interval. The algorithm takes care that the motion along the path lines is accurate. If in reality the robot goes out of the ε-aisle of path lines an additional correction is applied to recalculate the path lines.

The motion along path lines is provides by a proper choice of reactions at footholds. The reactions are determined at each time to an accuracy of the module value N and directed oppositely along the line connecting footholds. It is expedient to choose N so as to minimize a certain criterion of quality. In this paper N is chosen to minimize a maximal value of the required coefficient of friction at footholds.

The motion stabilization in the roll χ is achieved by varying the lateral leg outthrow in two next steps. The problem is solved under the assumption that in these two steps the reactions at footholds will be equal to the programmed ones.

The lateral outthrows of legs for (γ+1)-th and (γ+2)-th steps are determined at the beginning of the flight phase in the γ-th step to satisfy the following conditions:

(a) at the end of the (γ+2)-th step the difference between nominal and actual values of χ and $\dot{\chi}$ is minimal;

(b) restrictions on the lateral outthrow are fulfilled (the legs reach given foothold positions);

(c) the lateral outthrow values minimally differ from the nominal ones.

The problem of determining the leg outthrow values is reduced to a rather simple one of square programming, and a solution algorithm is constructed.

To make the task of motion stabilization in $\bar{\gamma}^*$ and χ easier one should provide most uniform distribution of load between fore and hind support legs. It can be done by varying the coordinates of foothold positions in the direction of motion and reconstructing the programmed motion in the pitch angle for the (γ+1)-th and (γ+2)-th steps. The problem is solved as above. The pitch motion obtained is used in the $\bar{\gamma}^*$ -stabilization algorithm.

The stabilization algorithm for <u>gallop</u> is constructed in the similar way. Here the roll stabilization is achieved by varying reactions and lateral outthrows, and the pitch stabilization by varying the coordinates of foothold positions in the motion direction.

The robot motion control algorithms were tested by computer simulation. For this a program complex was developed that included the control algorithms and a mathematical model of the robot's spatial motion dynamics.

The computational results showed the efficiency of the four-legged robot motion stabilization algorithms in the trot, amble and gallop cases under various disturbances (in initial conditions; a weight on the robot's body whose presence is unknown to the control system; disturbing forces and torques, etc.).

REFERENCES:

[1] Okhotsimsky, D.E., Platonov, A.K., Lapshin, V.V., Energetics investigation of the six-legged walking robot motion (Russian), Akad. Nauk SSSR Inst. Prikl. Mat. Preprint, (1981) No.96.

[2] Lapshin, V.V., Motion dynamics and control of a jumping robot (Russian), Izv. Akad. Nauk SSSR, MTT, (1983) No.5, 42-52.

[3] Beletskii, V.V., Bolotin, Yu.V., Energetics of spatial two-legged walking (Russian), Akad. Nauk SSSR Inst. Prikl. Mat. Preprint, (1981) No.118.

[4] Hayot, D.F., Taylor, C.R., Gait and energetics of locomotion in horse, Nature, v.292 (1981) No.5820, 239-240.

[5] Bolotin, Yu.V., Dynamic stabilization of statically unstable gaits of a walking robot (Russian), Akad. Nauk SSSR Inst. Prikl. Mat. Preprint (1983) No.63.

[6] Golubev, Yu.F., Novikova, I.A., Motion modes of a walking robot with violation of the static stability (Russian), Akad. Nauk SSSR Inst. Prikl. Mat. Preprint (1983) No.5.

[7] Larin, V.B., Control of a walking robot (Russian), (USSR, Kiev, 1980).

[8] Raibert, M.H., Sutherland, I.E., **Machines** that walk, Scientific American, v.248 (1983) No.1, 32-41.

[9] Alekseeva, L.A., Golubev, Yu.F., An adaptive algorithm for motion stabilization of a automated walking robot (Russian), Izv. Akad. Nauk SSSR, Tekhn. Kibernetika, (1976) No.5, 56-64.

ROBOTS - SKILL AND SENSITIVE BEHAVIOUR

Dan Mândutianu, Serban Voinea
Central Institute for Management and Informatics
Bucharest
ROMANIA

The paper refers to a planning system intended
to be used for intelligent robots. The planning
mechanism is driven by a set of special kind of
production rules, called demons. There are five
types of demons: if-requested, if-tested, if-
added, if-deleted and if-achieved. Each of these
kinds of demons is launched by a particular situation. The paper stresses on the capacity to fa-
ce complex planning problems and the ability to
respond to modifications of the knowledge base.

In the field of robot applications in industrial assembly processes
one can easily identify intermediate stages or ancillary tasks.
Each of them can be described by a production rule.

The proposed planning system is founded on an extended meaning of
a production rule which borrows some properties of PLANNER theorems
and some from the frame theory. We shall call demon the item used
in planning activity.

We define five types of demons:

        (1) if-requested
        (2) if-tested
        (3) if-inserted
        (4) if-deleted
        (5) if-achieved

Each demon has an associated assertion which plays an essential
role in its invokation. The difference among the five types of demons consists mainly in the context in which the assertion starts
the demon activation (or let it compete for).

A demon of type (1) is the classical production rule or the consequent theorem of PLANNER. If the associated assertion of the demon occurs as a subgoal in the plan refinement process, then the
demon becomes a candidate for activation with the aim to accomplish
the goal. This kind of demon is the most suitable to rewrite a
goal as a subgoal sequence. The demons of this type form the kernel of a planning system for a certain application field.

Before explaining the meaning of the others, we shall describe the
common demon structure with reference to the knowledge representation approach. A demon is identified by the associated assertion
and its type. The knowledge base is composed of a set of assertions.
The assertions may express goals, facts or robot actions.

A demon is composed of title and body. The title contains the type and the assertion. The body consists of four optional fields:

<demon-type> <assertion>
< relevance>
< preconditions >
<achieve-list>
<effects>

Relevance is a first criterion for the selection of the demon when it contends the opportunity for selection with other demons of the same type and assertion. Relevance is a positive integer not greater then 100 and behaves like a priority. Its declared value is the static (initial) value but it may be modified during plan development. The dynamic value of the relevance enables a flexible behaviour by adequate demon activation enhancing appropriate solutions to similar problems (events) occurring in different stages of a plan.

The preconditions are assertions (facts) that have to be true for the activated demon. If the type, assertion and relevance recommend the demon for activation then the assertions in the precondition list are checked in turn. Those which are not yet satisfied become subgoals. The fail in satisfying all the preconditions leads to demon dropping and the selection of another one with the same type, assertion, but with a less or equal relevance (if any).

In the achieve list one encounters goals to be satisfied after precondition fulfillment. Failure brings about planning leaving and may have two causes: either the original goal is unapproachable or the demon set is incomplete or oddly designed.

The effects of demon activation are expressed as a list of facts to be added or deleted from the knowledge base. This is the way to update the base to point the effects of the corresponding demon activation.

As mentioned above, the fields of the demon body are optional. The default relevance value is 50. The absence of preconditions makes the demon active when the type, assertion and relevance recommend it, irrespective to the existence of other demons with a smaller relevance. The actions can be absent when they are shifted to the precondition part. This is a means to provide backtracking when subgoal achievement is not sure. The effects of a demon may not be present in the demon description, they may manifest as side effects of the demons invoked during its activation.

Resuming the description of the other types of demons, we notice that an if-tested demon is invoked if its assertion occurs in the precondition list of a demon, when the truth value is tested and the assertion is not present in the knowledge base. This type of demon is useful when an assertion is not explicitly introduced in the base and its value can be inferred from the others. An optional effect of the demon is the insertion of the assertion into the base. The truth value can be calculated as a function of other assertions, present or not in the knowledge base, as follows:

- the logical conjunction of the assertions appearing in the precondition list of a demon;
- the logical disjunction of the precondition list of distinct if-tested demons with the same assertion and relevance.

For example, the expression:

Q=A+BCD+EF

can be calculated as follows:

```
IF-TESTED Q
    PRECONDITIONS A
    EFFECTS INSERT Q
IF-TESTED Q
    PRECONDITIONS B
                 C
                 D
    EFFECTS INSERT Q
IF-TESTED Q
    PRECONDITIONS E
                 F
    EFFECTS INSERT Q
```

The assertions A, B, C, D, E, F may be present or not in the knowledge base. We should notice that the effect:

```
INSERT Q
```

is optional, the demon designer having to choose between two alternatives. If the assertion Q is frequently tested and its truth value is relatively stable, then it is desirable to insert it into the base in order to avoid demon activation each time Q is tested. On the contrary, if Q is frequently changing, then it is not recommended to introduce the assertion, for keeping the base free of overloading with ephemeral data.

A demon of the if-inserted type is invoked everytime its assertion appears in the effect list of an active demon, preceded by the keyword INSERT. Such a demon is useful to update the knowledge base by inserting or deleting the assertions whose meaning (sense) is in connection with the associated assertion of the demon. For example, when an object A is set onto another object B, one inserts in the base the assertion:

```
A-ON-B
```

A demon with this assertion may be defined, for deleting:

```
B-FREE
```

and inserting:

```
B-OCCUPIED
```

and also, if the assertion:

```
C-ON-A
```

was true, for inserting:

```
C-ON-B
```

We shall define two demons with distinct relevances to constrain the attempt to apply first the demon with nonempty precondition list:

```
IF-INSERTED A-ON-B
    RELEVANCE 100
    PRECONDITIONS C-ON-A
    EFFECTS DELETE B-FREE
            INSERT B-OCCUPIED
            INSERT C-ON-B

IF-INSERTED A-ON-B
    RELEVANCE 50
    EFFECTS DELETE B-FREE
            INSERT B-OCCUPIED
```

In a robot control system where planning and execution take place simultaneously, the occurrence of an event (stimulus) is treated as follows: one interrupts the planning process and an insertion of the fact expressing the event is added at the top of the current goal list. A predefined demon handling such an insertion is then automatically activated.

If-deleted demons are quite similar to the if-inserted ones, but they are activated when the assertion is to be deleted from the knowledge base.

A demon of if-achieved type differs from the others because it is invoked by a primitive action occurring in the achieve list of an active demon. This kind of demon does not compete with the demons if-requested because it is activated by a different kind of assertion, prefixed by the keyword PRIMITIVE. Usually, the if-achieved demons are employed to simulate (by knowledge base updating) the effects of robot movements during planning. For instance, if in the achieve list of a demon is written:

   PRIMITIVE MOVE-ARM-FROM-A-TO-B

then we may define a demon as follows:

   IF-ACHIEVED MOVE-ARM-FROM-A-TO-B
    EFFECTS DELETE ARM-AT-A
      INSERT ARM-AT-B

In all the above examples the demons had an empty achieve list except the demon if-requested. This is rather natural for the demons used only for knowledge base updating. Nevertheless, nothing prevents us from using all demon types in the plan generation process. It is up to the demon designer to use other types of demons for plan refinement.

The planning system is implemented on PDP-11 computer. It may be used in connection with a VAL-like language to program a five joint robot. Further developments are directed towards language extension in order to enable a unitary description of both demons and the static knowledge.

REFERENCES

[1] McDermott, D., Planning and Acting, Cognitive Sciences, 2 (1978) 71-109.

[2] Nilsson, N.J., Some Examples of AI Mechanisms for Goal Seeking, Planning, Reasoning, in: Klix, F. (ed.), Human and Artificial Intelligence (VEB Deutscher Verlag der Wissenschafter, Berlin, 1978).

[3] Davis, R. and King, J., An Overview on Production Systems, Stanford Artificial Intelligence Laboratory, Memo AIM-271 (1975).

[4] Mândutianu, D., Planning Tasks in Advanced Robot Control, in: Proc. 2-nd International Conference Artificial Intelligence and Information - Control Systems of Robots (Smolenice, 1982) 139-142.

[5] Bobrow, D. and Raphael, B., New Programming Languages for Artificial Intelligence, Computing Surveys, 3 (1974) 153-174.

ROUND-S : AN EXPERIMENT WITH KNOWLEDGE DRIVEN
SEMANTICS IN NATURAL LANGUAGE UNDERSTANDING

Sanda Mânduţianu

Central Institute for Management
and Informatics
Bucharest, ROMANIA

A model for semantic representation is presented, using domain-specific knowledge, with a special interest in problems taken from real world setting. Grammar-oriented techniques for natural language understanding are used. The conceptual knowledge base is a model used as a source of suggestions about the content of the sentences; an expectation driven model of understanding is presented.

INTRODUCTION

ROUND-S (ROmanian UNDerstanding) has been conceived as an experiment in natural language understanding. The purpose of the research is to create a set of tools for investigating domain-specific knowledge bases freely using natural language.

For the present application, the universe of discourse is a collection of computer programs from the National Computer Library. The system is supposed to supply a human partner with desired information within this range.

The knowledge of the system is explicitly defined and reflects the expected content of the sentences. The characterization of the world is made by conceptual primitives of knowledge which describe the objects and their relationships. In this objectual model, understanding a question means to choose the appropriate primitive and assign values to it.

To achieve these aims, the system is provided with tools for the analysis of linguistic structures, a model of semantic representation, and a general problem solving procedure.

SYSTEM OVERVIEW AND FUNDAMENTALS

ROUND-S is now used for dialogue in Romanian on the basis of its knowledge about the collection of programs from the National Program Library.

The system is entirely implemented in DMLISP [4] on a PDP 11/45-like minicomputer.

The linguistic processing of a sentence is made by an ATN compiler [3]. The grammar specification is general enough to be used not only for this application, and with slight modification when changing the domains. The ATN compiler generator can also be independently used for ATN grammar refinements as an off-line task.

The ATN compiler has the goal to yield a deep structure consistent with the model of knowledge. Acting as a coroutine, the lexical analysis aims to discover some properties of the input words, as: grammatical category (noun, verb, etc.), basic form of the word (without inflexion), other properties valued as relevant (tense for the verbs, number for the nouns, etc.), and sometimes semantic information.

The semantic analysis and the solving of the problem raised by the sentence are separately dealt with in the process of understanding. The role of semantic analysis is to build a semantic representation of the utterance. This internal representation is used by the problem solver in order to give an answer using the knowledge base of the system. Understanding is then a matter of comparison between the model proposed by the sentence and the model of the world existing in the knowledge base. At the representational level, the knowledge base is a semantic network, which is used in a pattern-matching manner.

SYNTAX

The goal of the grammar, as a working model, is to formalize the structure of the most frequent utterances in a certain domain of discourse. The grammar has to fix those structures upon which the semantic analysis can work.

The considered corpus contains utterances which generally express the desire to be informed about the characteristics of objects, the components of a class of objects, etc. The sentences, taking into account the aims and the attitude towards the content can be interrogative, declarative or imperative (for the time being other types of sentences can be omitted).

Since the main purpose of the system is to understand the message and not to grasp syntactic inadequacies, one can neglect some syntactic features such as the agreement in number and gender (Romanian is a heavily inflected language), the cases of nouns, etc. Since the main bearer of semantic information is considered the noun, the grammar is noun-oriented, i.e. the syntactic structure reflects the dependencies between different noun groups in the sentence, ordered by a verb at a personal mode.

The deep structure is conceived so that to represent in the best way the nesting of the noun groups. Examples of sentences and their deep structure (in a list representation) are the following:

Which functions have the programs of class A ?
(function (program (class A)))

Which authors have the integration programs worked out at ICI ?
(author (program integration ICI))

SEMANTICS AND KNOWLEDGE

The object-model of the world is used by the system to characterize the expected meaning of the sentences to be processed. The formal frame according to which the linguistic structures are matched against the knowledge model is called here semantics.

The objects of the real world can be partitioned in concepts and their instances. Between concepts there is a finite set of

relationships. The role of semantic analysis is:
- to accept a certain message as being consistent with the system knowledge,
- to build up a semantic representation of the message.

It is presumed that the deep structure denotes objects of the real world. The grouping of the elements in the deep structure around nouns, reflects the ordering of some objects around a centre through specific relationships. For example, the noun group "program of integration by Runge-Kutta method" is a surface form for the semantic representation:

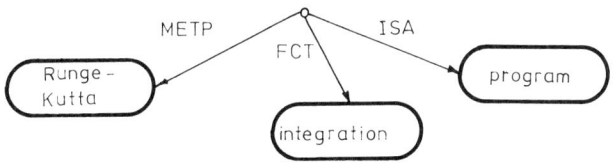

Figure 1

In a list form the same representation is:

(program(FCT integration)(METP Runge-Kutta))

The sample of Figure 1 is an instantiation of the concept "program":

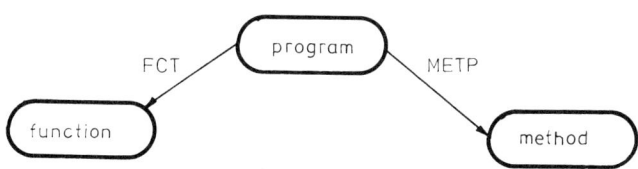

Figure 2

Every concept has a generic description which can be expressed as:

(concept(relation$_x$ concept$_x$)*)

For the concept "program" the generic description can be:

(program(FCT function)(METP method))

An instance has as semantic representation an instantiation of the generic description. For example, the semantic representation of BIBMAT, an instance of a program, is as following:

(BIBMAT(FCT function)(METP Runge-Kutta))

This model has some analogies with the semantic cases model [1], here the cases being related to objects and specific for the domain.

Proving the semantic consistency of the message is implicitly done by revealing the affinity to a generic description for every object.

The knowledge representation is based on the semantic net model. There are two levels of knowledge: conceptual and factual. At the conceptual level the concepts are represented in conformity with their generic description. The conceptual net is used for the identification of the relationships between the objects from the deep structure and for building semantic representation. For a specific application, the conceptual net has to contain the concepts considered as relevant for the domain. In the presented domain, concepts such as: program, method, function, author, etc. are known today. The factual net contains the instances of the concepts with their instantiated relationships.

The knowledge base is used in a pattern-matching manner. In very general terms, understanding is done by a comparison between the message and the conceptual model of knowledge.

CONCLUDING REMARKS

In its present version ROUND-S is used as dialogue system in Romanian about the programs from the National System Library. The main topics of the system have been:
- to experiment some general methods of designing linguistic processors;
- to establish a nucleus of an ATN grammar for Roumanian;
- to study an object-model of knowledge;
- to experiment an implementation of such a system in a real world.

REFERENCES

[1] Fillmore, Ch., The Case for Case, in: Bach, E. and Harms, R. (eds.), Universals in Linguistic Theory (1978).

[2] Findler, N. (ed.), Associative Networks. Representation and Use of Knowledge by Computers (Acad. Press, 1978).

[3] Mânduțianu, S., Augmented Transition Networks-Model and Tool for Linguistic Processors Implementation, Res. Report, ICI (1983).

[4] Sotirescu, D., Stefănescu, M., Report on the Interactive System DMLISP, IPB (1981).

A REASONABLE COMPROMISE BETWEEN STRAIGHTFORWARD
AND FEEDBACK LAWS IN A COMBINED SYSTEM FOR ROBOTS
CONTROL

Ognian B.Manolov   Nedko S. Shivarov

Institute of Industrial Cybernetics and Robotics
Bulgarian Academy of Sciences, Acad.G.Bonchev bl.2
1113 Sofia, BULGARIA

The dynamic mathematical model of spatial kinematic mechanism with a definite number of degrees of movement, based on the Lagrange method is used to obtain the inverse model, which is applied in a combined system for an optimal trajectory control. A linearized inverse model leads to a conventional regulator synthesis in the feedback loop. Some computational results achieved by means of the symplified simulation model of manipulator with definite degrees of movement are presented.

INTRODUCTION

During the last decade great attention has been devoted to industrial manipulators. The problems of analysis and synthesis of control for such machineries have been discussed by many authors, but usually in a kinetostatic sense. Taking into account inertial torques, masses, friction coefficients, Coriolis accelerations,ect.,the industrial manipulator is described by systems of interconnectional nonlinear time-variant differential equations, [1,2] . These equations allow the analysis of the manipulators and are a good basis for synthesis of suiteble control laws. The synthesis is a very cumbersome task due to the static and dynamic restrictions imposed on the closed-loop systems state and control vectors. In some papers another approach is described based on the inverse problem of dynamics, but it has been developed for a very simplified model [3] of manipulator movement, described by linear differential equations [4] and not including dynamics of manipulator but only that of the load in the gripper [5] .

PROBLEM STATEMENT

A.Optimal control problem. The mathematical model of a mechanical system is usually constructed either by D'Alambert's principle, Neuton-Euler method or second order Lagrangian equations. Following the well-known resilts [2] , the industrial manipulator like a spatial mechanism, having single degree of movement joints, can be described only by nonlinear matrix differential equations :

$$A(q) \cdot \ddot{q}(t) + B(q,\dot{q}) \cdot \dot{q}(t) = C(q) \cdot F + D(q) \cdot M + G(q) \cdot P + m_o(t) \quad (1)$$

under the constraints : $|\dot{q}(t)| = \bar{\dot{q}}$, $|m_o(t)| = \bar{m}_o$ (2)

resulting from the mechanical configuration of the manipulator, where $q(t) \in R^n$ is a generalized coordinates vector, $F \in R^n$ is an external force vector, M is an external torgue vector, $P \in R^n$ is a weight force vector, $m_o(t) \in R^n$ is a driving torque vector, $A(t)$, $B(q,\dot{q})$, $C(q)$, $D(q)$ and $G(q)$ are (nxn) coefficient matrices, whose elements depend on the metrical and force parameters of the manipulator, as well as an the angular shifts and velocities, t is a time and n is a number of kinematical chains members (degrees of movement).

Consider the problem of the gripper moving from a given initial to a given terminal point (q_0 and q_f resp.) **along** a piecewise required trajectory $q^*(t)$, $t \in [t_0, t_f]$ so that constraints (2) hold. In general, the actual trajectory $q(t)$ of the gripper will differ from $q^*(t)$, because of the mathematical model incorrectness, **disturbances** ect. A useful performance criterion that takes into consideration the trajectory error as well as control action energy is of the form :

$$J = \frac{1}{2} X'_i \cdot S(q^*) \cdot X_f + \frac{1}{2} \int_{t_0}^{t_f} \left[X'(t) \cdot Q(q^*,t) \cdot X(t) + u'(t) \cdot R(q^*,t) \cdot u(t) \right] \cdot dt \to \min \quad (3)$$

where : $X(t) = q^*(t) - q(t)$ is a system error vector, $u(t) = m_o(t) - m_c(t)$ is a control vector, m_c is a resistant torque vector, $S(q^*), Q(q^*,t)$ and $R(q^*,t)$ are diagonal, positive definite, the primes denote transposition weighting matrices.

By the relations (1)-(3) we can formulate the following problem (well-known in control theory [6]): Determine a control law $u(t)$ that minimizes the performance criterion (3) along the trajectory of the system (1), so that the constraints (2) hold.

The problem stated is nonlinear. Necessary and sufficient conditions for existence and uniqueness of the solution are not known. A natural and widely used approach to this problem is the linearization of (1), which may be accomplished along the desired trajectory, or a sliding piecewise linearization in the neighbourhoods of selected terminal points of the desired trajectory $q^*(t)$ - point-to-point linearization.

B. Inverse problems of dynamics. The design of the optimal control regulator has a very serious disadvantage. It is an iterative process of searching min J in (3) because it is not possible to find a direct relationship between the character of a required trajectory of movement and the value of matrix coefficients in the $S(.)$, $Q(.)$ and $R(.)$ in (3). Moreover, if we wanted to implement the point-to-point linearization with an optimal regulator design for robot trajectory control, it would consume a long computing time and "on-line" control would be impossible. A very fast result can be obtained, if we have parameters of the required system trajectory movement. In this case, by the method of the inverse problem of dynamics [4] it is possible to synthetize such control algorithms, which are providing necessary dynamic characteristics of close-loop system [5] . The structure properties of the control law are fully identical with structure properties of the classical optimal control law by quadratic criterions as (3). This method is very fast in terms of computing because it is using only algebraic operations, but control law is optimal only for the required trajectory.

C. Inverse model of manipulator. In some practical problems we can obtain the mathematical equations which are describing dynamics of the spatial mechanism. For real manipulators, one of the well-known methods [1,3] gives a mathematical model by differential equations in the following form :

$$\sum_{k=1}^{n} C_{ik} \cdot \ddot{q}_k + \sum_{k=1}^{n} \sum_{l=1}^{n} C_{ikl} \cdot \dot{q}_k \cdot \dot{q}_l + C_i = F_i \quad , \quad i=1,2,\ldots,n \quad (4)$$

where q, $\dot{q}$, $\ddot{q}$ are n-vectors of generalized coordinates, their velocities and accelerations ; C_i, C_{ik}, C_{ikl} are dynamic coefficients, depending on the q, on geometric parameters and on kinematic chain of the manipulator ; F are generalized external (control) torques. Taking into account the main conception of the inverse problem of dynamics we accept that it is the required trajctory $X^*(t)$. We also assume that there is a computing block, which is generating corresponding required vectors $q^*(t)$, $\dot{q}^*(t)$ and $\ddot{q}^*(t)$. Such a computing block is called the "program trajectory generator" (PTG) and is described in detail in [7]. Then we can easily compute the required control torques by using (4) and rearranging it to the following form :

$$F_i^* = \sum_{k=1}^{n} C_{ik}^* \cdot \ddot{q}_k^* + \sum_{k=1}^{n}\sum_{l=1}^{n} C_{ikl}^* \cdot \dot{q}_k^* \cdot \dot{q}_l^* + C_i^* \quad , \quad i=1,2,\ldots,n \qquad (5)$$

The algebraic equations system (5) will be named "inverse model of manipulator (IMM), and a control system with IMM will be correspondingly called "straightforward control system" for the trajectory control. In a real case, for manipulator with many numbers of degrees of movement $(n>3)$, it is a difficult and cumbersome work-consuming process to obtain equations (4),(5) in a "hand-made" procedure, and their analytical expression is very long and compicated. In [8,9] a programing package, named LPSMCM, for automated conversion and derivation the (4),(5) in symbol type is developed. Consequently, for any concrete manipulator with a given kinematic chain and phisical characteristics, package LPSMCM renders full dynamic equations (4) in addition to the dynamics of servosystems, equations of IMM (5), and expressions for C_i, C_{ik}, C_{ikl} in a maximim short form.

D. Combined (straightforward-feedback) approach for optimal trajectory control. A very good and satisfactory result may be achieved by the combined control system [7]. When equations (4), (5) are ideally inversed, the feedback loop control will be superfluous. In the real case there are many disturbance factors, so much the more we will carry out artificial reasonable, simplification of the IMM. In [8] a procedure of such simplification was described, based on physical considerations. On the other hand we were using the computer modelling techniques to simulate groups of required movements of new simplifing models IMM, where these members in IMM, which are not given a sensitive investment in computation of F_i^* in (5), were eliminated. Thus we can construct a simplified IMM, satisfying some compromise quality criteria. When we hawe such IMM, we can obtain the optimal controler coefficients in feedback loop, because in this case our object will be linear and time-invariant. After certain transformations of the (4) the linear model can be described in the form :

$A_1 \cdot \ddot{q}(t) + A_2 \cdot \dot{q}(t) + A_3 \cdot q(t) + A_4 + u(t) = 0$ and decomposed in :

$\dot{Z}(t) = W \cdot Z(t) + V \cdot u(t)$, where :

$$Z(t) = \begin{vmatrix} q(t) \\ ---- \\ \dot{q}(t) \end{vmatrix} + W^{-1} \cdot A_4 \quad , \quad W = \begin{vmatrix} 0 & I_n \\ ------------ \\ -A_1 \cdot A_2 & -A_1 \cdot A_3 \end{vmatrix} \quad , \quad V = \begin{vmatrix} 0 \\ ---- \\ H_1 \end{vmatrix} \qquad (6)$$

The performance criteria may be considered as :

$$J = \frac{1}{2} \int_0^\infty \left[Z'(t) \cdot Q \cdot Z(t) + u'(t) \cdot R \cdot u(t) \right] \cdot dt \qquad (7)$$

It is well known that the problem (6),(7) has a unique solution :

$$u(t) = -R^{-1}.V'.P.Z(t) \tag{8}$$

where P is the positive definite solution of the appropriate alegebraic matrix Riccati equation [6].

SIMULATION RESULTS AND CONCLUSION

The kinematic chain of manipulator has been used with concrete phisical parameters in the LPSMCM package for obtaining the equations (4) and (5). These models were included in our computer modelling compex ROBMAN [8] to simulate the full combined system for trajectory optimal control, described in Sect. D. The approximated simplifying variant of IMM included only some inertial and gravity members C_{ik}, C_i. After simulating tasks of trajectory movement, in the result of the experiments, it could be seen, that designed combined control system for robots performs satisfactorily along these trajectories.

REFERENCES :

[1] Bejczy,A.K., Robot Arm Dynamics and Control, NASA, JPL Techn. Memo, Calif.Inst. of Technol., Pasadena, Calif., Febr.15(1974), 33-669.
[2] Mahil, S.S., Mathematical Model of an Industrial Manipulator : A Close Form Solution Using Lagranges Method, Proc. 7th Jap. Nat. Conf. of Robots, (1977).
[3] Poul, R.P. Moddelling , Trajectory Calculation and Servoing of a Computer Controlled Arm, Standford Art.Int.Laboratory, Memo AIM - 177, Nov. (1972).
[4] Krutko, P.D.,Popov, E.P., Build-up of Movement Control Algorithms for Robots-Manipulators,Proc. USSR Acad.of Sc.,Vol.255, No 1, (1980)(in Russian).
[5] Krutko, P.D., Popov E.P., A Optimal Controller Design and Inverse Problems of Dynamics for Controllable Systems, Tech.Cybern., News USSR Acad. of Sc.3(1982) 182 - 193 (in Russian).
[6] Kalman, R.E., Contribution to the Theory of Optimal Control, Bol.Soc.Math.Mexicana 1 (1960) 102 - 119.
[7] Kogan, B.J., Petrov, A.A., Perfileva, I.M., Tulepbaev, V.B. Gybrid Algorithms for Robot-Manipulator Movement Control, Trans. on United Conf.Robotic Systems (Vladimir, Oct.1978) (in Russian)
[8] Manolov, O.B. , Computer Symulation of Manipulator-Robots Control Systems, Ph.D.Dissert.,Inst.of Control Sc.,Acad.Sc.USSR (Oct.1981)(in Russian).
[9] Manolov, O.B., Interactive Program for Robot Straightforward Control System Design Using Faster Build-up Algorithm, Comp. and Artif.Inteligense Jrnl. Vol. 3, No 4 (1984) (in print.).

ON THE INTELLECTUAL PROGRAM PACKAGES

V.M.Matrosov, S.N.Vassiljev, O.G.Divakov,
G.A.Oparin
Irkutsk Computer Centre of Siberian Branch
of the Academy of Sciences of the USSR,
Irkutsk, USSR.

Here are presented the intellectual program packages for mathematical regularities constructing ("PACKAGE MODELING"), the derivation of theorems on dynamical systems properties, the decision-making and the metasystem for the automatic production and for the support of program packages functioning. This software is produced in Irkutsk CS of SB of AS of the USSR.

PROGRAM PACKAGE "MODELING"

Mathematical models constructing was always the creative work, especially the constructing the original models. Program package "Modeling" represents an attempt to automatise the process of mathematical models constructing taking into account the following considerations.

1. As it is well-known the unity of the universe is expressed by the existence of general regularities of functioning of objects (and processes) in different object regions (the principles of conservation of matter, general principles of mechanics and etc.). These regularities are described by the same mathematical expressions (equations). That is why the same mathematical expressions may be used for the description of different objects functioning.

2. The mathematical regularity constructing with the help of analogy method is realized by the following scheme. An investigator studies an object of interest and makes a multiattribute choice from the well-known regularities, the one, to which the object functioning is subjected; then, he uses some mathematical description of the chosen regularity and after that he identifies the values of either these or those variables, parameters and etc.

The package [1] is developed for the specialists of some object regions, which are neither mathematicians, nor programmers, but who wish to use mathematical regularities and corresponding abilities of a computer. The input language of the package is developed as the fragment of russian restricted by syntax and lexics.

Information on the objects and their relations from some object region under consideration, on the regularities region and the corresponding mathematical regularities is stored in the knowledge base of the package.

Knowledge on the object region and on the relevant mathematical models are represented in the form of semantic network. Its nodes are the frames [2] together with the expressions of special language. It is the language for the description of frames transformation operations, the representation of some conditions of frames initialization and for the description of some mathematical regularities, possible values of arguments and actions over the semantic network.

Semantics of the language is provided by the knowledge on the object region and on the mathematical regularities located in the knowledge base of the package.

The input task for package consists of the informal description of the object under modeling and of the formulation of problem, which must be solved, using the selected model.

The package "Modeling" consistes of linguistic and semantic processors and of the processor of mathematical regularities constructing. Text of the task is subjected to syntactic and semantic analysis. The information from the knowledge base is used in order to find the relevant regularities.

Two later processors are realized as a program-interpretor, working over the semantic network and over the set of abovementioned language expressions. Processing the later ones, the interpretor produces a set of mathematical regularities. Here all the variables are connected with definite notions of the network, that enable one to formulate the comments in russian for them.

Additional desired information is requested from the investigator. Output of the package represents some set of mathematical expressions.

PROGRAM PACKAGE FOR THEOREM DERIVATION

The package [3] is assigned to specialists in the field of systems dynamics and control theory. Its assignment is the computer derivation(in the analytical form)of some conditions of existence of either these or those properties P in the studied mathematical model M. These conditions are obtained in terms of existence of suitable vector Lyapunov functions (VLF) V and, possibly, in terms of auxiliary mathematical models, more simple for study (comparison systems)M_c with certain properties P_c.

Formal-logical structure of the theorems obtained by the package is of the form

for the comparison theorem: $\widetilde{M} \, \& \, (\underset{i}{\&} \, D_i) \rightarrow (P_c \rightarrow P)$, (1)

for the theorem on properties: $\widetilde{M}^* \, \& \, (\underset{i}{\&} \, D_i^*) \, \& \, P_c^* \rightarrow P$. (2)

Here $\widetilde{M}$ is the characteristic condition overlapped by the definition on VLF V (for example, it means the majorization of V values on the motions of dynamical system M by corresponding solutions of comparison system M_c that is usually finite-dimensional), and the conditions D_i on V, M_c are formed by P and may have different informal sense (definite positivity, continuity, boundedness and etc. of V, existence and continuability of solutions in M_c and so on).
The definition P is given by a user from the terminal. The search of premisses sufficient in (I) for satisfiability of the property P is regulated by so-called conditions of subformulae correlation

which are found by means of careful analysis of known theorems and of experience of obtaining of new theorems of such type. They restrict the set of possible premisses M, D_i, P_c in equation (1). The mechanism of derivation of the (1) type theorems, which is called the comparison principle, consists of some composite permissible and derived inference rules with small fold in heuristic strategy of their usage. That is why, the uncertainty of derivation is sharply restricted though the pragmatically justified variety of conditions remains.

Theorems (2) are obtained by transition from the conditions of theorems (1) to more effectively verified conditions $\tilde{M}^*$, D_i^*, P_c^* . For this purpose the additional knowledge from the theories of models M and M_o is used (the theorems on differential and other inequalities, on properties of quasimonotone comparison systems and etc.), which is structurized by the special way. In spite of the certain specialization of classes of derivable theorems, the problems of their derivation are mass due to the variety of properties P definitions and of the models M, due to variety of V functions, and also due to the occurence of theorems of (1),(2) type in different sections of mathematics. On the base of developed mechanism the various theorems with analogs of Lyapunov functions and morphisms in the theory of differential equations, systems dynamics, control theory are obtained manually or by a computer. These theorems are either the modifications and generalizations of known theorems or the new ones. They are completely compatible with those published at present time in periodical or in dissertations. Computer time for proper derivation contains some minutes.

PACKAGE PROGRAM ON DECISION-MAKING

The package [4] provides the automatised realization of the decision-making process in the dialogue regime. This process represents the choice of one or some more rational versions of solutions (projects, plans, controls) from the set X of solutions by the vector criterion $f=(f_1, f_2, \ldots, f_m): X \to R^m$.

1. The general problem of the selection of the set X^P of non-dominated solutions with respect to Pareto preference relation is considered in two following forms of description.

1.1: when X is finite and the solutions $x \in X$ are given by tabular (by vector estimations of $f(x)$); 1.2: when X is the polyhedral set in R^n with the criterion $f(x)=((c^1, x), \ldots, (c^m, x)), c^i \in R^n$, $i=1,2,\ldots,m$.

Problem 1.1 is solved by a simple way. In order to solve the problem 1.2 the methods based on multicriteria simplex method [5] are developed.

There are solved also the following problems:
2. Problem of choice of more preferential solution;
3. Problem of ranking the solutions by preference;
4. Problem of qualitative description of solutions preference.
Problem 2 is solved by known methods of partial pairwise comparison of alternatives [6] , problem 3 is solved by the method ELECTRE [7] and etc. In order to solve problem 4 a method of scalarization of vector criterion in the class of second-order polynomials is devel-

oped, where the a priori subject estimations of the difference sign of the scalar function values for some pairs of alternative solutions are used.

When X,f are given as in problem 1.2 and preliminary selection of the set X^p is non-practible (for example, due to large dimension of restrictions system), then problem 2 is solved by a man-computer variant of conditional gradient method [8] and by the method of restrictions [9].

The package is successfully tested on the problems of multicriteria choice of versions of construction and evolution of energypower systems and the estimation of technical systems.

"SATURN" METASYSTEM

This metasystem [10] is the dialogue instrumental complex, which supports the functioning and the certain technology of the dialogue applied program package (APP) projecting for a computer BESM-6 with OS DISPAK and with the monitor system MONITOR-80. The usage of SATURN metasystem essentially minimizes the period of APP development; the participation of the system programmers is reduced to minimum in this process. At all stages the dialogue essentially increases the labour productivity of APP developers and users and the requirements to their qualification are minimized in programming. The metasystem includes:
- the administrative subsystem, which sanctions the access of the user (administrator, APP developer, i.e. problem programmer or APP user) to certain means of the metasystem;
- the means of description and the debugging of model of the problem region the problems of which must be solved by APP under development;
- the means of description of APP input language the dynamical part;
- the means for the automation of APP documentation production;
- the means of APP modification;
- the means for description of data archives configuration and the data prevention from non-sanctioned access;
- the means of APP integration;
- the monitor (control program) of the package.

The package monitor works in the combined (interpretation + compilation) regime of execution of computer processes schemes (CPS) and it provides the following means for the package user:
- the statement of APP problem by the procedure, non-procedure or combined (procedure - non-procedure) way;
- CPS design, including the static, static-dynamical and dialogue design;
- interpretation of CPS, obtained either in the result of problem statement by the procedure way or in the result of calculations design for the problem statement by the non-procedure or by the combined way;
- compilation (generation) of autonomous working program for CPS; besides, this program is realized in the package regime of a computer;
- usage of CPS as the package operation;
- flexible control of computer process;
- work with data as well in autonomous regime, as in the process of CPS execution;
- multivariation of data storage in archives;

- dynamical distribution of operating storage for data;
- reaction on non-standard and accident situations, which occur in problem operations.

LANGUAGE MEANS AND COMPUTER PROCESS DESIGN IN "SATURN"

It is supposed, that the problem region of APP, which is constructed by SATURN metasystem, may be specified by the pair of sets Z and V (where Z is the set of typed objects (parameters) of the problem region, and V is the set of operations performed over the objects from the sets Z), being the result of structural analysis of problem region and the increasing construction of complex objects and operations from simple basic ones. The formalized description of the problem region is introduced and stored in the system data base; it is possible to communicate with it in the dialogue regime.

Problem region specification determines the APP input language, which has the sufficiently simple structure and it is oriented to the user, i.e. to the specialist in the problem region, who is nonprogrammer.

It contains the means of computer process organization (L-language) and the means of description of dynamical objects of the problem region (M-language). L-language has the form: $L = \langle L_0, L_1, \ldots, L_k \rangle$, where $L_i = \langle Z_i, V_i, S \rangle$ is the input language of i-th subsystem. Here $Z_i \subseteq Z, V_i \subseteq V$ are correspondingly the sets of names of parameters and operations. Its language provides the complex usage of procedure and non-procedure means of problem statement in combination with the dialogue regime, that enables the user to prescribe only the node points of CPS by procedure way(points of branching, of cyclic processes organization and etc.); the designer must form only linear parts of the scheme on the base of non-procedure statements and check the correctness of CPS.

M-language is that of mnemonic denotations. It is constructed by the problem programmer for the description of mathematical models of the problem region objects, represented in the form of matrix-vector equations having definite type and structure. Here the elements of matrices and vectors are the functions of some parameters. Translator from M-language transforms this description into a set of base language procedures. The set represents the dynamical part of problem moduli library.

For the problems and subproblems stated in non-procedure form,the static design of linear chains of operations is realized before the stage of CPS performance;by a set of initial parameters these chains calculate the goal. The design is produced by mathematical models of problem subsystems of the package.These models are static complexes [11], which are automatically formed at the stage of design of problem subsystems. A designer checks the existence and uniqueness of problem solution and it realizes the solution construction in case of problem solvability.

The user has the possibility to transfer the design at the stage of CPS performance(static-dynamic design which is absent in known instrumental systems such as PRIZ and SPORA). In this case the the designer is able to trace the computer circumstances, which take place in the course of CPS interpretation (by the moment of design it knows the executed branches of computer process and also what values of the parameters are calculated).

REFERENCES:

[1] Divakov O.G., Kuz'min V.A., Madjarov T.I., Schurov Yu.V., Application program package for automatization of mathematical model construction, in: II International conference on artificial intelligence and information control systems of robots (Smolenice,CSSR, 1982).
[2] Minsky M., Frames for knowledge representation (M.,Power,1979).
[3] Matrosov V.M., Vassiljev S.N., Karatuev V.G. and others, Algorithms for derivation of theorems of vector Lyapunov functions method (Novosibirsk, Science, 1981).
[4] Vassiljev S.N., Selyodkin A.P., To construction of program package on decision-making, in : Packages of applied programs. Methods and developments (Novosibirsk, Science, 1981).
[5] Yu P.L., Zeleny M., The set of all nondominated solutions in linear cases and a multicriteria symplex method, J.Math.Anal.Appl., 49, 2 (1975), 430-468.
[6] Vinogradskaja T.M., Two algorithms for the choice of multidimensional alternatives, Automatics and telemechanics,3,(1977), 90-96.
[7] Roy B., Bertier P., La method ELECTRE II,SEMA, Note de travial, 142 (1971).
[8] Geoffrion A., Dyer G., Feinberg A., Solution of optimization problems on the base of man-computer procedures, in:Problems of analysis and decision-making procedure(M.,World,1976).
[9] Benajun R., Larychev O.I., de Montogolfje and others, Linear programming with many criteria. Method of restrictions, Automatica and telemechanics, 8(1971), 108-116.
[10] Oparin G.A., Feoktistov D.G., SATURN - metasystem for the applied program packages development, in: II-d All Union conference "Automation of program packages and translators production". Thesis of papers (Tallin,1983).
[11] Oparin G.A., To theory of the computer process design in the applied program packages, in: Applied program packages. Methods and developments(Novosibirsk, Science, 1981).

DATA OPTIMIZATION IN NATURAL LANGUAGE BASED SYSTEMS

Wolfgang Menzel

Central Institute of Linguistics
Academy of Sciences of the GDR
Berlin, GDR

Data optimization is considered to be the most important strategy to attain a higher level of computational effiency in natural language based systems. The basic idea is given and some techniques for storage reduction are presented which make use of the distinction between static and dynamic structures exclusively.

Computational efficiency is one of the serious problems in the design of natural language based systems, not only from a potential user's point of view, from which it is an essential criterion for a successful commercial utilization. Efficiency certainly should be of no less importance during the development of a system, even in its experimental stages.

Since the extremely high complexity of pretentious natural language applications, system developers are forced to make use of programming languages of a sufficient high level (usually LISP and its derivatives, PROLOG, SETL, REFAL, etc.) and their apparent inefficiencies are taken as a necessary evil. Last but not least due to the problem of efficiency many of today's natural language systems are in a strong sense demonstrational ones only, restricting themselves in several directions or showing a rather poor performance. Especially in small research groups the necessary man power is not at hand to work in both directions: the investigation of the basic principles the system is to be based upon, as well as the optimization of system components. Moreover, testing and verification of the general validity of a specific system requires extensive experimentation, what meets serious (efficiency-) obstacles in numerous contemporary software solutions. Consequently, we see a strong demand for the inclusion of tools for optimization into the customary programming environments of Computational Linguistics, to facilitate the system development as well as to make the transition into a commercial product more flexible.

Up to the moment research on automatic program optimization has limited itself almost exclusively to the analysis of the program text only (cf. the techniques to be applied in an optimizing SETL-compiler [6]). Unfortunately, in typical natural language based systems the ratio between the linguistic reference data and the programs reaches a level, where program analysis no longer can be considered to be the main source of information concerning optimization. In a linguistic string-to-string transformation [3], for instance, more than 80% of the memory are occupied by the reference knowledge of the system. Hence, at least a storage optimization first of all has to start from a detailed analysis of the data to be processed.

Generally, within the life cycle of a data item three main stages can be well distinguished:

(a) dynamic: Data on which constructive access functions (e.g. SET, ADD, UPDATE, INPUT) are still operating.

(b) static: Data only accessed by selective functions yet (e.g. GET, SEEK, OUTPUT).

(c) dead: Data not used anymore.

Whereas the transition from static to dead data usually can be exploited via a garbage collection or an explicit free command, the dynamic/static difference remains unconsidered in almost every programming system. This difference, however, allows considerable optimizations on the representation of static data using the fact of the reduced and thus simplified access functions for them. The importance of this kind of optimization becomes obvious if one takes into account that the portion of static data usually amounts to 90% and more. Due to the voluminous linguistic reference knowledge (dictionary entries, rules etc.) this situation seems to be a typical one in natural language applications[1] and here we find one of the major reasons for the unefficiency of todays pointer languages: The huge amount of static data is stored in data structures originally designed for dynamic ones.

Three kinds of information are necessary in principle to carry out an optimizing transformation changing a dynamic into a static data representation: the moment, the direction and the degree of the optimization. Whereas it is possible to detect the last occurrence of a constructor access on a specific data structure (i.e. the moment it becomes static) fully automatic [6], neither the direction nor the degree of the optimization can be determined by a program analysis. The results of different optimization techniques are contradictory to a degree that the system designer has to decide at any rate, which kind of optimization criteria should be taken as a basis:

(1) storage capacity

(2) access time (e.g. for search procedures)

(3) locality (if a virtual environment is used, where just for pointer languages a "working set" can hardly be established [1])

Furthermore, each optimization technique may be characterized by a specific cost/benefit ratio which first of all depends on the amount of data analysis necessary to carry out the optimization. Especially in the case of higher expenditures the application of a technique is worthwhile only under specific circumstances. Again the designer has to choose, up to which depth an optimization remains sensible.

---

[1] [1] reports 96% for a french data base query system; in the already mentioned string manipulation system [3] the figure is 94%, although expensive optimizations have already been applied.

Since storage limitations play an important role in many natural language based systems, the following considerations will focus mainly on storage reductions. Very similar results, however, can be obtained for other optimization criteria as well.

To the rather cheap techniques which can be applied on a data structure even without a detailed data analysis belong three very simple ones:

(1) Simplification: For certain data structures the constructive access functions (e.g. UPDATE or INPUT) can be omitted in the final version of the system.

(2) Separation: In a virtual environment static and dynamic data may be separated as to make the repeated read-out of a static and thus unchanged page unneccessary.

(3) Size-tuning: The fixed size of the address space of a static data structure may be used to reduce pointer (as well as length attributes etc.) down to the maximum needed. This is of especial significiance if hardware dependent boundaries are not yet exceeded (e.g. the boundary between a 16 and a 32 bit integer).

More far reaching optimizations become possible if the data structure will be rearranged according to a detailed and sometimes extremely expensive analysis of it, e.g.:

(4) Linearization: Sequential reordering of lists etc. to allow the omission of pointer, indicating always the immediate next record of the data structure. Given certain conditions, linear lists may be represented by arrays or even bit strings.

(5) Localization: Improvement of the locality by reordering the data structure to be able to install offset pointer instead of the ordinary absolute ones. In a virtual system improved localization additionally helps to avoid page defaults.

(6) Condensation: Diminuition of data redundancy by multiple use of entries using the relation of set- (string-, list-) inclusion.

In any case, these techniques imply the necessity of specialized selector functions for the optimized data. Thus, they are profitable only if applied to big enough data structures, as one could find them in any of today's programming systems in the form of pools for lists, strings, etc. [4].

Some more optimizations, especially to achieve a good local behaviour of a data structure, become possible, if an access statistics is available. Normally, access frequencies can be computed in a run time analysis on a sufficient amount of real data only. In the processing of natural language, however, sometimes simple regularities allow to derive rough access distributions from a pure static data analysis (e.g. ZIPF's law, which gives a good relation between the length of a string and its frequency of usage).

Traditionally, data oriented optimization techniques have been implemented only, if at all, in special purpose systems (e.g. [2]). De facto, these systems include higly specialized translators which compile the reference knowledge needed into an optimized internal code, in a strong analogy to an optimizing compiler for a higher level programming language: The incoming data (programs as well as static reference knowledge) are analyzed and optimized according to the build-in criteria.

In contrast to the traditional approach of "hand-made" data optimizers a scheme would be desirable where software tools for analysis and transformation of data structures are an integrated part of the programming system the natural language processor is imbedded in. Hence, a good programming system for the purpose of natural language research ought to support two demands:

(a) the design of the natural language based system itself and

(b) the design of data compiler for the reference knowledge.

The development of tools for the compilation of data can proceed in several steps, corresponding to different levels of comfort:

(1) The supply of alternative implementations for one and the same abstract data type (as already offered in some SETL-systems [5]) from which the system designer may choose an appropriate one according to his experience. Tools for data analysis remain to be written by means of the implementation language.

(2) The integration of data analysis and transformation functions (for the linearization of lists, the detection of redundant entries, etc.) in the programming system. The designer still has to decide upon the optimization technique and must invoke the desired functions.

(3) An automatic invocation of the optimizing functions according to an optimization criteria (e.g. speed, space, locality) and an upper limit for the cost/benefit ratio given both by the system designer.

Among the techniques for the reorganization of data structures, especially localization and condensation involve considerable expenses. Thus the cost/benefit ratio of an optimization always has to be transparent for the programmer in order to objectivize his decisions about the techniques to apply as well as to facilitate a necessary amount of experimentation to determine a sensible degree of the optimization.

Programming systems which supply tools for data analysis and transformation allow the creation of natural language systems on a higher level of quality while preserving the well known advantages of the very high programming languages: mental simplicity and flexibility in experimental environments. Optimizing data compilation, however, becomes a very difficult task in systems using a procedural knowledge representation. The scattering of data throughout the different system modules makes an automatic data analysis almost impractical. So, from the viewpoint of data optimization an old wisdom from the earlier days of mechanical translation gains new actuality: linguistic data should be carefully separated from the programs in order to compile both of them according to their specific properties.

[1] KANOI,H. and VAN CANEGHEM,M., Implementing a very high level language on a very low cost computer, Univ. Aix-Marseille 1979
[2] MENZEL,W., Die Implem. der GPU, Tagung ASV 81, Potsdam 1981
[3] MENZEL,W., A Grapheme-to-Phoneme Transformation for German, to appear in Počitace a umelá inteligencia
[4] NORDSTRÖM,M., LISP F3 - Implementation guide, DLU Uppsala, 1978
[5] PARTSCH,H. and STEINBRÜGGEN,R., TUM 18108, TU München 1981
[6] SCHWARTZ,J.T., Optimization of very high level languages, Comp. languages, 1 (1975), 161-194, 197-218

Artificial Intelligence and Information-Control Systems of Robots
I. Plander (editor)
© Elsevier Science Publishers B.V. (North-Holland), 1984

A FORMAL APPROACH TO VERB SEMANTICS

G. Mihailova
Institute for Bulgarian
Language

G. Gargov
Mathematical Logic Section
Institute of Mathematics

Bulgarian Academy of Sciences
Sofia, Bulgaria

This paper reports on a project for a systematic study of the
semantic structure of Bulgarian verbs in connection with
problems of applied linguistics and artificial intelligence
such as automatic natural language processing and knowledge
representation. A language for semantic representation based
on untyped lambda-calculus is presented and the readings of
two related lexical classes - "verbs of communication" and
"verbs of speech" - are discussed together with the main
procedures used to establish these readings.

INTRODUCTION

The importance of the lexical component is recognized in AI and contemporary
natural language processing relies heavily on such a component. Definitions of
lexical items are looked for which are to be appropriate for knowledge representation. And the central question of recent AI investigations undoubtly is the
building of more realistic system for handling knowledge. The language part of
such a system must be based on a profound linguistic theory, in partiqular on a
sound and comprehensive semantic theory.

Schefe stressed in [7] that knowledge representation needs logic. It is our
belief that there are a lot of very interesting and usable in AI logical techniques beyond first-order logic. One such technique is described below.

The problem of finding suitable languages for semantic representation is not a
new one. The requirements of theoretical justification and at the same time of
practical acceptability impose very strict limitations on the possible solutions.
One attempt in this direction is the formal language for word readings proposed
by Shalyapina in [3].

Large scale investigations of verb systems of different natural languages are
rare pursuits. We might mention the work of T.Ballmer and W. Brennenstuhl [4]
who gave a semantic categorization of German verbs based on the theoretical
foundation of frame theory. The notion of frame they used as an organizing principle to cast the 13 000 readings (of simple verb forms) into 40 frames, or
models, as they say. In the present exposition another organizing principle is
presented, but our aim is very much the same as theirs: we try to find the
general structure of the semantic space of all Bulgarian verbs. The outcome of
this pursuit is not yet clear, yet we hope that some of the already obtained
results could have applications in the area of AI language investigations.

VERB MEANINGS AND PROCEDURES FOR THEIR ESTABLISHING

Let us briefly review the fundamentals of the semantic theory we intend to use in
our investigation. The main goal of any such theory is to associate expressions

(words, sentences, etc.) with   m e a n i n g s , and to explain what sorts of
entities meanings are. There exist different answers to this problem but all of
them concern the structure of meanings and the methods to reduce the meanings
of complex linguistic units (e.g. sentences) to the meanings of simpler ones -
in the ideal case to the meanings of already indecomposable units (semantic
atoms). Such meaning reduction is supposed to be executable in a completely formal way and should lead to the level of single words (or idioms). The method of
decomposition seems appropriate in the field of word semantics too, but have been
rarely explored until recently.

We build the present analysis around the notion of a   s i t u a t i o n . Thus we
proceed in the spirit of the theory "Meaning ⟷ Text" (cf. [1] and [2]).
A situation is a "fragment of reality" reflected lexically, so situations are
associated with certain words. In such a case we say that the word names the situation. A situation can usually be named by many different words. It should be
mentioned that in fact we deal not with particular situation but rather with
classes of similar "fragments of reality", situation-schemata. This faces us
with epistemological problems concerning the foundations of such structuring of
the world. For the lack of space we leave aside these very interesting issues.

In situations some important components can be discerned - the participants in
the situation - we call them semantic   a c t a n t s . The number of actants of
a situation can be 0, 1, 2, ... - on this basis we distinguish n-actant situations for different values of n. Some of the actants can themselves be
situations (this fact is crucial for our choice of the language for semantic representation). Situations and their actants are elements of the world of meanings
(not the only ones) and to denote them we use the common term   s e m e. So meanings are composed of semes. The language of meanings must show the way they are
composed.

Verbs usually name situations and the relation of semantic similarity between
verbs,which generates the so-called semantic fields, is based on nearness of situations. This means a repetition of a seme in the meanings of groups of verbs
- such an invariant is used for delimiting of   l e x i c a l   c l a s s e s
of verbs and is sometimes termed   a r c h i - s e m e of the class. We present
as an example two classes of verbs: verbs of communication and verbs of speech.
An intuitive analysis of the "communication situation" shows that it requires
at least two agents X and Y and another situation S as actants: X causes Y to
know (about) S. This seme appears neccesserily in every verb of the class and is
the archi-seme. Of course there are other semes in the meanings of the verbs of
the class - these are called secondary and according to them the class is split
into 4 subclasses, which can be further divided into 15 subclasses of lower
rank according to the presence of tertiary semes and so on. As can be seen the
structure of the class is determined by the relation of h y p o n y m y . The
class of verbs of speech exibits analogous constitution - here the archi-seme
is "X uses his voice to produce pieces of a language Z". This seme is found in
verbs of communication too, but as a secondary seme. Thus   говоря   (speak)
is a member of both classes with two of its readings, which differ only in the
rank of the semes. This mechanism is an important addition to the priciple of
homonymic structuring of verb classes.

The intuitive comparison of meanings that leads to structuring of verb classes
needs linguistic justification. Here we briefly list four procedures (tests)for
such justification:
     - the deep syntactical structures test (cf. [1] and [2]);
     - the syntactic compatibility test ;
     - the compatibility on the level of text test;
     - the semantic distribution test.
These procedures can confirm the presence of semes but they leave open the problem of choosing the readings, in particular the choice of elementary semes.But

Formal approach to verb semantics   253

this is a problem in any lexical semantics theory that we know of (cf. for example
[6]). On Fig.1 we show the semantic graph of a reading of the verb speak. The
partitioning into main and secondary sub-graph is characteristic for our approach.

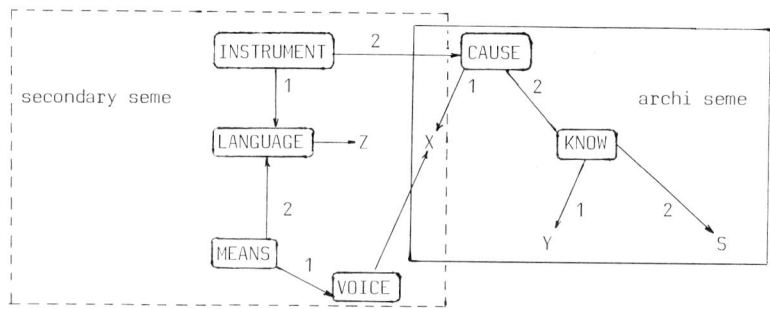

Figure 1
A semantical graph representation of one
reading of the verb говоря (speak)

THE LANGUAGE FOR SEMANTIC REPRESENTATION

Our formal language for semantic representation is a intensional logic language
(similar to Montague original one [5] but) based on a structure familiar from
untyped λ-calculus. It resembles very much the language proposed by Turner in
[9] for treating nominalization.

A central notion is the notion of semantic domain (SD).
Definition A partially ordered set (D, $\leq$) is complete if there exist least upper bounds for all ω-chains $d_0 \leq d_1 \leq \ldots \leq d_n \leq \ldots$ in D (denoted by $\sup d_n$). An SD is a complete partially ordered set with a least element.

Example BOOL is an SD, where BOOL = { True, False, Undefined } and $\leq$ is
such that Undefined $\leq$ True, Undefined $\leq$ False.

A function mapping one SD into another is continuous if it preserves sup-s. There
are several constructions that give new SD-s from old ones : sum, product, and
function-space (cf. [9]). The last one is denoted ($D_1 \rightarrow D_2$) and represents the
SD of all continuous functions f: $D_1 \rightarrow D_2$ ordered by point-wise domination.

D. Scott developed a method for solving recursive semantic domain equations in
[8]. Thus all such equations that appear below should be considered solvable.

For the definition of the language we need the notion of t y p e. We start from
a set of SD-s (the basic types) which contains BOOL and several other domains as
for example PERSON, and so on. Then we introduce the SD SIT (for situation) and
would like SIT to satisfy equations like the following:

$$SIT = (BOOL + (PERSON \rightarrow BOOL) + \ldots + (SIT \rightarrow SIT)).$$

Now we postulate a one-to-one correspondence between types and SD-s that can be
constructed from the basic ones by means of recursive definitions. Then we proceed to define the set of expressions for each type. We have constants of different types, for example we have the constant CAUSE of type ((PERSON x SIT) $\rightarrow$
$\rightarrow$ BOOL). Expressions are built from constants and variables by means of lambda-abstraction, application, logical connectives and quantifiers. If we interpret
basic types by some SD-s then every expression receives a (mathematical) meaning:

an element of the corresponding semantical domain in the interpretation of the type structure.
Now we declare some of the sub-expressions of an expression of different ranks. Call such marked expression a s e m a n t i c   f o r m u l a. The language of semantic formulae is currently being tested for writing down the readings of verbs.

It should be mentioned that this language is suitable for incoporating pragmatic information, too. In fact this was the original intention of the founder of this trend of modern formal linguistics R. Montague. An extension of the language to cover pragmatic aspects of language is quite straightforward.

REFERENCES

[1] Апресян, Ю. Д., Лексическая семантика /Наука, Москва,1974/
[2] Мельчук, И. А., Опыт теории лингвистических моделей "Смысл⟷Текст" /Наука, Москва, 1974 /
[3] Шаляпина, З.М., Формальный язык для записи толкований слов и словосочетаний, Проблемы кибернетики, 36/1979/, 247-278.
[4] Ballmer, T., W. Brennenstuhl, An empirical approach to frametheory: verb thesaurus organisation, in Eikmeyer, H.-J. and Reiser Z.(eds.) Words, Worlds, and Contexts (W. de Gruyter, Berlin, 1981)
[5] Montague, R., Formal Philosophy (Yale Univ. Press, New Haven, 1974)
[6] Sager, N., Natural Language Information Processing (Addison-Wesley, Reading, Mass., 1981)
[7] Schefe, P., Some fundamental issues in knowledge representation, in Wahlster, W. (ed.) , GWAI - 82 (Springer, Berlin, 1982)
[8] Scott, D., Continuous lattices, in Lawvere, F. W. (ed.), Toposes, Algebraic Geometry, and Logic (Springer, Berlin, 1972)
[9] Turner, R., Montague semantics, nominalization and Scott's domains, Linguistics and Philosophy, 6 (1983), 259 - 288 .

SM-4-"OMEGA" INTERACTIVE IMAGE PROCESSING SYSTEM IN SOLVING ARTIFICIAL INTELLIGENCE PROBLEMS

E.G. Mikhaltsov, V.P. Pjatkin

Computing Center, Siberian Branch of the USSR Academy of Sciences, Novosibirsk

> An interactive image processing system is described. It consists of a control computer SM-4 and a specialized grayscale colour terminal "OMEGA". System software has been created in the framework of the disk operating system "RAFOS". This software is oriented on representation and processing of graphical information, which is important for the applied problems of artificial intelligence.

Imagery is a perspective and adequate means of information representation for artificial intelligence systems since it possesses a number of advantages the main of which are the following: informational capacity, compactness and visuality. Future application of artificial intelligence robots will demand complex forms of imagery analysis. An immense quantity of information contained in images along with the need to nonlinearly transform them potentially makes digital image processing one of the most complicated branches of signal processing. The signal processing category includes the following pictorial information processing problems which are important for the applied problems of artificial intelligence [1]:

   Character recognition (print, hand)
   Image recognition (monochromatic, colour)
   Image processing
   Image analysis
   Image understanding
   Scene analysis
   Speech recognition (separate words and a merged speech)
   Natural language understanding

To develop and to debug the algorithms of solving the above problems it is hard to over-estimate the use of automatized image processing systems, which provide a dialogue and dynamic display of results of processing on a colour grayscale display screen [2].

In this paper, an interactive system of image processing is considered. It consists of a specialized colour grayscale terminal "OMEGA" attached to the SM-4 computer through a hardware-software interface. The general view of the system is shown in Figure 1. The SM-4 computer plays the role of a control computer. Information input-output, the system and image processing programs mode assignment are implemented by SM-4 computer.

Figure 1
General view of the system

The "OMEGA" terminal is a part of the system for digital image processing and displaying. The number of jointly processed images is 3 (possible extension up to 16). The maximum size of every input image is 512 x 512 pixels with density resolution up to 8 bits. The functional scheme of the "OMEGA" terminal is given in Figure 2.

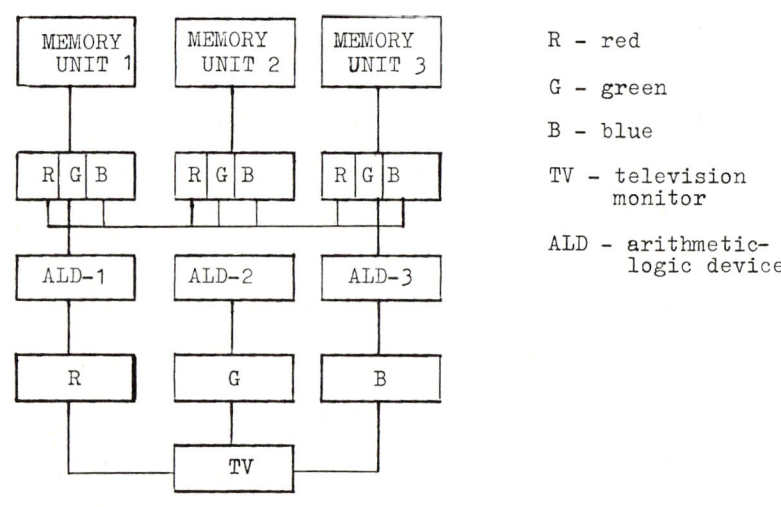

R - red

G - green

B - blue

TV - television monitor

ALD - arithmetic-logic device

Figure 2
Functional scheme of the "OMEGA" terminal

Image processing is performed in a pipelining way at the television scanning rate (clock frequency is 10 MHz, frame frequency is 25 Hz). Digital image data and control information transfer between the SM-4 computer and the "OMEGA" terminal is accomplished through the hardware interface. There are three restore memory units, each having 256 Kbyte capacity. The memory design is "biport" or bimodul. That simultaneously provides both high-speed data transfer to (from) the computer and continuous video channel servicing. The controller of each memory unit allows information reading with a vertical or horizontal shift (or with a shift along both coordinates) on any number of pixels. In addition, the controller allows one to enlarge a part of an image by a factor of 2, 4, 8. Functional transformers (FTs) together with arithmetical-logical devices (ALDs) provide execution of most frequently used operations on initial images (addition, subtraction, multiplication, division, linear and nonlinear transformation of pixel brightness). The FTs are high-speed programmable memories of 256 x 8 bit each. Combinational logical schemes perform algebraic addition in a digital manner from the FT outputs. Three combinational logic chains provide red, green, and blue video signals, respectively, for the colour television monitor. Every chain is connected with all the restore memory units through the FTs. Therefore, all the possible image commutations and combinations may be executed.

Start system software has been created within the framework of the disk operating system "RAFOS". Considerable information contents in the form of images where data prevail over processing procedures make it necessary to develop a special language, allowing data transformation on the level of description of objects and classes of objects. An image as an object is characterized by a number of properties:
- considerable data contents; an image presented in the form of a two-dimensional matrix or, for colour and multispectral data in the form of a multidimensional matrix, has from units to tens Mbytes;
- for many applications a particular image size and an accuracy of presentation of separate pixels do not play an essential role for processing algorithms; visual contents, evaluated as a rule by a person, is of importance.

Thus, an image processing language must allow image size variation to optimize the processing algorithm and the calls to external carriers. In this language, images are considered continuous multidimensional functions. If necessary, the compiler introduces interpolation of missing values and averages groups of values. These requirements are natural, they facilitate the development of software-hardware means, since they make it possible to change harmlessly sizes, accuracy of representation and data structures for applied program packages, and to introduce new hardware means, which quicken data processing. To achieve this, it is enough to change the processor and, correspondingly, the image file and to implement the algorithms most frequently used by special processors. The image data structures are implemented by the image system catalogue, which is used at the compilation stage and leads to working out a varying performable code depending on the image type and organization. A high-level image processing language disciplines a user, it makes him do programming not going into detail of algorithms implementation and data representation. Therefore, there appears a field of action for the hardware-software optimization of the processing procedure.

Basic ideas of this approach to the software organization of the interactive digital image processing system have been proved while implementing a particular programming system, connected with the representation and processing of graphical information, which is important for solving such artificial intelligence problems as scene analysis, robot or manipulator moving planning in a complex environment, etc.

REFERENCES

[1] Plander I. Parallel and Problem-Oriented Processors for Artificial Intelligence and Robotics, Computers and Artificial Intelligence, 1 (1982), 7-33.
[2] Kalantaev P.A., Kompankov B.V., Mikhaltsov E.G., Pjatkin V.P., Rjabchikova L.I., Salavatov R.M., Shakirov R.A. System of Interactive Image Processing. - In: Intercative Systems. Report Abstracts of the Fifth School-Seminar. Tbilisi, Metsniereba, 1983, 172-173 (in Russian).

Artificial Intelligence and Information-Control Systems of Robots
I. Plander (editor)
© Elsevier Science Publishers B.V. (North-Holland), 1984

UNIVERSAL SYSTOLIC ARRAY PROCESSORS FOR FAST MATRIX OPERATIONS

Jozef Mikloško, Bedrich Zaťko

Institute of Technical Cybernetics
Slovak Academy of Sciences
84237 Bratislava, Dúbravská 9
Czechoslovakia

The paper gives three new universal almost homogeneous systolic arrays (SLED, MID and SLEMID), which can solve on one array of processors some (or all) of these problems: system of linear equations (SLE), matrix inversion (MI) and determinant (D). Matrix multiplication for the array similar to SLED is also suggested. For the description of our systolic algorithms formal apparatus is formulated.

INTRODUCTION

Most of the signal and image processing algorithms can be formulated in terms of matrix operations which are well suited to parallel implementation on array processors with a number of simple identical processors parallel operating on the matrix elements. Such array processors are e.g. systolic arrays [1], which have received growing attention since 1981 because of new VLSI technology.

Systolic arrays (SA) are highly parallel computing networks of simple, almost identical, processors which rhythmically calculate in parallel and transfer data through simple, usually nearest neighbour connections, communication networks. Their input data flow into the input channels. Data regularly flow through processors in the array and without being stored in the memory, they are frequently reused in the calculation. Output data come out from the output channels. SA are therefore the ideal way to use the new VLSI technology for obtaining very high speed for suitable calculations.

Implementation of parallel architecture can be achieved by mapping desired algorithms on VLSI chips. Algorithms, which would be suitable for SA, must satisfy the following conditions [2]: the use of pipelining and parallelism, each data being multiply used, regular data flow consisting of several types of simple operations and, if possible, being universal. The last condition is not satisfied by most known SA since these systems are specialised only for silicon implementation of one algorithm.

In this paper a description is given of some universal SA which can solve on one array some (or all) of these problems: System of Linear Equations (SLE)

$$Ax = a \qquad (1)$$

where $A = (a_{ij})$ is a regular matrix of the n-th order, $x = (x_i)$, $a = (a_{i,n+1})$, $i,j = 1,2,\ldots,n$,

__Matrix Inversion__ (MI)
$$D = A^{-1} = (b_{ij}) \tag{2}$$
and the calculation of __D__eterminant (D)
$$d = \det|A|. \tag{3}$$
Although calculations of (1), (2) and (3) are crucial in solving various important problems, neverthelesess so far not many papers have been concerned with the solution of these problems on SA. Their survey is in [3] and briefly in [4], where there are also designs of specialised SA for (1) and for (2). Until now all known SA have been highly specialised.

In this paper we present three new almost homogeneous SA with some universal features for solution: (1) and (3) on n/n array (SLED), (2) and (3) on n/n array (MID) and (1), (2) and (3) on n/(n+1) array (SLEMID). All these SA are able to solve only the problems of size m where $m \leq n$.

Our SA will be composed of the matrix of processors with n rows and n (or n+1) columns which will be interconnected by the square communication network. Each processor p_{ij}, $i = 1,2,\ldots,n$, $j = 1,2,\ldots,n(n+1)$ has registers RA_{ij}, Rx_{ij} and Ry_{ij} on the contents of which multiplication and substraction is executed. The processor p_{11} computes moreover division and has also a special register Rz_{11} which = 1 at the begining of computation.

Having analyzed several types of elimination algorithms, for our implementation we have chosen Jordan's elimination: in (1) the matrix A is eliminated parallel by the columns to the unit matrix; in (2) the same operations are performed to get B from the unit matrix; determinant (3) is the product of leading elements in elimination. Although Jordan's elimination is not very homogeneous, our SA have, except p_{11} a homogeneous structure.

The following symbolics has been chosen to describe our systolic algorithms:
$\forall i$: $i=1,2,\ldots,n$; $\forall j$: $j=1,2,\ldots,n$ (n+1 on n/(n+1) array);
$\forall i(k)$: $i=1,2,\ldots,k-1,k+1,\ldots,n$;
for $\forall i \forall j$ parinput $\downarrow a_{ij} \Rightarrow Ra_{ij}$: input of a_{ij} from the top to the bottom into the Ra_{ij};
for $\forall i$ partransfer $\rightarrow Ra_{i1} \Rightarrow Rx_{ij}$ $\forall j$: transfer of the Ra_{i1} into the Rx_{ij} $\forall j$ (partransfer$_0$ means that after transfer $Ra_{i1}:=0$);
for $\forall i \forall j$ parcyclshift $\uparrow Ra_{ij} \Rightarrow Ra_{i-1,j}$: cyclic shift of the registers upwards, where $Ra_{0j} \equiv Ra_{nj}$;
for $\forall i \forall j$ parcyclshift$\leftarrow Ra_{ij} \Rightarrow Ra_{i,j-1}$: cyclic shift to the left, where $Ra_{i0} \equiv Ra_{in}$;
for $\forall i \forall j$ pardo $Ra_{ij} \Leftarrow Ra_{ij}$ op$_1$ Rx_{ij} op$_2$ Ry_{ij}: performance of arithmetic expression with operations op$_1$ and op$_2$ on the appropriate registers and the storage of the results into Ra_{ij};
for $\forall j$ parstore $Ra_{1j} \Leftarrow Rx_{1j}$: storing of Rx_{1j} into Ra_{1j};
do $Rz_{11} \Leftarrow Rz_{11}$ op$_1$ Rx_{11}: sequential execution op$_1$ on appropriate registers;
for $\forall i \forall j$ paroutput $\rightarrow Ra_{ij}$: output Ra_{ij} to the right.

output$_1 \leftarrow$ Rz$_{11}$: output Rz$_{11}$ to the left and set Rz$_{11}$ = 1.
$\downarrow \uparrow \rightarrow \leftarrow$, means direction of given operation, prefix par-
means its parallel execution. Symbol e $\wedge$ f means parallel realisation of the expressions e and f.

The kernel of our systolic algorithms executes elimination on the
submatrix (n-k+1) /(n-k+1), k=1,2,...,n. It consists of these operations:
KERNEL(k): Ry$_{11} \Leftarrow$ -1/Rx$_{11}$ $\wedge$ Rz$_{11} \Leftarrow$ Rz$_{11}$·Rx$_{11}$;
partransfer $\rightarrow$ Ry$_{11}$ $\Rightarrow$ Ry$_{1j}$ $\forall$ j $\wedge$ Rx$_{11} \Leftarrow$ 1 ;
for $\forall$ j pardo Ra$_{1j} \Leftarrow$ Ra$_{1j}$ - Rx$_{1j}$·Ry$_{1j}$;
for $\forall$ j (partransfer $\downarrow$ Ra$_{1j}$ $\Rightarrow$ Ry$_{ij}$ $\forall$ i(1)) ;
for $\forall$ i(1) $\forall$ j pardo Ra$_{ij} \Leftarrow$ Ra$_{ij}$ - Rx$_{ij}$·Ry$_{ij}$;
for $\forall$ i $\forall$ j parcyclshift $\leftarrow$ Ra$_{ij}$ $\Rightarrow$ Ra$_{i,j-1}$;
for $\forall$ i $\forall$ j parcyclshift $\uparrow$ Ra$_{ij}$ $\Rightarrow$ Ra$_{i-1,j}$;

KERNEL(k) computes in Ry$_{11}$ reciprocal value of leading element and
in Rz$_{11}$ prepares the value of determinant. After transfer of Ry$_{11}$
to all processors in the first row the algorithm performs elimination on submatrix and leading element of the next step is driven
by cyclic shifts into the p$_{11}$.

SYSTOLIC ARRAY SLED FOR SOLUTION (1) AND (3)

On the basis of our symbolics Jordan's elimination for (1) and (3)
will be implemented on SA SLED, composed of n/n processors, interconnected by the square communication network by this systolic algorithm:
for $\forall$ i parinput $\rightarrow$ a$_{i1}$ $\Rightarrow$ Rx$_{ij}$ $\forall$ j $\wedge$ for $\forall$ i parinput $\downarrow$ a$_{i,n+1}$ $\Rightarrow$ Ra$_{i1}$
$\wedge$ for $\forall$ i $\forall$ j(1) parinput $\downarrow$ a$_{ij}$ $\Rightarrow$ Ra$_{ij}$;
for k = 1 to n do
begin for $\forall$(if k = 1 then j(1) else j) partransfer$_o$ Ra$_{1j}$ $\Rightarrow$ Rx$_{1j}$
$\wedge$ if k >1 then for $\forall$ i(1) partransfer$_o \rightarrow$ Ra$_{i1}$ $\Rightarrow$ Rx$_{ij}$ $\forall$ j ;
KERNEL(k); end;
output$_1 \leftarrow$ Rz$_{11}$ $\wedge$ for $\forall$ i paroutput $\leftarrow$ Ra$_{i1}$;
In this case KERNEL(k) is without Rx$_{11} \Leftarrow$ 1.

Input of 1-st column of A is from the left into Rx$_{i1}$, right side of
(1) (j-th column of A, j=2,3,...,n) from the top into Ra$_{i1}$ (Ra$_{ij}$).
The structure of the systolic array SLED is given on this scheme

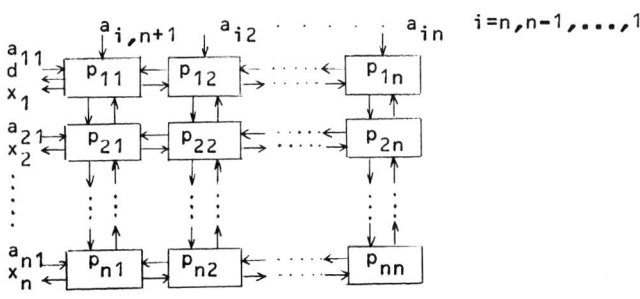

Processor p_{11} simultaneously calculates $Ry_{11}:= -1/Rx_{11}$ and $Rz_{11}:= Rz_{11} \cdot Rx_{11}$ and then elimination step $Ra_{11}:= Ra_{11} - Rx_{11} \cdot Ry_{11}$. All the other p_{ij} in the array compute only $Ra_{ij} := Ra_{ij} - Rx_{ij} \cdot Ry_{ij}$. Let the real implementation time of addition, multiplication, division, transfer, cyclic shift, assignment, parallel input and output of n elements be a, m, d, t, s, p, i, o and let d > m. Then the total time for SLED will be $T_{SLED}^{(n)} = n[d+i+2(a+m+s) + 3(t+p)] + o$.

SYSTOLIC ARRAY MID FOR SOLUTION (2) AND (3)

Jordan's elimination for (2) and (3) on n/n systolic array MID will be given by this systolic algorithm:
   for $\forall i \forall j$ parinput $\downarrow a_{ij} \Rightarrow Ra_{ij}$;
   for k = 1 to n do
   begin for $\forall j$ partransfer$_o$ $Ra_{1j} \Rightarrow Rx_{1j} \wedge$ for $\forall i(1)$ partransfer$_o \rightarrow Ra_{i1} \Rightarrow Rx_{ij} \forall j$;
       KERNEL(k); end;
   output$_1 \leftarrow Rz_{11} \wedge$ for $\forall i \forall j$ par output $\downarrow Ra_{ij}$;

The algorithm executes elimination on both matrix A and unit matrix in such a way that in the k-th cycle n-k columns of A and k columns of B are processed. The structure of MID is - except of input and output channels - equal to SLED. Input of a_{ij} is from the top into Ra_{ij}, output of b_{ij} is down from Ra_{ij}. The ratio of times for Jordan's elimination of (1) and (2) on serial computer is 2:1. For SA is this ratio 1:1 since $T_{MID}^{(n)} = T_{SLED}^{(n)} + (n-1)o$.

SYSTOLIC ARRAY SLEMID FOR SOLUTION (1), (2) AND (3)

The universal systolic algorithm for the simultaneous calculation (1), (2) and (3) is the following:
   for $\forall i \forall j$ parinput $\downarrow a_{ij} \Rightarrow Ra_{ij}$;
   for k = 1 to n do
   begin for $\forall j$ partransfer$_o$ $Ra_{1j} \Rightarrow Rx_{1j} \wedge$ for $\forall i(1)$ partransfer$_o \rightarrow Ra_{i1} \Rightarrow Rx_{ij} \forall j$;
       KERNEL(k); end;
   output$_1 \leftarrow Rz_{11} \wedge \forall i$ paroutput $\leftarrow Ra_{i1} \wedge$ for $\forall i \forall j(1)$ paroutput $\downarrow Ra_{ij}$;

It is performed on n/(n+1) systolic array SLEMID which is given on this scheme:

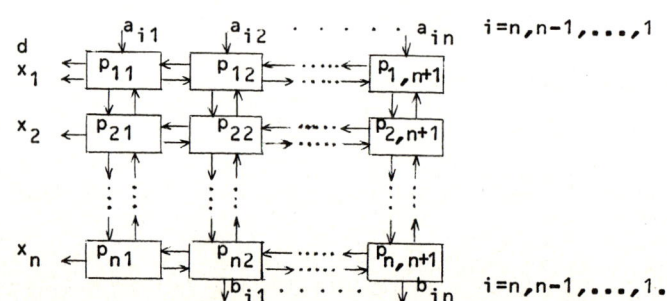

Universal systolic array processors

Total time for SLEMID is equal to $T_{MID}^{(n)}$ i.e. more calculations did not increase computational time with this algorithm.

Remarks:
1. In our algorithms we suppose that no division by 0 can occur. This id guaranteed e.g. if A is a positively definite or strictly diagonally dominant matrix. If any leading element in the eliminated matrix is ≈ 0, then our algorithms fail. This case can be avoided by cyclically shifting the lines upwards or columns to the left until the first appropriate element is found. E.g. in SLED some modification of partial pivoting can be implemented in which we shall continue with cyclic shifting upwards until new leading element in P_{11} will not be greater than a given constant c stored in some additional register Rc_{11} (for $\forall$ i $\forall$ j parcyclshift $\uparrow$ $Ra_{ij} \Rightarrow Ra_{i-1,j}$ while $Ra_{11} < Rc_{11}$) ; . Partial pivoting i.e. choosing the maximum element in column can be arranged by construction of some kind of associative memory from registers $Ra_{i,1}$, i=1,2,...,n in which the maximum can be quickly found and cyclically shifted upwards.

2. Since columns just eliminated in A for solution of (1) and (3) are useless for the next computation, SA SLED can be modified also on array n/(n+1) similar to SLEMID so, that in KERNEL(k) cyclical shift to the left is substituted by transfer i.e. in the new array no chanells for the cyclic shift of rows are. We also note that by some diagonal interconnection network we can substitute two cyclic shifts (left and up) by one diagonal shift.

3. SA n/n similar to SLED or MID can be constructed also for other matrix operations. E.g. for multiplication of n/n matrices C=A.B algorithm from [5] can be modified on systolic in this way:
for $\forall$ i $\forall$ j parinput $\downarrow$ $\bar{a}_{ij} \Rightarrow Rx_{ij}$ $\wedge$ for $\forall$ i $\forall$ j parinput $\rightarrow b_{ij} \Rightarrow Ry_{ij}$
$\wedge$ for $\forall$ i $\forall$ j pardo $Ra_{ij} \Leftarrow 0$;

for k = 1 to n do
begin for $\forall$ i $\forall$ j pardo $Ra_{ij} \Leftarrow Ra_{ij} - Rx_{ij} \cdot Ry_{ij}$;
  for $\forall$ i $\forall$ j parcyclshift $\leftarrow Ry_{ij} \Rightarrow Ry_{i,j-1}$;
  for $\forall$ i $\forall$ j parcyclshift $\uparrow$ $Rx_{ij} \Rightarrow Rx_{i-1,j}$; end;
for $\forall$ i $\forall$ j paroutput $\downarrow Ra_{ij}$;

$\bar{A} = (\bar{a}_{ij})$ ($\bar{B} = (\bar{b}_{ij})$) is obtained from A (-B) by cyclic shift of the i-th row (column) about i-1 columns (rows) i=1,2,...,n, to the left (upwards). At the end c_{ij} are in Ra_{ij}.

4. Control of SA can be performed that the systolic algorithm is splitted into tacts whereby each processors has in its own memory only the numbers and operations of its tacts. Control unit by global synchronisation sends to all processors the number of tact just performed in time of which each processor executes its own operation.

REFERENCE

[1] Kung,H.T.,Leiserson,C.E.: Systolic arrays for VLSI. In: Sparse Matrix Proc. 1978, SIAM, 1979, pp.256-282.
[2] Foster,M.J.,Kung,H.T.: The design of special-purpose VLSI chips. Computer, 1, 1980, pp.26-40.
[3] Tidén,E.,Lisper,B.,Schreiber,R.: Systolic arrays. Techn.rep.TRI-TANA-8315, Royal Inst. of Techn.,Num.Anal.and Comp.Sci.Dep., 1983, p.45.
[4] Mikloško,J.: Systolic systems for the linear aequation system and matrix inversion.Comp.and Artif.Intell.,2,4,1983, pp.361-372.
[5] Thurber,K.J.: Large scale computer architecture, parallel and associative processors. Rochelle Park,N.J.,Heyden Book Co.,1976.

HIERARCHICAL PARALLEL ALGORITHMS

N.N.Mirenkov

Institute of Mathematics
Siberian Branch of the USSR Academy of Sciences
Novosibirsk
USSR

The paper introduces a concept of the hierarchical parallel algorithm which is the problem parallelism description in the viewpoint of a few levels of abstracting. The relation of the problem executing rate to the number of parallel running actions is used in distinguishing the basis of the levels. The introduced concept is associated with the problem of the mathematical method portability for computing systems of various architectures.

Now a trend is formed in creating own algorithmic "industry" for every computing system architecture. So the portability question is raised not only for the programs, but for their more abstract representatives - algorithms (methods). That is, we would like to construct such parallel algorithms (p-algorithms) which could be rather easily transformed for a wide architecture class. The portability question may be schematically represented as follows. A problem is described in the p-algorithm language (task 1), a system architecture is described in the architecture language (task 2) and then, according to the descriptions of the problem and the architecture the most suitable computing processes are realized (task 3).

Today there is partial implementation experience of this scheme. Two approaches may be distinguished in it. In the first one the basis is to discover the problem parallelism represented in a conventional language, in the second one the basis is to express the computing system parallelism in the syntax of a language. These approaches' generalization is seen (for instance, by R.Perrot from Belfast University) in the construction (for pipeline and array processors) of a language which must represent the problem parallelism. This idea is attractive, but it is not clear yet - what is, in general, the inside parallelism of a problem. The matter is that, although it is objective, it can be understood only via some architecture hypothesis.

Before suggesting a generalized model for the problem parallelism representation we touch upon task 3 associated with the mapping of actions (modules) of a p-algorithm to processing elements (PE) of a computing system. Let $M_1, M_2, \ldots, M_m$ be some p-algorithm actions, and $P_1, P_2, \ldots, P_n$ be system PE. Among actions and among PE there are certain relations: intermodule and interprocessor communications.

We define, following [1], a set of matrices: matrix X such that

$x_{ik}=1$ if M_i is assigned to P_k, and otherwise $x_{ik}=0$; matrix Q where q_{ik} is the processing cost for M_i on P_k ($q_{ik}=\infty$, implies that M_i cannot be executed at P_k); matrix V where v_{ij} is the volume of data sent from M_i to M_j (if $v_{ij}=0$, then modules do not communicate with each other); matrix D where $d_{k\ell}$ is a measure of the communication cost between P_k and P_ℓ ($d_{k\ell}=\infty$ if PE are not connected).

Then the cost of the X assignment can be expressed as follows:

$$Cost(X) = \sum_i \sum_k \left\{ q_{ik} x_{ik} + \sum_{\ell < k} \sum_{j < i} w\, v_{ij} d_{k\ell} x_{ik} x_{j\ell} \right\}, \qquad (1)$$

where w is a scale factor. This expression may be accompanied by some constraints. For instance, for memory size: $\sum s_i x_{ik} \le R_k$, $k=1,2,\ldots,n$; where s_i is the amount of memory storage required by M_i, and R_k is the memory capacity at P_k; for realtime: $\sum u_i x_{ik} \le T_k$, $k=1,2,\ldots,n$; where u_i is processing time required by M_i, T_k is the required time limit to process the modules that reside in P_k. Other constraints may be added, for instance, those still more completely representing queueing delays in connection with the precedence relation among modules. Determination of X minimizing (1) may be very complicated. Nevertheless, it gives a formal foundation for the whole problem of portability and shows that we are in need of such problem parallelism descriptions which make this determination acceptable in the complexity and in the quality. In connection with this we suggest to design the hierarchical p-algorithms (hp-algorithms), whose descriptions represent explicitly or implicitly possible approaches to module uniting, construction of various parallelization levels, parallelism redistributing between levels and so on.

The important step in the hp-algorithm designing is the relation diagram construction of the algorithm running rate c from the PE number h. The typical picture of this relation is represented as follows.

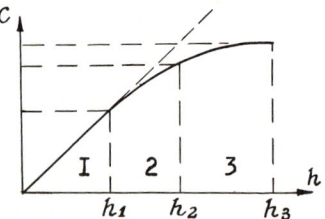

From it we can see that there are three scopes of supereffective (1), effective (2) and ineffective (3) parallelization. In scopes (1) and (2) the p-algorithm running rate is practically increasing in proportion to PE number, and, besides, in scope (1) the proportional coefficient is close to 1. For linear algebra problems these scopes, as a rule, are determined by the following inequalities: $h_1 \le N$, $N \le h_2 \le N^2$, $h_3 \ge N^2$, where N is the matrix size. From here a conclusion springs to mind. A p-algorithm must be at first designed in an orientation to the scope (1) or (2) parallelism, under the mapping assumption of it to rather powerful PE, and then - in the orientation to the scope (3) parallelism, under the assumption that every processing element may be interpreted as pipeline, data flow or another system with rather simple processing modules.

The representation of n level hp-algorithm Π we regard as an n-duple of p-algorithms:

$$\Pi = < \Pi_1, \Pi_2, \ldots, \Pi_n >,$$

where every Π_i represents a part of the inside parallelism of a problem and, besides, the algorithmic complexity of a single action (module) in Π_i is decreased with the increase of i. Today it is natural to consider $n \leq 3$.

A p-algorithm Π_1 is founded on the large-block strategy of parallelization [2]. Its essence is that the number of implied parallel modules is associated to the measure of the problem size (for instance, with the points number of difference grid along an axis). Every module is rather large; after allocating it to some processing element (maybe, to the local memory) the time of its execution will be more than that required for resulting data transference as input data to other modules. The p-algorithm Π_2 involves the parallelism with modules, containing up to a few arithmetic operations. The overhead of the parallel work organization is essential, but the calculation speed-up is proportional to the PE number. Finally, the p-algorithm Π_3 associates its execution with microactions which are arithmetic operation components.

Let us examine an example of an hp-algorithm construction for a mathematical physics problem. Let it be the boundary initial problem for the two-dimensional heat equation and the following splitting method is employed for it [3]:

$$\frac{u_{ij}^{n+1/2} - u_{ij}^{n}}{\tau} = \Lambda_{11} u_{ij}^{n+1/2} + f_{ij}^{1},$$

$$\frac{u_{ij}^{n+1} - u_{ij}^{n+1/2}}{\tau} = \Lambda_{22} u_{ij}^{n+1} + f_{ij}^{2},$$

$$f_{ij} = f_{ij}^{1} + f_{ij}^{2}; \quad u_{ij}^{n}|_{\Gamma} = u_{ij}^{n+1}|_{\Gamma} = g_{ij}; \quad u_{ij}^{0} = \bar{g}_{ij}.$$

Besides, the difference grid dimension is $N \times N$. Here the first level of parallelization involves modules which employ the chase-method for one or several lines of the grid, $h_1 \leq N$. For the distributed memory systems parallelization of this sort of problems is described in [4]. It employs a special production line scheme for the chase-method usage along vertical lines of the grid and does not require array transposition. A p-algorithm based on data distribution among modules not in strips (as in [4]), but in large-block-skewed segments, is described in [2]. Both papers represent the relations determining the p-algorithm efficiency in the dependence on the number of parallel execution actions, time of arithmetic operations and intermodule communication. These relations point out clear conditions when large-block parallelization gives a speed-up by $c \cdot h_1$ times with c close to 1. The other important result which was obtained there is that a p-algorithm may be described as several or even one basic module which is copied in dependence on the PE number and is tuned to problem size as to a parameter [5].

The second level parallelization base is given by the method from [3], oriented to parallel execution of the chase-method for a single line of the grid. The main idea is to choose from $\{u_{ij}, i = \overline{0,N}\}$ for $\forall j$ a part of unknowns $\{u_{\ell j}, \ell = 0, 1 \cdot n, \ldots, m \cdot n\}$ as the parameters, to construct the equation system for them, to solve this system and then to calculate the remainder of the unknowns.

The analysis shows that this method gives the maximal speed-up of calculation for $n = m = \sqrt{N}$. Then as h_2 one may take $N\sqrt{N}$. In this case p-algorithm description may be represented as the basic set description of multiplying modules.

Let us now proceed to the next level of parallelization. It is known that the method from [6] leads to the maximal speed-up of the solution of a tridiagonal linear system. This speed-up is proportional to $N/log_2 N$ with N PE. The method from [3] gives the same result, if it is employed at first to compute $N/2$ parametric variables, then for $N/4$, $N/8$ and so on. Hence it follows that for the problem under consideration h_3 equals N^2.

CONCLUDING REMARKS

The development of the methods for parallel data processing (we mean methods, not programs) must be accomplished by using the inside parallelism of a problem. However, this parallelism must be described in the viewpoint of a few levels of abstracting which would allow us to synthesize a p-program for a particular computing system from p-algorithm description. The principal moment in p-algorithm description is the representation of parametrically tunable and copied modules and also p-algorithm's quality functions. They allow us to transform the determination of the minimum $Cost(X)$ from (1) to not too complicated search for the corresponding parameters values.

Increase of "loading" for the method constructors seems to be a very important step on the way of a balanced approach to the parallel data processing organization.

REFERENCES

[1] Chu,W.W., Holloway,L.J., Lan,M. and Efe,K., Task Allocation in Distributed Data Processing, Computer, vo.13, 11 (1980)57-69.
[2] Mirenkov,N.N., Parallel algorithms for problem solving on homogeneous computer systems, in: Vycisl.Sistemy, 57 (Novosibirsk, 1973) 3-32.
[3] Janenko,N.N., Konovalov,A.N., Bugrov,A.N., Shustov G.V., About parallel computing organization and "parallelizing" of chase-method, in: Numerical mechanics of continua methods, vo.9, 7 (Novosibirsk, 1978), 139-146.
[4] Mirenkov,N.N., An implementation of alternating direction method on computer system "Minsk-222", in: Vycisl. Sistemy, 30, (Novosibirsk, 1968),26-33.
[5] Mirenkov,N.N., System parallel programming, Part 1, The Inst. of Math. Preprint OBC-05 (Novosibirsk, 1978) 3-35.
[6] Kogge,P.M., Stone,H.S., A parallel algorithm for the efficient solution of a general class of recurrence equations, IEEE Trans. on Computers, vo.C-22, 8 (1973), 786-792.

RESULTS OF IMPLEMENTATION OF THE FIRST VERSION OF MEDICAL EXPERT SYSTEM "CONSULTANT"

Olga S. Molokova, Mary Ju. Chernyakovskaja

Laboratory of AI methods for medicine
Automation and Control Processes Institute
Far-Eastern Research Center of Academy of Sciences
Vladivostok
U.S.S.R.

The software of the first version of medical expert system "CONSULTANT" realizes the following possibilities: the correct knowledge base creation, input, acceptability testing, and interpretation of the pacient data, decision-making in the most probable diagnostic hypotheses and generation of the explanation with required degree of detaility. In the process of projecting the first version of "CONSULTANT" the method of system's formal specification with the help of the frame model language was applied.

The implementation of the first version of medical expert system "CONSULTANT" forms a part of investigations directed to development of methodology, technology, and instrumental facilities for creation of expert systems [1,2]. Investigation of the mixed computations' technique of compiling the knowledge base into expert system software [2], acquirement of experience in building and debugging the knowledge base, generation of explanations and analysis of the expert system performance - are purposes of the implementation.

The knowledge base of the first version is experimental and it consists of descriptions of seven diseases and 32 observations and their interrelations. These descriptions concern the section of medicine - acute abdominal surgical diseases. As compared with [1], the knowledge base and data base schemas of the system's first version are considerably simplified. A disease is described with its clinical picture and with differential-diagnostic information. A clinical picture consists of many clinical manifestations. A clinical manifestation is implied as casual relation between the disease as being a cause and the value of observation as being an effect. Clinical manifestation can have some variants of effects, and each variant has its own typicalness l . In description of the differential diagnosis of disease with its competitive one, a set of differentiating manifestations is given, i.e. the values of observations testifying against the competitor. An observation is specified by possible values area and by normal values.

The data base schema specifies models of the case diagnoses. It determines structure of observation and disease models, of models interpretating the observed values as being normal, or clinical or differentiating disease manifestations. Knowledge base and data base schemas are matched, these schemas being a simple problem-oriented representation [3].

In the process of projecting the first version of "CONSULTANT" the method of system's formal specification with the help of the frame models language was applied [4], i.e., a frame model of matching relation between the knowledge base and data base schemas was developed. In order to implement the matching relation model there was developed an algorithm constructing a data base according to the knowledge base and the input information about a patient [5]. The software of the system's first version realizes the following possibilities: the knowledge base creation and testing the context conditions, input, acceptability testing, and interpretation of the patient data, decision-making in the most probable diagnostic hypotheses and generation of the explanations with required degree of detail.

The knowledge base of the first version of expert system "CONSULTANT" is described with the help of medical diagnostic knowledge representation language MEDIFOR [6]. The formation of the internal knowledge base representation is performed through translator of MEDIFOR. The translator consists of two blocs: the first one analyses the MEDIFOR-text and translates it into internal representation; the latter uses internal knowledge base representation in order to check up on context conditions. In this case the agreement relation between the notional structure of knowledge base and its schema, and a number of syntactic and semantic conditions of a knowledge base correctness are checked. An example of the syntactic condition is: the determining and the using entries of observation's values must be matched; the determining entry is a description of possible values area of observation, the using entries are the clinical and differentiating manifestations. An example of semantic condition is: for all observations being patologic symptoms, the normal value must be given in the form of "non-presence".

The patient data input can be effected in both batch and dialog. Each data is a result of observation or a set of such results. In the process of input, the control of data correctness occures; a data is considered to be incorrect, if a result of unknown observation is entered or if an observed value does not enter the possible values area; there is also a possibility of correcting the erroneous data.

Decision-making in the most probable hypotheses is performed on the basis of heuristic rules. These rules take into account just how well the each disease model explains the input data, and these provide the establishment of partial order on the set of disease models.

The explanation is made by the way of generating the texts describing results of computations, with needed degree of detaility [7]. In the first version of expert system "CONSULTANT", the explanation subsystem generates texts on topics "Diagnosis", "A diagnosis foundation", and "Why the certain diseases are non-diagnosis". For every topic, the texts with several degrees of detaility can be formed. In the first version of system "CONSULTANT" three degrees of detaility are separated out: the minimal, the normal, and the complete degrees. An interface with the system in order to obtain explanations may be performed in both batch and dialog.

The implementation of the first version of expert system "CONSULTANT" was made with the help of the data flow relation programming language RELYP in the framework of instrumental complex for creation of the expert systems [2].

The experimental use of the first version of system "CONSULTANT", being carried out currently, is intended for the man-machine process of debugging a medical diagnostic knowledge base to be investigated. Although the study is still far from being completed, already now it can be concluded that the expert systems of a similar class are adequate instrument to solve the task in view. In our opinion, this is provided with such expert system's features as the representation of the notional structure of medical diagnostic knowledge, the use of the problem knowledge descripting formalizm, which is natural to experts, and the possibility for obtaining the explanation with needed degrees of detaility.

REFERENCES:

[1] Černjahovskaja, M.Ju., Predstavlenie znanij v ëkspertnyh sistemah medicynskoj diagnostiki (DVNC AN SSSR, Vladivostok, 1983): in russian.
[2] Artemjeva, I.L., Gorbačev, S.B., Kleščev, A.S., Lifšic, A.Ja., Orlov, S.I., Orlova, L.D. and Uvarova, T.G., Instrumentalnyj kompleks dlja realizacii jazykov predstavlenija znanij, Programmirovanie 4 (1983) 78-89: in russian.
[3] Kleshchev, A.S., Problem-oriented representations for development of knowledge base for expert systems, 3-d International Conference "Artif. Intell. and Inform.-Control Systems of Robots" (North-Holland, Amsterdam, 1984).
[4] Kleščev, A.S., Frejmovye modeli i ih primenenie v predstavlenii znanij, in: Kleščev, A.S. and Černjahovskaja, M.Ju. (eds.), Jazyki predstavlenija znanija i voprosy realizacii ëkspertnyh sistem (DVNC AN SSSR, Vladivostok, 1983) 3-12: in russian.
[5] Molokova, O.S., Razrabotka programmnogo obespecenija pervoj versii medicinskoj ëkspertnoj sistemy "KONSULTANT", in: Kleščev, A.S. and Černjahovskaja, M.Ju. (eds.), Jazyki predstavlenija znanija i voprosy realizacii ëkspertnyh sistem (DVNC AN SSSR, Vladivostok, 1983) 77-95: in russian.
[6] Gorbachev, S.B., Kleshchev, A.S. and Chernyakovskaja, M.Ju., A problem-oriented language for medical diagnostic knowledge representation MEDIFOR-3, 2-nd International Conference "Artif. Intell. and Inform. Control Systems of Robots" (1982) 99-102: in russian.
[7] Molokova, O.S., Černjahovskaja, M.Ju., Voprosy sozdanija programmnoj sistemy generacii tekstov objasnenija v ramkah banka medicinskogo znanija, in: Eršov, A.P. (ed.), Problemy teoretičeskogo i sistemnogo programmirovanïja (NGU, Novosibirsk, 1982) 125-134: in russian.

ADVANCED CONTROL SYSTEM FOR INDUSTRIAL ROBOTS

L. Oprea, D. Nedelea, B. Udrea   A. Moangă

Automatica - Research & Design Division   Central Institute
Sos. Fabrica de Glucoză nr. 17   for Management and
72322 BUCUREȘTI 30   Informatics, Bd.
ROMANIA   Miciurin 8 București

This paper presents a software system - GENERA - for programming and control industrial robots with a minicomputer COMPA-4801 (DEC compatible). GENERA system is working with REMT family robots (electrically driven, five degrees of freedom, polar coordinates, romanian made robot). Algorithms for trajectory generation and movement control, programming facilities, hardware and software configuration are presented.

INTRODUCTION

The adaptability of industrial robots makes them potentially more attractive especially in the area of batch assembly however, current robots are of limited adaptibility.

We have developed a modular, flexible software system, GENERA, for programming and control of industrial robots, with the aid of a minicomputer. Both nontextual or textual methods can be used with the same control system. The control system can be developed to process force, proximity and visual information for assembly applications.

GENERAL PRESENTATION OF GENERA SYSTEM

The GENERA system can controll the robot joint coordinates (for point to point instructions: PPT, PPTI, PPTV, PPTR) and in cartesian coordinates (three straight line instructions: LINE, LINE T, LINE V).

During the teaching sesion, the operator can move the robot independently on every degree of freedom (with a selected speed), or in a coordonated straight line way: up-down, forward-backward.

Besides movement instructions, one can use the following instructions: REPEAT-END REPEAT for programming loops; CALL-RETURN for writing subroutines; JUMP, JUMP IF INPUT ON, JUMP IF INPUT OFF, JUMP IF FLAG ON, JUMP IF FLAG OFF for unconditional or conditional jumps in the program (the system has sixteen programmable flags and sixteen binary inputs for syncronisation with machine tools or other robots); OUTPUT ON, OUTPUT OFF, GRASP, UNGRASP for controlling the machine tools or other devices and the hand of the robot; The programs are written in memory, using push-buttons on the specialised console, and can be stored on the floppy-disc. Up to four programs can be read and linked from the floppy-disc and executed in the automatic mode.

TRAJECTORY GENERATION AND EXECUTION

The seven movement instructions of GENERA system have the following characteristics:

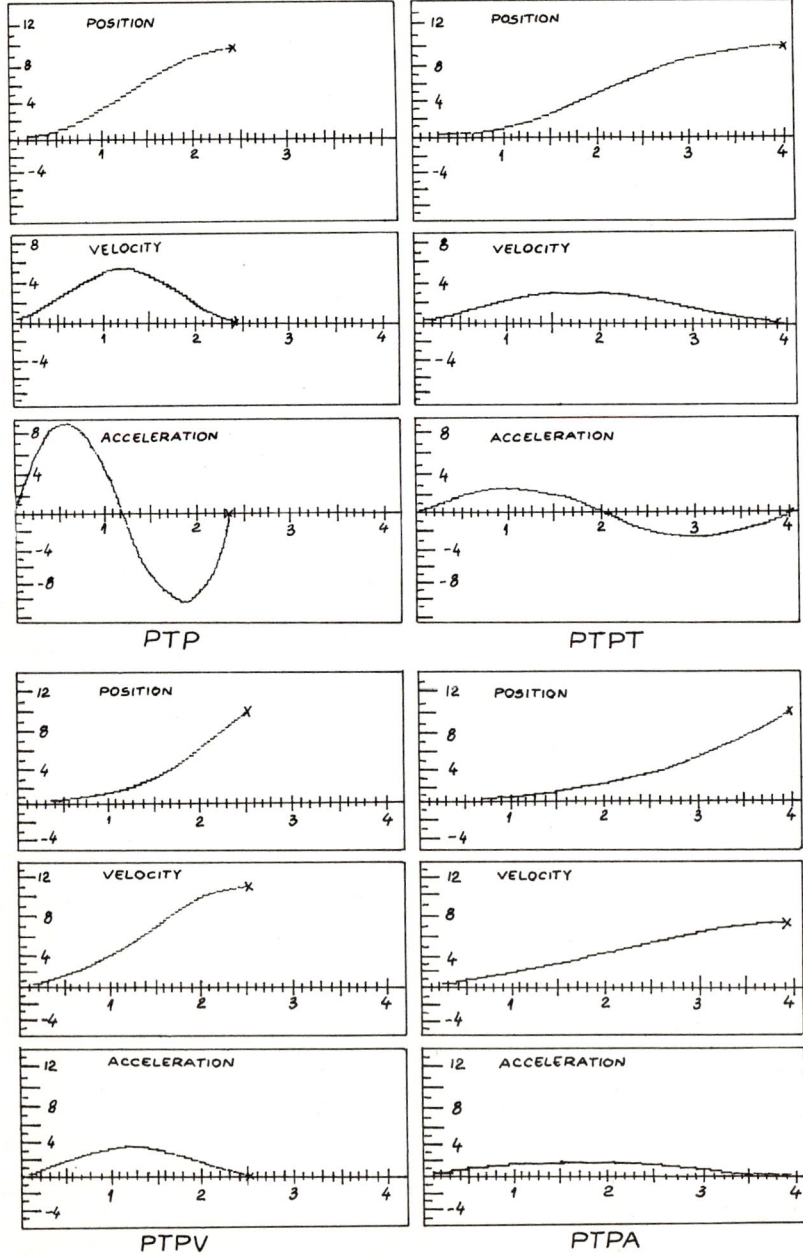

Fig. 1

PTP   - point to point movement in shortest time, without overflowing acceleration limits;
PTPT   - point to point movement in an imposed time;
PTPV   - point to point movement with imposed final velocity (V = K*Vmax/100; Vmax - velocity limit on every degree of freedom; K - the desired percentage of the velocity);
PTPA   - point to point movement with time and final velocity imposed;
LINE   - straight line movement, between two points, in carthesian coordinates, in shortest time, without overflowing acceleration limits;
LINE V - straight line movement, between two points, in carthesian coordinates, with constant velocity along the line;
LINE T - straight line movement, between two points, in carthesian coordinates, with imposed time;

Trajectory generation uses polinomial interpolation functions, direct and inverse geometrical models of mechanical structures.

For point to point movements the acceleration is interpolated using a three order polinom:

$$Q''(t) = A1(t/T)(1-t/T)(B-t/T) \quad ; \quad t \in (0,T)$$

where $Q''(t)$ is a joint acceleration, A1 and B are parameters. The acceleration is zero at $t=0$, $t=T$ and $t=BT$ (a chosen moment, to improve the movement quality).

Velocity and position - $Q'(t)$ and $Q(t)$ - are interpolated as follows:

$$Q'(t) = A1T((1/4)(t/T)^4 - ((1+B)/3)(t/T)^3 + (B/2)(t/T)^2) + A2$$

$$Q(t) = A1T^2((1/20)(t/T)^5 - ((1+B)/12)(t/T)^4 + (B/6)(t/T)^3) + A2T(t/T) + A3$$

where: $A2 = Q'(0)$; $A3 = Q(0)$

The four types of movement (time, velocity, none or both imposed) are presented in fig. 1.

The straight line motion is obtained by coordonating the first 3 degrees of freedom movements of the robot.

The initial and final points of the line are transformed from joints coordinates into carthesian coordinates, in the teaching phase. The results of interpolation in carthesian coordinates are on-line transformed into joint coordinates using the inverse geometrical model in an analitical form.

Position controlers are digitally implemented. Control structure of the CAMERA system is presented in fig. 2.

SOFTWARE IMPLEMENTATION

An 8 kwords CAMERA system running under four kwords real time operating system is used for programming (in a teaching by doing mode) and control industrial robots. The software structure is presented in fig. 3. The main functions of the CAMERA software system are:
- Generating the robot program;
- Executing the robot program step by step or in automatic mode;
- Read and write programs on a floppy-disc;
- Read and write data from (to) a specialised interface;
- Manual and automatic control of the robot;
- Trajectory generation for joint and carthesian movements;
- Trajectory execution;
All the programs are written in MICRO-11 language, using software floating point routines.

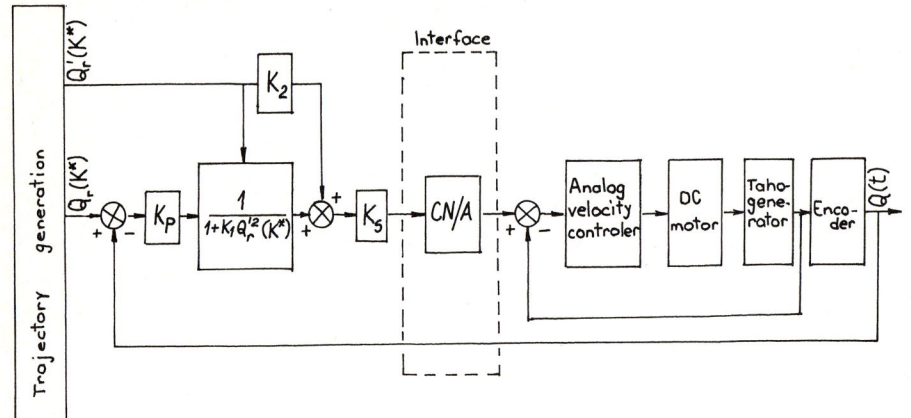

Fig. 2

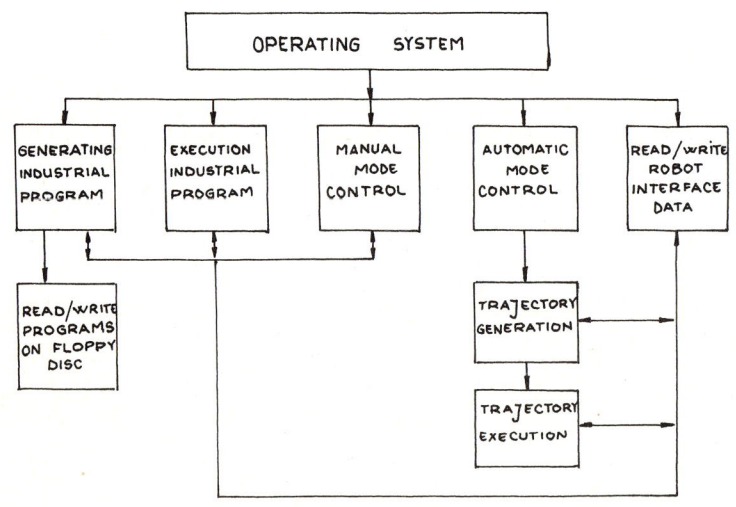

Fig. 3

CONCLUSIONS

The GENERA system can also work with an explicit programming language CAR (Carthesian Abstract Robot). The control system is succesfully used for manipulation, arc and spot welding applications. It will be rewritten for a multi-processor system. In a minicomputer version it will handle force, proximity and visual information.

NATURAL LANGUAGE INTERFACE TO AN EXPERT SYSTEM

Jarmila Panevová

Faculty of Mathematics and Physics
Charles University
Prague

For expert systems and for question answering not only a parser, but a grammatico-semantic analysis of natural language input is needed; such an analysis of Czech, the first version of which has already been implemented, accounts for the semantic functions of the dependency relation, for topic and focus, and (using valency frames and semantic features) finds ways how to disambiguate input sentences without an undesirable growth of the number of analyses.

The method TIBAQ, elaborated by the Prague group of algebraic linguistics, is primarily determined for automatic question answering; since it includes a procedure of inferencing, it can also be understood as an appropriate basis of an expert system. For such an aim the rules of inference have to be so formulated as to be sufficient for problem solving, and the linguistic processor has to ensure language comprehension (understanding). If the latter task is so conceived that the systems should not cover only a restricted area, but that it can be freely extended, then the questions of a grammatico-semantic analysis are to be solved in a general way, while the lexicon can be enlarged step by step, starting from a narrow nuclear set. The analysis has to meet similar requirements as those concerning a question-answering system, which are stronger than those of machine translation: the ambiguity of the input language should be resolved, whereas with translation this is not necessary, if the target language shares ambiguous expressions or constructions with the input language.

For this task a linguistic processor for Czech is under preparation, which should be able to transfer Czech sentences concerning electronics into representations of their meanings and vice versa. In this paper we concentrate on the questions of analysis, the required output of which is a labelled rooted tree representing the dependency-based semantic structure of the input sentence. The nodes of the tree are labelled by complex symbols each of which has four parts: lexical, syntactic (the participants or deep cases and the free modifications), morphological (the grammatemes or morphological meanings of tense, aspect, modality with verbs, number with nouns, degree of comparison with adjectives) and those of the topic/focus articulation denoted by L(eft) and R(ight), since the contextually bound (non-bound) items stand to the left (right) of their governing nodes, see point 3(c) below.

This output of the grammatico-semantic analysis can serve as input for the rules of inference, and also as a base of a procedure of intensional semantic interpretation. An example of a (simplified) representation of a meaning of a sentence is presented in Fig.1.

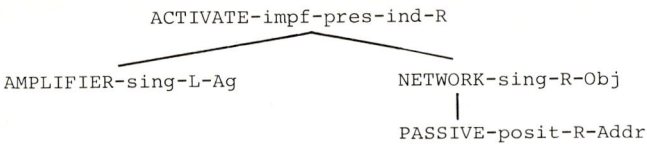

Fig.1.

One of the meanings of the (Czech equivalent of the) sentence "An amplifier activates a passive network" (in Czech also a passive paraphrase with the same deep word order is possible, lit. "By an amplifier (there) is activated a passive network"); the lexical meanings are represented here by graphemic shapes of the English words (for the sake of perspicuity); they are followed by the grammatemes, the boundness markers and the syntactic part (equal to zero with the head verb).

2. The means of implementation of the analysis is Colmerauer´s Q-language, a higher-type language that was first applied in the English-to-French machine translation system of the group T.A.U.M. in Canada.

The present version of the analysis handles the regular grammatical phenomena of Czech, as well as examples of those types of irregularities that are not quite rare. The whole procedure consists of four Q-systems (the rules within a Q-system are unordered and are applied whenever the conditions for their applications hold; the Q-systems are ordered). A rule changes a tree corresponding to its lefthand side into a tree determined by its righthand side, if the condition stated in the rule is met. The trees in Q-language are not identical to those characterized above, the main reason being that in the Q-language there are no complex symbols; furthermore, every lexical label is represented here as depending on a node corresponding to its word class, and various syntactic and semantic features are included, see Fig.2, containing one of the possible semantic representations of "The paper concerns the sources of current", the linearized form of which is:

#(V(CONCERN(V*,OPAT(2),V*1),N(PAPER(L($AG),Z*)),
N(SOURCE(R($PAT),W*),N(CURRENT(R($DET),U*)))),END)

where V*, V*1, Z*, W*, U* are variables for lists of features belonging to the "governing" word form,
OPAT(2) stands for "obligatory Patient (i.e.Objective) in the form of the form of Genitive case",
END marks the end of an indicative sentence.

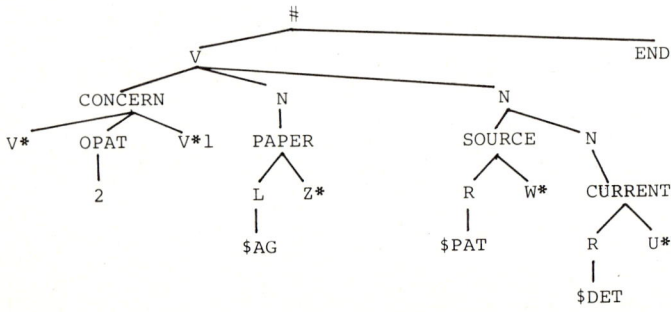

Fig.2.

The first Q-system handles such lexical information as gender of nouns, semantic features (abstract noun, name of a device, action verb, etc.), and especially the valency frames, where e.g.OPAT(4) denotes an obligatory Patient in the Accusative case, FEFF(NA(4)) - an optional (facultative). Effect in Accusative with the preposition na. With the adverbial modifications the morphemic form can be stated only with a certain preference, e.g. TAKE: OFROMWHERE(OD(2),Z(2)); the adverbial modifications are listed in the frames only with such verbs (or nouns) with which they are obligatory or frequent, the other occurences being analyzed on the basis of a general list of free complementations.

Such synonyms that share their syntactic properties are transferred to their primary counterparts by means of such rules as:
§(E,L,E,M,E,N,T,U*1) == Nl(*K,PRVEK) + HD(U*1)
where Nl denotes a gender, *K a semantic feature, U*1 a variable for an ending, and HD a morphemic paradigm.

The morphemic analysis, represented by rules of such a form, is contained in the second Q-system, which includes also rules for the identification of antecedents of relative pronouns and for its copying into the relative clause, as well as the relabelling of the participants of a passive verb.

In the third Q-system the basic types of noun phrases are handled (ADJ + N, N and N, ADJ and ADJ), the words filling the valency slots are identified and the ambiguity of Nominative and Accusative with transitive verbs is resolved in accordance with the preferences of semantic features. Those prepositional cases that do not fill any valency slots are determined as free modifications, their semantic roles being determined after individual contextual criteria, which can be illustrated by a partial algorithm for BEZ + Genitive ("without"),denoted here as B (the algorithm is carried out after the governing word of B was identified):

		Yes	No
(1) Is B followed by OHLEDU NA, ZŘETELE NA ("regards to")		Modif.of regard	2
(2) Does B depend on a noun?		Modif.of accompaniment(neg)	3
(3) Is there in the clause a modal verb (including LZE, JE MOŽNÉ - "is possible")?		Modif.of condition	4
(4) Is B preceded by I ("even")?		Modif.of concession	5
(5) Is the governing verb in the conditional mood (without ABY, KDYBY)?		Modif.of irreal condition	Modif.of accomp.(neg)

Similar algorithms were formulated, checked and partly implemented for other prepositional and simple cases, for the infinitive and for subordinating conjunctions. The identification of the clause governing an embedded clause is carried out by a preliminary, simplified set of rules in the present form of the program: the immediately preceding clause is chosen whenever the embedded clause does not stand at the beginning of the sentence. A noun in the Genitive case following immediately after another noun is treated as its adjunct, denoting the general relationship, $DET (though e.g. the Genitive in such groups as the director of a factory, a bottle of wine, or the city of Prague should be handled as denoting other kinds of modifications in a more detailed procedure, which is prepared for implementation).

The fourth Q-system transfers nominalizations to embedded predications (i.e. marks action nouns, infinitives, verbal adjectives as forms of verbs, etc.) and fulfils the slots of Actor and Patient by "general" items, if they still are empty (e.g. in This relationship is maintained = One maintains this relationship; This device is always necessary for filtering).

3. The analysis of Czech has certain advantages if compared with the usual natural language parsers:

(a) Not only the syntactic structure of the sentence is described (i.e. which lexical item depends on which governing word) , but also the semantic values, the kinds of the dependency relation (participants, free modifications).

(b) The valency (case) frames are used not only with verbs, but also with nouns, e.g. gain (Cz.zisk) having an optional, but frequent modification of origin in the form of z + Genitive, director governing a Patient, and adjectives (full having a Partitive, etc).

(c) Topic and focus are identified as two parts of the representation of the meaning of a sentence; the labels R and L do not always correspond to the surface word order, being determined (on the basis of empirical, operationally testable criteria) by contextual boundness (e.g. an adjective usually is non-bound, i.e. more dynamic than its governing noun, though this stands to the right). The lexical items directly depending on the main verb belong to the focus if they are non-bound, and to the topic if they are contextually bound; this holds also for the verb itself, which is non-bound in the primary case. The analysis assigns L to those modifications of a verb that stand to the left of the latter, R is assigned to the rightmost modification in the clause, and a rather complex algorithm is prepared for the modifications standing between the verb and its rightmost modification (a basic ordering of the kinds of modifications is used here as a clue). Cleft construction and such adverbs as even point out the focus (e.g. in Even amplifiers were employed the verb is in the topic). The boundary between topic and focus is relevant for knowledge representation, since in many cases it decides what can be inferred from a statement: thus from Operational amplifiers are used in active filter networks (with the primary intonation, i.e. with the in-phrase belonging to the focus) it follows that operational amplifier is a means used in that areas rather than that it is the single or main means used there, so that e.g. the question What is used in active filter networks? can be only partially answered on the basis of that statement.

(d) Certain known complications are caused by coordinated structures; without discussing the details here, we just want to remark that using rules of inferences from a surface construction of the form N and N (... and N) we arrive at a sentential coordination if no such words occur higher in the tree as combination of, relationship between.

(e) In our algorithms also a procedure handling prepositional cases as depending either on a preceding noun, or on a verb is included:

    (i) the slots in the valency frames of verbs are filled;
   (ii) the same for nouns and adjectives;
  (iii) the semantic features and their compatibility or preference in certain combinations of nouns and verbs are checked (to distinguish e.g. between to see a honest man with a red shirt - attribute, and ...with one´s own eyes - adverbial);
  (iv) the individual prepositions are characterized as for their frequency in this or that function (e.g. in, i.e. Czech v + Locative probably is an adverbial modification in the polytechnical texts of the studied type).

In this way it is possible to restrict the number of the outputs of the analysis of most sentences in the sample used for the first experiments in a reasonable way.

SOFTWARE SYSTEM OF ROBOTIZED MANUFACTURING SHOP

Pavlov V.A.
Leningrad Politechnic Institute
USSR

The approach to the organization of the software system of robotized manufacturing shop is discussed. The software of the upper level control computer solves the problems of operative production planning and automatic equipment dispatching. The software of the lower level computer realizes the real time control of the robotized production cell.

The software system of robotized manufacturing shop (RMS), developed in the Leningrad Politechnic Institute, is designed in accordance with the two-level structure of the control computing system. One part of the software system of RMS, realized on the upper level computer, is designed for the operative production planning and dispatching of the automatic computer-controlled equipment: robotized production cells (RPC), transport robots and automatic warehouses. Besides, data acceptance from the automatic technological information preparing system, storing of this data and sending the technological control programs to the automatic equipment control units are realized.

The software of the upper level computer consists of operative production planning subsystem and dispatching subsystem. The source data for the planning subsystem are the follows: production program, i.e. the plan of production for the planning period, the production time established standards for each automatic equipment during planning period, the information of the RMS equipment and technological data, concerning the products and including operation cycles of executions of technological operations for each RPC, operation cycles of container replacements from the warehouse to each RPC, operation cycles of RPC readjustments, types and holding capacities of containers have been used, codes of tools and industrial equipments etc. These data are recieved from a man-operator or from the automatic technological information preparing system just before the beginning of planning period.

The operative production planning subsystem distributes the production program among RPC and determines the sequence of products processing on each RPC on the base of the criteria of workplace capacity optimization. The standard-plan for RMS (i.e. the distribution of the production program among all RPC) and the shift-tasks for each RPC are the results of planning subsystem functioning.

Shift-tasks file contains all necessary source data for dispatching subsystem. Besides, the dispatching subsystem uses automatic warehouse state models built-up by one of its programs. This subsystem consists of the following programs: RPC Control Programs (the number of these programs is equal to the number of RPC), Transport Robots Control Programs, Automatic Warehouse Control Program, Warehouse State Registration Program and Shift-Task Processing Program. To initiate this subsystem a man-operator has to run Shift-Task Processing Program. The further subsystem functioning carries out in autimatic mode and in the case of emergency situations absence doesn't require any operator's interference.

Shift-Task Processing Program checks up the presence of necessary blanks, component units, tools and empty containers in the warehouse to fulfil the shift-task on each RPC and runs the corresponding RPC Control Programs. During execution Shift-Task Processing Program uses Warehouse State Registration Program, which ensures the building up and processing of the material and tool warehouse models. The warehouse models building up is carried out in accordance with load and unload lists inputted in the computer by operator. On the requests of Shift-Task Processing and Warehouse Control Programs, the Warehouse State Registrarion Program carries out the requested material objects codes searching in the warehouse models and returns the number of corresponding warehouse cell.

RPC Control Programs ensure the shift-tasks execution by the appropriate RPC. For this purpose each of these programs controls (by means of requests to Transport Robot Control Program) the timely bringing of empty containers, blanks, component units and tools to the appropriate RPC and the sending of products from RPC to the warehouse, rewrites the necessary technological program from the computer file memory to the RPC local control unit and sends the signal to start this program.

Transport Robot and Warehouse Control Programs ensure the synchronization of the warehouse stackers and RPC transport robots to provide the necessary material objects bringing from the warehouse to RPC and the products sending to the warehouse. Warehouse State Registration Program is used to find the necessary material object code in the warehouse model and to correct this model.

The dispatching subsystem provides the printing of shift-task execution reports for each RPC, production program execution summary list for the whole RMS, automatic warehouse check list etc. on the requests of a man-operator.

Nowadays two versions of the upper level RMS software system have been realized. The first one has been done for the disk-based real time operating system of the control computer ACBT M-6000, and the second one - for the real time operating system of the control computer CM-4.

The software of automatic equipment local control units is the second part of RMS software system. This part includes three typical software systems: RPC software system, transport robot software system and automatic warehouse software system. The Algorithmic Robot Control System "Bars" /1/ is used as a base for a construction of these three types of software systems. The "Bars" system includes its own operating system ensuring the time-sharing mode in the control computer. In this case automatic equipment, industrial robots and a man-operator are the "users" of the computer. Besides of sending the control programs to the automatic equipment, the "Bars" system provides the movement control of robots being supplied with various sensors, including the TV-based vision system.

The applied programs of the "Bars" system consist of three groups in accordance with three basic robot subsystems: (a) actuators control programs; (b) sensory information processing programs; (c) man-robot communication programs. Actuators control programs ensure the calculation of the control inputs for robot actuators and the sending of control programs and signals to the automatic equipment. The programs of (b) group process the information recieved from the sensors of robot and equipment. Nowadays the ultrasonic, photoelectric, tactile sensors and the TV-based vision system are used for robots. The last group includes the programs ensuring a dialogue between a man-operator and a control computer and the translator of the problem-oriented language ROCOL, which is used for robot programming.

Each program module of the "Bars" system is attributed with priority corresponding to its function importance and necessity of fast responce on the request for this module activization. In this system the preemptive resume priority discipline is used.

The "Bars" system developed nowadays includes the following set of modules pertained to the actuators control programs: 1) Controlling Inputs Calculation Module, in which the target point coordinates have been given in the Cartesian or in the robot characteristic coordinates transform into controlling inputs which must be sent to robot actuators to remove it to the target point; 2) Robot Control Module sending the calculated controlling inputs to robot actuators through the information exchange unit; 3) System Locking Module ensuring the emergency brake of robot on a man-operator request or on the emergency sensor signals; simultaneously the further execution of the robot program is also locked until recieving the appropriate instruction from a man-operator.

The group of the sensory information processing programs consists of two program modules: 1) Position Encoders Read-Out Module that reads out and transforms the information on current robot position in space; 2) Sensors Read-Out Module that feeds the "Bars" system with the information on the environment state, recieved from the robot sensors.

The man-robot communication programs realize the functions of the problem-oriented language ROCOL translator and include four program modules: 1) Statements Input Module recieves and analyzes the information from the terminal, including the problem-oriented language ROCOL statements; 2) Directives Decoding Module translates robot functioning programs from ROCOL language into machine codes; 3) Task Execution Module realizes a performance of assigned robot functioning program; this module operates in the mode of ROCOL statements interpretation; 4) Message Output Module types on the terminal the information on requests of the "Bars" system program modules.

The "Bars" system monitor consists of three program modules: 1) Interrupt Processing Module analyzes and classifies the interrupt signals from the peripheral equipment; 2) Program Selection Module ensures CPU time distribution among the "Bars" system program modules; 3) Timer Operation Module ensures the connection of the robot control with the real time.

Finally, the group of service modules includes the following program modules: 1) Library Subroutines Calling Module ensures the addressing of the program modules to the library subroutines; 2) File

Memory Access Module is intended for an information exchange between the "Bars" system and file memory units; 3) System Checking Module carries out the checking of system readiness for operation during its functioning.

The problem-oriented language ROCOL is used for robot programming and includes three groups of statements. The basic statements of ROCOL are used for the robot functioning program logic description and falls into three types. The basic statements of the first type perform arithmetical and logical operations over data arrays and branches in the program. The basic statements of the second type realize the elementary robot actions programming (opening and closing of a gripper, replacement in space in predetermined direction, replacement between two predetermined points etc.). The basic statements of the third type ensures the programming of interactions with the sensor system of robot, with the man-operator and the programming of outputs of control commands to the technological equipment.

The editing statements allow to edit the robot functioning programs in computer memory and control the program translation modes. The controlling statements of ROCOL language are used for setting the working modes of robots and control computer and for operator's interference to the process of robot functioning program execution.

The "Bars" system ensures the individual and group modes of industrial robots and technological equipment control. The existing versions of this system have been realized on the control computers ACBT M-6000, M-7000, CM-2 and micro-computer "Electronika-60".

REFERENCES

/1/ Jurevich E.I., Novatchenko S.I., Pavlov V.A., et al., Robots control via computer (Energia, Leningrad, 1980). (in Russian).

A DOMAIN INDEPENDENT FRAMEWORK FOR PROBLEM SOLVING

Boris Petkoff

Scientific Information Centre

Bulgarian Academy of Science

Sofia, Bulgaria

A domain independent framework for problem solving is offered,
which could be described incremenatlly in Petri-nets terms
and implemented as a Knowledge Based System to intensify
the research and development in specific domain.
The solution proposed is founded on the methodology of science
and the practice of scientific research, on the theory of control
systems and on the practical structure of knowledge employed
in Expert Systems.

INTRODUCTION

The building of a problem-solving framework in knowledge based systems appears
to be one of the most important research problems today. However a look at the existing expert systems (Erman (1983), Bond (1981)) gives some idea of the diversity
in knowledge-acquiring, -storing and -utilizing mechanisms. There are many pragmatical knowledge engineering approaches resp. families of systems:
* the top-down or MYCIN-type,
* the model-based or CASNET type,
* the blackboard or HEARSAY type,
* the bottom-up or R1-type, etc.
The research on expert systems has to focus on the architecture of large and complex knowledge bases, because the current systems are relatively simple, unflexible,
restricted to very narrow domains, and have no access to higher-level representations of the knowledge domain and their own problem solving activity.
The three-level model offered in this paper takes into consideration the complex
character of the cognition process as a multi-level phenomenon and tries to satisfy
the requirements of the formal reconstruction of intelligent behaviour with a powerful architecture, including parallel processing units.
The model is built up of three hierarchical levels of knowledge: strategic, tactical
and operative, which consist of similar fundamental elements and have the same structure of information processing:
* four declarative knowledge units (dku),
* four procedural knowledge units (pku),
graphically represented with circles, resp. boxes.
The constituents of the basic "molecular" structure of the model are pairs of dku/pku
elements, resp. pku/dku elements, i.e. circle-box or box-circle.
The levels are connected in the same manner by pairs of elements of different kinds.
Generalizdtion increases bottom-up and counter-clockwise, resp. specification increases top-down and clock-wise, i.e. the knowledge processes are running in both
directions.
The three levels define a hierarchy of problems, resp. meta-problems whose solutions determine their teleological behaviour or whose solution failures make them
pass the control to the next higher level, i.e. the model emphasizes the dynamic
properties of each knowledge acquisition process which is governed by the methodology and logic of a certain application area.

PETRI-NET INTERPRETATION

We can interpret the three-level model in terms of petri-nets (tool developed in the early 60-ies to describe the information flow in systems) because they have shown to be particularly adequate in describing distributed systems and concurrent processes and thus became a basic tool for a general systems theory (Genrich (1976), Mauri, Provera (1982)).
Thus, as a net, we can distinguish the following components of the model:
* set DKU of circles
* set PKU of boxes
* the connection between them represented by a relationship $F \subseteq DKU \times PKU \cup PKU \times DKU$
The versatility of this tool, its application in describing the most varied situations is related to the possibility of singling out in quite different areas triples of concepts which can be interpreted as the resp. components DKU, PKU and F; and to the fact that each of these interpretations determines in a natural way some dynamics of the net.
This proposal explicates the "horizontal" aspects (that is, the logical structure of the domain) and the "vertical" aspects as well (that is, the meta aspects of knowledge based systems).
In this context:
* the circles represent knowledge states
* the boxes represents knowledge acts
* the connection (DKU)⟶[PKU] means that the knowledge unit DKU has been used in the act [PKU]   The connection [PKU]⟶(DKU) means that the knowledge unit (DKU) has been generated by the act [PKU]. Thus:
* a class of structures is associated to each circle, e.g. frames of empirical knowledge are associated to (EM)
* the boxes are interpreted as structure transformers and/or generators, e.g. [IM] employs inductive methods to generate hypothesis from empirical structures.
They take already existing structures from the corresponding circles (input edges: (EM)⟶[IM]) and produce new ones (output edges: [IM]⟶(HP)

EXPLANATION OF THE MODEL   (Petkoff (1984))

Methodological problems - strategic level(Fig. 1)

(dku) The Domain Dependent Picture of the World (DDPW) integrates and generalizes all empirical and theoretical knowledge of the particular discipline in this scientific domain.
[pku] The Gnoseologic Aspect of the Interval Principle [GIAP] determines the conceptual pattern which is used by the expert as a filter to perceive and to partition the reality in order to find a mapping between its fragments and the created hierarchical systems of notions.
(dku) The Intervals of Abstraction (INAB) reflect the imposed from Nature constraints (which are implicit but objective), and outcome a framework for the determination of the hierarchical system of notions.
[pku] The Ontologic Aspect of the Interval Principle [OAIP] describes and determines the limit between important and subordinate properties resp. factors of the object of cognition, which have to be identified in its environment during the experiment.
(dku) The Differentiating Ability resp. Power (DADP) determines the motivated and efficient identification of the object of cognition within its environment, and at the same time this ability itself is dependent on constraints and limits, imposed from the nature of the object, out of which new cognition is not possible.
[pku] The Ontologic Aspect of the Relativity Principle [OARP] contrives the reduction of the object properties up to a set of relevant ones, because each object of cognition has a finite number of properties in respect to a system of reference.

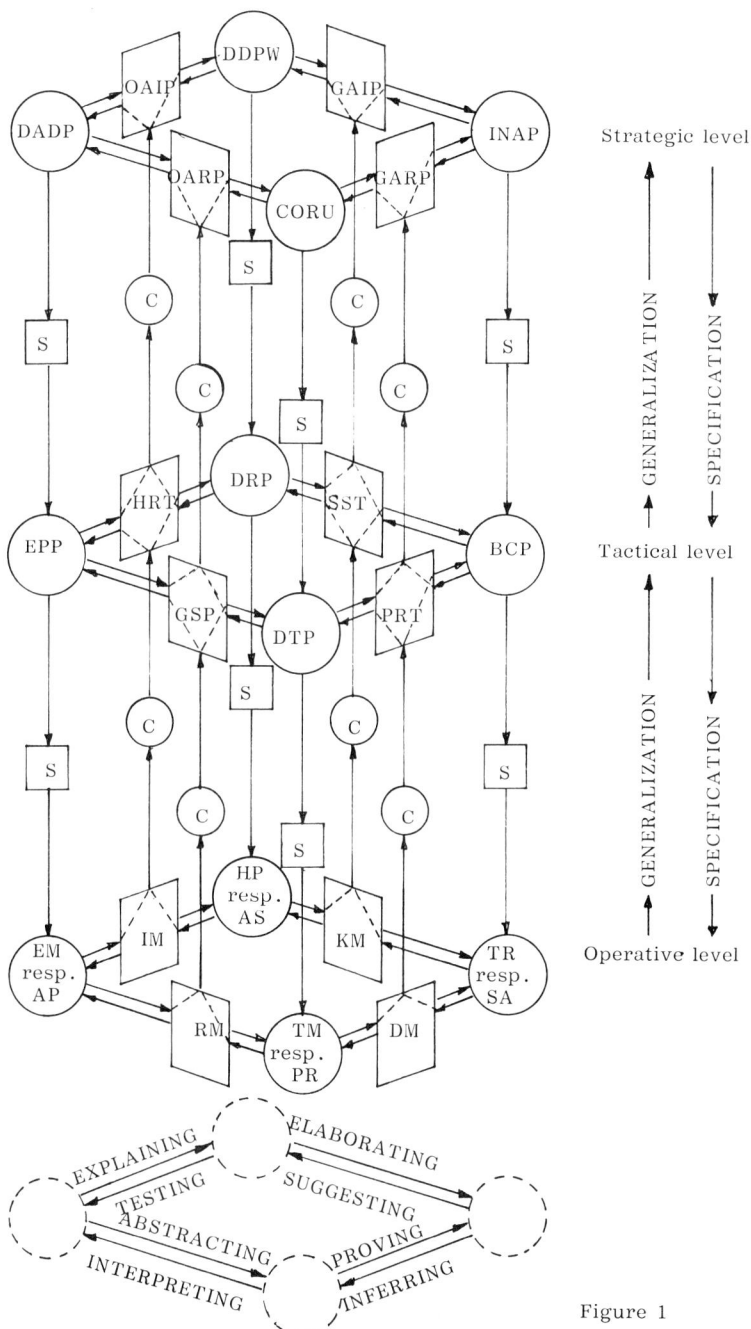

Figure 1

(dku) The Correspondent Rules (CORU) manage the mapping between the properties of the object and the intervdls of abstraction.
[pku] The Gnoseologic Aspect of the Relativity Principle [GARP] brings the results of the cognition process into line with the potential outcomes, constrained by the nature of the object of cognition, because sooner or later the limits are reached where nonrelevant becomes relevant, potential becomes actual etc.

Logical problems - tactical level (Fig. 1)

(dku) The Discipline Related Picture of the World (DRP) is a component of the domain dependent picture of the world.
(dku) The Baisc Conceptual Pattern (BCP) expresses the relations between the theoretical constructs and corresponds to the particular discipline related picture of the world.
(dku) The Derived Theoretical Patterns (DTP) are the inference closure of the basic conceptual pattern, but sometimes these patterns are primary and can be generalized to basic conceptual pattern.
(dku) The Experimental Plans and Procedures (EPP) have to isolate the disturbance and nonrelevant factors.
[pku] The Heuristics [HRT] are used to create a set of hypotheses according to the discipline related picture of the world and/or to test some of these.
[pku] The Substantiation Theory [SST] resp. Begruendungstheorie brings some of these hypotheses into line with the basic conceptual pattern and/or create some new hypotheses.
[pku] The Proof Theory [PRT] resp. Beweistheorie is used to infer many derived theoretical patterns from the basic conceptual pattern and/or to deduce the evidence of some theoretical patterns.
[pku] The Justification Theory [JST] resp. Bestaetigungstheorie is used to verify the derived theoretical patterns by ideal experiments and simulated measurements and/or to create some new theoretical patterns.

Problems of science - operative level (Fig. 1)

(dku) Empiry (EM) resp. Application (AP)
[pku] Inductive Methods [IM] are used for discovering object's characteristics.
(dku) Hypothesis (HP) resp. Assumptions (AS)
[pku] Constructive Methods [KM] are used for substantiation of proposed hypotheses.
(dku) Theory (TR) resp. Set of Axioms (SA)
[pku] Deductive Methods [DM] are used for interferring of possible consequences of proposed theory.
(dku) Theorems (TM) resp. Propositions (PR)
[pku] Reductive Methods [RM] are used for validation of selected theory.

Connections

(dku) Conditions -(C)
[pku] Specificators - [S]

CONCLUDING REMARKS

The present three-level model emphasizes dynamic properties of each knowledge acquisition process, which is governed by the logic and methodology of a certain research area. In this particular case attention should be paid to the fact that the role of deductive methods has been given in current AI-research unjustified priority over the other methods. The model can be incrementally described in formal terms and implemented as a knowledge acquistion mechanism in an expert system.

REFERENCES
[1] Erman, L., Expert Systems-Tutorial, Teknowledge Inc.(IJCAI-1983)
[2] Bond, A., Machine Intelligence (Pergamon Infotech Ltd., Maidenhead, 1981)
[3] Genrich,H.J.,The Petri Net Representation in Mathematical Knowledge (GMD 1976)
[4] Mauri,G., Provera E.,Knowledge Representation by means of Petri Nets in Teaching,(Instituto di Cibernetica, Universiteta di Milano, Private Information, 1982)
[5] Petkoff,B.,A Cybernetic Model of Scientific Research and Cognition,(Proceedings of the 7th European Meeting on Cybernetics and System Research, North Holland Elsevier Science Publishers B.V., Amsterdam, 1984)

FUNCTIONAL APPROACH TO KNOWLEDGE REPRESENTATION

Jaroslav Pokorný

Department of Computer Science
Charles University
Malostranské náměstí 25
Praha 1, Czechoslovakia

Pavel Materna

Design Institute PÚDIS
Lidových milicí 69
Praha 2, Czechoslovakia

The basic problem of Artificial Intelligence is
the development of a sufficiently precise notation
for representing knowledge (i.e., knowledge representation scheme). This paper is concerned with
the development of a new (functional) approach to
knowledge representation based on transparent
intensional logic. This logic gives the apparatus
with greater expressive power than 1st order
systems and with capability of analysing natural
language.

INTRODUCTION

In recent years there has been a growing agreement about the
usefulness of conceptual modelling in databases (DB) [1] . Its
tools such as semantic data models (e.g. [2], [3]) represent an
important contribution to the understanding of data in databases.
From the perspective of Artificial Intelligence (AI) reseaech, DB
results concerning DB models and query languages have influenced
research on knowledge representation ([4], [5]), some results about
the expressive power of programming primitives in query languages
have showed boundaries and drawbacks of the languages based on the
first-order logic [6].

Both DB and AI systems represent and process knowledge about the
real world. In both fields there is a need for a precise and
powerfull formalism to represent many aspects of knowledge. The
purpose of this brief paper is to describe a formal apparatus
based on the notion of function. We are not specifying any particular data model here, but the tool suitable for production of both
knowledge representation schemes in AI and data models in DB.
Moreover, two aspects of the functional approach are emphasized -
its expressivity (it is greater than that of the 1st order languages) and its satisfying capability of analysing sentences of
natural language. Both the aspects seem to be decisive in the
knowledge base constructing.

AN OVERVIEW OF TRANSPARENT INTENSIONAL LOGIC

When looking for an adequate logical tool which would underlie
research concerning knowledge representation one should take into
consideration two rather important points:
 i/ The natural languages through which we get the knowledge to be
represented do not behave as 1st order languages. Applying a 1st
order analysis to the expressions of natural languages one becomes
very unnatural, and it often happens that some information gets
lost. A mere sortalization does not help; we should be able to
deal not only with properties of individuals but also with proper-

ties of propositions ("incredibility", "falsity" etc.), with properties of properties (being a mourning color is an example) etc. Moreover, the standard 1st order languages do not make it possible to distinguish between classes and properties, relations-in-extension and relation-in-intension, truth-values and propositions, individuals and individual concepts, in general: between extensions and intensions.

ii/ One should distinguish between the meaning of an expression and the reference of this expression under some given circumstances. Thus the meaning of a sentence (say, "It rains in Prague") is a proposition (here: the proposition that it rains in Prague), whereas the truth-value of a sentence (i.e., its reference) is something which can change with circumstances (that it rains in Prague is true in some possible worlds and at some time moments only); the meaning of a description (say, "the most populous country") is an individual concept, whereas the object which happens - under the given circumstances - to satisfy the description is its (instantaneous) reference (here: in the actual world just now it is China), which can change with time and the possible worlds. Traditionally, extensionalists identify de facto meaning with reference, which is in good accordance with point i: properties of, say, individuals are represented as monadic predicates, i.e., as expressions with which the intended interpretation associates classes (of individuals).

Taking into account the two above points we consider (transparent) intensional logic ("TIL") by Tichy to be the most convenient logical tool for knowledge representation.

We shall briefly characterize TIL; as for details we refer to [7], [8]. TIL is a partial type theory, i.e., it is a (simple) type theory which treats partial functions "on a par with total ones" ([8], p.55). Types are - transparently - defined as sets of functions (including 0-ary functions):

Where B is a base, i.e., a collection of non-empty pairwise disjoint classes, the class of the <u>types over B</u> is the least class containing a/ the members of B,
b/ with $\eta, \xi_1, \ldots, \xi_n$ being already types over B also the class of (total and partial) functions from $\xi_1 \times \ldots \times \xi_n$ into η ; this class will be denoted by $(\eta \xi_1 \ldots \xi_n)$ here.

TIL is a good framework for logically analysing natural languages; the latter are considered to be related to epistemic bases (EB), which contain the following types:

o ... the set of truth-values,
τ ... the set of time moments (or: real numbers),
ι ... the respective universe of discourse (members: individuals),
ω ... the respective logical space (members: possible worlds).

Let η be a type over an EB. Any member A of η will be called an η-object (the fact will be expressed as A/η). For any type η, η-objects and η-variables (that give under a valuation v an η-object as their value) <u>are atomic constructions</u>. The **compound** constructions are just the following ones:

a/ applications; where Y is an $(\eta \xi_1 \ldots \xi_n)$-construction (i.e., where Y constructs - or v-constructs dependently on the valuation

v - an ($\eta\ \xi_1\ldots\xi_n$)-object), and $X_1,\ldots,X_n$ are ξ_1-,...., ξ_n-
constructions, respectively, $[YX_1\ldots X_n]$ is an η-construction
called application of Y to $X_1,\ldots,X_n$.
b/ λ-abstraction; where Y is an η-construction and $\underline{x}_1,\ldots,\underline{x}_n$ are
ξ_1-,...., ξ_n-variables, respectively, $\lambda \underline{x}_1\ldots \underline{x}_n Y$ is a λ-abstraction
of Y with respect to $\underline{x}_1,\ldots,\underline{x}_n$ (or: an $\underline{x}_1,\ldots,\underline{x}_n$-closure of Y).

Constructions are atomic constructions and **compound** constructions.
The way the constructions (v-)construct objects is desribed in [7],
[8]. A strong deductive apparatus is built over the above concepts
(see [8]), which may prove important when representing knowledges
by means of TIL (the most simple applications see [10]).

NATURAL LANGUAGE UNDERSTANDING

We can show now - through examples only - the way TIL analyses the
empirical expressions of natural language ("L-expressions").
Revealing meanings of simple and compound L-expressions has its
logical aspect: firstly, the type of the object denoted by an L-
expression must be determined (mastering the given language is a
necessary condition of this to be done). Secondly, the dependence
of the meaning of a compoud L-expression on the meanings of its
components is given through (compound) constructions: analysing an
L-expression equals finding such a construction.

An important feature of the TIL-analyses: the constructions expressed by L-expressions typically construct intensions, i.e., $((\eta\tau)\omega)$
-objects for some type η. (For exaple: whereas a property of
individuals is an $(((o\iota)\tau)\omega)$-object, a class of individuals is
an $(o\iota)$-object. The class of actual cats existing at the present
moment is the value of the property of being a cat in the actual
world at the present moment. In general, properties of η-objects
are $(((o\eta)\tau)\omega)$-objects, relations-in-intension of $\xi_1,\ldots,\xi_n$-
objects are $(((o\xi_1\ldots\xi_n)\tau)\omega)$-objects.)

Thus analysing an L-sentence one has to find an $((o\tau)\omega)$-construc-
tion, since sentences denote (i.e., their meanings are) propositions, which in turn are $((o\tau)\omega)$-objects. Therefore, any analysis of an L-sentence has the form $\lambda w \lambda t\ A$, where w is an ω-variab-
le, t is a τ-variable and A is an o-construction. Having, e.g.,
the sentence Charles believes that the French President is a smoker

we get: a/ type analysis: Ch/ι (Charles), B/$(((o\iota((o\tau)\omega))\tau)\omega)$
(Believe), Fr/$((\iota\tau)\omega)$ (the French President), S/$(((o\iota)\tau)\omega)$
(Smoker).
    b/ synthesis, whose result is
$\lambda w \lambda t [[\ [Bw]t]Ch\ \lambda w\ \lambda t [\ [\ [Sw]\ t]\ [\ [Fr\ w]t]]]$.
(It is easily seen that constructions can be viewed as trees.)

Let us introduce following abbreviations: $\eta_{\tau\omega}$ will stand for $((\eta\tau)\omega)$,
A_{wt} will stand for $[[Aw]t]$, π will stand for $((o\tau)\omega)$. Applications
of binary connectives and binary relations-in-extension will be
written in the infix notation.

Consider a concrete sphere of interest, say, school education; we
first perform a type-theoretical analysis of the "key words" of

which the sentences describing the sphere in question consist. As an example, consider the expressions "department", "student","grade" "course". All these words denote intensions. For "department", one can take the object for a property of a class of individuals, i.e., $(o(o\iota))_{\tau\omega}$ -object. "Course" denotes a property of classes of propositions, i.e., an $(o(o\pi))_{\tau\omega}$ -object. Finally, "Grade" denotes a world- and time-dependent function that takes the pairs <student, course> to numbers and is undefined on the other pairs < individual, class of propositions > : its type is $(\tau\iota(o\pi))_{\tau\omega}$.

Now we are expected to able to write down a construction which would correspond to the sentence /S/- The grade in the course of physic of most of the students of the department of philosophy is greater than 2.
We have: Phys/$(o(o\pi))_{\tau\omega}$ (the course of physic), Deph/$(o(o\iota))_{\tau\omega}$ (the department of physic), $>/(o\tau\tau)$, $2/\tau$.

Now, what about "most" ? To say what /S/ says in other words we can use the concept of cardinality. We have, of course, Cardi/$(\tau(o\iota))$. Futhermore we need conjunction $\wedge/(ooo)$ and negation $\sim/(oo)$.

A following structure may be taken for a (simplified) fragment of the structure of the sphere in question: With every department there is associated a class of students. In every world W at every time moment T this association is a function, say, S, of type $((o\iota)(o\iota))$, where the second occurence of $(o\iota)$ is the type of the particular department in W at T and the first occurence is the type of the class of the respective students in W at T. Similarly in W at T G of type $(\tau\iota(o\pi))$ is the grade of a student in the given course.

Now we already can analyse /S/ as follows:($\underline{x}$ is of type ι.)

$\lambda\underline{w}\ \lambda\underline{t}\ [[\underline{\text{Cardi}}\ \lambda\underline{x}\ [[[\underline{S}'_{wt}\ \underline{\text{Deph}}_{wt}]\ \underline{x}]\wedge [[\underline{G}'_{wt}\ \underline{x}\ \underline{\text{Phys}}_{wt}] > \underline{2}]]] >$
$\ \ \ \ \ \ \ [\underline{\text{Cardi}}\ \lambda\underline{x}\ [[[\underline{S}'_{wt}\ \underline{\text{Deph}}_{wt}]\ \underline{x}]\wedge \sim [[\underline{G}'_{wt}\ \underline{x}\ \underline{\text{Phys}}_{wt}] > \underline{2}]]]\ ]$.

Here $\underline{S}'$ and $\underline{G}'$ are functions whose values in particular world and time moment are $\underline{S}$ and $\underline{G}$. Generally, such functions $\underline{F}'$ and $\underline{F}$ are in [9] called **attributes** and **pseudo-attributes**, respectively. Finally, the (functional) knowledge base is a collection of pseudo-attributes and the pairs < construction,truth-value > giving the analysis of sentences in given W and T. In temporal versions we get tabels of the pairs

[1] ISO TC97/SC5/WG3, Concepts and Terminology for the Conceptual schema and Inform.Base,van Griethuysen, J.J.(ed.),1982.
[2] Mylopoulos, J. and Wong, H.K.T., Some Features of the Taxis Data Model, in: Proc.of V.L.D.B., Montreal, Canada, 1980.
[3] Prabudha De, et al, A new model for data base abstraction, Information Systems, 7, 1 (1982)1-12.
[4] Smith, J.M. and Smith, D.C.P., Principles on database conceptual design, DB Design techniques 1, Yao, S.B., et al (eds.) 1981.
[5] Proc.of the works.on data abstraction, DB and conept.modelling, Brodie, M.L. and Zilles, S.N.(eds.), Pingree Park, Colorado,1980.
[6] Chandra, A.K., Programming Primitives for Database Languages,in: Proc.of 8th ann.ACM Symp.on Princ.of PL,Wiliamsburg,Virg.,1981.
[7] Materna, P. and Pokorný, J., Applying simple theory of types to databases, Information Systems, 6, 4 (1981) 283-300.
[8] Tichý, P., Foundations of Partial Type Theory, Reports on Mathematical Logic, 14 (1982) 55-72.
[9] Materna, P., Theory of types and data description, Kybernetika 14 (1978) 313-327.
[10] Chrz,T., ADAM(overview&examples),RR.,Federal Statist.Off.,Praha, Czechoslovakia, 1982.

DYNAMIC CORRECTNESS OF CONTROL DEVICES
FUNCTIONS REALIZATION

Ponomarev V.M., Domaratsky A.N., Nikiforov V.V.

Leningrad Research Computer Center
Academy of Sciences
U.S.S.R.

The model of parallel computational process is considered to formalize the conception "phase of algorithm execution". The relations between this conception and "phases of function realisation" and relations between logical and dynamic correctness of computations are discussed. The function, which represents the dynamic requirements on computations in the case of control devices is defined. The dynamic requirements on special type of control device functions are given.

Wide automation of industry on the base of robots and other controlled equipment leads to the development of large variety of control devices (CD). The set of quality and quantity indexis, which characterize the CD functional possibilities improvement, is necessary for the increasing of CD efficient elaborations and use.

Each CD functional possibility is periodicaly appeared during its activity for specific time intervals. The begining of such interval (phase of present CD function realization) is connected with necessity of concrete act, corresponding to the function; the completion of this act ends the specific time interval (ends the phase of that function realization). Such an approach means that phases of CD function realization concern the category of outward appearence of this device acts and characterize its acts peculiarities from the point of view of an outward observer, for example - from the point of view of a user (a man-operator, working with the device) or "from the point of view" of controlled objects.

A concrete fragment of a computational process (a phase of execution of some component of general CD functioning algorithm) corresponds to each phase of concrete CD function realization, that is carried out by control device. The difference in conceptions "phase of CD function realization" and "phase of algorithm execution" is as follows: the first one concerns the outward appearence of the device activity, the second one concerns its inward organization forms.

An absolute CD functional possibilities characteristic must contain (for all functions are being executed by this device) indications of guaranteed (permissible) values of phases dinamic parameters of functions realization. As an example of such a dinamic parameter let us give the verge values of coming frequency of some CD function realization phases; another example - the value of time interval permissible duration from the moment of the necessity origin of the next CD function realization phase to the one, when this phase must be completed.

Limitations on values of CD function realization phase dynamic parameters lead to the requirements of CD algorithm exection phases speed. Such dependence is not trivial in developed systems, but in any case the formal model of computational process, oriented on computations dynamic peculiarity indication, must be used. The necessary formalization is to be carried out from the parallel algorithm formal model, because the developed CD are characterized by essential parallelizm of computations.

Any conception of parallel algorithm includes the notions extension about control transmission function of sequential type algorithms. The authors of works [1,2] suggest to put a "unchain function" - predicat $p_A(s)$ on the data states spase: the interval of execution e_i of operator A begins since the unchain function $p_A(s)$ takes its true value.

The efficient method of parallel algorithm structurization is to represent it as a set of asynchronous interactive sequential algorithms. Let us call the set of operators which enters in the asynchronous parallel algorithm and make up an independent (closed on control) sequential algorithm to be a sequential component of this asynchronous algorithm. Many CD functions are easily realized as independent sequential components.

To develop the model [1,2] for quasiparallel computation case let us represent the unchain function in the form of conjunction $p_A = s_A \& r_A$ of functional component s_A and component of priority r_A. The functional component is true when according to computation process development logic conditions for operator A execution appear; the component of priority is true when a processor may be given for operator A execution.

Let us pick out a local signal variable z_F (pointer) for each sequential component F, which points next operator being executed. The functional component is $s_A = q_A \& (z_A = A)$, where q_A - outward condition - predicat, which in general case depends on global variable values. Such structurization of unchain function leads to extraction of key operators of asynchronous algorithm (those operators, for which $q_A \not\equiv true$) and computation process phases for a separated sequential component (phase is fragment e_i, e_{i+1}, ... , e_{i+m} of sequential process, which includes the only key operator e_i and is completed by key operator e_{i+m+1}).

The key operator picking out, the use of phase conception as the extention unit of executions, corresponding to separate sequential component, gives the opportunity of distinguishing the interaction dinamic peculiarity of asynchronous algorithm sequential components, without taking into account the details of sequential component inward construction.

The representation of functionaly independent parts of algorithm as sequential components, consideration of execution phases as extension acts of parallel computation process makes easier the development of logically correct algorithms.

If some sequential component F has key operators, then F must be active periodically, the periods of this activity must concern with definite events, which are fixed by means of modifications of corresponding signal variables values. Special requirements are put to each phase (phase interval) as on realized computations nature, as on it's duration. Functional component s_A of unchain function represents the readiness of data, needed for these computations (ahd readiness of necessary system resources). The moment of putting of $s_A = \underline{true}$ may by naturally considered to be beginning moment T_β of corresponding computation phase (execution interval).

Signal bonds regulate the sequence of executed operations of information processing for asynchronous algorithm which is logical corrected; the duration of computation phases and execution of single operators is not connected with algorithm logical structure. The duration of computation phases of asynchronic algorithm sequential components may be changed from realization to realization arbitrary without logical violations.

In real time system case the requirement of only computations logical correctness is not enough: it is necessary to put limitations on duration of time intervals of single functions execution and permissible time of algorithm under execution, permissible time on reaction on outward signals; i.e. algorithm logical structure correctness requirements must be added by its realization dynamic correctness requirements.

Table 1. Spectrum of IR CD function realization hurryness values

Hurryness		Types of systems			
(1/sec)	Cycle	Pozition	Contour	Adaptive	
0.1		I / O	Files forming control-programms	Optimization fragments	
1			Corrections forming	Kinematics tasks Text editing operations	Situation estimation
10		I / O	Directives processing of desk messages	Handle control	
100		Technology	information	Interpolation Trajectory control processing	
1000		I / O of Control	technological information signals forming		
> 1000		Measurement		registration	

In general the character of requirements to the computation phase φ duration may be represented as function $\Theta(\varphi,t)$, which gives approximate value of phase realisation dynamic correctness (the correctness of phase φ completion by the time moment t).

Let $\Theta(\varphi,t)$ changes from 0 to 1, bigger values of $\Theta(\varphi,t)$ correspond to more correct situations: absolute dynamic correctness corresponds to value 1, absolute unacceptable phase φ execution duration corresponds to value 0; values in between may show the decrease of phase φ realisation quality (to the case of dynamicaly correct computations).

In the majority of practical tasks the requirements of dynamic correctness are expressed as monotonously nondecreasing time function; the important moment $D=\max\{t/\Theta(\varphi,t)=1$ represents either the estimation of phase φ completion top permissible moment, or the estimation of φ execution comletion top moment without the decreasing of system act quality.

The value $h=1/(D-T_g)$ is an important parameter, which characterize the requirement of dynamic correctness of phase φ realisation; it reflects the degree of hurryness of phase φ execution: with $D=\infty$ parameter h is zero, with short time interval for phase execution parameter h takes bigger values.

Parameter h may play an important role in real time systems classification: there is significant difference between various real time systems both in values range of h and in characteristical (typical for concrete system) values of that phase hurryness parameter.

As it mentioned beforehand, value of parameter h and is closely connected with limitations on permissible values of CD function realizaton phase durution. Table 1 demonstrates the value variation of this parameter for different industrial robot (IR) types.

The corresponding computation phases hurryness value are due to the values of function realization hurryness from this table. This dependence is largly determined by asynchronous algorithm structure.

For testing of CD acts algorithm dynamic correctness it is necessary to have estimations of computations volume v for different algorithm execution phases. In our notation the requirements of dynamic correctness are formalized as a system of relations of type hv<1; this conditions of dynamic correctness may be taken, for example, as a base for realization of service optimal discipline in the case of quasiparallel computations.

Literature.

[1] Нариньяни, А.С, Теория параллельного программирования, Кибернетика 3 (1974) I-16; 5 (1974) I-17.

[2] Котов, В.Е., Теория параллельного программирования, Кибернетика I (1974) I-16; 2 (1974) I-18.

Artificial Intelligence and Information-Control Systems of Robots
I. Plander (editor)
© Elsevier Science Publishers B.V. (North-Holland), 1984

CODEX: A COMPUTER-BASED DIAGNOSTIC EXPERT SYSTEM

M. Popper and F. Gyárfáš
Research Institute of Medical Bionics
Bratislava
Czechoslovakia

The paper introduces briefly some key elements of the CODEX - an empty diagnostic expert system. The systems knowledge bases are constructed as a diagnoses model net. Each object in this net is represented by a frame -like data structure called prototype. The reasoning engine of the system is based on a prototype driven backward and forward (associative) chaining inference mechanism. The system´s usage - as it was experimentally proven - is not limited to medical domain only.

INTRODUCTION

Nowadays, when according to [2] more than 1500 expert systems (ES) are known (approximatively a fifth of them are devoted to medical diagnostics), it may be not too interesting to announce a new one. However, there is not established any generally accepted expert system design style so that a new experiment and gained experience may still have a value. In the following as we introduce our CODEX expert system we are not going to repeat the known story about such systems. Instead we plea to see our medical diagnostic aid in the context of some well known diagnostic ESs as for example MYCIN, EMYCIN, NEOMYCIN, EXPERT, and (most of all) CENTAUR [1]. In the remaining very limited space available no comprehensive description of CODEX is possible. What follows is rather an attempt to sketch some of its principles hopefully giving a feeling to the reader.

BASIC CHARAKTERISTICS OF CODEX

CODEX is an empty expert system. Its architecture is in concordance with the most generally accepted structure of ESs. Besides of the knowledge base (KB) its most important part is the inference mechanism (IM) and naturally the explanation (EM) and communication (CM) modules are the inevitable components as well. The utilization of the system crucially depends on KB it works with. To create a functional KB is a hard job for a knowledge engineer. There are the following assisting components of the CODEX system available in KB design: the knowledge aquisition subsystem (enables the KB to be fed up with knowledge quanta), the KB maintenance and control subsystems (enabling to modify its content and control its consistency - those are important activities frequently performed in the course of KB development and debugging), and the utility subsystem (enabling in various ways to visualize the content of the KB, its structure, each element, and the possible inference traces).

THE KNOWLEDGE BASE PRINCIPLES

We avoid discussion of the conceptual background of the adopted KB design. Some of our related thoughts can be found in [5]. What follows is rather a syntactically viewed description.

```
PROTOTYPE
    (DECLARATIVE-PART
        (PROTOTYPE-NAME name)
        (PROTOTYPE-DEFINITION free-text)
        (VALUE-TYPE logical|numerical)
        (VALUE-ASSIGNMENT-MODE ask-for|search-for|infer-it)
        (STRUCTURE attributed|nonatributed
            (IF-ATTRIBUTED attribute-evaluation-priorities)))
    (VALUE-ASSIGNMENT-PART
        (IF-ASKED-FOR text-of-the-question
            (IF-ATTRIBUTED
                (ATTRIBUTE-1 attribute-question)
                (ATTRIBUTE-2 attribute-question)
                ... ))
        (IF-SEARCHED-FOR data-base-access
            (IF-ATTRIBUTED
                (ATTRIBUTE-1 data-base-access)
                (ATTRIBUTE-2 data-base-access)
                ... ))
        (IF-INFERRED
            (IF-CONFIRMED (CONFIRM-CRITERION criterion))
            (IF-DISCONFIRMED (DISCONFIRM-CRITERION criterion))
            (IF-ATTRIBUTED
                (ATTRIBUTE-1 (CONFIRM-CRITERION criterion))
                (ATTRIBUTE-2 (CONFIRM-CRITERION criterion))
                ... )))
    (ASSOCIATION-PART
        (PROTOTYPE-SET-1 (ASSOC-CRITERION criterion))
        (PROTOTYPE-SET-2 (ASSOC-CRITERION criterion))
        ... )
    (MESSAGE-PART
        (IF-NOTIFICATION
            (NOTE-1 free-text (NOTE-CRITERION criterion))
            (NOTE-2 free-text (NOTE-CRITERION criterion))
            ... )
        (END-RESULT
            (PREFIX free-text (SUPRESS-CRITERION criterion))
            (IF-ATTRIBUTED
                (INFIX-1 free-text (SUPRESS-CRITERION criterion))
                (INFIX-2 free-text (SUPRESS-CRITERION criterion))
                ...
                (SUFFIX free-text)))))
```

Fig. 1

The medical knowledge being used in CODEX knowledge base can be strictly divided into declarative and procedural parts. While the declarative one is being some kind of information serving mostly the needs of the KB user and designer the procedural knowledge serves either for infering a value or for triggering na action. The deep structure most of the procedural knowledge in the medical diagnostics may be seen in the *modus ponens* principle. On the surface, however, this principle takes the form of a *production rule*. Therefore, in each diagnostic ES a kind of a *production rules system* is being used. In the simplest form it is a pure *production system* which in nontrivial applications exhibits several known limitations. To overcome them in the CODEX system the production rules are *structuralized* in some groupings to separate rules used in a *prototypical situation*. The grouping is based on *logical and functional relations among the rules*. The rules in such a grouping are not homogenuous in their function: some are *for value assignments* and some for various kinds of *actions*, but all are tied together by a prototypical situation. The declarative knowledge associated to such situation is attached to them so that all this as a whole creates a frame-like data structure which we name *the prototype*. The Fig. 1 depicts its general scheme. Most of the texts used in this figure are self-explanatory, however, some deserve explanation.

An object being represented by a prototype may be present or absent, or sometimes - at a given moment - its presence is undecidable. The logically valued prototype is then TRUE, FALSE, or UNKNOWN, respectively. A numerically valued object manifests itself by a numerical value or by UNKNOWN value if it is unobservable or uninferable. Some of the composite (attributed) objects manifest their presence by logical or numerical values of at least some of their attributes.

Prescription of the prototype value assignment is the content of the value-assignment-part. Let us note that in case of infered value assignment for a nonattributed prototype at least the IF-CONFIRMED slot is required to be specified. In case of an attributed prototype besides the attribute slots the IF-CONFIRMED and IF-DIS-CONFIRMED slots are facultatively specified. If they are specified and the respective criterions are positively evaluated then they govern the resulting prototype value assignment. This feature is rather significant as it enables to specify for example the AKO relation to other prototypes.

The prototype association-part serves for triggering some other prototypes for evaluation. This feature allows to control the IM attention including the situation when some so called surprise or residual values occure (see [1]). It is important to recognize that triggering means activation, thus scheduling for evaluation, and not the evaluation itself.

The message-part evaluation potentially adds to the final end-result of the diagnostic process. The result of a prototype evaluation is generated as a message from the PREFIX, INFIX, and SUFFIX slots (the last two mentioned are applicable in attributed prototypes only). However, it may occure that such a message display in the whole end-result context is redundant or even confusing. Such situatins can be foreseen and their occurence tested by the content of the SUPRESS-CRITERION parts of related slots. Besides those messages it is useful to notify the CODEX user about the course of diagnostic process and to keep him informed about some situations occured in the course of this process. The display of the related messages is controlled by the IF-NOTIFICATION slots. The messages can be displayed to the user as the diagnostic process proceeds or as a part of the final end-result.

CRITERIA

Under the term criterion we understand the *antecedent* of a production rule. The *consequent of such a rule is implicitely given by the slot in which the criterion occures*. It is either a *value assignment* or an *action*. A unified definition of a criterion is as follows
```
<criterion> ::=<alternative> | <criterion> OR <alternative>
<alternative> ::= <expression> | <alternative> AND <expression>
<expression> ::= <clause> | -<clause> | *<clause> | TRUE | FALSE | UNKNOWN
<clause> ::= <propositional-term> | <relation> |<boolean-treshold-function> |
            |<logical-procedure>
<propositional-term> ::= PROTOTYPE | PROTOTYPE.ATTR
<relation> ::=<operand-1><rel-operator><operand-2>
<operand-1> ::=<numerical-term> | <numerical-procedure>
<operand-2> ::=<operand-1> | REAL-NUMBER
<numerical-term> ::= PROTOTYPE | PROTOTYPE.ATTR
<rel-operator> ::= < | > | =
<logical-procedure> ::= <procedure>
<numerical-procedure> ::= <procedure>
<procedure> ::= %{*}PROC-NAME(<actual-parameter>*)%
<actual-parameter> ::= {*}<propositional-term>
<boolean-treshold-function> ::= <treshoid>(<argument>+)
<treshold> ::= NATURAL-NUMBER
<argument> ::={*}<propositional-term> | {*}<relation>
```

To this definition at least two remarks should be given. The first concerns the unary operator ´*´. It has two meanings which are contextually recognised unequivocally. If the ´*´ occures in front of a clause it causes returning a FALSE value if the clause has been TRUE or FALSE evaluated and a TRUE value if it has been UNKNOWN evaluated. This use of the ´*´operator proved to be useful in triggering an action if some data is unavailable. The meaning of the ´*´ is different if used in front of a PROC-NAME. Then it signifies that the definite truth value (TRUE or FALSE) is not obligatory for all actual-parameters. If the ´*´ is located in front of an actual-parameter then only this one is not obligatory. The second remark concerns the boolean treshold function. It enables to specify a minimal number of conditions to be satisfied in the antecedent in order to assign a truth value to the consequent or to trigger an action. The use of this function is very natural and powerfull as well - it simplifies rather complex logical expressions.

THE INFERENCE MECHANISM

The diagnostic process itself (resolving a disease from given data) corresponds to the IM activities. They follow from criterion evaluation in the activated prototypes. Kleenes´ logic is used in the criterion evaluation. The basic IM philosophy is the *backward chaining*. It is governed by the value-assignment-part of the prototype. A kind of *forward (associative) chaining* is possible as well. It follows from the content of the prototype association-part. The intermixing both of those techniques is regularly performed by the IM. The IM is controlled by three control data structures creating an *agenda*. The first one correspond to the *user diagnostic plan*, the second one is a *deductive stack*, and the third one is a *queue to the systems´plan developed by associations*. For more details see [4]. The IM embodies several built in procedural heuristics as well as procedurally represented meta-knowledge serving for efficient control of the whole diagnostic process. Some of them are discussed in [3].

CONCLUDING REMARKS

The sketched diagnostic expert system CODEX has been written in the Standard MUMPS language. The system requires alternatively 4 or 8K words of the core memory to run, while the size of the whole program code is about 50K bytes. Naturally at least one disc cartridge is required - it hosts the KB as well. The size of KB are limited only by the used disc capacity and do not influence significantly the systems´ response time. Experiences were gained using the CODEX on SM 4/20 and PDP 11 computers. The system is in testing phase of its development. The testing concerns several important aspects, mainly the clinical applicability of the system as a whole, the KB design aids for medical specialists as well as for knowledge engineers, and the adequacy of particular knowledge bases - seven of them are in advanced stage of development. (Nonmedical KBs were successfully tested as well.) Besides the system proved to be a potentially useful diagnostic aid it is being appreciated as a tool for crisp structuralization of medical knowledge, too.

REFERENCES

[1] Aikins, J.S.: Prototypes and Production Rules: A Knowledge Representation for Computer Consultations. Comp. Sci. Dept. Rep. No. STAN-CS-80-814, 1980, 204pp.
[2] Kulikowski, C.A.: Progress in Expert AI Medical Consultation Systems. In Bemmel van, J.H., Ball, M.J., Wigertz, O. (eds.): Proceedings of the MEDINFO ´83, North-Holland, Amsterdam, 1983, (499-502)
[3] Gyárfáš, F., Popper, M.: CODEX: Prototypes Driven backward and forward chaining Computerized Diagnostic Expert System. To appear in Proceedings of the 7th European Meeting on Cybernetics and Research, Vienna, 1984.
[4] Popper, M. et al.: The Diagnostic Expert System CODEX. VÚLB-TR-6/83, Res. Inst. of Medical Bionics, Bratislava, 1983.
[5] Popper, M., Kelemen, J.: Levels of Diagnostics: An Essay Why and an Attempt How to Formalise Medical Diagnostic Reasoning. To appear in Computers and Artificial Intelligence, 3, 1984.

A LIMITED VOCABULARY SPEECH RECOGNITION SYSTEM

Josef Psutka

Department of Technical Cybernetics
Technical Institute, Plzeň
C.S.S.R.

The present paper summarizes partial results that we have got at recognition of a limited words set. The method of selection of basic attributes from the speech signal is here described. Reduction of number of measured attributes is ensured by both a suitable setting of the parameter of measuring T_i and by a following transformation and by a selection of information attributes. The classification rule is designed in the space with the metric L_∞. Our experiments were aimed at the recognition of words spoken by one speaker and by a greater number of speakers.

INTRODUCTION

The solved problem of speech recognition is not simple due to both time dependance and information redundancy of the speech signal. However, these circumstances bring about considerable difficulties by design of a system separating suitable attributes from the speech signal. We must always take a final effect into consideration - - volume of recognized vocabulary, number of speakers, area of utilization, etc. We can direct our effort therefore to recognition of isolated speech sounds, a few words, a wide vocabulary of different words or continuous speech. The problems of speech classification can be researched by using pattern recognition methods.

SPEECH SIGNAL PROCESSING

A suitable basic description of gaining (a primary measurable set of attributes) is most difficult part at speech recognition. It was designed and realized a laboratory analyzer that generates the basic description of desirable quality. The principle of working of analyzer is based on measuring of four parameters of speech signal. We get information of instantaneous frequency both by clipping of speech signal i.e. by comparing of acoustical signal in instants of its zero crossing and by comparing in points of local extremes. The two following parameters inform of properties of energy and they are obtained by measuring of energy in two frequency bounds - up to 650 [Hz] and above 650 [Hz]. The analyzer then ensures the preliminary treatment of acoustical signal, the alternative of integral constant of measuring T_i (time interval at which the mean values of measured frequency and energy are periodically given). We must here accent that designing the analyzer we largely used information got by studying of phonetic and formant structures of Czech language.

The aim of first experiments was to check the quality of obtained basic description at recognition of chosen sets of 21 words (NULA, JEDNA, DVA, TŘI, ČTYŘI, PĚT, ŠEST, SEDM, OSM, DEVĚT, VPŘED, VZAD, NAHORU, DOLU, PLUS, MINUS, VLEVO, VPRAVO, VEZMI, PUSŤ, STOP).

PRELIMINARY REDUCTION OF DIMENSION OF THE BASIC
DESCRIPTION BY SETTING T_i

At the first experiments, the requirement of classification in real time with the adaptation of recognizer possibility to the voice of one speaker or more speakers, if need be. We were got by the requirement of classification in real time to realize a most possibly simple classification rule with minimum of computing operation. We pursued, for these reasons, the possibility of optimal setting of the parameter measuring T_i. The problem consisted in the fact that at the minimum value of T_i we get a quality basic description, but, on the other hand, the decision rule has markedly higher demand on memory, and regarding the high number of computing operations the classification time is lengthening. On the other hand, the basic description is simple for too maximum value of T_i, but a part of information for good recognition is getting lost. If T_i increases, the individual properties of different classes patterns disappear and these patterns approximate to each other. The aim was to find a compromise between a number of measured data and their classification abilities. To find an optimal value of T_i, a method utilizing the probability estimation of the minimum distance between patterns of other classes was suggested. The method is based on properties of the IIIrd asymptotic distribution. Using training set of words prepared for setting-up of recognizer, an estimation of parameter ω in dependance on setting of T_i was made. The parameter ω is the low limit of metric distance between patterns of different classes. The dependance "knee" comes at increasing T_i over 50 [ms].

INFORMATION ATTRIBUTES SELECTION

The information attributes selection is executed, owing to computing reasons, through linear operations above parameters of the basic description. We search for such linear representation

$$\tau \; : \; H_S \rightarrow H_A \qquad (1)$$

which transforms the primary space H_S into H_A so that the dimension of the new attributes spaces will be A, where A is much smaller then S. This new minimal representation should keep the classifying capability on the approximately same level as the basic description. In the first phase, the basic description (measured by optimal T_i) was subjected to the normalization of the pattern space. This supposes such a transformation G^T after which the surfaces of constant dispersion are changed into the S-dimensional unit spheres. Invariance regarding any orthogonal transformations is the advantage of this transformation. For finding of the transformation matrix G^T it is necessary to compute the estimation of the covariance matrix $\hat{D}$. It can be expressed as

$$\hat{D} = \frac{1}{K}\sum_{k=1}^{K} \frac{1}{R}\sum_{r=1}^{R} (z_{kr} - \bar{z}_k)(z_{kr} - \bar{z}_k)^T \qquad (2)$$

where z_{kr} is the rth pattern of the kth class from the space of basic description ($z_{kr} \in H_S$), $\bar{z}_k$ is the mean of patterns in the kth class, K is the number of classes, R is the number of patterns in the class. Then we can write the matrix G^T as

$$G^T = \Lambda^{\frac{1}{2}} C^T \qquad (3)$$

where Λ is diagonal matrix which has the eigenvalues of the matrix $\hat{D}$ on the diagonal, the matrix C^T is orthonormal and its matrix rows are the eigenvectors of the matrix $\hat{D}$.

The second phase, the selection of the information attributes, is based on the best approximation of the original pattern from H_S to the patterns from H_A, where A < S. This technique of the selection of the minimal number attributes is deduced from the Karhunen-Loève expansion. For the classification in the space with metric L_∞, the expansion with matrix $\hat{T}_V$ was applied

$$\hat{T}_V = \frac{1}{K(K-1)} \sum_{q<p} \gamma_{qp}^2 (\bar{y}_q - \bar{y}_p)(\bar{y}_q - \bar{y}_p)^T \qquad (4)$$

where $\gamma_{qp} = |\bar{y}_q - \bar{y}_p|^{-\alpha}$, $\bar{y}_q$ is the normalized mean of patterns in the qth class, K is the number of classes, α is the optional exponent. Let us note that we must choose those eigenvectors that correspond to the largest eigenvalues of the matrix $\hat{T}_V$. The best attributes are based on a mean square error criterion of approximating the original prototypes with only A attributes. From the chosen eigenvectors, we can arranged a rectangular matrix $\tilde{B}^T$ which is AxS dimensions, and to transform the pattern x_{kr} from the original space H_S into a new H_A information attributes space

$$x_{kr} = \tilde{B}^T \Lambda^{-\frac{1}{2}} C^T z_{kr} = \tilde{W}^T z_{kr} \qquad (5)$$

where x_{kr} is r^{th} pattern of kth class from H_A, $\tilde{W}^T$ is the AxS transformation matrix.

CLASSIFICATION BY ETALON METHOD

The classification rule is based on the etalon method. A cover etalon for each class was designed, an inner etalon was designed for each pattern in the class. The cover etalon is the smallest, containing all patterns of own class, the size of the inner etalon is limited by the nearest pattern of other classes. The figure of these etalons depends on the used metric. In the space with metric L_∞, where the distance between two A-dimensional patterns x_a and x_b is defined as

$$\varrho(x_a, x_b) = \max_i |x_{ai} - x_{bi}|, \qquad (6)$$

the etalon is A-dimensional rectangular prism. A function of appurtenance to class is defined by means of the cover etalon and the inner one. This function determines the area of information attributes space that contains patterns of training set of own class. When we know the function of appurtenance to class we can minimize a number of inner etalons for each class (the coverage problem). The own classification rule functions so that we get a basic description of word after having processed the spoken word with analyzer with optimal T_i. This description is then time normalized and transformed into space of information attributes (A-dimension) with the help of the matrix $\tilde{W}^T$. In the information attributes space, the cover etalons and inner ones are designed. First we test the appurtenance of the tested pattern x_t to the cover etalon. So we are finding for which k is satisfied the relation

$$x_t \in O_k \qquad (7)$$

where O_k is the cover etalon of kth class, k= 1,2,...,K. If this relation is not satisfied for no k, we classify the pattern into NOT-RECOGNIZED class, if the relation is satisfied for only one $k = k^*$, we can say that the pattern was RECOGNIZED and we can classify it into the class k^*. If the tested pattern x_t belongs to more than one cover etalon (cover etalons intersect each other), we must pass to a lower level and make a classification according to the inner etalons.

CONCLUSION

We used results estimating the parameter ω to setting fundamental parameter of measuring T_i. The parameter T_i was set on 50 [ms] in order to ensure the compromise between a number of measured data of chosen words and their classifying abilities. In the following phase, our work was aimed to find a system of information attributes and to design a recognition rule. We have to point out that we succeeded to reduce the space dimension more than twenty times, by using both a suitable setting of the parameter T_i and a transformation of patterns into the information attributes space in which the recognition rule is designed.

Recognizing words spoken by a great number of speakers we got the following results: at T_i = 50 [ms] setting, the training set (21x40 words) was classified with 100 p.c. correctness, classifying the testing set (21x40 words) it was well recognized 82 p.c. of words. One word classification time was about Δt = 0,8 [s] on the average. Recognizing words spoken by one speaker, we got the following results: at T_i = 50 [ms] setting, the training set (21x10 words) was classified again with 100 p.c. correctness, classifying the testing set (21x10 words) it was well recognized 96 p.c. of words. One word classification time was about Δt = 0,37 [s]. The whole algorithm was realized on the computer ICL 4-72.

BIBLIOGRAPHY

[1] Gumbel,E., Statistics of extremes, New York, Columbia University Press, 1962.

[2] Turbovic,I.T., Opoznanije obrazov, Moskva, Nauka, 1971.

[3] Reddy,D.R., Speech Recognition, New York, Academic Press, 1975.

[4] Psutka,J., Rozpoznávání omezené množiny slov v reálném čase, in: Metody rozpoznávání obrazů, Praha, ČSVTS-FEL-ČVUT, 1982.

[5] Psutka,J., Systém pro rozpoznávání omezené množiny slov v reálném čase, Kandidátská disertační práce, Praha, FEL, 1979.

"LAOCON" CONTROL SYSTEMS OF ROBOTS

István G.Rákóczy; László Frittmann; Erika Kovács
Computer and Automation Institute
Hungarian Academy of Sciences
BUDAPEST
HUNGARY

LAOCON blends the best of today's computer techniques
- local area network, distributed intelligence,
parallel processing - in a new modular industrial
control system.
Central control unit is replaced by notebook-size
hermetically saled modules to be mounted diretly on
the controlled machine, next to the input (switches,
senson etc.) and output (motors, solenoids etc.)
devices.
Each module is based on a microcomputer that co-
operates in performing the control funkctions in a
high speed parallel processing system, there is no
need for a central unit.

1.1. GENERAL DESCRIPTION

LAOCON (Local Area Optimized COntrol Network) offers a unique new
concept in the control of medium size industrial processes and
systems. (Figure 1.) It is a family of packaged low cost interface/
processing units (DMC I/O's) that can be positioned remotely and
linked together with twisted pairs of wires to provide ready-to-use
control systems.

In the field of industrial controllers one can observe nowadays that
the cost of smaller systems is not represented by their electronic
hardware but rather the mechanical packaging and necessary I/O
interfaces. This trend is expected to be universal in a year or two.

The packaged blocks of LAOCON system can be positioned where the
actionis on the plant or on the machine to the origin of input signal
sources or to the place of power equipments. This method drastically
decreases the cost of cabeling and mechanical cabinets.

The new feature wich distingquishes LAOCON from the rest of packaged
remote data acquisition and control systems is that it requires no
"Master Station" or control Computer. Being a totally distributed
control system, all the processing work required to control a simple
machine or even the whole process of a plant is performed by the I/O
boxes themselves.

For smaller systems this offers considerable const savings-there is
no computer overhead. LAOCON provides economic solutions for
applications too, that only require 2-3.

For larger applications LAOCON has the unique feature of expanding
its computing/processing power with each I/O box added.

LAOCON without user intervention partitions application control program and distributes among the processors in I/O boxes and builds up the communication net to keep parallel processing running. This gives tremendous flexibility for applications having very different I/O numers and sizes.

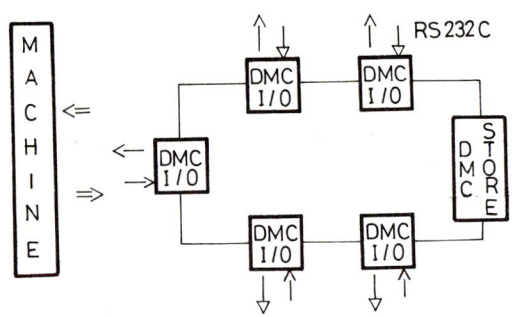

DMC : Distributed Micro Controller

Figure 1.

1.2. LAOCON FEATURES

Notebook-sized LAOCON units are packed in boxes of rugged mechanical construction, tolerating temperature, humidity, vibration and electro-magnetic interferences. There is no need for additional racks, terminals, fans, power supplies, etc. Cables from machinery are directly attachable to screwtype terminals. Besides them only a 24 VDC power cable and a twisted pair of communication cables are needed.

Each LAOCON is fully monitored, with LED's displaying the state of inputs and outputs, the result of self-diagnostics.

In case of error, there is no need for serviceman: based on self-diagnostic LED's even an untrained person can localize the faulty unit and replace it with a screwdriver. Small size and low cost makes a viable alternative for even small-scale users to have spare modules on stock. When installing a new modul no programming is required, not even address setting. Simply replace and switch on -LAOCON will do the rest.

Satisfying various application demands a set of further modules(24VDC power, PID control, position control, stepping motor control, +/-10V analog, 240VAC output, moreover, a small man-machine interface with one-line 16-segment display and CRT control line) can directly be attached to the PSCS (Proprietory Serial Communication System) link.

Information exchange among various units take place via a appx. 30.000 Baud serial communication link (PSCS).

Worst-case response time for a system with e.g. 300 I/Os is as low as 50 msec (typically 10 msec).

2.1. THE "PRODESTA" PROGRAMMING SYSTEM

The user programs the LAOCON system in such a way as if it were a single computer process controller. It is carried out on a home-computer (e.g. Apple II) based program developing station (PRODESTA) Figure 2.

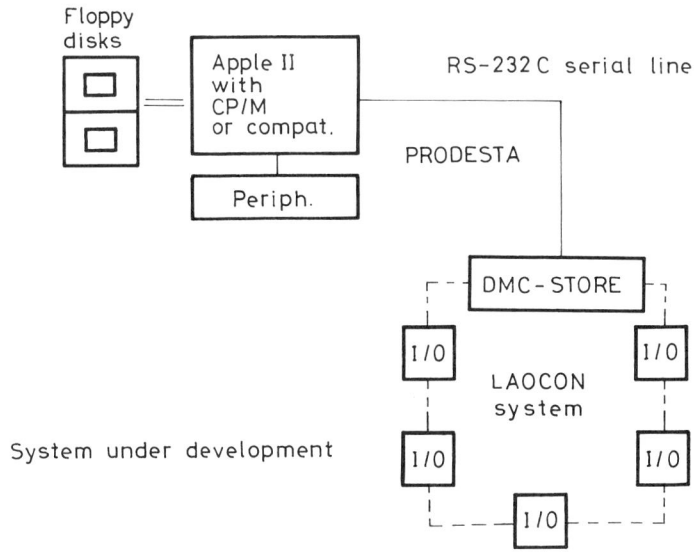

Figure 2.

The debugged user program is transmitted to the storage module via RS-232C serial line and stored in the EEPROM memory of the unit, thus the development computer is not required for regular control operation. The storage/monitor module will optimally distribute the funkctions among DMC I/O units, optimizing to minimal cycle period considering the time of information exchange as well.

2.2. PRODESTA FEATURES

- LANGUAGE:

This process control system has a BASIC-like COntrol LAnguage (COLA), that has the features as follows:
. Expressions are written as in any other high
  level programming languages.

- I/O variables have symbolic names
- Standard and user defined functions can be linked into the control program to carry out special control functions.

- EDITOR /OMPILER/ MONITOR:

The Editor/Compiler/Monitor (ECOMO) system proveds the user with a complete programming environment for development where every function needed for the developing work (program modification, translating and debugging) can be used at any moment without changing the environment.

> A high level algorithm automatically partitions the sequential control program into hazard-free sub-programs to be run on different LAOCON blocks. The distribution algorithm ensures optimal structures among LAOCON modules considering the total amount of time for local processing and system communication.

ECOMO system is a homogenious software tool that supports every task needed in the development process. ECOMO has been designed with definite aims in mind:

a.) Preparing control programs for machine or process control application requires no special computer skill, the system is easy to learn and use (approximately 8 hours training is enough).

b.) ECOMO keeps the user completely unewere of the fact that he or she uses a distributed multiprocessing system. During the process of program developing (program writing, -editing simulating, debugging and monitoring) the user works with the system as if it were a single monolithic process control computer.

- DEMOS is the DEbugging MOnitoring Subsystem of ECOMO. It is used for on-line and off-line debugging with the same user interface. DEMOS can be imagined as a communication window between the programmer and the process control program. Through this window the programmer can examine, modify not only values of system variables but even the control program itself. User can move the window over the control program and the variable field, moreover, can change the highlighted information. DEMOS has all the well known facilities have been used in a user friendly program debugging system. User can:

- Examine/modify values of variables and the control program.
- Define break points.
- Set variable values, thus the program does not change these user defined values.
- Back trace changes of the system variables.

-HARDWARE BACKGROUND:

The ECOMO program developing system including DEMOS can be run on any personal computer (Apple II, Osborne, etc) under CP/M operating system.

A PARALLEL COMPUTER SYSTEM SIMD

Karol Richter

Institute of Technical Cybernetics
Slovak Academy of Sciences
Dubravská cesta 84237 Bratislava
Czechoslovakia

The aim of this paper is to characterize briefly
a SIMD type parallel computer system which is
being developed at the Institute of Technical
Cybernetics of the Slovak Academy of Sciences.

INTRODUCTION

Parallel computer systems are capable, in many cases, of attaining a considerably higher computation speed than sequential computers do, therefore in the last decade intensive research of parallel computer systems has been observable.
At the Institute of Technical Cybernetics of the Slovak Academy of Sciences, research and development of the SIMD type (single instruction-multiple data) computer system is being carried out with the working name "Parallel Computer System SIMD". The system development is in the stage of functional model verification. In the paper the hardware and the system software are introduced.

OVERVIEW

Figure 1. shows a block diagram of the Parallel Computer System SIMD (PCS SIMD). There are eight major blocks from which seven belong to the parallel section and one to the sequential section. The sequential section is a SM 50/50 computer system, but any SM type computer system with unibus organization (SM 4/20, SM 52/11 etc.) can be used. Its major responsibility is to handle the peripherals, control the system from console commands, and perform diagnostic functions.
The parallel section is a SIMD type multiprocessor system (MS SIMD). It is made up of seven block: the control memory, the multiport connection system, the control unit, the associative modules, the interactive module, the interconnection module and the input/output processors.

CONTROL MEMORY

The control memory has a block structure. The blocks are used to store instructions for MS SIMD and data. The maximum adressable size of the control memory is 64 K words. In the functional model the block size is 2 K words. It exihibits read and write cycle times of less than 200 nsec, including a multiport connection system. When more than one block is available, it can be dedicated for instruction or data storing. The speed of MS SIMD in this case is higher by overlapping the instruction reading and data transfer between control memory and control unit. The control unit, SM 50/50 and host can transfer data fo/from control memory in parallel if they access different blocks of control memory.

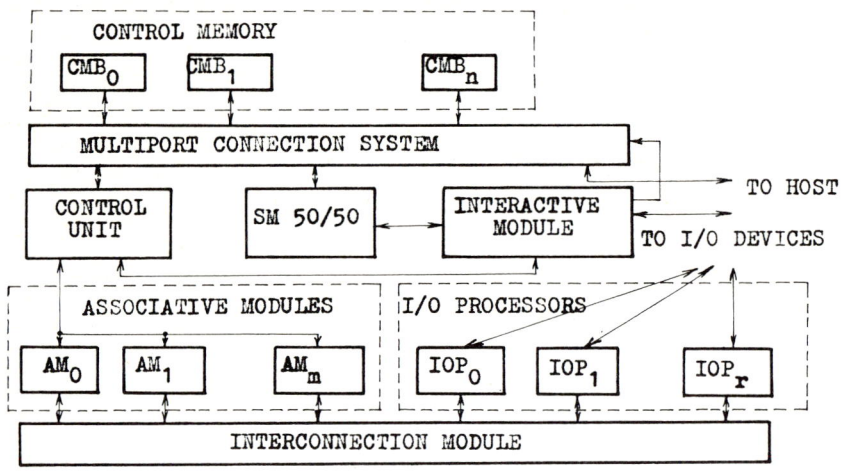

Fig.1
Block diagram of the PCS SIMD

The multiport connection system (MCS) has two parts: the port switch logic and bus logic. The port switch logic allows to choose for every control memory block the access mode and the priority of connected units. It enables to switch every control memory block to two different access modes. In the first of them the control memory block is dedicated fully to MS SIMD instructions storing. This mode enables to read the instructions with maximum speed. In the second mode the control memory block can be used for data and instruction storing. The access of connected units in this mode is ruled by their priority. The highest priority is assigned to data access from the control unit.
The bus logic connects the instruction path of control unit and the data paths of all connected units to port switch logic of every control memory block.

ASSOCIATIVE MODULES

To the control unit 1 to 32 associative modules may be connected. Each associative module contains a multi-dimensional access memory unit, one-bit processor units, parallel input/output unit (PIOU), interconnection unit and connection unit. Figure 2. shows the block structure of the associative module. Data in the associative module are stored in the multi-dimensional access memory unit. It has wide read and write busses for parallel access to a large number (64 in functional model) of memory unit bits. Data can be accessed in many different access model (bit-slice access mode, word access mode and mixed modes). Through the interconnection unit, data are transferred between units of the associative module. The interconnection unit enables data manipulation (permutations including shifts) during data transfer.
One bit processor unit contains registers and logic circuits. The

registers are used as temporary fast storage, and participate in logical operations. During the performance of the instruction, the data in all selected words (unmasked) of memory units are processed by processing units of all selected associative modules simultaneously.
The PIOU-s control the high bandwidth I/O transfers. The autonomous operation of PIOU-s enables to perform operations in some of the associative modules, controlled by the control unit, and in the same time to transfer data between specified associative modules controlled by PIOU-s. Detailed information on PIOU is given in lit[1]. The connection unit contains interface circuitry for interfacing the associative module with control unit.
The functional model of PCS SIMD contains associative modules with 64 processor units and 64 words x 1 K bits of multi-dimensional access memory.

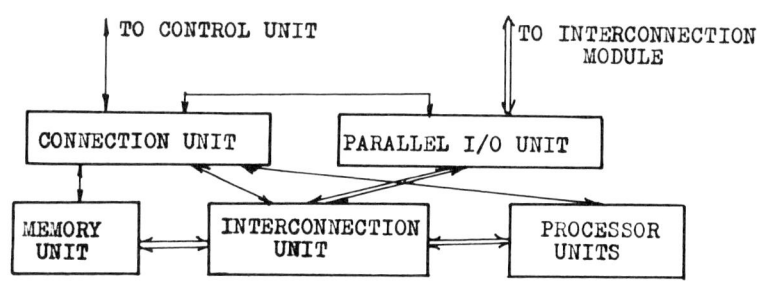

Fig.2
The block structure of associative module

CONTROL UNIT

The control unit controls the MS SIMD. Instructions are drawn from the control memory. The control unit contains various registers connected to internal input and output busses. Typical instructions not involving associative modules are the "load register from the control memory", "store register to register", "store register to control memory", "branch" and interactive module instructions. Typical associative module instructions are "load associative module/modules with 32 bit data from control unit register", "store 32 bit data from associative module to control unit register", "find first responder", "load processor unit register from memory unit","store processor unit register to memory unit", "store register to register". These instructions are executed on all unmasked words of selected associative modules in parallel. Special type instructions are PIOU instructions which specify the required block transfer.

INTERACTIVE MODULE

The interactive module has its own instruction set and autonomously controls their execution. The instructions to the interactive module are sent from SM 50/50, MS SIMD and host computer. The interactive module is equipped with priority logic for the case that more instructions are waiting for execution.
The interactive module enables :
- to gain information on the state of computation in MS SIMD,SM 50/50 and host by sensing information stored before in the inter**active** module

- to synchronize parallel computation of MS SIMD, SM 50/50 and host by sending and sensing information to/from the interactive module
- to set and clear interrupts to the SM 50/50, MS SIMD and host
- to switch every control memory block to the required access mode
- to get information on errors of MS SIMD
- to start, halt and specify the mode of MS SIMD operation (single step, continuous execution).

INTERCONNECTION MODULE

The interconnection module realizes the requested connection between associative modules mutually and between associative modules and IOP-s. Two interconnection module structures are investigated for PCS SIMD. The bus structure and the crossbar structure. In the functional sample the bus structure is used. Detailed information on the bus structure is given in lit [1].

I/O PROCESSOR

The I/O processor (IOP) is a specialized device designed mainly for high-speed data transfer between high-capacity storages, specialized peripherals and associative modules.

HOST COMPUTER

The design of PCS SIMD allows it to be connected to other computers as a special-purpose peripheral. As a host, SM type computers with unibus structure or EC type computers can be used. In the case of the EC type computer a specialized interface unit must be used. When PCS SIMD and host operate in an integrated fashion a single task can use both machines to satisfy its processing requirements.

PCS SIMD CONFIGURATION

The PCS SIMD allows to effectively supply the users´ needs by selecting the required type and configuration of the host (if any), the number of control memory blocks, the size and number of associative modules, the number of IOP-s and the type and configuration of the sequential section. The designed PCS SIMD enables to connect 32 associative modules with maximum configuration of each 256 processor units and multidimensional access memory unit with size 256 words x 64 K bits.

SYSTEM SOFTWARE

The system software of PCS SIMD is created by adding PCS SIMD related software to a standard SM type computer operating system. For the PCS SIMD loader, linker, program supervisor, debug module, control module, ASPL assembler, macro-processor and library of system macro instructions and subroutines are being developed. The integrated use of PCS SIMD and a host computer makes additional software necessary.
The user can write programs in the ASPL assembler language developed for PCS SIMD. Also a macro language is created to increase the users flexibility at assembly time.
The software used to convert source language programs into executable load modules includes ASPL assembler, macro-processor and linker. The loader moves the load module created by the linker into MS SIMD control memory beginning at the specified address.
The program supervisor is the software interface between the parallel and sequential section of the system. It makes the I/O instruc-

tions of the SM 50/50 operating system available, provides a programmable interrupt to a SM 50/50 routine, program overlay capability etc.
The debug module enables the user effectively to debug programs by giving him control of the execution of the program and access to all memory units and registers. Dumps of all memory areas are possible. The control module enables the user to control the execution of the PCS SIMD program. Commands as start, halt and continue execution are processed directly by the control module.
The library of the system macro instructions and subroutines is in the stage of development. The simulator of PCS SIMD [2], which enables in advance to debug the developed macro instructions and subroutines, has been implemented on the EC 4/20 computer. Detailed information on subroutines and macro instructions is given in lit [3].

PCS SIMD APPLICATIONS

The assumed application areas of PCS SIMD are image processing, large scale database management, information retrieval, signal processing, large scale matrix computations, on-line management information systems, sensor data processing systems.

CONCLUSION

In the paper a brief description of PCS SIMD is given. The system is a powerful SIMD type parallel computer system with modular organization. It can contain thousands of processing units and attain the speed of hundreds of milions of operations per sec.
It can be used in the stand-alone mode or as a software-programable peripheral, or special purpose processor, for attachment to SM or EC type conventional computer systems.

REFERENCES

1   Gašparík, I. and Richter, K., Organization possibilities and transfer subsystem structure of SIMD type parallel computer systems, Computers and Artificial Intelligence Jrnl.2 (1983).
2   Skákala, J., A Parallel Processor Simulator, Computers and Artificial Intelligence Jrnl. 4(1983), 61-75.
3   Mikloško, J. and Lucká, M., Fast parallel algorithms for associative computer, Artificial Intelligence and Information-Control Systems of Robots, Inter.Conf. (1982) 162-166.

SOLVING TASKS ON SEMANTIC NETWORKS AND GRAPHS
BY ACTIVE DISTRIBUTED STRUCTURES

Peter S. Sapaty

Mathematical Machines and Systems Special Design
Bureau of the Glushkov Cybernetics Institute of
the Ukr. SSR Academy of Sciences, Kiev
USSR

Efficient methods of structural solving of complex tasks on semantic networks and graphs are presented. They are based on a concept of active data networks without separating data representation and computation. The data networks find solutions in a self-organizing manner with high degree of performance when put into multiprocessor environment. Some hypothetical network computer is discussed for the direct interpretation of an active data network model.

INTRODUCTION

One of the most real approaches to unlimited growth of computer performance is to use distributed computer structures excluding common resources bottle-necks like global storage, communication structure or control. Their effective application needs fundamental revision of the traditional task solving methods according to the idea of distributed computing.

In this report we present a number of essentially new approaches to the organization of distributed parallel computations on complex data structures - networks and graphs. They are based on the direct representation of networks and graphs by topologically similar to them network computers whose nodes and sometimes arcs are active blocks with their own local storage. Such blocks besides keeping information about the data structure are able to do local computations and exchanges with neighbouring blocks. So a network or a graph being put into such distributed active environment becomes an active data base which can autonomously, without any external intervention, solve complex tasks on itself or another data structures.

Three main approaches where such active data network is used as an associative network processor, a self-organizing model working according to the analogous principle, a network-structured interpreter for information retrieval languages [1,2] are discussed.

ACTIVE DATA NETWORK AS AN ASSOCIATIVE NETWORK PROCESSOR

A structural realization of some operations on a pair of semantic networks S1 and S2 with named vertices and arcs is considered. One network, say S1, is directly introduced as a distributed network processor and the other S2 is considered as a text -

adjacency structure showing for each node a list of its immediate successors together with the names of corresponding arcs.

The desired solution is obtained as a result of associative, parallel reading of textually introduced network S2 by means of structurally introduced network S1. The result is retained in the structure of network S1 and may be autonomously copied and passed beyond S1, if necessary, as a resultant textual adjacency structure.

In case of intersection operation of networks S1 and S2 network S1 permits to traverse itself only for the common part of both networks, that is S1 ∩ S2. For the union operation network S2 omits in S1 their common part and the rest of S2 when being passed through S1 is supplemented by autonomously copied textual description of structure S1. So the result is S1 ∪ S2. The supplement operation of network S2 to network S1 when S1 includes S2 is executed through two stages: at first network S2 passing through S1 erases from S1 their common arcs, and then by means of retained arcs and their corresponding nodes the resulting network is composed, this being a supplement of S2 up to S1.

For such operations as testing the identity of two networks or inclusion of one network into another that do not require the resultant adjacency structure a single efficient operation is considered. It enables, after S2 passes through S1, by means of some signs being globally established by S1, to evaluate the desired result easily.

The time of structural execution of all described operations is linearly proportional to the volume of nets, and the result is obtained directly in the process of reading S2 by S1.

ACTIVE DATA NETWORK AS A DISTRIBUTED SELF-ORGANIZING SYSTEM

An autonomous solution of main tasks that usually take place on graphs and networks by means of an active network structure is considered. The method is based on a model as some integral active informational field. The computer network continuously supporting such integral field contains nodes with their own memories that correspond to nodes of a graph or a network on which the solution is to be found. These nodes communicate among themselves across distributed common memory blocks corresponding to the arcs or edges of graphs or networks.

In a number of cases the active nodes may have an access to the individual memories of adjacent nodes. Active nodes may also, on their own initiative, seize adjacent nodes forming with them new, united nodes, establish additional or delete existing connections with other nodes. The operation of every node is described by a simple set of local rules which allows essential non-determinism and at the same time guarantees bringing the whole network to the desired final state.

The tasks on such network model are solved similarly to the functioning of analogous devices. The solution is obtained in the result of the integral transitive process all over the structure which takes place because of inconsistencies in the data field.

Every node of the network is continuously balancing the values on adjacent arcs, without synchronization with the adjacent nodes on data, and constantly improving in such a way the local solution in its own point of informational field.

This makes it possible to find efficiently on graphs and networks connected components, points of connection and biconnected components, strongly connected components and one-way connected components, additional graph, ordinal function of a graph without contours, shortest paths tree, diameter, center and radius of a graph, minimum spanning trees, fundamental set of cycles, matchings and coverings, internally and externally stable subsets, cliques, chromatic number, and also to calculate network diagrams or to optimize the flow through networks.

The offered approach enables to solve the described kinds of tasks generally in the execution time of the order of diameters or radii of graphs. The unrigid character of informational bounds between nodes, the unity of data representation and computation, the absence of control in conventional terms altogether enable to obtain globally parallel non-deterministic network algorithms which are also stable to the environmental failures and delays.

A number of such network algorithms is based on their structural similarity to the inner processes of reaching the optimal states in natural, physical systems. For instance, in case of finding the total flow in a transport network the constant application in every node of simple set of rules on balancing the values on arcs leads to the development of the following global processes. Initially, the maximally possible flow is trying to traverse the network after placing on arcs proceeding from the starting node values of flows equal to their throughputs. If in some directions it is impossible for the whole flow to come forward, the rest of the flow is coming back to the minimal depth and trying to pass across the network in other directions.

Such processes create multiple pipelines of the forward and backward wave processes with illegible wavefronts all over the network. These structural transitive processes having been terminated, a self-establishing of the total flow takes place for all kinds of the network topology including the networks with contours.

ACTIVE DATA NETWORK AS A NETWORK INTERPRETER OF THE INFORMATION RETRIEVAL LANGUAGES

Computer networks under consideration constructed in accordance with the topology of the data graph may be used for the autonomous realization on active semantic networks of a number of complex search operations of some information retrieval language. Such a language consists of the two sublanguages - the language of search images (LSI) and the language of operations over search images (LOS). By setting some initial, creating sets of nodes of the network and special generator expressions which describe the conditions of spreading search waves across the network, LSI enables to select on the network the required substructures which are considered as operands of the LOS language.

The analysis showed that all operations of such retrieval language may be autonomously executed by means of an active semantic network spreading over itself, as the waves of messages, search images with the types of operations to be executed over the selected substructures. During the process of selecting subnets the generators which are transmitted on the wavefronts gradually lose their utilized parts until they exhaust their means for outlining the required fragments in the general network.

Thus the active data network works in a manner similar to the functioning of the data flow models but instead of data the instructions of LSI and LOS languages move across the network whereas the data themselves in the form of an active semantic network remain immovable. This approach enables to solve structurally such tasks on semantic networks as decomposition, assembly of the whole from components, pattern matching, context influences, different forms of properties inheritance mechanisms, etc., with high degree of concurrency.

CONCLUSION

The reported methods of solving tasks on networks and graphs structurally based upon the idea of active data networks may be efficiently interpreted by different kinds of multiprocessor systems with multiple instructions and data streams as well as by distributed networks of computers. However, in order to fully realize the potential possibilities of the active data network model it would be desirable to design the special network computer. Therefore some hypothetical network computer model for the direct support of active data network is briefly described. It may be based on the regular multimicroprocessor network having besides local connections between processors some special channels of global communications and control which permit analogous realization. Some auxiliary blocks may also exist in the network computer realizing such functions as loading the network, collecting the results flowing out of the network and listening to its activity in order to determine the moments of termination of transitive processes.

Active data network model is represented in such network computer as an active space-bounded list where the differences in volume and topology between processor network and active data network are smoothed by allocating more than one node of a network in a single processor, whose storage is divided into zones for different nodes, some zones being transitive. The processors share their computing power among the nodes allocated on them. Some questions on structure dynamics of active data networks allocated in the rigid regular structure of the multiprocessor network are also discussed.

REFERENCES

[1] Sapaty, P.S., A Structural Approach to Solving Tasks of Graph and Network Theory, in Proc. 5th All-Union School on Parallel Programming and High-Performance Systems. Vol.4, "Naukowa Dumka", Kiev, USSR, 1982.

[2] Sapaty, P.S., About Efficient Structural Realization of Operations on Semantic Networks, Proc. of the USSR Academy of Sciences. Technical Cybernetics, 5 (1983) 128-134.

HIGHLY PARALLEL ALGORITHMS AND THE ARCHITECTURE OF A COMPUTER SYSTEM FOR SOLVING LARGE MATRIX PROBLEMS

S.G.Sedukhin

Institute of Mathematics
Siberian Branch of the USSR Academy of Sciences
Novosibirsk
USSR

In the paper considered are the basic stages of designing and analysing flow computational schemes providing direct correspondence between mathematical expressions of algorithms and networks realizing those algorithms. Given are structural and time characteristics for a number of numerical algorithms for solving matrix formulated problems, and proposed is an architecture of a reconfigurable computer system oriented upon the optimal realization of the algorithms under consideration.

A great number of algorithms for solving matrix formulated problems are characterized by high degree of parallelism which, for the use of general-purpose computers, is compulsory transformed into a linear sequence of operations over a single data stream. The development of very large-scale integrated (VLSI) circuits makes it practically possible to create computational means with a great number of processing cells (processors). On the other hand, great communication cost of high-speed elements in VLSI circuits demands here topological locality, asynchronousness and regularity of concurrent processing, communication and control [1].

I. The basic stages of the synthesis of structural schemes of computations which make up a formal foundation for topology development of VLSI circuits are considered as the example of the algorithm of transitive closure of a graph having computer relation with the whole class of linear algebra methods [2]. The algorithm of the transitive closure of a graph $G=(V,E)$, where $V=\{v_1, v_2, \ldots, v_n\}$ is a set of nodes, and E is a set of arcs, is written as follows:

$$c_{ij}^{(0)} = c_{ij}, \quad 1 \leqslant i,j \leqslant n;$$
$$c_{ij}^{(\kappa)} = c_{ij}^{(\kappa-1)} + c_{i\kappa}^{(\kappa-1)} \cdot c_{\kappa j}^{(\kappa-1)}, \quad 1 \leqslant i,j \leqslant n, 1 \leqslant \kappa \leqslant n.$$

Here, the initial $(n \times n)$-matrix $C=[c_{ij}]$ is assigned as a sum of identity matrix and adjacency matrix of the graph G. The elements of the obtained $(n \times n)$-availability matrix $C^* = [c_{ij}^{(n)}]$ equal

$$c_{ij}^{(n)} = \begin{cases} 1, & \text{if the path from } v_i \text{ to } v_j \text{ does exist;} \\ 0 & \text{otherwise.} \end{cases}$$

Define a task R_{ij}^k as an indivisible unit of computational actions to determine the element $c_{ij}^{(\kappa)}$ at the processing step (stage) $\kappa \in \{1, 2, \ldots, n\}$. The range of values and the determination domain of the task R_{ij}^{κ} equal respectively

$$W(R_{ij}^{\kappa}) = \{c_{ij}^{(\kappa)}\}, \quad D(R_{ij}^{\kappa}) = \{c_{ij}^{(\kappa-1)}\} \cup \{c_{i\kappa}^{(\kappa-1)}: \kappa \neq j\} \cup \{c_{\kappa j}^{(\kappa-1)}: \kappa \neq i\}.$$

Then for a set of tasks of the κ-th stage $R^{\kappa} = \{R_{ij}^{\kappa}: 1 \leq i, j \leq n\}$ the set

$$X_{\kappa} = \bigcap_{1 \leq i,j \leq n} D(R_{ij}^{\kappa}) = \{c_{i\kappa}^{(\kappa-1)}: 1 \leq i \leq n\} \cup \{c_{\kappa j}^{(\kappa-1)}: 1 \leq j \leq n\}$$

assigns the common determination domain, i.e. elements X_{κ} are common operands for a set of tasks R^{κ}.

Introduce a transitive binary precedence constraint of the tasks, $\prec = (R, R')$ implying that the task R should precede the task R'. Precedence constraint of a set R^{κ} for the processing of common operands X_{κ} can formally be written as follows:

$$\prec_{\kappa} = \{(R_{ij-1}^{\kappa}, R_{ij}^{\kappa}): \kappa < j \leq n\}^{*} \cup \{(R_{ij+1}^{\kappa}, R_{ij}^{\kappa}): j < \kappa \leq n\}^{*} \cup$$

$$\cup \{(R_{i-1j}^{\kappa}, R_{ij}^{\kappa}): \kappa < i \leq n\}^{*} \cup \{(R_{i+1j}^{\kappa}, R_{ij}^{\kappa}): i < \kappa \leq n\}^{*},$$

where $*$ denotes the transitive closure of a set.

To a system of tasks $S_{\kappa} = \langle R^{\kappa}, \prec_{\kappa} \rangle$ there corresponds a partial ordering graph $\Gamma_{\kappa} = (R_{ij}^{\kappa}, \prec^{\kappa})$, whose nodes are the tasks $R_{ij}^{\kappa} \in R^{\kappa}$, and the arcs $\prec^{\kappa}$ expose the relation of tasks on common data X_{κ} processing. The graph Γ^{κ} uniquely identifies the structural scheme of the κ-th stage of computations. To the whole algorithm there corresponds the set of structural schemes $\{\Gamma_{\kappa}: 1 \leq \kappa \leq n\}$ presented in Fig. 1 for the case $n = 4$. Dark vertices of every graph Γ_{κ} denote the tasks R_{ij}^{κ} determining on the $(\kappa-1)$-th stage the common operands from X_{κ}.

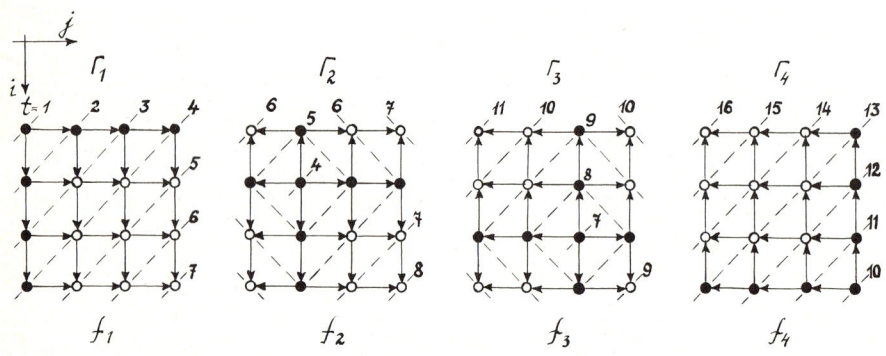

Fig. 1.

The precedence relation of tasks $\prec_{\kappa}$ induces on the set R^{κ} of the graph Γ_{κ} vertices the partition $[R^{\kappa}]$ into equivalence classes

$$[R^{\kappa}] = \{[R_{\rho_{\kappa}}^{\kappa}]: 0 \leq \rho_{\kappa} \leq \rho_{\kappa}^{max}\},$$

where $\left[R_{\rho_\kappa}^\kappa\right] = \left\{R_{ij}^\kappa : |\kappa-i|+|\kappa-j|=\rho_\kappa,\, 1\leq i,j\leq n\right\}$ is the class of mutually independent and, therefore, concurrently implemented tasks disposed in the system S_κ at the same distance $\rho_\kappa = 1, 2, \ldots, \rho_\kappa^{max}$ from the initial task of the κ-th stage of computations $R_{\kappa\kappa}^\kappa = [R_o^\kappa]$, $\rho_\kappa^{max} = max[2(\kappa-1), 2(n-\kappa)]$. For such a two-dimensional interpretation of structural schemes to every vertex R_{ij}^κ of the graph Γ_κ one can associate the (i,j)-th computational cell and to the arcs – the information interchange channels. The obtained array of n×n computational cells, orthogonally connected, can: (1) concurrently realize in time and space all the available in the system S_κ sequences of processing and communication of the tasks R^κ, and (2) overlap the processing of the following each other task systems S_κ.

If a unit step ρ_κ by the space in S_κ equals, for the network of processing cells, a unit step by the time t, then the implementation time of the κ-th stage of computations will change in the range $t_\kappa \leq t \leq t_\kappa + \rho_\kappa^{max}$ where $t_\kappa = 3\kappa - 2$. It is convenient to assume that the implementation of every κ-th stage concerns the propagation in the array of the wave front of computations and interchange $\mathcal{L}^\kappa$ whose position on different time steps $t = 1, 2, \ldots$ is drawn in Fig. 1 by dotted lines. Thus, time complexity of two-dimensional interpretation of the algorithm of n×n processing array makes up the quantity $T_2(n) = t_n + \rho_n^{max} = 5n - 4$. To compare, time (arithmetic) complexity of sequential interpretation of the method by a single computer is the quantity $T_o(n) = n^3$.

The obtained array of n×n processing cells can be estimated from the viewpoint of the realization optimality on the basis of VLSI circuits. Note, first of all, that the area of a unit processing cell of the array does not depend on the logical size of the problem (the initial matrix order) since for the storage, processing and data interchange in a processing cell it is necessary to have $O(1)$ registers. If now the physical size (area) of a chip $A(n)$ is measured by a number of processing cells in the array, i.e. $A(n) = O(n^2)$, then the condition connecting the area and the computation time chip in our case is equal to

$$A(n) \cdot T_2^2(n) = O(n^4),$$

which shows the optimality of the obtained array by the criterion AT^2 [3].

It is easy to demonstrate that time complexity of one-dimensional interpretation of an algorithm on the array of n linearly connected computers, each having the local memory of $O(n)$ words, makes up the quantity $T_1(n) = n^2 + O(n)$. The existing partitioned alternative of the algorithm allows one to effectively realize two-dimensional or one-dimensional interpretation in the array containing an arbitrary number of either N×N or N computers, where $1 < N < n$ (bounded parallelism). In this case, the initial (n×n)-matrix is partitioned into N×N submatrices where $N = n/r$ and r is an integer. In the general case, time complexity of m-dimensional interpretation of an algorithm of an N^m computers array is determined by the expression

$$T_m(n) = O(n^3/N^m),$$

where n is the logical size of the problem, N^m is the physical size of the array ($1 \leq N \leq n$); m is the size of interpretation space ($m = 0, 1, 2$).

II. Obtaining of the graph transitive closure is one of many algorithms which can be directly realized by the hardware on the basis of VLSI circuits. Structural and time characteristics of a number of algorithms for the solution of matrix formulated problems are given below for the case of unbounded parallelism. In the given list n is the logical size of the problem; K is the number of iterations; $\mathcal{L}$ is linear, C - cyclic, R - orthogonal, G - hexagonal connection types of processing cells in the array; $[B, \rho]$ is the array containing ρ processing cells connected as $B \in \{\mathcal{L}, C, R, G\}$.

1. Multiplication of two (n × n)-matrices: $T_1(n) = n^3$; $[\mathcal{L}/C, n]$ - array: $T_n(n) = n^2$; $[R/G, n \times n]$ - array: $T_{n^2}(n) = 3n$.

2. Triangularization

a) of (n × n)-matrix:

$T_1(n) = n^3/3$; $[\mathcal{L}, n]$ - array: $T_n(n) = n^2/2$; $[R/G, n \times n]$ - array: $T_{n^2}(n) = 3n$,

b) of positive definite symmetric (n × n)-matrix by Cholesky's method:

$T_1(n) = n^3/6$; $[\mathcal{L}, n]$ - array: $T_n(n) = n^2/2$; $[R/G, n^2/2]$ - array: $T_{n^2/2}(n) = 3n$,

c) of q band (n × n)-matrices of bandwidth $m = 2\rho - 1$, $m \ll n$:

$T_1(q, n) = q \rho^2 n$; $[R/G, m \times n]$ - array: $T_{mn}(q, n) = 3n + \rho q$; $[\mathcal{L}, n]$ - array: $T_n(q, n) = \rho n + \rho^2 q$; $[\mathcal{L}, m]$ - array: $T_m(q, n) = q m n$.

3. Reduction of (n × n)-matrix to two-diagonal form by Householder method: $T_1(n) = 4n^3/3$; $[C, n]$ - array: $T_n(n) = 9n^2/2$.

4. Solution of a linear recurrent n-order system:

$T_1(n) = n^2/2$; $[\mathcal{L}, n]$ - array: $T_n(n) = 2n$.

5. Solution of n linear algebraic equations system by:

a) direct method:

$T_1(n) = n^3/3$; $[\mathcal{L}, n]$ - array: $T_n(n) = n^2/2$; $[R/G, n^2]$ - array: $T_{n^2}(n) = 5n$,

b) Jacobi iteration method: $T_1(n) = n^2 K$; $[C, n]$ - array: $T_n(n) = n \cdot K$,

c) Zeidel iteration method: $T_1(n) = n^2 K$; $[C, n]$ - array: $T_n(n) = 2 n \cdot K$.

6. Inversion of (n × n)-matrix by the compact scheme:

$T_1(n) = n^3$; $[\mathcal{L}, n]$ - array: $T_n(n) = 2n^2$; $[R/G, n^2]$ - array: $T_{n^2}(n) = 7n$.

7. Determination of eigenvalues of (n × n)-matrix by:

a) Danilevsky method: $T_1(n) = n^3$; $[C, n]$ - array: $T_n(n) = 2n^2$,

b) Krylov method: $T_1(n) = n^3$; $[C, n]$ - array: $T_n(n) = n^2$.

8. Determination the first eigenvalue of (n × n)-matrix by scalar

product method: $T_1(n) = n^3 \cdot \kappa$; $[C, n]$ - array: $T_n(n) = n^2 \cdot \kappa$.

III. Since to a set of algorithms there corresponds a set of structural schemes, then the optimal solution of a wide class of matrix formulated problems can be provided in a computer system whose functional structure (architecture) contains a programmable network of locally connected processing cells (micro-computers) and a coordinated, by bandwidth, subsystem of matching and input/output(Fig.2).

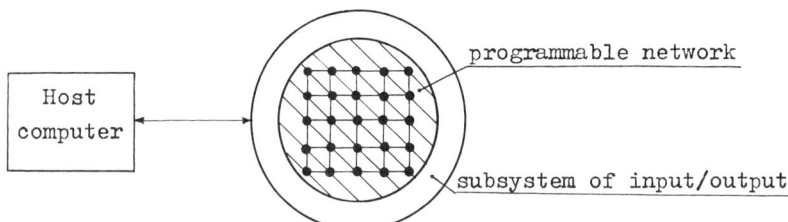

Fig. 2.

Programming matching makes it possible to create in the iterative structure of a network special-purpose communication-processing subsystems which are optimally adjusted to solve particular problems under particular conditions. In this case matching provides necessary for the solution of the problem performance level (by using a certain number of specially connected processors) and reliability level by exposure, isolation and by-pass of failure processors).
Note that the developed communication-processing structures of algorithms do not demand global synchronization which is the main obstacle to realize (on the basis of VLSI circuits) the known systolic algorithms [4]. Besides, the structures obtained are characterized by single-typeness and mass usage of computational cells, regularity of disjoint connections, simplicity of control, planarity, coordination with input/output, which directly meets the requirements of VLSI environment.

REFERENCES

[1] Mischin,A.I., Sedukhin,S.G., Computer systems and parallel computation with a local communication, Vychislitelnye sistemy 78 (1979), Novosibirsk, 90-103.
[2] Aho,A., Hopcroft,J., Ullman,J., The design and analysis of computer algorithms (Addison-Wesley, Reading, Mass., 1976).
[3] Savage, J.E., Area-time tradeoffs for matrix multiplication and transitive closure in the VLSI model, in: Proc. of the 17th Annual Allerton Conf. on Commun., Control and Comput., Oct. 1979.
[4] Kung, H.T., Why Systolic Architectures?, Computer, v.15, No 1, (1982) 37-46.

REPRESENTATION AND GENERALIZATION OF TRANSFORMATIONS BETWEEN RELATIONAL STRUCTURES

Joachim Selbig

Central Institute for Cybernetics and Information Processes
AdW der DDR
DDR - 1086 Berlin
Kurstr. 33

In the fields of learning heuristics to improve
problem solving expertise and of action sequences
for robot movements the generalization of transformations between relational structures is a
important topic. We describe an approach for solving that task, where transformations between relational structures are represented in a closed
form.

INTRODUCTION

Transformations between relational structures are descriptions of changes of structured objects. Structured objects are for example structural formulas of chemical compounds, scenes of children's blocks, and states of an assembly process. Changes of structured objects are discrete dynamical processes, where an original structured object is being transformed into a new one.

Generalization means to find a description, which is implied by an initial description. Every generalization procedure is based on certain generalization rules, which are related to special forms of descriptions /1/.

In our approach the generalization of transformations is realized by constructing a classification function with the help of a decision tree approach /3/, /4/. From the transformations of the training sample a hypothesis about the classification function is constructed.

Classification errors lead to a correction of the hypothesis. The mechanisms for correcting a hypothesis are realized as metaalgorithms for constructing classification algorithms.

REPRESENTATION OF TRANSFORMATIONS

Let L be a finite set of binary labels for properties and relations (we view properties as special reflexive relations). A binary relational structure over L is a pair of finite sets $\gamma = (X, E)$, where X is the set of nodes and $E \subseteq L \times X^2$ is the set of arcs. Let

$\gamma_1 = (X_1, E_1)$ and $\gamma_2 = (X_2, E_2)$ be binary relational structures over L, where γ_1 is the description of a structured object, which undergoes a change, and γ_2 is the description of the changed structured object. Furthermore let $T \subseteq X_1 \times X_2$ be a binary relation such that $(\forall x_i \in X_1)(\exists x_j \in X_2)((x_i, x_j) \in T)$ and $(\forall x_i \in X_2)(\exists x_j \in X_1)$ $((x_j, x_i) \in T)$. In general the sets X_1 and X_2 are not disjoint. We construct a binary relational structure $\gamma_2^* = (X_2^*, E_2^*)$, which is isomorph to γ_2, $\gamma_2 \tilde{\cong} \gamma_2^*$, such that $X_1 \cap X_2^* = \emptyset$.

Then we call the binary relational structure $\mathcal{T} = (X, E)$ over $M = L \cup \{T'\}$ the transformation between the relational structures γ_1 and γ_2, $\gamma_1 \xrightarrow{T} \gamma_2$, where $X = X_2 \cup X_2^*$ and $E = E_1 \cup E_2^* \cup T' \subseteq M \times X^2$. T' is derived from T by the bijective mapping $f: X_2 \rightarrow X_2^*$. The algorithm for constructing classification functions uses the triples at first, whose arc label corresponds to the distinguished transformation relation T'.

Given a transformation $\mathcal{T} = (X, E)$ over M. For $(x_i, x_j) \in X^2$ we put $y(x_i, x_j) = (y_0(x_i, x_j), \ldots, y_s(x_i, x_j))$ with $s = |M|$, where y_0 is the characteristic function of $D = \{(x, x) \mid x \in X\}$, and y_1 is the characteristic function of $R_1 \in M$. Let $Y = \{y(x_i, x_j) \mid (x_i, x_j) \in X^2\}$ be the set of all distinct (s+1)-tuples. By the surjective mapping $f_1: X^2 \rightarrow Y$ and the bijective mapping $f_2: Y \rightarrow W$ we get an indicator function $f_0 = f_2 \circ f_1$ of an indexed partition of X^2, $\mathcal{P} = \{P_w\}_{w \in W}$, where $P_w = \{(x_i, x_j) \in X^2 \mid f_0(x_i, x_j) = w\}$ with $w \in W$. In particular there is a $\bar{w} \in W$ such that $P_{\bar{w}} = T'$. Let $V \subseteq W$ such that $V = \{w \in W \mid P_w \subseteq D\}$ and $S_v = \{x_i \in X \mid (x_i, x_i) \in P_v\}$ with $v \in V$. Then $\mathcal{P}_X: \{S_v\}_{v \in V} \cap \{X_1, X_2^*\}$ is a partition of X with the indicator function f_X. $\mathcal{P}_X = \{Q_u\}_{u \in U}$.

We want to represent a transformation by substructures of a fixed size. Therefore we have to characterize nodes or arcs one-to-one. If this is not possible by the indexes of the partitions we have to introduce a number for distinguishing nodes or arcs. For $u \in U$ let $l_u = |Q_u|$. Furthermore let $\bar{U} = \bigcup_{u \in U} \{u\} \times \{1, \ldots, l_u\}$ and $\bar{T}_X: X \rightarrow \bar{U}$ with $\bar{T}_X(x_i) = (u, \lambda)$, where $u = f_X(x_i)$ and λ is a number from $\{1, \ldots, l_u\}$.

The indicator functions f_0 and f_X are the basis for constructing triples of the form $(w, (u_1, \lambda_1), (u_2, \lambda_2))$ with $w \in W - V$ and $(u_1, \lambda_1), (u_2, \lambda_2) \in \bar{U}$.

Let $Z = \{(f_0(x_i, x_j), \bar{T}_X(x_i), \bar{T}_X(x_j)) \mid (x_i, x_j) \in X^2 - D\}$. By the bijective mapping $\bar{f}_2: Z \rightarrow \bar{W}$ every triple from Z is conjugated to a number of $\overline{W}$ such that by $\mathcal{T}_1: X^2- D \rightarrow Z$ and $\mathcal{T}_0 = \mathcal{T}_2 \circ \mathcal{T}_1$ a one-to-one representation of transformations is possible.

GENERALIZATION OF TRANSFORMATIONS BY DECISION TREES

Given a classification problem $(\mathcal{L}, \mathcal{R})$, where $\mathcal{L} = \{\mathcal{T}_1, \ldots, \mathcal{T}_N\}$ is a finite set of transformations, the training sample, and $\mathcal{R} = \{K_i\}_{i \in I}$ is a partition of $\mathcal{L}$. The solution of the classification problem consists in the construction of a classification function for distinguishing the classes. Let Y now be the set of all (s+1)-tuples $y(x_i, x_j)$ with $(x_i, x_j) \in X_1^2$ and $l \in \{1, \ldots, N\}$ occuring in $\mathcal{L}$.

By sequential consideration of the transformations $\mathcal{T}_l \in \mathcal{L}$ we get an enumeration of all triples contained in $Z = \bigcup_{l \in \{1, \ldots, N\}} Z_l$ by means of the bijective mapping $\mathcal{T}_2: Z \rightarrow \overline{W}$. Before introducing new numbers for the enumeration of triples it is checked, whether there is a permutation of the node set such that triple set of a considered transformation may be mapped injective to the existing set of numbers. If this case is excluded we choose the permutation, which leads to the smallest set of triples, for which new numbers have to be introduced. The number of possible permutations is determined by the number of the equivalence classes of $\mathcal{P}_x = \{Q_u\}_{u \in U}$ and their powers, $a = \prod_{u \in U} l_u!$. In our approach we adopt a method for refining the partition $\mathcal{P}_x$, which leads to a reduction in the number of possible permutations of X_1. This method is based on an approach for detecting isomorphisms of graphs /2/. We put $\mathcal{P}^{(0)} = \mathcal{P} = \{P^{(0)}\}_{w \in W^{(0)}}$. For $i \geq 0$ let $\mathcal{P}^{(i)} = \{P_w^{(i)}\}_{w \in W^{(i)}}$ be a partition of X_1^2 with the indicator function $f_0^{(i)}: X_1^2 \rightarrow W^{(i)}$. For $1 \leq s, t \leq W^{(i)}$ we consider the partition $\{P_s^{(i)}(j) P_t^{(i)T}\}_{j \in \{1, \ldots, n\}}$ with the indicator function $f_{st}^{(i)}: X_1^2 \rightarrow \{1, \ldots, n\}$, where $f_{st}^{(i)}(x_u, x_v) = |\{x_j \in X_1 | f_0^{(i)}(x_u, x_j) = s \wedge f_0^{(i)}(x_v, x_j) = t\}|$. We put $y^{(i+1)} = (f_0^{(i)}, f_{11}^{(i)}, \ldots, f_{|W^{(i)}||W^{(i)}|}^{(i)})$. Let $Y^{(i+1)}$ be the set of all tuples $y^{(i+1)}$. As shown above we get a partition $\mathcal{P}^{(i+1)}$ of X_1^2 and it holds $(\exists g \geq 0)(\mathcal{P}^{(g+1)} = \mathcal{P}^{(g)})$. From $\mathcal{P}^{(g)}$ a partition $\mathcal{P}_x^{(g)}$ is derivable, which is under certain circumstances equal to the automorphism partition of X_1. In this way we get a set $\overline{W}^{(g)}$ of "names" for all triples containing in $\mathcal{L}$, where the labels occuring in the triples contain information about the surroundings of the nodes in the relational structures of a transformation. Let $\overline{W}_w^{(g)}$ be the set of triple names, for which the arc labels containing in

the triples were derived from the original relation named
$w \in W^{(o)} - V^{(o)}$. (In the following we omit the refining index g). Let
$Q_i^r = \{\mathcal{F} \in K_i | (\exists (x_u,x_v) \in X^2 - D)(\overline{f}_o(x_u,x_v) = r)\}$ with $i \in I$ and $r \in \overline{W}$.
Furthermore let $\mathcal{G}_i^w = \{Q_i^r : r \in \overline{W}_w\}$ be a family of subsets. This family is identifiable with a bipartite graph $G_2^w(m_i,n_i) = (V_1,V_2,E)$
with the node classes $V_1 = \mathcal{G}_i^w$ and $V_2 = K_i$ where $m_i = |V_1|$ and $n_i = |V_2|$. It holds $(Q_i^r, \mathcal{F}_s) \in E$ iff $\mathcal{F}_s \in Q_i^r$. Let $M_i = \{(Q_i^r1, \mathcal{F}_{s_1}),\ldots,(Q_i^rn, \mathcal{F}_{s_n})\}$ be a matching in $G_2^w(m_i,n_i)$. We use such matchings for defining tests of a decision tree together with a measure b_i for evaluating the meaning of a matching M_i to separate the classes.

Suppose $I = \{1,2\}$. For $i \in I$ we put $K_i^{(o)} = K_i$ and construct $G_2^{\overline{w}}(m_i^{(o)}, n_i^{(o)})$ and $M_i^{(o)}$. Now we determine $\max_{i \in I} b_i^{(o)} = b_j^{(o)}$ with $j \in I$ and use $M_j^{(o)}$ as the first test of a binary decision tree. There are two conditions to formulate the checking of that test.

Condition 1: $(\exists (x_u,x_v) \in X_1^2 - D_1)(\overline{f}_o(x_u,x_v) = r)((Q_j^r, \mathcal{F}_1) \in M_j^{(o)})$

Condition 2: $(\exists (Q_j^r, \mathcal{F}_s) \in M_j^{(o)})(\exists (x_u,x_v) \in X_1^2 - D_1)(\overline{f}_o(x_u,x_v) = r)$

Suppose $\mathcal{F}_1 \in K_1^{(o)} \cup K_2^{(o)}$. If (condition 1)$\vee$(condition 2) is true then $\mathcal{F}_1$ passes the 1-branch of the test; otherwise $\mathcal{F}_1$ passes the 0-branch of the test. We consider a branch of a test of the decision tree, at which we find a subproblem of the original classification problem. For $i \in I$ we construct $G_2^{\overline{w}}(m_i^{(k)}, n_i^{(k)})$ and $M_i^{(k)}$. We determine $\max_{i \in I} b_i^{(k)} = b_j^{(k)}$ with $j \in I$ and use $M_j^{(k)}$ as the next test at the considered branch of the decision tree. If no further matching exists in $G_2^{\overline{w}}(m_i^{(k)}, n_i^{(k)})$ we construct the greatest bipartite graph $G_2^w(m_i^{(k)}, n_i^{(k)})$ with $w \in W^{(o)} - (V^{(o)} \cup \{w\})$. To formulate the checking of the current test we have to modify condition 2.

The algorithm stops if there is no subproblem of the original classification problem at a branch of the decision tree.

REFERENCES

/1/ Dietterich, T. G., Michalski, R. S., Learning and Generalization of Structural Descriptions: Evalution Criteria and Comperative Review of Selected Methods, Report UIUCDCS-R-80-1007, University of Illinois (1980).

/2/ Hinteregger, J., Tinhofer, G., Zerlegung der Knotenmengen von Graphen zum Nachweis der Isomorphie, Computing, 18(1977)351-359.

/3/ Unger, S., Wysotzki, F., Lernfähige Klassifizierungssysteme (Akademie-Verlag, Berlin, 1981).

/4/ Wysotzki, F., Kolbe, W., Selbig, J., Concept Learning by Structured Examples - An Algebraic Approach, Proc. of IJCAI-81 (Vancouver, 1981) 153-158.

ARTIFICIAL INTELLIGENCE AND SEMANTICS

Petr Sgall

Faculty of Mathematics and Physics
Charles University
Prague

Fully automated question-answering systems as well
as approaches to knowledge representation attempting
at a universal character both require relatively complete
procedures of natural language comprehension,
in which the questions of semantics play a substantial
role. It is then necessary to include an adequate
description of natural language meaning, of reference
assignment and truth conditional semantics into systems
of artificial intelligence.

1. LINGUISTIC ASPECTS OF ARTIFICIAL INTELLIGENCE

If the systems belonging to the domain of Artificial Intelligence (AI) such as question answering (QA), a dialogue with a robot or with an expert system, etc., are to function as really automated systems, they should be so designed as to accept natural language (NL) texts (including questions, instructions, etc.) at their input, without any specific coding. AI systems should include procedures analyzing the input texts in the extent required by the given purpose (a preliminary linguistic analysis is to determine which sublanguage will occur at the input of the system). Also the level of the output of the analysis has to be decided on according to the given task: the analysis can only be understood as a translation of the NL input texts into a formal (disambiguated) language serving for the inner aims of the system. AI thus requires complex systems of NL comprehension, as has been broadly recognized; e.g. [30],[25,p.518],[16]; it is expected that the role of linguistic analyses in the future development of computers will continue to grow, cf. [6,p.115f],[23][1].

The first QA systems including NL comprehension were mostly limited to restricted sublanguages of English; the method TIBAQ, formulated by the Prague group [13],[28], has been elaborated since 1976 as an open general system; its main procedures are now implemented for the first experiments in a computer EC 1040 in PL/1, Q-language and Assembler (the linguistic analysis is discussed in the paper by Panevová in this volume). Another system of a more or less similar character is described in [8].

2. NATURAL LANGUAGE COMPREHENSION AND KNOWLEDGE REPRESENTATION

Various systems of knowledge representation (KR) were analyzed in [2, p.29], where it was pointed out that among the most appropriate types of semantic networks there are those working with a linguistic level. It has been noticed [22,p.36] that many approaches treated KR as an area of engineering, but now the time has come to integrate this domain with theoretical linguistics. Barr and Feigenbaum [1, p.186f.] state that "in semantic network representations there is ... no agreed-upon notion of what a given representational structure means," in other words that often the output of NL analysis is constructed in an ad hoc way, to be useful for a relatively narrow class of tasks.

To achieve a more universal level, with which the system of KR could be generalized and used for different tasks without creating new problems of principle, it is useful to bring KR to a basis as close to NL as possible. NL is universal in the sense that its structure always allows its users to create new means if these are necessary for newly found objects and relations to be named and spoken about (either complex denominations are formed then, or new lexical items are coined, without any necessity to change the grammar). NL pays a high price for its universality: its meanings are vague, and its structure is full of irregularities and a-symmetries (ambiguity, synonymy). However, linguistic research has yielded a relatively well established image of the internal (deep, underlying, tectogrammatical) structure of NL, which is free from asymmetries, regular and supplies a common patterning of meaning in various NL´s. If this structure is used as the basis for KR, then the latter may achieve the postulated universal character. By means of the system based on the method TIBAQ we wanted to substantiate the idea that such a task is feasible.

In this case KR can be based on semantic networks with which every statement would correspond to a meaning of a sentence, the necessary interconnections then being mediated by the lexicon (in which not only synonymy, but also such relations as hyponymy, i.e. semantic subordination, are reflected) and by a mechanism of reference assignment, Sect.3.2;[14]. The edges of the graph representing a statement can be labelled by different kinds of dependency relations: Actor, Objective, Addressee, Origin, Effect, and various free (adverbial) modifications such as Instrument, Cause, Locative, several temporal and other complementations, see Panevová[21],Sgall [27]; also the topic-focus articulation of the sentence, the scope of negation and presuppositions are reflected in such a graph [11], [12], the nodes of which are labelled by complex symbols each of which has a lexical part and other parts representing contextual boundness and morphological meanings (definiteness, number, tense, modality, etc.). For a framework handling also coordination and apposition, see [24].

3. NATURAL LANGUAGE SEMANTICS AND INTENSIONAL LOGIC

It can be objected that a language useful for the internal purposes of KR and AI should be more explicit in what concerns the scopes of operators (including such means as quantifiers, variables, etc.). It seems possible to construct such a language without giving up the universality of the NL basis, if procedures are used which transfer the representations of meanings to a formal language of intensional logic [18]. Extensional logic (e.g. predicate calculus) is not sufficient for such a purpose, as has been shown in logic, cf. the following discussion.

3.1. With many linguistic approaches there still is a gap between the "internal" semantics of NL (using such concepts as those we listed in Sect.2) and the "external" semantics based on truth values, possible worlds and models. This gap, stated as such in [7], is present also with Chomsky [4], who(p.165f) makes a distinction between the "logical structure" of sentences, which incorporates features of sentence structure determined by grammar, and their "semantic representations", which are not well accessible still, since they are co-determined by complex factors of cognitive faculties, beliefs, etc. With some approaches elaborating the intensional semantics of Montague [19], esp. [9], this gap is avoided in that every syntactic rule is immediately connected with a rule of semantic interpretation, the latter belonging to the "external" semantics; however, in this way the patterning of linguistic meaning is not described, since one proceeds from surface syntax directly to a formal language of logic, the structure of which is remote from that of NL.

3.2. A solution can be found if we understand linguistic meaning as a level if its own, which should be present in the theoretical framework, though not necessarily in every application to the questions of KR or AI, where various shortcuts are possible. The following framework can then be used, in which the 8-tuple (Sent, Mean, Ref, Sense, Prop, U, W, T) describes the relationship between "internal" and "external" semantics:

Sent is a set of strings interpreted as the outer forms of the sentences of the language described;
for every $\underline{s} \in$ Sent, Mean($\underline{s}$) is set of labelled graphs, interpreted as the meanings of $\underline{s}$; we write Mean(Sent) for the set of all meanings of the sentences of the language;
U is a class (not a set) containing as its elements all entities that can be referred to; there are sets U_i in U which are interpreted as the sets of objects to which a referring expression can refer (the set of all tables, of all meanings of the word light, etc.);
for every $\underline{m} \in$ Mean(Sent), Ref($\underline{m}$) = $U_1 \times U_2 \times \ldots \times U_{k(\underline{m})}$, where $\underline{k}(\underline{m})$ is the number of the referring elements in $\underline{m}$, and every $\underline{h} \in$ Ref($\underline{m}$) is interpreted as an assignment of reference;
Sense($\underline{m}$) = $\{\underline{m}\} \times$ Ref($\underline{m}$);
W is the set of possible worlds;
T = {true, false};
for every $\underline{h} \in$ Sense(Mean(Sent)), Prop($\underline{h}$) is a partial function from W into T (if the presuppositions of $\underline{h}$ are not met in $\underline{w}$, then Prop(h) assigns no truth value to $\underline{w}$, $\underline{w} \in$ W).

Thus Carnap´s concept of proposition is retained and the formalism is universal: the referential indices (I, you, here,...) can be rendered by free variables in Prop(h), see [19], [17], a belief sentence can be handled as concerning the sense of a sentence (since from Tom thinks that he has two hands it does not follow that Tom assumes the number of his hands to be the even prime number), metalinguistic contexts can be analyzed, such paradoxes as the Liar´s sentence are described as assigning no true value to any possible world, and such inconsistencies as a round circle can be appropriately treated. [2] A suitable basis for Winograd´s [30] procedural semantics is gained; sentences are interpreted by functions or procedures, cf. [29], an assertion is divided into topic and focus and interpreted as an instruction to the hearer what salient items in his memory should be picked out and what new relations should be assigned to them (cf. the "given-new" strategy in psychology and in cognitive science). Ways of combining this approach with an analysis of semantics as a behavioral system processing information [5] and as connected with formal nerve nets [26] are studied.

3.3. This approach is used also in a procedure (implemented in a microcomputer by J.Hajič) transferring the representations of meanings of sentences into formulas of a formal language used in the Institute of Technical Cybernetics of the Slovak Academy of Sciences for the description of the activities of a robot, e.g.:
    Cz.sentence: Může být krabice na odkládací ploše?
              ("Can a box be in a deposit space?")
    m: +(V-být-R-Inter-Possib(N-krabice-Ag,N-plocha-kde3(Adj-odkládací)))
    formula: "$um(ep2,eu1)?"

FOOTNOTES:
1 AI systems of QA should be distinguished from simpler NL front-end query systems, which are known esp. from the ZAPSIB-like systems produced first in the Novosibirsk laboratory led by Narinyani, then in the Prague group of algebraic linguistics (see Hajič [10]; his method KODAS is now used by several institutes interested in automatic control), and elsewhere. Such simple NL-interface systems are designed for communication with restricted data bases, so that the analysis they include need not cover all the levels of NL, only a lexical and a partial syntactic analysis being essential here; this idea (as well as other points of the approach) was also accepted in [3].

2 As Hayes [15] points out, both declarative and procedural aspects of the subject matter have to be included in KR; Narinyani [20] presents a way in which incomplete information can be handled, preserving the useful declarative features.

REFERENCES:

[1] Barr,A. and Feigenbaum,E.A.(eds.), The Handbook of AI, Vol.I (1981).
[2] Brachman,R.J., On the Epistemological Status of Semantic Networks, in Findler,N.V.(ed.), Associative Networks (New York. 1981) 3-50.
[3] Buráňová,E. et al., Systems of Contact with Database in NL, Computers and AI 2 (1983) 47-57.
[4] Chomsky,N., Essays on Form and Interpretation(New York-Amsterdam 1977).
[5] Cooper,W.S., Foundations of Logico-Linguistics (Dordrecht 1978).
[6] Feigenbaum,E.A. and McCorduck,P., The Fifth Generation, Reading (Mass. 1983).
[7] Fillmore,C.J., The Case for Case Reopened, in Cole,P. and Sadock,J.M. (eds.), Syntax and Semantics 8, Grammatical Relations (New York 1977) 59-81.
[8] Frey,W., Reyle,U. and Rohrer,Ch., Automatic Construction of a Knowledge Base by Analyzing Texts in NL, mimeo (Stuttgart 1982).
[9] Gazdar,G., Constituent Structures, mimeo (1979).
[10] Hajič,J., KODAS - A NL Interface to a Simple Database, Prague Bullet. of Mathem.Ling. 39 (1983) 65-76.
[11] Hajičová,E., Negation and Topic vs.Comment, Philologica Prag.16 (1973) 81-93.
[12] Hajičová,E. and Sgall,P., A Dependency Based Specification of Topic and Focus, SMIL 1/2 (1980) 93-140.
[13] Hajičová,E. and Sgall,P., Towards Automatic Understanding of Technical Texts, Prague Bullet. of Mathem.Ling. 36 (1981) 5-24.
[14] Hajičová,E. and Vrbová,J., On the Role of the Hierarchy of Activation in NL Understanding, Proceedings of COLING 82 (1982) 107-113.
[15] Hayes,P.J., In defence of Logic, Proceedings of IJCAI (1977) 559-565.
[16] Hofstadter,D.R., Gödel, Escher, Bach: An Eternal Golden Braid (New York 1980).
[17] Lewis,D., General Semantics, Synthese 22 (1970) 18-67.
[18] Materna,P. and Sgall,P., Optional Participants in a Semantic Interpretation, Prague Bullet.of Mathem.Ling. 39 (1983) 27-40.
[19] Montague,R., Formal Philosophy, ed.by R.Thomason (London 1974).
[20] Narinyani,A.S., Sub-Definiteness and Basis Means of Knowledge Representation, Computers and AI 2 (1983) 443-452.
[21] Panevová,J., NL Interface to an Expert System, in this volume.
[22] Percova,N.N., O sistemach ponimanija teksta na jestv.jaz., Projekt Vostok 3, 231 (Novosibirsk 1980).
[23] Plander,I., The Japanese Project of Fifth Generation Computer Systems, Computers and AI 1 (1982) 441-452.
[24] Plátek,M., Sgall,J. and Sgall,P., A Dependency Base for a Linguistic Description, to appear in Contributions to Functional Syntax, Semantics and Language Comprehension (Prague and Amsterdam, in press).
[25] Pospelov,G.S., Sistemnyj analiz i isskustvennyj intelekt, Computers and AI 2 (1983) 453-472, 513-530.
[26] Schnelle,H., Elements of Theoretical Net-Linguistics, Theoretical Linguistics 8 (1981) 67-100.
[27] Sgall,P., The Level of Linguistic Meaning, Prague Bullet.of Mathem. Ling. 35 (1981) 5-40.
[28] Sgall,P., Towards a Fully Automatic System of Commmunication with Data Bases, Computers and AI 1 (1982) 25-46.
[29] Wilks,Y., Some Thoughts on Procedural Semantics, mimeo, (Univ.of Essex 1980).
[30] Winograd,T., Understanding Natural Language (Edinburgh 1972).
[31] Winograd,T., Towards a Procedural Understanding of Semantics, Révue internat.de phil. (1976) 260-303.

DECISION-MAKING IN CONDITIONS OF FUZZY UNCERTAINTIES AND OPPOSING FACTORS, USING HUMAN SPECIFICS

D.I.Shapiro

Institute of Automatical Control Systems

USSR

In this work discussed the problems of Fuzzy Choise, the computing models and their applications

INTRODUCTION

In one of the most commonly occuring classes of decision-making problems the Decision Maker (DM) F_0, in the context of limited resources, must choose a strategy meeting the reguirements of his criteria in relationships with independent opposing objects F_1 which possess local criteria, constraints and strategies. In descriptions of such problems there are qualitative fuzzy uncertainties arising both from description of problems in a natural language (parametres, criteria,constraints) and from uncertainties peculiar to man in procedures of evaluation and selection. In such problems the need arises for determining and using the specifics of the unique DM F_0 both in normal operation conditions and in those of fatigue and stress, and for ascertaining the condition of the partner in communication F_i in the complex system of relationships F_i.

THE MODEL OF DECISION MAKING

In this system of relationships the DM F_0 and objects (partners in communication F_i) are represented respectively by a collection of characteristic parametres $X_0 = (x_0^i, \ldots, x_o^m)$ and $X_i = (x_i^i, \ldots, x_i^m)$, criteria Q_a, Q_i, constraints L_o, L_i, strategies $u \in U$, $v_i \in V_i$, as well as by evaluation scales of parametre changes $\{q_o^i\}$ and $\{q_i^i\}$. The sum total of parametres X^j makes up the collection of situational data $S_t = \{X\}_t$. The data describes the state of the system $\overset{\approx}{x}$, environment $\tilde{x}$ and man's condition $\overline{x}$ and can be represented in terms of quantity and quality (fuzzy). The DM's strategy $u^+ \in U$ in concrete Γ_i depends on the characteristics of the partner F_i evaluated by the DM. Procedures for decision-making in incompletely defined conditions with the use of the DM's specifics are realized through a situational model for developing rational recommendations. The model uses the concept of final decision being made by man on the basis of selecting from computer-supplied recommendations (under the given set of situational data criteria and constraints. The model consists of functional macroblocs responsible for concrete procedures: Presentation, Monitoring, Evaluation,Selection, Teaching, Asessment, Assessment of the DM's Condition, Perception, Control, etc.In the computer the macroblocs (or their larger independent bloc-parts and micro-blocs) are represented by program modules. The concrete combination of macroblocs and blocs.adequate to the problem, is evolved by the DM with the help of the Control macrobloc. Thus in problems involving decision-making in organizational management one would use the combination of macroblocs Presentation,Monitoring,Evaluation,Selection,Teaching (I), in problems involving the monitoring of the DM's condition the macroblocs Assessment and Assessment of the DM's Condition would be indicated ,while problems involving evaluation of sensory dara would call for the macrobloc Perception (3).

FUZZY CHOICE

In compliance with the general theory of choise (4),the external description of the selection procedure is characterised by a family of triades $\{X,Y,R\}$ where X is the space of states, Y -the space of evaluated parametres and R - the set of decisions. The internal description characterises the structure of choice, i.e. the mode of elaborating solution R for each $x \in X$. Two operators are considered: ϕ^{o4} which characterises the structure of the evaluation procedure, $\{q\}: X \to Y$; ϕ^B - characterises the structure of the procedure for choosing $Y = \{Re, M(Re)\}$. The existence of solutions of problems involving choice in fuzzily described data is connected with the fulfilment of the following conditions: Definition I. Strategy U(x) is the order $(R^I,...,R^t)$ of elementary decisions at moments of time t=I, ..., t=T, $R^3 \in \{R\}$; $\{R\}$ is the set of elementary decisions (in the particular case where $u(x) = R^1$). Definition 2. The permissible set of strategies U is such a set of strategies U ($U \in U$) whose elements meet the requirements of the existence of criteria and constraints $\mu_Q(x) > 0$; $\mu_L(x) > 0$. Definition 3. The problem whose description contains fuzzy elements (X, Y, U) where $\mu(x), \mu(y)$, $\mu(U) \in J(.); J(.) \neq 0$; ($J(.)$ - the set of membership functions) has solution U which belongs to the permissible class if $\mu(\bar{u}) > 0$ and $\bar{u} \in \bar{U}$. The problems with fuzzy desciptions may involve three types of classic (as per (4)) mechanisms of choice: according to the scaler criterium, multi-scale (according to the vector criterium) and according to relative superiority. In doing so the scales used in evaluation procedures may be represented by membership function of quality change $y = \mu(q)$ or a set of fuzzy equivalence classes $y = \{\mu_v(q,v)/q^v; \vartheta = 1,..., N v$, each element having its own membership. Evaluation procedures applied in concrete problems call for due consideration to their specifics. Examples of procedures realized in the form of program modules are cited in the report. The procedure for selecting $Y = \{Re, \mu(Re)\}$. Multiscale selection procedures belong to two types: Type I. Selection in multi-scale spaces of $w + r + I$ order (where m is the number of elements of the situational data set and r is the number of local criteria. This is a two-stage procedure. At its first stage the extent of meeting local criteria is determined, the latter being $Q_r(Y)$, while at the second stage the degree of meeting the global criterium $\mu Q_o(y) = Re, \mu(Re)$ is determined. In this procedure selection is made with the help of fuzzy membership surface $\mu Q_o(y) = \mu [\pi(y1,...,y^m)]_{y^j}$ constructed in the measured space m+r+I. The value of y^j is determined by the above-cited specifics of the evaluation procedure and can be represented by the value of the evaluation membership function according to the parametre $\mu q(x)$ or by the element of the scale - the fuzzy area $\mu_v(q,v)/q_v$. Type 2. Selection in multi-scale spaces with opposing factors. This multi-scale selection procedure is based on the use of fuzzy integral game /1/ and is also a two-stage one. At the first stage the data are formed which are necessary for staging and realizing the game

$$\Gamma_{ji} = \{ \Gamma_{ji} [X, Y, U, V_i], Q, L \} \quad (1)$$

where X is the space of state $x \in X$; Y is the space of evaluated parametres $y \in Y$; U is the space of inputs $u \in U$; V_i is the space of inputs $v_i \in V_i$;Q is the set of criteria (Q_o, Q_i); L is the set of constrants (L_o, L_i); Γ_{fi} is the local game F_o, F_i ; $f_{ji}: Y \times U \times V_i \to Y$

$$-L_o \leq u \leq L_o ; \quad -L_i \leq V_i \leq L_i \quad ; \quad (2)$$

$$Q_o(X) = -\bigcap_i Q_i(x) ; \quad (3)$$

Each vector y_i in space characterises the evaluated characteristics of objects F_i and the DM's (F_o) attitude towards them. In the space of evaluated parameters the importance may change of individual coordinates $(y_j) \dashv / \lrcorner j$ and the importance of concrete vectors $\psi_i \cdot y_i = W_i$. The DM stays within the system of relationships described by expressions (1÷3) with objects F_i, the latter having their own objectives and strategies $v_i \in V_i$, must choose a strategy $\bar{u}^* \in \bar{U}$ (belonging to the permissible class) which determines his rational behaviour in terms of Q_0 and L_0. The choise of strategies is determined by the condition

$$Max \; Q_o(W_i \; \bar{u}(W_i)) = MQ_o(W_\ell, \bar{u}^*(W\ell))$$

where W_1 is the value of W_i determining the largest value of $\mu \; Q_o \; (\ell = 1, 2, ...)$

Concrete procedures for presenting data, preliminary estimates, monitoring of parametre changes: evaluation, selection, etc. are realized in the form of program modules.

APPLICATIONS

In concrete applications the DM uses the Control macrobloc for forming the sum total of procedures which are adequate to the problem specifics. This approach is used in problems involving decisions in organizational, medical and technological systems. In(1) the problem is considered of elaborating rational recommendations in an organizational system realized through a three-stage procedure : (evaluation of parametres - evaluation according to local criteria - evaluation according to the global criterium) using the fuzzy membership surface. (5) consideres the problem of treating neirosis and assessing the DM's state, the DM being under stress, on the basis of monitoring heurohormone changes. The multi-stage procedure of decision-making is also used in the problem of urgent distribution of material facilities in relationships of DM F_0 with two independent objects F_I and F_2, with one of whom (F_I) cooperation is maintained in the framework of social division of labour while with the other (F_2) negotiations are under way on facilities allocation (e.g. on cooperation in R & D matters) (6). Local problems having clear (as opposed to fuzzy) descriptions with the help of non-coalition differential games are considered in (6). The considered multi-stage procedure using macroblocs Presentation, Monitoring, Evaluation, Teaching, Assessment can be used in scientific research for analysing research findings and planning new neurophysiological experiments. In doing so due consideration is given to objective characteristics of processes, data on the specifics of those under test and the researcher's idea as to the evaluation of parametre quality, the parametres characterizing the aims and results of experiments (7).

CONCLUSIONS

The paper considers some specific aspects of decision-making in uncertain conditions and with opposing factors on the basis of situationa model for developing rational recommendations.

BIBLIOGRAPHY

1   Shapiro D.I.,Model' postroenija reshenija v nechetkich uslovijakh, Tekchnicheskaja kibernetika 4 (1983) 40-49,
2   Shapiro,D.I. and Vasiljev,V.I.,O kommunikativnych protsessakch v cheloveko-mashinnykch sistemakch prinjatija reshenij, in: Tezisy IX vsesojuznogo seminara po kibernetike 3(Sukhumi, NSK, 1981) 149-150.
3   Shapiro, D.I., Prinjatije reshenij v organizatsionnykch i tekchnologicheskikch sistemakch s ispol'zovanijem osobennostej cheloveka,in: Mezhdunarodnyj simpozium po iskusstvennomu intellektu, (Leningrad,1983) 120-129.
4   Aizerman M.A., and Malyshevski A.V.,Problemy logicheskogo obosnovanija v obshchej teorii vybora (IPU,Moskva,1982).
5. Shapiro D.I., and Vasiljev,V.I.,Dialogovaja sistema prinjatija reshenij s kontrolem sostojanija LPR, Trudy Tartusskogo universiteta 551,Iskusstvennyi intellekt (Tartu ,TTU,1980) 129-135.
6   Vaisbord E.M., and Zhukovskij V.I.,Vvedenije v differentsisl' nyje igry neskol'kikch lits i ikch prilozhenija (Sovetskoje radio, Moskva,1980).
7. Shapiro D.I., Ob ispol'zovanii rasplyvchatykch obrazov kek sredstva izuchenija neosoznovajemoj psikchicheskoj dejatel' nosti in: Bessoznatel'noje: priroda, funksii, metody, issledovanija, 3(Metsniereba, Tbilisi,1978) 667-674.

APPLICATIONS OF A MICROCOMPUTER-BASED ROBOT
VISION SYSTEM

Andras Siegler and Miklos Bathor

Computer and Automation Institute, Budapest,
Hungary

The paper presents the following applications of a microcomputer-based vision equipment. Assembly robot with vison: a PUMA robot has been equipped with visual input. Object manipulation on a moving belt as well as identification (separation) of several objects seen at the same time are some of the tasks performed. Control of component paths along an automated assembly line: the position/orientation of small assembly parts which cannot be identified or ordered by traditional mechanical means is determined by the vision equipment. Paint spray robot with visual input: a programmable enamel-spraying robot works under the direction of a vision equipment.

INTRODUCTION

In the course of the past few years results of applied artificial intelligence research entered everyday practice. One of the scientific areas the achievements of which have close relation to present industrial activity is robot vision. By our days robot vision systems have become off-the shelf goods in industrially developed countries. Such systems are based now on microprocessors and special vision-oriented and robot control peripheries can now be purchased as single PC boards or even as single chips. The fast development in this field had an impact on artificial intelligence research in Hungary, too. In the Computer and Automation Institute, Budapest a general-purpose robot vision system based on a 16-bit microprocessor has been elaborated.

1. INTEGRATION OF ROBOT CONTROL WITH COMPUTER VISION

Simultaneously with scientific development in robotics and sensing technology industrial need for intelligent material handling devices has been growing continously. For this reason emphasis has been put on supplementing already existing robot control devices with intelligent sensing abilities. A significant step in this direction has been the integration of a PUMA robot with the microcomputer-based object recognizer. To solve the problem of communication between robot and vision equipment a straightforward method has been chosen: the Z8000 microcomputer has been plugged into the VAL controller of the PUMA in the place of its own terminal. This means that the vision equipment can pass information to the PUMA exactly as a human operator can. Typical terminal question-answer sequences are pre-programmed and played back with actual parameters at the right moments. This kind of arrangement is being used under industrial circumstances for performing random pick-and-place tasks with resting and with moving objects.

In on other robot vision application the camera is mounted on the end effector of the robot. The latter is used for scanning the whole working space while keeping the camera looking downwards. On the working table a couple of objects are randomly placed. During scanning the robot stops above each object, the vision program identifies the actual object and records its position, too.

A crucial problem in integrating robot control with computer vision is how to match the image seen by the TV camera with the physical workspace of the robot. For this purpose a calibration algorithm has been developed which makes use of the abilities of the VAL system. The result of this algorithm is the transformation of positions and orientations determined by the vision system into the coordinate system of the robot. The program which connects vision with robot control is running on the same microcomputer as vision programs do. It consists of the following steps:

1.1 SET-UP PHASIS

The controllable state of every module is checked automatically and the cause of any failure is printed out in the form of self-explanatory error messages. Such error can be that the TV camera is not switched on, the robot is not powered or not calibrated to its own frame. If every component is correctly working then control is passed to the vision module and "teaching" period starts. Parts to be recognized later on are placed one after the other in front of the camera and the vision system records all necessary features used for recognition and the name of the part in question. Thus a library of recognizable objects is created and the vision module is ready for operation (Chetverikov, 1983).

1.2 CALIBRATION PHASIS

Calibration is performed by pointing at "calibration points" on the visible working scene by using the robot and then locating the same points by the vision system as well. A special pointing tool is mounted on the end effector of the robot. (Fig.1.) The first step of calibration is thus to adjust tool parameters of the robot according to the size of the pointing device. This is done by the "TOOL" instruction of the PUMA robot. As a next step, the robot is removed from the visible part of the working scene and the first calibration point (called P_0) is placed to the origin of the image coordinate system. The vision system locates the position of this point on the image. Then the robot is guided by using the manual control box over this point in a way that the pointer points exactly to the calibration point. The position of the robot is then recorded by a "HERE P0" instruction. The some sequence of steps are performed for two other calibration points (P_1 and P_2) which have to be roughly on the x and y axis of the vision coordinate system respectively. (Fig. 2) These points have to be not very close to P_0.

We take the possible linear distortion of the camera in different directions also into account. This is the reason why we determine a separate transformation factor in the x and y directions. These are called "facx" and "facy" and we get them as

$$facx = \frac{x_{P_1} - x_{P_0}}{x_{V_1} - x_{V_0}} \quad \text{and} \quad facy = \frac{y_{P_2} - y_{P_0}}{y_{V_2} - y_{V_0}}$$

where x_{P_o} y_{P_o} are the Cartesian coordinates of P_o, x_{P_1} is the Cartesian x coordinate of P_1 and y_{P_2} is the Cartesian y coordinate of P_2. x_{V_o}, y_{V_o}, x_{V_1}, y_{V_2} are coordinates of the same points measured in pixels on the image coordinate system. Values read in by the camer in pixels can be transformed into mm-s by using the above factors. The transformation of the origin of the robot coordinate system into the origin of the visible scene is finally done automatically by "POINT V" instructions.

1.3 RECOGNITION AND ROBOT CONTROL

After having finished calibration the hand-eye system is ready for the required oparation. Recognition is initiated by a human operator or by an external signal. The vision system returns the identification code of the object on the image, the x, y coordinates of its weight center and the direction angle α of its main axis of inertia. The control program adds the constant z value and the constant ϑ angle (90°) required by the robot controller. Finally it sends out an "EX MANIP" instruction with an argument corresponding to the identity of the object on which a robot program of the same identification code has to be performed.

2. FURTHER APPLICATIONS OF THE ROBOT VISION SYSTEM

2.1. USE OF COMPUTER VISION ON AN AUTOMATED ASSEMBLY LINE

The control of the path of small assembly parts according to their type and/or position is a typical problem in automated batch assembly. A program running on the Z8000 microcomputer has been elaborated which can be used either with flat or with shaft-like assembly components. In a typical situation shafts are coming out from a vibratory bowl feeder and moving one after the other on a conveyor. The TV camera is monitoring the conveyor from a perpendicular direction and the vision module analyses its longitudinal contour. By analysing the contour shape the computer can decide e.g. which end of the shaft comes first or - if the shafts don't touch each other - which component is actually on the conveyor. According to the result gates along the path are controlled and e.g. all parts laying in the wrong position can be fed back into the vibrating bowl. The system is going to be used in the auto industry.

2.2. COMPUTER VISION FOR GUIDING A PAINT SPRAY ROBOT

Cover sheets of gas cookers are coated by enamel along an automated spraying line. In order to properly paint every detail of the sheets a paint-spray robot is used for pre-painting. The raw metal sheets are arriving on a conveyor line in hanging position. Identical sheets are coming in short series i.e. the spraying program has to be changed frequently. Sometimes two or more narrow sheets of the same type are hung above each other. These are the reasons why robot vision is needed. Without using it a person would be required just for watching the conveyor and guiding the robot according to the part arrived. The TV camera is looking at the line from aside. The parts are illuminated from the back thus the contour of each part can well be seen. After having recognized the actual part and determined how many of them are hung above each other the corresponding spraying program is selected and - with appropriate scheduling - the robot is started.

SUMMARY

In this paper we gave an overlook of the different uses of the robot vision equipment developed in the Computer and Automation Institute. Further efforts are concentrated on building a more reliable, single PCB version of this equipment with extended software capabilities in object recognition. Another project is in progress for using the same equipment for robot control purposes in a broader sense: it has to be able to control communication between man and robot and to do kinematic calculations as well.

REFERENCES

1   D.Chetverikov; An industrial object recognition system, Szamitastechnika, (November 1983) (In Hungarian)

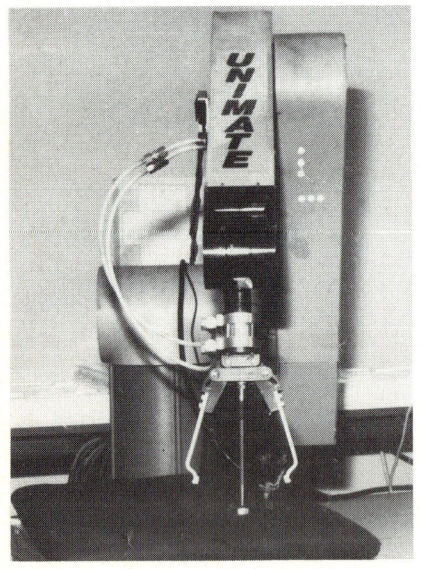

Fig. 1.   Fig. 2.

KNOWLEDGE PRESENTATION IN THE FORM OF ROLE STRUCTURES

I.Sildmäe, R.Käi

Laboratory of Artificial Intelligence
Tartu State University
Tartu, Estonian S.S.R.
U.S.S.R.

Grammar investigation in cognitive aspect has shown that grammar expresses the connections existing in reality. With the help of these connections is formed the thought of a text, and thoughts (but not meanings) form our knowledge. Reality, language and cognition have the similar structure of connections.

(1) Our purpose was the computer realization of such a system that would be based not on forward given semantic meanings but would be able to form knowledge on the basis of texts. We supposed that grammar executes two, not one function. Besides the formal linguistic function it executes the cognitive function as well. Connections existing in reality and cognized by a human being are expressed by grammar. Everything a person is eager to speak about is expressed by words in a sentence, and grammar means are used to show in what kinds of connections in reality exist objects and phenomena designated by words.

(2) Connections existing in reality are mainly expressed in such a way that words in a sentence are put in cognitive roles with the help of grammar means. Role expresses the position of a side of a connection. Each connection is characterized by its sides' roles. Relations between a role and an object or a phenomenon designated by words differ from those between features and this very object or the phenomenon. Role is not a feature characterizing an object or a phenomenon itself but a category exposing the connections between objects. A role doesn't 'belong' to an object designated by a word but characterizes the position of an object in the system of connections existing in reality. One and the same object or phenomenon of reality and the word designiting it may be met in different roles.

Role presentation of connections corresponds to the structure of reality. In reality connections also do not exist by themselves separately from objects being the sides of such connections. Connection takes place in the presence of sides and depends on their position in relation to each other.

A way of expressing connections by grammar means with the help of roles is the most rational way. Besides, role presentation of connections is more multisided and precize than the connection 'subject-predicate' used in logics that deals with all connections as connections between subjects and their predicates. The role way of presenting connections is versatile and flexible. It allows to scrutinize objects of cognition in different roles and with different fillers of other roles.

(3) It's possible to expose roles existing in language on a large amount of texts using the cognitive approach to grammar. There are approximately 40 roles in Russian /1/. Half of them characterizes the connections inside objects, phenomena, situations, spatial and temporal connections (r). Here also belong connections between words as concepts, i.e. formal logical connections. Their basis lies in the similarity of contents of concepts. In such a way are formed the connections of concepts on the basis of their contents and volume. One side of connection is a narrower concept, another side is a wider one, or the sides of connections may be concept and its feature. The other roles (R) express connections between objects in dynamic situations.

The analysis of texts and grammar in cognitive aspect allows also to define what kinds of grammar means are used in language for the expression of each role. It served as the basis for working out the rules of role definition for the computer realization. The rules operate with word forms and other grammar means one may come across with in a sentence. In some cases there is necessary to use such knowledge as: whether the object is material or non-material, animated or inanimate, etc.

(4) Role structures present thoughts. A thought consists of objects of thinking and cognitive connections between them.
A thought is born in a moment when no less than two objects of thought are bound in cognition by connections (roles) generated from reality. Larger role structure present 'longer' thoughts. The thought of a sentence is expressed by its role structure. Sentences in a complete text are found to be in the same roles of reality, thus forming, already on the level of the text, 'larger' thoughts. They may present descriptions of situations or events larger than those described by sentences; or simply we deal with spacial, temporal or causal rows.

Thus reality, language and cognition have similar structure of connections (roles). The level of cognition development defines the possible pretenders to the roles on the level of language and cognition.

Understanding of text consists of formation of its cognitive structure and recognition of objects (words) used in it on the basis of the former knowledge, i.e. knowledge about the role in which that object (word) has been met early and what kinds of fillers of other roles were possible. In case there is a contradiction between the coming structure and old knowledge, their reciprocal role correction takes place.

It's impossible to form a thought only of word 'meanings' based on features characterazing them. With such approach we miss the side expressing the connections of reality. These very connections unite objects and phenomena and in such a way create thoughts. Therefore it's quite groundless to identify 'meanings' and thoughts. Thought is a principally different phenomenon than 'meaning' or a sum of 'meanings'. We suppose that a machine translation is possible to realize using thoughts but not 'meanings'.

(5) Proceeding from the above-mentioned principles we have created the system 'DATUM'. The vocabulary of the system includes 5000 words. The basic knowledge of system consists of all forms of the words with their possible role (roles). The system is able (with some parts of speech) to form itself, on the basis of formal markers, all possible forms of new words and to define the possible roles of these forms.

The role homonimy in a concrete text is solved by rules based on cognitive understanding of grammatical markers. Using this knowledge the system is able within the vocabulary limits to make a role structure of different sentences unknown to system. The system makes these structures rapidly because it doesn't spend its time on morphological, syntactical or semantic analysis.

(6) The knowledge of the system is formed of cognitive (role) structures existing in sentences and texts. Knowledge is build with these very cognitive connections (roles) of reality. What is the role structure of an object and in what roles it may exist and what kind of pretenders there may be for other roles - all this is the essence of knowledge about this object. Roles characterizing static and dynamic situations form the so called situational knowledge. Logic connections (roles) between concepts form formal logic knowledge. It's the presence of these two side (situational and conceptual knowledge) that provides the unity of the individual and the general in our knowledge. As it has been already stated knowledge of a human being is organized as spacial, temporal and causal rows. Here also belongs the conceptual organization of knowledge.

Special (e.g. medical, juridical etc.) knowledge is found to be in the same cognitive connections (roles). Knowledge of doctors is organized by medical objects and concepts and knowledge of lawers by juridical ones. Education consists of explaining the role structure of this or that object or phenomenon in the given area as well as of pointing out the roles in which that object or phenomenon may be found and what fillers in that case have other roles. Since such knowledge is taken from texts it is contained in these texts as their role structure and consequently it is being exposed from texts.

(7) Thinking is the formation of thoughts and operation with them. The system 'DATUM' also performs such operations. Thought formation comes from the tasks put to the system (questions, problems, etc.). Operation by thoughts is based on the principle that each connection that is expressed by roles has the features that do not change depending on the pretender to the filler of this role and features that depend on pretenders. It allows from two thoughts expressed by roles to form the third one-role consequence /2/. The connections between concepts give the possibility to operate with sillogisms. It is the two sides of thinking.

The formation of conceptual structures from role structures describing situations and, if necessary, the operation by both of them allows the system to answer questions, to draw general conclusions, to infer and to form new knowledge.

/1/ И.Сильдмяэ, Познавательная структура знаний, Počitače a umelá inteligencia, Vol.1, No 5, October 1982.
/2/ Поспелов Д.А. О "человеческих" рассуждениях в интеллектуальных системах, "Вопросы кибернетики" АН СССР, Москва 1983.

FROM SENTENCES TO ATTRIBUTE NETWORKS[+]

Michael W. Sobolewski and Zenon Kulpa

Institute of Biocybernetics and Biomedical Engineering
Warsaw, Poland

The crucial problems in construction of knowledge-based systems are issues of knowledge representation and natural man/machine communication. In the paper, attribute-networks - a new representational scheme based on so-called attribute systems is explained and a method of translation from simplified natural language sentences into attribute networks representing their meaning is shown.

INTRODUCTION

Knowledge-based expert systems [1-3], to be efficient and useful, must be able to communicate with a user in a manner most natural to him in all modes of their use - getting answers to problems (and explanations), improving the system's knowledge, and "harvesting" the knowledge base. To achieve this, an expert system must be based on an efficient and homogeneous method of representig data on all various levels of the system, and it should be able to translate from a conversational language - e.g., sentences in some (simplified) natural language - into its internal representation of data (and back as well).

This translation process involves usually several levels of representation and processing. The first, syntactic level concerns representation and processing of input/output language sentences as structures made of words. Then they are further processed in order to extract their meaning, i.e. a representation of some states, events or queries in terms of elementary facts and goals. This representation constitutes the semantic level. The third level - the knowledge level - contains rules (facts in implicational form), used to process the meanings of the user statements in order to acquire new knowledge, answer a query, or explain action of the system. Mutual interdependence of these levels is shown in Fig.1 (adapted from a similar scheme used in [5] to describe the structure of pictorial communication systems).

To achieve homogeneity of the system, it seems reasonable to use the same knowledge-representation scheme on all the levels. The essential and natural manner of representig some knowledge seems to be in terms of objects (e.g., a toy block, a patient) described by a set of attributes (e.g., colour, body-temperature) with given values (e.g., red, 37.5°C). Therefore we propose an attribute-network scheme based on attribute systems, formally introduced in [4]. In the sequel we explain briefly the assentals of this representational scheme, and then we show how the process of translation from (simplified) natural language sentences into attribute network representation of their meaning might be organized. More details and examples of this process may be found in [6].

[+] The research reported here was supported by the Research Project No. 06.9.

ATTRIBUTE SYSTEMS AND ATTRIBUTE NETWORKS

An (elementary) attribute names (disjoint) sets of objects belonging to some description space. The attribute is given by:
1. Its name, serving to identify it unambiguously (e.g.: profession).
2. Its sort (a set of values of its descriptors; called also a set of values of the attribute, e.g., names of professions: lawyer, programmer, ..., etc.). The values serve to build names (descriptors) of the subsets of the description space. All sorts contain also an empty value (denoted $\perp$) naming an empty subset. A descriptor is an expression of the form i:v, where i is an attribute name and v is a value from the sort of i (e.g.: profession:lawyer).
3. Its semantics, i.e., a function mapping a set of descriptors into a family of disjoint subsets of the description space. It is usually defined by some more or less physical "measuring device" (in our example it might be a professional certificate). For compound attributes the semantics is defined indirectly, in terms of semantics of their component attributes. To define a compound attribute (e.g.: occupation), one should additionally specify:
4. Its component attributes (e.g.: (worker,profession)).
5. Its type, denoting a manner of composition.
6. A value-naming function establishing correspondence between values in the compound attribute and combinations of values in the component attributes (e.g.: if worker:Mary and profession:lawyer then occupation:Jones, ..., etc).

In [4], four types of compound attributes were distinguished:
1. Union type (denoted $\cup$): for composing together attributes with disjoint sets of described objects (e.g.: predicate = $\cup$(simple-predicate,compound-predicate)).
2. Meet type (denoted $\cap$): for using component attributes as features of objects described by the compound attribute (e.g.: toy-block = $\cap$(shape,size,colour)).
3. Product type (denoted $\sqcap$): for describing objects composed from their constituent parts (e.g.: sentence = $\sqcap$(subject-group,predicate-group)).
4. Set type (denoted $\sqcup$): for objects consisting of sets of elements of the component types (e.g.: drawing = $\sqcup$(line-segment,arc)).

The element representing some atom of knowledge in attribute formalism is called an usage. The basic type of usage is an elementary formula of one of the forms:
$v_1 = \cup i_1 : i_2 : \ldots i_n : v_n$ or $v_1 = \cup i_1 : i_2 : \ldots i_n : z$, where $i_1, i_2, \ldots, i_n$ are names of attributes such that i_j is a component attribute of i_{j+1}, $v_1 \in sort(i_1), v_n \in sort(i_n)$, and $i_n : z$ is an attribute variable ranging over the set of descriptors of the attribute i_n (informally, we might consider z_n as a variable ranging over $sort(i_n)$).
Sets of usages can be represented graphically as so-called attribute networks. Nodes of such a network represent occurences of values (v_1, v_n, etc.) and arcs - attribute names. E.g., to convey meaning of the sentence "Mary is a lawyer" we might use the compound attribute occupation = $\sqcap$(worker,profession) such that Mary $\in$ sort(worker), lawyer $\in$ sort(profession) and Jones $\in$ sort(occupation). The value Jones is an (arbitrary) name of the fact described by our sentence (given, e.g., by the context of the sentence - we were talking about Mary Jones). Then the meaning will be represented by usages: Mary = $\cup$worker:occupation:Jones, lawyer = $\cup$profession: occupation:Jones and the attribute network in Fig.2.

ENGLISH-LIKE LANGUAGE SENTENCES

As language expressions on the syntactic level (Fig.1) we take simple sentences from a so-called ELL(English-Like Language), used in several expert systems languages (e.g., RITA, ROSIE [1,3] and in the legal decision system LDS [1] written in ROSIE). The ELL contains five kinds of sentences with simplified English-like syntax:

1. Class membership, e.g.: "Mary is a lawyer".
2. Predication, e.g.: "Mary is wealthy".
3. Prepositions, e.g.: "Mary is in Chicago".
4. Intransitve verbs, e.g.: "Mary does commute".
5. Transitive verbs, e.g.: "John did give Mary the book".
Compound sentences can be also constructed - in this case, the interactive module should be able to decompose them into component simple sentences and recognize their kinds. Elementary sorts of this system (of attributes subject, preposition, verb, place, etc.) consist of English words serving as sub-vocabularies for the field of discourse of the expert system considered.
statement = $\bigcap$(sentence,kind),
sentence = $\bigcap$(subject-group,predicate,object,adverbials),
subject-group = $\bigcap$(saxon-genitive,subject),
predicate = $\bigcup$(simple-predicate,compound-predicate),
object = $\bigcap$(direct-object,indirect-object,propositional-object),
adverbials = $\bigcap$(of-place,of-manner,of-time),
simple-predicate = $\bigcap$(do-form,verb), compound-predicate = $\bigcap$(link,predicative),
prepositional-object = $\bigcap$(preposition,simple-object),
of-place = $\bigcap$(preposition,place), of-manner = $\bigcap$(preposition,manner),
of-time = $\bigcap$(preposition,time).
Depending of the value of the kind attribute, additional constraints on the values of the other attributes are imposed, e.g., if $\cup$kind:statement:S = intransitive-verbs, then $\cup$object:sentence:statement:S = $\bot$ (i.e., does not exist). Every sentence (given by the user) is described in terms of the above system of attributes by a production system operating on the syntactic level and having appropriate production rules for every of the five kinds of sentences.

FROM SENTENCES TO ATTRIBUTE NETWORKS

On the semantic level the meaning of the sentences is represented by structured objects (represented graphically by an attribute network) in a "semantic" attribute system, designed to convey sentence meanings. Depending on the kind of the sentence, different attributes are used to convey its meaning.

For example the first kind of sentences represents the class membership relation, so that the following compound attribute scheme is used to describe its meaning: membership = T(element,class) where T denotes the type of membership (here it might be $\bigcap$ or $\bigsqcap$, depending on the particular meaning of the class attribute). The names "membership", "element", and "class" denote "attribute name variables" for which particular attribute names are substituted, depending on contents of the particular sentences. The class attribute is derived from the predicative of the sentence (by the function named "cl"), and its component attributes and type depend on the exact meaning of the class, so they are supplied by the semantic-category functions of the class argument (named "mem", "elem", and "type"). One of production rules for this kind of sentences will look like:
PR1: if $\cup$kind:statement:z = class-membership $\wedge$
     $\cup$saxon-genitive:subject-group:sentence:statement:z = $\bot$
     then cv = $\cup$predicative:compound-predicate:predicate:sentence:statement:z $\wedge$
         class = cl(cv) $\wedge$ ev = $\cup$subject:subject-group:sentence:statement:z $\wedge$
         T = type(class) $\wedge$ membership = memb(class) $\wedge$ element = elem(class) $\wedge$
         mv = arbitrary.
Variables cv, ev, and mv range over values of attributes derived as substitutions for attribute name variables class, element, and membership respectively. The formula mv = arbitrary means that the variable mv takes some value (according to the value-ranging function of the compound attribute memb(class) in terms of its component attributes [4]) which is defined arbitrary by the system (implicitly) or by the user (explicitly, through additional dialogue with the system). To give a simple example, the sentence "Mary is a lawyer", when processed by the rule PR1, first produces substitution {lawyer/cv,Mary/ev},then if cl(lawyer) = profession, type(profession) = $\bigcap$, memb(profession) = occupation and elem(profession) = worker,

the substitutions {profession/class, ∩/T, occupation/membership, worker/element} are derived, and provided the additional (implicit or explicit) analysis produces {Jones/mv} we will end with the attribute network of Fig.2 as representation of the meaning of the sentence. Similar rules are given for other kinds of sentences. Names of sentences (i.e., of the facts representing their meaning) might also appear as parts of other sentences (explicitly or as a result of decomposition of compound sentences into simple ones). Then they might be used for "arbitrary" values by appropriate rules. E.g., using P1 to name the third example sentence "Mary is in Chicago", we might also process the sentence "P1 is from October". Adding to our examples one more sentence "John's address is 37 Maple St" (of the second kind) and processing all of them by the rules of the above type we might obtain the attribute network of Fig.3 as a representation of their joint meaning (provided the "arbitrary" values were chosen to be "Jones" also for the second and last sentences, "lawyer" for the fourth, "October" for the fifth, and "Mary" for the P1-referring one - see [6] for details).

REFERENCES

[1] Waterman, D.A., Rule-based expert systems, in: Bond, A.M. (ed), Machine Intelligence (Infotech State of the Art Rep., Pergamon Infotech Ltd, Mainhead, 1981).
[2] Michie, D., Knowledge-based systems, Rep. UIUCDCS-R-80-1001, Dept. of Comp. Sc., of Univ. of Illinois (1980).
[3] Waterman, D.A., Design of a Rule-oriented System for Implementing Expertise, Rand Note N-1158-1-ARPA (1979).
[4] Sobolewski M.W., Structured object representations in many-sorted attribute systems, in: Proc. Int. Symp. on Artificial Intelligence (Leningrad, Oct.1983).
[5] Kulpa, Z., Iconics: computer aided visual communication, in: Proc. 2nd Conf. on Image Analysis and Processing (Fasano, Italy, Nov.1982).
[6] Sobolewski, M.W., Od zdań do sieci atrybutowych (From sentences to attribute networks, in Polish), Inst. of Biocyb.&Biomed. Engng.Rep. (Warsaw, 1983).

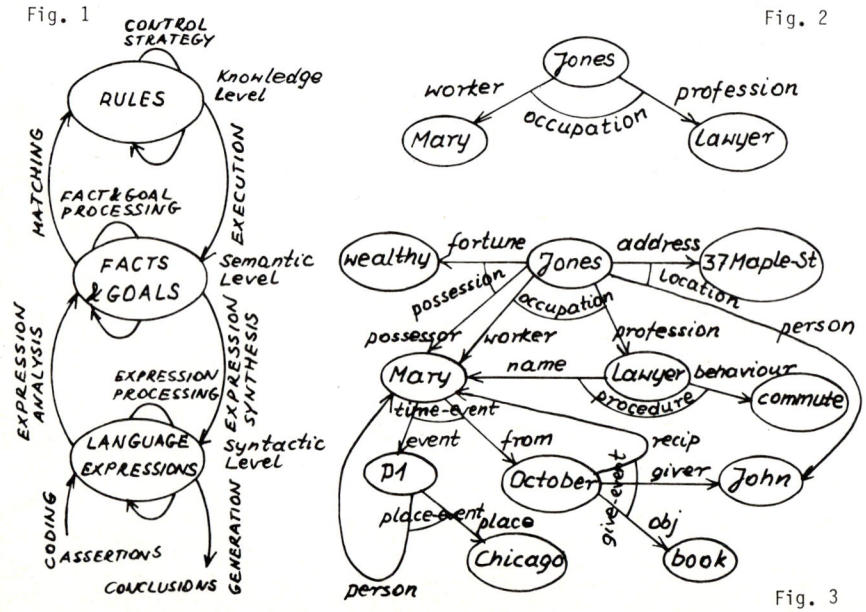

A METHOD OF THE EXECUTION OF FUZZY PROGRAMS

Zenon A. Sosnowski

Computing Centre
Technical University of Bialystok
Bialystok, Poland

The paper presents a general algorithm of finding of all possible performances of the fuzzy program. The fuzzy program is represented as regular expresion. It is shown how to construct finite-state machines executing the fuzzy programs. The said algorithm allows to solve the problems given on a very general way. Implementation of the algorithm in the programming language LISP is described.

INTRODUCTION

In [1] the fuzzy program is denoted by regular expresion on set Σ, which is the set of fuzzy instructions. In order to execute such a program it should be translated into a sequence of ordinary (not fuzzy) instructions, and the said translation is defined as execution of the fuzzy program. The process of translation of the fuzzy program into the ordinary one is controled with aid of two functions: function of possibility and preference. The first chooses the instruction to be executable in any situation, whereas the last subordinates any of chosen instruction the preference grade of performance.

To perform the ordinary instruction the finite-state machine is defined
$$M = (K, X, X_0, \Psi, T)$$
where:
- K - a finite nonempty set of instructions,
- X - a finite nonempty set of states,
- X_0 - an initial state,
- T - a set of final states,
- Ψ - the transition function, $\Psi : X \times K \to X$.

The execution of fuzzy program is performed with aid of the fuzzy machine
$$\hat{M} = (\Sigma, M, f, \lambda)$$
where:
- Σ - a finite nonempty set of fuzzy instructions,
- M - a finite-state machine as defined above,
- f - the feasibility function, $f : X \times \Sigma \times K \to [0,1]$,
- λ - the performance function, $\lambda : X \times \Sigma \times K \to [0,1]$.

The paper [2] shows a method how to perform the fuzzy program if the functions f and λ as well as description of machine instruction are given. In this algorithm a multiple repetition of the same fuzzy instruction is possible and the repetition number is undefined. However, it is known that the fuzzy program consists of n steps. The return's number to the previous instruction may be at most equal 2.

The application of this algorithm requires a cognizance of the functions f and λ which definition may be difficult when the set X and K consist of many elements. In the paper [3] the algorithm of a fuzzy program performance has been shown and its application does not require a cognizance, a priori, of the possibility function. Using this algorithm there is a sequence of instructions $\bar{\mu}$, which allows to attain the final state T, if such exists, proceeding from the state X_o and using instructions of the sequence $\bar{\mu}$, respectively. The effect of this algorithm may be represented in the following manner: (i -number of consecutive machine state, X_i- description of this state, $\Psi(X_i, M)$ - performance effect of the instruction μ in the state X_i) whereof:

$$\bigwedge_{i,j \in N} \bigwedge_{\substack{M \in K \\ X_i \in X}} \{X_j = \Psi(X_i, M) \in X\}$$

DESCRIPTION OF THE PROBLEM

In the algorithm of fuzzy program execution which has been reported by R. Jakubowski and A. Kasprzak ([2]) a cognizance of the functions f and λ is necessary. When the sets X and K contain many elements, the definition of these functions may be difficult. In the algorithm reported by E.Czogala and J.Ihnatowicz ([3]) it is necessary to know the function f describing which transitions from the state $X_i \rightarrow X_j$, $X_i, X_j \in X$ are possible and which instructions are to be applied. Both algorithms find one sequence of instructions which is a performance of the fuzzy program.

Since the analyzing of the machine of finite states number is an extremely difficult issue, it seems to be proper to construct the algorithm of fuzzy program performance which usage does not require not only a cognizance a priori of the possibility function value but also the preference function value. This algorithm is described in the present paper and includes all performances of the fuzzy program ensuring attainment of final states T of the machine M. The algorithm permits more general description of the problem which include solely one fuzzy instruction: "to attain the state from T, proceeding from the state X_o". In the case when the values of the functions f and λ are known a priori, this algorithm has its optimum performance of the fuzzy program.

DESCRIPTION OF THE ALGORITHM

The work of algorithm may be described as follows:
Let: i - denotes a successive number of the machine state,

X_i - is description of the i state of machine M,

$\Psi(X_i, M)$ - effect of instruction performance in the state X_i, (partial function is admissible).

Initially, the following data have to be introduced, namely: description of states X and T of the machine M, instructions $M \in K$ as well as the number N defining a maximal length of the sequence $\bar{\mu}$.

Subsequently, the first state of the machine M is admitted as the initial state X_0. Further proceeding is as follows:

Step 1: settlement of the list of possible instructions to be performed in the state X_i. If value of possibility function is known, the list includes only those instructions for which $f(X_i, a, \mu) = 1$. If not, the list contains whole set K. If value of the function λ is known, the order on the list of possibilities is in compliance with the criterion (i.e. cost of the instruction performance).

Step 2: if in the state X_i, an instruction is to be performed then go to step 3, otherwise go to step 9.

Step 3: if the function $\psi(X_i, \mu)$ is definite, then go to step 5, otherwise go to step 4.

Step 4: cancelation of instruction μ from the list of instructions possibly to performance in the state X_i and go to step 2.

Step 5: perform instruction μ in the state X_i, $i \leftarrow i+1$.

Step 6: if $X_i \in T$ then go to step 8, otherwise go to step 7.

Step 7: if $n < N$ then go to step 1, otherwise go to step 9.

Step 8: record of solution.

Step 9: decrease of possibility list. $i \leftarrow i-1$

Step 10: if $i \neq 0$ then go to step 2.

Step 11: if the list of solution is not empty, then go to step 12, otherwise go to step 13.

Step 12: success, print the list of all solutions. Stop.

Step 13: report failure. Stop.

The steps 9 and 10 ensure a possibility to return to the previous states of machine M and to perform other instruction choice μ than before. This procedure is repeted as long as all combinations possibilities are examined. If the list of solutions is nonempty then it contains all possible performances of the fuzzy program. It is possible to process this list in order to find the optimum performance.

The above described algorithm does not require a cognizance of the machine states number and it is unnecessary to analyze whether the transformation from the state X_i to X_j is possible and which instructions and transitional states are used. The number of all machine states is unknown, and their definition nor analysis is unnecessary. The only states being analyzed for which function ψ is definite whereas this examination is performed automatically.

IMPLEMENTATION

The program consist of a serie of procedures which realize particular fragment of the algorithm. The program is described in structural manner and its work is based on the recurrence functions development. Principal functions of the program are:

DO - realization of main processing loop,
BACK - return to previous state,
WORK - performance of instruction and final control,
END - printing of results.

Apart from these functions the program works basing of functions supplied by user:

CREATE - creation of list possible to perform instructions in the state X_i,
CHECK - check if function performance in the state X_i is possible,
EXECUTE - performance of instruction μ,
FINISH - control whether the final state is attained.

These functions operate basing on description of the machine M and
Ń which has to be supplied as a data to the program. The algorithm
has been implemented in LISP because of its sufficient generality
and assimilation for user. LISP has some mechanism rendering
possible the control of solutions search course and gives an
opportunity of direct work on searched objects and on procedures
representing the system knowlege, maintaining its procedural
knowlege representation.

CONCLUSION

The paper presents the algorithm of fuzzy program execution which
does not require an analyse á priori of values of the possibility
function f and performance function λ and it is easier in practice
than other algorithm reported in [2] and [3]. This algorithm enables
a return to any number of machine states in the case when performance
of any instruction seems to be impossible, or when the final state
has been attained, or the searched sequence is too long. The discovery
of all possible solutions is assured providing that such exist. In
the case when the function λ value is known, the algorithm includes
a simple criterion of optimization making at each step the choice
of the "cheapest" instruction. A possibility of the procedure
alteration CREATE, CHECK, FINISH and EXECUTE give application of
the algorithm for any process which may be described by the fuzzy
algorithm. Notwithstanding that algorithm is very general and may be
ineffective, the implementation of it in LISP enables the application
of the heuristics which limits considerably problem of the so-called
"explosion of combinations" being involved in all algorithm using
the backtracing technique.

REFERENCES

[1] Chang, S. H., On the execution of fuzzy programs using
finite-state machines, IEEE Trans. on Computers, C-21, 1972.
[2] Jakubowski, R., Kasprzak, A., Application of fuzzy programs to
the design of machining technology, Bull. Acad. Polon. Sci. Ser.
Techn., 21/1973.
[3] Czogała, E., Ihnatowicz, J., Some problems of automatic design
the sequence of technological instructions using fuzzy program,
Podstawy Sterowania, (8) 1978 303-316 /in Polish/.

A MAGNETIC SENSING MICROSYSTEM
FOR ASSEMBLING ROBOTS

Aurelian M. Stănescu
Mihai M. Atodiroaiei

Control and Computer Department
Politehnic Institute of Bucharest
76206 Bucharest, Splaiul Independenței 313
R O M A N I A

The sensing systems of adaptive robots are
incorporating different types of visual,
tactile, force, proximity, orientation sensors
to obtain more information about an incomplete
known environment. This work has an attempt to
foccuse the investigation on the magnetoresistance and Hall sensors, useful for assembling
robots. The measurement methods, developed in
our lab. are presented, as well as the microsystem hardware architecture and some software
facilities.

INTRODUCTION

Robotics is now-a-days a promising control technology, increasing
production flexibility, efficiency and goods quality and improving
the working conditions for dangerous, hard, unpleasant or uneffi-
cient industrial jobs. Due to robotics rush we are faced with a
complex social-economical phenomenon, involving system development.
The robots impact is not a technological one only. It is generating
a progress accelerating inner loop inside our social-economical
large scale system (Stănescu (1981)). The "robotics age" of our
civilization is seemed to be at very beginning. The first
generation robots are special machines only, characterized by an
increased "flexibility" due to both their mechanical architecture
and their programming facilities. Excluding the pick-and-place
manipulators, the robot "population" is still small, though some
technological lines implying object transfer, welding, painting,
a.s.o, were success fully robotized. The second generation robots
underline a more promising way of the adaptive, "inteligent"
machines. The objects recognition techniques and high level
planning open "the door" of exploiting a different type of robot/
environment interactions, increasing the machine autonomy.

Our research team activity is foccused on the following two main
directions: (i) to improve the robot "perception", that means the
using of the new sensors and fast, real-time, dedicated algorithmes
to preprocess the environmental information, (ii) to improve the
decisional level of the hierarchized control system by the
artificial inteligence algorithmes implementation. The main purpose
of this paper is to investigate some advantages of the galvanomagnetic sensors, used for assembling robots. During last years a
special attention has normally received the artificial robot vision
(Alecsander (1983)), as well as the tactile (Raibert (1982)) and

force sensing However, now-a-days sensors technology suggests us many other "non-human-like" solutions. Some good results has been obtained to implement navigation sensors as sonar, laser range finder, a.s.o. (Rovisec (1980,81,82,83)). By our knowledge Hall sensors are few times used as proximity elements only; the magnetic sensors could cooperate with the artificial vision (global scene analyzing system), as well as with local interactive tactile system to synthetize an optimum redundance perception system. Some advantages of these magnetic sensors are usefully for robotics: (1) industrial miniaturized sensors (Hall, magnetoresistance) availability, (2) magnetic field modelling, (3) local sensing (without contact) and control of robot hand position for optimum graspping, (4) magnetic forces development, (5) good mechanical resistance, (6) no illumination problems. Our first applications were connected with some object feature recognition, and a computing procedure of an optimum graspping. An improved application is planned for this, to assemble an electrical micromotor.

MAGNETIC SENSING METHODS

Different constructive types of galvanomagnetic sensors have been tested during our investigations. Some of them are commercially available like: (S1) Hall sensor produced by Siemens (KSY10), having a sensitivity of about 200V/AT, 7mA maximum current and 200mV output voltage at 0,2T; (S2) Permalloy magnetoresistance sensor delivered by RTC(CMR) as a full bridge circuit (four sensors mounted differentially) with high sensitivity and low temperature coefficient. It has also been developed two types of special magnetic sensors, namely: (S3) (InSb-NiSb) magnetoresistance of about (1,5x3x0,6)mm, having $R_o=400\Omega$ and $R_B=5000\Omega$ at B=0,6T, obtained by a specific technology recommended by Weiss (1967); (S4) (GaAs) sensor, sensitive to the magnetic field orientation.

Regarding (S4) sensor, both the volume effect sandwich probe and the epitaxial probe (Gunn diode-like) have been produced, having an area about $(0,35-1,17)mm^2$. Two electric connecting wires were applied by thermocompression. Ciupină (1980) and Stănescu (1982) have proved that their geometrical magnetoresistance is expressed by the equation:
$$R_m(\varphi,H) = a(H)/(1+b(H)\cos^2\varphi) + R_c$$
where φ the angle between the magnetic field ($\vec{B}$) and the surface unit vector ($\vec{n}$), H is the magnetic field intensity and R_c is the ohmic resistance. The a,b coefficients have been experimentally measured and their average values were determined by a mean-least-squarre erorr algorithme. As an example PEII probe has a=382,604971, b=21,278786, R_c=4,738969 at B=1,82T. Due to the finite dimensions of these probes, the resistance change should be derrived by a corrected formula $R/R_o=(R/R_o)\infty (1-0,543d/l)$, where $(R/R_o)\infty$ is the geometric magnetoresistance of an infinite theoretical probe and d/l are the real dimensions, as it is shown in Fig.1. By the same figure, there are presented the probe magnetoresistance in termes of the angle φ and V/A characteristics also. If the magnetic field is less than 0,8T, then the resistance change $\Delta R/R_o$ will depend on H^2 with a maximum error of 4,52%.

$$\frac{\Delta R}{R_o} = (\mu_m H)^2$$

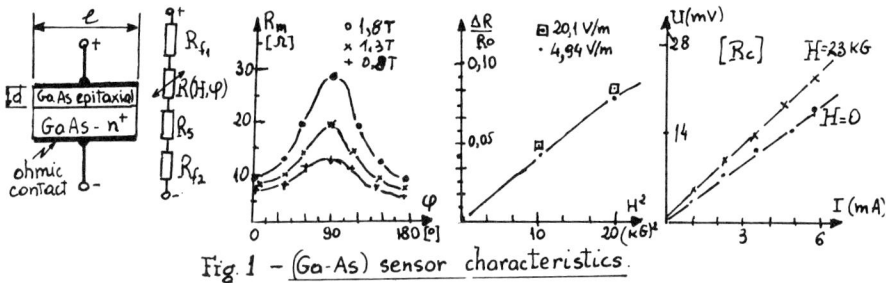

Fig. 1 - (Ga-As) sensor characteristics.

Excluding the Hall on-off proximity sensors, useful for stop detection or optimum distance detection, we refer for this work at the following measurement metods: (a) <u>Displacement method</u>: a square matrix of 8x8 pins, contacting the unknown object (as it is shown in figure 2a) are displacing 64 magnetoresistance (MR), which move across a constant, uniform magnetic field (B_o). According to the dependence R_m B(S(Z)) , each pin will measure the unknown object height. The ideea was proposed by Peruchon, who has used the differential transformers, and Swords and Hill with photoelectric cells. An improved characteristic can be obtain if a small, plate, permanent magnet is displaced in front of the fixed, differential connected, double MR, which is also premagnetized (figure 2n); (b) <u>distance method</u>: a magnetic gripper (figure 2b) moves over a ferromagnetic table with unknown object on it; a magnetoresistance matrix (16x4 for example) is measuring the different paths induction according to $B_o = (IN)(\delta/\mu_o + S_o f/Sf \cdot \mu_f)$, so that $R_m = B_o(\delta(Z))$. . This method was developed for 2-D objects and an error of maximum 4,82% was recorded for $\delta \in [0,5-5,5]$mm. A flux concentrator will improve the resolution and a Hall proximity sensor can control the maximum distance, (c) <u>field deformation method</u>: a uniform magnetic field, developed between the fingers of robot hand, is disturbed by introducing inside the field the unknown object. A 8x8 magnetoresistance matric is measuring the magnetic field intensity, while the opossite 8x8 matrix with field orientation S4 will determine φ_i angles. The searching is controled locally by hand rotating and closing, as necessary should be (figure 2c) The prismatic and cilindrical objects were successfully tested.

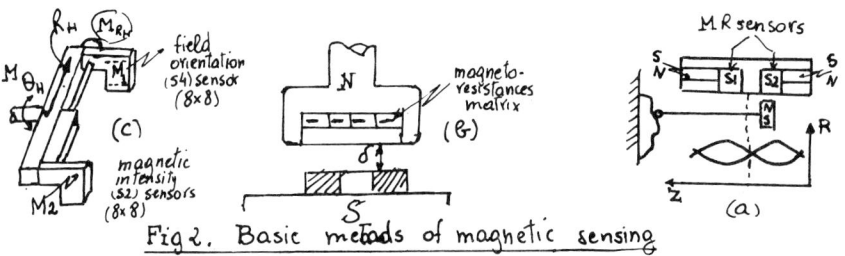

Fig 2. Basic metods of magnetic sensing

DATA PROCESSING MICROSYSTEM

Due to the matrix configuration of the magnetic sensing system, it has been designed a general interfacing circuit. It consists of (1) an individual operational amplifier array (not always necessary) for impedance matching, (2) an analog multiplexing unit, (3) a data acquisition unit. To reduce the circuit volume and to increase its reability, we have used some chips delivered by Burr Brown, namely: MPC16S analog multiplexer and SDM853 data acquisition system. The multiplexing unit is connected with sixteen single ended inputs of the op. amplifiers. The system can be expanded without limit by using (n+1) MPC16S and a 8 bit channel adress generator. Finally, a SDM853 (8/16 channels) can acquire and digitize low level or high level analog signals. A built-in high quality instrumentation amplifier allows input signals range of $\pm 10mV$ to $\pm 10V$. This expandable module accepts either 16 single ends of 8 differential inputs and converts the multiplexed data signals into 12 bit digital words with an accuracy of $\pm 0,025\%$. The interfacing circuit is presented in Fig.3. If. the sensing matrix has only 32/48 measuring points, it will be better to use a modified interface with 2/3 SDM853, connected to the op. amp. outputs and a digital multiplexer. This interfacing circuit allows the minimum number of chips and it avoids the analog multiplexers.

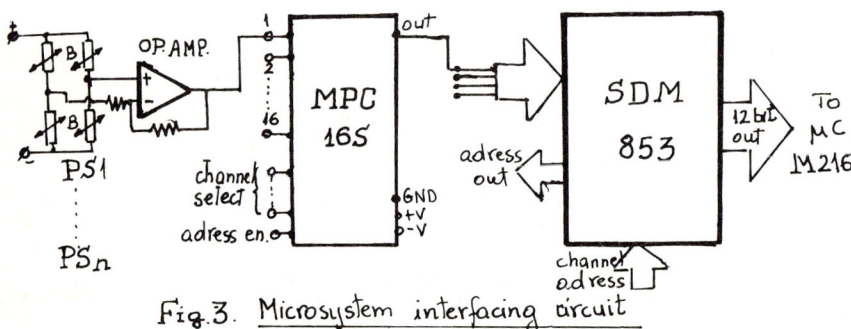

Fig.3. Microsystem interfacing circuit

As a general philosophy of the robot control system architecture, we think a distributed microcomputers network should offer some advantages of the software organizing and paralell processing. The real time high speed requirements and the memory capacity, necessary for the magnetic sensing system, are suggested us a second generation microcomputer M216, used as developping configuration. The modular M216 has an architecture based on two biprocessor CPU, one built around 8086 μP and the other built around 8080A μP. Its memory is expandable by modules of 128K (maximum eight). The other SLAVE modules are connecting peripherial units (dual floppy-disk, display, magnetic tape unit, DMA, plotting device, a.s.o.). MASTER and SLAVE modules are interconnected by a time-multiplexed, low-price, passive bus; its global capacity is constrained by 5MHz maximum transfer rate. The measurement data are processed by 8086 CPU, having a clock signal of 5MHz delivered by 8284 circuit. A bus controller 8288 is used to command the local and global system resources. The 8080 CPU module has a local memory of 2K RAM and 8K REPROM. It is used to control the polar movement of a local positionating system of two d.o.f. robot hand (rotating θ_H, closing R_H). A module IPLOT, generally used for XY ploter, are supplying two analog outputs for (Θ_H, R_H) within the range of 0-7V and a 10 bit resolution.

The microcomputer has an operating system (SFDX-18 or CP/M) on the floppy disk. A cross-software on 8080 is generating the programmes for 8086 (macroassembler ASM86,PL/M-86,LINK86). Pascal and Fortran IV with graphics facilities are also the available compilers. The real-time programme package is written in Pascal, ASM 86 for such an application of optimum graspping fingers position. The algorithme involves: (1) contour segmentation (2) primitives generation (3) primitives parametrisation (4) optimum positioning of the figures primitives.

CONCLUSION

A microsystem consisting of a matrix galvanomagnetic sensors, an interfacing circuit and a microcomputer are experimentally developed in our laboratory for assembling robots. This microsystem is simple,compact, reliable,hand placed and it has a lower price than an artificial vision or an artificial skin. The main robotic task is to extract the unknown object contour and to find the optimum graspping position of the robot hand. It is not intented to implement a "perfect" it self magnetic sensing, but we aim to use cooperatively this system with our artificial CCTV vision (Stănescu (1982)) Further work is necessary for improving magnetic sensing of complex objects as well as to optimize the last step of the grasspping algorithm.

REFERENCE

1 Stănescu A.M. Scenario-analysis of social-economical impact of industrial robots, Nat. Cybernetics Conf.,Buch; 1981.
2 Alecsander I. Artificial vision for robots, Kogan Ltd,London, 1983.
3 Raibert M.M. A VSLI tactile array sensor, Proc. of 12 th I.S.I.R.,Paris, June, 1982
4 Ciupină V. Electrical parameters determination of high mobility semiconductors by geometrical magnetoresistance studying, Phisics Ph.D,University of Bucharest, 1980.
5 x x x Robot Vision and Sensory Control Conference,1980, 1981,1982,1983
6 Stănescu A.M. and others.Architecture, control and software of a modular robot system with pneumatic stepping motors and vision, Proc. of 12 th ISIR Paris, June,1982.

ACQUISITION OF DATA FOR 3-D VISION SYSTEMS

G. Stanke and P. Florath

Central Institute for Cybernetics and Information Processes
1086 Berlin, Kurstr. 33
GDR

3-D vision is of increasing interest in research and development as well as in industrial and non-industrial applications. Appropriate data acquisition is the first main step in 3-D vision. Considering such criteria as analysing method, image coding and physical implementation of light projection and sensors different approaches are systematized. An attempt of valuation shows the two problems to overcome, image acquisition time and reference between image pixels and surface points. Two proposals are given how to avoid these problems for limited classes of applications. Both methods are based on relatively simple light pattern projections.

INTRODUCTION

The recognition of 3-D scenes becomes a necessity especially in connection with flexible automation. Instances are well known: intelligent robots, visual inspection, supervising of assembly, arc-welding. Additionally, such techniques win non-industrial fields as medicine and arts too. 3-D recognition needs algorithms to determine identity, location and orientation of objects in space. The basic problem is that only projections of 3-D objects are available. In order to overcome this difficulty all approaches try to extract so called 2 1/2-D information from the scene (e. g. distances, orientation of surface points). To accomplish this task with a resonable effort as much as possible apriori known parameters have to be put into the process of data acquisition (illumination, perception).

Even if the general progress in image understanding is not so high /1/ a broad spectrum of solutions is proposed for illumination and scanning. An estimation in /2/ says we have to wait about 5 - 10 years for wide spread industrial use of 3-D vision, a 100-fold computation power will be needed and the price will move around the 10-fold of today 2-D vision systems. Nevertheless first applications arise e. g. for welding /26/ or for very special inspection tasks/7/.

In /3, 4/ structures of 3-D vision systems are described. Generally the data acquisition process is considered as relatively independent. The direct contour tracking is an exeption /6/. In the following paragraphs a systematization and evaluation of approaches using different basic principles are given. The main bottle-necks are formulated. Two solutions are proposed which can yield to effective systems for limited classes of recognition tasks.

SYSTEMATIZATION OF 3-D DATA ACQUISITION SYSTEMS

A common feature of all approaches is to put into the acquisition process known parameters in order to reduce the number of inherent degrees of freedom. As criteria for their systematization can serve: principle of analysis, variable illumination (time and geometry),

Principle of analysis	Principle of coding	Sensors used	Time of Acquisition	Accuracy	Physical Implementation	Remarks
Direct range measuring	Time of flight	Photomultiplier	$N^2 \cdot T$; typical hundreds of points/s	some cm in range 1–3 m	Pulse modulated	Implementations with different parameters exist /11,23,5/. very expensive
		acoustic transducer		2 – 3 cm (over 0,3–10m)	ultrasonic pulses	Suitable for special applications and environments /24,25/
	Phase shift	Photomultiplier	$N^2 \cdot T$; typical hundreds of points/s	some cm in range 1–3 m	modulated beam/reference beam	Implementations with different parameters /10,14,20, 21,23,24/. expensive
Triangulation	Sequences of light points	TV or CCD-matrix camera	$N^2 \cdot T$; e.g. 512x512x20ms= 5000s e.g.300 points/s	proportional to N e.g. 1% in x,y 0,2% in z	rotating mirrors	Problems of mechanical and kinematical stability /13/
					controlled mirrors	Direct contour tracking by random access /6/
		Position sensitive photodetector	$N^2 \cdot T$; e.g. 512x512x0,5 $\mu s \approx 0,12s$	smaller 1 cm	electro optical crystals	No mechanical parts, no implementation known
		TV or CCD-matrix camera			Projector and scanner synchronized	Very fast solution, relatively compact /15/
	Contents of the points	TV or CCD-matrix camera	$CF \cdot T$ with CF=1+2 ld N e.g.10x20ms=0,2s e.g.16000points/s		electromechanical shutter in the light beam	The shutter is numerically controlled /12/. A contents-depending shutter depth is possible
		color sensitive TV or CCDcamera	T		each point has a multi spectral coding	No implementation known, only a theoretical possibility
	Sequences of light stripes	TV or CCD matrix camera	$NS \cdot T$ with NS=Number of stripes e.g. 10x20 ms	proportional to NS	Laser with cylindrical lense/slit in a slide	Many different solutions /e.g. 17,18/
	Projected single grid	TV or CCD matrix camera	typical 20 ms	depending on grid resolution	Laser beam array; grid-slide	The Problem lies in reference finding and ambiguity of grid stripes; low cost solution /16,19/
Moiré techniques	Gratings in the projected as well as the received beam	TV or CCD matrix camera	typical 20 ms	e. g. 2 mm	for high quality a source of parallel light is needed	Suitable for low distances between grid and object /22/

(N=Number of raster lines/columns
T=time for one sensor cycle)

structured scanning, physical principle of variable illumination or of sensors, technical effort needed, time requirements, depth resolution etc. For reasons of space only a subset is used in the table. The space and time variable illumination is stressed because it represents the basic possibilities how to make 2 1/2-D information available. Other well known possibilities of extracting 3-D data from images (shape from texture, shape from shading, depth from focus, depth from stereo, motion stereo) are not considered. A good survey is found in /5/.

In a certain point of view direct measuring seems to be the most appropriate method because the 2 1/2-D data are obtained immediately and the reached accuracy can often be sufficient. But the time needed for a single image is relativly high and the costs for equipment are not negligible. The sequential projection of point and repeated picture scanning is time consuming too, and it needs well working mirror systems /5/. Here the system proposed in /15/ reduce the number of scanned pictures for a logarithmic magnitude by shutter coding. In /14/ a very compact solution is described. The system refered to in /24/ can be mounted in a robot-hand. The development would be forced by cheeper laser diodes and special triangulation circuits, a great influence would be reached by non-mechanical randomly adressable laser projectors. All these systems support by help of the space/time resolution of projected and scanned information the correspondence between image and scene. The price for low acquisition time in light pattern systems illuminating whole scene at once is a higher amount of computation to solve the correspondence problem. Such systems allow a low cost solution.

APPROACHES WITH SPECIAL STRUCTURED LIGHT PATTERNS

The following two proposals are made to support the solution of the correspondence problem in scenes illuminated by a single light pattern, i. e., to combine the advantage of a single scanning with reduced computation.

First, the light pattern results from superimposing grids of different resolutions. The higher the resolution the finer the lines. The appropriate relations between two consecutive grid resolutions have to be determined by experiments in the investigated environment. Resonable relations would be: $N(i) = \sqrt{N(i-1)}$ or $N(i) = ld\ N(i-1)$.

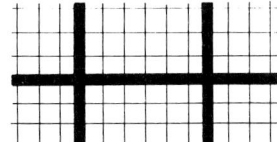

Example of a hierarchical grid sector

Appropriate window-operators can be used to detect crossing points of grid lines for further references. Operators for larger windows can often be implemented by means of a suitable combination of operators for smaller windows (e.g. 3x3). This is especially useful if special hardware is available /27/. Strongly distorted lines and shadows cause trouble.

Second, let the task be to verify a certain 3-D object in the camera field of view in a fixed position and orientation. For given camera and projector geometries a special task-dependent grid is computed in such a manner that projection of this grid onto the scene leads to a regular pattern in the image if the object is seen in the expected way. Fast optical or digital filtering and/or difference techniques allow a high speed verification. Digital film output devices are appropriate to produce arbitrary grid patterns.

CONCLUSION

For 3-D vision there is a number of mostly experimental solutions for data acquisition. These data have to be analysed by means of higher level recognition algorithms. If the variability of the scene is appropriately restricted and/or illumination and perception conditions are strongly controlled already today 3-D recognition tasks can be accomplished.

REFERENCES

/ 1/ Klette, R.,Konferenz "ComputerVision and Pattern Recognition",Bild und Ton, Vol.36,No.12(1983),379-380.
/ 2/ Villers, P.,Recent Proliferation of Industrial Vision Applications, Proc. 13. ISIR (1983) 3. 1-3.20.
/ 3/ Kanade, T., Representation and Control in Vision, in:Haralick,R.M. (ed.), Pictorial Data Analysis (Springer,New York,1983). 171-197.
/ 4/ Florath, P.,3-D Object Recognition with Location Constraints, in this Volume.
/ 5/ Jarvis, R.A.,A Perspective on Range Finding Techniques for Computer Vision, IEEE-PAMI-5,No.2,(1983),122-139.
/ 6/ Ishi, M.,Nagata,T.,Feature Extraction of Three Dimensional Objects and Visual Processing in a Hand-eye System Using Laser Tracker,PR 8 (1976),229-237.
/ 7/ Kinnucan, P.,Machines that See, High Technology; 3 (1983),No.4,30-36.
/ 8/ Woodham, R.J.,Analysing Images of Curved Surfaces, AI 17 (1981), 117-141.
/ 9/ Vamos, T. and Bathor,M., 3-D Complex Object Recognition Using Programmed Illumination,Proc.ICPR,(1980),1091-1093.
/10/ Duda, R.O.,Nitzan,P.and Barrett,P.,Use of Range and Reflectance Data to Find Planar Surface Regions, IEEE-PAMI-1,No.3,(1979),259-271.
/11/ Lewis, R.A. and Johnston,A.R.,A Scanning Laser Rangefinder for a Robotic Vehicle,Proc.5.IJCAI,(1979),762-768.
/12/ Altschuler, M.D.,et.al.,The Numerical Stereo Camera,Proc.of SPIE 283,15-24.
/13/ Connah,D.M.and Fishbourne,C.A.,Using a Laser for Scene Analysis,Proc.2.RoViSeC,(1982),233-240.
/14/ Nimrod, N.,Margolith,A.and Mergler,W.H.,A Laser-based Scanning Range Finder for Robotic Applications,Proc.2.RoViSeC,(1982),241-252.
/15/ Rioux, M.,3-D Camera Based on Synchronized Scanning,13.ISIR,17.48-17.60.
/16/ Will, P.M.and Pennington,K.S.,Grid Coding:A Novel Technique for Image Processing,Proc.IEEE 60,(1972),No.6,669-680.
/17/ Agin, G.I.and Binford,T.Q.,Computer Description of Curved Objects,Proc. IJCAI 73,629-640.
/18/ Shirai, Y.and Suwa,M.,Recognition of Polyhedrons with a Range Finder,Proc. IJCAI 71,80-87.
/19/ Röcker, F.and Kiessling,A.,Methods for Analysing Three Dimensional Scenes. Proc. IJCAI 75,669-673.
/20/ Pago, C.I.and Hassan,H.,Non-contact Inspection of Complex Components Using a Range Finder Vision System,Proc.1Int.Conf.on Robot Vision,(1983),245-254.
/21/ Rybak, W.I.et.al.,Visual Perception of Robots Environment-Methods and Techniques of Constructing,ISAI 83,Leningrad.
/22/ Chu, I.,Bloch,P.,Application of Moiré Patterns for Obtaining Surface Contour Information on Patients Receiving Radiotherapy,Proc.of SPIE 283,1981,2-6.
/23/ Levi, P.,Industrieroboter lernen räumlich sehen,Elektronik 16.6.83,93-98.
/24/ Agin, G.I.and Highnam,P.I.,Movable Light-Stripe Sensor for Obtaining Three-Dimensional Coordinate Measurements,Proc.of SPIE 360,326-333.
/25/ Schoenwald, I.S.et.al.,Acoustic Scanning for Robotic Range Sensing and Object Pattern Recognition,IEEE Ultrasonic Symposium,(1982),945-949.
/26/ Kremers, I.,et.al.,Development of a Machine-Vision-Based Robotic Arc-Welding System,Proc.13.ISIR,(1983)14.19-14.32.
/27/ Schwarze, G.and Vlček,J.,Realtime Image Processing for Robotic and Inspection Systems with Specialized Processors,Proc.2.AIICSR(1982),Smolenice,220-223

IMPROVING THE STRUCTURE OF LOGIC PROGRAMS

Petr Štěpánek

Department of Cybernetics
Charles University
Malostranské náměstí 25
118 00 Praha 1

Olga Štěpánková

Institute of Computational
Techniques, ČVUT, Horská 3
128 00 Praha 2
Czechoslovakia

Transformations of Logic Programs motivated by Structured Programming are described and their impact on the methodology of logic programming is discussed.Theoretical results are compared with the attempts to develop a practical methodology for the construction of logic programs.

INTRODUCTION

The stepwise synthesis of algorithms used in the discipline of structured programming uses the decomposition of goals to subgoals. Quite often, the resulting programs are preocupied with data flow and their logical structure remains hidden. This led D. Harel [H1] to propose a tree-like specification/programming language of And/Or Schemes which emphasizes the logical structure of algorithms determined by the decomposition of goals to subgoals. Harel [H2] proposed transformations of And/Or Schemes which allow to improve their structure.

Alternation of And/Or subgoaling is a prominent feature of logic programs. E.Shapiro [S] observed that And/Or Schemes and logic programs are based on similar principles. It was shown in [Š1] that every And/Or Scheme can be simulated by a logic program. The proof gives a clear insight to the relation between And/Or Schemes and logic programs. It allows to point out to certain syntactical restrictions in the definition of And/Or Schemes which are superfitial in the corresponding logic programs. It turns out that there are logic programs which do not have a natural conterpart in And/Or Schemes. In [Š2], there were developed transformations of logic programs and their computation trees which improve the local and global structure of programs and are generalizations of the transformations of And/Or Schemes from [H2] . These transformations made possible to prove a Normal Form Theorem for logic programs. The results of this kind represent the impact of Structured programming to the theory of logic programs. On the other hand, there were attempts to develop a practical methodology of logic programming influenced by the discipline of structured programming. Recently proposed language PRIMLOG [KKM] introduces a design methodology by means of syntactic constraints for logic programs in a PROLOG environment. PRIMLOG is in fact a subset of PROLOG which aims at control of complexity of the designer's work. PRIMLOG restricts the syntactical means used in decomposition of a goal. The resulting programs usually tend to require a larger number of levels of hierarchical decomposition than is necessary in PROLOG programs, increasing to some extent the memory space and run time. This is compensated by reduced error rate and improved quality of programs /see [KKM] and [MK]/.

The aim of this paper is to study the possibilities of improving the structure of logic programs by the above mentioned structural transformations. We shall use the Normal Form Theorem to show that certain restrictions of PRIMLOG are fully justified. We indicate some restrictions of PRIMLOG which seem to be problematic.

TRANSFORMATIONS OF LOGIC PROGRAMS

We shall describe three types of transformations of logic programs motivated by the concept of computation trees of logic programs. First, we shall recall the definition of a computation tree from [Š2] . If A is a predicate symbol of a first-order language L , we call an AND/OR-tree T a computation tree for A , provided that T has the following properties

/i/ the root of T is an OR-node labelled by $A(v_1,...,v_n)$, where $v_1,...,v_n$ is an appropriate tuple of distinct variables. Every OR-node of T is labelled by an atomic formula of L and the labels of internal /i.e. non-leaf/ OR-nodes consist of a predicate symbol and a tuple of distinct variables.

/ii/ If n is an OR-node with the label B , all its successors are AND-nodes labelled by Horn clauses the head of which contains the same predicate symbol as B . Every edge connecting n with its successor n´ is labelled by a substitution which unifies B with the head of the label of n´.

/iii/ To avoid multiplicity in defining predicates, the labels of different internal OR-nodes have different predicate symbols.

/iv/ If n is and AND-node labelled by the clause $B \leftarrow A_1,..., A_n$ then for every $i \leq n$ there is a successor node n_i of n the label of which contains the same predicate symbol as A_i. Moreover, if n_i is a leaf, its label is A_i.

/v/ Every AND-node labelled by an unconditional statement is a list.

We shall illustrate the concept by the example on Fig. 1a of the tree for the predicate FIB/x,y/ which denotes the relation "y is the x-th fibonacci number".

We distinguish two types of OR-leaves according to the attached predicate symbols. We call a leaf primitive provided that its predicate symbol is different from every predicate symbol attached to an internal OR-node, otherwise, we say that it is a call-leaf. The predicate symbol of a call leaf ℓ coincides with the predicate symbol of exactly one internal OR-node, which is a called node /called by ℓ/. Note that the computation tree from Fig.1a contains three call-leaves and two called nodes. They are connected by a dashed bow.

It is easy to see that the set of all clauses labelling the AND-nodes of a computation tree for A is a logic program computing A . On the other hand, if P is a logic program computing A , it is not difficult to construct a computation tree for A, which corresponds to the program P. We say that a computation tree is tidy iff every call leaf l has its called node on the path from the root to l. Note that the computation tree on Fig. 1a is tidy. A logic program P is tidy for a predicate A iff P has a tidy computation tree for A.

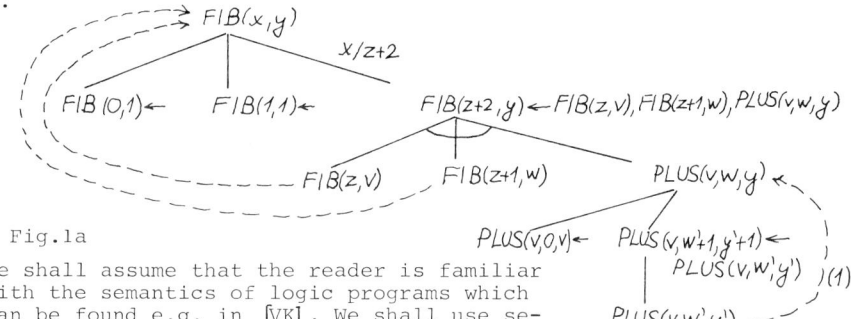

Fig.1a

We shall assume that the reader is familiar with the semantics of logic programs which can be found e.g. in [VK]. We shall use semantics to compare programs. If P and Q are logic programs, we say that P extends Q provided that for every predicate which occurs both in P and Q, the denotations of A in P and Q are the same. Note that nothing is claimed for predicates which do not occur in both programs.

It was shown in [§2] that for every logic program P and every predicate of P, there is a program Q which extends P and is tidy. The program Q is obtained by a transformation of the computation tree T_P of P which adds some isomorphic copies of certain subtrees of T_P labelled by new predicate symbols. Tidy trees and tidy programs are easier to handle and there are two important transformations of tidy programs which allow

/i/ to push the called nodes closer to the root
/ii/ to push upwards the nodes of OR-branching

We shall use /i/ to push the call /1/ from Fig.1a up to the root of the tree. To do this, we replace the predicate FIB by FIBB with two additional arguments b and u. Variable b serves as a switch for two types of calls of FIBB, variable u overtakes the value y´ during the simulation of the call PLUS/v,w, y´/, while it is a dummy variable for the calls inherited from the original FIB predicate.

We have the following computation tree for FIBB.

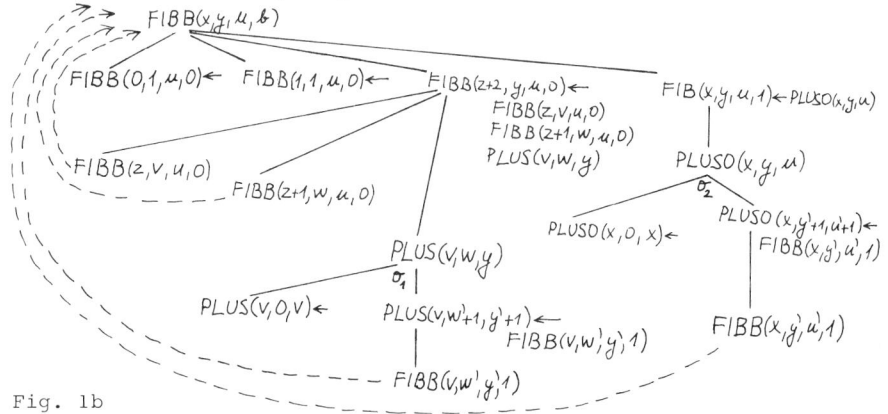

Fig. 1b

Combining the transformations /i/ and /ii/, it was shown in [§2] that every logic program P computing the relation A can be transformed to a tidy program Q computing the same relation which has at most one called node and at most two alternations of AND- and OR-nodes on every branch. In this case, we say that Q is in normal form. Note that the program from Fig. 1b is in normal from, but it computes the relation FIBB instead of FIB. We can remedy this by adding the clause FIB/x,y/⟵ FIBB/x,y,u,0/ to the program, but then we have to push up the OR-branching in the nodes o_1, o_2.

PRIMLOG: STRUCTURED PROGRAMMING IN PROLOG

The main feature of the PRIMLOG methodology is the severe restriction of the rate at which the designer is allowed to refine the structure of his task.
PRIMLOG identifies five possible ways of the structural decomposition - partitions, which are considered to be the building blocks of every PRIMLOG program: task, and, or, recursion and data base. The syntax of partitions specific to PRIMLOG, namely of and, or and recursion is given as follows

AND $R/t_1,t_2/$ ⟵ $A/s_1,s_2/$, $B/r_1,r_2/$

OR $R/t_1,t_2/$ ⟵ $A/s_1,s_2/$
            $R/p_1,p_2/$ ⟵ $B/r_1,r_2/$

RECURSION $R/t_1,t_2/$ ⟵
                                    $R/p_1,p_2/$ ⟵ $A/q_1,q_2/$, $R/r_1,r_2/$

Note that computation trees of PRIMLOG are at most binary and that the only allowed recursion in PRIMLOG is in the explicit type described by the recursion partition. PRIMLOG prohibits any implicit recursion e.g. A⟵B, B⟵C, C⟵A is not a legal construct of PRIMLOG.
Generally, there can be easily met the restrictions of PRIMLOG concerning the syntax of AND, OR partitions by introduction of some new predicates. This claim is illustrated by the transformation of the computation tree from Fig. 2a to that of Fig. 2b.

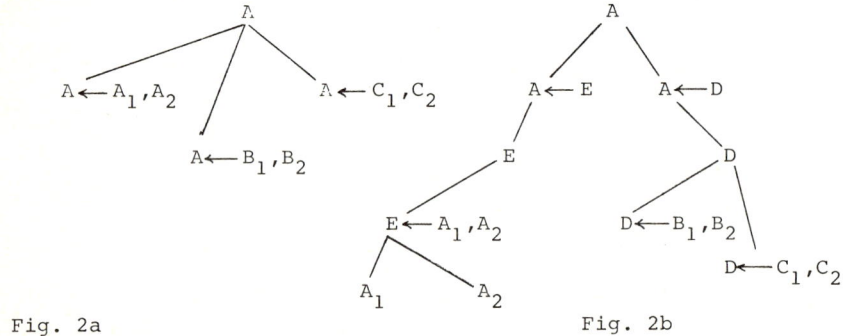

Fig. 2a   Fig. 2b

The resulting computation tree does not correspond to a PRIMLOG program yet. But one more modification of the similar type applied to the clauses D⟵B_1,B_2, D⟵C_1,C_2 would lead to the desired PRIMLOG program.
The most restrictive demand of PRIMLOG seems to be the limitation of the distance between the call leaf and the called node, which is al-

lowed to be two only /the explicite recursion in one clause/. It was shown in [ŠeŠ] that every recursive function can be computed by a stratifiable program, which allows the distance two between the call-leaf and the called node only, but more than three atoms are allowed in one recursion clause. The Normal Form Theorem extends this result to all computable relations. But there are usually several successors of the recursion node of the computation tree of any program transformed to the normal form /see Fig. 1b/.
Thus waht really limits the generality of PRIMLOG is the use of only two clauses for the description of the behaviour of the recursion predicate.
The experiments with PRIMLOG motivated the proposal of another version of a similar design methodology NEW PRIMLOG [KM] [MK]. This version modifies the definition of the AND, OR partitions and introduces new CASE partition:

AND $\quad A \leftarrow B_1, B_2, B_3$

OR $\quad A \leftarrow B_1, B_2$
$\quad\quad A \leftarrow C_1, C_2$

CASE $\quad A \leftarrow B_1$
$\quad\quad A \leftarrow B_2$
$\quad\quad .....$
$\quad\quad A \leftarrow B_n \quad$ where $\quad n \quad$ is arbitrary

Even this later version does not pay attention to the problem of recursion with multiple branching. We suggest the following generalization of RECURSION partition combining the strength of both CASE and RECURSION partitions:

CASE RECURSION $\quad R \leftarrow B_1$
$\quad\quad R \leftarrow B_2, R$
$\quad\quad ....$
$\quad\quad R \leftarrow B_n, R \quad$ where $\quad n \quad$ is arbitrary

The acceptance of such a partition in PRIMLOG would provide for full strength of PROLOG - any problem computable in PROLOG could be programmed in PRIMLOG, too.
It would be advisable to consider even the posiibility that some of $B_2, \ldots, B_n$ is R, too. This happens to be the case in FID. Though there are methods, which allow to avoid such double recursion, it is worth of considering, whether their cost is not too high.

REFERENCES
[H1] Harel,D. And/Or Programs, ACM Transact.Prog.Lang 2 /1980/,1-17
[H2] Harel,D. And/Or Schemes, in MFCS 80, LNCS 88 Springer-Verlag 1980
[KKM] Kaposi,A. Markusz,Z. PRIMLOG, in Informatica 79, Bled,Yugoslavia
[MK] Markusz, Z. Kaposi,A. A Desing methodology in PROLOG Programming, in Proc. 1st Int. Conf. on Log. Prog. Marseille 82, 139 - 145
[Š1] Štěpánková,O. Štěpánek,P. And/Or Schemes and Log. Prorams,(to appear) in Proc. Coll. on Alg. Comb. and Log. in Comp. Sci. Györ
[Š2] Štěpánková,O. Štěpánek,P. Computation Trees and Transformations of Logic Programs, submitted to 2nd Int. Conf. Logic. Prog. 84
[VK] Van Emden,M.H., Kowalski, R.A. The Semantics of Predicate Logic as a Programming Language, JACM 23 /1976/, 733 - 742
[ŠeŠ] Šebelík,J. Štěpánek,P. Horn clause Programs for Recursive Functions, in Logic Programming, ACADEMIC PRESS, London 1982

Artificial Intelligence and Information-Control Systems of Robots
I. Plander (editor)
© Elsevier Science Publishers B.V. (North-Holland), 1984

A FRAMEWORK FOR CONSTRUCTING KNOWLEDGE-BASED PLANNING SYSTEMS

Gheorghe Tecuci

Research Department
Central Institute for Management and Informatics
Bucharest, Romania

The paper describes work done at building a system to aid in easy implementation of interactive planning systems hierarchically generating nonlinear plans as partially ordered networks of actions.

INTRODUCTION

Our overall design goal is to develop knowledge representation, control, and knowledge acquisition facilities useful in constructing planning systems for different domains.

We are working in the hierarchic nonlinear planning paradigm, building directly on work done at NOAH (1), NONLIN (3) (10), SIPE (7) (16) and other planning systems. The planning process is viewed as an incremental instantiation of goals in networks of subgoals and processes, finally obtaining a partially ordered network of processes which achieve the proposed goal(s). Parallel action performance raises the difficult problem of detecting and removing the interactions. Apart from the goal and the situation in which the goal is to be achieved, some metaconstraints can be imposed on the plan to be generated (a maximum duration of the plan execution, for example) and some optimization criteria can be indicated (minimize the cost, for example). The metaconstraints and the optimization criteria are represented as metagoals whose achievement controls the planning process. Because the plan is hierarchically generated, the metaconstraints are evaluated at different levels of abstraction of the plan. The same applies to the optimization criteria.

The specific attributes of the system include (a) facilities for generating competing plans, (b) facilities for using constraints in the partial plans and for reasoning on these partial solutions, (c) facilities for the user to control the search for a solution, that is interactive planning facilities, (d) facilities for interactive knowledge acquisition, both in the stage of knowledge base construction and during interactive planning.

KNOWLEDGE REPRESENTATION

We adopted and integrated different formalisms for representing the different kinds of knowledge needed for a planning system.

We use prototypes to represent the objects used during plan execution. These prototypes are ordered in a class-subclass hierarchy in which a subclass prototype inherits the properties of its superclass prototypes. A special kind of objects are the resources (objects used during action performance and then released) which could be shared or unshared.

The planning, deduction, and metaplanning operators are represented as production rules. Each planning operator indicates a means of achieving a general goal (depending on, possibly constrained, variables) by a general plan (depending on the same variables) which is a network of goals and processes. Other information is also included in the operator, as for instance, when is the operator applicable (preconditions), how is the plan to be integrated in a larger plan when replacing the goal of the operator, the estimated cost or duration of the plan, etc. Deductive operators deduce new assertions from existing ones in the world model, if their preconditions are satisfied. A metaplanning operator indicates a metagoal and a metaplan which is appropriate for achieving it when the operator preconditions are satisfied. The metaplanning operators control the planning process. They are a natural means for encoding optimization procedures.

The result of the planning process is a hierarchy of networks. Each network is a plan at a certain level of abstraction. The effects of each plan step are recorded at that step (as first order predicates) so that the description of the current state of the world is distributed in the network. During the planning process, the system mantains global features of the current plan, which are used by the metaplanning operators to control the process.

CONTROL

The control problem is of fundamental importance in constructing efficient planners. We believe that autonomous planners cannot be powerful enough for practical applications. That is why we adopted a flexible control mechanism which allows a user to participate, as deeply as he wishes, in the planning process.

The system has a layered agenda control structure. In each agenda several tasks are competing for execution, one of them being selected and executed by an interpreter, on the basis of the partial solution and the metaoperators. The system allows the user to take the place of each interpreter. As a top level interpreter, the user can decide to refine the plan, to analyze it and fix any problems, or to reject the plan and look for an alternative one. The corresponding tasks have also agenda control structures and the user can take the place of their interpreters. To refine the plan, for example, the user (acting as interpreter) can decide to replace plan steps with subplans, to create new constraints on the plan variables, or to refine already existing constraints. After deciding to decompose a plan step, several lower level decisions are to be made, as for instance, what particular step to decompose and what planning operator to use for this purpose.

To analyze the plan and fix the problems, the user can invoke tasks which detect or eliminate harmful interactions (parallel processes have opposite effects, making the plan infeasible), detect or eliminate useful interactions (parallel processes have the same effects, making the plan inefficient), detect or eliminate resource interactions (unshared resources are used by parallel processes or the amount of resources used by parallel processes exceeds the available ones).

KNOWLEDGE ACQUISITION

A primary goal of our research is to provide tools for knowledge acquisition, both in the stage of knowledge base construction and during planning system operation.

The knowledge used by a planning system can be divided in competence knowledge (prototype objects, planning and deductive operators) and performance knowledge (metaplanning operators). This separation allows for the identification of different strategies for knowledge acquisition.

In the stage of knowledge base construction, an expert and the system analyze complete plans and the goals they achieve, in order to define planning and deductive operators and prototype objects. Their job is to fill the gap between a goal and a detailed plan, by defining several intermediate plans. This process is the reverse of the planning process. The user groups actions in the detailed plan and replaces them with higher level actions or goals. This way he implicitly defines planning operators. The system tries to correlate user decisions with previously defined operators. Similar operators are generalized under user supervision. In this cooperative generalization process, individual objects or resources are replaced by prototype objects. The process is repeatedly applied, the result being a hierarchy of planning operators and a hierarchy of prototype objects. In (12) we present some results in automatic generation of hierarchies of prototypes, from examples of individual object descriptions.

In the stage of interactive planning, the user and the system generate plans and define metaplanning operators. While trying to achieve a goal, the system indicates the planning operator it considers the best to be applied. The user is able to reject the operator in the favour of another one, from the knowledge base. In this case, the user and the system have to define a new metaplanning operator, or to modify an existing one, so that, in a future similar situation, the system apply the planning operator chosen by the user. The user can also indicate a planning operator which doesn't exist in the knowledge base. In this case, the system has to integrate the new operator in the knowledge base.

The adopted knowledge acquisition strategy is an intermediate one between that of defining knowledge base components by an expert and that of automatically generating knowledge base components from examples of plans.

REFERENCES

(1) Barr, A., Cohen, P., Feigenbaum, E., The Handbook of Artificial Intelligence (HeurisTech, Stanford, 1982).

(2) Benjamin, P. and Harrison, M., A production system for learning plans from an expert, in: Proc. National Conf. on Artificial Intelligence, pp. 22-26, Washington, D.C., August 1983.

(3) Daniel, L. and Tate, A., A Retrospective on the "Planning: a Joint AI/OR Approach" Project, DAI Working Paper 125,

Univ. of Edinburgh (October 1982).

(4) Erman, L.D., London, P.E. and Fickas, S.F., The design and an example use of Hearsay-III, in: Proc. 7th Int. Joint Conf. on Artificial Intelligence, pp. 409-415, Vancouver, August 1981.

(5) Fikes, R., Hart, P. and Nilsson, N., Learning and Executing Generalized Robot Plans, Technical Note 70, SRI International (July 1972).

(6) Kodratoff, Y. and Ganascia, J.G., Learning as a nondeterministic but exact logical process, in: Proc. Int. Machine Learning Workshop, Illinois, June 1983.

(7) Robinson, A. and Wilkins, D., An Interactive Planning System, Technical Note 245, SRI International (July 1981).

(8) Sotirescu, D.N. and Stefanescu, M., Report on the DM-LISP Interactive Programming System, Politechnical Institute of Bucharest (April 1981).

(9) Stefik, M., Planning and meta-planning, Artificial Intelligence 16(2), 1981, 141-169.

(10) Tate, A., Project Planning Using a Hierarchic Non-linear Planner, DAI Research Report 25, Univ. of Edinburgh (August 1976).

(11) Tecuci, G., Mânduţianu, D. and Voinea, S., A hierarchical system for robot programming, Comp. and Artificial Intelligence 2 (1983) 167-188.

(12) Tecuci, G., Learning Hierarchical Descriptions from Examples, Research Report AI-FD 27, Central Institute for Management and Informatics (February 1983).

(13) Tecuci, G., Robot learning and planning, in: Preprints Int. Conf. on Control Problems of Industrial Robots, Varna, October 1983.

(14) Vere, S., Inductive learning of relational productions, in: Waterman, D. and Hayes-Roth, F. (eds), Pattern-Directed Inference Systems (Academic, New York, 1978).

(15) Wilenski, R., Meta-planning, in: Proc. National Conf. on Artificial Intelligence, pp. 334-336, Stanford, August 1980.

(16) Wilkins, D., Domain-Independent Planning: Representation and Plan Generation, Technical Note 266R, SRI International (May 1983).

Artificial Intelligence and Information-Control Systems of Robots
I. Plander (editor)
© Elsevier Science Publishers B.V. (North-Holland), 1984

Area-Time Complexity for VLSI

Clark D. Thompson

Division of Computer Science
573 Evans Hall
U.C.Berkeley, CA 94720

A simplified model of VLSI computation is used to derive lower bounds on the area-time^2 [2] complexity of computation. Circuits for sorting and discrete Fourier transformation are proven to require area A and time T such that $AT^2 = \Omega(N^2 \lg^2 N)$.
Lower bounds on circuit area are also considered. This paper shows how lower bounds on circuit area can be obtained from AT^2 proofs.

1. MODEL OF VLSI COMPUTATION

In our formal model, we orient chips in the Cartesian plane. Labelling the axes l for length and w for width, we say that a chip is the L by W square defined by $0 \leq l \leq L$ and $0 \leq w \leq W$. The axes can be scaled so that at most k wires can be cut by any length-k segment in the plane of the chip, if $k > \mu$. Here μ is the small fixed constant representing the number of available wiring layers.

The area A of a chip is most naturally expressed as the product of its length L and width W. An alternative definition, considered briefly in Section 5, is to count only the area that is "occupied" by gates or wires. Our lower bounds are valid for either of these definitions of circuit area.

We introduce time T into our model as follows. A chip that has been in operation T time units is viewed as having swept out an area-time volume of L·W·T. That is, we add a third axis t to our Cartesian coordinate system in order to represent time [8]. The t-axis is scaled to correspond to the digital bandwidth available in the VLSI technology under consideration. One unit of time is just long enough to send one bit down a wire.

Achievable digital bandwidths currently range from a low of about 10^8 bits/second/wire (in CMOS) to a high of perhaps 10^{11} bits/second/wire (in IBM's Josephson junction Current Injection Logic [9]). Thus our unit of time for VLSI circuits is 10^{-8} to 10^{-11} seconds.

Considering, again, a length-k cut-segment in the plane of the chip: if this cut-segment remains in place for T time units, its information capacity is at most kT. This information capacity is numerically equal to the area of the surface swept out by the cut-segment in our area-time coordinate system.

Consider, now, a cut-surface perpendicular to the time axis. Such a cut separates a region of the chip at one time from itself, an instant later. The information flowing across this cut is the "state" of that region of the circuit. By the argument below, this information is upper-bounded by the area of the cut-surface. Thus, whether a cut-surface is perpendicular or parallel to the t-axis, the flow of information across that surface is bounded by the area of the surface.

Why do we assert that the storage capacity of a VLSI circuit is bounded by its area? The reason is that wires are the smallest features on a chip. Gates are formed of special types of wire crossings. For example, a metal wire over a polysilicon wire forms part of a MOS gate. There can be no more gates, and thus no more bits of state, than wire crossings.

Stating our information capacity assumption formally, we write

Assumption A-1. At most a bits of information can cross a rectangular cut-surface of area a, if the cut-surface is either parallel or perpendicular to the time axis, and if each dimension of the cut-surface is longer than the fixed constant μ.

(The reason we do not permit cut-surfaces to be skew to the time axis is that we are not sure how to bound information capacity in such cases. Without digging into the matter too deeply, it appears that the capacity of a skewed cut-surface of area a might be as much as $\sqrt{3}a$. Since we have no need of skewed cut-surfaces, we have chosen to define the scaling factors in the model as simply as possible.)

We now discuss circuit input and output, in order to define how information is produced and consumed in our model.

A circuit is said to perform a computation in a when- and where-oblivious [18] fashion if its input and output events occur at predetermined times and places, regardless of the input values being read. In this paper we ignore the more complex (and somewhat rarer) case of non-oblivious circuits.

We further restrict our attention to so-called semelective circuits [23] (coined from Latin: semel=once, lectus=read), in which each input bit is read exactly once. This restriction is almost universally observed in practice.

In a final idealization of the input/output behavior of real circuits, we associate each I/O event with a single point in the area-time coordinates of a circuit. Thus, the m-th bit of the n-th input word might be read at coordinate $(l_{n,m}, w_{n,m}, t_{n,m})$. Information about $x_{n,m}$ may then percolate throughout the chip as the computation proceeds.

Using Assumption A-1, we prove lower bounds on area and time by requiring that the circuit always produce the correct output values. This means that enough information must be present at the area-time coordinate of an output event to determine its value. As with inputs, we assume that output events are points in area-time space.

In actual practice, however, circuit inputs and outputs are not points in area-time. An input value is typically available for at least 10 time units, anywhere on an I/O pad of area 10^3 or 10^4. Similarly, a circuit must hold its output values stable over at least this much area-time volume. This obsevation does not invalidate our model. In fact, Assumption A-1 must hold a fortiori for I/O events because they have such little bandwidth per unit area.

Note that it is quite possible for an I/O event to occur in the plane of an area-time cut-surface, in some application of Assumption A-1. In such cases, we are justified in placing such events on either "side" of the cut-surface. Our reasoning is that, since the information involved in an I/O event must be constant over all points in a non-zero volume of area-time, Assumption A-1 must hold for any and all infinitesimal adjustments in the I/O events area-time coordinates.

Formally stating our assumption about when- and where-oblivious, semelective, pointcoordinate I/O, we write

Assumption A-2. Each input event $x_{n,m}$ is associated with a fixed point $(l_{n,m}, w_{n,m}, t_{n,m})$ in the area-time coordinates of a VLSI circuit. Output events are also points in area-time space. If any I/O events lie in the plane of a cut-surface, they may be assigned arbitrarily to either "side" of the plane: the information flow bound of Assumption A-1 must hold for any such assignment.

Note that our model assumptions do not require that information flow in the normal, forward-in-time, fashion. Indeed, an output event can occur before the input event that determines its value. Thus our model is intrinsically nondeterministic. We require only that our circuit's output "guesses" are proved correct, sooner or later, by information flowing from its inputs.

Our two assumptions are, however, strong enouht to prove tight lower bounds on area-time complexity. The following definitions and lemmas illustrate our proof technique.

Definition. A circuit has "temporal information flow" I if a cut-surface can be found, perpendicular to the t-axis, across which I bits must flow.

Lemma 1-1. The area A of any circuit with temporal information flow I must obey $A > I$.

Proof. The area A of the chip must be at least as large as the area of the cut-surface. By Assumption A-1, the cut-surface area is bounded from below by I. ▢

Definition. A circuit has "cross-chip information flow" I if two cut-surfaces can be found, one perpendicular to the l-axis and one perpendicular to the w-axis, across which I bits must flow.

Lemma 1-2. $AT^2 \geq I^2$ for any circuit with cross-chip information flow I.

Proof. Consider the cut-surface perpendicular to the l-axis. It has area at most WT and thus, by Assumption A-1, $WT \geq I$. Similarly, $LT \geq I$. Multiplying the two inequalities together, we obtain the Lemma. ▢

2. NOTATION

The following letters have special meaning:

A - circuit area, see § 1; B - the matrix defining a discrete Fourier transform, see § 4; L - circuit length, see § 1; μ - number of layers of wiring, see § 1; M - the number of bits in an input word, see § 3; N - the number of words of input, see § 3; q - the modulus of the arithmetic operations for the DFT, see § 4; T - circuit time, see § 1; W circuit width, see § 1; X - the vector of random input bits, see § 3 and § 4; $\check{X}$ - a particular value for X; $x_{n,m}$ - the m-th least-significant bit of the n-th input word, see § 3 and §4; Y - the vector of output bits, see § 3 and § 4; $\check{Y}$ - a paricular value for Y; and $y_{n,m}$ - the m-th least-significant bit of the n-th output word, see § 3 and § 4.

In addition, we use the following standard functional notation.

"probability distribution" for a discrete random variable X, Pr[X = $\check{X}$], constrained by

$$(\forall \check{X} \; 0 \leq Pr[X = \check{X}] \leq 1) \text{ and } (\sum_{\check{X}} Pr[X = \check{X}] = 1)$$

"entropy of X":

$$H(X) = \sum_{\check{X}} - Pr[X = \check{X}] \lg Pr[X = \check{X}]$$

"worst-case entropy of X":

$$H_W(X) = \lg \left| \{ \check{X} : Pr[X = \check{X}] > 0 \} \right|$$

The entropy function H(X) can be interpreted as the average length of a description of an event in X. The worst-case entropy function $H_W(X)$ is, by contrast, the length of the longest descriptor for an event in X. The latter definition is more useful for our purposes, since we study circuits with when-oblivious I/O. Hence we seek worst-case bounds on information and time.

3. LOWER BOUNDS FOR SORTING

The problem of sorting is to arrange a sequence of input values into increasing order. We assume that the inputs are expressed as M-bit integers, that 2^M grows proportionately with the number N of inputs, and that each input bit position actually represents one bit of (worst-case) information. More formally, we assume:

Definition S-1: The input to a sorting circuit is a vector X of NM boolean variables $x_{n,m} \in \{0,1\}$ for $1 \leq n \leq N$, $1 \leq m \leq M$. Each value of X is possible: $Pr(X = \check{X}) > 0$.

Definition S-2. $M \geq (1+\epsilon) \lg N$, for some fixed $\epsilon > 0$.

Definition S-3. The inputs X are interpreted as N words of M bits, encoded in straight binary. We refer to the n-th word as $x_{n,*}$; its value is given by

$$x_{n,*} = \sum_m x_{n,m} 2^{M-m}$$

Let $\mathcal{T}$ be any permutation of $\{1, 2, \ldots, N\}$ that brings the $x_{n,*}$ into nondecreasing order: $x_{\mathcal{T}(n),*} \leq x_{\mathcal{T}(n+1),*}$, for $1 \leq n < N$. Then the value of each bit in the output vector Y is defined by $y_{n,m} = x_{\mathcal{T}(n),m}$.

Definitions S-1 and S-2 can be used to express the entropy of the input vector as a function of N alone:

$$H(X) \geq (1 + \epsilon)(N \lg N)$$

We do not know whether definition S-2 is strictly necessary to prove strong lower bounds on the sorting problem. However, we have found counterexamples to our lower bound theorems if $M < .5 \lg N$. It seems that, if M is too small, the sorting problem reduces to a much easier "counting problem." This issue is discussed again at the end of this section.

We need to make one more definition before proving our first AT^2 theorem:

Definition. A chip has "bit-serial I/O" if all M bits of each input word $x_{n,*}$ enter the chip at the same place (l_n, w_n). Similarly, one place is associated with each output word $y_{n,m}$.

Note that the time $t_{n,m}$ at a bit-serial circuit receives the m-th bit of input $x_{n,*}$ is, in general, distinct from the time at which it gets the $(m+1)$st bit of this word. For lack of space the following theorem, and the subsequent ones, are presented without proofs.

Theorem 3-1. $AT^2 = \Omega(N^2 \lg^2 N)$ for any sorting chip with bit-serial I/O.

For sorting chips not obeying the bit-serial I/O restriction, we offer the following theorem due to Vuillemin [31].

Theorem 3-2. $AT^2 = \Omega(N^2)$ for any chip sorting N numbers.

To prove the above theorem we have to take advantage of the fact that our cut-surface was perpendicular to the time axis. Thus we demonstrate there is a temporal information flow of N/2 bits, as needed to apply Lemma 1-1:

Theorem 3-3. $A = \Omega(N)$ for any chip sorting N numbers.

Unfortunately, Lemma 1-1 does not apply to the $\Omega(N \lg N)$ information flow observed in the proof of Theorem 3-1. For that flow, it was important that all the bits of each input word lie on one side or the other of a cut-surface. The bit-serial I/O assumption was designed to assure that this is the case.

This suggests an interesting question: Is the bit-serial I/O assumption necessary to prove an $\Omega(N \lg N)$ information flow? If not then $AT^2 = \Omega(N \lg N)$ for unrestricted inputs, as well as $A = \Omega(N$

lg N). A sketch of these results was recently shown the author by Tom Leighton of M.I.T. [16]. The only defect of Leighton's proof technique is that it probably requires word lengths M of at least 4 lg N.

Thus an open question remains: What is the minimum word length for which the AT^2 complexity of sorting is $\Omega(N \lg N)$? The interesting range of word length is between .5 lg N and lg N, since sorting is certainly "easy" when $M \leq .5 \lg N$:

Theorem 3-4. A circuit can be built to sort N m-bit words, using area $A = O(NM)$ and time $T = O(2^M \lg N)$.

4. DISCRETE FOURIER TRANSFORMATION

The discrete Fourier transform (or DFT) on N elements, computed over a finite ring of modulus q, can be defined in the following fashion. Note the similarities to our definition of the sorting problem.

Definition D-1. The input to a DFT circuit is a vector X of NM boolean variables $x_{n,m} \in \{0,1\}$ for $1 \leq n \leq N$, $1 \leq m \leq M$. Each value of X is possible: $\Pr(X = \check{X}) > 0$.

Definition D-2. $M = \lceil \lg q \rceil$. Also, the prime factorization $p_1^{r_1} p_2^{r_2} \ldots, p_k^{r_k}$ of the ring modulus q must be such that N is evenly divisible by the least common divisor of $p_1 - 1$, $p_2 - 1, \ldots, p_k - 1$.

Definition D-3. Elements of the ring are coded as binary integers from the set $\{0, 1, \ldots, q - 1\}$. Ring multiplication and addition are then performed as integer multiplication and addition modulo q. Writing $x_{n,*}$ for the value of the n-th input word,

$$x_{n,*} = \sum_m x_{n,m} 2^{M-m}$$

and, similarly, writing $y_{n,*}$ for the n-th output word, the DFT is a simple matrix-vector multiplication $Y = BX$. The ij-th element of the matrix B is defined by

$$B[i,j] = \sqrt[N]{1}^{ij}$$

The restriction on q's factorization in Definition D-2 is necessary and sufficient to ensure that $\sqrt[N]{1}$ and N^{-1} exist in the ring. The matrix B is thus well-defined, and our DFT has the usual properties of invertibility, orthogonality, and cyclic convolvability [2].

Definition D-2 also implies that $q > N$, and thus that $M \geq \lceil \lg N \rceil$. As in the sorting problem, the entropy of the input vector is $H_w(X) = \Omega(N \lg N)$.

We approach our AT^2 theorem by means of the following lemma.

Lemma 4-1. [30], [28]. Let B_R be the square submatrix formed by selecting the first $\lfloor N/2 \rfloor$ rows and any $\lfloor N/2 \rfloor$ columns of the matrix

B of Definition D-3. If the ring modulus q is prime, then B_R is invertible.

Theorem 4-2. [24] . $AT^2 = \Omega(N^2 \lg^2 N)$ for the bit-serial computation of the DFT.

We do not know of any lower bound on information flow in a DFT computation that does not assume the inputs are presented in bit-serial fashion. However, Theorem 4-2 is strong enough to prove the following result:

Corollary 4-3. [25] . The area of a shuffle-exchange graph is bounded from below by $A = \Omega(N^2/\lg^2 N)$.

5. CONCLUSION

In this paper, we have shown that the finite width and bandwidth of wires in VLSI circuits imply lower bounds on area and on the area-time^2 product. Using the bit-serial I/O assumption, we were able to prove that $AT^2 = \Omega(N^2 \log^2 N)$ for both sorting and Fourier transformation. These bounds are tight, since circuits can be constructed to match this performance [26, 27]. Some of these circuits occupy only $O(N \lg N)$ area, showing that a lower bound of $A = \Omega(N \lg N)$ would be the best-possible result for these problems. Unfortunately, no such lower bounds are available in the published literature.

We are also unable to prove that $AT^2 = \Omega(N^2 \lg^2 N)$ for circuits which don't employ bit-serial I/O. Tom Leighton appears to have proved this theorem for the sorting problem [16]. Using the techniques of this paper, a simple corollary of Leighton's proof is that all sorting circuits have $A = \Omega(N \lg N)$. We conjecture that analogous bounds could be obtained for Fourier transformation.

Another open problem, mentioned in Section 4, is to understand the effect of word length on the area-time complexity of sorting. Word lengths between $(\lg N)/2$ and $(\lg N)$ bits are the most interesting. Circuits based on an enumeration strategy [20] work well on shorter words, and we have reasonably-tight bounds for longer words.

Research could of course be done to determine the area-time complexity of problems other than sorting and Fourier transformation. Ullman's recent book [29] is a good summary of the current state-of-the-art in VLSI complexity theory. In brief, tight or nearly-tight bounds have been proven for integer arithmetic, [1, 5, 32, 12] matrix multiplication, [31, 23, 4] boolean predicates and language recognition problems, [6, 18, 22] as well as for transitive closure and other graph-theoretic calculations [10, 11].

Another research direction is to determine the effect of varying model assumptions. For example, one might assume that information is transmitted at a maximum velocity, [7] that the circuit is allowed to have some forms of nondeterministic or random behavior, [19, 3] that circuits are three-dimensional, [21] or that circuit I/O is not semelective [13]. Also, one might consider different parameters of circuit performance, such as "occupied area" [25] or energy consumption [17, 14].

We can immediately extend the results of this paper in a couple of the directions mentioned above. Bounds on volume-time complexity can be obtained in a fashion analogous to the AT^2 proofs. We introduce a fourth spatial coordinate h, for height, to our area-time system. (This model will only be appropriate when the height H of a chip is allowed to grow with the size of the problem.) Assuming that wires have a finite cross-sectional area, the information capacity of a space-time cut is proportional to the volume of the cut. Now we observe that the cross-chip information flow of our proofs will occur across three surfaces, one perpendicular to each **of** the three spatial axes. We then write three inequalities: $HLT \geq I$, $HWT \geq I$, $LWT \geq I$. Multiplying the three together we find that $V^2T^3 \geq I^3$, where V is the volume of the chip.

A second extension is to a different notion of circuit area. The "bounding rectangle" definition of area used in this paper is something of an overstimate of the actual amount of wires and gates required by a circuit. A circuit with a nonconvex perimeter could have an arbitrarily small ratio between its "occupied area" A_O and its "bounding rectangle" A. This objection to our definition of A is, however, not of fundamental importance. Any circuit with holes or a nonconvex perimeter can be warped into a rectangular shape, stretching its wires only by an additive constant factor proportional to the size of the largest unwarpable "feature" of the chip. Thus, up to constant factors, nonconvex and hole-y circuits have no speed or area advantage. Rectangular (or even square) circuits are sufficiently general to cover the VLSI design space.

REFERENCES

[1] H. Abelson and P. Andreae, "Information Transfer and Area-Time Tradeoffs for VLSI Multiplication," Comm. ACM, vol. 23, no.1, pp. 20-23, January 1980.

[2] Ramesh C. Agarwal and Sidney C. Burrus, "Number Theoretic Transforms to Implement Fast Digital Convolutions," Proc. IEEE, vol. 63, no. 4, pp. 550-560, April 1975.

[3] A. V. Aho, J. D. Ullman, and M. Yannakakis, "On Notions of Information Transfer in VLSI Circuits," in Proc. 15th Annual ACM Symp. on Theory of Computing, pp. 133-139, April 1983.

[4] Dana Angluin, "VLSI: On the Merits of Batching," unpublished manuscript, Yale University, April 1982.

[5] R. Brent and H. T. Kung, "The Area-Time Complexity of Binary Multiplication," JACM, vol 28, no.3, pp. 521-534, July 1981.

[6] R. P. Brent and L. Goldshlager, "Some Area-Time Tradeoffs for VLSI," SIAM J. Comput., vol. 11, no. 4, pp. 737-747, November 1982.

[7] B. Chazelle and L. Monier, "Towards More Realistic Models of Computation for VLSI", in Proc. 11th Annual ACM Symp. on Theory of Computing, pp. 209-213, April 1979.

[8] Abbas El Gamal and King F. Pang, "VLSI Complexity of Functions with Certain Local Properties," extended abstract, November 1983.

[9] T.R. Gheewala, "Design of 2.5-Micrometer Josephson Current Injection Logic (CIL)," IBM J. Res. Develop., vol. 24, no. 2, pp. 130-142, March 1980.

[10] Susanne E. Hambrusch and Janos Simon, "Solving Undirected Graph Problems on VLSI," CS-81-23, Computer Science Dept., Pennsylvania State Univ., Univ. Park, PA 16802, December 1981.

[11] J. Ja'Ja', "The VLSI Complexity of Graph Problems," CS-81-25, Computer Science Dept., Pennsylvania State Univ., Univ. Park, PA 16802, October 1981.

[12] J. Ja'Ja' and V.K. Prasanna Kumar, "Information Transfer in Distributed Computing with Applications to VLSI," CS-82-17, Computer Science Dept., Pennsylvania State Univ., Univ. Park, PA 16802, August 1982.

[13] Zvi M. Kedem and Alessandro Zorat, "Replication of Inputs May Save Computational Resources in VLSI," in Proc. 22nd Symp. on the Foundations of Computer Science, IEEE Computer Society, October 1981.

[14] Gloria Kissin, "Measuring Energy Consumption in VLSI Circuits: a Foundation," in Proc. 14th Annual ACM Symp. on Theory of Computing, pp. 99-104, May 1982.

[15] F. T. Leighton, "Layouts for the Shuffle-Exchange Graph and Lower Bound Techniques for VLSI," Ph. D. Dissertation, MIT/LCS/TR-724, M.I.T. Lab for Computer Science, June 1982.

[16] F. T. Leighton, private communication, November 1983.

[17] Thomas Lengauer and Kurt Mehlhorn, "On the Complexity of VLSI Computations", in VLSI Systems and Computations, ed. H.T. Kung, Bob Sproull, Guy Steele, pp. 89-99, Computer Science Press, October 1981.

[18] Richard J. Lipton and Robert Sedgewick, "Lower Bounds for VLSI," in Proc. 13th Annual ACM Symp. on Theory of Computing, pp. 300-307, May 1981.

[19] Kurt Mehlhorn and Erik M. Schmidt, "Las Vegas is better than Determinism in VLSI," in Proc. 14th Annual ACM Symp. on Theory of Computing, pp. 330-337, May 1982.

[20] D.E. Muller and F.P. Preparata, "Bounds to Complexities of Networks for Sorting and for Switching," JACM, vol. 22, no. 2, pp. 195-201, April 1975.

[21] Arnold L. Rosenberg, "Three-Dimensional VLSI, I: a case study," in VLSI Systems and Computations, ed. H.T. Kung, Bob Sproull, Guy Steele, pp. 69-79, October 1981.

[22] J. Savage, "Planar Circuit Complexity and the Performance of VLSI Algorithms," in VLSI Systems and Computations, ed. H.T. Kung, Bob Sproull, Guy Steele, pp. 61-68, Computer Science Press, October 1981.

[23] J. Savage, "Area-Time Tradeoffs for Matrix Multiplication and Related Problems in VLSI Models," Journal of Comput. and Syst. Sci., vol. 22, no.2, pp. 230-242, April 1981.

[24] James B. Saxe, private communication, October 1978.

[25] C.D. Thompson, "A Complexity Theory for VLSI," Ph.D. Dissertation, CMU-CS-80-140, Computer Science Dept., Carnegie-Mellon University, August 1980.

[26] C.D. Thompson, "Fourier Transforms in VLSI," IEEE Trans. Comput., October 1983.

[27] C.D. Thompson, "The VLSI Complexity of Sorting," IEEE Trans. Comput., December 1983.

[28] Martin Tompa, "Time-Space Tradeoffs for Computing Functions, Using Connectivity Properties of Their Circuits," in Proc. 10th Annual ACM Symp. on Theory of Computing, pp. 196-204, May 1978.

[29] J. Ullman, Computational Aspects of VLSI, Computer Science Press, 1984.

[30] Leslie G. Valiant, "Graph-Theoretic Properties in Computational Complexity", Journal of Computation and Systems Sciences, vol. 13, pp. 278-285, 1976.

[31] J. Vuillemin, "A Combinational Limit to the Computing Power of VLSI Circuits," IEEE Trans. Comput., vol. C-32, no. 3, pp. 294-300, March 1983.

[32] A.C. Yao, "The Entropic Limits of VLSI Computations," in Proc. 13th Annual ACM Symp. on Theory of Computing, pp. 308-311, May 1981.

A FAST SVD IMAGE RESTORATION ON AN ASSOCIATIVE PARALLEL COMPUTER

Marián Vajteršic

Institute of Technical Cybernetics
Slovak Academy of Sciences
84237 Bratislava, Dúbravská 9
Czechoslovakia

The paper presents a fast parallel algorithm for the restoration of images using the singular value decomposition /SVD/ method. The algorithm proposed is advantageous for implementation on an associative computer of the SIMD type. The blur matrix of order N is decomposed by orthogonal rotations in only $O(N)$ parallel steps and the restored image is obtained in $O(\log N)$ additional operations, using N^2 processors.

INTRODUCTION

With the advent of parallel computers /e.g. STARAN, ICL DAP, MPP/, algebraic approaches in image processing become attractive for practical computation. In digital image processing, the restoration represents one of most computer time and space consuming problems. To restore the ideal image, rather complicated mathematical computations are performed on a measured image field in order to remove the influence of degradation in an imaging system. One of the effective direct restoration approaches uses the SVD decomposition of the degradation matrix [1]. The major limitation of using this method is a computational one. Even if the matrix is circulant and the Fast Fourier Transform can be used, the sequential computational complexity is $O(N^2 \log N)$. Generally, for a real NxN matrix the sequential SVD requires $O(N^3)$ operations. Therefore, growing attention is paid to parallel methods. Most recently, parallel algorithms for VLSI structures have been developed [2].

In this paper, a fast parallel SVD algorithm is presented as a crucial block within a restoration algorithm for an associative SIMD computer. The restoration principle is described in the next section. The parallel SVD algorithm is presented in section 3. The algorithm is of Jacobi-type, where the matrix is diagonalized by rotations from both of its sides. An efficient ordering of rotations is proposed where each row and column is rotated in each of N iterations exactly once. The algorithm is formulated for the parallel associative computer in section 4. It is shown that only one fast re-ordering of data by the permutation network is required in each iteration. Since each iteration is obtained with N^2 processors in a constant number of arithmetical steps, the total complexity $O(N)$ has been achieved.

THE SVD IMAGE RESTORATION PRINCIPLE

The imaging model in a discretized form can be expressed by
$$g = Bf + n \qquad (1)$$
where B is NxN blur matrix, g contains the

measured values of the image f and n is the additional noise. The SVD concept to restore f from (1) is based on the decomposition

$$B = UDV^T \qquad (2)$$

where the matrices U and V are each orthogonal and D is a diagonal matrix. The columns u_i and v_i of NxN matrices U and V are respectively left and right singular vectors and elements $d(1) \geq d(2) \geq ... \geq d(N) \geq 0$ of D are singular values of B. Since $UU^T = VV^T$ the generalized inverse $\tilde{B}$ of B is

$$\tilde{B} = VD^{-1}U^T = \sum_{i=1}^{r} d(i)^{-1} v_i u_i^T \qquad (3)$$

where r is the rank of B. Hence, the restored image $\tilde{f}$ can be obtained by

$$\tilde{f} = \tilde{B}g = VD^{-1}U^T g = \sum_{i=1}^{r} (d(i))^{-1} (u_i^T g) v_i . \qquad (4)$$

THE PARALLEL SVD ALGORITHM

Our attention will be focused on the two-by two SVD procedure [3], which can be parallelized efficiently. In this method, the rotation matrices J_{pq}^L and J_{pq}^R are formed in order to annihilate elements b_{pq}, b_{qp} ($p<q$) of the matrix B. Both matrices are the same as the identity ones, except the elements c_{pq}^L, c_{pq}^R (in both positions $(p,p),(q,q)$), s_{pq}^L, s_{pq}^R (in the position (p,q)) and $-s_{pq}^L$, $-s_{pq}^R$ (position (q,p)). These elements can be evaluated as follows [2]:

for i = 1,2 do
  if i = 1 then a: = $b_{qq} - b_{pp}$, b: = $b_{pq} + b_{qp}$
            else a: = $b_{qq} + b_{pp}$, b: = $b_{qp} - b_{pq}$
  r: = a/b
  s: = $\text{sign}(r)/(|r| + \sqrt{1+r^2})$ (5)
  t(i): = $1/\sqrt{1+s^2}$, u(i): = t(i)s

$$c_{pq}^L := t(1)t(2) + u(1)u(2), \quad s_{pq}^L := u(1)t(2) - t(1)u(2) \qquad (6)$$

$$c_{pq}^R := t(1)t(2) - u(1)u(2), \quad s_{pq}^R := u(1)t(2) + t(1)u(2). \qquad (7)$$

The corresponding rotation of the matrix B is $(J_{pq}^L)^T B J_{pq}^R$, i.e. only its rows $\bar{b}_p$, $\bar{b}_q$ and columns b_p, b_q are transformed by

$$\bar{b}_p := c_{pq}^L \bar{b}_p - s_{pq}^L \bar{b}_q , \quad \bar{b}_q := s_{pq}^L \bar{b}_p + c_{pq}^L \bar{b}_q \qquad (8)$$

$$b_p := c_{pq}^R b_p - s_{pq}^R b_q , \quad b_q := s_{pq}^R b_p + c_{pq}^R b_q \qquad (9)$$

The columns u_i and v_i of U and V are transformed analogically by

$$u_p := c_{pq}^L u_p - s_{pq}^L u_q , \quad u_q := s_{pq}^L u_p + c_{pq}^L u_q \qquad (10)$$

$$v_p := c_{pq}^R v_p - s_{pq}^R v_q , \quad v_q := s_{pq}^R v_p + c_{pq}^R v_q . \qquad (11)$$

In the annihilation process, the transformations (8),(9) are performed for all pairs (p,q), $p,q=1,...,N$ $p \neq q$. It has been observed in [4] that some of these N(N-1) rotations can be computed concurrently. The most effective parallel computational scheme for N^2 processors consists in dividing these rotations into N-1 phases where in each of them all N rows and columns are rotated once. The following ordering schema ORD with these characteristics can be proposed for N=4

$$\begin{array}{llll}(1,2) & (2,1) & (3,4) & (4,3)\\ (1,4) & (2,3) & (3,2) & (4,1)\\ (1,3) & (2,4) & (3,1) & (4,2)\end{array} \qquad (12)$$

where the pairs (p,q) in its i-th row (i=1,2,3) denote the pairs of numbers of rows /columns/ of the matrix which are rotated in i-th phase concurrently. Parallel execution of rotations in the i-th row of the scheme can be expressed by $(J_i^L)^T B J_i^R$, where the matrices J_i are direct sums of matrices J_{pq} corresponding to this row. Hence, one sweep of the diagonalization process is $(J_1^L J_2^L \ldots J_N^L)^T$. $B.(J_1^R J_2^R \ldots J_N^R)$ where N is the order of B. Then one sweep of evaluating the matrices U and V is respectively $UJ_1^L J_2^L \ldots J_N^L$ and $VJ_1^R J_2^R \ldots J_N^R$ whereby at the beginning of the orthogonalization U=V=I. The rotation sweeps are computer for a given $\epsilon > 0$ until

$$\sum_{i \neq j} b_{ij} < \epsilon . \qquad (13)$$

THE RESTORATION ALGORITHM FOR AN ASSOCIATIVE PROCESSOR

In this section, the fast SVD image restoration algorithm for an associative parallel computer of the SIMD type will be formulated. To give the explanation of the algorithm, a detailed architectural characterization of the computer system under consideration[5] may be omitted here. We assume only that it is composed of one or more associative modules, each of them containg an orthogonal memory block. One elementary processor capable of performing operations in a bit-serial manner is assigned to each word of the memory. The fields of the memory are assumed to be a lenght of $N^2 = 2^{2n}$ (and hence, each of them is compossed of N blocks of a lenght $N=2^n$). Then parallel execution of an arithmetic-logical operation O over data located in corresponding words of fields P and Q can be denoted by $F \leftarrow P \circ Q(M)$ where M is a mask and F is a field of results.

The interconnection network allows fast permutation of data in order to support parallel computations. Our aim is to use only permutations with a pameter which is a power of 2 because such regular re-orderings of data can be realized by the permutation network in one step only. The cyclic shift of a field P with a parameter 2^i within its blocks of a lenght 2^p ($0 \leq i < p \leq 2n$) will be denoted by $P(2^i, 2^p)$. As an example, the following scheme represents $P(2^2, 2^3)$ where P contains indexes ij, i,j=1,...,4:

P: 11 12 13 14 21 22 23 24 31 32 33 34 41 42 43 44

$P(2^2,2^3)$: 21 22 23 24 11 12 13 14 41 42 43 44 31 32 33 34.   (14)

Considering the elements of P devided by the first index i into 4 blocks (denoted by 1-4), 14 corresponds to the first row of the example (12) of the ordering scheme ORD. Denoting an i-th permutation of P /corresponding to i-th row of ORD/ as P[i], the scheme (12) can be expressed by

$$P = P[0] \xrightarrow[0]{} P[1] \xrightarrow[1]{} P[2] \xrightarrow[0]{} P[3]$$

where a number between $P[l]$ and $P[l+1]$, $l=0,1,2$ represents a value of the parameter j, for which holds $P[l+1] = P[l](2^{n+j}, 2^{n+j+1})$. Thus, the permutations corresponding to the scheme ORD can be represented for arbitrary $N=2^n$ as a string of numbers. To make this ordering more transparent, for $N=16$ the following permutation parameters are obtained

       0 1 0 2 0 1 0 4 0 1 0 2 0 1 0

We note that the permutation scheme ORD can be adapted in the same manner also for fields with N elements only. The algorithm uses a mask M which can be represented as a row-wise ordered identity matrix I and a mask $\bar{M}$ which is complementary to M. Then the algorithm can be formulated for $N=2^n$ in main programming blocks A and B as follows:
begin
/A. The SVD reduction block/
 Input fields: PR1, PRC1, PR2, PRC2 - row-wise located matrix B
              PU1, PU2, PV1, PV2 - row-wise located matrix I
              EPSILON - value of ε located in each word of the
                        field
 Output fields: PR1 - the eigenvalues $d(i)$ located in $(i+N(i-1))$-th positions
               PU1,PV1 - the matrices U and V respectively ordered
                         column-wise
PR1← B, PRC1← B, PR2←B, PRC2←B /a row-wise location of B/
PU1← I, PU2← I, PV1← I, PV2← I, M← I /a row-wise location of I/
S:for $j=1,2,\ldots,N-1$
  P1← 0, P2← 0, P3← 0, P4← 0
  PRC1← PRC1[i] /i-th permutation of PRC1 by ORD within blocks/
  PR2← PR2[i]   /i-th permutation of PR2 by ORD/
  PRC2← PRC2[i] /i-th permutation of PRC2 by ORD/
  PRC2← PRC2[i] /i-th permutation of PRC2 by ORD within blocks/
  PU2← PU2[i], PV2← PV2[i] /i-th permutation of PU2 and PV2 by ORD/
  P1← PR1(M), P2← PRC1(M), P3← PR2(M), P4← PRC2(M)
  for $j=0,1,\ldots,n-1$
   P1← P1 + P1($2^j,2^{j+1}$), P4← P4 + P4($2^j,2^{j+1}$) /spread of b_{pp} and b_{qq}/
   P2← P2 + P2($2^j,2^{j+1}$), P3← P3 + P3($2^j,2^{j+1}$)/spread of b_{pq} and b_{qp}/
  P5← P4 - P1 /$a=b_{qq}-b_{pp}$ and $(-a)$ in p-th and q-th blocks/
  P6← P2 + P3 /$b=b_{pq}+b_{qp}$ in each word of p-th and q-th blocks/
  evaluation of respectively $t(1)$ and $\pm u(1)$ in P5 and P6 according
  to (5)
  P7← P1 + P4 /$a=b_{pp}+b_{qq}$ in p-th and q-th blocks/
  P8← P3 - P2 /$b=b_{qp}-b_{pq}$ and $(-b)$ in p-th and q-th blocks/
  evaluation of respectively $t(2)$ and $\pm u(2)$ values in P8 and P9
  according to (5)
  P9← P6 . P8, P10← P6 . P7, P6← P5 . P8, P8← P5 . P7
  P5← P8 + P9, P7← P10 - P6 /evaluation of (6) /
  P8← P8 - P9, P10← P10 + P6 /evaluation of (7) /
  P6← P5 . PR1, P9← P7 . PR2, PR1← P6 - P9 ⎫
  P6← P5 . PR2, P9← P7 . PR1, PR2← P6 + P9 ⎬ transformation of
  P6← P5 . PRC1, P9← P7 . PRC2, PRC1← P6 - P9 ⎬ PR1,PR2,PRC1 and
  P6← P5 . PRC2, P9← P7 . PRC1, PRC2← P6 + P9 ⎭ PRC2 according to (8)
  P6← P5 . PU1, P9← P7 . PU2, PU1← P6 - P9 ⎫ transformation of co-
  P6← P5 . PU2, P9← P7 . PU1, PU2← P6 + P9 ⎭ lumns of U by (10)
  P6← P8 . PV1, P9← P10 . PV2, PV1← P6 - P9 ⎫ transformation of co-
  P6← P8 . PV2, P9← P10 . PV1, PV2← P6 + P9 ⎭ lumns of V by (11)
  P8← O($\bar{M}$), P10← O($\bar{M}$)

```
    for j=0,1,...,n-1
      P8 ← P8 + P8(2^(n+j), 2^(n+j+1)),  P10 ← P10 + P10(2^(n+j), 2^(n+j+1))
                                                  (spread of c_pq^R and ±s_pq^R )
    P6 ← P8 . PR1,  P9 ← P10 . PRC1,  PR1 ← P6 - P9  ⎫(transformation
    P6 ← P8 . PRC1, P9 ← P10 . PR1,   PRC1 ← P6 + P9 ⎬ of PR1,PRC1,PR2,
    P6 ← P8 . PR2,  P9 ← P10 . PRC2,  PR2 ← P6 - P9  ⎪ PRC2 according to
    P6 ← P8 . PRC2, P9 ← P10 . PR2,   PRC2 ← P6 + P9 ⎭ (9))
    P5 ← PR1,  P5 ← O(M)                      ⎫
    for j=0,1,...,n-1                         ⎪
      P5 ← P5 + P5(2^j,2^(j+1))               ⎪
    for j=0,1,...,n-1                         ⎬ (criterion (13))
      P5 ← P5 + P5(2^(n+j),2^(n+j+1))         ⎪
    if P5 > EPSILON go to S                   ⎭
  /B. The restoration block/
  Input fields: PR1,PU1,PV1-from the programming block A
                PG-values of the measured image g located in each
                   its block
  Output field: PF-values of the restored image f̃ located in each
                   its block
    P1 ← O,  P1 ← PR1(M)
    P2 ← PU1 . PG
    for j=0,1,...,n-1
      P1 ← P1 + P1(2^j,2^(j+1))
      P2 ← P2 + P2(2^j,2^(j+1))
    PF ← P2/P1
    for j=0,1,...,n-1
      PF ← PF + PF(2^(n+j),2^(n+j+1))         (evaluation of (4))
end.
```

The number of arithmetical operations is constant within the loop
for i. Due to the theoretical observations [4,2], the number of
sweeps /i.e. the number of jumps to the label S/ is also constant.
Hence, the number of parallel operations is $O(N)$ for block A. The
restoration block requires $O(\log N)$ operations. Thus, the total number of parallel arithmetical steps of the algorithm is $O(N)$ only.
We note that for the efficient realization of data permutations and
the two-side orthogonalization procedure, some redundant arithmetical operations are introduced /evaluation of PR2,PRC1,PRC2,PU2,PV2/
which do not increase the $O(N)$ estimation. Due to the efficient ordering ORD, within each orthogonalization phase only one permutation
cycle is performed. Moreover, it has been achieved using "a power
of 2" permutations only, which are simply realizable on the considered associative computer. The other advantage of this algorithm
consists in the fact that despite the row-wise ordering of B in PR1,
PR2,PRC1,PRC2, the right-hand side transformation (9) can be done
without transpositions of them. Thus, $O(N)$ matrix transposes are saved in each sweep.

REFERENCES

[1] Pratt,W.K., Digital Image Processing /J.Wiley and Sons, New York, 1978/.
[2] Brent,R.P., Luk,F.T and Loan,Ch.V., Computation of the singular value decomposition using mesh-connected processors, Techn.Rep. 82-528, Dept. of Comp. Sc., Cornell Univ. /March 1983/.
[3] Forsythe,G.E. and Henrici,P., The cyclic Jacobi method for computing the principal values of a complex matrix, Trans.Amer.Math. Soc. 94 /1960/ 1-23.
[4] Sameh,A.H., On Jacobi and Jacobi-like algorithms for a parallel computer, Math.Comput 25 /1971/, 579-590.
[5] Richter,K., Parallel computer system SIMD, in: This Proceedings.

Artificial Intelligence and Information-Control Systems of Robots
I. Plander (editor)
© Elsevier Science Publishers B.V. (North-Holland), 1984

DEDICATED NUMERICAL COPROCESSOR FOR MATRIX HANDLING
THROUGHPUT ENHANCEMENT

Karel Vlček

TESLA Valašské Meziříčí k. p.
757 63 Valašské Meziříčí, Hemy 2
Czechoslovakia

Unraveling of a dedicated Numerical Coprocessor design takes
its bearing towards modern high throughput signal processors.
The hardware requirements of the fixed point as well as the
floating point arithmetics are compared. The discrete control
marginal tasks are emphasized on the matrix multiplication
and the transcendental function values calculation. The amount
of necessary hardware for the implementation of the discrete
control is evaluated.
The architecture of the Numerical Coprocessor is dedicated to
the Digital Dynamic Control and Digital Signal Processing.
The function of the processor can be changed with a multimode
control word. A basic pipeline structure is fitted by programm-
ably operating registers and a flexible data path. The Coprocessor is compatible with both 8-bit and 16-bit microcomputers
by means of the programmable data interface.

INTRODUCTION

Many recent advances in the implementation of the digital signal processing /DSP/
is refered in [1] . A lot of authors were inspired to take advantages of signal
microprocessors or other supporting digital signal processing LSI for the implementation of the digital dynamic control /DDC/ [3] , [4] , [5] . The outstanding study [2] deals with similarities and differences in philosophy, goals, and analytical
techniques of the both mentioned branches of the discrete signal applications.

In DSP the most important problem is the design of an *implementable* system meeting
given frequency or time responses. The reguest of short computation time and the
necessity to process a wide data word have a considerable influence upon architecture and performance of the processor. This attention is motivated by the need for
extremely efficient systems to perform complex signal processing tasks at very high
data rates.

In DDC the emphasis has been pointed far less on implementation and more on developing methods for *determining* system design specifications.

In DSP one is interested in the issue of implementation of a system with a specified *input-output behavior*. On the other hand the DDC issue of implementation is
not considered up to nearly the same extent. We can see some fundamental differences in the two disciplines. The important role is played by the *state-space model*
for a given physical system.

STATE-SPACE MODEL CONTRIBUTION

It will be shown the digital filter can be dessigned by both the input-output and
the state-spece techniques. In the first case we obtain /by factoring a transfer

function/ a well known product of lower order transfer functions.

$$H(z) = \frac{(1 + bz^{-1})(1 + dz^{-1})}{(1 - az^{-1})(1 - cz^{-1})} \tag{1}$$

The overall filter is minimal. The state-space model technique gives on variety minimal forms

$$x(k+1) = \begin{bmatrix} f_{11} & f_{12} \\ f_{21} & f_{22} \end{bmatrix} x(k) + \begin{bmatrix} g_1 \\ g_2 \end{bmatrix} u(k)$$

$$y(k) = \begin{bmatrix} h_1, & h_2 \end{bmatrix} x(k) + u(k) \tag{2}$$

Prescribing the relation 1 to the state space model form algorithm we obtain the state-space description of the cascade form:

$$x(k+1) = \begin{bmatrix} a & 0 \\ a+b & c \end{bmatrix} x(k) + \begin{bmatrix} 1 \\ 1 \end{bmatrix} u(k)$$

$$y(k) = \begin{bmatrix} a+b, & c+d \end{bmatrix} x(k) + u(k) \tag{3}$$

That is relatively easy to go from an algorithm to a state-space description; but neither it is at all natural or clear how to go the opposite way. However that is fact the relationship between state-space modelling and digital system structures presents the way to develop a useful filter structures for *multivariable systems*.

The state-space model control theory relies heavily on mathematical relationship involving matrices and vectors [5]. However the matrix calculations are not in accordance with a general purpose processor architecture in regard to both the number precision or the time consuming requests. A dedicated numerical coprocessor with a proper numerical representation can duly fulfil the task.

NUMERICAL REPRESENTATION

The most fundamental decision is whether to use the *fixed-point* or the *floating point* numerical representation. Well, in a lot of the classical tutorial papers is preferred the fixed point arithmetic for digital filters except special cases having a due long cascade of elementary filter sections [6]. However, matrix operations have just a great number of "elementary sections". This point of view shows that matrix operations are processed more advantageously in floating point arithmetic.

The first generation of the signal microprocessors [7] applies exclusively the fixed point arithmetic in the 2nd complement code. The author of the study [8] concerns the fixed point, the floating point as well as the block floating point arithmetics.

As a representative opinion about fixed or floating point arithmetic, it is possible to take the practical experience with a high-performance digital signal processor (HSP) [9]. The HSP includes a parallel multiplier as well as supporting circuits for the exponent processing. The floating point adder/subtractor occupies a substantial area of silicon.

The data format of HSP floating point arithmetic is shown in Fig. 1.

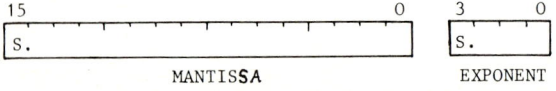

Fig. 1 Floating point data format

Presented floating-point data format is a model for the Numerical Coprocessor data format. The following text described the architecture of the Numerical Coprocessor designed for the DDC applications. The system design is accomodated to its dynamic range rather then the speed. The serial-parallel arithmetic unit implementation is designed to comply with todays technology.

At first the arithmetic unit is referred. Lately, the programmable data path and other supporting functions of the Numerical Coprocessor are mentioned.

A "BARREL SHIFTING" ALU

The familiar type of the supporting arithmetic unit of microcomputer is characterised by a simple arithmetic unit having stackcontrolled registers. Thus ALU makes it possible to easy programme ever sophisticated algorithm. However, its speed is limited by the necessity of very frequent data transfers.

On the other hand, a *pipeline ALU* is characterised by predeterminated operating registers. This type of ALU minimizes the number of data transfers. However, the programmability is limited regarding the register incorporation into the architecture.

The function of operating registers of the ALU being a model of the architecture of a pipeline arithmetic unit, is determinated by its incorporation into the ALU structure. But various algorithm types require the programmability of registers. This has led to the creation a merged structure by the pipeline ALU and the set of programmable registers [10].

An improved type of an arithmetic unit for floating point data processing is based on the vector multiplier with supporting a four-bit adder and a comparator for exponent data processing. The ALU is enabled by a "barrel shifting" subsystem to the accumulation function.

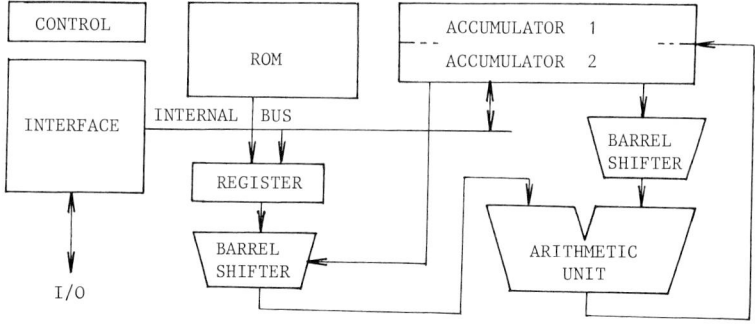

Fig. 2 Numerical Coprocessor improved by "barrel shifting" ALU

The mantissa can be shifted for accumulation in the extent of the 32-bit accumulator by an exponent value. The requests for accumulating the data format by Fig. 1. are ensured by this way. The hardware overhead of the floating point number processing modificated vector multiplier is approximately 30 %.

COMPACT AND TIGHLY ENCODED

To satisfy the needs of both the current and the future systems the Numerical Coprocessor provides a flexible data interface to be compatible with either a 16-bit data bus or an 8-bit one.
The 16-bit bus is connected directly to the 16 data pins (D$\emptyset$ ÷ D15) . In the alternative cooperation the 8-bit data bus is required to be connected to both the lower

data pins (D∅ ÷ D7) and the higher ones (D8 ÷ D15) at the same time. After loading the lower bits of the second operand an internal sequential operation is started. When the second portion of operand is loaded the operation is finished. This way is suiteble for the cooperation of the Numerical Coprocessor and the 8-bit host microcomputer. The interface operation the 16-bit or the 8-bit mode is programmed by control word.

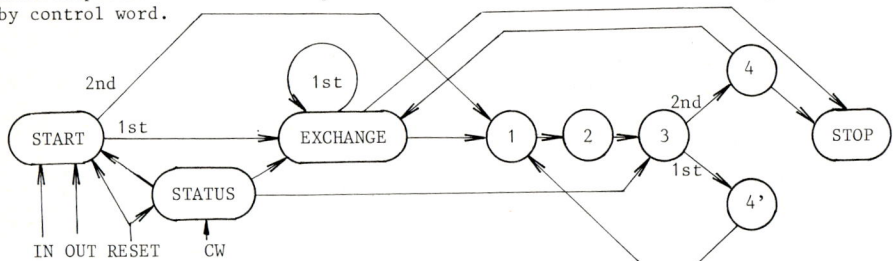

Fig. 3　The flow-diagram of the INPUT/OUTPUT data handling
　　　　1st .... first data pass　　　　　CW ... control word
　　　　2nd .... second data pass　　　　IN,OUT ... control lines
　　　　1,2,3,4,4' ... internal clock steps

ACKNOWLEDGEMENT

The author wishes to thank Professor I. Plander, DrSc. for his support and interest in my work.

REFERENCES

[1] J. Schloss: Some New Developments Concerning Digital Signal Processing. The 2nd European Signal Processing Conference EUSIPCO-83, Erlangen, Germany, Sept. 12 - 16, 1983 (North-Holland, Amsterdam, 1983) p. 787 - 792

[2] A. S. Willsky: Relationship Between Digital Signal Processing and Control and Estimation Theory. Proceedings of the IEEE, vol. 66, no.9 (Sept. 1978) p. 996 - 1017

[3] R. H. Cushman: Digital-processing tools present design challenges. EDN (May 13, 1981) p. 103 - 109

[4] R. H. Cushman: Signal-Processing Design awaits digital takeover. EDN (June 24, 1981) p. 119 - 128

[5] T. Dintersmith, P. Toldalagi: Apply modern control theory to optimize digital systems. EDN (April 28, 1983) p. 165 - 179

[6] S. L. Freeny: Special-Purpose Hardware for Digital Filtering. Proceedings of the IEEE, vol. 63, no.4 (April 1975) p. 633 - 648

[7] K. Vlček: The aspects of signal Microprocessor architectures. Proceedings of the Sixth Summer Symposium on Circuit Theory 1982 SSCT 82 Prague, Czechoslovakia, July 12 - 16, 1982 p. 181 - 185

[8] R. Block, A. Lacroix: Signal Representation in Digital Signal Processing. Internat. Conf. on Digital Signal Processing, Florence, Italy, Sept. 2 - 5, 1981 p. 240 - 247

[9] Y. Hagiwara, Y. Kita, T. Miyamoto, Y. Toba, H. Hara, T. Akazawa: A Single Chip Digital Signal Processor and Its Application to Real-Time speech Analysis. IEE J. of Solid-State Circuits vol. SC-18, no.1, (Feb. 1983) p. 91 - 99

[10] K. Vlček: Multiplier-Accumulator with Directed Data Flow. The 2nd European Signal Processing Conference EUSIPCO-83, Erlangen, Germany, Sept. 12 - 16, 1983 (North-Holland, Amsterdam, 1983) p. 833 - 836

THE COMPUTATION OF THE WEAK VISIBILITY POLYGON

Günter Werner

Institut of Mathematics
Friedrich-Schiller-University
6900 Jena, GDR

There are many concepts of visibility. The weak external visibility defined by Valentine includes some open problems. The strong hidden line problem might be termed as the jail house problem: What part of a polygonal region a patrolling guard can see? Is it possible to compute this part in linear time? We present an $O\ N \log N$ time algorithm for computing the weakly externally visible polygon.

INTRODUCTION

The notion of visibility in geometric objects is one that appears in many applications: the hidden line problem of graphics [1], in image processing [2], surveillance, and control of robots [3]. There are many papers concerning the problem of visibility in a polygonal region from a fixed point [2,4,5,6,7,8]. In this paper we discuss the weak external visibility [12] of polygons.

Many algorithms in image processing are correct only on a small set of images. Sklansky's algorithm [9] for computing the convex hull of a simple polygon is elegant but it works correct only on weakly externally visible polygons, shown by Toussaint and Avis [10]. The same authors published a paper where an optimal algorithm for determining the weak external visibility is described [11]. If a simple polygon isn't weakly externally visible it is a natural extension to ask which part of polygon is weakly externally visible. Is it possible to compute this part in linear time might be termed as the strong hidden line problem [7]. In this paper we present an $O(N \log N)$ time algorithm for computing the weakly externally visible polygon in two dimensions. The optimality of this algorithm wasn't shown but we suppose that the strong hidden line problem has to be answered negative.

DEFINITIONS AND PRELIMINARY RESULTS

Let $\mathcal{P} = (P, E)$ denote a simple planar polygon which is represented by a set of N points $p_1, \ldots, p_N$ in the Euclidean plane. We assume that the points are given in clockwise order, so that interior of the polygon lies to the right as the boundary of the polygon is traversed. A line segment lies outside $\mathcal{P}$ if the line segment doesn't intersect the interior of the polygon.

We say that a point p of the boundary of $\mathcal{P}$ is weakly externally visible if there is a line segment joining p and a point of the convex hull of $\mathcal{P}$ and lieing outside $\mathcal{P}$. The set of all weakly externally visible points of $\mathcal{P}$ is the boundary of the (weak) visibility

polygon $V(\mathcal{P}, CH(\mathcal{P}))$ of $\mathcal{P}$.
Let x, y, z be points of the Euclidean plane and x_i, y_i (i=1,2,3) their Cartesian coordinates. Let
$T = (x_3-x_2)(y_1-y_2) - (y_3-y_2)(x_1-x_2)$.
The points x, y, z describe a right (left, no) turn, if T is positive (negative, zero) and we write (x,y,z) r.t. (1.t., r.t., 1.t.) if x,y,z is a right (left, right left, right or no, left or no) turn.
$\overline{xy}$ denotes the straight line with points x and y, $\overrightarrow{xy}$ the radius with start point x through y and $\overline{xy}$ the line segment with endpoints x and y. Henceforth p_1 is a point of the convex hull of $\mathcal{P}$.
Let further p_i be a fixed point of the polygon.
p_i has a left half tangent iff there is a point $p_j \in \mathcal{P}$, j < i and for all segments $\overline{p_r p_s} \in E$ with r < i, s < i and $\overline{p_r p_s} \cap \overline{p_i p_j} \neq \emptyset$ hold (p_i, p_j, p_r) 1.t.$^+$ and (p_i, p_j, p_s) 1.t.$^+$. $\overrightarrow{p_i p_j}$ is the left half tangent of p_i. The definition of a right half tangent we get by changing the orientation of the enumeration of points and substituting 1.t.$^+$ by r.t.$^+$ in the definition above. The definition of right half tangents and left half tangents respectively is an essential part of the algorithm for computing the visibility polygon: A point p of the boundary of $\mathcal{P}$ is weakly externally visible iff p has both right and left half tangents with fixed orientation or $p=p_1$. For the algorithm we need some further technical definitions. Let i,j be integers, $i \leq N$, $j \leq N$:
$i[j] = 10^{\lceil \lg N \rceil}$. i+j inductive defines a code of a sequence of numbers.
i is a part of j ($i \sqsubseteq j$) iff there are numbers $j_1, \ldots, j_n$ ($j_1 \leq N$) and $j = i[j_1] \ldots [j_n]$.
For $i \sqsubseteq j$ $j^{i/}$ denotes the integer of j without part i:
$j^{i/} = j_1[j_2] \ldots [j_n]$. first(j) is the smallest first part of integer j, i.e. for $j = j_1[j_2] \ldots [j_n]$ and $j_1 \leq N$ holds first$(j) = j_1$.
Let $k = k_1 \cdot 10^{n-1} + \ldots + k_n \cdot 10^0$, $r = \left\lfloor \dfrac{n}{2\lceil \lg N \rceil} \right\rfloor \cdot \lceil \lg N \rceil$.

$\Upsilon(k) = k_{n-r} \cdot (\lceil \lg N \rceil - 1) \cdot 10^{\lceil \lg N \rceil - 1} + \ldots + k_{n-r-1} \cdot 10 + k_{n-r} \cdot 10^0$
is the middle part of the integer k. At least π_i x,y,z denotes the i-th component of the triple (x,y,z), and $\pi(P_i) = p_i$.

THE ALGORITHM LHATAN

Input: A circular linked list L
$P_1, P_2, \ldots, P_N$ of three dimensional vectors containing in the first component the number i and in the second and third component the x- and y-coordinates of the vertex p_i in clockwise order. p_i is the vertex with coordinates $\pi_2(P_i)$ and $\pi_3(P_i)$. p_1 is a point of the convex hull of $\mathcal{P}$. N is the quantity of vertices of $\mathcal{P}$.
Method: The algorithm examines the vertices of $\mathcal{P}$ in clockwise order, updating a stack T and functions s and f. If a vertex p_i has a left half tangent, then $s(P_i)$ defines a triple P_i with p_i is a vertex on $\mathcal{P}$ and $\overrightarrow{p_i p_j}$ is the left half tangent of p_i^j.f(i) is a code of a convex curve between p_1 and p_j containing p_j.
Initially T is empty. After scanning P_i the stack is as follow. T contains all triples P_j ($j \leq i$) with vertices p_j of $\mathcal{P}$ which are not hidden from edges $\overline{p_k p_{k+1}}$ with $j \leq k \leq i$. If during the scanning

Computation of the weak visibility polygon

will be detected that some vertices are hidden these elements will be eliminated from the stack and a Steinerpoint has to be inserted in the stack.
Remark: After clockwise scanning the whole polygon $\mathcal{P}$ it is possible that T contains hidden points. These points are eliminated in a second scan in anticlockwise order.
procedure LHATAN

```
( initialization )
    PUSH(T) ← P₁;
    PUSH(T) ← P₂;
    s(P₂) ← P₁;
    f(2) ← 1 [2];
( general step )
    FOR j=3 TO N DO
        IF (𝒯₂(s(P_{j-1})) ,P_{j-1},P_j) r.t.⁺ and (P_{j-2},P_{j-1},P_j) r.t.⁺ THEN
            BEGIN
            PUSH(T) ← P_j ;
            s(P_j) ← P_{j-1} ;
            f(j) ← f(j-1) [j] ;
            END
        IF (𝒯(s(P_{j-1})) ,P_{j-1},P_j) l.t. THEN
1           BEGIN
            k ← 1;
            WHILE (𝒯(s^{k+1}(P_{j-1})) ,𝒯( s^k(P_{j-1})) , P_j) l.t. DO k ← k+1;
            PUSH(T) ← P_j ;
            s(P_j) ← s^k(P_{j-1});
            f(j) ← f(𝒯₁( s^k(P_{j-1})))[j] ;
            END
        IF (𝒯(s(P_{j-1})) , P_{j-1},P_j) r.t.⁺ and (P_{j-2},P_{j-1},P_j) l.t. THEN
            BEGIN
            POP(T);
2           P ← POP(T);
            WHILE P_j,P_{j-1} ∩ 𝒯(P), 𝒯(s(P)) ≠ ∅ DO P ← POP(T);
            PUSH(T) ← P;
            k ← 𝒯₁(s(P_{j-1})) [f(𝒯₁(s(P))) f(𝒯₁(s(P_{j-1}))) / ];
            1 ← φ(k);
3           WHILE (𝒯(s(P₁)) , P₁,P_j) l.t. DO
                BEGIN
                k ← 𝒯₁(s(P_{j-1})) [f(1)^{f(𝒯₁(s(P_{j-1})))} / ] ;
                1 ← φ(k);
                END
            IF (P₁,P_{first(f(𝒯(s(P))) f(1)/)},P_j) l.t.⁺ THEN GOTO 4;
            WHILE (𝒯(s(P₁)) , P₁,P_j) r.t.⁺ DO
                BEGIN
                k ← 1[f(𝒯₁(s(P))) f(1) /];
                1 ← φ(k);
```

```
            END
    IF($\overline{\pi(s(P_1))}$ , $p_1,p_j$) l.t.   THEN GOTO 3;
4   PUSH(T) ← $P_j$;
    $s(P_j)$ ← $P_1$;
    f(j) ← f(1)[j];
    j ← j+1;
    IF ($p_{j-1}$, $\overline{\pi(s(P_{j-1}))}$, $p_j$) l.t.$^+$  THEN GOTO 2
       ELSE IF ($p_{j-2},p_{j-1},p_j$) r.t.  THEN
            BEGIN
            PUSH(T) ← $\overline{\pi(P)}$, $P_{\overline{\pi}_1(P)+1} \cap \overline{\pi(s(P_{j-1}))}$, $p_{j-1}$ ;
            GOTO 1 ;
            END
          ELSE
            BEGIN
            k ← j-1;
            j ← j+1;
            WHILE $\overline{p_{j-1},p_j} \cap \overline{p_k, \pi(s(P_k))}$ = ∅ DO
               BEGIN
               j ← j+1;
               END
            GOTO 2;
            END
    END
```

After clockwise scanning the polygon with algorithm LHATAN we examine the polygon containing in the stack T. Let Q_i denote the i-th element of the stack, i.e. Q_i=POP^i(T) and N$^\bullet$ the quantity of T.

We get the algorithm RHATAN by changing LHATAN only substituting the terms   r.t. by l.t.
                r.t.$^+$ by l.t.$^+$
                l.t. by r.t.
                l.t.$^+$ by r.t.$^+$
                N by N$^\bullet$
                P_i by Q_i and p_i by q_i.

THE ALGORITHM VISPOL

Input: See input LHATAN.
Method: After preprocessing and scanning the polygon in two directions T contains the incident vertices of the visibility polygon V($\mathcal{P}$, CH($\mathcal{P}$)).
```
procedure VISPOL
    FOR i=1 TO N DO compute $10^i$ and ⌈lgi⌉;
    CALL LHATAN;
    FOR i=1 TO N$^\bullet$ DO $Q_i$ ← POP(T);
    CALL RHATAN
```

It is easy to verify that VISPOL runs in O(N log N) time. Thus we may state the main result of the paper.

THEOREM: The procedure VISPOL computes the visibility polygon
$V(\mathcal{P}, CH(\mathcal{P}))$ in time $O(N \log N)$.
To verify that we remark, that all circles of the procedure LHATAN
and RHATAN respectively run in linear time and only the two WHILE-
circles of Lable 3 run in time $O(N \log N)$.

CONCLUSIONS

It was not posible to show the optimality of the algorithm VISPOL
up to now, i.e. this algorithm is no answer to the strong hidden
line problem.
It is easy to see, that the computation of the weak visibility po-
lygon $V(\mathcal{P}, \overrightarrow{uv})$ [12] is time equivalent to the computation of
$V(\mathcal{P}, CH(\mathcal{P}))$. A simple modification of the algorithm VISPOL computes the polygon $V(\mathcal{P}, \overrightarrow{uv})$.

REFERENCES

[1] H.Freeman, P.P.Loutrel, An algorithm for the solution of the two dimensional hidden line problem, IEEE Trans. Electron. Comput. EC-16, No. 6, 784-790.
[2] L.S.Davis, M.L.Benedikt, Computational models of space: Isovists and Isovist Fields, Comp. Graph.Image Proc.11 (1979).
[3] N.J.Nilsson, A mobile automaton: An application of artificial intelligence techniques, Proc. IJCAI, 1969, 509-520.
[4] M.I.Shamos, Problems in Computational Geometry, Carnegie-Mellon University, 1975, revised 1977.
[5] D.T.Lee, F.P.Preparata, An optimal algorithm for finding the kernel of a polygon, Journ.Ass.Comput.Mach., vol.26, No.3, 415-421.
[6] H.El Giny, D.Avis, A linear algorithm for determing the visibility polygon from a point, J.Algorithms, 1981, 186-197.
[7] G.T.Toussaint, Pattern recognition and geometrical complexity, Proc. 5th Int. Conf. Pattern Recog., Miami Beach, Fl., 1980.
[8] G.Werner, Zwei Algorithmen zur Berechnung des Sichtbarkeitspolygons von einem Punkt, Forschungsergebnisse der Friedrich-Schiller-Universität Jena, 1982.
[9] J.Sklansky, Measuring concavity on a rectangular mosaic, IEEE Trans. Comput. C-21, 1355-1364, 1972.
[10] G.T.Toussaint, D.Avis, On a convex hull algorithm for polygons and its application to triangulation problems, Pattern Recog. 15, No.1, 23-29, 1982.
[11] D.Avis, G.T.Toussaint, An optimal algorithm for determing the visibility of a polygon from an edge, IEEE Trans.Comp., Vol. C-30, No.12, 910-914, 1981.
[12] F.A.Valentine, Minimal sets of visibility, Proc.Amer.Math.Soc. 4, 917-921, 1953.

A PLAN GENERATING SYSTEM OF AN INTELLECTUAL ROBOT
USING A FRAME REPRESENTATION OF THE INFORMATION

Nely P. Zlatareva

Institute of Industrial Cybernetics & Robotics
Bulgarian Academy of Sciences, Acad.G.Bonchev Str.
bl.2, 1113 Sofia, Bulgaria

Traditionally, the task of the plan generating system is defined as the task of heuristic search, where the initial model of the environment is formulated, followed by the final model in which the desired aim is considered to be reached and a set of operators which transform one environmental model into another. Formally, this task may be represented as a fourtuple (M_o, M, O, T) (1), where $M=\{M_i\}$ - a set of environmental models, $M_o=\{M_{oj}\}$ - a set of initial models, $T=\{T_k\}$ - a set of final models, and $O=\{O_l\}$ - a set of operators.

The solution of the task, appears to be a series of operators $O_1, O_2, \ldots, O_n$ at $O_1 \circ O_2 \circ O_3 \circ \ldots O_n(M_{oj}) \to T$, where $O_1 \circ O_2 \circ O_3 \circ \ldots \circ O_n(M_{oj})$ is a composition of functions $O_n(O_{n-1}(\ldots(O_2(O_1(M_{oj})))\ldots))$ of $M_{oj} \in M_o$.

The description of every $M_{oj} \in M_o$ consist of the description of particular objects and the relations between them.

Let assume, that each object influences only the objects placed in its working subspace[1]. Then each working subspace can be described, with the help of the frame F_i, which has the following structure:

name of the slot	body of the slot
name	⟨atom⟩
type	⟨active, passive⟩
description	⟨a list of atoms⟩
pointer	⟨atom⟩
actions	⟨a list of production rules⟩
controlling parameters	⟨$\tilde{M}_1, \tilde{M}_2, \tilde{M}_3$⟩

where on the slot "name" is written the name of the concrete

---

[1] We consider that, the working space of the robot is devided into separate subspaces, each of which is identified by the name of its lower plane. Due to that, father down, the term "working subspace" we shall use together with the term "working plane".

working plane; slot "type" consists of information whether the concrete plane plays the role of "basic object" in the current model. Under "basic" we shall understand the object, which has the property "active", i.e. it determines the planning process during one or more iterations. The introduction of such a notion restricts considerably the searching space, which on the other hand increases the rapid action of the planning system. Slot "description" comprizes an ordered set of objects ($PL_{i1}, IP_{i2}, IP_{i3}, \ldots, IP_{in}$) found on the working plane PL_{i1} in the current environmental model. Through the information in the slot "pointer" the frames are connected in the form of a net which characterizes the current environmental model M_j and it is interpreted as a metaframe $M_{ti} = \{F_i, R_i\}$, where $F_i \in F$, F - a set of frames, and $R_i \in R$, R - a set of binary orientated arcs, between two neighbour frames. Each metaframe can contain only one active frame and exactly that frame takes the initiation to generate a production rule in the model M_{ti}. A list of production rules is recorded in the slot "actions". These rules make possible the realization of the actions of the objects, belonging to the working space of the basic object. Each production rule consists of two parts:

- left, comprises the conditions, which must exist in the current model, in order to utilize the given production rule;

- right, a description of the changes, that had taken place in the base knowledge (2). As a result of the usage of the given production rules, the effect of the already applied action is described.

In this realization we have used three production rules:

- DEIST(IP,X,Y), where IP - object, changes its place as a result of the action of the given production rule over the current environmental model; X is the identifire of an object or the working plane on which the object IP is found in the model M_{ti}; Y - identifire of an object or a working plane over which IP moves to the model M_{t+1}

- DECOM(IP,IPP,PL_{y1}), where IPP - object is found under IP in the model M_{ti} and PL_{y1} - identifire of the working place over which IP is placed as a result of the influence of the given production rule in the model $M_{(t+1)i}$.

- REANG(IP,PL_{z1},PL_{y1}), where PL_{z1} - identifire of a working plane over which the object IP is found in the model M_{ti}, and PL_{y1} - a plane on which the object IP is placed as a result of the influence of the production rule.

The slot "controlling parameters" contains a list of three
elements $(\tilde{M}_1,\tilde{M}_2,\tilde{M}_3)$ controlling the planning process, where $\tilde{M}_1$
becomes a value equal to one, if the corresponding frame contains
in the slot "description" an ordered list of objects, overlapping
with those in the final metaframe. In the opposite case $\tilde{M}_1$ will have
the value zero; $\tilde{M}_2$ is the number, which points to the number of
objects found in the given working subspace; $\tilde{M}_3$ becomes a value
equal to one, when an action is realized by an object from the given
subspace and as a result, that very object takes the same place in
the description of the final metaframe.

Lets introduce the following notions:

- "direct action" - direct action of the object IP is important
only when such conditions in the model M_{ti} exist, which allow the
application of the production rule DEIST(IP,X,Y), as a result of
which IP will take the place described in the final metaframe.

- "unloading" - if the conditions for application are not obeyed
by any of the production rules DEIST(IP,X,Y), after the successive
actualization of all frames in the current environmental model, the
first frame, which contains the conditions $(\tilde{M}_2 \geqslant 2)\&(\tilde{M}_3 \neq 1)$, and
satisfied the production rule DECOM(IP,IPP,PL_{y1}) is activized again
and realizes the action "unloading" of the object IP over the free
working plane. It is considered that the introduction of the additional condition $\tilde{M}_2 = \max_{F_i}(\tilde{M}_2)$ will allow the liberation of the largest
number, which were later studied by the planning algorithm in order
to make possible the realization of direct action. If none of these
frames had not performed the conditions for the application of the
production rule DECOM(IP,IPP,PL_{y1}) (in each working subspace can be
found only one object and with no objects an action can not be
realized) then an operation for rearrangement of basic elements takes
place.

A special procedure is introduced in the planning algorithm.
It realized the necessary condition for the application of the production rule REANG(IP,PL_{z1}, PL_{y1}). This procedure is connected with the
transmission of the activity over the frame, which will garantee the
continuation of the planning process, approaching the final environmental model.

The actual planning can be represented as a sequence of the
following stages:

1. The examination of the truthness of the input task. Each

object, taking part in the initial metaframe, must be described in the final metaframe too.

2. Calculating the element values $\tilde{M}_2$, which determine the frame candidates for activization.

3. Among the frame candidates for activization we must look for those in which the conditions for the application for the production rule DEIST(IP,X,Y) is realized and it is activized. If there is no such a frame, we must look for a frame during which activation the conditions for the application of the production rule DECOM(IP,IPP,PL$_{y1}$) are realized, i.e. we are looking for a frame which will use the conditions $(\tilde{M}_2 \geqslant 2) \& (\tilde{M}_3 \neq 1)$.

4. If all frames in the current metaframe have $\tilde{M}_2=(0,1)$, the first frame is activized, where the conditions for the accepted production rule REANG(IP,PL$_{z1}$,PL$_{y1}$) take place.

5. As a result of the application of the production rule over current environmental model which is viewed by the system, as a metaframe generates a new metaframe, containing the changes, which had occured as a result of the influence on the part of the production rule.

6. Checking is done for the end of the planning process and the condition for checking is that all frames in the current model must contain $(\tilde{M}_1=1)$.

7. If the condition for the end of the planning process is not realized, a list of frame candidates for activization is regenerated and the described process is repeated.

8. The realization of the condition for the end of the planning process includes a special procedure, which determines whether the optimization of the resulting plan is necessary, and if is necessary, the system generates a new model from the set of the of the initial models. If the system decides that the generated plan is optimal, it is lieble to work in the lower level of the planning system, where the planning of the trajectory of the action of the robot in the coordinative space (X,Y,Z) is realized.

The described system is modeled on a programm language PL-1. The experiments, that were done, show the fast action of the system, which allows the operation to take place in large scale in real time. The volume of the programm is 30 Kbytes, which allows, by no problems the transmission of the system on mini or personal computers for achivment of transplantation process for the industrial environment. The possible application of the system is for the usage of robot assembly operation.

REFERENCES:

1. Э.В.Попов, Г.Р.Фирдман, Алгоритмические основы интеллектуальных роботов и искусственного интеллекта, Наука, Москва, 1976.

2. N.Zlatareva, A model of interactive hierarchical system for making decision and planning the behaviour of intellectual robot, in Тезисы докладов Международного семинара по современным методам принятия решений, июнь, София, 1983.

A NEW APPROACH TO THE DESIGN OF EXPERT SYSTEM ARCHITECTURES

Giovanni Guida, Carlo Tasso

University of Udine
Udine, Italy

This paper presents some new proposals in the field of expert system architectures. A short outline of the state-of-the-art is first presented, and some of the main limitations of current technology are discussed. The paper then focuses on a novel two-level architecture in which it is possible to clearly distinguish operation from planning. This structure allows disciplined and effective representation and use of meta-knowledge. The impact of this architecture on matching, conflict resolution and inference mechanisms is then analysed, and the expected advantages in terms of flexibility, skill, and efficiency are evaluated.

STATE-OF-THE-ART IN EXPERT SYSTEM TECHNOLOGY AND PERSPECTIVES FOR FUTURE DIRECTIONS

By the term expert system we refer here to that class of high-performance problem solvers able to operate in complex domains, built up by means of a rule-based deduction technology - other types of non rule-based systems will not be addressed to here (Davis and King, 1977; Stefik et al., 1982). The first expert systems were designed in the seventies, mainly with application-oriented aims, as the result of the merging of classic problem solving methods with the area of knowledge representation (Feigenbaum, 1977). The area of expert systems has developed very rapidly in the last decade, and has shown a strong impact on applications. Expert systems capable of providing functionality and efficiency at or near the level of human experts have been constructed in several subject domains (medicine, geology, chemistry, system configuration, mathematics, etc.), and they are now in operation both in research laboratories and industrial sites. To date expert systems can show skilled deduction capabilities, they are able to deal with uncertain and judgmental knowledge, they can explain their conclusions to the user and help him in formulating his problem and needs. (Hayes-Roth, Lenat, and Waterman, 1983; Erman, 1983).

Despite their success both in research and industry; expert systems still rely on a quite small set of established methodologies, and current technology in the area of rule-based systems is still far from the achievement of its ultimate possibilities. Inference mechanisms (based on the classical <matching - conflict resolution - action> loop) are generally poorly effective and control strategies (forward, backward, mixed) are fixed. The use of meta-knowledge to direct the inference process is still lacking a clear structuring. Knowledge about time and space is not easy to represent. The knowledge bases available to the system are not allowed to be as large as it would be required to address several areas of actual interest. Knowledge acquisition from human experts (including, knowledge evaluation, maintenance, etc.) still lacks adequate tools and constitutes a real bottleneck of system design. More precisely, the limitations of the current technology and the shortcomings of current applications may be organized in three classes (Waltz, 1983).

1. Intrinsic technical limitations

   - the basic control and inference mechanisms now in use for expert system design are not skilled and effective enough to allow development of systems operating with very large knowledge bases and in real time, as it would be required in several application areas;
   - knowledge available to expert systems is almost empirical and does not include a general (mainly model-theoretical) description of the subject domain; therefore, deriving missing knowledge from general principles is not possible;
   - models of inexact and uncertain reasoning currently in use are often very naive and do not allow adequate representation and use of judgmental knowledge;
   - mechanisms for verification of the expert system activity for plausibility are not available; so the conclusions they propose may sometimes be naive, or even misleading;
   - only very poor tools exist to support the process of knowledge acquisition from human experts (including validation, consistency, redundancy, completeness, etc.), for maintaining the knowledge bases, and for improving system capabilities through learning.

2. System design and development limitations

   - constructing an expert system may require several man-years of effort of a high specialized task-force (including a technical manager, artificial intelligence system designers, knowledge engineers, domain experts, programmers with artificial intelligence background), which is often difficult to assemble;
   - the practice of expert system design is still lacking a sound methodology;
   - tools for improving the productivity of expert system design and construction (such as, meta-systems, expert system building packages, knowledge representation languages, etc.) are still scarce, their performance is limited, and their use is restricted to small classes of suitable domains;
   - most of the expert systems which are now in operation are the result of special single-customer projects; viable technologies for large-scale production of experts systems do not exist yet.

3. Use limitations

   - expert systems currently produced are suitable only for classes of specific application domains;
   - the knowledge acquisition bottleneck constitutes one of the main impediments to the development of several applications;
   - current technology expert systems often provide limited performance (skill and efficiency) in comparison to human experts;
   - the technological and personnel resources needed to develop and maintain an expert system operating in a real environment are not easy to assemble and they are generally very expensive;
   - cost/benefit evaluations are often uncertain and their results are not always in favour of the adoption of an expert system.

An overall appreciation of the expert system area shows two contrasting facets: on one side progress in research and development has led to a number of practical applications and to a strong interest by industry, on the other side the available technology is still in a very early stage of development (Waltz, 1983). In the next years, advancements in basic research are expected to go much further than refining and completing existing technology: a real jump forward is needed to push expert systems to a substantially higher level of performance. Several research efforts of the recent years indicate this trend towards new-generation expert systems (Furukawa et al., 1982; Suwa et al., 1982; Sauers and Walsh, 1983), which will include most of the capabilities of skill and efficiency which are out of reach of current technology. When basic research results in this direction will be established, their impact on applications will surely be dramatic: higher performance and lower cost will push expert systems towards a large-scale technology.

Among the most promising research directions which will basically contribute to the development of a new-generation technology in the area of rule-based expert systems we mention:

- knowledge acquisition and evaluation (including consistency, redundancy, completeness, etc.);
- learning (both control and domain knowledge) from experience and remote (or general) knowledge;
- representation languages suitable for both expert knowledge (uncertain, fragmentary, anedoctal, etc.) and organized knowledge (model-theoretical, taxonomic, etc.) on the subject domain;
- inference methods, including flexible management of several classes of reasoning schemas (decomposition into subproblems, by contraddiction, by analogy, by default, case analysis, etc.);
- control strategies for planning and monitoring the inference process, including the representation and use of meta-knowledge;
- interfaces (to the user, the expert, the knowledge engineer), including both language aspects (graphics, natural language, friendly dialogue, etc.) and conceptual aspects (co-operative behaviour, introduction to appropriate use of the sysyem, explanation, etc.).

Note that several of the above research tasks are closely interdependent: a substantial advancement in one area can not take place without involving other related areas. This strongly reinforces the above claim of the establishment of a trend towards a new-generation technology.

AIM AND SCOPE

In a previous paper (Guida and Tasso, 1983) we have developed some issues related to knowledge acquisition and, also, we have briefly outlined a set of requirements that a new-generation expert system should be able to implement. We also have raised the exigency for new expert system architectures supporting a more flexible management of control and deduction mechanisms. This paper, going further along this line, focuses on skill and effectiveness of control and deduction mechanisms and proposes a novel meta-level architecture which should enhance both flexibility and efficiency.

The specific goals of our research directly derive from an analysis of a class of shortcomings of existing systems:

- control strategies (depth-first, breadth-first, etc.) are fixed;
- deduction mechanisms (forward, backward, mixed) are also fixed;
- representation and use of meta-knowledge generally lacks a clear methodology;
- mechanisms for speeding up matching (such as partitioning) are static, i.e. they can not vary during the operation of the system;
- conflict resolution is usually based on very general principles and does not evaluate candidate rules in the specific context to which they should be applied;

- there is no general mechanism for a long run planning of the system operation, distinct from operation itself (i.e., the use of knowledge and meta-knowledge takes place at the same level).

The aim of this paper is to propose a unitary solution to this set of problems which can constitute the basis for the design of a novel expert system architecture.

THE META-LEVEL ARCHITECTURE: DIVIDING OPERATION FROM PLANNING

An expert system utilizes two kinds of knowledge: domain knowledge and meta-knowledge. The first one concerns the specific application domain of the expert program, and it is usually expressed through condition-action rules. It should encompass all the information necessary to deal with the several different situations related to specific tasks. By meta-knowledge we refer here to "knowledge about domain knowledge", that is about the content, structure, and use of domain knowledge (Davis and Buchanan, 1977; Davis, 1980). It includes reasoning, deducting, and judgmental methods employed in an application domain during the problem solving process. Meta-knowledge also encodes information about selection, organization, and scheduling of the activities to be performed for solving a specific task.

Only rarely meta-knowledge is treated as an independent entity, and expert systems are not modular with respect to it. Often, meta-knowledge is not embedded explicitly (in declarative form) in expert systems, but it is inserted into the algorithm. This gives a very rigid structure, especially for what concerns the general problem solving techniques utilized. It is therefore possible to recognize meta-knowledge in the inference methods adopted, in the rule base partitioning criteria, and in the conflict resolution algorithms. In other approaches, meta-knowledge is formulated through production rules (meta-rules). This provides a far more flexible tool for system design and operation, even though knowledge and meta-knowledge are still dealt with by the inference engine at same level. Moreover, the concept of meta-knowledge is generally conceived in a quite restricted sense, as it only concerns the task of improving the performance of the system, without deeply affecting its mode of operation. Our proposal focuses, in a very general sense, on the capability of overall controlling in a flexible way the inference activity of an expert system. From this point of view, we can distinguish two levels of activity within an expert system: i) the <u>operation-level</u>, which utilizes domain specific knowledge in order to perform basic tasks required for solving a particular problem, and ii) the <u>planning-level</u>, which aims at managing and monitoring through meta-knowledge all the activities performed in the lower operation level, such as inferencing, matching, and conflict resolution. These two levels communicate through:
- the <u>current problem description</u>, which contains the state of the problem solving process;
- the <u>goal</u>, which is a piece of knowledge managed by the upper level and used to direct operation-level activities (Hatvany, 1983).

At the planning-level the expert system may be viewed as a <u>goal management system</u>, which utilizes a <u>strategy-rule base</u> embedding meta-knowledge in order to generate goals to be assigned to the underlying level. Its activity is rule-based and takes into consideration both the current problem description and the previous goals issued, in order to check when and how a goal is reached, to suspend not promising goals, to resume suspended goals, to kill goals considered useless (because they are already achieved or their achievement is no more interesting for the task at hand). Furthermore, the planning level stops operation of the expert system when no more goals can be generated and no suspended goals remain. All the knowledge utilized at this upper level is contained in the strategy-rule base, which supplies mechanisms for guiding the reasoning process, for evaluating possible alternative inference paths, and for effective implementation of the chosen deduction strategy (Barnett, 1984).

At the operation-level the expert system behaves very similarly to a classic rule-based system, but it receives in input from the upper level a goal to be achieved, which is utilized to choose the current inference strategy and to direct both matching and conflict resolution.

The general architecture here proposed is illustrated in Figure 1, which shows the two levels with the related knowldge bases.

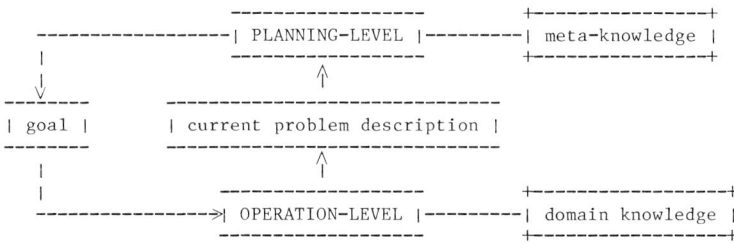

Figure 1. Overall architecture of a two-level expert system.

A crucial point in the above architecture is the structure designed for the notion of goal. In fact, the correct and effective link between the two levels and the possibility of a disciplined organization of meta-knowledge is solely committed to the goal. In our proposal the goal structure contains three parts:
- <u>partitioning driver</u>, which is constituted by a pattern to be matched with the set of block descriptors utilized for dynamic partitioning;
- <u>control and inference driver</u>, which can suggest the most appropriate inference mechanism to adopt, by defining how to link elementary deduction steps together to build up a strategy;
- <u>ordering driver</u>, which is devoted to rank rules in the conflict set in order to facilitate the choice of the most promising rule to fire next.

(See next two sections for a precise definition of the notions above utilized in an informal way).

MATCHING AND CONFLICT RESOLUTION WITH GOALS

Matching and conflict resolution are the kernel of a rule-based system. The requirements for good matching and conflict resolution algorithms are very straightforward: efficiency and skill, respectively. Matching should be able to retrieve all relevant rules in very short time, even when the rule base and the current problem description are very large and the rule structure is complicated. Conflict resolution should be able to choose, at each step of the deduction process, the most promising rule to fire next in order to reach the current goal. Both these activities have a dramatic impact on the performance of the inference engine. One of the most recent advances in this area is represented by the Rete Match Algorithm (Forgy, 1982) - see also (McDermott, Newell, and Moore, 1978).

In our, approach we aim at making matching and conflict resolution more effective by taking advantage from the new notion of goal. We split each of these two activities into two parts: a goal-dependent phase followed by a goal-independent one. Therefore we obtain:

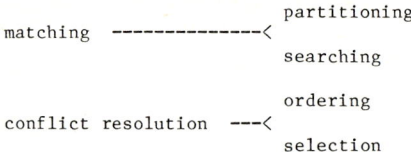

Searching and selection are goal-independent and can inherit all experience so far available for matching and conflict resolution. Partitioning and ordering are conceived as preprocessing activities which should make substantially faster and more skilled the subsequent elaboration. We deal with each of them separately.

The notion of partitioning of the rule base in order to speed up matching is not new in the literature. A usual way of partitioning (McDermott, 1980) consists in a static division of the rule base into separate non-overlapping parts (partitions), each containing knowledge relevant to a different subject or to a different stage of the deduction process. During system operation the matcher addresses not the entire rule base but only that partition which is considered relevant to the current deduction phase. The expected advantages of this indexing strategy are obvious. However, this kind of partitioning suffers from several shortcomings:

- partitioning is static, i.e., it must be decided a priori and is fixed;
- good partitions are not easy to find out at the moment of knowledge acquisition;
- partitions generally relate to specific phases of the deduction process and require that at least the overall line of operation of the system is determined and fixed a priori.

Our proposal inherits this basic idea of dividing the rule base into parts, but utilizes a different dynamic technique of partitioning and, also, it assigns to partitioning a far more important role than indexing the rule base. Rules are organized, at the moment of knowledge acquisition, into blocks, each one containing rules relating to some common subject. To each block, a block descriptor is given which contains a symbolic representation of the specific task the rules refer to. Blocks are supposed to be of variable size but, in any case, far smaller than the usual static partitions. During system operation the current goal (more precisely the <partitioning driver>) is first matched with the set of block descriptors. The blocks which correctly match the goal are merged together to form the current partition to be used for searching candidate rules. Therefore, partitioning is now goal-dependent and dynamic. It is no more connected to any fixed organization of the deduction process into sequential phases. Moreover, it is reasonably easy to perform at the moment of knowledge acquisition, since it only depends on knowledge about the domain and does not presupposes to know about the expected system operation.

An important point related to the task of matching is dealing with partial and best matching (Guida and Tasso, 1983). This topic, however, will not be dealt with here, and it will be the subject of a future work.

The result of matching is the retrieval of a set of candidate rules (the conflict set) from which the next rule to fire can be chosen. Ordering deals with the task of evaluating the expectation for the rules in the conflict set to produce the most desirable and valuable effect upon execution. Simple, fixed criteria are generally adopted for this crucial task or, in more sophisticated cases, conflict resolution is heuristically guided by meta-rules. In our approach ordering is intended as a process which evaluates the rules in the conflict set with respect to the current goal, and ranks them into a partial order. This is done by using the <ordering driver> of the goal, either in a very simple way through matching with the RHS and LHS of the rules in the conflict set, or, in a more sophisticated way, through an interpretation of the expected effect of the rules.

BASIC INFERENCE MECHANISMS

Independently of how matching and conflict resolution are carried out, control and inference mechanisms play a crucial role in the design of the inference engine. Currently, fixed quite elementary strategies are used for this task, including forward and backward chaining, etc. The shortcomings of these techniques mainly relate to the impossibility of having a sufficiently large variety of deduction methods which can cover at least in part the spectrum of human reasoning.

Our proposal is to add flexibility to the inference process in order to allow several different strategies to be implemented according to the specific features of the current problem to be solved. We deal here with this subject in two steps: i) first we analyse and decompose the basic inference mechanisms of production rules into elementary components; ii) afterwards we will propose strategies for a skilled dynamic assembly of these elementary components into different deduction mechanisms, according to the exigency expressed by the current goal.

Let us introduce the following terminology. A rule is a pair A --> B, where A (left-hand-side, LHS) and B (right-hand-side, RHS) are clauses made up by elementary terms and logical connectives (the specific form of A and B is immaterial here). The meaning of a rule is that of logical implication. The current problem description is made up by a set of terms, called facts (FACT), assumed to hold altogether (i.e., their conjunction is true), and by a set of terms, called hypotheses (HYPO), whose truth-value is unknown but is supposed to be true. A term is true (T) in a given moment if it belongs to FACT, false (F) if its negation belongs to FACT, undefined (U) otherwise. A target condition, expressed by a predicate on FACT, is assigned. The task of the inference engine is to expand FACT, using available rules or by directly acquiring new facts from the user, until the target condition becomes true. To this purpose rules applying to the current problem description have to be chosen and then executed. This involves the process of matching the LHS or RHS of the rules with the current problem description (FACT or HYPO) in order to assign to them an appropriate truth-value and to choose candidate rules to fire. Let us introduce the predicate MATCH of two arguments, X belonging to {LHS, RHS} and Y belonging to {FACT, HYPO}, defined as:

$$MATCH(X, Y) = \begin{cases} T \text{ if X evaluates to T in Y} \\ F \text{ if X evaluates to F in Y} \\ U \text{ if X cannot receive a truth-value in Y} \end{cases}$$

Four classes of actions may now be identified, each containg several elementary deduction steps, which can be used to expand FACT:

1. Deduce new facts from existing ones. This can be done in two ways:

   1. if   MATCH(LHS, FACT)=T   2. if   MATCH(RHS, FACT)=F
      then   add RHS to FACT   then   add not(LHS) to FACT

2. Generate new hypotheses from already existing ones. This can occur in six ways:

    1. if   MATCH(LHS, FACT)=F   4. if   MATCH(RHS, FACT)=T
       then   add not(RHS) to HYPO   then   add LHS to HYPO

    2. if   MATCH(LHS, HYPO)=T   5. if   MATCH(RHS, HYPO)=T
       then   add RHS to HYPO   then   add LHS to HYPO

    3. if   MATCH(LHS, HYPO)=F   6. if   MATCH(LHS, HYPO)=F
       then   add not(RHS) to HYPO   then   add not(LHS) to HYPO

3. Validate or refute hypoteses using facts. This can be done in two ways:

    1. if   MATCH(hypo, fact)=T   2. if   MATCH(hypo, fact)=F
       then   delete hypo from HYPO   then   delete hypo from HYPO

where the variables hypo and fact belong to HYPO and FACT respectively, and the predicate MATCH is extended accordingly.

4. Acquire new facts from outside, through a dialogue with the user.

Putting these elementary deduction steps together, it is possible to obtain a very large and flexible variety of inference strategies. For example, the classical forward and backward chaining mechanisms may be obtained in the following way:
forward :   [1.1]
backward: 2.4 + [2.5] + {4} + 3.1 + [1.1]
where, [ ] denote possible iteration of the enclosed deduction step, + denotes concatenation of deduction steps, and { } denote an optional deduction step.

Several other inference strategies can now be built up by composing elementary deduction steps. For example, the usual technique of 'hypothesis refutation by contraddiction' may be obtained as: [2.2] + {4} + 3.2 + [1.2].

How to obtain the most appropriate strategy for the current problem description is specified by the <control and inference driver> of the goal.

CONCLUSIONS AND PERSPECTIVES

In the paper a novel structure of expert system has been described, which proposes itself as a contribution in the field of meta-level architectures. The advantages of this proposal are to be found both in the expected performance (skill and efficiency), and in the design methodology suggested for collecting and organizing meta-knowledge in a rational and disciplined way.

The design of an experimental system (in the area of safety of road transportation of hazardous materials) supporting most of the features above introduced is to date ongoing (Guida and Tasso, 1983).

REFERENCES

    1. Barnett, J.A., How much is control knowledge worth? - A primitive example, Artificial Intelligence 22 (1984) 77-89.
    2. Davis, R., Meta-rules: Reasoning about control, Artificial Intelligence 18 (1980) 179-222.

3. Davis, R. and Buchanan, B., Meta-level knowledge. Overview and applications, in: Proc. 5th Int. Joint Conf. on Artificial Intelligence, Cambridge, MA, August 1977, 920-927.
4. Davis, R. and King, I., An overiew of production systems, in: Elcock, E.W. and Michie, D. (eds.), Machine Intelligence 8 (John Wiley, New York, 1977) 300-332.
5. Erman, L.D., Expert systems, in: Ritchie, G. and Albers, G. (eds.) IJCAI-83 Tutorial on Artificial Intelligence, Karlsruhe, FRG, August 1983.
6. Feigenbaum, E.A., The art of artificial intelligence: Themes and case studies of knowledge engineering, in: Proc. 5th Int. Joint Conf. on Artificial Intelligence, Cambridge, August 1977, 1014-1029.
7. Forgy, C.L., Rete: A fast algorithm for the many pattern/many object pattern match problem, Artificial Intelligence 19 (1982) 17-37.
8. Furukawa, K. et al., Problem solving and inference mechanisms, in: Moto-oka, T. (ed.), Fifth Generation Computer Systems (North-Holland, Amsterdam, 1982) 131-138.
9. Guida, G. and Tasso, C., The issue of knowledge acquisition in the design of rule-based expert systems, in: V.M. Ponomaryov (ed.), Proc. 1st IFAC Int. Symposium on Artificial Intelligence, Leningrad, USSR, October 1983 (Pergamon Press, Oxford, 1984).
10. Hatvany, J., The efficient use of deficient knowledge, in: V.M. Ponomaryov (ed.), Proc. 1st IFAC Int. Symposium on Artificial Intelligence, Leningrad, USSR, October 1983 (Pergamon Press, Oxford, 1984).
11. Hayes-Roth, F., Lenat, D.B., and Waterman, D.A., Building expert systems (Addison-Wesley, Reading, MA, 1983).
12. McDermott, J., Newell, A., and Moore, J., The efficiency of certain production system implementations, in: Waterman, D.A. and Hayes-Roth, F. (eds.), Pattern-Directed Inference Systems (Academic Press, New York, 1978) 155-176.
13. McDermott, J., R1: A rule-based configurer of computer systems, Dept. of Computer Science, Carnegie-Mellon University, Rept. CMU-CS-80-119, April, 1980.
14. Sauers, R. and Walsh, R., On the requirements of future expert systems, in: Proc. 8th Int. Joint Conf. on Artificial Intelligence, Karlsruhe, FRG, August 1983, 110-115.
15. Stefik, M. et al., The organization of expert systems - A tutorial, Artificial Intelligence 18 (1982) 135-173.
16. Suwa, M. et al., Knowledge base mechanisms, in: Moto-oka, T. (ed.), Fifth Generation Computer Systems (North-Holland, Amsterdam, 1982) 139-145.
17. Waltz, D. (chairman), Artificial Intelligence : An assessment of the state-of-the-art and recommendations for future directions, The AI Magazine 4,3 (1983) 55-67.